D1105694

HANDBOOK OF

RACIAL-CULTURAL PSYCHOLOGY AND COUNSELING

HANDBOOK OF

RACIAL-CULTURAL PSYCHOLOGY AND COUNSELING

Theory and Research

Volume One

Edited by

ROBERT T. CARTER

WILEY

John Wiley & Sons, Inc.

Published by John Wiley & Sons, Inc., Hoboken, New Jersey.
Published simultaneously in Canada.

Library of Congress Cataloging-in-Publication Data:

Handbook of racial-cultural psychology and counseling : theory and research, volume 1 / edited by
    Robert T. Carter.
        p. cm.
    Includes bibliographical references.
    ISBN 0-471-38628-6 (cloth : v. 1) — ISBN 0-471-38629-4 (cloth : v. 2) —
    ISBN 0-471-65625-9 (set)
        1. Psychiatry, Transcultural—Handbooks, manuals, etc. 2. Psychology—Cross-cultural
    studies—Handbooks, manuals, etc. 3. Cross-cultural counseling—Handbooks, manuals, etc.
    I. Carter, Robert T., 1948–
    RC455.4.E8H368 2004
    616.59—dc22

                                                                    2004042222

Printed in the United States of America.

10 9 8 7 6 5 4 3 2 1

Christopher, Sidney, Bryant Jr., Jasmine, Brianna, and Ricardo

Acknowledgments

I would like to thank all the people who helped make the *Handbook* possible. First and foremost I would like to thank the contributors because without their thoughts and hard work there would be no *Handbook*. Alex Pieterse served from the beginning as the editorial assistant helping me keep all the details organized. A deep and heartfelt thanks goes to him; he was invaluable. Later during the project, Bryant Williams and Amanda Sommerfeld joined Alex. They were wonderful, and contributed a great deal. They were assisted at various points by others who were part of my research group: Joanna Bailey, Noah Collins, Mari Li Hsu, Carol Wan, Sidney Smith, Schekeva Hall, Silvia Mazzula, and Jessica Forsyth. I am indebted to the editorial professionals at John Wiley & Sons: Peggy Alexander, Isabel Pratt, and Linda Witzling, and the production personnel at Publications Development Company of Texas: Pam Blackmon and her staff. I cannot overlook my wife, Adrienne Millican Carter, who always had words of encouragement and reassurance when I wanted to give up. Thanks to all of you for your support. It helped make a lonely and solitary process feel more like a collaboration.

Contents

Contributors

Benjamin P. Bowser, PhD
California State University–Hayward
Hayward, California

Angela M. Byars-Winston, PhD
University of Wisconsin–Madison
Madison, Wisconsin

Susan Chavez Cameron, PhD
Howard University, School of
   Education
Washington, DC

Robert T. Carter, PhD
Teachers College, Columbia University
New York, New York

William R. Concepción, BA
Teachers College, Columbia University
New York, New York

Madonna G. Constantine, PhD
Teachers College, Columbia University
New York, New York

Catarina I. Costa, MSEd
Fordham University at Lincoln Center
New York, New York

Juris G. Draguns, PhD
Pennsylvania State University
University Park, Pennsylvania

Nadya A. Fouad, PhD
University of Wisconsin–Milwaukee
Milwaukee, Wisconsin

Jairo N. Fuertes, PhD, ABPP
Fordham University at Lincoln Center
New York, New York

Kathy A. Gainor, PhD
Montclair State University
Montclair, New Jersey

Janet E. Helms, PhD
Boston College, Lynch School of
   Education
Chestnut Hill, Massachusetts

Mindy Hersh, PsyD
Ohlone College
Fremont, California

Carla D. Hunter, MA
Teachers College, Columbia University
New York, New York

Farah A. Ibrahim, PhD
Oregon State University
Corvallis, Oregon

Sam D. Johnson Jr., PhD
Baruch College, City University of
    New York
New York, New York

Heather L. Juby, EdM
Teachers College, Columbia University
New York, New York

Kwong-Liem Karl Kwan, PhD
Purdue University
West Lafayette, Indiana

Eric L. Kohatsu, PhD
California State University
Los Angeles, California

Marie L. Miville, PhD
Teachers College, Columbia University
New York, New York

Lisa N. Mueller, MSEd
Fordham University at Lincoln Center
New York, New York

Paul Pedersen, PhD
University of Hawaii
Honolulu, Hawaii

Alex L. Pieterse, MA
Teachers College, Columbia University
New York, New York

P. Scott Richards, PhD
Brigham Young University
Provo, Utah

Timothy B. Smith, PhD
Brigham Young University
Provo, Utah

Caroline E. Shin, MS
University of Houston Counseling
    Center
Houston, Texas

Joy Stephens, MS
Ohio State University, Counseling and
    Consultation Services
Columbus, Ohio

Chalmer E. Thompson, PhD
Indiana University
Bloomington, Indiana

Joseph E. Trimble, PhD
Western Washington University
Bellingham, Washington

Anika K. Warren, PhD
Teachers College, Columbia University
New York, New York

Sherry K. Watt, PhD
University of Iowa
Iowa City, Iowa

Bryant Williams, MA
Teachers College, Columbia University
New York, New York

Leo Wilton, PhD
Binghamton University
Binghamton, New York

Christine J. Yeh, PhD
Teachers College, Columbia University
New York, New York

Uprooting Inequity and Disparities in Counseling and Psychology: An Introduction

Robert T. Carter

A visit to my office by Jennifer Simon of John Wiley & Sons one afternoon was both unexpected and welcomed. I have always felt positive toward Wiley since the publisher accepted my first book, *The Influence of Race and Racial Identity in Psychotherapy: Toward a Racially Inclusive Model* (Carter, 1995). I was not prepared for what she asked of me, nor did I think I could complete the project at the time. Ms. Simon, who has since left the company, asked if I would be willing to edit a reference handbook on cultural issues that would set the stage for research and scholarship for the coming decade. Editing a reference handbook would be, at the very least, a daunting task, and I could not envision how such a handbook could add to the existing volumes in the field of psychology. I begged off by asking for time to contemplate her request. I began to think about what was needed in the growing literature of cultural counseling and psychology.

I wondered what type of content would build both on the work of existing scholars and at the same time contribute a distinct and new perspective that did not currently exist in the field. I mulled over the request for several months, and during a subsequent visit, I heard myself saying that what seemed to be needed was a book that advanced the field beyond the focus on the needs of "ethnic minority" groups. It seems that my ideas and thoughts at the first meeting had been only electrical charges or impulses in my brain, and I was surprised by my own words. I went on to say, perhaps the field needed a concept- or construct-based volume that explored and discussed key and critical concepts common to the field of cultural counseling and psychology. But a volume that explored ideas alone without research seemed limited and insufficient. It seemed equally important to know what had been learned from research and scholarship regarding the key or critical concepts and constructs.

The result of our conversation was the notion of a handbook with two volumes, the first of which would be devoted to conceptual and theoretical concepts as well as research and scholarship associated with racial-cultural psychology. The second volume would address practitioner and training needs for guidance on emerging issues in our racially and culturally diverse society. The project in its conception was enormous and daunting; to bring it to fruition required the contributions of leading scholars and researchers as well as up-and-coming scholars and practice-based scholars. I was not sure at first if I could assemble such a group. As I review the list of contributors, I am honored and proud to have worked with such distinguished scholars and researchers. Some have given much to the field, and many have much more to offer. The ideas I have chosen to highlight in this *Handbook* focus on what I have come to call racial-cultural psychology.

Today, one can find many terms used to refer to issues of culture in psychology and other disciplines, such as diversity-sensitive, ethnocultural, cross-cultural, intercultural, working-across-cultures, counseling special populations, culture-specific psychotherapy, culturally different, the culturally diverse, transcultural psychiatry, multicultural, cultural diversity, and many others. Of these terms, we are probably most familiar with multicultural, cross-cultural, and cultural diversity. More often than not, the terms define cultural difference broadly to include a variety of group memberships. The various group memberships I call reference groups; others call them social identity groups. When terms like cultural diversity or multicultural are used, one might be referring to ethnicity, gender, social class, race, sexual orientation, age, or disability. It is possible for the speaker or writer to refer to all reference groups. For instance, when cross-cultural counseling competencies were introduced, defined, and described in the 1980s (Sue et al., 1982), *cross-cultural* was defined as any counseling interaction that involved any reference group difference between the client and the counselor. Thus, broad and encompassing terms are used today to address issues of various types of reference group differences. Because the terms *multicultural* and *cultural diversity* lack specificity, I find them confusing and hard to understand.

I have written about my confusion elsewhere (Carter & Qureshi, 1995) and proposed a model as a way to clarify what might be meant by the different terms. I identified assumptions about cultural difference that I thought were being overlooked and unstated and thus were hidden in the various terms used today. I briefly review the model here, in part to again clarify the tacit or underlying meaning associated with the use of terms such as multicultural and cultural diversity and also to indicate the conceptual foundation for my use of the race-based term *racial-cultural*.

The assumptive types presented here are adopted from the work that Qureshi and I completed in 1995 (Carter, 1995, 2000; Carter & Qureshi, 1995). We presented five assumptions that we argued were embedded in the various meanings used to define cultural differences: Universal, Ubiquitous, Traditional, Race-based, and Pan-national. It is important to point out the difference between basic assumptions and strategies used to write and teach about cultural difference. I believe that regardless of the strategies (i.e., approaches, content, and so forth) used, one works from basic and fundamental assumptions about the nature of cultural difference. It is possible for teaching or counseling strategies to be mistaken for one's basic assumptions or biases. The following description of the types of assumptions about cultural differences is intended to highlight basic beliefs, implied by terms such as cultural diversity or multicultural:

Universal—This assumption equates culture with individual differences. The essential assumption is that humans are alike and differ primarily as unique people. Therefore, only secondarily does our experience and identity derive from group memberships (e.g., ethnicity, race, gender). Culture (in terms of reference groups) is noted and understood as characteristics of that specific person. Much of traditional psychological and counseling theory and practice is guided by the Universal assumption of differences. The Universal approach takes a color-blind view of racial and cultural differences, wherein group differences are of little or no relevance.

Ubiquitous—This assumption holds that all differences associated with group membership(s) are salient. All forms of social or group identity are considered cultural. Culture can be a function of geography, income, gender, age, race, religion, ethnicity, and sexual orientation. The Ubiquitous approach contends that there is a fundamental cultural difference between a gay White male and a straight White male. The Ubiquitous assumption is prevalent in many of the definitions of cultural diversity and multicultural counseling and psychology. The view of difference as common experience or identity presumes that one's shared group membership cuts across dominant cultural group patterns. Thus, White or Asian or Black men and women share a culture (based on race) and at the same time are considered culturally different from one another due to their gender group membership.

Traditional—This (anthropological) assumption of cultural difference defines culture as deriving from a country with a common language, values, beliefs, rituals, and so forth. One is a member of a cultural group by birth and country influence. Central to beliefs about culture is common experience as a function of socialization and environment.

Race-based—This assumption holds that race is the primary form of culture in North America, that is, cultural groups are identified on the basis of race. People are classified into races by skin color, language, and physical features. Race-based theorists hold that the definitive aspects of culture, for example, cultural values (see Carter, 1991), vary ultimately according to psychologically (i.e., racial identity) and socially based racial categories. The Race-based approach assumes that the experience of belonging to a racial group transcends/supersedes all other experiences in the United States. Because race is the most visible of all "cultural differences" and because of the history of racial segregation and racism in the United States, race has been and continues to be the ultimate measure of social exclusion and inclusion.

Pan-national—This assumption views race in the global context as definitive of culture. The focus of this assumption about cultural difference is on the role of oppression and violence rendered by the legacy of colonialism and slavery primarily directed at people of Color throughout the world. Whites are viewed as the dominant group who reinforce their dominance through a culture and social structures that are based on denial, denigration, violence, and exploitation (Wallace & Carter, 2003).

The race as culture or race-based assumptive perspective is a more viable approach to understanding cultural differences because it is historically and sociopolitically based. Moreover, recent scholarship (e.g., Bell, 2004; Clark, Anderson, Clark, & Williams, 1999; DHHS, 2001, Williams & Williams-Morris, 2000), regarding employment, education, health, and political participation show that there continues to be gross disparities along racial lines wherein non-White people (regardless of ethnic background) fair far worse than Whites (regardless of the White person's ethnic group membership). This model of unstated assumptions is helpful, yet it is not clear why it is necessary. For much of American history, the basis of difference was assumed to be due to race and culture. How did the effort to address race, racism, and race relations in psychology and counseling and in American life become a focus on cultural diversity and multicultural issues? I articulate what I think race means in my chapter with Alex Pieterse. In essence, I, as well as many other scholars (Feagin, 2000; Sue, 2003), believe our society is and has been structured on the basis of racial group membership. In North America, notions and attitudes regarding race drive society's beliefs about people and their culture. Thus, we are socialized to think that people's abilities and access to institutions should be guided by attributes that are assigned because of their race and presumed culture.

Duckitt (1992) pointed out that between 1920 and the 1980s, much of psychological research directed at understanding prejudice was conducted during decades that were characterized by White domination of so-called backward people, a designation that many social scientists, including psychologists, used to justify White domination. During the later part of this period, psychologists recognized that White racism was a part of the structure of American society as a whole, not just in the South.

Prior to the 1950s, scholars considered non-White racial groups in North America to be less than civilized or devoid of culture. The view that non-Whites lacked culture was specifically directed at Blacks, although other racial groups were also targeted. Common beliefs of this period were that members of all non-White groups were unintelligent, lazy, cowardly, and immoral, primarily because of racial characteristics and unquestioned stereotypes ascribed to members of each group (Marger, 2000, 2002). Justification for their lower social status, in the form of economic restrictions and denial of education and civil rights, was based on commonly held beliefs that non-Whites were biologically and genetically inferior to Whites. Black people struggled in various ways during the 1920s through the 1960s to gain the rights that they earned in society. Blacks' efforts and struggle for racial justice gained national attention in the 1950s and 1960s, when some of the victories regarding racial equality came along with fierce White resistance against letting go of their power over other racial and cultural groups.

Blacks, after fighting and contributing to the war efforts at home and abroad during World War I and II, began to claim their rights as citizens, many who had moved from the South to the North between the 1900s and mid-century, started political, social, and civic organizations that led the fight for racial justice. The activism of the era set in motion the civil rights movement first in the South and then throughout the country. One of the first and most well-known victories was the

1954 *Brown v. Board of Education* Supreme Court decision that began the removal of legal segregation in the South but did not alter the less formal racially divisive structures in other parts of the country. In 1956, the Supreme Court struck down segregation on buses. Today, racial hostility is less often expressed openly, however, the separation continues in a different form—education and opportunity still are unequal for people of Color.

The 1960s was the decade in which the actions and changes of the 1950s were expanded through more direct confrontation in the form of civil disorder, like sit-ins at White-only lunch counters, riding interstate buses, and using the White-only waiting rooms and bathrooms combined with efforts to integrate schools. Much of the activism was met with physical attacks by White citizens. For instance, after one freedom ride—White and Black riders were attacked by a mob of Whites. It took some 400 federal marshals to restore order. The nature of racism was revealed with glaring clarity. It became harder for most Americans to deny its harsh reality. The historical march on Washington took place in 1963 and the activism led to the passage of the 1964 Civil Rights Act and the 1965 Voting Rights Act.

Social scientists, psychologists, and educators contributed to race relations in varied ways. For instance, Kenneth Clark's expert testimony helped in the *Brown v. Board of Education* case. There were three other significant reports issued in the 1960s that social scientists participated in producing. The Moynihan Report on the Black Family, The Coleman Report on Educational Equity, and the Kerner Commission Report on Civil Unrest in the Nations Cities (Jones, 1972).

All the reports were issued in the late 1960s. Two of the three were used to shape government policy and the third received less attention and response. The Moynihan Report on the Black Family set out the principles of cultural and social deficit models used to explain lack of social development on the part of Black people. According to the Moynihan Report, the Black family was in crisis and caught in a tangle of pathology because women headed many families. Thus, the Black family was unstable due to discrimination and prejudice. Yet, racial bias was not the focus of the report; rather it was the deprivation and loss of cohesion brought about by the female-headed families and the poor connection to mainstream cultural norms. Jones (1972) noted, "the general acceptance of [Moynihan's] point of view led many social scientists to argue that Black culture is no more than lower-class culture (p. 52)." Coleman, in his report on educational equity in public schools, argued for school integration because he found from his study that Black educational achievement could be enhanced if Blacks were in the same schools with White students. Thus, educational equity depended on Blacks being moved into schools with Whites since many of the Blacks schools and families had few resources. The resources at home seemed to matter most in educational achievement. So Blacks and members of other racial groups began to be accepted or bused to what were previously White-only schools and workplaces. Yet, in spite of the changes (busing and court orders), race-based educational inequity remains a feature of American society (Bell, 2004).

The influx of Blacks and Hispanics that entered American institutions presented some difficulty for counselors, educators, and psychologists who were accustomed to working with mostly White students and clients. In the late 1960s and 1970s, scholars led by Vontress (196) began to write about the counseling and psychological needs of Black and Hispanic students who were now present in colleges and universities, mental health clinics, and other institutions. The deficit models that characterized national policy dominated the early work of psychologists and counselors. The negative aspects of using White society and culture as the norm for standards of behavior, thought, and feelings was revealed by scholars like Vontress and led to a change in language. The language in psychology and counseling was first focused on cross-racial counseling or counseling minorities. Texts, journal articles, and courses for mental health professionals were presented on how to work with specific culturally disadvantaged groups like counseling Blacks and Hispanics and so on. But by the late 1970s, the language shifted from disadvantaged to culturally different.

The calls for equality and rights in the 1970s led scholars to argue that people of Color were not inferior or culturally disadvantaged, rather they were culturally different. The difference was not simply one based on skin-color, rather the cultural differences emerged from segregation and isolation due to custom and legal discrimination. Each group identified on the basis of race was segregated into their own communities and housing restrictions kept the groups isolated from the White mainstream. Historians argued that isolation in separate communities and neighborhoods facilitated the retention of each group's traditional cultural patterns as reflected in kinship networks, gender roles, cultural values, language systems, interpersonal styles, and communication systems. Some psychologists and educators argued that such differences were attributed to cultural disadvantage—a belief that focused blame on the victims of oppression (Harper & McFadden, 2003). But the 1960s ended with the release of the Kerner Commission Report that identified racism as a cause for non-White anger and lack of social and political progress. A recognized area of concern today is the writing of many scholars and professional associations' guidelines for dealing with racial and cultural differences (e.g., APA, 2001).

In 1968 Kerner noted that the country was heading toward "two nations one Black, one White" and that "White racism" was the major and most significant factor in the civil unrest that had erupted in the nation's cities. The view expressed in the report was a departure from the view of mainstream Americans who did not think their attitudes and behaviors were responsible for the unrest. Nor did they like the idea that they were called racists. Thus, the recommendations of the Kerner Commission, which were far reaching and suggested that racism be dismantled in most American institutions, were never implemented. Many called for the nation to accept responsibility for leaving Americans of Color behind and recommended that remedies be put in place to reverse the history of exclusion. But the focus of the nation was shifting to the war in Vietnam, antiwar protests, an economic recession, women's rights, and demands by other ethnic groups for "minority" status. Thus, systemic racism continues to be responsible for health and educational inequities in society. Many inequities contribute to poor mental health (DHHS, 2001).

The civil rights movement also stirred other groups' racial consciousness (e.g., Native Americans, Hispanics), and they joined Blacks in seeking redress to racial oppression and discrimination. Other groups also fought to shrug off the types of oppression that created limits for them. White ethnics (Italian, Irish, Polish, etc.), women (primarily White women), gays and lesbians, and the disabled began movements of their own.

The struggle for equality raised awareness about some of the truths regarding racism and race relations in North America. Psychologists, educators, counselors, and other social scientists began to document and write more openly about racism and its effects on individuals, groups, and society as a whole. Jones (1972) identified various forms of racism, such as individual, institutional, and cultural, that significantly contributed to mental health scholars' efforts to understand how race and racism affected mental health service provision and therapy.

In the 1970s, scholars in counseling and psychology focused more time and attention on the neglected needs of ethnic minorities and other non-White groups. But by the mid-1970s and early 1980s, there began to be a shift in language and terminology used in psychology and counseling, from reference to specific racial (deemed cultural groups) to terms like cross-cultural, counseling across cultures, and counseling the culturally different (Harper, 2003). Thus, by the 1980s, the cultural movement in psychology, counseling, and other disciplines was well underway. The culturally different emphasis initially did not include a larger range of differences; rather, its emphasis initially was on race as the primary source of cultural difference. In most articles and books, the race-as-culture emphasis focused on the specific needs of members of racial (sometimes called ethnic minority) groups.

By the 1990s, as scholars developed models of psychology and counseling based on the notion of cultural difference, the idea of counseling and helping relationships that were cross-cultural tended to be defined in terms of multiple sources of difference, such as gender and ethnicity. Cross-cultural became multicultural and came to include many aspects of difference—age, sexual orientation, religion, disability, and so on— each considered equal in importance. Thus, race has become one of many aspects of difference. Helms and Cook (1999) contend that terms such as culture, cultural diversity, and multicultural are substitutes for race and that the use of the terms disempowers historically disenfranchised Americans (Blacks or African Americans, Native Americans, Hispanics or Latinos, and Asians). It is because the terms refer to many social demographic groups "that they become virtually useless for explaining the ways in which the therapy process is influenced by racial or cultural factors" (p. 29). Moreover, the use of ambiguous language makes it easy to encourage acceptance of cultural pluralism of various types "without actually acknowledging it" (p. 29). In essence, Helms and Cook suggest that the terms are less threatening to Whites and allow all people to think of themselves in some way as an oppressed "minority." As happened in the 1970s and since that time, there are now many more oppressed groups who are making demands on limited economic, social, and political resources. Thus, racial-cultural groups who have been historically shut out of social access have to compete with one another for far fewer social, political, and economic resources.

I have chosen to define the focus of the *Handbook* as racial-cultural. It does not seem possible to address effectively the complexity of cultural differences when the sources of separation and subjugation in our society are treated as one of many factors. Race has been and is a central aspect of difference in our social system (Feagin, 2000). Moreover, I think it is imperative that race, ethnicity, and culture not be confused with one another nor be treated as social categories but as meaningful components of each person's psychological makeup. Moreover, the idea that race does not include other reference groups is misleading and inaccurate.

For those within a racial group who psychologically identify with that group and culture (others may identify with the dominant culture), there are variations and differences both group-based and psychologically based (i.e., racial, gender, ethnic, class identity) due to gender, socioeconomic class, religion, sexual orientation, and ableness. Our understanding of the reference groups is best informed through the lens of race and culture as defined above, given the central role race plays in our society. Only in this way will scholars and researchers be able to understand the various ways in which social class, gender, language, sexual orientation, and other aspects of one's identity interact and influence health and mental health.

THE ORGANIZATION AND OVERVIEW OF THE HANDBOOK

The perspective and core concepts of this volume were defined and explained to contributors in a letter that stated:

> I am going to ask you and all other contributors to follow the conceptual schema and overview of the book. The *Handbook* is intended to be one that focuses on Racial-Cultural Psychology, which in my view is a perspective on cultural difference that uses race as the context for understanding culture. However, it does not mean that one should focus on specific racial groups. Rather, the focus should be on how race, and through race, culture, affects psychological and social functioning. The conceptual idea of race is reflected in skin color, language, and physical features and its sociopolitical use. Ethnicity is thought of as one's country of origin and is loosely connected to one's heritage and family background. Culture is thought of as learned patterns through socialization.
>
> I recognize that it is ambitious of me to strive for cohesion of concepts and content for such a large and extensive work with many different authors; however, I am committed to trying to do so. I ask that you work with me in an effort to achieve coherence and consistency around these important constructs. In addition, I request that you use the conceptual schema outlined above with regard to race, culture, and ethnicity and that you use the racial-cultural frame for the development of your chapters. The chapters should be comprehensive, substantive reviews of the literature, including a focus for future inquiry in the specific area.

Not all contributors followed my instructions, as should be expected, but enough did. The use of the term *multicultural* was hard to eliminate, so some authors used it. I was pleased that so many joined me to produce excellent and thoughtful chapters for the *Handbook*.

Part I: Core Racial-Cultural Concepts, Ideas, and Theories

Volume One consists of 20 chapters and is divided into two parts. Part I is focused on core racial-cultural concepts, ideas, and theories in that contributors discuss the meaning of core concepts and constructs such as culture, ethnicity, and race and provide historical background and future directions.

In the opening chapter, Paul Pedersen places the development of theory in cultural psychology in the context of the disciplines of psychology and anthropology. What is of particular significance is the way he moves the reader from the origins of cultural psychology to its current place in psychology. He sheds light on the complexity of terminology and conceptual issues that evolved over time in psychology, cross-cultural psychology, and related disciplines.

Pedersen highlights that Western scholars have been taught to ignore and so underestimate the power of our cultural filters. He reminds us also of the power of what he calls the "force of multicultural issues" in psychology. He argues that a multicultural framework represents an expanding paradigm shift in psychology. He also shows us that just as the movement for racial justice and civil rights met considerable resistance, so does the effort to advance racial-cultural psychology. He identifies the source of resistance from mainstream psychologists, educators, and social scientists to a paradigm shift in psychology driven by racial-cultural scholars and researchers.

The chapter by Sam D. Johnson Jr. discusses the core concept of culture. He traces the development of the concept in anthropology through to its use in psychology. He points out that culture has many definitions that differ depending on one's focus. For instance, whether the focus is historical, setting group norms, establishing behavioral standards, or setting out psychological structure, the context shapes the definition. Thus, the concept, Johnson argues, lacks clarity and focus. For Johnson, culture as a concept is best understood as being shaped by our "context" and serves as the basis for communication. He argues that grasping the significance of context for culture and communication will clear some of the confusion and help us find focus in our effort to understand and define culture.

Heather L. Juby and William R. Concepción explore the origins of the concept "ethnicity." They explain how the construct has been defined in various social science disciplines, what the term means from various conceptual and disciplinary models, and its current usage. They also show the sources of ambiguity associated with the term *ethnicity* in psychology and other social science disciplines. The discussion of how the term's definitions have shifted and changed is particularly powerful. The historical and contextual uses of the term contributed to its shifting usage and meaning. Ethnicity has been related to ancestry, culture, and nations, among others. It has been used as a flexible and fluid construct depending on the theory in which it is used. What Juby and Concepción bring to our understanding of racial-cultural psychology is the manner in which other social sciences influence and have contributed to our ideas and conceptions. We see from their writing how our current use of ethnicity has been influenced by social, anthropological, economic, and other considerations. They remind us of the limitations of trying to understand complex concepts and constructs through the lens of one discipline. At the same time, the authors point to the resistance by scholars and practitioners in the mental health clinical and research areas to acknowledge ethnicity and its potential role in psychological health and distress. They argue that only by distinguishing ethnicity from race and culture can we advance our knowledge about how that aspect of identity can help and/or hinder one's life.

Robert T. Carter and Alex L. Pieterse discuss the meaning and significance of race from psychological and social frameworks. They trace the historical evolution of the concept of race and link its use and meaning to how the term has evolved. They argue that race is not the same as ethnicity for many reasons. They contend that it is important to distinguish the two concepts because race has a distinct meaning and attitudes connected to it. Ethnicity is clearly less visible and is not externally defined, as is the case with race. The authors present an analysis of how the ideas surrounding race have become manifested, over many centuries, into the subordination of groups identified as less desirable races. What stands out in their analysis is the consistent social stratification that is determined by race. Yet, the authors argue for the need to go beyond social and demographic uses of race. They argue for the importance of understanding race as a psychological construct that has significance for all racial groups. Racial identity (i.e., psychological orientation toward one's racial group membership) is presented as the future venue for understanding how racial dynamics affect people's lives.

Madonna G. Constantine and Leo Wilton place the role of racial-cultural concepts and theories into historical perspective. They show how such concepts undergird the multicultural or racial-cultural movement. In particular, the discussion of the foundational work of Black psychologists and their contribution to the formation of Black psychology, the work of Asian scholars who focused on cross-racial communication patterns, and the emergence of Black racial identity in the 1970s are highlighted and identified as providing the foundation on which cultural work today stands. Also in their chapter, we see the evolution of competence in cross-racial counseling to what is presently called multicultural counseling competency.

In their chapter on socialization across and within cultures, Christine J. Yeh and Carla D. Hunter provide a perspective on how ideas and lessons about who we are get communicated. They remind us that the self is constructed in a cultural context. They show that one of the major objectives of a society is to teach its members what it means to be a member. As we grow up in our family systems we learn what is important and what is not; it is in this process that self is formed. Yeh and Hunter discuss the literature on the cultural influences on the socialization process and point out that depending on the values and norms of a culture, self may take on many forms, a reality not often recognized or acknowledged in Western psychology and social institutions. We assume our Western notion of individualism is universal, a belief that is shown to be false. Moreover, we learn that we need to broaden our notion of self as the single, unique individual to one that includes multiple aspects of self that are relational and constructed from situation to situation.

The next two chapters discuss some aspect of psychologically based racial-cultural identity development. Madonna G. Constantine, Sherry K. Watt, Kathy A. Gainor, and Anika K. Warren illustrate the impact of racial-cultural theories and describe how the theories and research that evolved from them influenced the development of other identity models for various social groups. They summarize the theories and show how other group-based models were fashioned after the race-based theories of William Cross and the research of Janet E. Helms and her colleagues (see Helms, 1990). Models of biracial, ethnic, womanist, gay and lesbian, and social class identity are described.

Kwong-Liem Karl Kwan's chapter on racial salience of racial-ethnic identity development explores the centrality of race and racial experience. He compares and contrasts race and ethnicity and notes how physical features play a prominent role in identity issues. He defines and describes the salience of race in social policy and demographic categories and shows how stereotypes come from racial concepts. He also addresses how racial stereotypes affect psychological explanations of cultural difference.

Timothy B. Smith and P. Scott Richards shift the focus to the role of spiritual and religious issues in racial-cultural psychology and psychotherapy. They note that religion and spiritual beliefs have been ignored in psychology and argue for greater inclusion of religious and spiritual experiences in racial-cultural psychology and practice.

Part II: Critical Issues in Racial-Cultural Research, Measurement, and Ethics

The second part of Volume One, which is focused on research in racial-cultural psychology, opens with a chapter by Juris G. Draguns. Draguns revisits the history of anthropology as it relates to understanding human behavior. He does so by examining and presenting research regarding human behavior and its cultural context and how researchers have defined culture. He shows how research traditions have evolved and compares and contrasts etic (universal) and emic (culture-specific) research paradigms; more important, he shows what type of knowledge has come from the various studies and research traditions. The chapter is an excellent review of research in racial-cultural psychology and provides a strong foundation for Part II.

Benjamin P. Bowser examines the research on socialization and places it in a cultural framework. He reviews the way social scientists have studied socialization and indicates how race and culture have been considered or ignored in the psychological and cultural literature. What is important about his review is the integration of class, culture, and race in his analysis of research on socialization.

As people in society grow up or enter the country they must adapt to the demands and expectations of the occupational and cultural features of the dominant mainstream American institutions. Three chapters address different aspects of life in our society, all of which have important implications for mental and physical health. The areas addressed are work, acculturation, and what happens to people who seek mental health services.

Eric L. Kohatsu demonstrates that as people need to find ways to navigate the institutions of the society they also must learn the language and ways of the dominant racial-cultural group to be accepted into the formal or informal structures of the society. He presents an analysis of the way scholars and researchers have tried to understand acculturation. He argues for the development of multidimensional models and measures of acculturation and reviews what we know from research about specific racial-cultural groups' acculturation experiences and processes.

Nadya A. Fouad and Angela M. Byars-Winston focus on the role of work in people's lives. They review the occupational and cultural literature to show what is known about racial-cultural people's experiences as they encounter the world of work. In their summary of the theory and research on vocational psychology, they show what we know and the possibilities for further research and theory development regarding work and learning for nondominant racial-cultural group people.

As people negotiate the stresses and strains of everyday life, they may need to seek mental health services. It is important to know what research tells us about what happens to racial-cultural people when they receive psychological services and to know if therapy is effective. Jairo N. Fuertes, Catarina I. Costa, Lisa N. Mueller, and Mindy Hersh report on the state of psychotherapy research as it pertains to the process and outcome of mental health practice. In their meta-analysis of the literature, it becomes clear that many scholars and researchers still do not include or incorporate the racial-cultural contexts and experiences of non-White people as they study what happens to people in therapy (process) and what occurs as a result of therapy (outcome). Although much is written about the effectiveness of psychotherapy, that knowledge is based on the experiences of one racial-cultural group. Scholars and researchers appear to make universal assumptions about how what they find apply to members of other racial-cultural groups.

Next, Chalmer E. Thompson, Caroline E. Shin, and Joy Stephens review the research literature on race and find that for more than 30 years race has been studied comparatively, absent theory and for the most part indirectly. These authors contend that the tendency to confuse or deny race while using other characteristics is partly to blame for the state of the research. When theory was used to study race, the majority used models of acculturation, cultural mistrust, and racial identity.

Marie L. Miville sheds light on research regarding biracial identity. Her chapter reveals the state of knowledge in an area of increased interest given the changes in public policy regarding racial categories (e.g., census options to identify more than one race). The research literature is growing and, as Milville points out, is in need of greater methodological rigor. Some believe that interviews are the best method with which to study biracial people's experiences, yet there are limits to what can be learned from this method. She points out that multiple methods would serve researchers' and scholars' interest in advancing knowledge about biracial identity issues and experiences.

Joseph E. Trimble focuses on issues of measurement in racial-cultural psychology, with some emphasis on racial and ethnic identity instruments. His review is broad in scope and touches on many instruments. One central theme is the role of the person's perception in constructing his or her identity. His discussion of cultural equivalence in measurement should set the stage for future research in the field. He argues that researchers should not rely on conventional and traditional psychometric strategies.

Janet E. Helms presents a meta-analyses of White racial identity studies in which she examines how issues of scale reliability and validity are dealt with in most studies. Central to the chapter is the discussion of a source of criticism and concern by many researchers of racial-cultural instruments: how to understand the meaning of reliability and validity of racial identity scales in particular and racial-cultural measures in general. One main point she raises is that researchers overlook the characteristics of samples in interpreting the reliability and validity of instruments. Also, researchers minimize evidence for validity and behave as if reliability is more important than validity. She reminds us of the significance of validity and shows us how to assess it from our research.

Farah A. Ibrahim and Susan Chavez Cameron outline critical issues relating to ethical practices in conducting racial-cultural research. The authors remind us of the harm done by various researchers and the numerous ethnical violations that have occurred over time in communities of Color. We learn about the current standards for ethical research and the limits of the standards currently in place. These writers offer recommendations to future and current researchers about how they can work in ways that respect and honor racial-cultural people and communities.

In the final chapter, Robert T. Carter, Alex L. Pieterse, and Bryant Williams summarize the central themes from the chapters in Volume I and highlight some of the common points raised by the contributors. They also show that the authors are making a call or demand to the profession to do a better job of capturing the human experience by lessening the biases inherent in the use of a mono-racial-cultural framework to comprehend human experience.

The *Handbook* fulfills the vision that the contributors and editor had for the project. The chapters shape and direct scholars and researchers thinking about racial-cultural psychology, and the contributors set a clear agenda for research and scholarship for the coming decades. The *Handbook* will be of value to mental and health professionals as well as educators in disciplines where race or culture is the topic of interest. Furthermore, the *Handbook* can be used in advanced training and course instruction across the social science disciplines in an effort to increase thoughtful consideration of race and culture.

REFERENCES

American Psychological Association. (2003). Guidelines on multicultural education, training, research, practice, and organizational change for psychologists. *American Psychologists, 58*(5), 377–402.

Bell, D. (2004). Silent Covenants: Brown v. Board of Education and the unfilled hopes for racial reform. New York, NY: Oxford University Press.

Clark, R., Anderson, N. B., Clark, V. R., & Williams, D. R. (1999). Racism as a stressor for African Americans: A biopsychosocial model. *American Psychologist, 54*, 805–816.

Carter, R. T. (1991). Cultural values: A review of empirical research and implications for counseling. *Journal of Counseling and Development, 70*, 164–173.

Carter, R. T. (1995). *The influence of race and racial identity in psychotherapy.* New York: Wiley.

Carter, R. T. (2000). Reimagining race in education: A new paradigm from psychology. *Teachers College Record, 102*(5), 864–896.

Carter, R. T., & Qureshi, A. (1995). A typology of philosophical assumptions in multicultural counseling and training. In J. Ponterotto, M. Casas, L. Suzuki, & C. Alexander (Eds.), *Handbook of multicultural counseling* (pp. 239–262). Newbury Park, CA: Sage.

Duckitt, J. (1992). Psychology and prejudice: A historical analysis and integrative framework. *American Psychologist, 47,* 1182–1193.

Feagin, J. R. (2000). *Racist America.* New York, NY: Routledge Press.

Harper, F. D. (2003). Background: Concepts and history. In F. D. Harper & J. McFadden (Eds.), *Culture and counseling: New approaches* (pp. 1–19). Boston: Allyn & Bacon.

Helms, J. E. (1990). *Black and White racial identity: Theory, research, and practice.* Westport, CT: Greenwood Press.

Helms, J. E. (1996). Toward a methodology for measuring and assessing racial as distinguished from ethnic identity. In G. R. Sodowsky & J. C. Impara (Eds.), *Multicultural assessment in counseling and clinical psychology* (pp. 143-192). Lincoln, NE: Buros Institute of Mental Measurements.

Helms, J. E., & Cook, D. A. (1999). *Using race and culture in counseling and psychotherapy.* Boston: Allyn & Bacon.

Jones, J. M. (1972). *Prejudice and racism.* New York: McGraw-Hill.

Marger, M. (2000). *Race and ethnic relations: American and global perspectives* (5th ed.). Belmont, CA: Wadsworth.

Marger, M. (2002). *Race and ethnic relations: American and global perspectives* (6th ed.). Belmont, CA: Wadsworth.

Sue, D. W. (2003).*Overcoming our racism: The journey to liberation.* San Francisco, CA: Jossey-Bass.

Sue, D. W., Bernier, J. B., Durran, M., Feinberg, L., Pedersen, P., Smith, E., et al. (1982). Position paper: Cross-cultural counseling competencies. *Counseling Psychologist, 10,* 45–52.

U.S. Department of Health and Human Service. (2001). *Mental health: Culture, race, and ethnicity—A supplement to mental health: A report of the surgeon General.* Rockville, MD: U.S. Department of Health and Human Services, Substance Abuse and Mental Health services Administration, Center for Mental Health Services.

Wallace, B. C., & Carter, R. T. (Eds.). (2003). *Understanding and dealing with violence: A multicultural approach.* Thousand Oaks, CA: Sage.

Williams, D. R., & Williams-Morris, R. (2000). Racism and mental health: An African American experience. *Ethnic Health, 5,* 243–268.

PART I

Core Racial-Cultural Concepts, Ideas, and Theories

CHAPTER 1

The Importance of Cultural Psychology Theory for Multicultural Counselors

Paul Pedersen

The psychological study of culture has conventionally assumed that there was a fixed state of mind whose observation was obscured by cultural distortions. The underlying assumption is that there is a single universal definition of normal behavior from the psychological perspective. A contrasting anthropological position assumed that cultural differences were clues to divergent attitudes, values, or perspectives that were different across cultures, based on culturally specific perspectives. The anthropological perspective assumed that different groups or individuals had somewhat different definitions of normal behavior resulting from their unique cultural context. Anthropologists have tended to take a relativist position when classifying and interpreting behavior across cultures. Psychologists, by contrast, have linked social characteristics and psychological phenomena with minimum attention to the different cultural viewpoints. When counseling psychologists have applied the same interpretation to the same behavior regardless of the cultural context, cultural bias has resulted (Pedersen, 1997, 2000a).

Try to imagine a dimension with conventional psychology anchoring the extreme end of the scale on one end and conventional anthropology anchoring the extreme other end. The area between these two extremes is occupied by a variety of theoretical positions that tend to favor one or the other perspective in part but not completely. While there is a great deal of controversy about the exact placement of these theoretical positions, there is a tendency to place cross-cultural psychology toward the side of conventional psychology and social constructivism toward the side of conventional anthropology. Cultural psychology is generally perceived to be approximately in the middle, acknowledging its debt to both anthropology and psychology. This chapter examines the features of cultural psychology relative to the other alternatives.

Counseling and therapy have a history of protecting the status quo against change, as perceived by minority cultures (i.e., racial minorities, women, and those who perceive themselves as disempowered by the majority). These attitudes are documented in scientific racism and Euro-American ethnocentrism (D. W. Sue & Sue, 1999). Cultural differences were explained by some through a "genetic deficiency" model that promoted the superiority of dominant cultures. This was matched to a "cultural deficit" model that described minorities as deprived or disadvantaged by their culture. Minorities in the United States were underrepresented among professional counselors and therapists, the topic of culture was trivialized at professional meetings, minority views were underrepresented in the research literature, and, consequently, the counseling profession was discredited among minority populations because they viewed counseling as a tool to maintain the differences between those who had power and access to resources and those who did not.

CULTURAL PSYCHOLOGIES

Adamopoulos and Lonner (2001) trace the connection between culture and psychology as a professional field back to Wilhelm Wundt's writing on Volkerpsychologie. Since that time, a stream of psychological research has focused mostly on the psychologized "first world" of Western-based psychology (Moghaddam, 1987), with less attention to the psychology of the rest of the world. Psychological research in other countries served merely to extend the variation and generalizability of these original psychological perspectives as the function of cross-cultural psychology (Berry, Poortinga, Segall, & Dasen, 1992). This involved (1) selecting a psychological principle, test, or model; (2) testing it to see if the pattern could be generalized; and (3) discovering factors unique to the new cultural context. Other cultures are treated as independent variables, assuming that cultures cannot be manipulated. The central task of cross-cultural psychology was the search for psychological universals. While cross-cultural psychology has focused on the objective study of non-Western "others" and cultural anthropology has moved away from any objective definition of culture, the field of cultural psychology has emerged as a combination of these other two extremes. Jahoda and Krewer (1997) provide the best comprehensive overview of historical background in the study of culture and psychology as an emerging field. As the field of psychology has spread around the world, this diversification has continued to increase and develop.

This chapter focuses primarily on cultural psychology charting the most promising future direction in the study of culture and psychology. J. G. Miller (1997) provides the best single source for an overview of cultural psychology as an emerging field in psychology by contrasting it to cross-cultural psychology. Cultural psychology may focus on many different cultures and may even depend on empirical methods but still be in the tradition of cultural psychology. On the other hand, other psychological research may focus on one culture, using ethnographic techniques, but be in the tradition of cross-cultural psychology:

> The dominant stance within cultural psychology is to view culture and psychology as mutually constitutive phenomena, i.e., as phenomena which make up each other or are integral to each other. In such a view, it is assumed that culture and individual behavior cannot be understood in isolation yet are also not reducible to each other. Such a stance contrasts with the tendency, particularly in early work in cross-cultural psychology, for culture and psychology to be understood as discrete phenomena, with culture contextualized as an independent variable that impacts on the dependent variable of individual behavior. (p. 88)

Harry Triandis is probably the foremost spokesperson for cross-cultural psychology and Richard A. Shweder is probably the foremost spokesperson for cultural psychology.

Cultural psychology, by contrast, has no clear organizational or methodological structure, making it difficult to tell where cross-cultural psychology ends and cultural psychology begins. Cultural psychology is less goal-directed in its identity and more broadly ecumenical in conceptualizing or conducting research. J. G. Miller (1997) describes the core perspective of cultural psychology as the belief that culture and individual behavior are inseparable components. Cross-cultural psychology by contrast understands culture and psychology as clearly separate, where culture is the independent variable that changes the dependent variable of individual behavior. Shweder (1990) goes so far as to describe traditional cross-cultural theory as just another branch of mainstream, logico-empirical psychology.

Social constructionism shares many aspects with cultural psychology. This perspective treats psychological processes exclusively as cultural phenomena. Features common to social constructionism and cultural psychology are a focus on the importance of cultural meanings in psychology, the role of cultural communication in the origin of ideas, the need for relativistic views, and a focus on psychological diversity. "The argument is made that cultural meanings, as expressed in cultural symbols and as embodied in cultural practices, form an essential source of patterning of human psychology" (J. G. Miller, 1997, p. 94). A core assumption of social constructionism is that psychology exists as a product of culturally based discourse rather than as the study of internal processes of the individual. All knowledge can be understood only through cultural meanings and practices, rejecting the need for a concept of an independent "self." To this extent, social constructionism is more radical toward anthropology than other versions of cultural psychology.

Psychological anthropology provides still another theoretical basis through anthropological investigations that use psychological concepts and methods. This perspective recognizes the mutual relevance of anthropology and psychology both from a methodological perspective and a conceptual perspective (Campbell & Naroll, 1972). Psychological anthropology has sponsored research on culture and dreams, culture and mental illness, cognitive anthropology, development of children, innovations in field research, and many other culture-centered orientations (Adamopoulos & Lonner, 2001).

INDIGENOUS PSYCHOLOGIES

Another orientation closely related to cultural psychology has evolved into the field of indigenous psychologies, or the indigenization of psychology. While they do not seek to abandon scientific objectivity, the experimental method, and the search for universals, adherents to this orientation contend that a truly rigorous science needs to be grounded in the indigenous human perspective of each cultural context, a perspective shared by cultural psychology. Culture is seen not as an independent variable but as the property of individuals interacting with their indigenous environment (Kim & Berry, 1993). For example, Yang (1995) conceptualizes the Chinese social orientation in two ways, first as a system of social-psychological interactions and second as a pattern of inclinations or "natural" tendencies based on past experience. This interaction between the person and the environment is demonstrated in the tension between autonomous and homonomous tendencies, each of which may be strong or weak. Four psychological perspectives emerge from the interaction of autonomous and honomomous trends: (1) strong conflict when the two perspectives clash, (2) social orientation when the homonomous trend dominates, (3) individual orientation when the autonomous trend dominates, and (4) weak conflict when neither trend dominates.

Family orientation, rather than the individual, constitutes the core of Chinese society, in contrast to Western cultures:

> The Chinese people simply generalize or extend their familistic experiences and habits acquired in the family to other groups so that the latter may be regarded as quasi familial organizations. Chinese familism (or familistic collectivism), as generalized to other social organizations, may be named generalized familism or pan familism. (Yang, 1995, p. 23)

This family perspective is significantly different from Western psychology's focus on the scientific study of individual behavior.

Yang (1999) had the dream of turning Western psychology, inappropriate to Chinese society, into a genuinely indigenous Chinese psychology. Yang describes the consequences of imposing Western psychology on non-Western cultures:

> What has been created via this highly Westernized research activity is a highly Westernized social science that is incompatible with the native cultures, peoples and phenomena studied in non-Western societies. The detrimental over-dominance of Western social sciences in the development of corresponding sciences in non-Western societies is the outcome of a worldwide academic hegemony of Western learning in at least the last hundred years. (p. 182)

Liu and Liu (1999) point out that the Eastern focus on interconnectedness is a more difficult concept to pin down than the Western search for truth because it involves synthesizing opposites, contradictions, paradox, and complex patterns that resembles the dynamic self-regulating process of complexity theory: "In Eastern traditions of scholarship, what is valued most is not truth. In broad outline, the pursuit of objective knowledge is subordinate to the quest for spiritual interconnectedness" (p. 10).

Yang (1997) describes his thinking as it evolves toward understanding North American psychology as its own kind of indigenous psychology, developing out of European intellectual traditions but much influenced by American society. Yang has developed a list of "seven nos" that a Chinese psychologist should avoid so that her or his research can become indigenous:

1. Do not habitually or uncritically adopt Western psychological concepts, theories, and methods.

2. Do not overlook Western psychologists' important experiences in developing their concepts, theories, and methods.

3. Do not reject useful indigenous concepts, theories, and methods developed by other Chinese psychologists.

4. Do not adopt any cross-cultural research strategy with a Western-dominant imposed etic or pseudo-etic approach.

5. Do not use concepts, variables, or units of analysis that are too broad or abstract.

6. Do not think through research problems in terms of English or any other foreign language.

7. Do not conceptualize academic research in political terms, that is, do not politicize research.

Along with the "seven nos," Yang also suggests 10 "yes" assertions to guide psychologists in a more positive direction:

1. Tolerate vague or ambiguous conditions and suspend decisions as long as possible in dealing with conceptual, theoretical, and methodological problems until something indigenous emerges in one's phenomenological field.

2. Be a typical Chinese when functioning as a researcher, letting Chinese ideas be reflected in the research.

3. Take into careful consideration the psychological or behavioral phenomenon to be studied and its concrete specific setting.

4. Consider the details of a behavior and its context before applying a Western conceptual theory, method, or tool.

5. Give priority to the study of culturally unique psychological and behavioral phenomena when studying Chinese people.

6. Make it a rule to begin any research with a thorough immersion into the natural setting.

7. Investigate, if possible, both the specific content (or structure) and the involved process (or mechanism).

8. Let research be based on the Chinese intellectual tradition rather than Western intellectual traditions.

9. Study not only the traditional aspects or elements but also modern applications.

10. Study not only the psychological functioning of ancient Chinese and relationships but contemporary Chinese people as well.

Chinese indigenous psychologists have worked to adapt Americanized individualism to make it applicable in both the Western individualistic and the Asian collectivist context. David Ho (1999) uses the term "relational counseling" to describe the uniquely Asian indigenous perspective based on a relational self in the Confucian tradition:

This relational conception takes full recognition of the individual's embeddedness in the social network. The social arena is alive with many actors interacting directly or indirectly with one another in a multiplicity of relationships. It is a dynamic field of forces and counter-forces in which the stature and significance of the individual actor appears to be diminished. Yet, selfhood is realized through harmonizing one's relationship with others. (p. 2)

The process of indigenizing psychology has become a powerful force for psychological change in counseling (Kagitcibasi, 1996). Western counseling and psychology have promoted the separated self as the healthy prototype across cultures, making counseling and psychology part of the problem, rather than part of the solution, through an emphasis on selfishness and lack of commitment to the group. Sinha (1997) describes the indigenizing perspective as advocating that (1) psychological knowledge is not to be externally imposed, (2) psychology needs to address everyday activities outside experimentally contrived laboratories, (3) behavior is best understood from the local frame of reference, and (4) psychology must reflect the reality of its sociocultural context. "The ultimate goal of indigenous psychology is the development of a universal psychology that incorporates all indigenous (including Western) psychologies. . . . It only asserts that panhuman psychological principles and theories cannot be taken for granted or assumed merely because they are developed in the West" (p. 160). Indigenization may be one step toward discovering true universals in the converging patterns of psychology, culture, and counseling (Kim & Berry, 1993).

To a great extent, conventional psychology carried the influence of European and American cultures, where it was "invented," particularly with its preference for an individualistic perspective. Cooper and Denner (1998) review the literature linking culture and psychology as they both strengthen and challenge the validity of psychological theories and their applications. They examine seven theoretical perspectives: individualism-collectivism, ecological systems, cultural-ecological systems, social identity, ecological and sociocultural systems, structure-agency, and multiple worlds. Although there is complementarity across theories, there are also distinctly separate viewpoints.

We argue, first, that bringing concepts of culture into psychological theories is an abstract, disputed and inherently unresolvable process, yet that doing so is crucial to both social science and policy in multicultural societies, particularly democracies. Second, we argue that explicit interdiciplinary, international and intergenerational discussions of culture and psychological processes—addressing issues of theories and application—advance global, national and local goals. (p. 563)

These complementary systems are evolving toward an understanding of culture in human development that neither overemphasizes nor ignores the individual or the group. Cultures are seen as developing systems of individuals, relationships, social contexts, and institutions. Theories link culture and psychological process as distinct but also complementary, similar but also different in the global context.

Oskamp (2000) describes how environmental psychology has challenged Westernized/modernized assumptions. To prevent an ecological disaster, urgent changes are needed in Westernized values that became popular in the nineteenth and twentieth centuries and that sponsored destructive attitudes and lifestyles. Howard (2000) identifies nine "killer attitudes" based on Westernized psychological values and assumptions:

1. Consumption produces happiness.
2. We don't need to think/worry about the future.
3. Short-term rewards and punishments are more important than long-term goals.
4. Growth is good.
5. We should all get as much of life's limited resources as we can.
6. Keeping the price of energy low is a good thing.
7. If it ain't broke, don't fix it.
8. We don't need to change behavior until science proves it necessary.
9. We will always find new solutions in time to expand limited resources.

The dangers of these dominant-culture values have led psychologists to better understand the values of other, contrasting cultures. For example, D. T. Miller (1999) examined the self-interest motive and the self-confirming role of assuming that:

> a norm exists in Western cultures that specifies self-interest both is and ought to be a powerful determinant of behavior. This norm influences people's actions and opinions as well as the accounts they give for their actions and opinions. In particular, it leads people to act and speak as though they care more about their material self-interest than they do. (p. 1053)

The more powerful this norm of self-interest is assumed to be, the more self-fulfilling psychological evidence will be found to support that premise.

As Stanley Sue (1999) points out, the emphasis in psychological research is more on internal than external validity. Internal validity leads to causal inference, whereas external validity estimates the degree to which results can be generalized. The lack of external validity may render findings meaningless, and the emphasis on internal validity has led to domination of majority/dominant culture values in textbook psychology. Lewis-Fernandez and Kleinman (1994) and Berry et al. (1992) document culture-bound assumptions of egocentricity of the self, mind/body dualism, and the view of culture as a superimposition on otherwise "knowable biological reality." There is a consistent pattern of the cultural encapsulation of textbook psychology by Wrenn (1962, 1985), Albee (1994), Samuda (1998), Paniagua (in press), D. W. Sue and D. Sue (1999, 2003), and Pedersen (2000a).

Psychological factors that result from socialization within any culture and that influence diagnosis are of particular interest because culturally based psychological factors affect perceptions and attributions used in diagnosis. To function appropriately, culture-centered health professionals need to be aware of their own and their clients' culturally learned assumptions.

Culture is complex but not chaotic. There are patterns that make it possible to manage cultural complexity. The functional precursors of mental health services have been documented in a wide variety of cultures, although usually not differentiated as separate counseling specialties. The labels "counseling," "therapy," and "human services" are relatively new, but the functions described by those labels have a long history, going back to the beginning of recorded relationships.

MULTICULTURALISM AS A FOURTH FORCE

We are only beginning to understand the ways that psychology has been changed in this decade (Mahoney & Patterson, 1992) in what has come to be called a paradigm shift. The underlying assumptions about psychology are moving from a monocultural to a multicultural basis, with profound consequences for counseling. The old rules of psychology focused on dissonance reduction. The new rules focus on the tolerance of ambiguity (Pedersen, 1998).

Smith, Harré, and Van Langenhove (1995) contrast the new with the old paradigm. The new paradigm emphasizes (1) understanding and describing the context more than just measuring variables; (2) predicting consequences, not just causes; (3) social significance, not just statistical significance; (4) language and discourse, not just numbers; (5) holistic perspectives, not just atomistic trivia; (6) complex interacting particulars, not simplistic universals; and (7) subjectively derived meaning, not objectively imposed meanings. Mahoney and Patterson (1992) describe the new paradigm as a cognitive revolution with an interdisciplinary perspective in which human behavior is described as reciprocal and interactive rather than linear and unidirectional. Wrightsman (1992) describes the new paradigm as beginning with George Kelly's personal construct theory, based on collectivistic and non-Western indigenous psychologies.

The newly popular methods of chaos theory and complexity theory in the hard, and more recently, in the soft sciences provide alternatives to the "linear, reductionistic thinking that has dominated science since the time of Newton—and that has now gone about as far as it can go in addressing the problems of our modern world" (Waldrop, 1992, p. 13). Butz (1997) borrows from chaos theory to explain how the self organizes complex experiences into coherent thought. Self is viewed as the coherence or integrity of each individual's complex cultural experiences. Culture provides us with transitory models of our self-identity, part of which is always changing and part of which remains the same. The self is dynamic like other self-organizing, nonlinear, and steady states, where stability becomes a stage of the system's developmental process. Culture becomes the perfect metaphor for understanding this new complex concept of self and its modern applications to culture and psychology (Pedersen, 2000b).

Thompson, Ellis, and Wildavsky (1990) describe cultural theory as providing the basis of a new perspective, dimension, or force in psychology and counseling:

> Social science is steeped in dualism: culture and structure, change and stability, dynamics and statics, methodological individualism and collectivism, voluntarism and determinism, nature and nurture, macro and micro, materialism and idealism, facts and values, objectivity and subjectivity, rationality and irrationality, and so forth. (p. 21)

Although these dualisms are convenient for analysis of behavior, they too often obscure how phenomena are interdependent. Needless controversies result from taking one side of the dualism and making that most important.

The basis of cultural theory is that we do not need to choose between the opposite ends of a dimension; indeed, we need to resist that temptation as overly simplistic. People can be both similar and different at the same time through the complementarity of quantum thinking models. Shore (1996) describes how cultural models are empirical analogues of society, understood as knowledge where the public and private models are combined in patterns of shared perspective.

There is considerable resistance to characterizing multiculturalism as a "fourth force." Tart (1975) claimed that transpersonal psychology was the fourth force in psychology, and transpersonal psychologists sometimes resent the movement to describe multiculturalism as a fourth force. Stanley Sue (1998) identified other sources of resistance to the term "multiculturalism" as a fourth force:

1. Some see multiculturalism as competing with already established theories of psychology in ways that threaten the conventional professions of counseling and psychology. However, making culture central strengthens rather than weakens conventional psychological theory.

2. The terms *multiculturalism* and *diversity* are closely associated with affirmative action, quotas, civil rights, discrimination, reverse discrimination, racism, sexism, political correctness, and other highly emotional terms. However, the competition for limited resources in a global context is necessarily controversial and emotional, and multiculturalism serves only to increase the visibility of these emotional factors.

3. To the extent that multiculturalism is connected with postmodernism, the arguments against postmodernism as a valid theory are also applied to multiculturalism. However, there is some evidence that postmodernism, by challenging conventional theories and methods, has at least some validity.

4. Those favoring a universalist perspective contend that the same practices of counseling and therapy apply equally to all populations without regard to cultural differences. However, both the similarities and the differences across cultures must be acknowledged for an accurate perspective.

5. Others contend that there are no accepted standards for describing multiculturalism as a theory in practice and that it is too loosely defined to be taken seriously. However, the work of defining multicultural standards and multicultural theory is in the process of being developed.

6. There are no measurable competencies for multicultural applications of counseling or adequate standards of practice. However, competencies are currently being tested, refined, modified, and validated.

7. Multiculturalism is too complicated and it would be unrealistic to expect counselors to attend to such a range of factors simultaneously. However, a complex perspective of reality would seem preferable to an artificial simplistic perspective, at least as an aspirational goal of counselors.

8. More research is needed on multicultural competencies, standards, methods, and approaches because the amount of research on cultural variables has grown by geometric proportions in the past 10 years.

9. Multicultural standards cannot be incorporated into the counseling profession until all groups have been included. However, the purpose of training counselors in multiculturalism is so that biased tests and theories can be interpreted in ways that are helpful to culturally different clients from the full range of cultural groups.

10. Some believe that multiculturalism represents reverse racism and quotas and is anti-White. Clearly, the transition from a monocultural to a multicultural perspective is likely to result in some trauma as power is redistributed according to fair and equitable standards.

Stanley Sue (1998) pointed out the tendency to misunderstand or misrepresent the notion of multiculturalism and the dangers of that misunderstanding. Because all behaviors are learned and displayed in a particular cultural context, accurate assessment, meaningful understanding, and appropriate intervention require attention to the client's cultural or, perhaps better yet, multicultural context. All psychological service providers share the same ultimate goal of accurate assessment, meaningful understanding, and appropriate intervention, regardless of cultural similarities or differences.

A CULTURE-CENTERED ALTERNATIVE APPROACH

Because a culture-centered perspective is complicated, it makes research, teaching, and direct service more inconvenient, which has caused cultural differences to be overlooked or viewed negatively. The monocultural perspective of psychology has served the purposes of a dominant culture in many specific ways (Gielen, 1994). Counseling in particular has often been guilty of protecting the status quo against change. With the increase in political activism, affirmative action, and articulate special interest groups, the cultural biases of conventional psychology have been illuminated. This illumination will ultimately increase the accurate, meaningful, and appropriate competence of psychologists, but only after the painful process of reexamining our underlying culturally biased assumptions has occurred.

A culture-centered perspective that applies cultural theories to the counseling process is illustrated in the book on multicultural theory (MCT) by D. W. Sue, Ivey, and Pedersen (1996). This approach is based on six propositions that demonstrate the fundamental importance of a culture-centered perspective:

1. Each Western or non-Western theory represents a different worldview.

2. The complex totality of interrelationships in the client-counselor experiences and the dynamic changing context must be the focus of counseling, however inconvenient that may become.

3. A counselor's or client's racial/cultural identity will influence how problems are defined and dictate or define appropriate counseling goals or processes.

4. The ultimate goal of a culture-centered approach is to expand the repertoire of helping responses available to counselors.

5. Conventional roles of counseling are only some of the many alternative helping roles available from a variety of cultural contexts.

6. MCT emphasizes the importance of expanding personal, family, group, and organizational consciousness in a contextual orientation.

As these MCT propositions are tested in practice, they will raise new questions about competencies of multicultural awareness, knowledge, and skill in combining cultural factors with psychological process. How do you know that a particular psychological test or theory provides valid explanations for behavior in a particular cultural context? What are the cultural boundaries that prevent generalization of psychological theories and methods? Which psychological theories, tests, and methods can best be used across cultures? Which psychological theories, tests, and methods require specific cultural conditions?

Culture is emerging as one of the most important and perhaps most misunderstood constructs in the contemporary counseling literature. Culture may be defined narrowly as limited to ethnicity and nationality or defined broadly to include any and all potentially salient ethnographic, demographic, status, or affiliation variables. Given the broader definition of culture, it is possible to identify at least a dozen assets that are available exclusively through developing a multicultural awareness of culture-centered psychology:

1. *Accuracy,* because all behaviors are learned and displayed in a cultural context.

2. *Conflict management,* because the common ground of shared values or expectations will be expressed differently in contrasting culturally learned behaviors across cultures, and reframing conflict in a culture-centered perspective will allow two people or groups to disagree on the appropriate behavior without disagreeing on their underlying shared values.

3. *Identity* as we become aware of the thousands of culture teachers, we have accumulated in our own internal dialogue from both friends and enemies.

4. A *healthy society* through cultural diversity, just as a healthy biosystem requires a diverse gene pool.

5. *Encapsulation protection,* where we will not inappropriately impose our own culturally encapsulated self-reference criteria on others.

6. *Survival,* with the opportunity to rehearse adaptive functioning across cultures for our own future in the increasingly global village where we will live.

7. *Social justice,* where applying measures of justice and moral development across cultures helps us differentiate absolute principles from culturally relative strategies.

8. *Right thinking* through the application of quantum thinking and complementarity, where both linear and nonlinear thinking can be applied appropriately.

9. *Personalized learning,* where all learning and change involve some culture shock when perceived from a multicultural perspective.

10. *Spirituality,* where the multicultural perspective enhances the completeness of spiritual understanding toward the same shared ultimate reality from different paths.

11. *Political stability* in developing pluralism as an alternative to either authoritarian or anarchic political systems.

12. *Robust psychology* as psychological theories, tests, and methods are strengthened by accommodating the psychological perspective of different cultures.

The culture-centered perspective describes the function of making culture central rather than marginal or trivial to psychological analysis (Pedersen, 2000b; Pedersen & Ivey, 1993). Much of the political controversy surrounding the term multicultural can be avoided by the culture-centered description without diminishing the central importance of culture to psychology.

CONCLUSION

Cultural psychology presents "a broad range of approaches representing a revival of phenomenology in reaction to the dominant positivistic paradigm of the mid twentieth century" (Poortinga, 1997, p. 353). Culture presents a model and framework for understanding the new paradigm emerging in psychology as a fourth force focusing on issues that psychology has been unable—or unwilling—to solve. The connection between culture and psychology has deep historical roots, perceiving culture in the mind of the people (Geertz, 1973). These emerging theories have made clear that culture and behavior are fundamentally connected. The trends toward cultural psychology have emerged in our own historical context to fill a gap otherwise left empty by conventional psychology.

REFERENCES

Adamopoulos, J., & Lonner, W. J. (2001). Culture and psychology at a crossroad: Historical perspective and theoretical analysis. In D. Matsumoto (Ed.), *The handbook of culture and psychology.* Oxford: Oxford University Press.

Albee, G. W. (1994). The sins of the fathers: Sexism, racism and ethnocentrism in psychology. *International Psychologist, 1,* 22.

Berry, J. W., Poortinga, Y. H., Segall, M. H., & Dasen, P. (1992). *Cross-cultural psychology: Research and applications.* Cambridge, England: Cambridge University Press.

Butz, M. R. (1997). *Chaos and complexity: Implications.* Washington, DC: Taylor & Francis.

Campbell, D. T., & Naroll, R. (1972). The mutual methodological relevance of anthropology and psychology. In F. L. Hsu (Ed.), *Psychological anthropology* (pp. 435–468). Cambridge, England: Schenkmane.

Cooper, C. R., & Denner, J. (1998). Theories linking culture and psychology: Universal and community-specific processes. *Annual Review of Psychology, 49,* 559–584.

Geertz, C. (1973). *The interpretation of cultures.* New York: Basic Books.

Gielen, U. P. (1994). American mainstream psychology and its relationship to international and cross-cultural psychology. In A. I. Communian & U. P. Gielen (Eds.), *Advancing psychology and its applications: International perspectives* (pp. 26–40). Milan, Italy: Franco Angeli.

Ho, D. Y. F. (1999). Relational counseling: An Asian perspective of therapeutic intervention. *Psychologische Britragg Band, 41,* 99–112.

Howard, G. (2000). Adapting human lifestyles for the 21st century. *American Psychologist, 55*(5), 509–515.

Jahoda, G., & Krewer, B. (1997). History of cross-cultural and cultural psychology. In J. W. Berry, Y. H. Poortinga, & J. Pandey (Eds.), *Handbook of cross-cultural psychology: Theory and method* (Vol. 1, pp. 1–42). Boston: Allyn & Bacon.

Kagitcibasi, C. (1996). *Family and human development across cultures.* Mahwah, NJ: Erlbaum.

Kim, U., & Berry, J. (1993). *Indigenous psychologies: Research and experience in cultural context.* Newbury Park, CA: Sage.

Lewis-Fernandez, R., & Kleinman, A. (1994). Culture, personality and psychopathology. *Journal of Abnormal Psychology, 103,* 67–71.

Liu, J. H., & Liu, S. H. (1999). Interconnectedness and Asian social psychology. In T. Sugiman, M. Karasawa, J. H. Liu, & C. Ward (Eds.), *Progress in Asian social psychology: III. Theoretical and empirical contributions.* Seoul, Korea: Kyoyook-Kwahak-Sa.

Mahoney, M. J., & Patterson, K. M. (1992). Changing theories of changes: Recent development in counseling. In S. D. Brown & R. W. Lent (Eds.), *Handbook of counseling psychology* (2nd ed., pp. 665–689). New York: Wiley.

Miller, D. T. (1999). The norm of self interest. *American Psychologist, 54*(12), 1053–1060.

Miller, J. G. (1997). Theoretical issues in cultural psychology. In J. W. Berry, Y. H. Poortinga, & J. Pandey (Eds.), *Handbook of cross-cultural psychology: Theory and method* (Vol. 1, pp. 85–128). Boston: Allyn & Bacon.

Moghaddam, F. M. (1987). Psychology in the three worlds. *American Psychologist, 42,* 912–920.

Oskamp, S. (2000). A sustainable future for humanity. *American Psychologist, 55,* 496–508.

Paniagua, F. A. (in press). *Diagnosis in a multicultural context: A casebook for mental health professionals.* Thousand Oaks, CA: Sage.

Pedersen, P. (1997). Recent trends in cultural theories. *Applied and Preventive Psychology, 6,* 221–231.

Pedersen, P. (1998). *Multiculturalism as a fourth force.* Philadelphia: Brunner/Mazel.

Pedersen, P. (2000a). *Handbook for developing multicultural awareness* (3rd ed.). Alexandria, VA: American Counseling Association.

Pedersen, P. (2000b). *Hidden messages in culture-centered counseling: A Triad Training Model.* Thousand Oaks, CA: Sage.

Pedersen, P., & Ivey, A. E. (1993). *Culture-centered counseling and interviewing skills.* Westport, CT: Greenwood/Praeger.

Poortinga, Y. H. (1997). Toward convergence. In J. W. Berry, Y. H. Poortinga, & J. Pandey (Eds.), *Handbook of cross-cultural psychology: Theory and method* (Vol. 1, pp. 347–387). Boston: Allyn & Bacon.

Samuda, R. J. (1998). *Psychological testing of American minorities: Issues and consequences* (2nd ed.). Thousand Oaks, CA: Sage.

Shore, B. (1996). *Culture in mind: Cognition, culture and the problem of meaning.* New York: Oxford University Press.

Shweder, R. A. (1990). Cultural psychology: What is it? In J. W. Stigler, R. A. Shweder, & G. Herdt (Eds.), *Cultural psychology: Essays on human cognitive development* (p. 1043). New York: Cambridge University Press.

Sinha, D. (1997). Indigenizing psychology. In J. W. Berry, Y. H. Poortinga, & J. Pandey (Eds.), *Handbook of cross-cultural psychology: Theory and method* (Vol. 1, pp. 129–170). Boston: Allyn & Bacon.

Smith, J. A., Harré, R., & Van Langenhove, L. (1995). *Rethinking psychology.* London: Sage.

Sue, D. W., Ivey, A. E., & Pedersen, P. B. (1996). *Multicultural counseling theory.* Belmont, CA: Brooks/Cole.

Sue, D. W., & Sue, D. (1999). *Counseling the culturally different: Theory and practice* (3rd ed.). New York: Wiley.

Sue, D. W., & Sue, D. (2003). *Counseling the culturally different: Theory and practice* (4th ed.). New York: Wiley.

Sue, S. (1998). In search of cultural competencies in psychology and counseling. *American Psychologist, 53,* 440–448.

Sue, S. (1999). Science, ethnicity and bias: Where have we gone wrong? *American Psychologist, 54*(12), 1070–1077.

Tart, C. T. (1975). Some assumptions of orthodox, Western psychology. In C. T. Tart (Ed.), *Transpersonal psychologies* (pp. 59–112). New York: Harper & Row.

Thompson, M., Ellis, R., & Wildavsky, A. (1990). *Cultural theory.* San Francisco: Westview Press.

Waldrop, M. M. (1992). *Complexity: The emerging science at the edge of order and chaos.* New York: Touchstone Books.

Wrenn, C. G. (1962). The culturally encapsulated counselor. *Harvard Educational Review, 32,* 444–449.

Wrenn, C. G. (1985). Afterword: The culturally encapsulated counselor revisited. In P. Pedersen (Ed.), *Handbook of cross-cultural counseling and therapy* (pp. 323–329). Westport, CT: Greenwood Press.

Wrightsman, L. S. (1992). *Assumptions about human nature: Implications for researchers and practitioners.* Newbury Park, CA: Sage.

Yang, K. S. (1995). Chinese social orientation: An integrative analysis. In T. Y. Lin, W. S. Tseng, & E. K. Yeh (Eds.), *Chinese societies and mental health* (pp. 19–39). New York: Oxford University Press.

Yang, K. S. (1997). Indigenizing Westernized Chinese psychology. In M. H. Bond (Ed.), *Working at the interface of cultures: Eighteen lies in social science* (pp. 62–76). New York: Routledge.

Yang, K. S. (1999). Towards an indigenous Chinese psychology: A selective review of methodological, theoretical and empirical accomplishments. *Chinese Journal of Psychology, 41*(2), 181–211.

CHAPTER 2

Culture, Context, and Counseling

Sam D. Johnson Jr.

Culture, context, frame of reference, perspective, heritage, background, language group; each of these words has served as analogues for some variant of culture. When applied in service of psychology and education, we have come a long way in this century in our understanding of culture's consequences for healthy human development. The word culture, which comes from *cultus,* the Latin term for "worship," originally meant respectful homage. Later on, culture was used to describe the practice of improving the soil. The concept was later extended to the cultivation of intellect and conduct. *Cultura* originally meant "cultivation." Cato's treatise on agriculture, *De agri cultura,* written about 160 B.C.E., is likely the oldest written work in Latin using the term. About two hundred years later, Cicero applied the term when he spoke about *cultura animi,* "the cultivation of the spirit."

A modern dictionary provides the following:

[1]cul·ture, Pronunciation: 'kəl-chər, Function: *noun, Etymology :* Middle English, from Middle French, from Latin *cultura,* from *cultus,* past participle

Date: 15th century. **1 :** CULTIVATION, TILLAGE   **2 :** the act of developing the intellectual and moral faculties especially by education, **3 :** expert care and training <beauty *culture>*   **4 a :** enlightenment and excellence of taste acquired by intellectual and aesthetic training **b :** acquaintance with and taste in fine arts, humanities, and broad aspects of science as distinguished from vocational and technical skills   **5 a :** the integrated pattern of human knowledge, belief, and behavior that depends upon man's capacity for learning and transmitting knowledge to succeeding generations   **b :** the customary beliefs, social forms, and material traits of a racial, religious, or social group **c :** the set of shared attitudes, values, goals, and practices that characterizes a company or corporation: cultivation of living material in prepared nutrient media; *also :* a product of such cultivation (Merriam-Webster, 2002)

In anthropology, the initial definition of culture was offered by Edward Burnett Tylor, in the first paragraph of his *Primitive Culture* (1871):

Culture or civilization, taken in its wide, ethnographic sense, is that complex whole which includes knowledge, belief, morals, law, custom and any other habits and capabilities acquired by man as a member of society.

The modern technical definition of culture, as socially patterned human thought and behavior, originally proposed by Tylor, is an open-ended list, which has been extended considerably since he first proposed it. Some researchers have attempted to create exhaustive universal lists of the content of culture, usually as guides for further research. Others have listed and mapped all the culture traits of particular geographic areas (E. T. Hall, 1977).

The first inventory of cultural categories was undertaken in 1872 by a committee of the British Association for the Advancement of Science, which was assisted by Tylor. The committee prepared an anthropological field manual that listed 76 culture topics, in no particular order, including such diverse items as cannibalism and language. The most exhaustive list is the "Outline of Cultural Materials," first published in 1938 and still used as a guide for cataloguing great masses of worldwide cultural data for cross-cultural surveys. Like the table of contents of a giant encyclopedia, the outline lists 79 major divisions and 637 subdivisions. For example, "Food Quest" is a major division, with such subdivisions as collecting, hunting, and fishing (Bodley, 2000).

There has been considerable theoretical debate by anthropologists since Tylor over the most useful attributes that a technical concept of culture should stress. For example, in 1952, Alfred Kroeber and Clyde Kluckhohn, American anthropologists, published a list of 160 different definitions of culture. Kroeber and Kluckhohn's *Culture: A Critical Review of Concepts and Definitions* acknowledged that culture is "learned, derived from biological environment, psychological and historical components of human existence." The specific culture concept that particular anthropologists work with is an important matter because it may influence the research problems they investigate, their methods and interpretations, and the positions they take on public policy issues.

Likewise, the work of other applied social scientists is constrained or enhanced by the culture constructs that they choose to use. The consequence of the wide range of diverse cultural concepts available for research and practical application is a lack of clarity and focus. Counseling psychologists have suffered this effect as it has embraced cultural diversity.

> All cultures embody the static and dynamic elements, necessary for [human psychological] development. Hence, if culture is the matrix in which the identity of the society is made and remade, development is the full name for the process of making or remaking. In that case, culture becomes the only fundamental framework that provides the basic context in which all other factors of human development are measured. It is the basis as well as the resource for development. (Mangaraj, 2001)

Table 2.1 summarizes our modern understanding of the characteristics of culture.

CULTURE AS CONTEXT

Perhaps the most significant writing about contexts is that of Gregory Bateson (1979), who offered insight into the role of contexts in understanding culture and

Table 2.1   Culture's Characteristics

1. *Culture marks a difference between humans and other animals:*
   Human-centered
   Tool using versus tool making
   Opposable thumb
   Humans and great apes are the only animals to make and use tools

2. *Culture is learned behavior:*
   Imitative learning
   Other learning: language
   Signs and symbols: language and art
   Culture is an artifact

3. *Culture is a social product:*
   Of an interacting group of organisms of the same species
   Of human use of language in context
   Of social behavior

4. *Culture is a context for behavior:*
   Culture with an uppercase *C;* culture with a lowercase *c*
   Culture is hierarchical.
   Culture is a system.

5. *Culture is a process:*
   Culture is adaptive.
   Culture is dynamic and evolving.

6. *Culture requires:*
   People
   Language
   Communication
   Social structure (family, community, society)

culture contact. Culture can be thought of as a context, that in Bateson's view is "the pattern over time . . . which fixes meaning" (p. 15). This temporal context is analogous to spatial context that locates and defines meaning. For example, an elephant's trunk is a nose "because it is located between the eyes and north of the mouth" (p. 16). The context for noses is typically a location between the eyes and above the mouth, so if the trunk is in that location, it must be a nose. Likewise, context defines the relationship between "concepts" and "words expressed" in the mind of the communicator and gives meaning to the words. Context makes communication possible by fixing the relationship between words and meaning over time. According to *Webster's Dictionary:*

con·text: 'kän-‚teks Middle English, weaving together of words, from Latin *contextus* connection of words, coherence, from *contexere* to weave together, from *com-* + *texere* to weave— more at technical

Date: circa 1568

1 : the parts of a discourse that surround a word or passage and can throw light on its meaning

2 : the interrelated conditions in which something exists or occurs: environment, setting

All context is part of a class of contexts. That is to say, individuals may fix meaning in an idiosyncratic fashion that incorporates a cultural context, but that individual context is not the same as the cultural context. Rather, both the individual and the cultural context are part of the class of contexts. For example, William's identity as a Swede incorporates the culture of Sweden but is not the same context as the culture of Sweden, which is a national context rather than an individual context.

Contexts function as cultural systems that operate at each level of human organization, from the intrapsychic to the interplanetary. Contexts have been represented as continua as well as layered interactive systems. Thinking contextually is a major part of developing skill as a cross-cultural counselor.

When E. T. Hall (1959) wrote about cultures, he described the Chinese language and culture as "high context" because the meaning of a character in Chinese language is highly dependent on the circumstances in which it occurs: One character can have widely different meanings depending on the context of its usage. Hall characterized cultures and some of their elements as low or high context based on their characteristics. In a low-context culture, people rely on spoken words and written communications for gathering clues to behavior. In a high-context culture, nonverbal signs, family status, age differences, and social setting add a lot more meaning to written or spoken words. The context in which the communication occurs may alter the meaning of the message. In the case of counseling, the interview setting is a context defined by the presence of a counselor, a client, and an office or consulting room. Diplomas, licenses, and certificates of training may also contribute to defining the context of a counseling interview. Clients whose cultural disposition is high or low context will attend to different features of the relationships and their attendant meanings. Any counseling interview has the potential to be a cross-cultural counseling interview, but some may be more cross-cultural than others. Differences in ethnicity, race, class, language, gender, and so on all contribute to the character of the context of a counseling session as cross-cultural.

Both the client and the counselor are cultural products. Each brings a subjective cultural context to the session. In addition, their interaction via communication creates the cultural context of the interview as an event. Just as the individual's context incorporates the cultural context and defines meaning for the individual, so the culture, the context of the social group, defines meaning for the group. Client and counselor are at once individuals and exemplars of their cultural groups. The culture of the counseling interview exists for Joe and Dr. Schmidt at 2 P.M. on Tuesdays and Thursdays. The context of that relationship is defined by the patterns it contains that fix meaning in the roles and statements in the culture of their counseling relationship.

Cultures, then, are represented in our experience by a variety of patterns specific to particular times and places. Ethnic groups are cultural groups that have established themselves as cultural exemplars of national cultures in diaspora. They may be described by the general characteristics used in cultural profiles, with the obvious distinction that the group is no longer in its context of origin, but rather in the context of the third culture of the country that has received them.

In cross-cultural counseling practice, counselors are primarily interested in the individual as a cultural exemplar. At minimum, they should be able to distinguish the context of the individual from the context of the group by understanding that the individual shares the group in a unique fashion, but the individual context is not the same as the context of the group.

Culture is a context, a pattern over time that fixes meaning. That pattern can have a temporal frame from several minutes to centuries. More often than not, when social scientists speak of culture the temporal frame is measured in multiple years. For example, a counseling psychologist may be using context and the culture it defines as a long-term construct to examine a client's development or as a short-term construct to examine the therapeutic relationship established with a client. Both are contexts and can be analyzed in cultural terms. In many respects, the work of the counselor involves assessing the contexts of a client's development and current circumstances and establishing a facilitative, culturally relevant relational context for the conduct of treatment.

CULTURE AND COMMUNICATION

Culture depends on language and communication for transmission and the establishment of shared meanings and understanding. The word "communication" derives from the Latin word *communico,* meaning sharing and union. John Dewey (1916), captured this relationship as follows:

> Society not only continues to exist *by* transmission, *by* communication, but it may fairly be said to exist *in* transmission, *in* communication. There is more than a verbal tie between the words common, community, and communication. Men live in a community in virtue of the things they have in common; and communication is the way in which they come to possess things in common. What they must have in common in order to form a community or society are aims, beliefs, aspirations, knowledge—a common understanding—like-mindedness as the sociologists say. (p. 5)

Implied in Dewey's conceptualization is the idea that a society communicates its *culture.* Culture and communication seem to exist in a perpetual linkage. Robert E. Park, a close associate of Dewey, wrote in 1938:

> Communication creates, or makes possible at least, that consensus and understanding among the individual components of a social group which eventually gives it and them the character not merely of society but of a cultural unit. It spins a web of custom and mutual expectation, which binds together social entities. . . . Family group or labor organization, every form of society except the most transient has a life history and a tradition. It is by communication that this tradition is transmitted. It is in this way that the continuity of common enterprises and social institutions is maintained, not merely from day to day, but from generation to generation. (pp. 191–197)

Communication is, first and foremost, a transmission and dissemination of meanings. The connection between communication and culture makes the objective of cross-cultural communication one of achieving conceptual transferability or equivalence across contexts. Likewise, the notion of a cross-cultural psychology implies the same transferability of psychological practices and principles across the social contexts that culture represents. Applied psychological practices such as counseling and psychotherapy are fundamentally language dependant. Effective communication is a core competency for counselors and psychotherapists regardless of the possibility of cultural or ethnic differences that may exist in their relationships.

RACE IN THE CONTEXT OF CULTURE

The flawed science of simple race-based causal thinking obtains into the present. Race is an easy answer in accounting for differences in behavior because it is coincident and associated with cultural difference in many circumstances. However, assuming that culture is the context that provides meaning over time suggests that the meaning of skin color or race is culturally dependent or contextually dependent. Without a specified context, it could be argued that race has no meaning. In fact, the biological basis of a socially constructed "race" has, to a large extent, been found to have no validity, and the current consensus is that there is no biological association between race and behavior within groups of humans (Villarosa, 2002).

Still, race as a social construct has tremendous illustrative value in certain types of sociological and psychological research. Because race is not a psychological construct, it has taken the development of means of assessing how people feel about race, both their own and that of others, to really begin to clarify this long-standing issue.

THE CULTURAL CONTEXT OF TREATMENT

Applied psychology is a cultural product of the Western way of knowing. The feasibility of exporting American applied psychology beyond the cultural context of the United States to non-Western cultures has been a historic question in the field (Gergen, Massey, Gulerce, & Gerishwar, 1996). What, if any, human psychological universals exist to support the applicability of mainstream American psychology in other cultural, ethnic, or linguistic contexts?

Regardless of the debate, efforts to make applied psychology culturally sensitive and its practitioners culturally competent have continued over the past 30 years. Initial efforts at incorporating difference into counseling were framed in racial terms that treated race as if it had some behavioral consequences beyond accounting for skin color. The counseling literature of the 1960s is replete with articles such as "The Negro Worker and the White Client: A Commentary on the Treatment Relationship" (Curry, 1964) and *Black Students and the school Counselor* (Bolden, 1970). Attempts to account for psychological differences between the races occupied a prominent position in the applied comparative psychology of the day. Earlier (Johnson, 1983), I wrote that three paradigms for interpreting difference have coexisted in the counseling literature: the Inferiority Paradigm, a race-based approach that attributed psychological differences between the races to biological and genetic factors; the Deficit Paradigm, a race-based approach that attributed the causes of "racial difference to social deviance or cultural deprivation[;] and the Multicultural Paradigm, that attributed psychological differences between the races to cultural and ethnic factors instead of race" (Johnson, 1990).

ACKNOWLEDGING CULTURE'S IMPACT ON COUNSELING

In the United States, counseling and psychotherapy have been questioned with regard to their value outside the context of the mainstream culture. Much of this critique has been derived from the basic issue of the transferability of applied psychological practices to ethnic and racial groups other than White Americans. Out of the aforementioned criticism there has emerged a movement to reframe applied psychological practice in cross-cultural terms with the intent of extending its general effectiveness to a full range of ethnic and racial groups.

The very notion of counseling, seeking the help of a counselor for personal emotional concerns, is a behavior that is culture bound. Across the planet, priests, shamans, medicine men, herbalists, and others perform the culturally ascribed role that counselors play in the United States. Back in the early 1980s, a former student came to visit me in my office after returning to the States from Trinidad. She had been trained a few years earlier in counseling psychology. She said the following: "The people in my country know what to do with a priest, and they know what to do with a doctor, but they don't have any idea what to do with a counselor." In fact, in addition to clients in other countries, significant portions of American minority group populations also share the characteristic of not knowing what to do with a counselor. Sue and Sue (1971) studied the utilization of mental health centers by Chinese Americans and found culture-bound variables to be implicated in the quality of services afforded these clients at a community mental health center.

MAKING CULTURE OPERATIONAL FOR COUNSELING

Paul Pedersen (1974), who coined the term "cross-cultural counseling," was among the first counselor educators to highlight the cultural problems of psychological practice. By 1977, he had begun using the Triad Model of cross-cultural counselor training in his classes at the University of Minnesota. Alan Ivey (1977) began to operationally define cultural expertise in counseling that same year. Up until that time, most counseling training and research dealt with differences in racial terms, with all of the attendant problems that have accompanied that practice. Pedersen worked with international students and realized that culture made a significant difference in his work with them. Both Pedersen and Ivey highlighted knowledge, awareness, and skill as the outcomes they sought.

These early efforts began a trend of using culture as an analogue for the developmental contexts and subjective consequences of development in those contexts for the clients of counseling. The desired outcomes of knowledge, awareness, and skill continue into the present as core outcomes and competencies of training in cross-cultural counseling.

The recent history of counseling is replete with efforts to train counselors to effectively understand and apply culture and all it represents to their work. Counselor training is a very frequent focus whenever the issue of cultural diversity is raised. How do we train counselors to use cultural information? How do we know they are effective at it? What outcomes are most desirable from cross-cultural counselor training? Currently, the complexity and validity of the heuristic efforts of early theorists and researchers are being put to empirical and clinical tests that will frame the future of work in this area. The current volume brings the best of that work together under a single cover. The synthesis and integration of formerly marginal notions of difference has begun in earnest. This author and many others are eager to see where it takes us.

REFERENCES

Bateson, G. (1979). *Mind and nature: A necessary unity.* New York: Ballantine Books.

Bodley, J. H. (2000). *Cultural anthropology: Tribes, states, and the global system* (3rd ed.). Mountain View, CA: Mayfield.

Bolden, J. A. (1970). Black students and the school counselor. *School Counselor, 7*(3), 204–208.

Curry, A. E. (1964, March). The Negro worker and the White client: A commentary on the treatment relationship. *Social Casework,* 131–136.

Dewey, J. (1916). *Democracy and education.* New York: Macmillan.

Gergen, K. J., Massey, A. L., Gulerce, A., & Gerishwar, M. (1996). Psychological science in cultural context. *American Psychologist, 51,* 496–503.

Hall, E. T. (1959). *The silent language.* Garden City, NY: Anchor Press/Doubleday.

Hall, E. T. (1977). *Beyond culture.* Garden City, NY: Anchor Press/Doubleday.

Ivey, A. (1977). Cultural expertise: Toward systematic outcome criteria in counseling and psychotherapy. *Personnel and Guidance Journal, 55,* 296–302.

Johnson, S. D. (1983). The Minnesota multiethnic counselor education curriculum: The design and evaluation of an intervention for cross cultural counselor training. (Doctoral dissertation, University of Minnesota, 1982). Dissertation Abstracts International.

Johnson, S. D. (1990). Toward clarifying culture race and ethnicity in the context of multicultural counseling. *Journal of Multicultural Counseling and Development, 18*(1), 41–50. Columbia University.

Kroeber, A. L., & Kluckhohn, C. (1952). *Culture: A critical review of concepts and definitions.* (Papers of the Peabody Museum of Harvard Archeology and Ethnology, Harvard University, Vol. 42, 1). Cambridge, MA: Museum Press.

Mangaraj, B. K. (2001). Management of development in the framework of culture. In *COMPASS: A journal of thought, quest and analysis,* R. K. Pand (Ed.), and Web-published by the Centre for Organizational Management, Policy Analysis and Socio-Cultural Studies (COMPASS) http://www.expage.com/gacompass, Bhubaneswar, Orissa, India.

Merriam-Webster Online Dictionary. (2002). Springfield, MA. Available from www.Merriam-Webster.com.

Park, R. E. (1938, September). Reflections on communication and culture. *American Journal of Sociology,* 191–197.

Pedersen, P. (1974). Cross-cultural communications training for mental health professionals. *International and Intercultural Communication Annual, 1,* 53–64.

Pedersen, P. (1977, October). The triad model of cross-cultural counselor training. *Personnel and Guidance Journal.*

Sue, S., & Sue, D. W. (1971). Chinese-American personality and mental health. *Amerasia Journal, 1,* 36–49. (Reprinted from *Roots: An Asian-American reader,* by A. Tachiki, E. Wong, F. Odo, & B. Wong, Eds., 1972, Los Angeles: Continental Graphics.)

Tylor, E. B. (1871, reprint 1958). *Primitive culture.* New York: Harper & Row.

Villarosa, L. (2002, January 1). A conversation with Joseph Graves: Beyond Black and White in biology and medicine. *New York Times,* Sec. F., p. 5.

CHAPTER 3

Ethnicity: The Term and Its Meaning

Heather L. Juby and William R. Concepción

The increasing ethnic and racial diversity in the United States and research showing ethnic disparities in the delivery of mental health services has resulted in a call
for culturally competent counseling. This call has stimulated a great deal of psychological research on the role of ethnicity in mental health and counseling. This
has been reflected in an increase in the past two decades in the number of articles,
books, and journals devoted to the study of ethnicity.

However, despite the abundance of research on ethnicity, there remains some
ambiguity around the definition of the term. Although there is general acknowledgment that ethnicity is a complex concept, there is a lack of consensus on how ethnicity should be understood, defined, and measured (Helms, 1996; Phinney, 1996).
There is currently no standard definition of *ethnicity,* and the choice of terminology
varies and tends to reflect the ideology and theory of each researcher as well as current trends and policies. Furthermore, other variables, such as nationality, race, and
religion, are often confounded with ethnicity in studying this variable. The terms
used to describe ethnic groups are also inconsistent. The terms race and ethnicity
are often used interchangeably; for example, they may be used in the same article
to describe the same groups. Other terms commonly used are racial/ethnic groups,
ethnic minority groups, and cultural groups. Such confusion around the definition
of ethnicity has serious implications for the validity of counseling research. This
chapter reviews conceptualizations of ethnicity in the social sciences, including sociology, anthropology, and psychology. In addition, the ways ethnicity has been operationalized in counseling research are examined, including a discussion of the
implications for various conceptualizations of ethnicity. Finally, the distinction between race and ethnicity is drawn and a definition of ethnicity for future counseling research is offered.

APPROACHES TO ETHNICITY IN THE SOCIAL SCIENCES

The fields of sociology and anthropology have vigorously debated theories of ethnicity. However, these debates have not yielded a consensual definition of the term. The
term *ethnic group* has been used to identify anything from small kinship groups to
large categories of people grouped according to basic shared characteristics (e.g.,
Hispanics; Yinger, 1985). Theorists have found it difficult to define ethnicity, arguing

that ethnicity is a multidimensional construct (Banton, 2001). As a result, definitions of ethnicity have most often been imprecise and ambiguous, often reducing ethnicity to being equated with culture (Kaufmann, 2000). The terms *ethnicity, culture, ancestry, nationality,* and *country of origin* are often used interchangeably, and most research on ethnicity does not define the way the term is used (Isajiw, 1974).

In general, theorists in sociology and anthropology have focused on the following themes: ethnicity as a group phenomenon, ethnicity and class, assimilation and pluralism, ethnic identity, discrimination and ethnic stratification, the content and boundaries of ethnicity, and the relationship between race and ethnicity (Sollors, 1996). Whereas anthropologists have been mostly concerned with the meaning of ethnicity globally (with a particular focus on developing nations), sociologists have mostly studied ethnicity in the United States and Europe. Sociological inquiry has looked at ethnicity at the societal level, focusing on the creation of ethnic groups (ethnogenesis) and their maintenance and dissolution, the social and political behavior of ethnic groups, and interethnic conflict and cooperation. Sociologists tend to focus on structural factors in ethnicity, such as residential patterns, occupational opportunities, migration/immigration patterns, and institutional participation. In addition, sociologists focus on structural inequalities and the ethnic stratification system. Political science concerns itself with the relationship of ethnicity to nations and ethnic conflict and such variables as voting behavior.

Derivation of the Term

The term ethnicity did not appear in the dictionary until the 1960s (Glazer & Moynihan, 1975). Previously, social scientists used the terms *races, nations,* or *tribes* when studying what we now call ethnic groups (Marger, 2003). Ethnicity appeared later in anthropological literature when, in the 1970s, it began to replace the term tribe (Cohen, 1978).

Ethnicity versus Related Constructs

Some researchers equate ethnicity with ancestry. Alba (1990) wrote:

> Ethnicity is inherently a matter of *ancestry,* of beliefs about the origins of one's forebears . . . ethnicity is oriented toward the past, toward the history and origin of family, group, and nation (p. 37). Kaufmann (2000) further amplified this definition by claiming "the term ethnic group should be reserved for communities which possess a belief in their shared genealogical descent and meet a threshold requirement that distinguishes them from smaller-scale phenomena like clans and tribes. . . ." (p. 6)

However, this definition has become problematic as more and more Americans claim a mixed ancestry.

Other theorists have conceptualized ethnic groups as primarily cultural groups. This notion, however, has also been criticized. Kaufmann (2000) writes, "Cultural attributes must . . . be distinguished from both ethnic groups and nations . . . cultures can exist without possessing a (collective) sense of self-consciousness." (p. 7).

"Nations" have also been used as definitions for ethnicity. Banton (2001) asserts that "nationality often overlaps with . . . ethnicity to such a degree that it is pointless to distinguish them" (p. 185). However, Calhoun (1993) argues that although intimately related, they are not the same thing. The difference, according to Calhoun, lies in the fact that nations seek political sovereignty, whereas ethnic groups' desire for recognition is not necessarily related to territorial boundaries or claims to self-determination.

Ethnicity as Fixed versus Fluid Construct

In sociology and anthropology, the classic debate around the nature of ethnicity has played out between the primordialist and the instrumentalist schools. The oldest definition of ethnicity reflects the primordialist approach; most other definitions of ethnicity have arisen in response to this approach. Primordialists assert that ethnicity is a fixed, categorical identity that is ascribed at birth (Geertz, 1963; Isaacs, 1975; Stack, 1986). In this way, ethnicity is seen as "extended kinship," a bond that cultivates strong emotions and loyalties (van den Berghe, 1981). Embedded deep within the psyche, the primordial bond is the "longing not to belong to any other group" (Geertz, 1963).

According to Geertz (1963), the ties were usually around any or all of the following: blood ties or kinship, race, language, region, custom, or religion. Geertz emphasized the divisive nature of these primordial bonds, describing them as overwhelming forces that threatened to tear apart new states in the modern world. Proponents of primordialism claimed that this theory explained the rise of ethnic violence in postcolonial states (van den Berghe, 1981). Primordialism was also used to explain the persistence of ethnicity, which social scientists had predicted would wane in the face of modernity. Marxian thinkers had predicted that class divisions would become more salient than ethnicity, and assimilationists in the United States had expected new immigrants to willingly give up their ethnicities in exchange for a new national identity.

Max Weber's (1968) definition of ethnicity echoed the primordialist stance. He defined an ethnic group as a group whose members

> entertain a subjective belief in their common descent because of similarities of physical type or of customs or both, or because of memories of colonization and migration . . . it does not matter whether or not an objective blood relationship exists. (p. 389)

Weber emphasized ethnicity as a social phenomenon and argued that members of an ethnic group interact with each other based on some type of common consciousness grounded in a shared history (Alba, 1990). In Weber's definition, the key criterion of ethnicity changed from actual shared lineage (such as that of kinship groups, tribes, and clans) to a more subjective sense of belonging to a group—what Kaufmann (2000) called the "myth of ancestry." This distinction was to become very important in the modern world, where previously isolated small kinship groups increasingly found themselves scattered throughout diverse cities and diasporas far from their homelands.

Barth (1969) departed from the primordialist stance, challenging the notion of ethnic group as a fixed category, asserting that ethnicity is shaped by the social context (Kaufert, 1977). According to Barth, ethnic groups are not defined by shared history or blood ties but through the establishment and maintenance of boundaries. These were not territorial boundaries, but psychological boundaries, consisting of shared perceptions of the criteria for membership and exclusion. Through his focus on boundaries, Barth emphasized the structural nature rather than the contents of ethnicity (e.g., culture). Barth also stressed the mutable and situational quality of ethnicity, arguing that the boundaries of ethnicity are constantly being renegotiated. Thus, ethnicity can change according to particular situations. Barth's definition changed the perspective of ethnicity from one based on relationships to one emphasizing similarities among members and influenced a whole new generation of social scientists who emphasized the fluid, situational character of ethnicity (Calhoun, 1993).

Influenced by Barth's characterization of ethnic groups as dynamic and ecological, a new school emerged: instrumentalism. In the 1970s and 1980s, the instrumentalists emphasized the political nature of ethnicity, conceptualizing ethnic groups as interest groups competing for scarce resources. According to the instrumentalists, the existence of social inequalities is a better explanation for the maintenance of ethnic groups than loyalties based on blood ties or common history. Shared experiences promote ethnic group mobilization toward common goals (Banton, 1983; Cohen, 1978; Hechter, 1986).

Thus, ethnicity is "a means of asserting one's rights in a political community in which ethnicity is a recognized element" (Cohen, 1978). Instrumentalist theories contributed the idea of ethnicity as socially constructed, a notion that has been generally accepted and expanded on in modern social science literature. However, this approach focuses more on the functional purpose of ethnicity as opposed to actually defining the term.

Assimilation versus Pluralism

Another classic debate in the sociological literature focused on the perspectives of assimilation versus pluralism, a debate that emphasized the cultural aspects of ethnic groups (Yancey, Ericksen, & Juliani, 1976). The assumption of the assimilationist perspective in the United States was that the importance of ethnic ties and differences among ethnic groups will diminish as a result of intermarriage, occupational achievement, and changes in residential patterns (Alba, 1990; Yancey et al., 1976). Pluralists challenged the notion that assimilation was the inevitable fate of all ethnic groups, highlighting the persistence and resurgence of ethnic identification in the 1970s (Glazer & Moynihan, 1975; Greeley, 1971). Alba studied this ethnic revival among Whites in upstate New York and noticed that the new interest in ethnic origins seemed to occur mainly in the third generation. Hansen (as cited in Sollors, 1996) had described this type of generational difference in ethnic identity. Whereas the first and second generations of immigrants are usually focused on the problems of adapting to a new culture, the third generation, already more American than not, has the luxury of recalling their ethnic origins with nostalgia. As Hansen put it, "What the son wishes to forget, the grandson wishes to remember" (p. 206).

Subjective versus Objective Approaches to Ethnicity

Theorists in the social sciences have also differentiated between the subjective and objective dimensions of ethnicity. Some feel that ethnicity is determined by the individual's self-definition; others emphasize that one's ethnic group membership is constrained by objective criteria. The postmodernists, at the most extreme end of the subjectivist camp, argue for the deconstruction of ethnicity and reject all attempts to objectively define the term (Levine, 1999). Barth's work as well as the empirical studies on third-generation return to ethnicity were two major influences on the development of the subjective approach to ethnicity (Isajiw, 1993).

Gans (1979) proposed the notion of "symbolic ethnicity" to characterize modern ethnicity among White Americans. Although intermarriage, acculturation, and social mobility have for the most part broken down cultural ties to their ancestors, White Americans retain a nostalgic loyalty to their ethnic heritage. Because these Americans do not have knowledge of their ancestral culture or speak the language, Gans calls this type of ethnic identification symbolic or voluntary. In other words, individuals can choose when and how they wish to identify with their ethnic group without having to pay the cost of actual membership or incorporate it into their everyday lives (Alba, 1990). For example, individuals may attend ethnic festivals, eat certain foods, or be members of social organizations particular to their self-described ethnic group. Alba asserts that:

> this symbolic identification with the ethnic group allows individuals to construct personal identities that contain some ethnic "spice." But at the same time, it represents a personalization of ethnicity and frequently amounts to little more than a token acknowledgment of ethnic background. (p. 30)

Critics of the subjectivist approach to ethnicity argue that external constraints (such as outgroup members' perceptions and formal policies) affect the availability and range of options one may use to label oneself. In addition, the subjectivist definition makes the categorization of ethnic groups difficult and thus the study of ethnicity practically impossible. For example, how "ethnic" does one have to be to be considered a member of an ethnic group? How does one deal with divergent criteria for ethnic group membership (i.e., ingroup versus outgroup members' perspectives)?

Objectivists tend to hold categorization by nonmembers as more important, whereas subjectivists claim that self-identification of members is more valid. Several theorists have combined both objective and subjective criteria in their definitions of ethnicity. Nagel (1994) argued that defining one's ethnicity is a "dialectical process" involving "what *you* think your ethnicity is, versus what *they* think your ethnicity is" (p. 154).

Ethnic Identity

Subjectivist theories of ethnicity as well as the growing reality of people with mixed heritage have led social scientists to investigate the ways individuals make sense of ethnicity (Alba, 1990). Studies have shown that people identify their ethnicity differently based on the situational context and how questions about ethnic background are formulated (e.g., Ornstein, 2000). Much of this work has come about as a result of the debate around census categories (Wallman, Evinger, & Schechter, 2000). Sociologists and anthropologists have begun to assert that in order to conduct rigorous research on ethnicity, it is imperative to study the meaning, use, and consequences of various ethnic labels. Much of this writing relies on psychological theories that will be discussed later in this chapter.

The issues concerning ethnic identity center around such questions as the following: In what situations does one's ethnicity become salient? In cases of mixed ethnicity, how does one decide which ethnic group to identify with, and does this change according to situation? To answer such dilemmas, researchers have asserted that levels of ethnic identification are important to take into consideration (Isajiw, 1993; Plax, 1972). Isajiw, for example, differentiates between external and internal aspects of ethnicity. External factors include behaviors such as speaking the language or practicing the traditions and customs of the group. Internal aspects include cognitive, attitudinal, and affective dimensions. The two aspects of ethnic identity can vary independently so that, for example, a person may have a high affective connection with his or her ethnicity but low behavioral manifestations of his or her ethnicity. Isajiw conceptualized a typology of various forms of ethnic identity. For example, a person exhibiting the prior example (low practice of customs with high emotional connection to the group) would be labeled as having an *ideological identity*. Plax (1972) called this type of minimal ethnic affiliation "passive identification." The converse (high level of practice with low emotional connection) would be considered a *ritualistic ethnic identity*.

Sociological and anthropological research and theory on ethnicity has ranged from a definition of ethnicity as ascriptive and given at birth to one that is based purely on one's self-definition. Currently, much of the focus in the literature centers around ethnic identity and the meaning individuals give their ethnicity. It is here that psychological theories have much to offer.

THE VIEW OF ETHNICITY IN PSYCHOLOGY

Research on ethnicity in psychology has become increasingly popular in the past several years but, like other fields, has not arrived at a clear consensus on how it should be conceptualized and studied. This has resulted in vague and inconsistent definitions of ethnicity and additional confusion about the concept. This section highlights the difficulties in capturing the meaning of ethnicity through discussion of the various ways it has been conceptualized in psychology and how such conceptualizations have been used to inform psychological research and practice.

Definitions of Ethnicity in Psychological Literature

Scholars have attempted to define ethnicity in various ways. For example, Betancourt and Lopez (1993) reported that ethnicity typically constitutes a group of individuals that share a common nationality, culture, or language. They related ethnicity to the Greek concept *ethnos*, referring to people of a nation or tribe, and *ethnikos*, which stands for national. Ethnicity was therefore conceptualized to be "the ethnic quality or affiliation of a group, which is normally characterized in terms of culture" (p. 631). They also stated that one's culture may be a determinant of one's ethnic group identification, which may also be reversed (i.e., one's ethnic identification can determine culture). They distinguished between two forms of culture: physical culture and subjective culture. Physical culture has been identified as directly observable creations, such as roads, buildings, and tools. Subjective culture includes the social norms, roles, beliefs, values, and communication patterns within a particular group of people.

Ethnicity has also been thought to be definitive on both broad and narrow levels (D. W. Sue et al., 1998). At the broad level, Sue and colleagues would have ethnicity encompass both cultural and physical features, overlapping with the conceptualization of race. The narrower (and their preferred) definition examines ethnicity from the perspective of individuals sharing a common ancestral origin on the basis of at least one national or cultural characteristic. Not involving any ties with biological or genetic traits, an ethnic group would be "one in which the members share and transmit a unique cultural and social heritage passed on from one generation to the next" (p. 10).

Similarly, S. Sue (1991) considers ethnicity as consisting of a group of individuals that share a unique cultural and social heritage (e.g., values, attitudes, behavioral patterns) that are passed on through generations. Sue acknowledges that although differences exist within ethnic groups, there are still general commonalities unique to specific groups that distinguish them from others. Further, for ethnicity and culture to have meaning, these differences need to be highlighted.

In Phinney's (1996) conceptualization of ethnicity, she proposed that ethnicity may best be understood as clusters of dimensions, rather than as categories (something that someone either has or does not have), an independent variable assumed to influence psychological outcomes, or as a nuisance variable to be controlled. At least three independent and overlapping aspects of ethnicity (that vary within and across ethnic groups) may account for its psychological importance, as well as provide some explanations for the existence of variation among groups. More specifically, ethnicity may be divided into (1) the cultural values, attitudes, and behaviors that distinguish ethnic groups; (2) the subjective sense of ethnic group membership held by group members (i.e., ethnic identity); and (3) experiences associated with minority status (including powerlessness, discrimination, prejudice).

To the extent that ethnicity has been thought of as being synonymous with culture, Phinney (1996) explained that the common assumption about the meaning of ethnicity focuses on the cultural characteristics of a particular group (e.g., norms, values, attitudes, beliefs) that stem from a common culture of origin and are transmitted across generations. Ethnic identity, or the degree to which one makes sense of and identifies with one's ethnic group, has also been considered a definitive component of ethnicity and can influence psychological functioning (Phinney, 1996).

Characterized by lower status and experiences with discrimination, minority standing in society has also been proposed to influence one's level of ethnic identification (Phinney, 1996; S. Sue, 1991). The extent to which this experience will impact an individual's psychological state depends on many factors, such as the history and present status of one's group in society, one's personal experiences with prejudice, and one's responses to perceptions of stereotypes and discrimination. According to Sue, the historical and contemporary forms of prejudice and discrimination some ethnic groups have experienced in the United States are shared phenomena that are necessary to account for in properly capturing ethnic group membership. Examining cultural characteristics alone is not sufficient in distinguishing ethnic groups, especially because many of them share the common experience of being exploited and oppressed in the United States (S. Sue, 1991).

In essence, the view of ethnicity in psychology is one that examines the shared characteristics that exist among groups of individuals, which are thought to take place on both physical and subjective levels. Related to culture, ethnicity provides us with information about a particular group's social norms, beliefs, and patterns of behavior that are unique to that group. One's sense of connectedness to one's ethnic group, which is often influenced by the messages one receives from society, is also thought to represent an aspect of ethnicity. Furthermore, shared experiences with oppression and discrimination can play an influential part in an individual's ethnic group identification.

Scholars have written further about ethnicity and its relationship to group and individual experience. For example, Nagel (1994) conceptualized ethnicity as a social construction that is continually being defined and modified by individuals in response to social, economic, and political influences as well as consistently evolving group ideologies. It functions as a way for groups to define themselves and maintain boundaries that unify and divide one group from another. Ethnicity, according to Nagel, is composed of two elements: ethnic identity and culture. Ethnic identity takes place on both internal and external levels. More specifically, the degree to which one feels a sense of connectedness to one's identified ethnic group, as well as how others view one's ethnic membership, constitute ethnic identity. Following this, a negotiation takes place between the level of connection one feels with a particular ethnic group and the messages society provides regarding what it deems that individual's ethnic membership to be.

Similarly, Pinderhughes (1989) related ethnic identification to one's self-definition in relation to societal factors. For example, one may be more or less inclined to claim or address one's ethnicity based on positive or negative evaluations society has imposed on one's ethnic group. In addition, societal inconsistencies in the way people are asked to define themselves can bring confusion regarding one's ethnic identification. Further, one's ethnic identity can become a source of ambivalence or discomfort, especially if it stirs up negative feelings about oneself. Consequently, individuals may use denial and avoidance mechanisms to compensate for the uncomfortable feelings that may come in addressing this topic. For example, some people may choose to relate to others only as human beings because addressing differences in people may constitute a form of racism or prejudice.

Ethnicity, according to Pinderhughes (1989), involves personal dynamics and socially inherited definitions of the self. Ethnicity captures both identification with one's group and one's view of the self that are influenced by the value society places on the group. One's level of ethnic identification may vary according to such things as nationality, country of origin, and religion. Ethnic identification may also remain outside of one's consciousness throughout one's life development.

To summarize, scholars in psychology have considered individuals' perceptions of themselves as members of specific ethnic groups to influence their level of ethnic group membership. Individuals' affiliation with their designated ethnic group is influenced by the extent to which they feel connected to it. This connectedness is influenced by external messages that individuals receive from their environment. External influences, such as the media and experiences with discrimination, also play a role in shaping one's level of affiliation with one's designated ethnic group, regardless of what that group may be.

We now turn our discussion from the theoretical conceptualizations of ethnicity to how ethnicity has been studied in psychological research and literature.

VIEWS OF ETHNICITY IN PSYCHOLOGICAL RESEARCH

Studies examining racial/ethnic issues in psychology have recently been attracting widespread interest. However, research actively committed to investigating racial/ethnic issues does not appear to support this interest. Carter, Akinsulure-Smith, Smailes, & Clauss (1998) observed in three premier counseling psychology journals that research dedicated to expanding and contributing to the growth of knowledge concerning racial/ethnic issues has been minimal. More specifically, less than 10% of the empirical research between 1982 and 1991 avoided using Whites as a normative population, used culture-specific measures and/or within-group variation, or offered any information that extended knowledge about the groups being investigated (Carter, 1998).

In racial/ethnic research in psychology, the study of ethnicity has experienced its own share of difficulties. For example, the literature examining ethnicity has been fraught with inconsistent and unclear terminology, where ethnicity is often used interchangeably with other variables, such as race and culture (Betancourt & Lopez, 1993; Phinney, 1996). Measures examining ethnic identity have been unreliable and lacked validity and the research has been unclear in distinguishing components of ethnic identity that are commonly shared across groups from those that are group-specific (Phinney, 1990). Cross-cultural researchers have examined ethnicity at the individual, group, and societal levels (S. Sue, 1991) but have consistently neglected to clearly define its meaning and explain which aspects of it are thought to influence behavior (Betancourt & Lopez, 1993). The frequent inconsistencies in the conceptualization and measurement of ethnicity consequently leave researchers with vague and unclear ideas as to what ethnicity is.

The Use of Professional Guidelines in Addressing Ethnicity

Psychological associations have provided guidelines to aid scholars and researchers alike in using clearer definitions of ethnicity in both research and clinical practice. Two widely referenced texts in these areas, the *Publication Manual of the American Psychological Association* (2001) and the American Psychiatric Association's

Diagnostic and Statistical Manual of Mental Disorders, fourth edition, text revision (*DSM-IV-TR,* 2000), are discussed here to share what has been written on this topic.

The *Publication Manual* (American Psychological Association, 2001) has addressed the issue facing scholars of identifying the terms race and ethnicity consistently. Two possible reasons for these inconsistencies have been proposed: scholars' personal preferences in how they are used and society's determination of what terms are considered acceptable during specific time periods. People tend to name racial and ethnic groups according to the way they want to label them. Additionally, some terms, commonly accepted during a certain time period, may later be viewed as dated and/or pejorative (e.g., Negro, Oriental) and are no longer acceptable (Raspberry, 1989).

To aid scholars in minimizing these inconsistencies, the *Publication Manual* (American Psychological Association, 2001) has proposed two guidelines. These guidelines encourage scholars to be specific and to be sensitive to reduce bias in their work. The guideline addressing sensitivity encourages scholars to consult with their participants regarding how they choose to designate themselves both racially and ethnically, while keeping in mind the importance of the other guideline, which is maintaining precision in terminology in scholarly work. Given this, the *Publication Manual* recommends using specific rather than broad terminology. For example, in a study examining Asians, it is preferable to identify the various Asian subgroups composing the sample (e.g., Chinese American, Vietnamese American) rather than use the broader label "Asian." Further, it may be more helpful to identify the national or geographical origins of subject participants rather than using umbrella terminology (e.g., using terms such as Cuban or Central American rather than Hispanic).

Authors of the *DSM-IV-TR* (American Psychiatric Association, 2000) have acknowledged the challenges clinicians face in their diagnostic assessment of mental illness in light of the increasing diversity of clients receiving treatment. Holding wide international acceptance as a diagnostic tool for mental disorders, the *DSM-IV-TR* encourages clinicians to practice greater sensitivity to cultural and ethnic factors in their clinical work. Further, the authors stress the importance of understanding and appreciating that what is considered pathological in one cultural group may be considered normative in another.

To provide a guide for practicing greater sensitivity to ethnic and cultural issues in therapy, authors of the *DSM-IV-TR:* (1) included a section regarding cultural variations in the manifestation of illnesses described in the *DSM-IV* classifications, (2) included an index to illustrate culture-bound syndromes not addressed in *DSM-IV* classifications, and (3) included an outline designed to aid the clinician in systematically formulating and understanding the impact of the client's cultural context on his or her mental illness. While this appears to address cultural differences in understanding mental illness, nowhere in the *DSM-IV-TR* has the definition of culture or ethnicity been offered. It appears that the two terms were used interchangeably, which implies that they are the same and ignores their specific nuances.

Thus, even official psychological guidebooks do not offer much guidance in defining ethnicity. While attempts have been made in identifying the variable, there is still a substantial lack of precision in capturing its essence, which will consequently lead to continuing inconsistency and confusion about its meaning.

RACE VERSUS ETHNICITY

The predominant mode of thinking in the social sciences, and in psychological theory and research in particular, is that race and ethnicity are overlapping and for the most part interchangeable constructs (Phinney, 1996). Thus, in most studies, ethnicity is merely another term for race (Hutchison, 1988; Yinger, 1985). In a content analysis of articles in prominent psychology journals over a period of 30 years, Beutler, Brown, Crothers, Booker, and Seabrook (1996) found that researchers have begun to use the term ethnicity when describing subjects while still relying on the five racial groups to categorize their subjects: White/Caucasian, Black/African American, Asian or Asian American, Hispanic/Latino, and Native American. This adoption of the term ethnicity has not happened serendipitously but is in fact a response to a strong call for such a change. The term ethnicity has been deemed "less emotionally laden and biased" and "less subject to stereotypic views" (Aspinall, 2001) than the term race. In addition, this change has been applauded for its seeming shift away from biological explanations for differences among groups to more culturally based differences (Beutler et al., 1996; Oppenheimer, 2001).

However, Helms and Talleyrand (1997) argued that allowing ethnicity to serve as a proxy for race limits further exploration of the construct of ethnicity, which in turn impedes understanding of the effect of ethnicity on individual and group attitudes and behavior. They promote the separation of the two constructs, with ethnicity referring to "dimensions of cultural socialization and expression."

Confusing race and ethnicity also obscures the reality of racism in the lives of people of Color in the United States and shifts attention away from research on how racism affects access to and quality of mental heath service delivery. Instead, any differences in utilization of services as well as in counseling process or outcome is attributed to cultural factors (such as a client's attitudes toward help-seeking) or cultural (e.g., worldview) differences between client and therapist. While such research is essential, elimination of research on racial variables avoids the discussion of structural factors affecting service delivery and runs the risk of "blaming the victim" (Aspinall, 2001).

Some researchers have found that members of the same racial group share similar cultural values (Carter & Helms, 1987). Due to the realities of racism, the history of segregation, and differential racial socialization, racial groups can also be conceptualized as ethnic groups (Taylor, 1979). However, rather than see this as further evidence for replacing the term "race" with "ethnicity," we propose that researchers clarify when they are studying a group in terms of ethnicity or in terms of race.

From a scientific perspective, Helms (1996) asserts that ethnicity and race should be maintained as separate constructs for research results to be externally valid. Ethnicity has seldom been treated as a scientific construct (Oppenheimer, 2001). We argue that to truly understand the nature of ethnicity, it must be isolated from other related constructs and studied rigorously, as is any other scientific variable. This would enable the study of potential interrelationships between ethnicity and similar variables.

Ethnicity Defined

Ethnicity is a complex construct that can overlap with many other concepts, such as ancestry, culture, race, family background, and religion. This has led researchers to use these terms interchangeably, leading to results with questionable validity. While most theorists agree that ethnicity is a multidimensional construct, containing both objective (or external) and subjective (or internal) facets, we contend that these dimensions must also be studied separately. Thus, ethnicity should be isolated from ancestry, culture, race, family background, and religion. Ethnicity should also be considered separately from ethnic identity, and any investigation of ethnicity should also take ethnic identity into account in order to access the subjective dimension of ethnicity (i.e., the extent to which one identifies with one's ethnic group). Specifically, we argue for a definition of ethnicity as categorical, namely, as country of origin. Inherent in our definition is the focus on shared culture as a result of socialization and a group's particular historical experience. For example, a man who was born in the United States and whose parents were born in Puerto Rico would be considered American by most outside observers. Thus, according to our proposed definition, he would be called American in terms of ethnicity and Puerto Rican in terms of heritage. Culturally, he may be more American, more Puerto Rican, or bicultural, depending on how he was raised. Depending on his subjective experience of his ethnicity, he may choose the label Puerto Rican, American, or Puerto Rican American, among others. This example separates the objective and subjective dimensions of ethnicity into three separate variables: ethnicity, heritage, and ethnic identity. This example does not take race into account, which can be added as yet another variable.

We recognize that our definition may appear reductionistic. Clearly, this definition of ethnicity does not reflect the way average people view themselves. However, we believe that by isolating and objectifying the variable ethnicity, the result will be a more rigorous scientific analysis and thus clearer understanding of the construct. Contrast the example above, of the American-born Puerto Rican, with a person born in Puerto Rico who has only recently arrived in the United States. If both are considered Puerto Rican in terms of ethnicity and studied as part of the same group, we run the risk of losing a great deal of important information about each of these people. The experience of being raised in different countries and cultural contexts may not be fully captured by merely controlling for acculturation. In addition, researchers would miss learning about the American aspects of the individual born in the United States while lumping him into a category with Puerto Ricans only. Studying ethnicity in this more traditional way also runs the risk of assuming that only so-called ethnic minority individuals "have" ethnicity or culture. This leads to a gap in our understanding of the "American" ethnicity, thus rendering American as a culture or ethnicity invisible.

CONCLUSION

A great deal of important research has been conducted on ethnicity in relation to various mental health constructs. However, the ambiguity that surrounds the term ethnicity and its confounding with other demographic variables has made it nearly impossible to generalize across research studies to advance understanding of the construct. Although many argue that ethnicity serves as an umbrella variable incorporating a set of interdependent variables, we propose that ethnicity be separated out as a discrete, categorical variable that can be easily identified and studied in conjunction with other variables, such as ethnic identity and heritage. We believe this would lead to a more consistent definition of ethnicity in research and thus more useful, valid research conclusions to guide counseling, research, policy, and training. With its focus on multicultural research, individual differences, and human development, counseling psychology is in a unique position to offer insight into the complex meaning of this construct.

REFERENCES

Alba, R. D. (1990). *Ethnic identity: The transformation of white America.* New Haven, CT: Yale University Press.

American Psychiatric Association. (2000). *Diagnostic and statistical manual of mental disorders* (4th ed., text rev.). Washington, DC: Author.

American Psychological Association. (2001). *Publication manual of the American Psychological Association* (5th ed.). Washington, DC: American Psychological Association.

Aspinall, P. J. (2001). Operationalising the collection of ethnicity data in studies of the sociology of health and illness. *Sociology of Health and Illness, 23,* 829–862.

Banton, M. (1983). Racial and ethnic competition. Cambridge, UK: Cambridge University Press.

Banton, M. (2001). Progress in ethnic and racial studies. *Ethnic and Racial Studies, 24,* 173–194.

Barth, F. (1969). *Ethnic groups and boundaries.* Boston: Little, Brown.

Betancourt, H., & Lopez, S. R. (1993). The study of culture, ethnicity, and race in American psychology. *American Psychologist, 48*(6), 629–637.

Beutler, L. E., Brown, M. T., Crothers, L., Booker, K., & Seabrook, M. K. (1996). The dilemma of factitious demographic distinctions in psychological research. *Journal of Consulting and Clinical Psychology, 64,* 892–902.

Calhoun, C. (1993). Nationalism and ethnicity. *Annual Review of Sociology, 19,* 211–239.

Carter, R. T., Akinsulure-Smith, A., Smailes, E. M., & Clauss, C. (1998). The status of racial/ethnic research in counseling psychology: Committed or complacent? *Journal of Black Psychology, 24,* 322–334.

Carter, R. T., & Helms, J. E. (1987). The relationship between Black value orientations and racial identity attitudes. *Measurement and Evaluation in Counseling and Development, 19,* 185–195.

Cohen, R. (1978). Ethnicity: Problem and focus in anthropology. *Annual Review of Anthropology, 7,* 379–403.

Gans, H. J. (1979). Symbolic ethnicity: The future of ethnic groups and cultures in America. *Ethnic and Racial Studies, 2,* 1–20.

Geertz, C. (1963). The integrative revolution: Primordial sentiments and civic politics in the new states. In C. Geertz (Ed.), *Old societies and new states* (pp. 105–157). New York: Free Press.

Glazer, N., & Moynihan, D. P. (Eds.). (1975). *Ethnicity: Theory and experience.* Cambridge, MA: Harvard University Press.

Greely, A. (1971). *Why can't they be like us.* New York: Dutton.

Hechter, M. (1986). Rational choice theory and the study of race and ethnic relations. In J. Rex & D. Mason (Eds.), *Theories of race and ethnic relations* (pp. 264–279). Cambridge, UK: Cambridge University Press.

Helms, J. E. (1996). Toward a methodology for measuring and assessing racial as distinguished from ethnic identity. In G. R. Sodowsky & J. C. Impara (Eds.), *Multicultural assessment in counseling and clinical psychology* (pp. 143–192). Lincoln, NE: Buros Institute of Mental Measurements.

Helms, J. E., & Talleyrand, R. M. (1997). Race is not ethnicity. *American Psychologist, 52,* 1246–1247.

Hutchison, R. (1988). A critique of race, ethnicity, and social class in recent leisure-recreation research. *Journal of Leisure Research, 20,* 10–30.

Isaacs, H. P. (1975). *Idols of the tribe: Group identity and political change.* New York: Harper & Row.

Isajiw, W. W. (1974). Definitions of ethnicity. *Ethnicity, 1,* 111–124.

Isajiw, W. W. (1993). Definition and dimensions of ethnicity: A theoretical framework. In Statistics Canada & U.S. Bureau of the Census (Eds.), *Challenges of measuring an ethnic world: Science, politics and reality: Proceedings of the joint Canada–United States conference on the measurement of ethnicity, April 1–3, 1992.* Washington, DC: U.S. Government Printing Office.

Kaufert, J. M. (1977). Situational identity and ethnicity among Ghanaian university students. *Journal of Modern African Studies, 15,* 126–135.

Kaufmann, E. (2000). Liberal ethnicity: Beyond liberal nationalism and minority rights. *Ethnic and Racial Studies, 23,* 1086–1119.

Levine, H. B. (1999). Reconstructing ethnicity. *Journal of the Royal Anthropological Institute, 5,* 165–180.

Marger, M. N. (2002). *Race and ethnic relations: American and global perspectives (6th ed.).* Belmont, CA: Wadsworth.

Nagel, J. (1994). Constructing ethnicity: Creating and recreating ethnic identity and culture. *Social Problems, 41,* 152–176.

Oppenheimer, G. M. (2001). Paradigm lost: Race, ethnicity, and the search for a new population taxonomy. *American Journal of Public Health, 91,* 1049–1055.

Ornstein, M. (2000). The specificity of ethnicity. Institute for Social Research Newsletter, 15.

Phinney, J. S. (1990). Ethnic identity in adolescents and adults: Review of research. *Psychological Bulletin, 108,* 499–514.

Phinney, J. S. (1996). When we talk about American ethnic groups, what do we mean? *American Psychologist, 51,* 918–927.

Pinderhughes, E. (1989). *Understanding race, ethnicity, and power: The key to efficacy in clinical practice.* New York: Free Press.

Plax, M. (1972). On studying ethnicity. *Public Opinion Quarterly, 36,* 99–104.

Raspberry, W. (1989, January 4). When "black" becomes "African American." *Washington Post,* p. A19.

Sollors, W. (Ed.). (1996). *Theories of ethnicity: A classical reader.* New York: New York University Press.

Stack, J. J. (1986). *The primordial challenge: Ethnicity in the contemporary world.* New York: Greenwood Press.

Sue, D. W., Carter, R. T., Casas, J. M., Fouad, N. A., Ivey, A. E., Jensen, M., et al. (Eds.). (1998). *Multicultural counseling competencies: Individual and organizational development.* Thousand Oaks, CA: Sage.

Sue, S. (1991). Ethnicity and culture in psychological research and practice. In J. D. Goodchilds (Ed.), *Psychological perspectives on human diversity in America: The master lectures* (pp. 51–85). Washington, DC: American Psychological Association.

Taylor, R. (1979). Black ethnicity and the persistence of ethnogenesis. *American Journal of Sociology, 84,* 1401–1423.

van den Berghe, P. L. (1981). *The ethnic phenomenon.* New York: Elsevier.

Wallman, K. K., Evinger, S., & Schechter, S. (2000). Measuring our nation's diversity: Developing a common language for data on race/ethnicity. *American Journal of Public Health, 90,* 1704–1708.

Weber, M. (1968). *Economy and society* (Vol. 1, pp. 3–38). G. Roth & C. Wittich (Eds). New York: Bedminister Press.

Yancey, W. L., Ericksen, E. P., & Juliani, R. N. (1976). Emergent ethnicity: A review and reformulation. *American Sociological Review, 41,* 391–403.

Yinger, J. M. (1985). Ethnicity. *Annual Review of Sociology, 11,* 151–180.

CHAPTER 4

Race: A Social and Psychological Analysis of the Term and Its Meaning

Robert T. Carter and Alex L. Pieterse

Racial classification is an enduring, complex, and controversial phenomenon that affects every aspect of life in North America. Race, its meaning and use in society, is a topic that continues to receive considerable attention in academic, economic, social, psychological, health, and political arenas. The concept and application of race in daily life historically has been shaped and deeply influenced by the physical and social science disciplines. In view of the continued significance of race in American life, this chapter provides a discussion of race from a sociopsychological perspective, highlights the mechanisms through which the significance of race is maintained, and argues for the need to view race as a psychological construct in the social sciences.

We begin by providing a brief historical review of the development of race as an idea and as used in social, economic, and political stratification systems that in essence limits life opportunities of the people who are not members of the preferred racial groups. The overview of the historical development of race is followed by a discussion of how race is used in contemporary life. The chapter concludes with an approach for understanding race as both a social and a psychological aspect of a person's daily life.

HISTORY OF RACE: THE WORD AND ITS MEANING

There is a great deal of confusion surrounding the meaning of the term race because it is often used interchangeably with ethnicity. The use of race and ethnicity as words with the same meaning obscures any distinction each term may convey.

In the United States, ethnicity is used to refer to national origin, and to race or religious group solidarity of Jewish Americans (Carter, 1995). The confusion about race arises because ethnicity is used as a euphemism for race when referring to people of Color and as a nonracial designation for Whites (Betancourt & Lopez, 1993; Helms & Cook, 1999). For example, Blacks, Asians, and Native Americans are often referred to as members of ethnic groups, as are Italian, Jewish, Irish, and Polish Americans. The tendency to ignore race by using ethnic group obscures for all groups their country (ethnic heritage) or culture of origin. The use of ethnicity to denote race disregards the ethnic variations among people of Color. Blacks are also American, Jamaican, English, and African, as Asians are Koreans, Chinese, Japanese, and Vietnamese, and Native Americans are Hopi, Seneca, Navajo, Miami, Sioux, and Blackfeet. The use of the term "ethnic group" has gained popularity, in part, because it is believed that it carries fewer negative or emotional connotations.

We contend that all groups in North America belong to both a racial and an ethnic group. Ethnic group membership or designation does not have the same meaning as racial group membership. As Helms (1996) points out, there are important distinctions between race and ethnicity. Ethnicity has not been used to nor does it define a place in the social hierarchy, whereas race does locate a group in the social hierarchy. One's ethnic group can change over time; one's racial group membership does not. Race does not define a specific or singular culture; people who belong to the Asian racial group represent many cultures. In contrast, ethnic group membership usually means membership in a singular culture.

Ethnic group membership means that one is socialized into one's culture. Racial group membership involves knowledge of racism and racial stereotypes. Law and traditional customs have determined who belongs to a particular racial group, while ethnic group membership is usually determined by in-group customs and desires. One's ethnic group status in many societies is no longer salient after three generations. On the other hand, racial group membership lasts over many generations. One's racial group membership is observable by others, whereas ethnic group membership is seldom recognized or observed by others. One is a member of a racial group through no action of one's own since it is an external designation. However, ethnic group membership requires active involvement in the group, usually learned through socialization (Yeh & Hunter, this *Handbook,* Volume One; Bowser, this *Handbook,* Volume One). Ethnic groups require new members from one's country of origin for the group to maintain itself. Racial group membership does not require infusion of immigrants from the home country.

Race, like ethnicity, has associated with it considerable confusion. Nevertheless, race is typically determined on the basis of skin color and physical features and, for Hispanics in the United States, language. Language has been used to define and identify Hispanics and Latinos as a functional racial group to distinguish them from Whites. Race has been defined in multiple ways, each reflecting a particular perspective, including biological (genetic), social (social construction), and psychological (identification with one's racial group; Carter, 1995; Jones, 1991; Smedley, 1999). A common and popular understanding of race, as seen in the dictionary definition, is that racial groups share physical and cultural characteristics: "a breeding stock of animals, a family, tribe, people or nation belonging to the same stock—a category of humankind that shares certain distinctive physical traits, an inherited temperament or disposition" (*Merriam Webster's Collegiate Dictionary,* 2003, p. 1024). Based on the dictionary definition, one's actions, social behavior, and attributes are linked to biological and genetic aspects of racial group membership. Therefore, race has been used to make psychological and cultural inferences about one's ascribed membership in a designated group (e.g., White, Asian, Native Indian, American). Today, the meaning attached to race still carries most, if not all, of its earlier elements for many who use the term. Yet, there is evidence to suggest that in fact race is a social construction with little connection to biology and genes (Graves, 2001), yet with strong connections to the psychological reality of most Americans (Carter, 1995; 2000b; Feagin & McKinney, 2003; Plotkin, 1993). The importance of the meaning associated with race is highlighted by Marger (2000), who observed:

> Most people attach significance to the concept of race and consider it a real and important division of humanity. And, as long as people believe that differences in selected physical traits are meaningful, they will act their beliefs. What is perhaps most important regarding the social classification of races (people) is that the perceived physical differences among groups are assumed to correspond to social and behavioral differences. Thus, Blacks, because they are black, are assumed to behave in certain ways and to achieve at certain levels because they are black. Whites are assumed to behave and achieve in other ways because they are white, and so on. (p. 167)

RACE: THE ROOTS OF ITS MEANING

Smedley (1999) discussed the work of scholars who sought to identify the use and roots of the word race. According to Smedley, Dover thought that "race" began to be used in "Latin-based languages" and eventually was used in the English language. Trevor took exception to Dover's line of reasoning about the origin of "race"; he claimed that "race" came from the Latin word *ratio,* meaning "classification," and could have been used to refer to species or kind. Trevor believed that ratio developed into the Italian *razza.* Spitzer supported Trevor's belief that *razza* was used in relation to animals and group classification. Race was also used at this time in history to refer to "a group of persons, animals, or plants, connected by common descent or origin. Having some common feature or features" (p. 38).

More important, Allen (1994) pointed out that the root of the concept race, with its derivative meanings, has evolved as a worldview. It was in the seventeenth century that race began to be used as a word to describe humans. The English translation of the Italian *razza* was race, and the word was applied to people encountered in the New World. Prior to this application, race was grounded in English attempts to conquer and oppress the Irish:

> Irish resistance . . . enraged many of the English, who persisted in viewing the Irish as rude, beastly, ignorant, cruel and unruly infidels. . . . Some Englishmen argued what was to become a familiar strain in European attitudes toward Indians and Africans in the New World during the coming century: that the Irish (who were thought of in racial terms) were better off as slaves of the English than they were retaining the brutish customs of their traditional culture. (Smedley, 1999, p. 57)

What is often not well understood about the power of the concept and use of race is its association with the breeding of animals. Intertwined in the definition and use of the word is the belief that the attributes and characteristics that identified distinct racial groups were heritable, inbred, unalterable, and permanent. The types of attributes and characteristics associated with racial group membership (and breed animals) included body size and build, skin and hair color, and such traits as aggressiveness, dullness, and intelligence as well as psychological and emotional characteristics.

So the concept and use of race carries the powerful notion that differences that are presumed to characterize particular racial groups cannot be changed. On the other hand, characteristics associated with ethnicity and cultural group membership are believed to be fluid and flexible. Jones (1997) and Smedley (1999) noted that the historical impact of events such as the Spanish Inquisition, the expansion of trade via sea merchants, the process of colonization, and the establishment of a slave trade are considered to be the most influential developments in the idea and use of race (Feagin & McKinney, 2003).

Religious institutions were dominant during the historical period of initial European exploration and contact with previously unknown groups of peoples, and as such, Christian and religious theories were invoked to help explain physical and cultural differences and to justify subjugation of some racial and cultural groups (Graves, 2001). Therefore, in seeking to understand the development of such attitudes that accompanied the growing use of racial categorization, the impact of Christian ideology cannot be overlooked. Europeans attempted to understand the differences among the diverse peoples they encountered on their journeys to the East and the New World. Christian dogma provided a paradigm that equated difference with deficiency and evil. The Spanish Inquisition, which equated purity with race and culture, and the Protestant Reformation were key historical events that were influential among European people in shaping their view of people in the New World. Additionally, European explorers equated civilization with Christianity and provided the seeds of what would later become a scientific justification of the deficiencies of non-White and non-European people with regard to morality and intellect.

Furthermore, religious ideas drawn from various interpretations of the Bible held that some people were cursed by God to be servants. The mark of the curse was believed widely to be dark or Black skin, according to many versions of Christian belief. Thus, by using biblical verse, racial classification was justified. However, Graves (2001) pointed out that a close reading of the Bible shows no specific reference to Black people as cursed servants. However, as noted by Fanon (1967) the color black was viewed by Europeans as synonymous with evil, sin, war, and Black people were viewed as the embodiment of evil.

Transalantic contact with different cultures and peoples had a significant impact on the European psyche (Graves, 2001), which can be seen in the thinking of the English philosopher David Hume, who wrote:

> I am apt to suspect the Negroes, and in general all the other species of men (for there are four or five different kinds) to be naturally inferior to whites. There never was a civilized nation of any complexion other than white, nor any individual eminent either in action or speculation.

On the other hand, the most rude and barbarous of the white, such as the ancient Germans, the present Tartars, have still something eminent about them, in their valor, form of government, or some other particular. (quoted in Fryer, 1984, p. 10)

These historical movements and philosophical stances provided a platform on which scientific efforts to understand race would later be built.

GENETIC AND OTHER EXPLANATIONS FOR RACIAL DIVERSITY

Other efforts to explain racial groups and physical differences have been advanced throughout history. Based on physical differences, it was proposed that people could not have descended from the same source (e.g., Adam and Eve, or a common ancestor). Thus, ideas of polygenesis were used to explain human variations and also served as the rationale for beliefs in the superiority of European people. In its original scientific use, race referred to a biological classification presumed to be associated with genetic transmission (Allen, 1994; Gould, 1981; Littlefield, Lieberman, & Reynolds, 1982; Smedley, 1998). The inferiority paradigm assumed that visible racial/ethnic group people are biologically limited and genetically inferior compared to Whites. This paradigm has a long history, both among the populace and in many scientific and academic disciplines, including psychology (Carter, 1996; Feagin, 2000; Fernando, 1998; Gossett, 1998).

After being hotly debated, the validity of race as a purely biological variable has been rejected, as there is no way to distinguish groups defined by race solely on the basis of genetic material (Graves, 2001). For instance, in North America, the current gene pool emerges from the mixing of Europeans, Africans, Black Americans, and Native people from various ethnic and national groups. Some would argue that all descendants in the United States are from a mixed-race gene pool and therefore are racially mixed (Bamshad & Olson, 2003; Carter, 1995; Graves, 2001; Jones & Carter, 1996; Yee, Halford, Fairchild, & Wyatt, 1993).

Because there is a compelling tendency to categorize individuals into groups based on visible makers, such as skin color, and because the phenotypical racial factors are easily detected, race is one of the most salient grounds for social categorization (Jones, 1991). Race therefore has become the basis for expectations regarding social roles, ability, performance, social and cultural values, and norms and mores for group and nongroup members (Alderfer, 2000; Darling-Hammond, 2000; Fine, 2000). The practical result of these beliefs is clearly seen in the following statement by Abraham Lincoln, an individual who is widely regarded as a champion of racial equality:

I am not, nor ever have been, in favor of bringing about in any way the social and political equality of the white and black races. I am not, nor ever have been, in favor of making voters or jurors of Negroes or qualifying them to hold office. . . . I will say in addition to this that there is a physical difference between the white and black races, which I believe, will ever forbid the two races living together on terms of social and political equality. And in as much as they cannot so live while they do remain together, there must be the position of superiors and inferior, and I as much as any other man am in favor of having the superior position assigned to the white race. (quoted in Nicolay & Hay, 1894, pp. 369, 370)

During the nineteenth century, as Haller (1971) has pointed out, "almost the whole of scientific thought in both America and Europe . . . accepted race inferiority" (p. 77). The idea of the superiority of White over Black races was well established, and the concept of White prejudice or White racial attitudes was not a scientific issue of any significance. Attitudes of racial superiority or antipathy to Blacks were widely accepted as inevitable and natural responses to the seemingly obvious inferiority and "backwardness" of Blacks and other colonial peoples (p. 1185). It is evident that the historical development of race allowed for the scientific employment of race to categorize groups of people as superior or inferior (Duckitt, 1992; Feagin & McKinney, 2003). Smedley (1999) believed that race:

> was the cultural invention of arbitrary meaning applied to what appeared to be natural division within the human species. The meaning has social value, but no intrinsic relationship to the biological diversity itself. Race has a reality created in the human mind, [but is] not a reflection of objective truth. . . . The most critical element of all was the belief that each exclusive group so differentiated was created unique and distinct by nature or God so that the imputed differences, believed fixed and unalterable, could never be bridged or transcended. (p. 22)

Michael Banton (1998) has argued that the development of racial theory cannot be fully appreciated without understanding the purposes that such a theory would serve and the social milieu in which the theory was developed. So the development of races as subspecies takes place in the context of a growing acceptance of Darwin's classification of species, while race as type was developed at a time when classification systems supported the economic structure and justified the existence of slavery (Feagin, 2000).

Given the historical review of both the social and scientific developments of race, we now turn to the social implications of race and its continuing relevance in contemporary society.

SOCIAL-POLITICAL IMPLICATIONS: THE RELATIONSHIP OF SOCIAL STRATIFICATION AND RACE

A significant relationship has been noted between the construction of race and the presence of social stratification. Marger (2000), in describing the process of assimilation of various racial and ethnic groups in the United States, notes the critical importance of visibility and its accompanying impact on the degree and rate of assimilation in to the dominant White culture. Building on the historical development of race, one can argue that attributions of inferiority and savagery based on visible difference are at the core of systems of social hierarchy that were and are supported by the development of various forms of racism: individual, institutional, and cultural (Feagin, 2000; Jones, 1997; Sue, 2003).

African Americans and Native Americans continue to be on the lower rungs of the social ladder. While this can be understood in the context of slavery and conquest/genocide, it is also noted that various attributions have been associated with Native Americans and Blacks as a reflection of their physical difference in relation to the dominant White group. It is true that many groups coming to America have experienced various forms of discrimination and oppression (e.g., southern Europeans, Jews), but most of these groups have been able to assimilate and climb the social ladder. With the establishment of social hierarchies both from a historical perspective and as an ongoing reality, others, especially non-Whites, have not been able to move up the social ladder, in spite of the fact that they have been in the country for many more generations. We argue that the lack of assimilation by Hispanics, American Indians, and people of African descent is largely related to the impact of physical difference, that is, their racial designation. The social construction of race therefore carries with it very real implications and consequences (Feagin, 2000; Feagin & McKinney, 2003).

The definition of race that we believe most aptly describes its use and meaning is one that has defined race as a sociopolitical designation in which individuals are assigned to a particular racial group based on presumed visible characteristics, such as skin color, physical features, and, in some cases, language. "Hispanic," for instance, is used as a functional race category that is not based on skin color, because people of Latin descent vary in skin color. Instead, language and culture are used to distinguish them from White Americans; the designation is White non-Hispanic (Carter, 2000b).

We now turn to a discussion of the system of human classification and stratification. Our objective is to emphasize elements associated with race that distinguish it from ethnicity and culture and that account for race's enduring qualities.

As we have shown, the race construct was used to distinguish groups on the basis of skin color, physical features, and language. From such distinctions racial classification systems evolved in which physical differences were associated with biological and genetic traits and characteristics. Notions of some racial groups being superior and others inferior dominated scientific and lay thinking, attitudes, and behavior for more than four centuries. The issue of genetics being associated with race has not been completely laid to rest (Bamshad & Olson, 2003; Hernstein & Murray, 1994; Rushton, 2000). Nevertheless, Bamshad and Olson contend that although geographic and distinct regions of the world can identify people, "self-reported ancestry is not necessarily a good predictor of genetic composition of a large number of Americans. Accordingly, common notions of race do not always reflect a person's genetic background" (p. 83).

The most compelling use of race that reflects its meaning comes from the imposition of legal and social customs that have set the worldview of race and racial groups firmly into the fabric of American institutions, social relationships, and individual belief systems. Consider, for instance, the system of racial stratification that was created with the imposition of slavery, forced migration of Native Americans and

Hispanics, and immigration laws that restricted the life opportunities of Asians (Feagin, 2000).

The status of Whites, rich and poor, was elevated and justified in myriad ways in everyday life. More important, racial language was developed and used in which White was set to be a marker for social status and power in relation to those not so designated. Yet the ending of slavery brought about change and some loosening of the divided opportunities for people of Color, former slaves in particular. For a brief time during Reconstruction Blacks began to participate in and contribute to society economically and politically (Packard, 2002). The gains did not last long, as Whites found it hard to accept Black progress. Slowly and with the federal government's blessing, Black people's rights were stripped again under the guise of state and federal laws that promoted segregation (Packard, 2002). For more than 100 years (1865–1965) after being freed as slaves, Blacks were denied the right to vote and were denied access and opportunity to most areas of life in American society. Denied rights as citizens and blocked from participating in most areas of social and economic life, Blacks were kept at the lowest social status. As Jaynes and Williams (1989) noted, "Most Black Americans could not work, live, shop, eat, seek entertainment or travel where they chose. A large majority of Blacks lived in poverty and few Black children had the opportunity to receive a basic education" (p. 3).

In a report that examined the status of Blacks in America from 1939 to 1989, Jaynes and Williams (1989) considered the status of Black participation in social institutions, residential segregation, and social life. They also studied racial attitudes and behavior during the 50-year period, as well as changes in the identity of Blacks and how Black identity influenced community and institution building. Other areas studied were politics, economics, education, health, the state of children and families, and crime and the administration of criminal justice. Jaynes and Williams noted some areas of change and improvement in Blacks' status during this period, which was due in part to economic prosperity, changes in social and racial attitudes, and social activism primarily by Blacks in the 1950s and 1960s.

The social and racial attitudes of Americans changed dramatically between 1939 and 1989. The overt racial attitudes that supported segregation, denial of rights, and legal discrimination shifted to attitudes that expressed support for equality. The new attitudes led to the dismantling of the legal system of segregation and discrimination. Principles of equality and fairness became more pronounced in the public's racial and social attitudes. However, regarding racial attitudes and behaviors, the researches noted that "the foremost conclusion is that race still matters greatly in the United States" (Jaynes & Williams, 1989, p. 155). While the ideals of fairness, equality, and justice were strongly expressed as well as principles of fair treatment, evidence of resistance was still significant. For example:

> Principles of equality are endorsed less when social contact is close, of long duration, or frequent and when it involves significant numbers of Blacks; Whites are much less prone to endorse policies to implement equal participation of [B]lacks in society. Evidence of the systemic nature of racism and its manifestation in everyday life. (Feagin, 2000, p. 155)

The study also found that although Black participation in American society (i.e., in the arts, education, religion, and other major institutions) increased after 1940, the greater level of participation did not result in significant or substantial integration. The report shows that even after legal enactments outlawing the subordination of Blacks and other people of Color to Whites, the idea that race determines one's value and worth has remained a strong aspect of American behavior, even while people express principles of equality and fairness. Many scholars now would argue that the meaning of race is more accurately understood in terms of economic or other factors. Some suggest that how a group comes to be part of the society is also an important factor it determining its subsequent social status.

Marger (2000) points out that the manner in which a group enters a society has powerful implications for its subsequent status and for how the group relates to the dominant group. Many people of varied racial, cultural, and ethnic groups were already in North America; others came to the colonies and later to the United States. It is striking to see that some groups along racial lines have gained access and opportunity to mainstream society, yet non-White groups have remained marginal (Sue, 2003). The study by Jaynes and Williams (1989) regarding Blacks shows their continued marginal status. If the characteristic that mattered most was race, then one would expect a similar fate for members of other racial groups.

Marger (2000, 2002) argued that one's status is not determined by one's race as much as by whether a group's social origins were voluntary or involuntary. If a people were beaten in battle (American Indians), had land taken (Mexican Americans), or were bought against their will (Africans), a subordinate status is likely to hold for many generations. Additionally, Marger describes social attainment along two dimensions: cultural assimilation and structural assimilation. Psychologists think of cultural assimilation as acculturation wherein one group adapts the cultural traits (i.e., language, religion) of another, usually the dominant group (Kohatsu, this *Handbook*, Volume One). For our purposes, cultural assimilation involves complete immersion into the culture of the dominant group, and acculturation involves adaptation of selective cultural elements without losing elements of one's culture of origin.

Structural assimilation takes place on two levels: formally, which is called secondary assimilation, and informally, which is primary assimilation. Secondary structural assimilation involves access on equal terms with the dominant group to power and privilege within major social institutions: economic, political, educational, and so on. Primary structural assimilation has to do with interaction among racial/ethnic group members within personal networks, such as neighborhoods, clubs, friendships, and family (marriage). Indicators of primary assimilation include marriage, club participation or membership, and mixed housing patterns. The greater the level of interaction with the dominant group, the higher the level of primary assimilation.

The dominant racial/ethnic group in North American society is White Anglo-Saxon Protestant. Marger (2000) notes:

> It was this group, the defining ethnic features of which were its north-western European and Protestant origins, that became the core group and subsequently set the tone of the

society and established its major economic, political, and social institutions. Their concentrated social power is evident in their over-representation in political and economic circles of power. (p. 147)

Time has created a broader national base of the group in power, but its White Protestant features remain. Moreover, the cultural values on which much of society and its institutions are based are grounded in Anglo- or European American cultural values. Our language, laws, education system, public policies, and religious systems are based on preferences of the dominant racial/ethnic group (Carter, 2004). Moreover, even though the nation is one of immigrants, national pressure and preference have been for conformity to the core dominant group's cultural values and preferences.

If one considers the status of various racial groups in terms of the cultural and structural features described above, Whites from various ethnic groups have the highest levels of cultural, primary, and secondary structural assimilation. Marger (2000) notes that Asians, Native American Indians, and Hispanics have attained moderate cultural assimilation, and Blacks are quite high in terms of acculturation or cultural assimilation. Asians have moderate levels of secondary structural assimilation (i.e., access to institutions) but are ranked low in primary structural assimilation, while Blacks, American Indians, and Hispanics are ranked low in both primary and secondary structural assimilation. In relative terms, Blacks are ranked the lowest of racial groups, followed by American Indians, Hispanics, and Asians. As Marger pointed out, each of the three racial groups is involved in considerable and continuing conflict with dominant group members and institutions.

Thus, for most groups of Color, status in the social structure remains close to the bottom on many indicators. *The point here is that during the twentieth century and the early years of the twenty-first century, the meaning, attitudes, and behaviors surrounding race have changed, yet the fact of race's significance has not.* What is harder to discern are the contours and features of race and its meaning (Feagin & McKinney, 2003).

Researchers discovered that race relations were shifting during the 1960s and 1970s at the same time racism and the meaning associated with one's race began to be less overt and more covert or symbolic (Dovidio & Gaertner, 1998; Dovidio, Gaertner, Kawakami, & Hodson, 2002; Jones, 1998). A new form of racism was identified, called modern or symbolic racism, in which one would not express negative racial attitudes openly but would do so indirectly. So, although people supported the ideals of equality, at the same time they resisted any effort at implementing programs designed to address historic exclusion based on race (e.g., affirmative action programs, reparations for descendants of slaves). Also, the language associated with race and racism began to change (Alderfer, 2000). Increasingly, people opted to use "ethnicity" for "race" and to contend that the relationships among historically disenfranchised Americans and Whites were less salient given the influx of immigrants from various countries around the world. What was more salient was ethnicity and culture. One of the sources for the argument of the importance of culture came from disenfranchised American "minorities" (Carter, this *Handbook,* Volume One).

Prior to the 1950s and 1960s (and for some today), members of non-White groups in North American society were considered biologically and genetically inferior to Whites, thus the justification for their lower status and the denial of education and civil rights. Once opportunities began to open for people of Color in the late 1960s and 1970s, many were able to earn college and graduate degrees; they then argued that inferiority was a false paradigm. In the 1970s, a new model was proposed to explain non-White progress: the cultural deprivation or culture of poverty paradigm (Harper & McFadden, 2003). The cultural deprivation theory was, and in some forms continues to be, used by psychologists and other social scientist as an alternative to the claims of biological inferiority. It replaced biology with environment, and its proponents argued that people of Color were denied the proper and appropriate setting or environment in which to learn, work, and live and therefore were held back from full participation in society.

By the mid-1970s, scholars of Color and other researchers in the social sciences argued that the cultural deprivation theories assumed that White culture was normative and treated people of Color as devoid of their own cultural patterns, traditions, and values. In psychology, many (Harper & McFadden, 2003) began to argue that minorities were not inferior or culturally deprived or disadvantaged; they were culturally different. Thus, by the 1980s the cultural movement in psychology and counseling and other disciplines was well underway. The culturally different emphasis initially did not include a larger range of differences; rather, its emphasis was on race alone as the primary source of cultural difference. As scholars developed models of psychology based on the notion of cultural difference, the idea of counseling and helping relationships as being cross-cultural began to emerge. But "cross-cultural" was initially defined in terms of multiple sources of difference, such as gender, age, and religion. Cross-cultural became *cultural diversity,* and multicultural perspectives evolved that included many aspects of difference as equal in importance, such as age, social class, sexual orientation, gender, and religion. Thus, race has become one of many aspects of difference (Sue & Sue, 2003).

In other areas of American life, various aspects of race-based experiences were being isolated and disconnected from a systematic set of polices and experiences associated with race (Feagin, 2000). In this way, the meaning associated with race and racism was being dismantled and fragmented. Prior to the shifting of the meaning of race, one achievement of scholars was the identification of three forms of racism: individual, institutional, and cultural (Jones & Carter, 1996). Individual racism is prejudice held by a specific person who believes that members of a different racial group are inferior to his or her own group. Institutional racism, on the other hand, has been defined as the intentional or unintentional outcomes that result from organizational policies and practices that affect members of racial groups disproportionately, for instance, in education, graduation rates, poor heath outcomes, and low employment rates for people of Color. Institutional racism is reflected in the gross differences in social participation and outcomes that exceed the group's numbers in the population. Cultural racism is reflected in the norms, values, language, and forms preferred or denied (the cultural styles of non-Whites) by dominant cultural group members.

Scholars and other researchers have been able to show the cultural and institutional patterns of racism that affect the lives of people of Color in efforts to secure housing, education, jobs, health care, and political representation (Williams, Neighbors, & Jackson, 2003). One side effect, or, some would argue, form of resistance to the identification of systemic racism, was to fragment each element or aspect of racism to words or forms that remove it from the whole (Feagin, 2000; Fine, 2000). Thus, for instance, remedies for racism in education and employment have been discussed as affirmative action and quota systems. As the existence of bias and hate crimes has become more common, individual acts of racism are treated not as manifestations of a system of meaning and accepted action based on the idea of dominant group superiority and power, but as isolated acts of hate and bias, whereby the systematic elements are lost and the focus becomes the act or feelings of an individual person. The actions of members of official institutions such as the police and the criminal justice system and how they use race as a way to focus investigations and punishment has been referred to as racial profiling or racial bias—again, terms that separate the action from the histories and systematically held and enacted set of beliefs about what it means to be a member of a particular racial group. Much of what was said and written about racism lacked complexity in that seldom did people consider psychological variation within racial groups. How one might resolve psychologically one's understanding of, rejection of, or involvement in racism was often simplistic at best.

Race as a Psychological Construct and the Role of Racism

A central question in evaluating the psychological impact of race is the notion of who benefits from racial categorization and its antecedents of oppression and racism. Are there psychological costs and benefits to being a victim or victimizer? The vast majority of literature on the subject has documented the effects of oppression and racism on the victims. Little has been written about the oppressors and the effects on them (Bowser & Hunt, 1996; Feagin, Vera, & Batur, 2001). In addition, the mental health literature has tended toward the use of sociological terms and phenomena such as the social- and group-based experiences of people of Color, in particular, Black people. The assumption seems to be that the racist conditions in which people are forced to live have negative psychological consequences. Scholars have spent centuries documenting the various mental health consequences of living under the ravages of racism. We would like to make three points about the psychological manifestations of racism:

1. The first is the need to focus on the impact of these practices on White Americans who have maintained and sustained a system of oppression through the development of cultural, institutional, and personal racism in North America.

2. Second, as we discuss the impact of racism as a form of oppression, we would like to extend that discussion beyond the individual level of analysis. We contend that it is essential to look beyond the beliefs and behaviors of individuals who may hold on to notions of the superiority of the White racial group in relation

to other racial groups. This type of belief is defined by Jones and Carter (1996) as individual racism, yet, in addition to individual racism, we argue that it is imperative to consider the impacts of racists' beliefs and practices as they have become institutionalized and core elements in North American culture. That is, we must examine the effects of racism on individuals and the group on both an institutional and a cultural level. Most people are familiar with descriptions of prejudice and acts of discrimination that usually are reported and described as beliefs held and acts taken by individuals (i.e., hate or bias). Less attention has been given to systemic and non-individualized aspects of racism. Jones and Carter define institutional racism as "those established laws, customs, and practices that systematically reflect and produce racial inequalities in American society . . . whether or not the individuals maintaining those practices have racist intentions" (pp. 2–3). Cultural racism is the conscious or subconscious conviction that White Euro-American cultural patterns and practices as reflected in economics, music, art, religious tenets, and so forth are superior to those of other racial groups (p. 3). Moreover, they noted that:

> racism is a complex concept which has the identifying characteristic of systematically unequal outcomes for people of different races. The concept of racism used here emphasizes ideology . . . and attitudes of racial superiority (individual racism), institutional power as a means of implementing ideological biases (institutional racism), and the broad-based cultural support of . . . (racists') [socialization and institutional] practices and beliefs (cultural racism). (p. 4)

3. The third point is to examine how each type of racism is manifested in the psychological structure of Whites and how people of Color are psychologically affected by racism and how one's psychological functioning varies with respect to how one resolves and copes with one's racial group membership.

Race and what it meant was clear prior to the 1950s, when racial stratification was legal and justified. The civil rights movement challenged the basis for the system of racism and shattered that clear picture of race. Now race has been fragmented into euphemistic language and disconnected terms such as "inner city," "at risk," "bias," "hate," all used to distort and hide the unspoken yet no less real impact of racial—not cultural or ethnic—beliefs (Feagin, 2000).

Despite the changes in language and meaning associated with race there has been one constant; that is, most writing about and use of race or ethnicity has treated the group as monolithic or homogeneous. The beliefs, ideas, and stereotypes held about a group were applied to all its members; moreover, characteristics, attributes, and one's membership in the group were seldom questioned. Any Black person, it was thought, could speak for the group because all Blacks (or American Indians or Hispanics) were thought to be the same. The social movement of the 1950s and 1960s revealed a significant shift in Americans' psychological and social beliefs. Scholars captured the psychological equivalent of the social movement's transformation from colored people to Black people, from Oriental to Asian, from tribes to nations, from

Hispanic to Latino. Social identity shifted from being externally imposed and de-fined to being internally developed and self-defined. "Colored" became "Black," and the psychological transformation was applied to individual Blacks in the form of theory called "racial identity." Models emerged that described the psychological process and variability of racial group identification. Racial identity theory offers a psychologically based understanding of race and presents a complex way to under-stand race and its meaning.

RACIAL IDENTITY THEORY

The term *racial identity,* not *race identity,* refers to one's psychological response to one's race; it reflects the extent to which one identifies with a particular racial or cultural group and how that identification influences perceptions, emotions, and behaviors toward people from other groups (Carter, 1995, 2000b; Helms & Cook, 1999).

In the psychological literature, there are three models of racial identity: White, Black, and people of Color. Each model is comprised of several distinct racial iden-tity statuses. The racial identity ego status is an aspect of personal identity that is expressed and integrated through a person's personality structure. It represents in-dividual, in-group, and out-group psychological resolutions. The racial identity ego statuses themselves contain a constellation of beliefs, thoughts, emotions, and be-haviors centered on one's membership in one's racial group. Although the statuses are similar for each racial group, variation exists as a result of the social position of the respective racial group; for example, each group has a distinct sociopolitical history that affects the expression of each status. It is important to point out that al-though each status is presented separately and discussed as a predominant status, the reader should not take that to mean that racial identity is about stages. The sta-tuses operate together, and it is believed that each person has available to him or her all of them in his or her personality structure. A person can develop sequentially from a less differentiated, externally derived, and less mature status to a more in-ternally based, complex, and differentiated mature status. Moreover, the profile or status configuration can have blends of various statuses or none of the statuses present within a person can be dominant. Thus, reflecting an undifferentiated or flat racial identity profile (see Carter, Helms, & Juby, 2004).

The following sections provide an overview of the models of racial identity for Blacks, people of Color, and Whites. Racial identity models for Blacks and people of Color are described together. We encourage the reader to consult other works for more detail (Carter, 1995, 2000a; Helms, this *Handbook,* Volume One; Helms & Cook, 1999; Thompson & Carter, 1997).

Whites' Psychological Responses to Race and Racism: White Racial Identity

We approach the discussion about the psychological manifestations of racism for Whites from an individual- and group-level analysis. The organizing constructs that we employ are White racial identity theory (Carter, 1995; Thompson & Carter,

1997) and the resulting emotional and behavioral effects of various resolutions on the part of each White person regarding how he or she expresses an understanding of race as part of his or her personality. The individual resolutions in turn culminate in a group coalition, which, taken together, represent Whites' dominant psychological orientations to race (i.e., racial identity operates as a profile wherein each status is present with lesser or greater distinct influences or statuses are blended) (Carter, 2000b). The group profile represents a coalition that serves as the filter used by Whites to understand the meaning and significance of race, racism, and oppression for the group as well as for members of other racial groups.

Each White person in the United States is socialized with implicit and explicit racial messages about themselves as members of a group who oppress others on the basis of race. In addition, the racial messages provide information about members of visible racial/ethnic groups (i.e., American Indians, Asians, Hispanics or Latinos, and Black Americans) who are the victims of oppression. Therefore, each type of racism becomes an integral component of each White person's ego structure or personality. Evolving a nonracist White identity means accepting one's Whiteness and recognizing the ways one participates in and benefits from individual, institutional, and cultural racism. There are six White racial identity ego statuses: Contact, Disintegration, Reintegration, Pseudo-independence, Immersion-Emersion, and Autonomy.

Externally defined and unsophisticated notions about one's White race characterize the Contact status of White racial identity. One is taught not to see race and to treat all people the same. This type of racial identity status when it is dominant or blended with other statuses might be thought of as the color-blind status or influence, in which one denies the existence of racism, but one's behavior and attitudes are guided by racist principles that have never been questioned. The person is not aware of how he or she benefits from institutional and cultural racism. Consider the psychological and emotional energy needed to deny and ignore the manner in which one's life is constructed. The psychological defense of denial and repression are strong in this status. The White person characterized by a predominately Contact ego structure is someone who is racist without knowing it. He or she reveres White culture and is an active and enthusiastic participant in its institutions. He or she may also think that the sociopolitical systems and institutions treat all citizens the same.

Blindness (especially when one is unaware) can sometimes lead to bumping into objects in the environment. To extend the analogy, in time people usually bump into the societal norms that govern cross-racial interaction, and when they open their eyes they come to see that Blacks and many other people of Color are not treated the same in the United States, no matter their accomplishments or social status. The awareness of racial inequities allows for the emergence of the Disintegration ego identity status. This White identity status evokes conscious awareness of one's Whiteness and feelings of conflict and, typically, guilt regarding that awareness. A personal moral crisis emerges. As a result, emotional turmoil accompanies this discovery. To quiet the emotional storm, persons can flee into their safe, predominantly White world, or they may choose to demonstrate that people of Color are not really inferior to Whites and set out to fix and save the victims, who just need some help overcoming the social obstacles created by racism. Another option is to decide that racism does not exist, or argue that, if it does, Whites today had nothing to do with what is usually associated with the past. Disintegration status persons are slightly aware that Whiteness does matter but are simply confused and have not yet changed their fundamental beliefs about themselves as members of the White race or about members of other races.

The power of group acceptance, coupled with the sociocultural depth of beliefs in White racism and Black and visible racial/ethnic group inferiority, make it more likely that one will come to believe that racism doesn't exist or, if it does, is a remnant of the past. Thus, for one with these ideas the next White racial identity status grows to be more distinct and exerts greater influence: Reintegration. The Reintegration status of White racial identity operates such that individuals see their Whiteness as a fact and recognize that their life circumstances are different from and in most instances better than those of non-Whites. However, this recognition is shielded with considerable defensiveness, characterized by denial and distortion. At this level, the White person actually accepts the notion of White racial superiority and Black or visible racial/ethnic group inferiority. These views may be held openly, as is the case with White supremacists, or be outside of consciousness, as is typical of large numbers of Americans (White and non-White). Reintegration is the White racial identity status most similar to what most think of as prejudiced. Such people are likely to choose to engage in discriminatory acts in the name of self-interest.

American society's norms regarding race make it possible for many Whites to be fixated at the Reintegration identity status. It may take some powerful event, with either Blacks or Whites, for a person to question and begin to abandon this type of White racial identity status. Such an event may trigger an examination of long-held beliefs about race or some highly publicized current racist event. This type of questioning may lead the person to decide that he or she wishes to abandon racism and begin the process of developing a nonracist White identity.

The process of defining a positive White racial identity begins when Pseudo-independence status becomes more differentiated. Here, one begins to reexamine ideas and knowledge about race. They question the prevailing notions about Blacks and people of Color that suggest they are innately inferior or deprived or deviant from Whites, and they begin to understand that Whites have responsibility for racism. Consequently, individuals become uncomfortable with being a White person and start to alter their outlook. However, these changes are primarily cognitive and lack emotional content. This ego identity status is primarily intellectual and ideological. Most individuals at this level alter racism from a safe distance or from positions of power and influence. However, the Pseudo-independent status is characterized by a sense of marginality: One is not as strongly identified with Whites but is not openly or emotionally accepting of or accepted by Blacks or people of Color.

At the Pseudo-independent status, the person has begun to understand individual racism but has not yet come to terms with institutional and cultural racism. He or she is still likely to evaluate people from other racial groups using criteria drawn from his or her own background and experiences. It is not until the individual's next identity status becomes more salient that his or her racial perspective becomes complex enough to incorporate emotional as well as structural information about the mechanism of racism. The resolution is to join with other like-minded Whites, a realization that allows for the emergence of the Immersion-Emersion White identity status.

For Whites, the Immersion-Emersion ego status is distinct from the other statuses in that, here, individuals do not reject people of Color but embrace Whites. They change myths and misinformation about Blacks, people of Color, and Whites, and replace them with accurate information about the historical and current significance and meaning of racial group memberships. They also start a process of integrating emotional and cognitive information and experiences, a process fueled by questions about race and racism at many personal and interpersonal levels, for instance, how can I feel proud of my race without being racist? These questions lead down a path of learning and soul searching. Other Whites are sought out and become the source and locus for answers to the Immersion questions. Changing Blacks or fighting for people of Color is no longer the goal; individuals at this level are more focused on changing Whites.

Autonomy emerges with greater salience in the ego structure when the person internalizes, nurtures, and applies the new meaning of Whiteness and does not oppress, idealize, or denigrate people based on racial group membership. Because race is no longer a psychological threat, individuals are able to have a more flexible worldview, and it is possible to abandon much cultural, institutional, and personal racism. Helms (1996) suggests that the person at this level of White racial identity development is open to new information about race and, consequently, is able to operate more effectively across races. He or she is better able to benefit from racial exchanges and sharing between members of various races and cultures. The person who has such a White identity status also values and seeks out cross-racial experiences.

Blacks and People of Color: Psychological Responses to Race and Racism

One racial identity status is Pre-encounter or Conformity characterized by beliefs that denigrate one's race, culture, and values and idealizes White culture and traditions. For an individual whose Pre-encounter status is dominant one may seek the approval of White society. The Encounter or Dissonance, ego identity status, is characterized by a personal and challenging experience with White or non-White society that leads the person to questions about his or her race and its meaning. Thus, wondering about the meaning of race indicates that this status has emerged and become more salient. One might consider these statuses as reflecting internalized racism. The person essentially comes to see members of his or her own group in the same way it is seen by the oppressors. The attributions about the reasons for the group's low and devalued social position are adopted and promoted as a mechanism to distance oneself from the group. The Encounter and Dissonance status is somewhat more transitional, but nevertheless is dominated by the worldview of the dominant sociorace group. The Immersion-Emersion status begins to emerge due to the search for answers to questions from the Encounter experience and involves learning the meaning and value of one's race and unique culture. The individual works actively to reject (immersion) the old views and replace (emersion) them with new ones. This is done by idealizing one's group and surrounding oneself exclusively with information and feelings associated with information about the group's history and experiences of oppression and racism. As emersion takes hold the foundation for the development of the fourth status, Internalization or Integrative Awareness is established, the individual's race and culture are experienced as valued aspects of himself or herself. When Internalization is dominant, an individual has pride in his or her race and culture, yet grasps that strengths and weaknesses exist in both his or her racial group's culture as well as White culture.

The racial identity models described previously suggest that Blacks, people of Color, and Whites come to varying resolutions about how they understand themselves as members of a racial group. For each person in the group, the process of development from an essentially external and socially determined status to a more internal and personal status resolution is in part socially determined. It is the process of questioning or examination of the societal messages about the relative worth of the dominant and nondominant groups that signals a shift in statuses. In this way, the messages and their content become internalized, and one examines how one came to hold and promote the process of oppression regardless of whether one is a member of the dominant or the nondominant group. The internal resolutions are more resistant to unexamined and internalized forms of oppression, primarily because the individual challenges, examines, and questions the truth and veracity of the messages about the relative groups. He or she comes to see the flaws and distortions in the rationale and process used to maintain the oppression of the designated group, in this case, Blacks and other people of Color. Also the weakness of and costs to the oppressor group become apparent. In summary, racial identity ego statuses (White and people of Color) are present within each person. The statuses may be undifferentiated, one or two statuses, may be dominant thus exerting greater influence or there may be blends of statuses with some having greater salience than others depending upon the strength of endorsement of that status (Carter, Helms, & Juby, 2004).

We began this discussion with the individual, but a societal analysis needs a group-level perspective. Individuals are the basic element of groups; as individuals come together to form groups, their racial identity statuses converge to form racial identity coalitions. These coalitions are composed of each individual status. The individual statuses add together and culminate into a dominant set of coalitions that reflect the various statuses. The prevailing views can be thought to reflect a dominant racial identity coalition. Evidence of such group-based racial identity statuses can be seen in the racial attitude or opinion research surveys that show over several decades marked differences in attitudes about social and racial issues by racial group (Dovidio et al., 2002). Consider the two types of statuses as external and internal, where the first four White racial identity statuses are basically external, as are the first two Black racial identity statuses. These external statuses can be thought of as a phase; the second phase would be internal statuses that are characterized by personal and internal resolutions. The first phase, regardless of the racial group, accepts and promotes racism and oppression as a group coalition; the second, internal phase rejects racism and oppression as a group coalition.

As Jones and Carter (1996) have noted, "Institutions can be characterized by the various racial identity coalitions. An institution can be color blind, confused, or prefer Whites" (p. 16); that is, an institution can ignore racial differences, or it can value them and integrate them into its practices and polices. Whites as a group benefit by believing that their race is not salient and that the status and resources they enjoy in society come to them by way of effort and merit. They have not been taught how they live as oppressors and the social and personal costs to them. Thus, they are able to feel moral superiority and may hold up the advantages or privileges as benefits.

A sense of personal pride and self-esteem may also be a benefit to members of dominant groups. But these benefits come at a cost. One cost is the loss of group pride: "Collective pride, which is a form of nourishing, group self-love, is an emotional experience that many White people find elusive. . . . Whites easily identify themselves as individuals, but not as members of a group" (Ross, 1996, p. 43). Some of the psychological costs are associated with the loss of a clear and consistent past and history. In addition, there is a loss in the capacity for general human intimacy. As Fernandez (1996) notes:

> A white-centered, superior attitude leaves the people holding it isolated, confused, and mentally underdeveloped. Racism produces false fears in Whites and allows these fears to control where they live, where they go to school, where they travel, where they work, with whom they socialize, where they play, and whom they love and marry. Whites develop unhealthy mechanisms, such as denial, false justification, projection, disassociation, and transference of blame, to deal with their fears about minorities. (p. 164)

It is not possible to connect to all humans while holding that some are not quite human. Whites who employ these psychological mechanisms, knowingly or not, also must project onto others to maintain their sense of worth and deny their own beliefs and practices as unjust in order to justify them. Whites lose compassion, the ability to hear and feel others' experiences, the ability to be kind, and the ability to be just. These losses are masked by the denial of reality and the creation of a world that is constructed on the basis of race and pretense of the existence of equality, fairness, and justice (Feagin & McKinney, 2003).

The cost to the victims of racism is well documented; it causes psychological, emotional, and physical injury (Carter, Forsyth, Mazzula, & Williams, in press). Victims often internalize their own oppression by coming to believe the myths and distortions about them that are created to maintain the oppression. Such beliefs create patterns of self-destruction in the victims, as evidenced in high rates of psychological disorder, crime, alcoholism and drug use, and high incidence of physical illness (Braithwaite & Taylor, 2001).

The benefits come in terms of collective pride, a deep sense of history, and a connection to members of oppressed groups. This pride can often serve as a core of personal strength and toughness that is used by many who are oppressed to overcome tremendous obstacles and achieve their goals in spite of the social pressure to hold them down (Franklin, 2004).

CONCLUSION

We contend that race and racism must not be an add-on to or simply understood in the context of racial theory, but must be integrated as aspects of personality in the core concepts of psychological theory. Race is often dismissed in the clinical literature as irrelevant to Whites because many Whites do not think of themselves in racial terms. Race seems to be reserved for Blacks and other non-Whites. However, to assume that race does not have meaning to all American people, including Whites, reflects a typical ahistorical understanding of the meaning of race and racism and denies Whites' credit for their invention of race as a form of social stratification (Allen, 1994). Kovel (1984) puts it this way:

> Prejudice is the surfacing of racism. Racism is the activity within history and culture through which races are created, oppressed, and fantasized about without the aid of bigots. . . . It pervades the history of our culture at the deepest of levels at which the primary fantasies are generated. The problem of racism is part of the problem of Western culture. (p. 95)

Our discussion has sought to outline the development and maintenance of race as an ideology and as a core aspect of both historical and contemporary American society. While some scholars and clinicians acknowledge race and racism as integral aspects of American society and culture, human development and personality theorists whose work forms the foundation for psychology seldom, if ever, include race or the system of racism as something that has implications for personality and psychological development and functioning. We think it is imperative that race and its meaning as a social and cultural mechanism for order and advantage be addressed directly and that race be used as a psychological construct and aspect of personality that we all have and should value. Then the meaning of race will become a valued and accepted part of each person's personality, rather than a mechanism for ongoing oppression.

REFERENCES

Alderfer, C. P. (2000). National culture and the new corporate language for race relations. In R. T. Carter (Ed.), *Addressing cultural issues in organizations: Beyond the corporate context* (pp. 19–34). Thousand Oaks, CA: Sage.

Allen, T. W. (1994). *The invention of the White race* (Vol. 2). London: Verso.

Bamshad, M. J., & Olson, S. E. (2003, December). Does race exist? *Scientific American,* 78–85.

Banton, M. (1998). *Racial theories* (2nd ed.). Cambridge University Press: New York.

Betancourt, H., & Lopez, S. R. (1993). The study of culture, ethnicity and race in American psychology. *American Psychologist, 48*(6), 629–637.

Bowser, B. P., & Hunt, R. G. (1996). *Impacts of racism on White Americans* (2nd ed.). Thousand Oaks, CA: Sage.

Braithwaite, R. L., & Taylor, S. E. (2001). *Health issues in the Black community* (2nd ed.). San Francisco, CA: Jossey-Bass.

Carter, R. T. (1995). *The influence of race and racial identity in psychotherapy.* New York: Wiley.

Carter, R. T. (1996). Exploring the complexity of racial identity attitude measures. In G. R. Sodowsky & J. C. Impara (Eds.), *Multicultural assessment in counseling and clinical psychology* (pp. 193–224). Lincoln, NE: Buros Institute of Mental Measurements.

Carter, R. T. (Ed.). (2000a). *Addressing cultural issues in organizations: Beyond the corporate context.* Thousand Oaks, CA: Sage.

Carter, R. T. (2000b). Reimagining race in education: A new paradigm from psychology. *Teachers College Record, 102*(5), 864–896.

Carter, R. T. (2004). *Disaster Response to Communities of Color: Cultural responsive intervention.* Technical report for the Connecticut Department of Mental Health and Addiction (DMHAS). Available from http://www.dmhas.state.ct.us.

Carter, R. T., Forsyth, J., Mazzula, S., & Williams, B. (in press). Racial discrimination and race-based traumatic stress. In R. T. Carter (Ed.), *Handbook of racial-cultural psychology and counseling: Training and practice* (Vol. 2). Hoboken, NJ: Wiley.

Carter, R. T., Helms, J. E., & Juby, H. L. (2004). The relationship between racism and racial identity for White Americans: A profile analysis. *Journal of Multicultural Counseling and Development, 32,* 2–17.

Darling-Haqmmond, L. (2000). Social contexts and learning: Organizational influences on the achievement of students of Color. In R. T. Carter (Ed.), *Addressing cultural issues in organizations: Beyond the corporate context* (pp. 69–88). Thousand Oaks, CA: Sage.

Dovidio, J. F., & Gaertner, S. L. (1998). On the nature of contemporary prejudice: The causes, consequences and challenges of aversive racism. In J. L. Eberhardt & S. T. Fiske (Eds.), *Confronting racism: The problem and the response.* Thousand Oaks, CA: Sage.

Dovidio, J. F., Gaertner, S. L., Kawakami, K., & Hodson, G. (2002). Why can't we just get along? Interpersonal biases and interracial distrust. *Cultural Diversity and Ethnic Minority Psychology, 8,* 88–102.

Duckitt, J. (1992). Psychology and prejudice: A historical analysis and integrative framework. *American Psychologist, 47,* 1182–1193.

Fanon, F. (1967). *Black skin, white masks.* New York: Grove Press.

Feagin, J. R. (2000). *Racist America.* New York: Routledge Press.

Feagin, J. R., & McKinney, K. D. (2003). *The many costs of racism.* Lanham, MD: Rowman & Littlefield Publisher.

Feagin, J. R., Vera, H., & Batur, P. (2001). *White Racism* (2nd ed.). New York: Routledge Press.

Fernando, D. (1998). *Race and culture in psychiatry.* London: Croom and Helm.

Fine, M. (2000). Whiting out social justice. In R. T. Carter (Ed.), *Addressing cultural issues in organizations: Beyond the corporate context* (pp. 35–50). Thousand Oaks, CA: Sage.

Franklin, A. J. (2004). *From brotherhood to manhood: How Black men rescue their relationships and dreams from the invisibility syndrome.* New York: Wiley.

Fryer, P. (1984). *Staying power: The history of Black people in Britain.* London: Pluto Press.

Gossett, T. F. (1998). *Race: The history of an idea in America.* New York: Oxford University Press.

Gould, S. J. (1981). *The mismeasure of man.* New York: Norton.

Graves, J. L., Jr. (2001). *The emperor's new clothes: Biological theories of race at the millennium.* New Brunswick, NJ: Rutgers University Press.

Haller, J. (1971). *Outcasts from evolution: Scientific attitudes of racial inferiority: 1859–1900.* Urbana: University of Illinois Press.

Harper, F. D., & McFadden, J. (2003). *Culture and counseling: New approaches.* Boston: Allyn & Bacon.

Helms, J. E. (1990). *Black and White racial identity: Theory, research, and practice.* Westport, CT: Greenwood Press.

Helms, J. E. (1996). Toward a methodology for measuring and assessing racial as distinguished from ethnic identity. In G. R. Sodowsky & J. C. Impara (Eds.), *Multicultural assessment in counseling and clinical psychology* (pp. 143–192). Lincoln, NE: Buros Institute of Mental Measurements.

Helms, J. E., & Cook, D. A. (1999). *Using race and culture in counseling and psychotherapy.* Boston: Allyn & Bacon.

Hernstein, R. J., & Murray, C. (1994). *The bell curve: Intelligence and class structure in American life.* New York: Free Press.

Jaynes, G. D., & Williams, R. M. (Eds.). (1989). *A common destiny: Blacks and American society.* Washington, DC: National Academy Press.

Jones, J. M. (1991). *Psychological models of race: What have they been and what should they be?* Washington, DC: American Psychological Association.

Jones, J. M. (1997). *Prejudice and racism* (2nd ed.). New York: McGraw-Hill.

Jones, J. M. (1998). Psychological knowledge and the new American dilemma of race. *Journal of Social Issues, 54*(4), 641–662.

Jones, J. M., & Carter, R. T. (1996). Racism and racial identity: Merging realities. In B. P. Bowser & R. G. Hunt (Eds.), *Impacts of racism on White Americans* (2nd ed., pp. 1–24). Newbury Park, CA: Sage.

Kovel, J. (1984). *White racism: A psychohistory.* New York: Pantheon Books.

Littlefield, A., Lieberman, L., & Reynolds, L. T. (1982). Redefining race: The potential demise of a concept in physical anthropology. *Current Anthropology, 23*(6), 641–555.

Marger, M. (2000). *Race and ethnic relations: American and global perspectives* (5th ed.). Belmont, CA: Wadsworth.

Marger, M. (2002). *Race and ethnic relations: American and global perspectives* (6th ed.). Belmont, CA: Wadsworth.

Merriam-Webster's Collegiate Dictionary. (11th ed.). (2003). Springfield, MA: Merriam-Webster, Inc.

Nicolay, J. G., & Hay, J. (Eds.). (1894). *Abraham Lincoln, complete works.* New York: Century Company.

Packard, J. M. (2002). *American Nightmare: The history of Jim Crow.* New York: St. Martin Press.

Plotkin, P. C. (1993). The psychological reality of social constructions. *Ethnic and Racial Studies, 16,* 633–656.

Rushton, J. P. (2000). *Race, evolution, and behavior: A life history perspective* (2nd ed.). Port Huron, MI: Charles Darwin Research Institute.

Smedley, A. (1998). "Race" and the construction of human identity. *American Anthropologists, 100,* 690–702.

Smedley, A. (1999). *Race in North America: Origin and evolution of a worldview* (2nd ed.). Boulder, CO: Westview Press.

Sue, D. W. (2003). *Overcoming our racism: The journey to liberation.* San Francisco, CA: Jossey-Bass.

Sue, D. W., & Sue, D. (2003). *Counseling the culturally diverse: Theory and practice* (4th ed.). New York: Wiley.

Thompson, C. E., & Carter, R. T. (Eds.). (1997). *Racial identity development theory: Applications to individual, group and organizations.* Hillsdale, NJ: Erlbaum.

Williams, D. R., Neighbors, H. W., & Jackson, J. S. (2003). Racial/ethnic discrimination and health: Findings from community studies. *American Journal of Public Health, 93*(2), 200–208.

Yee, A., Halford, H., Fairchild, F. W., & Wyatt, G. E. (1993). Addressing psychology's problems with race. *American Psychologist, 48,* 1132–1140.

CHAPTER 5

The Role of Racial and Cultural Constructs in the History of the Multicultural Counseling Movement

Madonna G. Constantine and Leo Wilton

Over the past few decades, multicultural scholars in the field of counseling psychology have dedicated considerable energy to conceptual and empirical writings that provided the foundation for the contemporary multicultural counseling movement. For example, prior to the late 1960s, little attention was paid to the role of race and culture as they affect the counseling process. Since then, several culturally based variables (e.g., racial-cultural identity development models, acculturation, cultural values, and multicultural counseling competencies) have been offered that greatly advance the area of multicultural counseling. Moreover, the increasing racial and ethnic diversity of the United States, due to immigration and differential birthrates between people of Color and Whites, has made it essential for counselors to acquire the necessary competencies for providing effective mental health services to diverse cultural populations (D. W. Sue & Sue, 1999, 2003).

In this chapter, we discuss the role of various racial and cultural constructs in the history of the multicultural counseling movement. These constructs have been vital in helping to shape the current foci on cultural considerations in counseling and psychotherapy. Following this discussion, we present a brief overview of the various versions of the multicultural counseling competencies to date. Finally, future directions for multicultural counseling practice and research are delineated.

RACIAL AND CULTURAL VARIABLES AND THE MULTICULTURAL COUNSELING MOVEMENT

With the advent of various sociohistorical and sociopolitical influences during the 1950s and 1960s (e.g., the civil rights and Black power movements, the Civil Rights Act of 1964, affirmative action legislation), race and culture became germane considerations in the practice of effective counseling and psychotherapy with culturally diverse clients (D. W. Sue et al., 1998). During this period, much of the scholarship initiated by Black psychologists (e.g., Guthrie, 1970; Harper, 1973; Harper & Stone,

1974; Pinderhughes, 1973; Vontress, 1967, 1968, 1969, 1971; White, 1970) challenged the relevance to Black people of traditional counseling theories grounded in Eurocentric or Western conceptual paradigms. Furthermore, many of the earlier Black pioneers posited that these theories were fundamentally oppressive to Black clients (Guthrie, 1998). The emergence of scholarship by Black psychologists during this era contributed enormously to the current focus on multicultural issues in the field of counseling psychology.

Joseph L. White (1970), a prominent Black scholar during this period, questioned the applicability of traditional Eurocentric theories to the life experiences of Black people. He noted that Black people's behavior was often pathologized in the context of traditional psychological theories. White stridently advocated for the importance of developing a theoretical perspective of Black psychology in the context of Black philosophy, Black families, and Black dialect:

> It is . . . important that we develop, out of the authentic experience of Black people in this country, an accurate workable theory of Black psychology. It is very difficult, if not impossible, to understand the lifestyles of Black people using traditional theories by White psychologists to explain White people. (p. 44)

Following the initial contributions by Black psychologists, the basis for the development of the contemporary multicultural counseling movement can be traced to multicultural theorists and researchers in the 1970s who highlighted the importance of recognizing cultural differences in counselor-client therapeutic relationships. For example, Vontress (1971) delineated the role of racial attitudes/dynamics, sociopolitical influences in counseling dyads, cross-cultural communication styles, and racial transference and countertransference with regard to rapport development between White counselors and Black clients. In another conceptual paper, Vontress (1974) contended that a multitude of racial and ethnic considerations often affect the provision of counseling services. He asserted that the development of rapport, the structure of the counseling sessions, transference, language and communication styles, self-disclosure, and misdiagnosis were essential variables that may influence the counseling process.

D. W. Sue and D. Sue (1977) discussed the role of cross-cultural communication patterns as potential barriers to effective cross-cultural counseling. They asserted that Western cultural values, such as language (e.g., standard English and verbal communication), class-bound values (e.g., adherence to strict time boundaries), and culture-bound values (e.g., individualism; preferences for emotional, verbal, and behavioral expressiveness) may conflict with non-Western cultural values. Moreover, D. W. Sue and D. Sue's formative work, indicating that high premature counseling termination rates for people of Color (as compared to Whites) related to cross-cultural differences in interpersonal interactions, appears to be consistent with current research findings in this vein (e.g., S. Sue, Zane, & Young, 1994). In addition, D. W. Sue and D. Sue raised issues about the appropriateness of counseling theories and techniques in the provision of mental health services to people of Color.

The 1970s also witnessed the emergence of scholarship that focused on theoretical conceptualizations of Black racial identity development (e.g., Cross, 1971, 1978; Gibbs, 1974; B. Jackson, 1975; C. G. Jackson & Kirschner, 1973; Milliones, 1973; Thomas, 1971; Vontress, 1971). It is beyond the scope of this chapter to provide a comprehensive overview of the Black racial identity theories (for reviews, see Carter, 1995; Constantine, Richardson, Benjamin, & Wilson, 1998; Helms, 1990). In essence, the Black racial identity theories were developed to focus on racial issues that were assumed to have an impact on the counseling process. For instance, Vontress (1971) conceptualized a Black racial identity model characterizing Black people into three types: Black, Negro, and Colored. Persons labeled "Black" were described as being ideologically located in Blackness, having a positive Black self-perception, and identifying with an African cultural heritage and a common experience of racial oppression. Individuals in the Black category were also typically younger, were educated, challenged White racism, and resided in urban communities, particularly in the North. People in the "Negro" category were characterized as accommodating Whites, being ambivalent about their racial self-perceptions, being trusting of Whites, being middle class, being reasonably well educated, and being more complacent with White society. Individuals in the "Colored" category were characterized as identifying with the term Colored (a racial classification of Blacks by White society), viewing themselves in relation to White norms and standards, and being unable to relate to the sociopolitical struggles of people of African descent. According to Vontress, White counselors were anxious and demonstrated difficulty in working with Blacks, related to Negroes with "little difficulty," and easily established rapport with Coloreds.

Cross (1971) also conceptualized a Black racial identity theory, called Nigrescence theory, which has five stages: Pre-encounter, Encounter, Immersion-Emersion, Internalization, and Internalization-Commitment. In the Pre-encounter stage, Blacks embrace White values and ideologies and denigrate Blackness. During the Encounter stage, Blacks have an experience or a series of experiences that challenge their Eurocentric worldviews or beliefs about race. During the Immersion-Emersion stage, Blacks engage in a racial identity transformation characterized by embracing Blackness (e.g., Black is beautiful). In the Internalization stage, Blacks accept their racial identity on intellectual and emotional levels, and in the Internalization-Commitment stage, Blacks are more firmly rooted in their Blackness. Parham and Helms (1981) later developed the Black Racial Identity Attitudes Scale to assess many of the attitudes captured by Cross's conceptual model.

In a reconceptualization of his earlier work on Black racial identity development, Cross (1991) thoroughly reexamined the landmark studies of Negro identity, most notably the doll studies conducted by Eugene and Ruth Horowitz and Kenneth and Mamie Clark. Based on his findings, he challenged the notion that self-hatred functioned as a dominant theme in Black identity. Cross (i.e., Cross & Vandiver, 2001) revised his Black racial identity model to focus on race salience for the Pre-encounter stage, which is characterized by the Pre-encounter Assimilation and Anti-Black identities. The Pre-encounter Assimilation identity describes a pro-American identity, and the Pre-encounter Anti-Black identity devalues Blackness. The Immersion-Emersion stage has been reconceptualized to create two distinct identities, pro-Black and anti-White, rather than juxtaposing both identities in one stage. The Internalization-Commitment identities are meshed into one identity, which is reconceptualized as the Internalization stage.

In the late 1970s, racial-cultural scholars developed racial and ethnic identity theories to focus on the attitudes and behaviors of other people of Color in the United States (i.e., Asians, Latinos, and Native Americans). For example, S. Sue and Sue (1971) formulated a theory of Asian American identity development by delineating differences in racial attitudes of Chinese Americans. In their model, the three phases of Asian American identity development include the Traditionalist (internalization of traditional Chinese cultural values), Marginal Person (assimilation and acculturation into the dominant White society), and Asian American (development of a positive bicultural identity). Atkinson, Morten, and Sue (1979) also formulated the minority identity development (MID) model to address the identity development experiences of people of Color. The fundamental premise of the MID model is that people of Color collectively experience oppression and hold attitudes in relation to the development of self and group identities. The stages of the MID model (i.e., Conformity, Dissonance, Resistance and Immersion, Introspection, and Synergetic Articulation and Awareness) focused on attitudes toward oneself, attitudes toward others in the same racial or cultural group, attitudes toward members of other racial or cultural groups, and attitudes toward the White racial group. According to Atkinson, Morten, and Sue (1998), the MID model was critical in developing an understanding of the attitudes and behaviors of people of Color as a collective group in engaging in non-Western cultures and in navigating the tensions associated with being bicultural (i.e., having both non-Western and Euro-American cultural perspectives). The MID model also sought to underscore the role of oppression in the racial or cultural identity development of people of Color, group differences in racial or cultural identity development, and the potential for racial or cultural groups to experience positive racial or cultural identity development.

By the early 1980s, the field of counseling psychology incorporated much of the formative racial and cultural conceptual frameworks into research and clinical practice, which largely formed the basis for the specialty of cross-cultural counseling. Racial-cultural scholars during this era continued to advance the production of cross-cultural counseling scholarship in several areas, such as (re)conceptualizing racial and cultural identity development models, the development of instrumentation to assess racial and cultural identity development, and conceptualizations of effective cross-cultural counseling practice. In particular, D. W. Sue and D. Sue's (1981) landmark work, *Counseling the Culturally Different: Theory and Practice,* provided a comprehensive discussion of sociopolitical and sociohistorical influences in counseling and psychotherapy, racial and cultural identity development models, the role of cultural worldviews in the counseling process, and other variables believed to be salient to effective cross-cultural counseling.

Their work, in part, laid some groundwork for the development of D. W. Sue et al.'s (1982) position paper outlining 11 cross-cultural counseling competencies. Specifically, the authors asserted that counselors' cross-cultural attitudes and beliefs, knowledge, and skills were important for competent therapeutic practice with people of Color. This paper served as the primary impetus for the present-day multicultural counseling competencies and is discussed in greater detail later in this chapter.

The 1980s also gave rise to the identification of vital issues in counseling American Indians (e.g., LaFromboise, 1988; LaFromboise & Rowe, 1983; Trimble & LaFromboise, 1987). Much of the work in this area examined acculturation, cultural values, and underutilization of mental health services (e.g., Indian Health Service, Bureau of Indian Affairs; university- and community-based counseling services) by American Indians. Specifically, LaFromboise discussed how differences in cultural values between counselors and American Indian clients could affect the counseling process. Similarly, Trimble and LaFromboise maintained that American Indians reported higher levels of credibility toward counselors when counselors employed a culturally appropriate counseling style as opposed to counselors who used either a directive or a nondirective counseling style.

The period of the 1980s also served as an important decade for the development of a plethora of many other racial-cultural identity development models, including ethnic (Phinney, 1989), Asian (Kim, 1981; Lee, 1991; Sodowsky, Kwan, & Pannu, 1995), Latino(a)/Hispanic (Bernal & Knight, 1993; Casas & Pytluk, 1995; Ruiz, 1990; Szapocznik, Santisteban, Kurtines, Hervis, & Spencer, 1982), Native American (Choney, Berryhill-Paapke, & Robbins, 1995), White (Helms, 1984; Ponterotto, 1988), biracial (Kerwin & Ponterotto, 1995; Root, 1992), feminist (Downing & Roush, 1985; McNamara & Richard, 1989), womanist (Helms, 1990), and gay/lesbian/bisexual (Cass, 1979; Fassinger & Miller, 1996; McCarn & Fassinger, 1996; Mohr & Fassinger, 2000) identity development models. Most of the racial and cultural identity development models represent a progression wherein individuals move from being generally unaware of racial or other cultural issues (especially oppression) to increased awareness of such issues. These models have been essential in helping mental health practitioners to understand racial and cultural identity development processes of both their clients and themselves and how racial and cultural dynamics influence the counseling process.

It was also during this period that the term "multicultural" became increasingly used in reference to many racial, ethnic, and other types of cultural issues (e.g., gender) because it was viewed as representing the complexities and intersections of individuals' various cultural identities with regard to their experiences and lives. It is important to note, however, that some racial-cultural scholars have viewed the term multicultural as potentially problematic in terms of its ability to shift attention away from important racial issues in the counseling process and because it is difficult to operationalize scientifically (Helms, 1994).

From the mid-1980s to the early 1990s, Janet Helms and her colleagues wrote extensively about people of Color and White racial identity development models and their application to counseling and psychotherapy (e.g., Helms, 1990, 1995; Helms & Carter, 1990). According to Helms (1995), the people of Color racial identity ego statuses have four phases: Conformity (a devaluing of own racial/ethnic group and adherence to Eurocentric standards/values), Dissonance (feelings of anxiety and ambivalence about own racial/ethnic group), Immersion (an idealization of own racial/ethnic group and a devaluing of all aspects of Euro-American culture), and Integrative Awareness (a valuing of own racial/ethnic group and Whites). In contrast, the White racial identity ego statuses constitute a six-phase model: Contact (a lack of awareness and/or denial about race), Disintegration (feelings of anxiety, confusion, and conflict about race), Reintegration (an idealization of Whiteness/White racial superiority, with a concurrent devaluing of people of Color), Pseudo-independence (an initial and intellectual understanding about race), Immersion-Emersion (having an understanding of Whiteness, racism, and White privilege), and Autonomy (an awareness of Whiteness and White privilege and the assumption of a nonracist White identity). These racial identity development models have been operationalized through the people of Color Racial Identity Attitude Scale (Helms & Carter, 1986) and the White Racial Identity Attitude Scale (Helms & Carter, 1990).

From the late 1980s to early 1990s, the development of cultural worldviews as a conceptual framework for counseling and psychotherapy also influenced the contemporary multicultural counseling movement. In particular, Carter (1995) asserted that assessment of cultural worldviews should be regarded as a critical element in the counseling process with culturally diverse clients. Building on the work of Kluckhohn and Strodtbeck (1961), several multicultural theorists (e.g., Carter, 1990, 1991; Carter & Helms, 1987; Ibrahim, 1984; Ibrahim & Kahn, 1987) identified various cultural worldview perspectives as important means for understanding cross-cultural differences in beliefs, values, and assumptions between clients and counselors. For example, Carter (1991) contended that cultural values influence four components of the counseling process: counselors' racial or cultural backgrounds; clients' racial or cultural backgrounds; assumptions about counseling relationships, nature of illness, and the origin of presenting problems; and therapeutic settings. Work in the area of cultural values has been substantially influential in helping mental health practitioners to understand how these values may both facilitate and impede the counseling process.

In the early to mid-1990s, based on D. W. Sue et al.'s (1982) position paper on the multicultural competencies of counselors, a multitude of self-report measures were developed to assess such competencies in mental health practitioners. For instance, the Cross-Cultural Counseling Inventory-Revised (LaFromboise, Coleman, & Hernandez, 1991) was developed for supervisors' assessment of their supervisees' multicultural counseling competencies; the Multicultural Awareness/ Knowledge/Skills Survey (D'Andrea, Daniels, & Heck, 1991) was designed to measure the effectiveness of multicultural counseling training; the Multicultural Counseling Inventory (Sodowsky, Taffe, Gutkin, & Wise, 1994) was developed to assess multicultural counseling awareness, knowledge, skills, and relationship; and the Multicultural Counseling Knowledge and Awareness Scale (Ponterotto, Gretchen, Utsey, Rieger, & Austin, 2002) was created to measure general knowledge related to multicultural counseling and subtle Eurocentric worldview bias. Many of these scales served as important means to attempt to operationalize the cross-cultural competencies outlined by D. W. Sue et al.

THE DEVELOPMENT OF MULTICULTURAL COUNSELING COMPETENCIES IN THE PAST 20 YEARS

In D. W. Sue et al.'s (1982) position paper delineating the cross-cultural competencies of counselors, the authors described three dimensions that characterize such competence. The first dimension, attitudes/beliefs, speaks to the professional need to examine personal biases and stereotypes, an orientation toward the value of multiculturalism, and an awareness of how counselors' preconceptions may stymie effective service delivery. The second dimension, knowledge, describes counselors' understanding of their own worldview, the development of their worldview, specific knowledge of the cultural groups they serve, and a broad understanding of historical and present-day sociopolitical influences on their clientele. Skills, the third dimension, relates to interventions and strategies on individual and institutional levels that are helpful and valuable in working with specific groups. This tripartite model served as the foundation for the original and subsequent multicultural counseling competencies.

The second version of the multicultural counseling competencies (i.e., D. W. Sue, Arredondo, & McDavis, 1992) was developed out of a professional initiative of the Association of Multicultural Counseling and Development under the presidency of Dr. Thomas Parham. D. W. Sue et al. generated the revised competencies to propose more specific standards for multiculturally competent practice and to outline specific plans for implementation of these proposed standards. The authors crossed the attitudes/beliefs, knowledge, and skills dimensions with three desired counselor characteristics: actively becoming more aware of personal assumptions about human behavior; understanding the worldview of culturally diverse clients without judgment; and actively practicing culturally sensitive and relevant intervention strategies and skills with culturally diverse clients. This configuration then formed a three-by-three matrix in which the authors presented 31 competencies. However, in enumerating these multicultural counseling competencies, several broad concepts were often utilized without specific definitions. Included in these nebulous constructs were the terms "multiculturalism," "diversity," "multicultural counseling," and "culture." Moreover, the term "culturally competent counselor" was defined in terms of sensitivity to racial and ethnic issues, although the authors had adopted an inclusive definition of culture (e.g., race, ethnicity, sexual orientation, gender, age, religion).

Arredondo et al. (1996) produced a supplement to D. W. Sue et al.'s (1992) competencies that served to formally define constructs and competencies that had been hard to implement in the previous version. Specifically, the terms *multicultural* and *diversity* were clarified and differentiated, and the phrase *multicultural counseling* was defined more concretely. Multicultural was defined as differences based on race, ethnicity, and culture, whereas diversity included other individual characteristics such as age, gender, and sexual orientation. Diversity was further illustrated through the Dimensions of Personal Identity Model (Arredondo, 1999). This model asserts that all individuals are multicultural; that individuals have personal, political, and historical cultures and are affected by such events; and that race and ethnicity interface with these factors of diversity. Arredondo et al.'s operationalization of the competencies also outlined specific criteria by which multicultural counseling competence could be measured.

The fourth version of the multicultural counseling competencies built on the three prior versions by focusing on multicultural organizational development. D. W. Sue et al. (1998) noted that a multiculturally inclusive organization is actively committed to diverse representation in all strata of the organization; maintains a supportive and responsive environment; purposefully includes elements of diverse cultures in instituting policies and practices; and is genuinely devoted to responding to issues that block diversity. Moreover, the authors highlighted the importance of counselors focusing on initiating multicultural competencies and social change within organizational contexts, businesses and industries, educational institutions, and professional organizations. The fourth version of the multicultural competencies also reflected major empirical and theoretical contributions in the literature, particularly research related to racial and ethnic identity development models (e.g., Helms, 1995) and potential helping roles of counselors and other mental health professionals (e.g., Atkinson, Thompson, & Grant, 1993). This focus is evident in the inclusion of three new competencies under the skills dimension, two of which speak to racial-cultural identity models, and the third of which addresses mental health professionals adopting a broader range of helping roles in working with culturally diverse clients (e.g., advocate or consultant).

The most recent delineation of the multicultural counseling competencies was published in 2003 under the title "Guidelines on Multicultural Education, Training, Research, Practice, and Organizational Change for Psychologists" (American Psychological Association [APA], 2003). These guidelines were developed primarily to provide psychologists with the rationale for the need to address issues of multicultural diversity in education, training, research, practice, and organizations. The guidelines also reflect the continuing evolution of the field of psychology in terms of addressing the different needs of historically marginalized individuals and groups in society based on racial or ethnic heritage and social group identity or membership (APA, 2003).

FUTURE DIRECTIONS FOR MULTICULTURAL COUNSELING PRACTICE AND RESEARCH

With regard to future directions for multicultural counseling practice, it is important to note that there are existing models of multicultural counseling that may represent optimal models by which to produce multiculturally competent counselors (Constantine, Kindaichi, Arorash, Donnelly, & Jung, 2002). In particular,

Atkinson et al.'s (1993) three-dimensional model of multicultural counseling can provide a structure for understanding certain client variables or issues within the helping process, and it identifies eight important helping roles that counselors might assume in working with culturally diverse individuals. These roles are advisor, consultant, advocate, change agent, facilitator of indigenous support systems, facilitator of indigenous healing methods, counselor, and psychotherapist. It is important that counselors become more flexible in adopting various roles in working with clients to meet their mental health needs more effectively. Currently, most counselor training programs neglect to teach students to develop helping skills employed in professional roles other than those of counselor and psychotherapist. Hence, it is crucial that these programs consider ways to prepare future practitioners to assume a broader range of helping roles in working with culturally diverse individuals.

It is also critical that counselors better understand how unique client variables might be related to or might affect their own multicultural competence. For example, clients' motivation for pursuing treatment could greatly determine the extent to which their counselors are effective in addressing clients' presenting concerns (Constantine & Ladany, 2001). Furthermore, clients' personality traits and values are presumably important factors to consider in the context of evaluations of multicultural counseling competence. The effects of a broad range of unique client variables may need to be recognized as important to the assessment of counselors' multicultural counseling competence (Constantine & Ladany, 2001).

There is also a need for counselors to identify the specific types of multicultural competencies that may be needed and utilized across various professional practice situations. That is, counseling is a multifaceted field, and the goals and responsibilities of counselors in mental health, school, career, and rehabilitation counseling settings may differ significantly, depending on the context. Thus, it is vital that mental health professionals identify the degree to which both universal and context-specific types of multicultural competencies can be applied to a range of counseling settings and environments.

In terms of future research directions for the area of multicultural counseling, there is a need for researchers to determine whether D. W. Sue et al.'s (1982, 1992, 1998) tripartite conceptualization of multicultural counseling competence fully encompasses this construct. Although some preliminary research has revealed that multicultural counseling competence may overlap significantly with general counseling competence (e.g., Coleman, 1998; Constantine, 2002; Fuertes & Brobst, 2002), it is important that future researchers identify *specific* components of each construct that might be both similar and different. Moreover, incorporating both clients' and counselors' perspectives of counseling may be key to formulating a more comprehensive conceptualization of multicultural counseling competence (Constantine, 2002). In particular, obtaining information from both members of counseling dyads could allow researchers to gain more accurate data about counselors' ability to address their clients' concerns in a culturally competent manner (Constantine et al., 2002).

REFERENCES

American Psychological Association. (2003). Guidelines on multicultural education, training, research, practice, and organizational change for psychologists. *American Psychologist, 58,* 377–402.

Arredondo, P. (1999). Multicultural counseling competencies as tools to address oppression and racism. *Journal of Counseling and Development, 77,* 102–108.

Arredondo, P., Toporek, R., Brown, S. P., Jones, J., Locke, D. C., Sanchez, J., et al. (1996). Operationalization of the multicultural counseling competencies. *Journal of Multicultural Counseling and Development, 24,* 42–78.

Atkinson, D. R., Morten, G., & Sue, D. W. (Eds.). (1979). *Counseling American minorities: A cross-cultural perspective.* Boston: McGraw-Hill.

Atkinson, D. R., Morten, G., & Sue, D. W. (Eds.). (1998). *Counseling American minorities: A cross-cultural perspective* (5th ed.). Boston: McGraw-Hill.

Atkinson, D. R., Thompson, C. E., & Grant, S. K. (1993). A three-dimensional model for counseling racial/ethnic minorities. *Counseling Psychologist, 21,* 257–277.

Bernal, M. E., & Knight, G. P. (1993). *Ethnic identity: Formation and transmission among Hispanics and other minorities.* Albany: State University of New York Press.

Carter, R. T. (1990). Cultural value differences between African-Americans and White Americans. *Journal of College Student Development, 31,* 71–79.

Carter, R. T. (1991). Racial identity attitudes and psychological functioning. *Journal of Multicultural Counseling and Development, 19,* 105–114.

Carter, R. T. (1995). *The influence of race and racial identity in psychotherapy: Toward a racially inclusive model.* New York: Wiley.

Carter, R. T., & Helms, J. E. (1987). The relationship of Black value-orientation to racial identity attitudes. *Measurement and Evaluation in Counseling and Development, 19,* 185–195.

Casas, J. M., & Pytluk, S. D. (1995). Hispanic identity development. In J. G. Ponterotto, J. M. Casas, L. A. Suzuki, & C. M. Alexander (Eds.), *Handbook of multicultural counseling* (pp. 155–180). Thousand Oaks, CA: Sage.

Cass, V. C. (1979). Homosexual identity formation: A theoretical model. *Journal of Homosexuality, 4,* 219–235.

Choney, S. K., Berryhill-Paapke, E., & Robbins, R. R. (1995). The acculturation of American Indians: Developing frameworks for research and practice. In J. G. Ponterotto, J. M. Casas, L. A. Suzuki, & C. M. Alexander (Eds.), *Handbook of multicultural counseling* (pp. 73–92). Thousand Oaks, CA: Sage.

Coleman, H. L. K. (1998). General and multicultural counseling competency: Apples and oranges? *Journal of Multicultural Counseling and Development, 26,* 147–1156.

Constantine, M. G. (2002). Predictors of satisfaction with counseling: Racial and ethnic minority clients' attitudes toward counseling and ratings of their counselors' general and multicultural counseling competence. *Journal of Counseling Psychology, 49,* 255–263.

Constantine, M. G., Kindaichi, M., Arorash, T. J., Donnelly, P. C., & Jung, K.-S. K. (2002). Clients' perceptions of multicultural counseling competence: Current status and future directions. *Counseling Psychologist, 30,* 407–416.

Constantine, M. G., & Ladany, N. (2001). New visions for defining and assessing multicultural counseling competence. In J. G. Ponterotto, J. M. Casas, L. A. Suzuki, & C. M. Alexander (Eds.), *Handbook of multicultural counseling* (2nd ed., pp. 482–498). Thousand Oaks, CA: Sage.

Constantine, M. G., Richardson, T. Q., Benjamin, E. M., & Wilson, J. W. (1998). An overview of Black racial identity theories: Limitations and considerations for future theoretical conceptualizations. *Applied and Preventive Psychology, 7,* 95–99.

Cross, W. E., Jr. (1971). The Negro-to-Black conversion experience: Toward a psychology of Black liberation. *Black World, 20,* 13–27.

Cross, W. E., Jr. (1978). The Thomas and Cross models of psychological nigrescence: A literature review. *Journal of Black Psychology, 4,* 13–31.

Cross, W. E., Jr. (1991). *Shades of Black: Diversity in African-American identity.* Philadelphia: Temple University Press.

Cross, W. E., Jr., & Vandiver, B. J. (2001). Nigrescence theory and measurement: Introducing the Cross Racial Identity Scale (CRIS). In J. G. Ponterotto, J. M. Casas, L. A. Suzuki, & C. M. Alexander (Eds.), *Handbook of multicultural counseling* (2nd ed., pp. 371–393). Thousand Oaks, CA: Sage.

D'Andrea, M., Daniels, J., & Heck, R. (1991). Evaluating the impact of multicultural counseling training. *Journal of Counseling and Development, 70,* 143–150.

Downing, N. E., & Roush, K. L. (1985). From passive acceptance to active commitment: A model of feminist identity development for women. *Counseling Psychologist, 13,* 695–709.

Fassinger, R. E., & Miller, B. A. (1996). Validation of an inclusive model of sexual minority identity formation on a sample of gay men. *Journal of Homosexuality, 32,* 53–79.

Fuertes, J. N., & Brobst, K. (2002). Clients' ratings of counselor multicultural competency. *Cultural Diversity and Ethnic Minority Psychology, 8,* 214–223.

Gibbs, J. T. (1974). Patterns of adaptation among Black students at a predominantly White university: Selected case studies. *American Journal of Orthopsychiatry, 44,* 728–740.

Guthrie, R. V. (1970). *Being Black: Psychological and sociological dilemmas.* San Francisco: Canfield Press.

Guthrie, R. V. (1998). *Even the rat was white: A historical view of psychology.* New York: Allyn & Bacon.

Harper, F. D. (1973). What counselors must know about the social sciences of Black Americans. *Journal of Negro Education, 42,* 109–116.

Harper, F. D., & Stone, W. O. (1974). Toward a theory of transcendent counseling with Blacks. *Journal of Non-White Concerns in Personnel and Guidance, 2,* 191–196.

Helms, J. E. (1984). Toward a theoretical explanation of the effects of race on counseling: A Black and White model. *Counseling Psychologist, 12,* 153–165.

Helms, J. E. (Ed.). (1990). *Black and White racial identity: Theory, research, and practice.* Westport, CT: Greenwood Press.

Helms, J. E. (1994). How multiculturalism obscures racial factors in the therapy process: Comment on Ridley et al. (1994), Sodowsky et al. (1994), Ottavi et al. (1994), and Thompson et al. (1994). *Journal of Counseling Psychology, 41,* 162–165.

Helms, J. E. (1995). An update of Helms's White and people of Color racial identity models. In J. G. Ponterotto, J. M. Casas, L. A. Suzuki, & C. M. Alexander (Eds.), *Handbook of multicultural counseling* (pp. 181–198). Thousand Oaks, CA: Sage.

Helms, J. E., & Carter, R. T. (1986). *Manual for the Visible Racial/Ethnic Identity Attitudes Scale.* Unpublished manuscript.

Helms, J. E., & Carter, R. T. (1990). Development of the White Racial Identity Attitude Scale. In J. E. Helms (Ed.), *Black and White racial identity: Theory, research, and practice* (pp. 67–80). Westport, CT: Greenwood Press.

Ibrahim, F. A. (1984). Cross-cultural counseling and psychotherapy: An existential-psychological perspective. *International Journal for the Advancement of Counseling, 7,* 159–169.

Ibrahim, F. A., & Kahn, H. (1987). Assessment of worldviews. *Psychological Reports, 60,* 163–176.

Jackson, B. (1975). Black identity development. In L. Golubschick & B. Persky (Eds.), *Urban social and educational issues* (pp. 158–164). Dubuque, IA: Kendall-Hall.

Jackson, G. G., & Kirschner, S. A. (1973). Racial self-designation and preference for a counselor. *Journal of Counseling Psychology, 20,* 560–564.

Kerwin, C., & Ponterotto, J. G. (1995). Biracial identity development: Theory and research. In J. G. Ponterotto, J. M. Casas, L. A. Suzuki, & C. M. Alexander (Eds.), *Handbook of multicultural counseling* (pp. 199–217). Thousand Oaks, CA: Sage.

Kim, J. (1981). The process of Asian American identity development: A study of Japanese American women's perceptions of their struggle to achieve personal identities as Americans of Asian ancestry. *Dissertation Abstracts International, 42,* 1551A. (UMI No. 81-18080)

Kluckhohn, F. R., & Strodtbeck, F. L. (1961). *Variations in value orientations.* Evanston, IL: Row, Petersen.

LaFromboise, T. D. (1988). American Indian mental health policy. *American Psychologist, 43,* 388–397.

LaFromboise, T. D., Coleman, H. L. K., & Hernandez, A. (1991). Development and factor structure of the Cross-Cultural Counseling Inventory-Revised. *Professional Psychology: Research and Practice, 22,* 380–388.

LaFromboise, T. D., & Rowe, W. (1983). Skills training for bicultural competence: Rationale and application. *Journal of Counseling Psychology, 30,* 589–595.

Lee, F. Y. (1991). *The relationship of ethnic identity to social support, self-esteem, psychological distress, and help-seeking behavior among Asian American college students.* Unpublished doctoral dissertation, University of Illinois, Urbana-Champaign.

McCarn, S. R., & Fassinger, R. E. (1996). Revisioning sexual minority identity formation: A new model of lesbian identity and its implications for counseling and research. *Counseling Psychologist, 24,* 508–534.

McNamara, K., & Richard, K. M. (1989). Feminist identity development: Implications for feminist therapy with women. *Journal of Counseling and Development, 68,* 184–193.

Milliones, J. (1973). *Construction of the Developmental Inventory of Black consciousness.* Unpublished doctoral dissertation, University of Pittsburgh, Pittsburgh, PA.

Mohr, J., & Fassinger, R. E. (2000). Measuring dimensions of lesbian and gay male experience. *Measurement and Evaluation in Counseling and Development, 33,* 66–90.

Parham, T. A., & Helms, J. E. (1981). The influence of Black students' racial identity attitudes on preference for counselor's race. *Journal of Counseling Psychology, 28,* 250–256.

Phinney, J. S. (1989). Stages of ethnic identity in minority group adolescence. *Journal of Early Adolescence, 9,* 34–49.

Pinderhughes, C. A. (1973). Racism and psychotherapy. In C. V. Willie, B. M. Kramer, & B. S. Brown (Eds.), *Racism and mental health* (pp. 61–121). Pittsburgh, PA: University of Pittsburgh Press.

Ponterotto, J. G. (1988). Racial consciousness development among White counselor trainees: A stage model. *Journal of Multicultural Counseling and Development, 16,* 146–156.

Ponterotto, J. G., Gretchen, D., Utsey, S. O., Rieger, B. P., & Austin, R. (2002). A revision of the Multicultural Counseling Awareness Scale. *Journal of Multicultural Counseling and Development, 30,* 153–180.

Root, M. P. P. (1992). *Racially mixed people in America.* Newbury Park, CA: Sage.

Ruiz, A. S. (1990). Ethnic identity: Crisis and resolution. *Journal of Multicultural Counseling and Development, 18,* 29–40.

Sodowsky, G. R., Kwan, K.-L. K., & Pannu, R. (1995). Ethnic identity of Asians in the United States. In J. G. Ponterotto, J. M. Casas, L. A. Suzuki, & C. M. Alexander (Eds.), *Handbook of multicultural counseling* (pp. 123–154). Thousand Oaks, CA: Sage.

Sodowsky, G. R., Taffe, R. C., Gutkin, T. B., & Wise, S. L. (1994). Development of the Multicultural Counseling Inventory: A self-report measure of multicultural competencies. *Journal of Counseling Psychology, 41,* 137–148.

Sue, D. W., Arredondo, P., & McDavis, R. J. (1992). Multicultural counseling competencies and standards: A call to the profession. *Journal of Multicultural Counseling and Development, 20,* 64–68.

Sue, D. W., Bernier, J. E., Durran, A., Feinberg, L., Pedersen, P. B., Smith, E. J., et al. (1982). Position paper: Cross-cultural counseling competencies. *Counseling Psychologist, 10,* 45–52.

Sue, D. W., Carter, R. T., Casas, J. M., Fouad, N. A., Ivey, A. E., Jensen, M., et al. (1998). *Multicultural counseling competencies: Individual and organizational development.* Thousand Oaks, CA: Sage.

Sue, D. W., & Sue, D. (1977). Barriers to effective cross-cultural counseling. *Journal of Counseling Psychology, 24,* 420–429.

Sue, D. W., & Sue, D. (1981). *Counseling the culturally different: Theory and practice.* New York: Wiley.

Sue, D. W., & Sue, D. (1999). *Counseling the culturally different: Theory and practice* (3rd ed.). New York: Wiley.

Sue, D. W., & Sue, D. (2003). *Counseling the culturally different: Theory and practice* (4th ed.). New York: Wiley.

Sue, S., & Sue, D. W. (1971). Chinese American personality and mental health. *Amerasian Journal, 1,* 36–49.

Sue, S., Zane, N., & Young, K. (1994). Research on psychotherapy with culturally diverse populations. In A. E. Bergin & S. L. Garfield (Eds.), *Handbook of psychotherapy and behavior change* (4th ed., pp. 783–817). New York: Wiley.

Szapocznik, J., Santisteban, D., Kurtines, W. M., Hervis, O. E., & Spencer, F. (1982). Life enhancements counseling: A psychosocial model of services for Cuban people. In E. E. Jones & S. J. Korchin (Eds.), *Minority mental health* (pp. 293–329). New York: Praeger.

Thomas, C. W. (1971). *Boys into men.* Beverly Hills, CA: Glencoe Press.

Trimble, J. E., & LaFromboise, T. D. (1987). American Indians and the counseling process: Culture, adaptation, and style. In P. Pedersen (Ed.), *Handbook of cross-cultural counseling and therapy* (pp. 127–133). New York: Greenwood Press.

Vontress, C. E. (1967). The culturally different. *Employment Science Review, 10,* 35–36.

Vontress, C. E. (1968). Counseling Negro students for college. *Journal of Negro Education, 37,* 37–44.

Vontress, C. E. (1969). Counseling the culturally different in our society. *Journal of Employment Counseling, 6,* 9–16.

Vontress, C. E. (1971). Racial differences: Impediments to rapport. *Journal of Counseling Psychology, 18,* 7–13.

Vontress, C. E. (1974). Barriers in cross-cultural counseling. *Counseling and Values, 18,* 160–165.

White, J. L. (1970). Toward a Black psychology. *Ebony, 25,* 44–52.

CHAPTER 6

The Socialization of Self: Understanding Shifting and Multiple Selves across Cultures

Christine J. Yeh and Carla D. Hunter

Understanding the relationship between socialization experiences and individuals' functioning is the core of Western psychological theory and practice (Bandura, 1965; Erikson, 1963; Freud, 1943; Wiggins, 1973). Who am I? What is my role in my family, in society? How do I relate to other people? What types of behaviors are socially acceptable? How do I understand who I am in relationship to others? The answer to these questions lead many to have diverse life experiences. Despite such diversity of experiences, "the person" is a central component in the socialization process. Yet, most definitions of socialization focus on its goal: to effectively participate within one's cultural frame of reference. Schneider (1988) defines socialization as "the process of learning how to behave effectively in groups and adjust to particular cultures" (p. 238). Kagitcibasi (1996) states, "Human development is socialization, together with maturation. It encompasses the lifelong process of becoming social, becoming a member of society" (p. 19). Eggan (1970) considers socialization the primary method through which persons receive information about cultural norms. These definitions of socialization convey what the socialization process involves: specifically, knowledge of rules, knowledge of cultural norms, and effectively using social skills to interact with others through shared systems of meaning.

In Western psychology, personhood is central to the understanding of socialization. Therefore, the primary methods of building theory and carrying out research to understand the process of socialization have been through the study of individuals and their behaviors (e.g., Allport, 1950; Bandura, 1965; Erikson, 1963; Freud, 1943; Kohlberg, 1976; Wiggins, 1973). For example, in their study of racial socialization, Caughy, Randolph, and O'Campo (2002) state, "Measures of racial socialization have been limited to those in which the respondent, either parent or child, reports on the types of racial socialization practices engaged in by parents" (p. 48). In research and theory, persons are viewed as the embodiment of their socialization experiences. Thus, the self is considered an important participant and observer in his or her socialization.

During the 1970s, psychologists suggested the need to take a step back from the individual perspective of understanding socialization. Between 1970 and 1980 the assumptions of American psychologists regarding the individual nature of person-hood (or self), which are the basis for theories of socialization, were criticized. The-orists such as Gergen (1973), Hogan (1975), Lasch (1979), Rotenberg (1977), Sampson (1977), and Smith (1978) criticized the emphasis in American psychology on the individual self and assumptions that views of the self as independent and au-tonomous are universal. Research in anthropology on culture and personality and in-creased focus on indigenous perspectives of mental health gave rise to concepts such as "relational self" (Berry, 1976; Berry, Poortinga, Segall, & Dasen, 2002; Whiting & Child, 1953) and "indexical self" (Gaines, 1982; Grills & Ajei, 2002). These con-cepts are the focus of current research, theory, and conceptualization, which has ex-tended our understanding of cultural selves (Kagitcibasi, 1996; Markus & Kitayama, 1991; Triandis, 1989).

Research in the past few decades across the fields of cultural, social, and coun-seling psychology, African psychology, and anthropology, sociology, philosophy, and religion has indicated that conceptualizations of the self as well as socialization vary across cultural contexts and social settings. This chapter reviews past and pres-ent research on socialization as it pertains to cultural conceptualizations of the self. We first discuss socialization from a Western perspective and highlight correspond-ing notions of self. Next, we provide examples of early and current research that demonstrate conceptualizations of self among different cultural groups. In particu-lar, we address how cultural context impacts notions of self and influences multidi-mensional and shifting ways of being. Crain (1992) states that socialization is "the process by which societies induce their members to behave in socially acceptable ways" (p. 178). What it means to behave in socially acceptable ways varies across cultures and especially with regard to the expectations of the self. A review of so-cialization and self holds implications for understanding differing conceptualiza-tions of self and the reciprocal interaction between culture and self. Our hope is that through understanding differing conceptualizations of self we continue to extend existing theory on socialization and selfhood, which may then impact our under-standing of socialization in various cultures, for example, racial, gender, and ethnic socialization (Yeh & Hwang, 2000b).

RESEARCH ON SOCIALIZATION AND DEVELOPMENT OF THE SELF

Socialization is considered to be the primary method through which the skills and knowledge needed to live and be a social being within a culture are transmitted. So-cialization equips individuals with knowledge about the roles, expectations, cognitive skills, and strategies necessary to manage in society (Hutcheon, 1999; Jambunathan, Burts, & Pierce, 2000). Depending on one's cultural reference point, the process of socialization may take differing forms. For example, in the West, parents, caregivers, and family units are considered primary socializing agents of children. The role of parents and caregivers in the socialization of children is the foundation of our under-standing of social learning theory, attachment, moral development, and personality development (Crain, 1992).

In social learning theory (Bandura, 1969, 1973, 1977), learning through imitating others is emphasized. Through observation of others' behaviors children learn how to behave and the consequences associated with their actions. In attachment theory (Ainsworth, 1973; Bowlby, 1953, 1969), a breakdown in the attachment style between parents or primary caregivers and their children may have consequences for the child's capacity to be social and form intimate relationships while growing up and as an adult (Schneider, 1988). An important aspect of socialization also involves learning the culture's moral rules. In fact, Grills and Ajei (2002) posit that "the concept of God, in every culture, indicates the values and ideals of human functioning upheld by that culture" (p. 79). Last, theories of personality development also rely on the role of early parental figures in the development of children. Positive or abnormal personality development is associated with poor or dysfunctional early socialization experiences (Corey, 2005; McWilliams, 1994).

Theories of socialization are embedded in the culture in which they are developed. Simply stated, "How the self is construed in a cultural context has direct implications for socialization" (Kagitcibasi, 1996, p. 69). Assumptions embedded in the aforementioned theories are that the self that is being socialized is independent, autonomous, and self-contained and possesses stable internal attributes and values (Kagitcibasi, 1996; Markus & Kitayama, 1991; Triandis, 1989). In Western cultures such as the United States, the goal of socialization is the development of an independent and autonomous adult, termed a referential self (Grills & Ajei, 2002). Although autonomy in an adult is an expectation that is consistent with the norms of Western culture, sociologists and psychologists also recognize that individuals are social beings. Hutcheon (1999) states, "To exist as a social being is to be forever emmeshed in some form of social interaction—in addition to the inevitable transactions with one's physical surroundings" (p. 45). Such a view of personhood in a relational context extends our conception of self and furthers our understanding of the influence of social groups and social interactions. However, the self that is discussed, even as a social being, is an individualistic self and is qualitatively different from a self that is connected to other selves, spirit, and nature, the self upheld in non-Western cultures.

Geertz's (1973, 1975) seminal research with people in Bali highlights a different conceptualization of self as one that is connected to others through kinship, birth order, and social status. Geertz describes the variety of ways by which individual Balinese are referred. For example, each person is provided a name, yet birth order is given precedence over the specific name. Furthermore, the Balinese rely on *teknonyms,* which are assigned to adults at the birth of the first child. Teknonyms are cultural referential points that take the form of "mother or father of Jim" (Schneider, 1988, p. 115). Teknonyms intimately and enduringly connect children to the adults in the family. Discussing Geertz's work with the Balinese, Schneider summed it up best when he stated:

> Imagine yourself in this society. Shortly after birth you would be named say, "Masjof," but most people would refer to you as "Firstborn." When you married you would keep your name until you had your first child, when you would become known as "mother of Roshed."

This would be your name until Roshed or one of his siblings produced a child, when your name would change again to "grandmother of Nowkan." (p. 115)

In comparison to the Balinese example, Western notions of self are quite different. In American culture, terms such as grandmother and mother designate roles and are not culturally embedded as part of the self. Kagitcibasi (1996) notes that in parent education classes in the United States, mothers are taught to separate themselves or "let go" of infants and their tendency to "merge" is considered harmful. Providing further evidence of differing conceptualizations of self, Choi (1992) found differing interaction styles between Korean and Canadian middle-class mothers and their young children. Choi found that Korean mothers tended to speak for their children, whereas Canadian mothers encouraged their children to be autonomous. Research conducted by Choi is consistent with early research by Caudill and Schooler (1973), in which communication styles between American and Japanese mothers also differed with respect to the emphasis on autonomy. American mothers encouraged their children to express their needs and desires, whereas Japanese mothers perceived their children's needs and desires to be connected with their own. Hence, early socialization practices seem to have strong implications for the realization of diverse conceptualizations of self and expectations for individual functioning in a social world. Using an example from African psychology, Obasi (2002) notes that in the African experience, health is connected to one's soul, one's spirit, the creator, and knowledge of one's destiny. Thus, sickness represents a disconnection in the relationship among these interconnected experiences, which are the essence of the African concept of personhood. Furthermore, in our qualitative research (Yeh, Hunter, Madan-Bahel, Chiang, & Arora, in press) with indigenous healers, notions of self as multidirectional and multilinear are linked to indigenous healers' understanding of persons and the causes of illness.

The results of experimental research with young adults and adults provide further evidence of differences in cultural understandings of self. Using the Twenty Statements Test (TST), an open-ended questionnaire that consists of 20 sentence completions that begin "I am . . . ," Cousins (1989) demonstrated that Japanese high school and college students tended to describe themselves according to their social roles and their relationships to their social units; European American high school and college students described themselves using internal attributes. When the TST was modified to include a specific context, Cousins found that Japanese respondents used more internal attributes than American subjects. Cousins hypothesized that Japanese respondents were able to use internal attributes because they were provided with social contexts for their responses, highlighting that the self exists in relation to others and may also be context-specific. Although long considered to be universal, Western notions of self as autonomous are culturally specific. Racially and ethnically diverse groups possess different conceptualizations of the self, which include one's role in the family of origin (Nsamenang, 1992), connectedness with others through shared relationships (Bond, 1986; Hsu, 1985), and connectedness to nature and spirit (Grills & Ajei, 2002; Heelas & Lock, 1981; Hunter & Lewis, in press; Marsella, DeVos, & Hsu, 1985; Nsamenang, 1992; Obasi, 2002; Shweder & Levine, 1984).

Historically, socialization has been discussed as a one-way process in which cultural norms are transmitted to individuals, usually from parent to child. Parents are considered primary socializing agents for children in the transmission of cultural norms. Furthermore, socialization is considered to occur primarily through verbal expression and overt behavior, in comparison to other means of socialization that are based on the use of affect, such as shame and guilt (Eggan, 1970). But this view of socialization that entails the perceptions of humans as passive receivers does not account for the construction of social reality (Corsaro & Eder, 1995) and shared cultural meaning (Heppner, Kivlighan, & Wampold, 1999). A view of socialization and socializing agents as passive also does not account for the shaping and reshaping of cultural norms (Hutcheon, 1999).

The socialization process is a complex system of ongoing reciprocal interaction (Hutcheon, 1999). For which Western notions of a stable, autonomous, and unique self seem insufficient. If we consider the self as existing outside the boundaries of linear time, we may view socialization as occurring simultaneously in the past, present, and future. Thus, to view socialization as multidirectional is to understand the concept of the shifting selves, multiple selves, and the idea of selfways. Therefore, a dynamic theory of self is necessary to address the differing ways socialization takes place and how meaning is transmitted and recreated in a cultural system. The social constructivist perspective is particularly helpful in furthering our understanding of the dynamic nature of socialization.

SOCIAL CONSTRUCTIVISM AND SELF

An important idea undergirding the literature on socialization and self is the notion of social constructivism. Specifically, according to the constructivism paradigm, notions of truth and reality are abandoned in favor of the notion that ideas about the world, especially in the social world, are constructed in the minds and experiences of individuals (Heppner et al., 1999). These constructions are shaped by culture, media, customs, traditions, social interactions, roles, and deeply rooted belief systems. Although such constructions exist and can be described to others, they are not necessarily representations of truth.

Social constructivism is based on four assumptions: (1) cultures create and share ways of understanding reality; (2) understanding is a social product; (3) understandings are persistent because they're useful (they reinforce social structures), not because they represent truth; and (4) understanding provides a map for social action and behavior (Heppner et al., 1999). To be able to conceptualize cultural selves in terms of these assumptions contributes to a deeper appreciation for the necessity of a shifting selves paradigm.

Constructions may be simple, complex, naïve, or sophisticated and may change over time, across context, or as a result of education, experience, or maturation (Heppner et al., 1999). In the context of understanding cultural selves, reality is created and recreated by cultural participants in various cultural systems and groups. Although there may be agreement that a particular event occurs, it is the *meaning* attributed to that event that is relevant. If we accept the assumption that selves are shaped by context and culture, then selves must continually shift, adapt, and change.

Understanding social constructivist perspectives of self is especially relevant in the counseling field because clients' perceptions and understandings of experience often conflict with a counselor's assumptions and worldviews (Sue & Sue, 2003). For example, if a client refuses to talk about her family, there are clearly numerous possible explanations. The client may be avoidant, resistant, private, or, in certain cultural frameworks (see Kondo, 1992, for an excellent discussion of this), she may be protecting the privacy and honor of her family by not revealing personal matters. A particular challenge in working across cultures is understanding how clients "construct" their experiences. This is especially difficult for counselors who are not aware of their own worldviews and who cannot separate their perspectives from their client's (Sue & Sue, 2003).

The idea that cultures share understandings of reality or truth is not new. Previous literature indicates that many cultural groups have shared worldviews (Carter, 1991; Sodowsky & Johnson, 1994; Sue & Sue, 2003). Specifically, based on the cultural value orientations model by Kluckhohn and Strodtbeck (1961), Carter describes how particular cultural groups have shared understandings of time, relationships with nature, nature of people, and activity. For example, certain cultural groups, such as Puerto Ricans (Garcia-Preto, 1996; Inclan, 1985), tend to endorse a present time value, whereas European Americans exhibit more emphasis on the future.

Social constructivists do not disagree about the actual occurrence of an event (e.g., the client not talking about her family). Rather, they believe that it is the *interpretation* of the occurrence that is pertinent to social interactions and in conceptualizations of self. And socialization plays a key role in one's interpretation. Given the tremendous increase in clients from different cultural backgrounds in the counseling setting, the existence of multiple constructions and multiple truths is very common. In fact, it is the growth of multiple realities that may contribute to cultural misunderstandings and conflicts in the cross-cultural counseling process and social interactions (Heppner et al., 1999). For example, in the case of the client who does not talk about her family, it may be due to the fact that in her culture, it is a sign of maturity to keep family issues within the bounds and privacy of the family circle. This perspective may contradict the counselor's socially constructed assumptions that the client is exhibiting resistant or avoidant tendencies. The counselor may be socialized to make sense of the client's behavior by seeing it as negative, while the client is behaving according to her cultural norms.

Because constructions do not represent universal truths or realities, events, experiences, and perceptions are bound to one another through interpretive lenses. Social constructions have longevity because they reinforce social structures, positions, and relationships, not necessarily because they represent truth (Heppner et al., 1999).

THE CO-CONSTRUCTION OF CULTURE AND SELF

Social constructivism is related to the notion of mutual constitution in social psychology, which emphasizes that we are social and cultural beings. For example, research has found that around the world, people smile. Yet, although this is a common ritual, it has different meanings (Bruner, 1990) and different consequences depending on the social and cultural context (Yrizarry, Matsumoto, Imai, Kooken, & Takeuchi, 2001). Similarly, understandings of self are informed by context, relationships between the people interacting, and cultural belief systems. Often, these understandings are tied to how we have been socialized to understand cultural norms. Individuals cannot be understood as separate from their settings. Instead, both individuals and contexts coexist in a process of mutual constitution (Bruner, 1990; Fiske, Kitayama, Markus, & Nisbett, 1998). Biology, genetics, and heredity are certainly critical aspects of social behavior and self, but research has highlighted that the self can shift depending on the situation and setting (Cousins, 1989; Kondo, 1992; Markus & Kitayama, 1991; Yeh, 1996; Yeh & Huang, 1996).

Thus, cultural values and how one is socialized to interpret events influence behaviors, thoughts, and emotions. Individuals in turn help give shape and meaning to their experience within a cultural context. Differential meanings are attached to behaviors depending on the cultural context in which the behavior has occurred, and individuals act within the parameters of appropriate behavior as deemed by the cultural context. As a result, the same behavior may have different meanings in different cultural contexts (Fivush & Buckner, 1997) according to how one is socialized.

It is important to explore how various cultural artifacts (e.g., proverbs, media images, stories, rituals) shape the relationships between selves and the social world. In particular, cultural artifacts influence beliefs, ideas, and how meaning is made of events and people. Thus, socialization to one's culture holds important implications for the development of self. Those in the West view socialization as one-directional and developmental; the assumption is that children are socialized and that socialization ends when one becomes an adult. Yet socialization is an ongoing, multidirectional process, which influences a person's ways of being.

Markus and colleagues describe socially and culturally embedded selves as selfways (Markus, Mullally, & Kitayama, 1997). Selfways involve being able to shift across multiple "sociocultural patterns of participation" (p. 16) and characteristic manners of interacting as a person in the world. Hence, selfways incorporate an understanding and internalization of socialization and culture as multidirectional and ongoing, rather than unidirectional and developmental. Specific features of selfways include "sociocultural historical ideas and values," "sociocultural-historical processes and practices," "social episodes in local worlds," and "psychological tendencies" (pp. 17–21). Sociocultural-historical ideas and values are religious, philosophical, and historical, such as those demonstrated in the Declaration of Independence, Protestantism, and Cartesian philosophy in the United States and in Buddhism, Shintoism, and Confucianism in Japan (Markus et al., 1997).

According to Markus et al. (1997), sociocultural-historical processes and practices include everday practices and influences, such as linguistic practices, proverbs, employment practices, and aspects of the legal system. For example, in the United States, common proverbs include "Pull yourself up by your boot straps"; "The early bird gets the worm"; and "Be true to yourself." These reflect a strong cultural emphasis on autonomy, assertiveness, and individuality. In contrast, in Asian cultures such as Japan and China, common sayings include "An elder in the house is a treasure in the house"; "Five hundred years ago, all came from the same family"; and "To take care of your body is the beginning of loving one's parents." Such sayings reflect the psychological tendencies of respect for elders, family unity, and filial piety in Asian cultural values.

Social episodes in local worlds refer to relational interactions that reflect embedded values and beliefs. Markus et al. (1997) describe practices in the United States that encourage autonomy, such as telling guests to "help themselves." In contrast, social episodes in Japan highlight the significance of group harmony. For example, children are expected to do school chores as a group, eat and serve lunch as a group, and learn to interact as interconnected members of a group. Numerous other examples of everyday events and social interactions reflect norms and values that are culturally constructed. Kim and Markus (1999) contrasted ordering a decaffeinated cappuccino with nonfat milk at a café in San Francisco with placing the same order in Seoul. In San Francisco, the practice of ordering such a specific cappuccino has an underlying meaning of uniqueness and standing out, which is consistent with Western cultural norms. In Seoul, the cultural expectation is that individuals order in ways that represent connectedness to others. Thus, ordering such a specialized drink may be frowned upon. In the United States, individuals are expected to be unique; in Korea, individuals are expected to conform to group norms.

Differential expectations of the person in varying cultural contexts have implications for the development of emotions, thoughts, behaviors, and perceptions (Fivush & Buckner, 1997) while cultural values reinforce group norms. Likewise, individuals' behaviors, thoughts, and emotions have meaning in a cultural context. Thus, interaction in a cultural context provides meaning to individuals and reinforces or changes cultural patterns. Such a dynamic interaction between individual and culture is the foundation of mutual constitution and of the development and socialization of self. Kim and Markus (1999) note that behavior, for example, among East Asians, occurs within the prescribed norms that are reinforced by cultural context. Essentially, individuals learn appropriate behavior while understanding of their core self occurs according to the norms established by their respective cultures.

Hence, it may be posited that the self is constructed in a cultural context and the self in turn shapes the cultural context. For example, connection to others is one of the primary reasons for conformity to group norms (Kim & Markus, 1999). Socialization can be thought of as occurring in a cultural context that triggers cognitions regarding appropriate behavior, whether conformity or uniqueness. In Western societies, independent self systems are constructed within a cultural norm that values uniqueness and independence, and interdependent self systems are constructed within a cultural norm that values conformity to the group.

MULTIPLE SELVES

Historically, Western conceptualizations of self have focused on individual personality traits, the stability of internal attributes, and an emphasis on being and becoming an individual who has mastery over his or her actions (Epstein, 1973).

Cross-cultural perspectives of self have challenged this perspective as the dominant and sole theoretical conceptualization for understanding persons and their behaviors, thoughts, and perceptions (Markus & Kitayama, 1998; Markus et al., 1997; McGuire, McGuire, & Cheever, 1986). Increased understanding of the ways one can be a person has given rise to several new theoretical conceptualizations of personhood (i.e., spirit, relational). We focus specifically on how the self is understood from the perspective of either individualism or collectivism (Triandis, 1989). This is not to say that there are not within group differences among Americans, for example, women are generally more relationally oriented and connection to others is an important part of the self-system (Cross, Bacon, & Morris, 2000). Likewise, spiritual persons may access a spiritual self in which connection to the universe, God, or a higher power is a major component of the self-system (Hunter & Lewis, 2004; Obasi, 2002). For ease of discussion, we have chosen to remain within the traditional individual and collectivism frameworks.

Individualistic cultures, such as those in the West, promote the development of independent selves. Personhood is viewed from the perspective of being an individual, one's internal attributes are given worth and are believed to guide behaviors, and individuals are expected to be unique, while social role and social context are deemphasized. Cultures in the East promote interdependent selves such that relationships, group expectations, and cultural contexts contribute to personhood. Thus, behaviors and thoughts occur within the norms of the culture, and relationships among others in the group are emphasized. One's way of being a person is intricately linked to others through social relationships, group norms, and cultural context (Markus & Kitayama, 1998; Markus et al., 1997; Yeh & Huang, 1996; Yeh & Hwang, 2000a). In addition, cultural context may be viewed as a prime for the accessibility of multiple selves, such as a public self, a private self, and a collective self. Relative accessibility of one's self system depends on the cultural norms and values in which one is raised. For example, in the United States, individuals are expected to be unique and value personal goals above the goals of the group. Relatedly, Americans may access self systems that are private, in contrast to Koreans, who may be primed by their cultural contexts to access a collective self.

The effects of priming on cognitive attributions for a novel event have been demonstrated experimentally among bicultural Chinese living in Hong Kong who have also been influenced by Western culture and Chinese Americans who were born in China but live in the United States. Cultural priming has also been experimentally demonstrated with European American and Korean high school students. In these experiments, European American students behaved consistently with cultural norms that represent individuality, uniqueness, and differentiation from others; Korean high school students made choices that represented conformity to the group. In essence, Korean high school students made choices that did not deviate from the majority.

SHIFTING SELVES

Bicultural competence is another theoretical perspective used to consider selves across varying cultural domains (LaFromboise, Coleman, & Gerton,

1993). Bicultural competence involves the integration of two cultures without experiencing the tension between the two (Domanico, Crawford, & Wolfe, 1994). According to the alternation model of bicultural competence (LaFromboise et al., 1993), an individual adjusts his or her behavior to a particular cultural or social context, without having to make a commitment to a specific cultural identity. Underlying the theory is that the person is socialized to respond to and make meaning of two different cultures. The ability to adapt the self across situational contexts may require using different languages, coping strategies, interpersonal communication, and motivational styles of interaction (Ramirez, 1984). Theories of bicultural competence differ from notions of shifting selves (see Yeh & Hwang, 2000a) in that bicultural competence acknowledges only two main cultural identities (dominant and culture of origin), whereas shifting selves theory allows for multiple ways the self can be expressed and understood across numerous relational and situational contexts. Shifting selves also holds implications for understanding socialization in multiple contexts. For example, research in the area of racial socialization may explore under which circumstances and in which contexts racial socialization attitudes are strongest and weakest. In line with this, research studies may also explore how the self adapts and changes (shifts) to cope within various cultural contexts and in relationship to other racial and cultural beings. Yeh (1999) provides an example of this in her discussion of shifting self theory and invisibility among African American males.

Shifting selves are contextually and situationally informed, malleable, adaptable, and evolving. A recurring idea in most research and theory on the interdependent self has been the relational and contextual emphasis on conceptions of the self. In particular, in a cross-cultural study of self in Japan and the United States, Yeh (1996) describes the Japanese self as multidimensional and situationally based. The Japanese shifting self shapes and expresses itself in terms of important interpersonal obligations. The shifting self is integrated with one's social and relational, not individual, responsibility and responds and adapts according to influences such as feelings, place, time, and social situation. Yeh determined that the most significant influence on how the Japanese self is expressed is the present social relationship and attendant obligatory patterns of social interaction. Due to these factors, Japanese selves are not consistent across situations; rather, Japanese selves are defined by social and relational contexts.

In collectivistic cultures, the notion of interdependent and shifting selves has arisen as a way of understanding the multiple ways the self is expressed across varying social roles and cultural contexts (Yeh & Hwang, 2000a). Yeh and Hwang have discussed that one of the hallmarks of multiple and shifting selves in collectivistic societies is that meaning is given to the self through relationships and social interaction, an interdependent self-construal (Markus & Kitayama, 1991). Thus, the self is meaningful in varying social contexts and social roles, which differs from how the self is expressed in individualistic cultures, where individuals develop an independent self-construal (Kanagawa, Cross, & Markus, 2001; Markus & Kitayama, 1991). Socialization of the self in differing cultural contexts is also believed to give rise to how the self samples information from the environment, makes meaning out of cultural experiences, and determines which cognitions are used to perceive and interact with the world (Hong, Morris, Chiu, & Benet-Martinez, 2000; Markus & Kitayama, 1991).

Hong et al. (2000) used cultural icons such as the U.S. flag and a Chinese dragon, the Capitol building and the Great Wall, and Superman and Stone Monkey, respectively, as primes in two experimental conditions and a control condition. When shown a picture of a school of fish, participants in the U.S. prime condition attributed behavior to internal explanations, for example, "The fish in front is the leader." Participants in the Chinese prime condition were more likely to attribute behavior to external reasons, such as "The fish is being chased." In the control condition, in which primes were not used, participants attributed behavior equally to internal and external attributions. Bicultural individuals are believed to contain both cultures; the accessibility of the self that is utilized is primed by cultural contexts. Similar results have been found in studies conducted by Triandis (1989), Trafimow, Triandis, and Goto (1989), Kim and Markus (1999), and Hong et al. (2000). The results from these studies provide insight into how the shifting self may function and how culture serves as a prime for the development of independent and interdependent self systems (Markus & Wurf, 1987). In other words, priming provides experimental evidence for how culture shapes and maintains the accessibility of independent and interdependent self systems.

CONCLUSION

Traditional views of the self have been explored and explained using Western views of the self as stable, unique, and consistent across varying social contexts. Western views have influenced socialization and self theories and the ways we think about the relationship between culture and self. Such a perspective assumes that how culture is communicated to self through the process of socialization is unidirectional rather than multidirectional and ongoing. The cross-cultural psychology perspective has provided another model with which to view the self-system. In a non-Western approach, relationships to other persons, spirit, nature, and the creator are given importance as critical aspects of the self-system. Among cultural groups such as Koreans, Japanese, Chinese, Africans, and Latinos, the self is relational. Behaviors, thoughts, and cognitions occur from the perspective of relationships to other persons and are not individualistic. In addition, cultural norms and practices provide meaning to interactions and individuals' behaviors reinforce and/or change cultural meaning through the dynamic interaction of mutual constitution. Thus, reality is shaped and reshaped and the self is able to shift across contexts.

Socialization is an integral aspect of understanding the ability of the self to shift in a variety of social contexts. The process of socialization is considered by many Western theorists to be the key to understanding how persons learn to be persons. The cultural psychology and African psychology perspectives highlight that differing conceptualizations of personhood do exist. According to one's socialization experiences, a dynamic changing self, an interrelated self, and an interconnected self are consistent with cultural norms. The notion of a stable and independent self may be viewed as maladaptive in cultural norms outside the United States. In American psychology, the tendency has been to view Western norms as universal and individuals who differed from the American cultural norms were perceived negatively. Through understanding the socialization experiences of diverse people, the tendency in American psychology to pathologize may be decreased. Selfhood may also be viewed as inextricably linked to culture and the ability of the self to shift as an expression of one's culture.

The self is socialized in a cultural context, and so individuals' behaviors, thoughts, and emotions must be understood from a cultural perspective. The notion of selfways provides us with another perspective for understanding culture's and socialization's impact on the self. Understanding the cultural context helps to understand individuals' attributions, psychological needs, and actions. It is equally important to understand that the accessibility of the differing self systems can be primed or activated through the communication of implicit cultural messages. This is not to say that we must simply understand culture to understand the individual; rather, we must understand that cultural practices and individuals' self systems in a culture are co-constructed.

REFERENCES

Ainsworth, M. D. S. (1973). The development of infant and mother attachment. In B. M. Caldwell & H. M. Ricciuti (Eds.), *Review of child development research* (Vol. 3, pp. 1–94). Chicago: University of Chicago Press.

Allport, G. W. (1950). *The nature of personality.* Cambridge, MA: Addison-Wesley Press.

Bandura, A. (1965). Influence of model's reinforcement contingencies on the acquisition of imitative responses. *Journal of Personality and Social Psychology, 1,* 589–595.

Bandura, A. (1969). *Principles of behavior modification.* New York: Holt, Rinehart and Winston.

Bandura, A. (1973). *Aggression: A social learning analysis.* Englewood Cliffs, NJ: Prentice-Hall.

Bandura, A. (1977). *Social learning theory.* Englewood Cliffs, NJ: Prentice-Hall.

Berry, J. W. (1976). *Human ecology and cognitive style: Comparative studies in cultural and psychological adaptation.* New York: Sage.

Berry, J. W., Poortinga, Y. H., Segall, M. H., & Dasen, P. R. (2002). *Cross-cultural psychology: Research and applications.* (2nd ed.). Cambridge, England: Cambridge University Press.

Bond, M. H. (1986). *The psychology of Chinese people.* New York: Oxford University Press.

Bowlby, J. (1953). *Child care and the growth of love.* Baltimore: Penguin Books.

Bowlby, J. (1969). *Attachment and loss. Volume I: Attachment* (2nd ed.). New York: Basic Books.

Bruner, J. S. (1990). Culture and human development: A new look. *Human Development, 33,* 344–355.

Carter, R. T. (1991). Cultural values: A review of the empirical research and implications for counseling. *Journal of Counseling and Development, 70,* 164–173.

Caudill, W. A., & Schooler, C. (1973). Child behavior and child rearing in Japan and the United States: An interim report. *Journal of Nervous and Mental Diseases, 157,* 323–338.

Caughy, M. O., Randolph, S. M., & O'Campo, P. J. (2002). The Africentric Home Environment Inventory: An observational measure of the racial socialization features of the home environment for African American preschool children. *Journal of Black Psychology, 28,* 37–52.

Choi, S. H. (1992). Communicative socialization processes: Korea and Canada. In S. Iwawaki, Y. Kashima, & K. Leung (Eds.), *Innovations in cross-cultural psychology* (pp. 103–121). Lisse, The Netherlands: Swets & Zeitlinger.

Corey, G. (2005). *Theory and practice of counseling and psychotherapy* (6th ed.). Belmont, CA: Wadsworth/Thompson Learning.

Corsaro, W. A., & Eder, D. (1995). Development and socialization of children and adolescents. In K. S. Cook & J. S. House (Eds.), *Sociological perspectives on social psychology* (pp. 421–451). Needham Heights, MA: Allyn & Bacon.

Cousins, S. (1989). Culture and selfhood in Japan and the U.S. *Journal of Personality and Social Psychology, 56,* 124–131.

Crain, W. (1992). *Theories of development: Concepts and applications* (3rd ed.). Englewood Cliffs, NJ: Prentice-Hall.

Cross, S. E., Bacon, P. L., & Morris, M. L. (2000). The relational-interdependent self-construal and relationships. *Journal of Personality and Social Psychology, 78,* 791–808.

Domanico, Y. B., Crawford, I., & Wolfe, A. S. (1994). Ethnic identity and self-concept in Mexican-American adolescents: Is bicultural identity related to stress or better adjustment? *Child and Youth Care Forum, 23,* 197–207.

Eggan, D. (1970). Instruction and affect in Hopi cultural continuity. In J. Middleton (Ed.), *From child to adult: Studies in the anthropology of education* (pp. 109–133). Garden City, NY: Natural History Press.

Epstein, S. (1973). The self-concept revisited or a theory of a theory. *American Psychologist, 28,* 404–416.

Erikson, E. H. (1963). *Childhood and society* (2nd ed.). New York: Norton.

Fiske, A. P., Kitayama, S., Markus, H. R., & Nisbett, R. E. (1998). The cultural matrix of social psychology. In D. T. Gilbert, S. T. Fiske, & G. Lindzey (Eds.), *The handbook of social psychology* (4th ed., Vol. 2, pp. 915–981). Boston: Oxford University Press.

Fivush, R., & Buckner, J. (1997). The self as socially constructed: A commentary. In U. Neisser & D. A. Jopling (Eds.), *The conceptual self in context* (pp. 176–181). New York: Cambridge University Press.

Freud, S. (1943). *A general introduction to psychoanalysis* (J. Riviere, Trans.). Garden City, NY: Garden City.

Gaines, A. D. (1982). Cultural definitions, behavior, and the person in American psychiatry. In A. J. Marsella & G. M. White (Eds.), *Cultural conceptions of mental health and therapy* (pp. 167–192). London: Reidel.

Garcia-Preto, N. (1996). Latino families: An overview. In M. McGoldrick, J. Giordano, & J. K. Pearce (Eds.), *Ethnicity and family therapy* (2nd ed., pp. 141–154). New York: Guilford Press.

Geertz, C. (1973). *The interpretation of cultures.* New York: Basic Books.

Geertz, C. (1975). On the nature of anthropological understanding. *American Scientist, 63,* 47–53.

Gergen, K. J. (1973). Social psychology as history. *Journal of Personality and Social Psychology, 26,* 309–320.

Grills, C., & Ajei, M. (2002). African-centered conceptualizations of self and consciousness. In P. Pedersen (Series Ed.) & T. A. Parham (Vol. Ed.), *Multicultural aspects of counseling* series: Vol. 18. Counseling persons of African descent: Raising the bar of practitioner competence (pp. 75–99). Thousand Oaks, CA: Sage.

Heelas, P., & Lock, A. (Eds.). (1981). *Indigenous psychologies: The anthropology of the self.* London: Academic Press.

Heppner, P. P., Kivlighan, D. M., & Wampold, B. E. (1999). *Research design in counseling* (2nd ed.). Belmont, CA: Wadsworth.

Hogan, R. (1975). Theoretical egocentrism and the problem of compliance. *American Psychologist, 30,* 533–540.

Hong, Y., Morris, M. W., Chiu, C., & Benet-Martinez, V. (2000). Multicultural minds: A dynamic constructivist approach to culture and cognition. *American Psychologist, 55,* 709–720.

Hsu, F. L. K. (1985). The self in cross-cultural perspective. In A. J. Marsella, G. DeVos, & F. L. K. Hsu (Eds.), *Culture and self* (pp. 24–55). London: Tavistock.

Hunter, C. D., & Lewis, M. E. L. (2004). Healing the impact of racism using the African American spirit. In J. L. Chin (Ed.), *The psychology of prejudice and discrimination.* Praeger Publishers.

Hutcheon, P. D. (1999). *Building character and culture.* Westport, CT: Praeger.

Inclan, J. (1985). Variations in value orientations in mental health work with Puerto Ricans. *Psychotherapy: Theory, Research, Practice, and Training, 22,* 324–334.

Jambunathan, S., Burts, D. C., & Pierce, S. (2000). Comparisons of parenting attitudes among five ethnic groups. *Journal of Comparative Family Studies, 31,* 395–406.

Kagitcibasi, C. (1996). *Family and human development across cultures: A view from the other side.* Mahwah, NJ: Erlbaum.

Kanagawa, C., Cross, S. E., & Markus, H. R. (2001). "Who am I?" The cultural psychology of the conceptual self. *Personality and Social Psychology Bulletin, 27,* 90–103.

Kim, H., & Markus, H. R. (1999). Deviance or uniqueness, harmony or conformity? A cultural analysis. *Journal of Personality and Social Psychology, 77,* 785–800.

Kluckhohn, F. R., & Strodtbeck, F. L. (1961). *Variations in value orientations.* Evanston, IL: Row, Peterson.

Kohlberg, L. (1976). Moral stages and moralization: The cognitive-developmental approach. In T. Lickona (Ed.), *Moral development and behavior: Theory, research, and social issues* (pp. 31–53). New York: Holt, Rinehart and Winston.

Kondo, D. K. (1992). *Crafting selves: Power, gender, and discourses of identity in a Japanese workplace.* Chicago: University of Chicago Press.

LaFromboise, T. D., Coleman, H. L. K., & Gerton, J. (1993). Psychological impact of biculturalism: Evidence and theory. *Psychological Bulletin, 114*(3), 395–412.

Lasch, C. (1979). *The culture of narcissism: American life in an age of diminishing expectations.* New York: Norton.

Markus, H. R., & Kitayama, S. (1991). Culture and self: Implications for cognition, emotion, and motivation. *Psychological Review, 98,* 224–253.

Markus, H. R., & Kitayama, S. (1998). The cultural psychology of personality. *Journal of Cross-Cultural Psychology, 29,* 63–87.

Markus, H. R., Mullally, P. R., & Kitayama, S. (1997). Selfways: Diversity in modes of cultural participation. In U. Neisser & D. A. Jopling (Eds.), *The conceptual self in context* (pp. 13–61). New York: Cambridge University Press.

Markus, H. R., & Wurf, E. (1987). The dynamic self-concept: A social psychological perspective. *Annual Review of Psychology, 38,* 299–337.

Marsella, A. J., DeVos, G., & Hsu, F. L. K. (Eds.). (1985). *Culture and self: Asian and Western perspectives.* New York: Tavistock.

McGuire, W. J., McGuire, C. V., & Cheever, J. (1986). The self in society: Effects of social contexts on the sense of self. *British Journal of Social Psychology, 25,* 259–270.

McWilliams, N. (1994). *Psychoanalytic diagnosis: Understanding personality structure in the clinical process.* New York: Guilford Press.

Nsamenang, A. B. (1992). *Human development in cultural context: A third world perspective.* Newbury Park, CA: Sage.

Obasi, E. M. (2002). Reconceptualizing the notion of self from the African deep structure. In P. Pedersen (Series Ed.) & T. A. Parham (Vol. Ed.), *Multicultural aspects of counseling series: Vol. 18. Counseling persons of African descent: Raising the bar of practitioner competence* (pp. 52–74). Thousand Oaks, CA: Sage.

Ramirez, M., III. (1984). Assessing and understanding biculturalism-multiculturalism in Mexican-American adults. In J. L. Martinez & R. H. Mendoza (Eds.), *Chicano psychology* (pp. 77–94). San Diego, CA: Academic Press.

Rotenberg, M. (1977). Alienating-individualism and reciprocal-individualism: A cross-cultural conceptualization. *Journal of Humanistic Psychology, 3,* 3–17.

Sampson, E. E. (1977). Psychology and the American ideal. *Journal of Personality and Social Psychology, 35,* 767–782.

Schneider, D. J. (1988). *Introduction to social psychology.* Austin, TX: Harcourt Brace Jovanovich.

Shweder, R. A., & LeVine, R. (1984). *Culture theory.* New York: Cambridge University Press.

Smith, M. B. (1978). Perspectives on selfhood. *American Psychologist, 33,* 1053–1063.

Sodowsky, G. R., & Johnson, P. (1994). Culturally lessened assumptions and values. In P. Pedersen & J. C. Carey (Eds.), *Multicultural counseling in schools: A practice handbook* (pp. 59–79). Needham Heights, MA: Allyn & Bacon.

Sue, D. W., & Sue, D. (2003). *Counseling the culturally diverse: Theory and practice* (4th ed.). New York: Wiley.

Trafimow, D., Triandis, H. C., & Goto, S. G. (1989). Some tests of the distinction between the private self and the collective self. *Journal of Personality and Social Psychology, 60,* 649–655.

Triandis, H. C. (1989). The self and social behavior in differing cultural contexts. *Psychological Review, 96,* 506–520.

Whiting, J. W., & Child, I. (1953). *Child training and personality.* New Haven, CT: Yale University Press.

Wiggins, J. (1973). *Personality and prediction: Principles of personality assessment.* Reading, MA: Addison-Wesley.

Yeh, C. J. (1996). A cultural perspective on interdependence in self and morality: A Japan-U.S. Comparison (Doctoral dissertation, Stanford University, 1996). *Dissertation Abstracts International, 57,* 162B.

Yeh, C. J. (1999). Invisibility and self-construal in African American men: Implications for training and practice. *Counseling Psychologist, 27,* 810–819.

Yeh, C. J., & Huang, K. (1996). The collectivisitic nature of ethnic identity development among Asian-American college students. *Adolescence, 31,* 645–661.

Yeh, C. J., Hunter, C. D., Madan-Bahel, A., Chiang, L., & Arora, A. (in press). *Indigenous and interdependent perspectives on healing: Implications for counseling practice and research.* Manuscript submitted for publication.

Yeh, C. J., & Hwang, M. Y. (2000a). Interdependence in ethnic identity and self: Implications for theory and practice. *Journal of Counseling and Development, 78,* 420–429.

Yeh, C. J., & Hwang, M. Y. (2000b). The sociocultural context of Asian Pacific American ethnic identity and self: Implications for counseling. In D. S. Sandhu (Ed.), *Asian and Pacific Islander Americans: Issues and concerns for counseling and psychotherapy* (pp. 127–138). Commack, NY: Nova Science.

Yrizzary, N., Matsumoto, D., Imai, C., Kooken, K., & Takeuchi, S. (2001). Culture and emotion. In L. L. Adler & U. P. Gielen (Eds.), *Cross-cultural topics in psychology* (2nd ed., pp. 131–147). Westport, CT: Praeger Publishers.

CHAPTER 7

The Influence of Cross's Initial Black Racial Identity Theory on Other Cultural Identity Conceptualizations

Madonna G. Constantine, Sherry K. Watt, Kathy A. Gainor, and
Anika K. Warren

Previous writings (e.g., Constantine, Richardson, Benjamin, & Wilson, 1998; Helms, 1995) have summarized the contributions of various Black racial identity theories to the understanding of the identity development process of Black Americans. In particular, Cross's (1971) initial nigrescence model has been cited as a significant influence in the formulation of subsequent cultural identity theories over the past three decades. Cross's model characterizes the process by which Blacks move from the idealization of Whites and the concurrent denigration of their own racial group, to a place where Blacks positively embrace their cultural identity and affirm the existence of other cultural identities.

This chapter summarizes the influence of Cross's (1971) initial Black racial identity theory on models of racial, ethnic, feminist, sexual orientation, spiritual, social class, and multiple identity development. In general, the cultural theories discussed in this chapter reflect several assumptions that parallel those of Black racial identity development theory as discussed by Helms and Piper (1994). The first assumption is that society rewards and punishes individuals for being members of certain cultural groups. Second, cultural group membership becomes a critical aspect of psychosocial identity due to the reward structure of society. Third, cultural identity development is a maturation process in which individuals eventually shed external, negative, societal images of self for more positive, internal definitions. Moreover, most of the cultural models outlined in this chapter share two foundational concepts: (1) they are delineated in a sequential stage format, and (2) they assume that self-concept is composed of reference group orientation and personal identity (Cross, 1971, 1991, 1995).

GENERAL U.S. RACIAL AND ETHNIC IDENTITY DEVELOPMENT MODELS

Since Cross's (1971) initial conceptualization of Black racial identity development, many general racial and ethnic and minority identity models have emerged. It is generally believed that developing a positive racial or ethnic identity is more complex for people of Color than it is for dominant racial groups such as White Americans (Rotheram-Borus & Wyche, 1994). The complexities of identity development for people of Color are linked to familial, sociopolitical, and psychosocial environmental influences that frequently compete with their ability to establish a healthy identity (Helms, 1995; Helms & Cook, 1999; Reynolds & Pope, 1991). The earlier stages of many of these models illustrate how people of Color must contend with oppressive dominant group influences in their attempts to establish healthy racial and ethnic identities. Helms and Cook asserted that identity development models depicting various cultural groups as exposed to similar oppressive conditions are examples of etic-universal models.

Influenced by Cross's (1971) Black identity model, Atkinson, Morten, and Sue (1979, 1983, 1989, 1993) conceptualized the minority identity development (MID) model as a five-stage curvilinear process with fluid boundaries. Atkinson et al. contended that although all people of Color may not experience every stage, there are four attitudes that persist across all levels of oppressed people's identity: self-views, views of members of the same minority group, views of individuals of a different minority group, and views of the dominant group. The first developmental stage of the MID model is *conformity,* wherein minority group members identify with the values and culture of the dominant racial group. In this stage, people of Color experience (1) feelings of shame, depreciation, and discrimination and (2) denial of minority afflictions toward self, members of the same group, and different minority groups. In the second stage of identity development, *dissonance,* people of Color are likely to attribute personal problems to their cultural identity. This attribution is the result of experiencing confusion or discovering discrepancies between previously held beliefs about self, members of the same and different minority groups, and dominant groups. During the third stage of development, *resistance and immersion,* people of Color tend to view personal problems as a consequence of their oppression. In this stage, views of their own minority group are respected, valued, and enacted. In addition, depreciating attitudes are expressed toward the dominant group. The fourth stage, *introspection,* is characterized by feelings of concern for personal autonomy, allegiance to other minority group members, and ethnocentric distrust toward the dominant culture. In the fifth stage, *synergetic articulation and integrative awareness,* the confusion and conflict that people of Color experienced in previous stages are replaced with their ability to value themselves, their own racial group, and other racial and ethnic groups.

Banks (1981) also constructed a five-stage ethnic identity model. Stage 1, *ethnic psychological captivity,* is similar to Cross's (1971) pre-encounter stage in that individuals in this stage have internalized society's negative views of their ethnic group. The *ethnic encapsulation* stage occurs when individuals largely participate in and idealize their own ethnic group. *Ethnic identity clarification,* stage 3, occurs when individuals learn self-acceptance. The fourth stage, *biethnicity,* results when individuals are able to function in their own ethnic group and in White America. In this stage, individuals possess a healthy sense of their ethnic identity. Finally, as individuals become self-actualized and are able to function across many different cultures, they are in the *multiethnicity* stage.

Underpinnings of Cross's (1971) Black racial identity theory are also present in Gay's (1984) three-stage ethnic identity model. Stage 1 of Gay's model is *pre-encounter,* where individuals' ethnic identity is subliminally dominated by White American conceptions of their own group. Stage 2, *encounter,* occurs when an event or experience causes individuals to identify new conceptions about their ethnic group reference. *Postencounter* is the final stage, wherein individuals view their ethnic group with pride and self-confidence and possess a sense of inner security.

Phinney (1989) constructed a three-stage ethnic identity development model that explicates how ethnic minority adolescents use various experiences to understand and accept their ethnic identity. The first stage of this model is *diffusion/foreclosure,* wherein adolescents' own ethnic identity has not been examined and they adopt the values and attitudes of the dominant group. This stage is similar to Cross's (1971) pre-encounter phase. *Moratorium,* the second stage, occurs when individuals begin to explore their ethnic identity in response to oppressive experiences or new cultural information. The *achievement* stage occurs when individuals come to terms with their ethnic identity and continue exploring this ethnicity.

In expanding Phinney's earlier (1989, 1993) work, Phinney and Kohatsu (1997) discussed how adolescents advance through the ethnic identity stages. They posited that there are three facets of ethnic identity formation that consist of four phases: the initial, transition, intermediate, and final phases. In the *initial* phase, adolescents are aware of their ethnic group membership but have not examined the cultural aspects of their group membership. The *transition* phase occurs when adolescents question their existing views and cultural values as a result of exposure to positive role models or encounters related to ethnic stereotyping, prejudice, or racism. As exploration, examination, and potential rejection of current views occur, adolescents move into the *intermediate* phase. The *final* phase of identity achievement occurs when adolescents experience a commitment and sense of direction that guide their future decisions.

Helms (1995, 2001) formulated a people of Color identity development model for individuals of African, Asian, and European indigenous descent in the United States. The model's five statuses or components are parallel to Cross's (1971) model and are believed to evolve in the following order. The first status, *conformity,* is reflected when people of Color value White culture and denigrate their own group. The *dissonance* status occurs when persons of Color experience ambivalence and confusion about their identity as they encounter new cultural information and question previously held cultural attitudes and beliefs. The third status is *immersion/emersion,* which results when people of Color have a heightened awareness of racial occurrences, experience marked discontent with Whites, and express allegiance, loyalty, and commitment to their own cultural group. The *internalization* status occurs when people of Color hold positive attitudes about their own group and are able to access and respond objectively to members of the dominant group. The final status is *integrative awareness,* wherein people of Color value members of their own group, other persons of Color, and White Americans.

U.S. BIRACIAL AND BIETHNIC IDENTITY DEVELOPMENT MODELS

According to Carter (1995), biracial individuals are either born to parents from two different racial groups or are transracially adopted by White parents. He asserts that choosing one racial group over the other can sabotage the biracial identity development process. Additionally, the development of a biracial identity for first-generation offspring of parents of different races is often viewed as more complex than for individuals from same-race parents (Kerwin & Ponterotto, 1995). The racial identity development process is vastly different from that of single-race persons because biracial individuals (1) may choose to identify with one racial group over the other, (2) automatically have membership in two different cultures, and (3) have the option to integrate more than one racial identity (Poston, 1990). However, to truly achieve a biracial identity, individuals must incorporate and value both components of their racial makeup (Root, 1990). The integration of both racial group identities is further complicated by the possibility that neither racial group will fully represent or accept all aspects of biracial individuals' identity. Thus, achieving a biracial identity is significantly impacted by individuals' environments, their likelihood of being oppressed by the higher-status racial group, and becoming or remaining marginalized by both groups (Poston, 1990; Root, 1990).

Influenced by Cross's (1971) conceptualization of Black racial identity development, several models have been proposed to describe biracial identity development. Poston (1990) proposed a five-stage model, suggesting that individuals develop a reference group orientation that includes their racial identity, group identity, race awareness, racial ideology, race evaluation, race esteem, race image, and racial self-identification. According to Poston's model, the first stage, *personal identity,* usually occurs in childhood, when biracial individuals are not cognizant of their mixed-race heritage. During the second stage, *choice of group categorization,* numerous societal, communal, and parental influences compel individuals to choose one racial or ethnic group identity. Carter (1995) suggested that physical features, personality, age, and political affiliation often influence individuals' choice of group categorization. The third stage, *enmeshment/denial,* is characterized by feelings of guilt about choosing one racial group over the other. That is, biracial individuals become enmeshed with one group and feel disloyal to the parent in the other group. Unable to resolve feelings of guilt and disloyalty, these individuals attempt to deny the racial separation and identify with both groups. In the fourth stage, *appreciation,* Poston asserted that individuals may remain committed to one racial group, but may explore the previously ignored racial group as they experience increased awareness and knowledge of the ignored group. In the fifth stage, *integration,* individuals may still identify with one racial group but value the integration of their multiple racial identities. Overall, Poston's model suggests that all biracial individuals will experience some conflict and subsequent periods of maladjustment during the identity development process.

According to Root (1990), biracial individuals achieve a healthy racial identity when they accept both sides of their racial lineage, disclose their identification choice, and develop coping strategies to deal with potential social resistance. Root's biracial identity development includes the following four phases: (1) acceptance of the racial designation assigned by society, (2) identification with both racial groups, (3) identification with a single racial group, and (4) identification with a new racial group. Root's phases are considered fluid and are not mutually exclusive as individuals move between them. Furthermore, Root notes that individuals' movement should remain stable if no parts of their identity are denied and if oppressions are not internalized.

Jacobs (1992) proposed three stages of biracial identity in children. During the first stage, biracial children are believed to acquire an understanding of skin color as a lasting characteristic. In the second stage, these children become aware of societal racial inequity and experience ambivalence about their biracial identity. During the third stage, biracial children recognize that skin color does not determine their racial group membership, and they gain a greater understanding and appreciation of their biracial status.

Kich (1992) presented a developmental model of biracial identity development that may be applicable across biracial groups. In the first stage of his model, *awareness of differentness and dissonance,* individuals between the ages of 3 and 10 become aware of differences between self-perceptions and others' perceptions of them. The next stage, *struggle for acceptance,* occurs between the age of 8 and young adulthood and is characterized by biracial individuals' struggle to gain self-acceptance and acceptance from others. The third stage of Kich's model, *self-acceptance and assertion of an interracial identity,* results when adult biracial individuals are able to define themselves racially rather than being defined by others. It is also characterized by biracial individuals' acceptance of their biracial or bicultural identities. Kich asserted that the integration of different, and sometimes contradictory, heritages is an ongoing process for biracial and bicultural individuals.

LaFromboise, Coleman, and Gerton's (1993) model of bicultural competence posited that single-race individuals possess the capacity to become biculturally competent. Their model asserts that it is possible for individuals to gain competence in two distinct cultures without losing their cultural identity or having to choose one culture over the other. To successfully navigate two cultures, individuals must acquire competence in six areas: (1) knowledge and awareness of cultural beliefs, values, and practices; (2) positive attitudes toward bicultural competence and toward the two cultural groups; (3) the belief that it is possible to live effectively in more than one culture; (4) effective verbal and nonverbal communication skills across cultures; (5) culturally appropriate behaviors and roles in interacting with each group; and (6) sufficient social support that may provide vital culturally related information.

Kerwin and Ponterotto's (1995) six-stage model of biracial identity development outlines the complex process that biracial individuals experience in their efforts to achieve a healthy racial identity. In the *preschool* stage, biracial individuals become increasingly aware of racial issues, including similarities and differences in people's appearances. During the *entry to school* phase, biracial children may classify themselves racially according to social and/or familial categories. Biracial individuals in the *preadolescence* stage recognize that their own and others' racial group member-ships are related to physical appearance factors, but they may make racial distinc-tions based on reference group affiliations rather than these physical descriptors. Peer pressure and ambivalence related to their racial identification may character-ize biracial individuals in the *adolescence* stage. In the *college/young adulthood* stage, biracial persons may immerse themselves in one culture while rejecting the other, and may acknowledge the advantages and disadvantages of biracial heritage. In the *adulthood* stage, biracial individuals continue to integrate different aspects of their racial identity by exploring interests in their own cultures and in different cultures. Integrated biracial individuals are believed to function successfully in various cultures and situations and experience an enhanced sense of self in inter-personal relationships (Kerwin & Ponterotto, 1995).

U.S. Immigrant Racial and Ethnic Identity Development Models

Although Cross's (1971) initial conceptualization of Black racial identity develop-ment has been instrumental to the development of many other cultural identity mod-els, there are currently few U.S. immigrant racial and ethnic identity development models that cite Cross's influence. Literature in the area of immigrant identity devel-opment has focused primarily on issues related to enculturation (i.e., ethnic social-ization) and acculturation (i.e., socialization into a different cultural group; Berry, 1997; Sodowsky & Kwan, 1997; Zimmerman, Ramirez-Valles, Washienko, Walter, & Dyer, 1996). Identity formation is a primary psychological issue in many immigrant populations because these individuals are often forced to make a choice about the primary culture with which they will identify (Berger, 1997).

Literature on Hispanic identity development models is extremely limited. However, general ethnic identity development models have been applied to mem-bers of various Hispanic subgroups. For example, Bernal, Knight, Ocampo, Garza, and Cota (1993) described Hispanic children's identity development as consisting of the following five components: (1) ethnic self-identification (children's catego-rization of themselves as members of their own ethnic group); (2) ethnic constancy (children's knowledge of their ethnic characteristics as permanent); (3) ethnic role behaviors (children's participation in behaviors that reflect their ethnic customs, values, language); (4) ethnic knowledge (children's knowledge that certain tradi-tions, customs, and values are salient to their own ethnic groups); and (5) ethnic feelings and preferences (children's feelings about their ethnic group and prefer-ences for their own ethnic group's behaviors). Bernal et al. asserted that children's ethnic identity development is affected by issues such as their social learning expe-riences provided by their families, their communities, and the dominant society. Casas and Pytluk (1995), however, noted that universal ethnic identity models, such as the one described by Bernal et al., are often inadequate to capture the diverse ex-periences of Hispanic subgroups and individuals who differ by numerous demo-graphic, socioeconomic, sociopolitical, sociohistorical, and sociopsychological variables.

According to Sodowsky, Kwan, and Pannu (1995), 37% of U.S. immigrants are of Asian descent, with the largest numbers of Asians migrating from China, Vietnam,

India, and the Philippines. More than 29 different Asian cultural groups have been identified in the United States (Fujita, 1990). Thus, like Hispanics, Asian American groups have many unique intra- and intercultural values. Kitano and Maki (1996) have noted that assimilation and ethnic identity are the most critical variables to consider when assessing how Asian Americans self-identify, and they developed a four-category model to capture this identification process. *Type A* Asian Americans are characterized as being highly assimilated and having low or no ethnic identification. *Type B* Asian Americans are viewed as being highly assimilated and having high ethnic identity (i.e., they demonstrate comfort in both their own and the dominant culture). Low assimilation and high ethnic identity describe *Type C* Asian Americans, who demonstrate strong Asian cultural ties and avoid assimilation. Asian Americans who have low assimilation and low ethnic identity are categorized as *Type D*. Type D individuals may feel the greatest amount of acculturative stress and marginalization in the United States and may suffer from severe psychological and social problems (Kitano & Maki, 1996).

Feminist and Womanist Identity Development Models

Drawing partially from Black racial identity development theory (Cross, 1971), Downing and Roush (1985) created a model of feminist identity development. They proposed a five-stage model based on the premise that in order for women to achieve an authentic and positive feminist identity, they must first recognize and struggle with the prejudice and discrimination they experience as women. Downing and Roush's feminist identity development model moves from traditional passive acceptance of gender roles to an active commitment to feminist and egalitarian societal ideations.

The first stage of Downing and Roush's (1985) model, *passive acceptance,* is marked by women's acceptance of traditional sex roles and notions of the superiority of men compared to women. Such women view traditional gender roles as advantageous and may seek out experiences and peers that allow them to maintain this belief. In the second stage, *revelation,* women begin to realize the negative societal images of women, and their previous denial of this phenomenon is broken down through a series of crises or contradictions. Examples of such "encounter" experiences include denial of credit, discrimination against female children, and participation in a consciousness-raising group. During the revelation stage, primary feelings of anger and secondary feelings of guilt emerge as women become aware of oppressions they experienced in the past, as well as their own participation in oppression. Intense self-examination and questioning of previous roles are accompanied by dualistic thinking in which all men are seen as negative and all women as positive.

In the third stage, *embeddedness-emanation,* women develop close emotional connections with other, similar women, providing them with opportunities to discharge their anger in a supportive environment. Other women are selected who are capable of providing women in this stage with reflections of their new and emerging frames of reference, opportunities to discharge their anger, and affirmations of their new identity. In addition, interactions with men are executed cautiously. Much like the immersion/emersion stage for Blacks emphasizing the "Black is Beautiful" culture, the embeddedness-emanation stage begins with submersion into a "Female is Beautiful" (Downing & Roush, 1985) or a "Sisterhood is Beautiful" (McNamara & Rickard, 1989) subculture, to an initial openness to alternative viewpoints or relativistic perspectives. Downing and Roush speculated that the embeddedness phase of this stage might be more difficult for White and heterosexual women than for Black women and lesbians, as the former are so integrally and intimately involved with the dominant White male culture.

The fourth stage, *synthesis,* is characterized by the development of a positive feminist identity, wherein oppression-related explanations for events and other casual factors are considered in making accurate attributions (McNamara & Rickard, 1989). Women in this stage no longer view sexism as the cause for all social and personal ills. Instead, they are able to take a stand that may separate them from many other feminists, and yet still maintain their identity as a feminist. Like the internalization stage of Black racial identity, there is an integration of personal and feminist values that results in an authentic feminist identity (McNamara & Rickard, 1989). Stage 5, *active commitment,* is characterized by the translation of the newly developed consolidated feminist identity achieved in the previous stage into meaningful and effective action (Downing & Roush, 1985). Like the internalization-commitment stage of Cross's (1971) Black racial identity theory, women in the active commitment stage possess a deep and pervasive commitment to social change. Issues are selected and prioritized base on women's unique talents, as well as the possibility for personal gratification and for effecting social change. Downing and Roush indicate that women's readiness to progress through the stages of development depends on many different types of interpersonal and environmental factors, and they acknowledge that the process of developing a feminist identity may be different for Black women and other women of Color.

Helms's womanist identity development model (WIDM; Ossana, Helms, & Leonard, 1992) was heavily influenced by Cross's (1971) initial Black racial identity development theory. Not only do the names of each stage resemble those of Cross's (1971, 1991) Black racial identity model, but movement through the four levels of identity development is also similar. The WIDM begins with women's passive acceptance of societal definitions of what it means to be a woman, to a more active synthesis of their own views of womanhood (Carter & Parks, 1996). In the first stage of Helms's womanist model, *pre-encounter,* women deny societal biases against women and passively accept the traditional roles without question. Pre-encounter women behave in a manner that favors men and devalues women (Carter & Parks, 1996; Parks, Carter, & Gushue, 1996). The *encounter* stage of womanist identity development is initiated by an external event or series of events that challenge the worldviews of pre-encounter women. These events give rise to confusion and questioning about the nature and expectations of gender roles in society as women begin to explore alternative views of men and women and their societal roles, and seek different ways to resolve role conflicts (Carter & Parks, 1996; Parks et al., 1996).

Named after the third stage of Cross's (1971) Black racial identity theory, the third stage of Helms's WIDM, *immersion-emersion,* is conceptualized as having two phases. In the first phase, women resolve the confusion and discomfort of encounter-like experiences by actively rejecting traditional male-dominated gender roles. They are often hostile toward men and idealize women. Although opposite from the traditional societal framework, their worldviews or perspectives in the immersion-emersion stage are still externally determined (Carter & Parks, 1996; Parks et al., 1996). In the second phase of the immersion-emersion stage, women begin to embrace a more internally derived womanist identity by seeking and developing intense interpersonal relationships with positive, self-determined female role models and other women (Carter & Parks, 1996; Parks et al., 1996). The last stage of the WIDM, *internalization,* is characterized by a more internally defined and fully integrated identity based on women's own personal standards of womanhood that are independent of traditional or feminist (i.e., political) views of womanhood (Carter & Parks, 1996; Parks et al., 1996). Women in the internalization stage of womanist identity may be labeled feminists, in the popular sense of the term, although their conceptualizations of womanhood may incorporate several traditional behaviors or values (Carter & Parks, 1996). One of the strengths of Helms's (Ossana et al., 1992) WIDM is that it acknowledges that environmental issues may strongly affect psychosocial development.

Gay and Lesbian Identity Development Models

Much like Black Americans and ethnic groups who lack social power in U.S. society, gay men, lesbians, and bisexual individuals must also work to develop a positive identity in the wake of societal oppression. Similar to Cross's (1971) Black identity model, many lesbian, gay, and bisexual identity development models stress the importance of individuals eventually achieving self-acceptance and self-definition in the face of such oppression. The emergence of sexual identity models and, more specifically, coming-out models has been significant since Cross's initial Black racial identity development model.

Cass (1979) has been credited with developing the first, and perhaps most widely cited, model of identity development for gays and lesbians (McCarn & Fassinger, 1996). Based on her work, several subsequent sexual identity models were developed. According to Cass, developing a gay or lesbian identity arises from individuals' attempts (i.e., affectively, cognitively, and behaviorally) to resolve the incongruence between their perceptions of themselves and others' perceptions of them that result from interactions between individuals and their environment.

Cass's (1979) homosexual identity development model encompasses six stages in which individuals move from nonhomosexual and heterosexual views of self to personalized views of self as homosexual. In the first stage, *identity confusion,* gay individuals encounter information about gays and homosexuality that is assigned some personal meaning, perhaps for the first time in their life. The stage involves gay individuals questioning their own assumptions about their sexual orientation and is accompanied by confusion and turmoil resulting from this experience of incongruence. According to Cass, gay individuals may attempt to manage their confusion by perceiving their behavior as correct and acceptable, correct but undesirable, or incorrect and undesirable. Identity foreclosure occurs when the latter two perceptions are held. Thus, gay individuals may adopt a strong antihomosexual stance or redefine and disown responsibility for their behavior through cognitive restructuring (e.g., being "taken advantage of" sexually by other gay individuals through sexual experimentation; Cass, 1979).

Identity comparison, the second stage of Cass's (1979) model, occurs only if a lesbian or gay identity has not been foreclosed in the previous stage. Although gay individuals are not able to view themselves as heterosexual, they experience feelings of isolation and alienation from both gay and heterosexual individuals. Geographical location and access to certain social groups may increase or decrease this sense of alienation. These individuals may continue to "pass" as heterosexual, view their same-sex behavior as unique to their current gay/lesbian relationship, adopt an asexual self-image, or seek to change their sexual orientation out of a sense of self-hatred (Cass, 1979).

In Cass's (1979) *identity tolerance* phase, gay individuals seek other gay people as they become more and more able to view themselves as gay. However, this gay or lesbian identity is simply tolerated, as these individuals work to reduce their sense of alienation by seeking out others who are "different." Positive contacts with gay and lesbian people can decrease isolation and self-hatred and may lead to acceptance of their same-sex sexual orientation (Cass, 1979). Stage 4, *identity acceptance,* involves gay individuals selectively revealing their sexual orientation. Much like the immersion-emersion stage of racial identity for Black Americans, associations with other gay people become an increasingly important part of these individuals' lives and provide structure for the emerging philosophy of legitimization (i.e., full legitimization, in which a gay/lesbian identity is viewed as publicly and privately valid, versus partial legitimization, in which same-sex orientation is seen as only privately valid but should not be "displayed" in public; Cass, 1979). This incongruence may be managed with an acceptance of passing as a coping strategy for reducing exposure to negative reactions of heterosexuals. As individuals enter the fifth stage, *identity pride,* they are aware of the incongruence between their own acceptance of their gay/lesbian identity and society's rejection of that identity. These individuals may cope by becoming immersed in gay/lesbian culture and having a strong sense of pride and commitment to gay/lesbian issues. If anger is present as they continue to confront societal expectations of heterosexuality, gay and lesbian persons may choose to purposely confront expressions of heterosexism by exercising their freedom to disclose their sexual orientation. In the final stage, *identity synthesis,* gay or lesbian identity matures into an aspect of self. As reported in the internalization stage of Cross's (1971) model, gay and lesbian individuals at this stage are capable of having more positive contacts with members of the socially dominant group (i.e., heterosexuals). This contact enables gay and lesbian individuals to integrate their sexual orientation with other aspects of their self-concept.

In one of the few studies conducted on her model, Cass (1984) found that, at least for Australian research participants, the predicted linear stages of gay and lesbian identity development could be distinguished. However, she found that the earlier and later stages tended to blur, suggesting four rather than six developmental stages.

Coleman (1982) also developed a coming-out model of gay identity development. His five-phase model was influenced by Cross (1971) and consisted of the following stages: (1) pre-coming out, (2) coming out, (3) exploration, (4) first relationships, and (5) integration.

Although several researchers examined the identity development process of lesbian women in the 1970s and early 1980s (e.g., Cass, 1984; Ettore, 1980; Moses, 1978; Ponse, 1978), Sophie (1985–1986) is credited with the first sexual identity development model that was applied exclusively to lesbian women. Her four-stage model consists of (1) first awareness, (2) testing and exploration, (3) identity acceptance, and (4) identity integration. After proposing her model, Sophie empirically tested the four stages and found that many experiences of the women who participated in her study seemed to fit the early stages of her model.

Chapman and Brannock (1987) formulated a second model of lesbian identity development. The five stages of Chapman and Brannock's model are (1) same-sex orientation (women feel connected to other women but do not attach a particular label to these feelings); (2) incongruence (women recognize that their feelings for other women are different from many of their friends' and may lack the desire to date men); (3) self-questioning/exploration (women's initial thoughts that they may be lesbian, which results in an exploration of lesbian and gay communities); (4) identification (lesbian women's self-identification as lesbian); and (5) choice of lifestyle (lesbian women's conscious choice to have relationships with women or seek other options). Chapman and Brannock tested their theoretical model and concluded that sexual orientation preceded awareness of same-sex attractions, and that awareness was the first step in self-labeling as lesbian.

Morales (1989) developed an identity model that attempted to encompass the dual statuses of gay and lesbian people of Color. The five identity states proposed by Morales are (1) denial of conflict, (2) bisexual versus gay/lesbian, (3) conflicts in allegiances, (4) establishing priorities in allegiance, and (5) integrating various communities. Morales's model acknowledges the struggle of gays and lesbians of Color by highlighting salient racial, ethnic, and familial issues that may impact these individuals' identity development.

Troiden (1989) developed a sociological model of lesbian and gay identity formation that consists of four stages: (1) sensitization (individuals consider themselves to be heterosexual but may have some social experiences that cause them to feel different or marginalized); (2) identity confusion (individuals consider the possibility that they may be gay); (3) identity assumption (individuals shift into a coming-out process); and (4) identity commitment (individuals assume a degree of comfort with and commitment to a homosexual self-identity).

Walters and Simoni (1993) empirically examined the identity development process of gay and lesbian individuals using a modified version of Parham and Helms's (1981) Black Racial Identity Attitude Scale. After controlling for sex, education, and age, they reported that self-esteem was significantly predicted by the group identity attitudes of gay men and lesbians. Specifically, higher group identity attitudes were significantly associated with higher levels of self-esteem, whereas preencounter group identity attitudes were significantly related to lower self-esteem.

Walters and Simoni's study was clearly influenced by Cross's (1971) Black racial identity theory and represented an important step in the development and validation of instruments to assess the identity development experiences of lesbian women and gay men.

McCarn and Fassinger (1996) proposed a model of lesbian identity formation that directly parallels several aspects of Black racial identity theory (Cross, 1971). First, McCarn and Fassinger clearly articulate the separate but related processes associated with both the personal and reference group aspects of identity discussed by Cross (1991). Second, consistent with Helms's (1995) reconceptualization of racial identity as consisting of ego statuses versus stages, McCarn and Fassinger use the term phases in discussing particular aspects of their model. Further, these phases are viewed as continuous and circular, with every new relationship or context having great potential to raise new issues and awareness. Although individual sexual identity and group membership identity processes are presented within each phase, they do not necessarily occur simultaneously in individuals.

In the first phase of McCarn and Fassinger's (1996) model, *awareness,* there is recognition of feeling or being different on an individual level and the existence of different sexual orientations on the group membership level. On an individual level, that which had previously been unconscious becomes conscious. However, this new consciousness does not translate into self-identification as lesbian. In the second phase, *exploration,* individuals actively examine the questions emerging in the first phase. Erotic feelings toward women or a particular woman are explored but do not necessarily translate into sexual behavior. On the group membership level, women in the exploration phase actively seek information about lesbian/gay people as they explore the possibility of belonging to this group. This exploration can be accompanied by feelings of anxiety, fear, anger, guilt, or even curiosity and joy. In the *deepening/commitment* phase, self-knowledge deepens as women begin to make some choices with regard to their individual sexuality (e.g., lesbian, bisexual). On a group level, association and involvement with lesbians and gays comes with increasing awareness of lesbian and gay oppression and the subsequent consequences of their choices. This may be accompanied by an intense identification with lesbian culture and rejection of heterosexual society. The last phase, *internalization/synthesis,* is marked by more acceptance of a lesbian identity as part of ongoing resolution and clarification of emotional and sexual self-exploration. Integration of sexuality into these individuals' concept of self is achieved as they make choices regarding disclosing their sexual orientation. Being a member of a sexual minority group is integrated into their overall self-concept, in which feelings of fulfillment, security, and consistency exist across contexts.

A Model of Spiritual Identity Development

Indirectly influenced by Cross's (1971) initial Black racial identity model, Linda James Myers developed a spiritual conceptualization of identity development that is rooted in Afrocentric values and perspectives. According to Myers's (1988, 1993) theory of optimal psychology, the ultimate purpose of life is to achieve peace, and peace is ultimately achieved by adopting an "optimal" worldview. An optimal worldview recognizes that spirit and matter are one and the same, and that any attempts to separate the spiritual from the material will result in failures to achieve harmony and peace; in contrast, a suboptimal worldview values quantification and competition and leads to societal "isms" (e.g., racism, sexism) that exist throughout Western society (Constantine et al., 1998). Similar to Cross's theory, an individual's search for self-knowledge is at the foundation of Myers's optimal theory, and Myers suggests that there are negative societal influences that individuals must shed to reach higher levels of consciousness about oppression.

A Social Class Identity Development Model

Social class includes the objective (e.g., income, education, occupation, and lifestyle) and subjective (e.g., individuals' perceptions of their social class and social identity) indicators of social status (Hoyt, 1999). Related to social class is class consciousness (Hoyt, 1999), a process of coming to know the reality social class plays in individuals' lives. Social class is considered to be a backdrop to or a salient construct in most studies of sociopolitical identity (Cross, 1991; Kiely, 1997; Munford, 1994).

Roffman and Cathcart (1996) presented a six-stage model of class identity that reflects a similar progression to other cultural models influenced by Cross's (1971) work. In the first stage, *passive acceptance,* individuals accept the domination of White, middle-class values, including the myth of meritocracy. In the second stage, these individuals *encounter* events in which an awareness of class membership develops; this awareness is accompanied by feelings of anger, shame, and guilt about participating in the class structure. During the third stage, *reintegration,* individuals attempt to resolve the dissonance resulting from the negative feelings of the previous stage by blaming the poor for their own poverty. This worldview enables them to avoid examining the oppressive implications of a capitalist distribution of wealth. This belief in White middle-class superiority is abandoned in the fourth stage, *pseudo-affiliative,* as individuals search for new ways to be "downwardly mobile." The next stage, *immersion/emersion,* is marked by the replacement of the myths and stereotypes about social class with more accurate information. Individuals learn about role models and new ideas for change. In the final stage, *commitment,* individuals develop a critical analysis of class and alliances with others who work toward social and economic justice (Roffman & Cathcart, 1996).

A Model of Identity Development for Persons with Disabilities

Cross's (1971) Black racial identity theory has also laid the foundation for the conceptualization of an identity development model for individuals with disabilities. The conceptualization of disability identity development is fairly recent to the identity development literature, and the model discussed below illustrates how positive identity development may occur for persons with disabilities (Gilson, Tusler, & Gill, 1997). Specifically, Gill (1997) conceptualized disability identity development as occurring through four types of integration: (1) coming to feel we belong, (2) coming home, (3) coming together, and (4) coming out. Integration is "defined as the act of incorporating or combining into a whole" (p. 39). According to Gill, integration is a central theme in the process of development in classic human development theory. People often understand themselves better after experiencing a disorder or crisis, and the actual process of synthesizing the disorder or crisis results in these individuals becoming stronger (Gill, 1997).

The ultimate task for persons with disabilities in the *coming to feel we belong* integration stage is to develop a comfortable identity with a social role despite being socially marginalized. In this type of integration, individuals strive to be included in society. In the second integration stage, *coming home,* individuals with disabilities struggle with their feelings related to associating with other disabled people. Gill (1997) reports that by associating with other disabled people, individuals with disabilities may have fears of rejection, of noninclusion in the mainstream of society, of being perceived by others as weak, and of the collective memories of the negative aspects of being disabled. In the third stage of integration, *coming together,* the concept of wholeness in understanding oneself is the focus. Integrating the physical, psychological, and emotional aspects of a disability is a major task in this type of integration. More specifically, the influence of the medical construction of disability has often caused individuals with disabilities to focus on one aspect of their physical or cognitive selves. Gill suggested that individuals' task in this type of integration is to bring together all parts of the self into a whole. The last stage of integration, *coming out,* is the final step toward a positive identity development; this stage involves persons with disabilities integrating private knowledge about themselves into public presentations of themselves. This type of integration requires that persons with disabilities embrace themselves, which involves honestly representing themselves with their disability as a fully integrated part of the public presentation. "Understanding how disabled people perceive themselves and how they wish to be perceived by others is essential in defining the emerging identity of [persons with disabilities]" (Gilson et al., 1997, p. 8).

Dominant Group Identity Development Models

The majority of models addressing the identity development process have focused on cultural groups that have experienced oppression in U.S. society. However, a number of theories have been developed to examine the process of cultural identity development for members of traditionally privileged groups, and these models have been influenced, either directly or indirectly, by Cross's (1971) initial Black racial identity theory.

For example, according to Helms (1984, 1990, 1995), White racial identity development is a process that entails Whites moving from an abandonment of racist attitudes (i.e., contact, disintegration, and reintegration) toward a nonracist White identity (i.e., pseudo-independence, immersion/emersion, and autonomy). In the *contact* phase or status, White individuals are unaware of racism and their role in it. White individuals operating primarily from the *disintegration* status develop an awareness of their Whiteness and experience guilt, confusion, and disorientation as a result. The *reintegration* status is marked by an idealization of Whiteness coinciding with denigration, intolerance, and negative distortion of people of Color. These three ego statuses typify the process of shedding the normative strategies

Whites have learned for dealing with race (Helms, 1995). *Pseudo-independence,* the first step in the process of adopting a nonracist White identity, consists of Whites' intellectual understanding of racism and how they may contribute to it, along with subtle feelings of superiority and intolerance toward other racial and ethnic groups. Similar to the immersion/emersion status of Helms's (1990) Black racial identity development model, the *immersion/emersion* status of White racial identity is characterized by a hypervigilant search to understand racism and the unearned privileges and benefits Whites may receive due solely to their racial group. When White individuals have reached the *autonomy* status, they use their own standards (rather than those of society) to define Whiteness, including relinquishing their privileged status and adopting a pluralistic worldview (Helms, 1995).

Rowe and his colleagues (i.e., Rowe, Behrens, & Leach, 1995; Rowe, Bennett, & Atkinson, 1994) developed a theory of White racial consciousness in an attempt to explain the various attitudes that White people hold about people of Color and their own racial group. In their original conceptualization, Rowe et al. (1994, 1995) proposed seven White racial consciousness types organized in terms of exploration of and commitment to racial and ethnic issues. Three types (i.e., avoidant, dependent, and dissonance) were considered to be "unachieved" racial consciousness statuses, whereas the other four types (conflictive, dominative, integrative, and reactive) represented "achieved" statuses.

Avoidant racial consciousness, indicative of neither exploration nor commitment to racial concerns, is demonstrated by ignoring, minimizing, or denying the existence or importance of racial issues. Whites with high *dependent* attitudes look to others for what their own superficially held racial attitudes should be (i.e., commitment to racial consciousness but no exploration). Another unachieved status, *dissonance,* is characteristic of Whites who are uncertain about what to think as a result of a lack of experience, information, or "congruence between previously held racial attitudes and recent personal or vicarious experience" (Rowe et al., 1995, p. 229). Dissonance attitudes are often held by individuals in transition from one set of racial attitudes to another.

Achieved statuses are characterized by both exploration of and commitment to currently held racial attitudes. Whites who hold *conflictive*-type attitudes usually support equality and fairness but are opposed to programs designed to decrease discrimination because they believe that discrimination no longer exists. *Dominative* racial attitudes are characterized by a belief in the inherent superiority of Whites, which entitles them to dominate people of Color, who, they believe, are somehow defective. Individuals with *integrative* racial attitudes are comfortable with their Whiteness and interacting with people of Color. They value a racially pluralistic society, believing that racism can be eradicated through goodwill, rational thought, and democratic processes. However, they tend to take a pragmatic approach to their sense of moral responsibility to effect change. Finally, Whites with high *reactive* racial consciousness attitudes are militant in their responses to recognized racism. Whites who hold reactive attitudes may identify with people of Color or romanticize their issues, and they may even feel guilty about being White. They may also sometimes engage in paternalistic behavior.

Using Helms's (1990, 1995) model of White racial identity as a basis for understanding another privileged or dominant group in society, Simoni and Walters (2001) developed a model of heterosexual identity development. Simoni and Walters proposed that heterosexuals can be (1) oblivious to issues of sexual orientation and heterosexual privilege (*contact*); (2) become aware of sexual orientation but experience confusion and disorientation about heterosexual privilege (*disintegration*); (3) idealize heterosexuality and degrade gays, lesbians, and bisexuals (*reintegration*); (4) intellectually acknowledge their heterosexuality but minimize heterosexual privilege (*pseudo-independence*); and (5) develop a positive, antiheterosexist heterosexual identity and fully acknowledge their heterosexual privilege (*autonomy*).

Preliminary research (Simoni & Walters, 2001) has indicated that disintegration and reintegration heterosexual identity attitudes were positively associated with heterosexism, whereas pseudo-independence attitudes were negatively correlated with heterosexism. These findings support the need for heterosexuals to examine their learned attitudes and beliefs about sexual orientation if we are to make significant progress in eliminating discrimination and oppression of lesbians, gay men, and bisexual men and women.

MULTIPLE IDENTITY DEVELOPMENT MODELS

Myers et al.'s (1991) optimal theory applied to identity development (OTAID) model is based largely on Myers's (1988, 1993) theory of optimal psychology. Hence, Myers et al.'s theory is founded on the premise that humans' ultimate purpose is to gain self-understanding, and that self-understanding requires identity development. The OTAID model is not linear or categorical; rather, it is an expanding spiral (Myers et al., 1991). Thus, the beginning and end of the identity development process are similar. The OTAID model is an existential model in that individuals are accepted for who they are in the moment, and the definition of self is not confined to one dimension. Individuals are empowered to hold multiple identities (without limits) when defining themselves.

The multiphase OTAID model captures the complexities and richness of individuals holistically, rather than categorizing specific aspects of culture (e.g., race, sex, social class). Myers et al.'s (1991) model begins at phase zero, *absence of conscious awareness,* wherein individuals' lack of awareness is associated with infancy. In this phase, their ability to separate themselves from others is not developed. In the *individuation* phase, the world is accepted at face value without question, and individuals' families determine their views of themselves and their values. Phase 2, *dissonance,* occurs when individuals begin to explore aspects of themselves that others have devalued. In this phase, conflicts between beliefs about themselves and the false images of themselves create feelings of anger, guilt, confusion, isolation, insecurity, or sadness. In phase 3, *immersion,* individuals learn to appreciate the devalued aspects of themselves by consciously seeking out others who are similarly devalued. Feelings of excitement, belonging, and joy are common in this phase. *Internalization,* phase 4, occurs when individuals feel increasingly secure about effectively integrating salient aspects of their identity. Following a deepened sense of self-worth, phase 5, *integration,* begins. In this phase, people begin changing their worldviews, and subsequent feelings of inner peace and security are felt. The final stage is *transformation,* wherein individuals define themselves as extensions of their ancestors, the unborn, nature, and community. It is at this point that reality is no longer based on external circumstances but is determined through harmony, spiritual awareness, and a holistic understanding of all humankind and life.

Similarly, Reynolds and Pope (1991) assert that the multiple dimensions of identity must be integrated in order to achieve a healthy identity resolution. Their multidimensional identity model (MIM) was developed to facilitate conceptualization and understanding of the impact of more than one oppressed group affiliation on individuals' identity development. The MIM was greatly influenced by Cross's (1971) Black racial identity theory and Root's (1990) biracial identity development model. According to Reynolds and Pope, one of four potential identity resolutions may occur for individuals who are members of societally oppressed groups: (1) passive acceptance of societal identification, (2) conscious identification with one aspect of self, (3) segmented identification with multiple components of self, or (4) intersecting identification with the multiple components of self.

CONCLUSION

Cross's (1971) initial Black racial identity development theory has served as a stimulus for the development of many other cultural identity models. The identity development models presented in this chapter illustrate the complexities and importance of understanding cultural identity development issues in relation to various aspects of self. It is clear that Cross's theory will continue to influence future conceptualizations of the identity development process for many cultural groups for years to come.

REFERENCES

Atkinson, D. R., Morten, G., & Sue, D. W. (1979). *Counseling American minorities: A cross-cultural perspective.* Dubuque, IA: Brown.

Atkinson, D. R., Morten, G., & Sue, D. W. (1983). *Counseling American minorities: A cross-cultural perspective* (2nd ed.). Dubuque, IA: Brown.

Atkinson, D. R., Morten, G., & Sue, D. W. (1989). *Counseling American minorities: A cross-cultural perspective* (3rd ed.). Dubuque, IA: Brown.

Atkinson, D. R., Morten, G., & Sue, D. W. (1993). *Counseling American minorities: A cross-cultural perspective* (4th ed.). Madison, WI: Brown & Benchmark.

Banks, J. A. (1981). The stages of ethnicity: Implications for reform. In J. A. Banks (Ed.), *Multi-ethnic education: Theory and practice* (pp. 129–139). Boston: Allyn & Bacon.

Berger, R. (1997). Adolescent immigrants in search of identity: Clingers, eradicators, vacillators, and integrators. *Child and Adolescent Social Work Journal, 14,* 263–275.

Bernal, M. E., Knight, G. P., Ocampo, K. A., Garza, C. A., & Cota, M. K. (1993). Development of Mexican American identity. In M. E. Bernal & G. P. Knight (Eds.), *Ethnic identity:*

Formation and transmission among Hispanics and other minorities (pp. 31–46). Albany: State University of New York Press.

Berry, J. W. (1997). Immigration, acculturation and adaptation. *Applied Psychology, 46,* 5–68.

Carter, R. T. (1995). Biracial identity and questions and concerns about racial identity status development. In R. T. Carter (Ed.), *The influence of race and racial identity in psychotherapy: Toward a racially inclusive model* (pp. 115–125). New York: Wiley.

Carter, R. T., & Parks, E. E. (1996). Womanist identity and mental health. *Journal of Counseling and Development, 74,* 484–489.

Casas, J. M., & Pytluk, S. D. (1995). Hispanic identity development: Implications for research and practice. In J. G. Ponterotto, J. M. Casas, L. A. Suzuki, & C. M. Alexander (Eds.), *Handbook of multicultural counseling* (pp. 155–180). Thousand Oaks, CA: Sage.

Cass, V. C. (1979). Homosexual identity formation: A theoretical model. *Journal of Homosexuality, 4,* 219–235.

Cass, V. C. (1984). Homosexual identity formation: Testing a theoretical model. *Journal of Sex Research, 20,* 143–167.

Chapman, B. E., & Brannock, J. C. (1987). Proposed model of lesbian identity development: An empirical examination. *Journal of Homosexuality, 14,* 69–80.

Coleman, E. (1982). Developmental stages of the coming out process. In J. Gonsiorek (Ed.), *Homosexuality and psychotherapy: A practitioner's handbook of affirmative models* (pp. 31–44). New York: Haworth Press.

Constantine, M. G., Richardson, T. Q., Benjamin, E. M., & Wilson, J. W. (1998). An overview of Black racial identity theories: Limitations and considerations for future theoretical conceptualizations. *Applied and Preventive Psychology, 7,* 95–99.

Cross, W. E., Jr. (1971). The Negro-to-Black conversion experience: Toward a psychology of Black liberation. *Black World, 20,* 13–27.

Cross, W. E., Jr. (1991). *Shades of Black: Diversity in African-American identity.* Philadelphia: Temple University Press.

Cross, W. E., Jr. (1995). The psychology of nigrescence: Revising the Cross model. In J. G. Ponterotto, J. M. Casas, L. A. Suzuki, & C. M. Alexander (Eds.), *Handbook of multicultural counseling* (pp. 93–122). Thousand Oaks, CA: Sage.

Downing, N. E., & Roush, K. L. (1985). From passive-acceptance to active commitment: A model of feminist identity development for women. *Counseling Psychologist, 13,* 695–709.

Ettore, E. (1980). *Lesbians, women, and society.* London: Routledge.

Fujita, S. (1990). Asian/Pacific-American mental health: Some needed research in epidemiology and service utilization. In F. C. Serafica, A. I. Schwebel, R. K. Russell, P. D. Isaac, & L. B. Myers (Eds.), *Mental health of ethnic minorities* (pp. 249–278). New York: Praeger.

Gay, G. (1984). Implications of selected models of ethnic identity development for educators. *Journal of Negro Education, 54,* 43–52.

Gill, C. (1997). Four types of integration in disability identity development. *Journal of Vocational Rehabilitation, 9,* 39–46.

Gilson, S. F., Tusler, A., & Gill, C. (1997). Ethnographic research in disability identity: Self-determination and community. *Journal of Vocational Rehabilitation, 9,* 7–17.

Helms, J. E. (1984). Toward a theoretical explanation of the effects of race on counseling: A Black and White model. *Counseling Psychologist, 12,* 153–165.

Helms, J. E. (Ed.). (1990). *Black and White racial identity: Theory, research and practice.* Westport, CT: Greenwood Press.

Helms, J. E. (1995). An update of Helms's White and people of Color racial identity models. In J. G. Ponterotto, J. M. Casas, L. A. Suzuki, & C. M. Alexander (Eds.), *Handbook of multicultural counseling* (pp. 181–198). Thousand Oaks, CA: Sage.

Helms, J. E. (2001). An update of Helms's White and people of Color racial identity models. In J. G. Ponterotto, J. M. Casas, L. A. Suzuki, & C. M. Alexander (Eds.), *Handbook of multicultural counseling* (2nd ed., pp. 181–198). Thousand Oaks, CA: Sage.

Helms, J. E., & Cook, D. A. (1999). *Using race and culture in counseling and psychotherapy: Theory and process.* Boston: Allyn & Bacon.

Helms, J. E., & Piper, R. E. (1994). Implications of racial identity theory for vocational psychology. *Journal of Vocational Behavior, 44,* 124–138.

Hoyt, S. K. (1999). Mentoring with class: Connections between social class and developmental relationships in the academy. In A. J. Murrell, F. J. Crosby, & R. J. Ely (Eds.), *Mentoring dilemmas: Developing relationships within multicultural organizations* (pp. 189–210). Mahwah, NJ: Erlbaum.

Jacobs, J. H. (1992). Identity development in biracial children. In M. P. P. Root (Ed.), *Racially mixed people in America* (pp. 190–206). Newbury Park, CA: Sage.

Kerwin, C., & Ponterotto, J. G. (1995). Biracial identity development: Theory and research. In J. G. Ponterotto, J. M. Casas, L. A. Suzuki, & C. M. Alexander (Eds.), *Handbook of multicultural counseling* (pp. 199–217). Thousand Oaks, CA: Sage.

Kich, G. K. (1992). The developmental process of asserting a biracial, bicultural identity. In M. P. P. Root (Ed.), *Racially mixed people in America* (pp. 304–317). Newbury Park, CA: Sage.

Kiely, L. J. (1997). An exploratory analysis of the relationship of racial identity, social class, and family influences on womanist identity development. *Dissertation Abstracts International, 58*(6-A), 2086.

Kitano, H. L., & Maki, M. T. (1996). A model for counseling Asian Americans. In P. B. Pedersen, J. G. Draguns, W. L. Lonner, & J. E. Trimble (Eds.), *Counseling across cultures* (4th ed., pp. 124–145). Honolulu: University of Hawaii Press.

LaFromboise, T. D., Coleman, H. L. K., & Gerton, J. (1993). Psychological impact of biculturalism: Evidence and theory. *Psychological Bulletin, 114,* 395–412.

McCarn, S. R., & Fassinger, R. E. (1996). Revisioning sexual minority identity formation: A new model of lesbian identity and its implications for counseling and research. *Counseling Psychologist, 24,* 508–534.

McNamara, K., & Rickard, K. M. (1989). Feminist identity development: Implications for feminist therapy with women. *Journal of Counseling and Development, 68,* 184–189.

Morales, E. S. (1989). Ethnic minority families and minority gays and lesbians. *Journal of Homosexuality, 17,* 217–239.

Moses, A. E. (1978). *Identities management in lesbian women.* New York: Praeger.

Munford, M. B. (1994). Relationship of gender, self-esteem, social class, and racial identity to depression in Blacks. *Journal of Black Psychology, 20,* 143–156.

Myers, L. J. (1988). *Understanding an Afrocentric world view: Introduction to optimal psychology.* Dubuque, IA: Kendall/Hunt.

Myers, L. J. (1993). *Understanding an Afrocentric world view: Introduction to optimal psychology* (2nd ed.). Dubuque, IA: Kendall/Hunt.

Myers, L. J., Speight, S. L., Highlen, P. S., Cox, C. I., Reynolds, A. L., Adams, E. M., et al. (1991). Identity development and worldview: Toward an optimal conceptualization. *Journal of Counseling and Development, 70,* 54–63.

Ossana, S. M., Helms, J. E., & Leonard, M. M. (1992). Do "womanist" identity attitudes influence college women's self-esteem and perceptions of environmental bias? *Journal of Counseling and Development, 70,* 402–408.

Parham, T. A., & Helms, J. E. (1981). The influence of Black students' racial identity attitudes on preferences for counselor's race. *Journal of Counseling Psychology, 28,* 250–257.

Parks, E. E., Carter, R. T., & Gushue, G. V. (1996). At the crossroads: Racial and womanist identity development in Black and White women. *Journal of Counseling and Development, 74,* 624–631.

Phinney, J. S. (1989). Stages of ethnic identity development in minority group adolescents. *Journal of Early Adolescence, 9,* 34–49.

Phinney, J. S. (1993). A three-stage model of ethnic identity development in adolescence. In M. E. Bernal & G. P. Knight (Eds.), *Ethnic identity: Formation and transmission among Hispanics and other minorities* (pp. 61–79). Albany: State University of New York Press.

Phinney, J. S., & Kohatsu, E. L. (1997). Ethnic and racial identity development and mental health. In J. Schulenberg, J. L. Maggs, & K. Hurrelman (Eds.), *Health risks and developmental transitions during adolescence* (pp. 420–443). New York: Cambridge University Press.

Ponse, B. (1978). *Identities in the lesbian world: The social construction of self.* London: Greenwood Press.

Poston, W. S. C. (1990). The biracial identity development model: A needed addition. *Journal of Counseling and Development, 69,* 152–155.

Reynolds, A. L., & Pope, R. L. (1991). The complexities of diversity: Exploring multiple oppressions. *Journal of Counseling and Development, 70,* 174–180.

Roffman, E., & Cathcart, D. (1996). *Using identity development models as an approach to addressing issues of race, class, and gender in graduate clinical training and educational programs.* Workshop presentation at the annual conference of the Association for Women in Psychology, Indianapolis, IN.

Root, M. P. P. (1990). Resolving "other" status: Identity development of biracial individuals. In L. S. Brown & M. P. Root (Eds.), *Complexity and diversity in feminist theory and therapy* (pp. 185–206). New York: Harrington Park Press.

Rotheram-Borus, M. J., & Wyche, K. F. (1994). Ethnic differences in identity development in the United States. In S. L. Archer (Ed.), *Interventions for adolescent identity development* (pp. 62–83). Thousand Oaks, CA: Sage.

Rowe, W., Behrens, J. T., & Leach, M. M. (1995). Racial/ethnic identity and racial consciousness: Looking back and looking forward. In J. G. Ponterotto, J. M. Casas, L. A. Suzuki, & C. M. Alexander (Eds.), *Handbook of multicultural counseling* (pp. 218–235). Thousand Oaks, CA: Sage.

Rowe, W., Bennett, S. K., & Atkinson, D. R. (1994). White racial identity model: A critique and alternative proposal. *Counseling Psychologist, 22,* 129–146.

Simoni, J. M., & Walters, K. L. (2001). Heterosexual identity and heterosexism: Recognizing privilege to reduce prejudice. *Journal of Homosexuality, 41,* 157–172.

Sodowsky, G. R., & Kwan, K.-L. K. (1997). Internal and external ethnic identity and their correlates: A study of Chinese American immigrants. *Journal of Multicultural Counseling and Development, 25,* 51–67.

Sodowsky, G. R., Kwan, K.-L. K., & Pannu, R. (1995). Ethnic identity of Asians in the United States. In J. G. Ponterotto, J. M. Casas, L. A. Suzuki, & C. M. Alexander (Eds.), *Handbook of multicultural counseling* (pp. 123–154). Thousand Oaks, CA: Sage.

Sophie, J. (1985–1986). A critical examination of stage theories of lesbian identity development. *Journal of Homosexuality, 12,* 39–51.

Troiden, R. R. (1989). The formation of homosexual identities. *Journal of Homosexuality, 17,* 43–73.

Walters, K. L., & Simoni, J. M. (1993). Lesbian and gay male identity attitudes and self-esteem: Implications for counseling. *Journal of Counseling Psychology, 40,* 94–99.

Zimmerman, M. A., Ramirez-Valles, J., Washienko, K. M., Walter, B., & Dyer, S. (1996). The development of a measure of enculturation for Native American youth. *American Journal of Community Psychology, 24,* 295–310.

CHAPTER 8

Racial Salience: Conceptual Dimensions and Implications for Racial and Ethnic Identity Development

Kwong-Liem Karl Kwan

Race and ethnicity are ambiguous concepts with no consensual definitions. Psychologists and other social scientists have challenged the interchangeable use of the two terms (Helms & Cook, 1999; Schaefer, 2000; D. W. Sue & Sue, 1999, 2003). In particular, the extent to which physical features, language, religion, national origins, and cultural patterns and practices are subsumed under the respective terms remains fuzzy. Psychologists (Helms & Talleyrand, 1997; Phinney, 1996; Smith, 1991) have disagreed on the preferential use of terms when applied to group categorization (i.e., racial group versus ethnic group) in a culturally heterogeneous environment with differential representation of visible racial and ethnic groups, such as the United States. Yet, psychologists and other social scientists have generally agreed that race should cease to be conceptualized as a biological entity and that both race and ethnicity should be considered socially constructed (Helms, 1995; Schaefer, 2000).

Beyond exacting the definitions of race and ethnicity, models of racial (Helms, 1992), ethnic (Phinney, 1996), racial/cultural (Atkinson, Morten, & Sue, 1998), and minority (Smith, 1991) identity development offer more meaningful and empathic understanding of the intrapersonal and psychosocial implications of the labeling and categorizing effects of race and ethnicity on the psychosocial experiences, identity conflicts, and cross-racial relationships of individuals in a multicultural society. Yet, psychologists relegate differential emphasis on race and ethnicity when applying these terms to delineate the identity development process and experience (i.e., racial identity versus ethnic identity) of individuals in societies with various visible racial and ethnic groups (Atkinson et al., 1998; Helms, 1996; Phinney, 1996; Smith, 1991; Sodowsky, Kwan, & Pannu, 1995).

The shifting dominance of race/racial identity and ethnicity/ethnic identity in a culturally heterogeneous society is a function of the salience of visible racial characteristics (primarily skin color) adopted by the majority in the society to label and categorize the population. In a given U.S. societal context with various visible racial and ethnic groups, the ethnic identity of English, German, Irish, and Italian

Americans (the four most reported ancestries of origins; U.S. Bureau of the Census, 2000) is often obscured by the "White" demographic label that society uses to categorize their racial group membership. Similarly, the collective racial group identity of Asian American is often more conspicuous among members of Chinese, Filipino, and Asian Indian ethnic origins (the three largest Asian American subgroups; U.S. Bureau of the Census, 2000) in a multiracial environment, whereas the ethnic group membership of the respective Asian American subgroups is likely to be more differentiated in a predominantly Asian social context.

Racial group membership, however, does not necessarily characterize an individual's racial identity. According to Helms and Cook (1999), racial identity refers to the psychological process of identifying with a demographic group externally ascribed by the dominant culture to members with shared visible characteristics *allegedly* of a racial nature. It connotes a group identity that is socially constructed and an outgroup identity that is externally ascribed. Beyond skin color, it is the subjective affiliation with shared cultural heritage and values that define ethnic identity. However, given that ethnic groups with similar skin color are often ascribed a social collective, "race interacts with ethnicity, so that at any given point, either factor may assume pre-potency. The factor of race becomes submerged when ethnicity is the more salient factor and vice versa" (Smith, 1991, p. 187).

In this chapter, the continuing discussions of the preferential use of race versus ethnicity is reviewed. The ambiguous relationship of race and ethnicity is further illustrated by their applications in the U.S. Bureau of the Census, 2000. A major thesis of the chapter is that perceived racial salience in the immediate environment mediates the shifting dominance of racial identity and ethnic identity. The conceptual dimensions of racial salience and their implications for research and practice in counseling and psychology are delineated.

RACE VERSUS ETHNICITY

As Schaefer (2000) noted, despite the many meanings, the only thing about *race* that is clear is that we are confused about the proper use of the term. Race has been studied as a biological concept (Gordon, 1976). At the end of the twentieth century, race was defined as "a geographic variety or subdivision of a species characterized by a more or less distinct combination of [morphological, behavioral, physiological] traits that are inheritable" (Rushton, 1995, p. 40). Inherent in the biological approach is that human beings can be categorized according to the phenotypic characteristics, such as skin color, facial features, eye color, and hair texture, that are presumed to reflect genetic makeup. Given that skin color has been used as one of the indicators of racial designation in the U.S. census (i.e., White versus all non-White groups), one implication of the biological definition is that racial classification is genetically and biologically determined. In other words, White Americans and all other non-White Americans are genetically different, and White Americans from various countries of origin (e.g., Ireland, Italy, Poland, United States) are genetically similar.

Social scientists, however, have found more differences within the so-called racial groups than between them (e.g., Zuckerman, 1990). Psychologists and sociologists, in particular, have questioned the validity of societal racial categories being genetically defined and reflecting biological difference. As Helms (1996) noted, The long history of voluntary and involuntary miscegenation in the United States has resulted in so-called mutually exclusive "racial" groups that share biological and genetic ancestry in typically unassessed amounts. According to data from Census 2000 (U.S. Bureau of the Census, 2000), approximately 2.4% of the general population, 2% of White Americans, 0.6% of American Indians and Asian Americans, and 0.3% of African Americans considered themselves bi/multiracial. Schaefer (2000) even argued that pure genetic types have not existed for some time, if they ever did (p. 12). The genetic basis of race, therefore, has been considered insignificant, and the contention that race is a purely biological variable has generally been rejected.

In addition to physical characteristics, a social relationship component has been incorporated in the definition of race. According to Cox (1948), *race* refers to "any people who are distinguished or consider themselves distinguished, in social relations with other peoples, by their physical characteristics" (p. 402). This definition encompasses several aspects of *ethnicity,* which has conventionally been used to refer to a group of people who are seen by others and themselves as having a clearly defined sociocultural history and distinct cultural features that are transmitted across generations (Smedley, 1993). Phinney (1996) observed that "a central theme that runs through the writings of anthropologists, cross-racial psychologists, and others concerned with understanding ethnicity is the need to identify the specific components that may account for observed cultural differences" (p. 920). Common indicators of observed differences include language, food, dress, and religion (Schaefer, 2000), which are considered objective, ethnocultural indicators of ethnicity (Berry, Poortinga, Segall, & Dasen, 1992; Schaefer, 2000). Berry et al. also delineated a subjective facet of ethnicity, which refers to a sense of attachment and a feeling of belonging to the group that leads individuals to work to maintain their group membership. This perspective treats ethnicity as equivalent to culture, assumes that certain cultural characteristics exist among people of the respective group, and conceptualizes ethnicity in terms of relevant cultural features that distinguish various groups.

Along with sociocultural aspects, ethnicity has also been used to refer to people who share common ancestries and national origins (Atkinson et al., 1998; Helms & Cook, 1999; Schaefer, 2000). According to Berry et al. (1992), ethnicity includes another objective facet: descent, or being an offspring and a derivative of an earlier cultural group. In addition to ethnocultural indicators (e.g., language, food), people of a given ethnic group can be identified by biological and visible indictors such as name and genealogy. From this perspective, ethnicity does not preclude the biological or genealogical aspect of group membership, which is often associated with the definition of race.

RACIAL GROUP VERSUS ETHNIC GROUP

It is apparent that there is an ambiguous relationship between the definitions of race and ethnicity. Whereas race and ethnicity may be treated as somewhat distinct in cross-national studies, the conceptual boundary between the two terms is especially blurred in the United States in light of the historical miscegenation, the increasingly immigrant nature of some non-White populations (notably, Asian and Pacific Islander and Hispanic Americans; U.S. Bureau of the Census, 2000), and the growing number of interracial marriages (Root, 2001; "Sunday Q&A," 2001). Yet, race and ethnicity continue to be used to label and classify the U.S. population. Psychologists share different perspectives on the preferential use of racial group and ethnic group as a demographic proxy for group classification.

Phinney (1996) proposed that ethnicity be used to encompass race and culture of origin. According to Phinney, ethnicity includes (1) cultural values, attitudes, and behaviors that distinguish ethnic groups; (2) a subjective sense of group attachment and belongingness held by members; and (3) the experiences associated with minority status, including powerlessness, discrimination, and prejudice (p. 919). While recognizing the social and psychological consequences of visible racial features (e.g., skin color) on identity development, Phinney contended that these implications of race could be subsumed as aspects of ethnicity, and that the term "ethnic groups" be used when referring to members of nondominant groups of Color from non-European origins.

Smith (1991) also considered ethnicity a more generic term in scope. As an example, Smith noted that it is the various aspects of ethnicity (e.g., language, ethnic signs and symbols, family structure) that distinguish the White American subgroups of Italian Americans, Irish Americans, and Jewish Americans. Similarly, Asian Americans can be differentiated along their countries of origin (e.g., Chinese Americans, Korean Americans, Vietnamese Americans) and their respective cultural practices and patterns. It is posited that a person is born into an ethnic group and becomes related to it through emotional and symbolic ties, and that ingroup-outgroup boundaries are primarily drawn according to an individual's self-identification with an ethnic-racial membership group as a salient reference group (p. 182). Healthy ethnic identity development requires a person to accept his or her ethnic membership group as a positive reference group (p. 186). Thus, Smith contended that ethnic group membership includes but is not limited to race, and that race may not be the most salient determining factor for identity development (p. 181).

Atkinson et al. (1998, p. 9) also considered ethnicity to be a more useful term because it is descriptive of people who share a common nationality and/or culture. Yet, due to differential rate and mode of acculturation, people from the same national origin or who share the same ancestry may not share the same cultural values. For example, within a given Hmong American family, the immigrant parents and their children may differ in the extent to which they identify with their original culture and the host culture. There are also variations in the extent to which racial self-identification is important to ethnic group members. Thus, Atkinson et al. elected to use the term "race/ethnicity" to signify groups of people who share a common ancestry and culture.

In culturally heterogeneous environments where visible physical characteristics (skin color, in particular) are used for social categorization, the invisible ethnicity aspects of cultural origin and group affiliation are often obscured. In other words, the unique ethnicity of a Polish American is masked by the White demographic identity imposed by the society. By the same token, a Black person who strives to reject his or her ethnic and cultural heritage and aspire to be White (as is characteristic of the conformity/pre-encounter racial identity status; Helms, 1995, 2001; D. W. Sue & Sue, 1999, 2003) cannot evade the Black/African American demographic category ascribed by the society. As Smith (1991) noted:

> In racially and ethnically pluralistic societies wherein race is the major determiner of one's status, ethnic identity development proceeds first along racial lines and second along ethnic lines. Although one's ethnicity constitutes a major status or a superordinate identity, it may, depending on the situation, be considered secondary to race. (p. 187)

Noting that societal power and resources in the United States are distributed according to the visible physical attribute of skin color (Helms, 1995), and that "advantageous or disadvantageous treatment occurs according to phenotypic characteristic," Helms and Talleyrand (1997, p. 1247) argued that race plays a more salient role in group categorization (e.g., White or Black) and concomitant racial socialization experience (e.g., White privilege, internalized racism among non-White groups). Helms and Cook (1999) noted that "when a person is perceived as being a member of a racial group [based on certain modal phenotypes such as skin color], the person's 'racial' demographic identity typically obliterates his or her membership in other demographic categories or social affiliations" (p. 16). In contrast, ethnicity (e.g., specific White ethnic subgroups) is largely invisible in the American society, and the term has "no meaning apart from its status as a proxy for racial classification or immigrant status" (Helms & Talleyrand, 1997, p. 1246). Helms and Talleyrand (1997) reinforced the notion that race is a social construction, and that discussions about people labeling themselves as "mixed" or people have "distinct racial features" have no meaning if race does not exist. Specifically, Helms and Talleyrand (1997) commented that:

> Comparison of Whites . . . with other racial or ethnic groups border on the nonsensical if one thinks of these larger collectives as reflecting single ethnic cultures, but they make considerable sense if one acknowledges the meaningfulness of fictive (or "as if") racial groups in American society. (p. 1247)

Therefore, Helms and Talleyrand (1997) contended that race is not ethnicity, and that it is ill-advised to subsume race under ethnicity. Given that racial group membership and socialization are invariably tied to salient racial appearance, Helms (1996; Helms & Richardson, 1997) recommended that the terms "sociorace" and "psychorace" be used to designate the social construction of race and its impact on identity experience. "Sociorace" refers to race-related processes at an interpersonal or societal level, and "psychorace" refers to person-level, intrapsychic attributes a person develops in response to racial socialization. Based on a review of psychology abstracts that reported measures or results involving race, ethnicity, or race and ethnicity, Helms and Talleyrand (1997) content analyzed abstracts that occurred in combination with measures. It was found that 29% of ethnicity and 100% of race-and-ethnicity abstracts overlapped with race abstracts, whereas only 11% of the race abstracts were the same as those listed under ethnicity or race-and-ethnicity abstracts. Results further supported race as a more distinctive construct in psychology and American society at large.

It is apparent that psychologists have differential preferences for using race and ethnicity to describe people in a culturally heterogeneous environment, and that there is considerable intersection and interaction, rather than a clear conceptual boundary, between the terms. In addition, visible characteristics loosely defined as race continue to be used to classify the U.S. population. Race and ethnicity are considered socially constructed, rather than biologically or genetically determined. The social construction of race and ethnicity has implications for the potential conflict between an individual's racial group and ethnic group identification.

RACE/RACIAL GROUP VERSUS ETHNICITY/ETHNIC GROUP: THE CASE OF THE U.S. CENSUS

Psychologists have often called for sensitivity to the heterogeneity among visible racial and ethnic group members whose identities are differentiated by various sociocultural characteristics, such as country of birth (i.e., U.S.- or foreign-born), mode of entry into the United States (i.e., voluntary or involuntary; immigrant or refugee), and generation status. In the U.S. census (U.S. Bureau of the Census, 2000), attempts were made to gather ethnicity-specific data regarding national origin and sociocultural groups to "reflect the increasing racial and ethnic diversity of the U.S. population" (p. 10). Yet, at the institutional level, the U.S. population is categorized first along the visible feature of skin color (i.e., a race component), national or geographical origins, and languages spoken (i.e., objective ethnicity components), which are all subsumed under race. The U.S. census, therefore, uses race to encompass ethnicity.

Skin color (i.e., White versus non-White) is used by the U.S. census (U.S. Bureau of the Census, 2000) as a primary taxonomic label to distinguish White from all other groups and among other non-White groups. Despite differences in various aspects of ethnicity, such as countries of origin (e.g., Hispanics from Mexico, Cuba, or Puerto Rico), ancestries (e.g., Asian Americans from Chinese, Vietnamese, or Asian Indian descent), language spoken, and cultural practices, these groups are collectively distinguished from White Americans on the basis of skin color. Census 2000 did include a question (i.e., Question 10: "What is this person's ancestry or ethnic origin? For example: Italian, Jamaican, Cambodian, . . . Norwegian, Dominican, French Canadian") that allowed information regarding White Americans' ethnic origin and multiple ancestry (e.g., German-Irish) to be reported, as well as defining "White" as "people having origins in any of the original peoples of Europe, the Middle East, or North Africa" (U.S. Bureau of the Census, 2000). However, separate ethnicity categories were not designated for European immigrants and their descendants, who would have to consider themselves as belonging to the White racial category because skin color was used in the census to distinguish them from other ethnic groups. Non-White Americans who are descendents of immigrant parents from, for example, Korea or Cuba would probably not consider themselves White, but would choose a designated racial category on the census form. Skin color, therefore, marks a racial boundary by which White ethnic groups are consolidated and non-White ethnic groups are differentiated.

Along with skin color, the U.S. census further distinguished the non-White groups by their *presumed* national origin and language used. National (e.g., Asian Indian, Chinese, Japanese, Korean, Vietnamese) and geographical (e.g., Native Hawaiian, Guamanian, Samoan) regions, often considered components of ethnicity (Schaefer, 2000), are used to designate the *race* of Asian and Pacific Islander and African American subgroups, as well as to classify the Spanish-speaking subgroups (e.g., Puerto Rican, Cuban). Despite attempts to gather information on country of origin, their differentiated ethnic affiliations are collectively subsumed under a racial category (e.g., Chinese, Filipinos, and Asian Indians were designated as Asian Americans; Mexicans, Puerto Ricans, and Cubans were designated as Spanish/Hispanic/Latino). Furthermore, language, often considered an ethnicity component (Barresi, 1990), was used to combine and categorize people (i.e., Spanish/Mexican/Latino) from Spanish-speaking countries.

RACIAL IDENTITY VERSUS ETHNIC IDENTITY

The Census 2000 classification system, based primarily on visibly discernable characteristics of skin color and the *presumed* association with another country of origin and language spoken, has implications for racial and ethnic identity development. At the institutional level, both White and non-White Americans are confronted with the issue of relating to a racial identity that is externally ascribed (e.g., White, Spanish/Hispanic/Latino) and defined primarily according to the salient characteristic of skin color. Racial identity development, therefore, involves a psychological process of coming to terms with the collective demographic identity that is socially ascribed based on salient race-related characteristics.

Along with a collective racial identity (e.g., Black, Asian American, Hispanic/Latino), non-White individuals are also accorded an ethnic identity based on their affiliation, be it actual or presumed, with another country or region of origin (e.g., African American, Japanese American, Mexican American), which was considered a racial category in the U.S. census. In other words, whether or not the different generations of Japanese Americans have personal and cultural ties with their ancestral origin, their affiliation with the ethnic reference group is presumed. Ethnic identity development, therefore, pertains to a process of coming to terms with an ethnic reference group (e.g., Chinese American) that is differentiated from other ethnic groups (e.g., Filipino, Vietnamese American) within a similar racial category (e.g., Asian American) that is externally designated (e.g., by the U.S. census) primarily on the basis of visible race-related characteristics (e.g., skin color).

Unlike Asian and Hispanic Americans, whose presumed ethnic identity is categorically designated, the self-reported ethnic identity of European and North Americans is submerged by an imposed White demographic label. Census data have shown that the most reported responses to the question "What is this person's ancestry or ethnic origin?" were German ($N = 46,488,992$), English ($N = 28,264,856$), Irish ($N = 33,067,131$), and Italian ($N = 15,942,683$), with 14 of the 17 reported ethnic origins being European (U.S. Bureau of the Census, 2000). Yet, unlike non-White individuals, acknowledgment of ethnic affiliation is largely voluntary for White individuals, whose ethnic diversity (e.g., German American, Italian American, Irish American) is not specifically delineated. The census classification system, therefore, designates a demographic identity to non-White individuals while obliterating the ethnic group membership of White people. Regardless of their salient or submerged status, it is apparent that both racial and ethnic identities are socially constructed. The shifting dominance of racial identity and ethnic identity in a culturally heterogeneous environment is a function of the individual's salience of visible racial characteristics, particularly skin color, adopted by the society to label and categorize the population.

CONCEPTUALIZATION OF RACIAL SALIENCE

Racial salience is defined as the extent to which one's racial and ethnic features are perceived and experienced as conspicuous during cross-racial interactions. Perception and experience of racial salience is likely to be heightened in racially and ethnically heterogeneous environments with a differential representation of visible racial and ethnic people (Smith, 1991). The "Asianness" of an Asian American student, for example, is likely to be conspicuous in a predominantly White university in the rural Midwest. In contrast, in monocultural environments, people are less likely to be aware of the racial and ethnic aspects of their identity. The "Asianness" of another student in a university in southern California with significant representation of Asians, for example, will be less acutely perceived. Thus, an individual is predisposed to experience racial salience when his or her skin color is conspicuous in the immediate environment.

As a result of visible race-related salience (e.g., skin color), ethnicity-specific (e.g., country of origin, language, food preference) and non-ethnicity-related (e.g., inferred traits, such as Asians being good at science) stereotypes may be provoked and used as attributional, emotional, and attitudinal referents by which a person in a cross-racial interpersonal encounter is categorized, evaluated, and subsequently treated (Brown, 1995; Feagin, 1989). These associated stereotypic images, in turn, lead to subsequent interpersonal behaviors, be they verbal or nonverbal, which would not be elicited or would be different if racial features were not perceived as salient during the interaction. In other words, certain interpersonal behavior is a consequence of the stereotyping that is provoked by perceived racial salience in a cross-racial contact situation. D. W. Sue (1992), for example, recalled an incident in which a high school teacher mentored him toward winning a prestigious science award because "you people" (i.e., Asians) are "good at it" (i.e., science). The prescribed action (i.e., behavioral outcome) reflected the stereotypes (i.e., attributional or attitudinal referents) that were attached to visible Asian appearance (i.e., racial salience). Stereotypes and subsequent interpersonal behaviors triggered would likely not occur when race-related characteristics are not perceived as salient in the cross-racial contact situation. Numerous biographic narratives (e.g., Lee, 1992; McBride, 1996; Schoem, 1994) and reports ("Redefining Race," 2000) have documented the mediating effects of these salience characteristics on interpersonal and intrapersonal processes and outcomes during cross-racial interactions.

Ethnicity-Specific and Non-Ethnicity-Related Stereotypes

One of the predominant ethnicity-related stereotypes that can be attributed to the societal classification system is the perception that non-White individuals are foreign-born or immigrants. As D. W. Sue and Sue (1999) noted, "Skin color and obvious physical differences . . . continue to warp the perception of White Americans in that persons of Color are seen as aliens in their own land" (p. 106). Reports in the news media, for example, repeatedly implied that Michelle Kwan, a figure skater born and raised in California who represented the United States at the 1998 and 2002 Winter Olympics, is not an American ("American [Tara Lipinski] Beats Out Kwan," "American [Sarah Hughes] Outshines Kwan"; see Fancher, 2002). Although it has been estimated that 18.4% of the foreign-born population in the United States was from Europe ($N = 4,772,270$) and North America ($N = 836,068$; U.S. Bureau of the Census, 2000), White immigrants or their descendants of European origin often elude such perception. The institutional classification system, therefore, facilitates integration of White individuals while differentiating non-White individuals from the dominant culture. Whereas the immigrant or alien characteristics of White Americans subsided over the generations, that of non-White Americans persist due to their racial salience. These perceptions, in turn, induce identity stress, especially among members of later generations of non-White Americans who do not have cultural and personal affiliation to the national origins of their immigrant ancestors. An experience reported by Ronald Takaki, renowned professor of American history, serves to illustrate such identity dilemma:

> I had flown from San Francisco to Norfolk [Virginia] and was riding in a taxi to my hotel to attend a conference on multiculturalism. Hundreds of educators from across the country were meeting to discuss the need for greater cultural diversity in the curriculum. My driver and I chatted about the weather and the tourists. . . . The rearview mirror reflected a white man in his forties. "How long have you been in this country?" he asked. "All my life," I replied, wincing. "I was born in the United States." With a strong southern drawl, he remarked: "I was wondering because your English is excellent!" Then, as I had many times before, I explained: "My grandfather came here from Japan in the 1880s. My family has been here, in America, for over a hundred years." He glanced at me in the mirror. Somehow I did not look "American" to him; my eyes and complexion looked foreign. . . . Questions like the one my taxi driver asked me are always jarring, but I can understand why he could not see me as American. He had a narrow but widely shared sense of the past—a history that has viewed American as European in ancestry. (Takaki, 1993, pp. 1–2)

Racial salience can trigger stereotypes or images that are non-ethnicity-related. When these non-ethnicity-related stereotypes are negative, racist or discriminatory behaviors or treatments may ensue. For example, despite the substantial disparity in levels of educational achievement and socioeconomic status, Asian Americans are often portrayed as the model minority (D. W. Sue & Sue, 1999, 2003); yet, in times of national and economic crises, the images of aliens, foreigners, and enemies may prevail (Lott, 1998). For African Americans, Stephens, Kwan, Pope, and Paquette (1999) found that, during interactions with White individuals, African American graduate students often have to confront verbal comments reflecting stereotypes that Black people are academically inferior and antagonistic. Niemann (2001) has observed that Chicano/a students were often described as lazy, uneducated, criminal, hostile, and dropouts in the research literature. In some extreme cases, certain violent behaviors were triggered specifically by perceived racial salience. For example, the fatal beating of Vincent Chin (a Chinese American) in 1982 (see Tajima & Choy, 1988) and target shooting of Won-Joon Yoon (a Korean international student at Indiana University) and members of other racial and ethnic minorities (see "Clinton Calls Shooting Spree," 1999) would not be prompted if their Asian appearance was not conspicuous in the contact situation. These incidents illustrate that both the process and outcome of intercultural relationships are mediated by the perceived implications of racial salience during cross-racial interactions. Interpersonal treatments triggered by perceived racial salience, be they conscious or unconscious, create an ingroup-outgroup boundary and perpetuate the perception of "difference" during the cross-racial contact situation.

External and Internal Catalysts

Experience of racial salience can be triggered by both external and internal catalysts. External catalysts refer to an individual's verbal or nonverbal behaviors that heighten another individual's awareness of the perceived cultural difference during a cross-racial interpersonal encounter. In a series of consensual qualitative studies with Black Americans (Stephens et al., 1999) and Asian Americans (Kwan, Pacquette, & Pope, 1999) in predominantly White communities, participants were asked to recall experiences in which comments about the participant would not have been made if the participant were White (i.e., the participant's Black or Asian racial features were not salient) during the interaction. Kwan et al. found that more than half of the Asian American respondents reported experiences of racial salience and difference when White people made comments or raised questions related to Asian Americans' country of origin, accent or fluency of spoken English, food preferences, and number of years in the United States (see Appendix A). Among a sample of Black students in a predominantly White university, Stephens et al. found that experience of racial salience was triggered when White people raised questions regarding academic ability, skin color and hairstyle, and verbal ability (see Appendix B).

Internal catalysts, on the other hand, refer to an individual's self-consciousness of and conditioned sensitivity to the potential implications of racial salience during White–non-White interactions. As a result of such perception, the person may engage in certain interpersonal behaviors that otherwise would not occur. Non-White people who have experienced repeated racist treatment, for example, may develop cultural paranoia that is manifested through guarded, nondisclosing, and distancing behaviors toward White people (Ridley, 1995). Although cultural paranoia is considered a healthy defensive mechanism against potential racist and discriminatory treatments by White people (Grier & Cobbs, 1968; Ridley, 1984), it creates psychological distance that impedes the development of meaningful intercultural relationships.

In sum, racial salience is perpetuated by both the discernible racial characteristics (notably skin color) and the race-related stereotyping potential of individuals in a cross-racial contact situation. It connotes a psychological experience of difference, whether real or perceived, which can be attributed to the visibility of race during cross-racial interactions. Racial salience experience, whether triggered by behaviors directed at the individual or the individual's self-consciousness, can be considered a psychological predisposition by which race, ethnicity, and the perceived implications of associated stereotypes interact to influence the process and outcome of cross-racial interactions. Therefore, in addition to the physical (i.e., race-related characteristics) and contextual (i.e., racial and ethnic composition of the immediate environment) dimensions, racial salience encompasses a psychological dimension and should be studied as a psychological phenomenon.

Mediator of Racial Identity and Ethnic Identity Development

The extent to which racial or ethnic identity emerges as a predominant aspect of identity is a function of the racial salience in the immediate environment. When the non-White person is a numerical minority in a given social context, racial identity becomes the more salient aspect. When one is surrounded by people with similar skin color (e.g., in an Asian American association meeting), ethnicity (e.g., Korean American) becomes the more salient aspect. Thus, the predominance of racial and ethnic identity shifts according to the racial makeup and potentiality of racial salience in the social context.

Yet, as a psychological construct, the extent of an individual's experiences and awareness of racial salience is indicative or reflective of racial identity development status. Visible race-related characteristics often predispose a person to certain stereotypic treatments. In Kwan et al.'s (1999) study, for example, Asian Americans believed that comments that reflected the stereotype that Asian Americans are immigrants who speak English with an accent would not be triggered had their Asianness not been salient when interacting with White people. Reaction to racial salience experience, however, is likely to be different for people at various levels of racial identity development. According to theories of racial and cultural identity development (Helms, 1995, 2001; D. W. Sue & Sue, 1999, 2003) non-White persons with a predominant *pre-encounter/conformity* status may not (want to) perceive their non-White ethnicity as salient given their attempt to aspire to the White group and to identify with the dominant status, whereas another individual in *immersion* status may be vigilant toward interpersonal behaviors that induce racial salience experience.

At the same time, racial salience experiences may serve as catalysts for racial and ethnic identity development. As discussed in Smith's (1991) theory of ethnic identity development, given that racial and ethnic group members have varying degrees of psychological accommodation toward one another, people may receive mixed messages regarding their reference group identification, reinforcing in some occasions and nonreinforcing in others, from various racial and ethnic reference groups. These differential messages may lead to identity confusion and conflict, which could be catalytic for an individual's racial and ethnic identity development. For example, according to racial identity models conceptualized by Cross (1995) and Helms (1995, 2001), non-White members who adopt a predominant *pre-encounter* or *conformity* racial identity status often aspire to the White group and reject their ethnic reference group. Yet, stereotypic treatment triggered by the person's physical racial salience may induce a psychological sense of racial salience in which the person experiences incongruity between his or her invisible, self-defined identity (i.e., a false sense of being White) and a stereotyped, group identity externally ascribed on the basis of the person's racial salience (i.e., being Black). Therefore, differential experiences of interpersonal acceptance or rejection due to racial salience enable people to examine and evaluate their identification with and differentiation from potential racial and ethnic reference groups. Similarly, a White person with a predominantly *contact* racial identity status (Helms, 1992) is oblivious to the significance of skin color in the allocation of societal power, privilege, and status. Whereas racial salience experiences may likely not be evident when a contact status White individual interacts with another contact status White person or a person of Color with a predominantly pre-encounter/conformity status, a White individual in contact status may feel a sense of interpersonal boundary when interacting with a *resistance* status person of Color or another White individual with a predominant *immersion* White racial identity status. Racial salience experience, therefore, may be catalytic for White people to realize the implications of skin color on interpersonal relationships that is necessary for a nonracist White identity to develop (Helms, 1992, 1995, 2001).

IMPLICATIONS FOR RESEARCH AND PRACTICE

Knowledge of the sources and consequences of racial salience experiences is important in the counseling process. During a cross-racial counseling encounter, a counselor may exhibit verbal or nonverbal behaviors that impose race-related stereotypes on a client of Color. Such behaviors may induce the client's psychological racial salience, decrease the counselor's achieved credibility in the cross-racial encounter (S. Sue & Zane, 1987), and create interpersonal boundaries that are counterproductive to the counseling process. Therefore, it is important to identify behaviors that would likely induce racial salience experience and impede meaningful interracial relationships. As previously reported, Kwan and colleagues have identified several White people's verbal and nonverbal behaviors during White–non-White interactions that induced racial salience experiences of African Americans (Stephens et al., 1999) and Asian Americans (Kwan et al., 1999) who were sampled in predominantly White communities. More than half of the Asian American participants reported that a racial salience experience was accompanied by feelings of "isolation/unaccepted/different" and "angry/mad/hurt," and feelings of "anger," "disbelief," "upset," and "isolation" were reported in all the cases in the African American sample. Qualitative explorations of the racial salience experiences enable researchers and clinicians to delineate dimensions of the construct that are common for and unique to various racial and ethnic groups, as well as to understand the process of interaction. Consequently, dimensions of racial salience derived from qualitative explorations can be translated into research instruments to explore conceptual relationships among racial identity, ethnic identity, and various cultural adjustment variables.

Similar awareness of and reactions to behaviors that trigger racial salience experience, however, may not be shared by all African Americans and Asian Americans in the same contact situations with White Americans. According to Helms (1995), people of Color who have not abandoned internalized racism (i.e., socialized negative conceptions of one's racial group) are not developmentally ready or mature enough to recognize incidents that trigger racial salience and to confront its implications. When an individual becomes more aware of the social and psychological implications of physical racial salience, the catalytic experiences may lead the individuals to question their existing reference group identification and to reconfigure their relationships with potential racial and ethnic reference groups. Therefore, a racial salience experience can be considered a process variable that mediates racial and ethnic identity development (Helms & Piper, 1994) and other psychological adjustment issues, such as defense mechanisms, perceived prejudice, and acculturative stress (e.g., Kwan & Sodowsky, 1997).

The capacity to understand the triggers of and empathize with the consequences of people of Color's racial salience experiences is indicative of a White person's racial identity status. Assessment of White counselors' reactions to non-White clients' report of racial salience experiences, therefore, provides information about the racial identity status of White counselors. Such information has implications for understanding multicultural counseling and supervision processes, as well as multicultural counseling competency training. Kwan, Nyman, and Paquette (2003), for example, administered a set of statements commonly reported as increasing racial salience experiences of African Americans and Asian Americans during their interactions with White people (e.g., "I can't believe that kid thinks I got into this school just because I am Black," "I'm sick and tired of always hearing that Asians are all smart and hard working") to a sample of trainees in multicultural education. These trainees were then asked to provide verbatim responses to these statements, as well as to report their thoughts and feelings provoked by these statements. The predominant White racial identity status (Helms, 1995) of these responses was determined, and their relationships with measures of multicultural counseling variables, such as racial attitudes and defensiveness, were investigated. Kwan et al. (2003) found that White trainees who moved toward reintergration status (characterized by denial of existence of racism, hostility, and anger toward people of Color, and focus on enhancement of White privilege) were more unaware of racial privilege, institutional discrimination, and blatant racial issues, than trainees who moved beyond reintegration status. Exploring awareness of and reactions to racial salience experiences, therefore, facilitates studies of its conceptual relationships with counseling process variables, such as White racial identity status and cultural empathy.

SUMMARY

Race and ethnicity encompass more than the demographic categories designated on the census form. Although cultural heritage and patterns define the various ethnic groups, the U.S. census uses a classification system that is first based on visible characteristics allegedly of a racial nature. In particular, skin color and the presumed association with national/regional origins and language were used as racial categories to classify the U.S. population. Despite the heterogeneity within various racial and ethnic groups, at both the institutional and interpersonal levels, people continue to be categorically differentiated and collectively stereotyped primarily on the basis of skin color.

In this chapter, the fuzzy constructs of race and ethnicity were reviewed. The conceptual dimensions of racial salience were delineated and its mediating effect on racial and ethnic identity development was discussed. It is proposed that dimensions of racial salience be further explored and studied in relation to racial and ethnic identity development, adjustment experiences, and conflicts, and multicultural counseling process variables.

APPENDIX A

Examples of Domains, Categories, Frequencies, and Exemplary Core Ideas for Asians' Experience of Racial Salience during Asian-White Interactions

Domain and Category	Frequency	Exemplary Core Ideas
What did White people say?		
Questions about aspects of Asian culture	Typical	"The nurse asked which Chinese restaurant I would recommend."
Questions about national origin	Typical	". . . ask me where I am from." "The driver asked me if I was born here."
How did Asians react?		
Affective Responses: I feel . . .		
Isolated/unaccepted/different	Typical	"I felt neglected and isolated." "I felt very unaccepted."
Angry/mad/hurt	Typical	"I was very hurt and offended." "I was very sad and angry."

Note: $N = 11$; Typical = Category applied to at least half of the cases. Categories with one or two participants were not reported.

Source: Kwan, K.-L. K., Paquette, T., & Pope, R. (1999, August). *Experience of ethnic salience: A qualitative exploration of Asian Americans' majority-minority interactions.* Symposium presented at the 107th annual convention of the American Psychological Association, Boston.

APPENDIX B

Examples of Behaviors of White People That Induced African American Students' Experience of Racial Salience

Domain and Category	Frequency	Exemplary Core Ideas
What did White people say?		
Comments that associated African Americans with negative/inferior personality or class statuses	General	"You people are so rude and obnoxious."
Suspicions directed at Black people	General	"How do you pay the bills on that truck?" (questioned by police at gas station)
Derogatory nonverbal or offensive verbal behaviors	Typical	"I've been cursed at by White customer."
Questioning/comments about African Americans' skin color and hair	Typical	"What do you do to your hair?"

Note: $N = 10$; General = Category applied to all cases; Typical = Category applied to at least half of the cases.

Source: Stephens, J., Kwan, K.-L. K., Pope, R., & Paquette, T. (1999, August). *Perception of salience of ethnicity: Qualitative investigation of African American students in a predominantly White university.* Presented at the 1999 annual convention of the American Psychological Association, Boston.

REFERENCES

Atkinson, D. R., Morten, G., & Sue, D. W. (1998). *Counseling American minorities* (5th ed.). Boston: McGraw-Hill.

Barresi, C. M. (1990). Ethnogerontology: Social aging in national, racial, and cultural groups. In K. F. Ferraro (Ed.), *Gerontology: Perspectives and issues* (pp. 247–265). New York: Springer.

Berry, J. W., Poortinga, Y. H., Segall, M. H., & Dasen, P. R. (1992). *Cross-cultural psychology: Research and applications.* New York: Cambridge University Press.

Brown, R. (1995). *Prejudice: Its social psychology.* Malden, MA: Blackwell.

Clinton calls shooting spree "a rebuke" of America's ideals. (1999, July 6). *CNN* [Electronic version]. Available from http://www.cnn.com/US/9907/06/illinois.shooting.01.

Cox, O. C. (1948). *Caste, class, and race.* Garden City, NY: Doubleday.

Cross, W. E., Jr. (1995). The psychology of nigrescence: Revising the Cross model. In J. G. Ponterotto, J. M. Casas, L. A. Suzuki, & C. M. Alexander (Eds.), *Handbook of multicultural counseling* (pp. 93–122). Thousand Oaks, CA: Sage.

Fancher, M. (2002, March 3). *Times* won't forget readers' reminder on Kwan headline. *Seattle Times.*

Feagin, J. R. (1989). *Racial and ethnic relations.* Englewood Cliffs, NJ: Prentice-Hall.

Gordon, M. (1976). The subsociety and the subculture. In A. Dashefsky (Ed.), *Ethnic identity in society* (pp. 25–35). Chicago: Rand McNally.

Grier, W., & Cobbs, P. (1968). *Black rage.* New York: Basic Books.

Helms, J. E. (1992). *A race is a nice thing to have: A guide to being a White person or understanding the White persons in your life.* Topeka, KS: Content Communications.

Helms, J. E. (1995). An update of Helms's White and people of Color racial identity models. In J. G. Ponterotto, J. M. Casas, L. A. Suzuki, & C. M. Alexander (Eds.), *Handbook of multicultural counseling* (pp. 181–198). Thousand Oaks, CA: Sage.

Helms, J. E. (2001). An update of Helms's White and people of Color racial identity models. In J. G. Ponterotto, J. M. Casas, L. A. Suzuki, & C. M. Alexander (Eds.), *Handbook of multicultural counseling* (2nd ed., pp. 181–198). Thousand Oaks, CA: Sage.

Helms, J. E. (1996). Toward a methodology for measuring and assessing racial identity as distinguished from ethnic identity. In G. R. Sodowsky & J. Impara (Eds.), *Multicultural assessment in counseling and clinical psychology* (pp. 285–311). Lincoln, NE: Buros Institute of Mental Measurements.

Helms, J. E., & Cook, D. A. (1999). *Using race and culture in counseling and psychotherapy.* Boston: Allyn & Bacon.

Helms, J. E., & Piper, R. E. (1994). Implications of racial identity theory for vocational psychology. *Journal of Vocational Behavior, 44,* 124–138.

Helms, J. E., & Richardson, T. (1997). How "multiculturalism" obscures race and culture as differential aspects of counseling competency. In D. Pope-Davis & H. Coleman (Eds.), *Multicultural counseling competencies: Assessment, education, and training and supervision* (pp. 60–79). Thousand Oaks, CA: Sage.

Helms, J. E., & Talleyrand, R. M. (1997). Race is not ethnicity. *American Psychologist, 52,* 1246–1247.

Kwan, K.-L. K., Nyman, S., & Paquette, T. (October 2003). White racial identity status, color-blindness, and verbatim interracial responses: Testing their corresponding relationships. Paper presented in a symposium at the 3rd annual Diversity Challenge conference at the Institute for the Study of Race and Culture, Boston College, MA.

Kwan, K.-L. K., Paquette, T., & Pope, R. (1999, August). *Experience of ethnic salience: A qualitative exploration of Asian Americans' majority-minority interactions.* Symposium presented at the 107th annual convention of the American Psychological Association, Boston.

Kwan, K.-L. K., & Sodowsky, G. R. (1997). Internal and external ethnic identity and their correlates: A study of Chinese American immigrants. *Journal of Multicultural Counseling and Development, 25,* 51–67.

Lee, J. (1992). *Asian Americans: Oral histories of first to fourth generation Americans from China, the Philippines, Japan, India, the Pacific Islands, Vietnam, and Cambodia.* New York: New Press.

Lott, J. T. (1998). *Asian Americans: From racial category to multiple identities.* Thousand Oaks, CA: Altamira Press.

McBride, J. (1996). *The color of water: A Black man's tribute to his White mother.* New York: Riverhead Books.

Niemann, Y. F. (2001). Stereotypes about Chicanas and Chicanos: Implications for counseling. *Counseling Psychologist, 29,* 55–90.

Phinney, J. S. (1996). When we talk about American ethnic groups, what do we mean? *American Psychologist, 51,* 918–927.

Redefining race in America. (2000, September 18). *Newsweek, 136,* 38–65.

Ridley, C. R. (1984). Clinical treatment of the nondisclosing Black client. *American Psychologist, 39,* 1234–1244.

Ridley, C. R. (1995). *Overcoming unintentional racism in counseling and therapy.* Thousand Oaks, CA: Sage.

Root, M. P. P. (2001). *Love's revolution: Interracial marriage.* Philadelphia: Temple University Press.

Rushton, J. P. (1995). Construct validity, censorship, and the genetics of race. *American Psychologist, 50,* 40–41.

Schaefer, R. T. (2000). *Racial and ethnic groups* (8th ed.). Upper Saddle River, NJ: Prentice-Hall.

Schoem, D. (Ed.). (1994). *Inside separate worlds: Life stories of young Blacks, Jews, and Latinos.* Ann Arbor: University of Michigan Press.

Smedley, A. (1993). *Race in North America: Origin and evolution of a world view.* Boulder, CO: Westview Press.

Smith, E. J. (1991). Ethnic identity development: Toward the development of a theory within the context of majority/minority status. *Journal of Counseling and Development, 70,* 181–188.

Sodowsky, G. R., Kwan, K.-L. K., & Pannu, R. (1995). Ethnic identity of Asians in the United States. In J. G. Ponterotto, J. M. Casas, L. A. Suzuki, & C. M. Alexander (Eds.), *Handbook of multicultural counseling* (pp. 123–154). Thousand Oaks, CA: Sage.

Stephens, J., Kwan, K.-L. K., Pope, R., & Paquette, T. (1999, August). *Perception of salience of ethnicity: Qualitative investigation of African American students in a predominantly White university.* Presented at the 1999 annual convention of the American Psychological Association, Boston.

Sue, D. W. (1992). *Cultural identity development* [Videotape]. Available from Microtraining and Multicultural Development, P. O. Box 9641, North Amherst, MA 01059–9641.

Sue, D. W., & Sue, D. (1999). *Counseling the culturally different* (3rd ed.). New York: Wiley.

Sue, D. W., & Sue, D. (2003). *Counseling the culturally diverse* (4th ed.). New York: Wiley.

Sue, S., & Zane, N. (1987). The role of culture and cultural techniques in psychotherapy. A critique and reformulation. *American Psychologist, 42,* 37–45.

Sunday Q&A. (2001, May 27). *New York Times* [National desk], pp. 1, 24.

Tajima, R. (Producer) & Choy, C. (Director) (1988). *Who killed Vincent Chin?* [Videotape]. Available from Filmakers Library, 124 East 40th Street, New York, NY 10016.

Takaki, R. (1993). *A different mirror: A history of multicultural America.* Boston: Little, Brown.

Thompson, C. E., & Neville, H. A. (1999). Racism, mental health, and mental health practice. *Counseling Psychologist, 27,* 155–223.

U.S. Bureau of the Census. (2000). *United States Census 2000: Basic facts about us.* Washington, DC: Author.

Zuckerman, M. (1990). Some dubious premises in research and theory on racial differences: Scientific, social, and ethical issues. *American Psychologist, 45,* 1297–1303.

CHAPTER 9

The Integration of Spiritual and Religious Issues in Racial-Cultural Psychology and Counseling

Timothy B. Smith and P. Scott Richards

The Society for the Study of Ethnic Minorities convened a special program on spirituality at the 2000 National Convention of the American Psychological Association, with Joseph Trimble delivering a presidential address entitled "Spiritual Affinity and Its Influence on Acculturation and Ethnic Identification." In that message, Trimble emphatically stated, "We can no longer ignore what is so basic and fundamental to three-fourths of the world's population. . . . The academy has ignored spirituality. As of today, that ends!" His address received a prolonged standing ovation.

A new movement has begun. Spirituality and religion are being integrated into racial-cultural psychology and counseling. This chapter reviews the literature that is the basis of that movement. We first describe the historical forces alluded to by Trimble (2000) that until only recently have minimized the relevance of religion and spirituality to psychological research and practice. We then summarize the potential benefits and concerns about incorporating spiritual and religious perspectives into research and practice that have been suggested in publications of the past 30 years. To demonstrate that religion and spirituality are central to racial-cultural psychology and counseling, literature describing the complex relationship between mental health, race and culture, and religiosity/spirituality is reviewed, as well as the literature investigating the relationship between religion and racism. Recommendations for future scholarship are provided in the concluding section of the chapter.

Some authors define religiousness as an individual's degree of involvement in an organized religion and its accompanying system of worship, rituals, and doctrines and spirituality in terms of private/personal transcendent beliefs and actions (e.g., Kelly, 1995; Richards & Bergin, 1997). In this chapter, we assume that religiousness and spirituality are highly interrelated and that both are salient to racial-cultural issues and to mental health. Given that the term faith can describe "the spiritual apprehension of . . . realities beyond the reach of sensible experience or logical proof" (*Oxford English Dictionary,* 2002), the generic term faith will sometimes be used to describe the combination of the religious and spiritual (see also Fowler, 1981).

As we present this review of the literature relevant to issues of faith, we acknowledge that many consider spiritual and religious experiences sacred, beyond description, or intensely personal. In our desire to appreciate all perspectives, we acknowledge the limitations in our coverage of the topic. Nevertheless, we hope that this chapter will facilitate future scholarship needed for faith to become a defining force in the field.

REVIEW OF THE PROFESSIONAL LITERATURE

Historical Trends of the Literature Addressing Religion and Spirituality

As publications in racial-cultural psychology and counseling have so clearly demonstrated, the assumptions and values of European and European American cultures have constrained the validity of mental health practices and research since their foundation (Carter, 1995; Helms & Cook, 1999). One of those foundational assumptions is that human behavior can be completely explained by observable natural phenomena. All alternative explanations have been considered untenable, including the existence of spiritual reality. The formation of psychology as an academic discipline in the late 1800s in Europe and North America was partly a reaction *against* religious approaches to the study of human behavior (Haque, 2001; Richards & Bergin, 1997).

Given that historical context, for many decades spirituality and religion were largely considered irrelevant to mental health, dismissed from serious discussion, and even scorned by professionals in the field (Bergin, 1980). Some scholars went so far as to portray religion as harmful to mental health. Most notably, Freud (1927), Watson (1924), Skinner (1971), and Ellis (1971) sought to liberate individuals professing faith in spiritual or religious beliefs with strong doses of rationalism, skepticism, and determinism. Throughout most of the previous century, during which time psychology and counseling developed and flourished, religion and spirituality were either ignored or repudiated by the profession.

In such a critical climate, few professionals defended the relevance of religion and spirituality to mental health. Notable exceptions, however, are found in the work of William James (1936), Carl Jung (1933), Gordon Allport (1950), Erik Erikson (1985), Abraham Maslow (1964), and Rollo May (1982), all of whom recognized that spirituality is a fundamental component of human experience. James undertook a philosophical approach to the study of religion, delineating the benefits and limitations of religiosity and emphasizing the spiritual aspects of human experience. Jung took an analytic approach to faith, acknowledging spirituality as a source of meaning and psychic wholeness. Allport took a social psychological approach, emphasizing differences between religiosity for intrinsic means and religiosity for extrinsic means. Erikson asserted that religion helps children internalize the faith, trust, and ego for healthy development and provides meaning, certainty, and hope throughout the life span. Maslow encouraged scientific study of religion so as to better understand the process of self-actualization and spiritual "peak experiences."

May also emphasized the need for spiritual meaning and self-transcendence. A review of current publications relevant to religion and spirituality emphasizes the importance of these scholars, with current writings on the topic still reflecting many of the ideas and concepts they advanced.

Although these notable scholars and their followers referred to the importance of religion and spirituality to mental health in theoretical terms, there was little empirical research on the topic until the second half of the twentieth century. This research was inconsistent and limited in scope and quality. In the 1970s, several reviews appeared (Argyle & Beit-Hallahmi, 1975; Malony, 1977; Strommen, 1971) that set the stage for an increase in the quality of scholarship, catalyzed further by Allen Bergin's call to the profession in 1980, theoretical work by James Fowler (1981), and reviews by Batson and Ventis (1982) and Bergin (1983), among others. The figurative floodgate to publication opened during the 1980s and was swept away in the 1990s, with literally hundreds of subsequent empirical studies (re)affirming the salience of religiosity and spirituality to mental health research and treatment (Batson, Schoenrade, & Ventis, 1993; George, Larson, Koenig, & McCullough, 2000; Koenig, McCullough, & Larson, 2001; McCullough, 1999; Payne, Bergin, Bielema, & Jenkins, 1991; Smith, McCullough, & Poll, 2003; Worthington, Kurusu, McCullough, & Sandage, 1996). A deluge of empirical research challenged decades of criticism that the study of religious and spiritual influences on mental health was neither scientific nor productive.

Although recent research findings are complex and sometimes inconsistent, the clear majority of empirical studies during the past two decades have observed positive associations between faith and wellness (e.g., Koenig et al., 2001). For example, numerous studies exploring the relationship of religious commitment to psychological adjustment and life satisfaction have found that people who are religiously devout but not extremists tend to report greater subjective well-being and life satisfaction, greater marital satisfaction and family cohesion, more ability to cope with stress and crises, less depression, and less worry and guilt than others (Batson et al., 1993; Gartner, 1996; George et al., 2000; Payne et al., 1991). Similarly, a large number of studies have explored the relationship of religious affiliation and commitment to various indicators of social conduct. In general, the findings indicate that religiosity is inversely related to alcohol and drug abuse, delinquency and criminal behavior, suicide, teen pregnancy, and divorce (Gartner, 1996; Koenig et al., 2001; Payne et al., 1991).

Not all of the research findings on religion and mental health have found a positive relationship. There is some evidence that religiosity may be positively associated with authoritarianism, dogmatism, rigidity, suggestibility, and dependence (Batson et al., 1993; Gartner, 1996). Due to inconsistent findings, the relationships of religiosity to self-esteem and anxiety are unclear (Batson et al., 1993; Gartner, 1996). There is also a marked absence of research examining the relationship of religious devotion to serious mental illness or impairment (Payne et al., 1991).

Some researchers have challenged the negative and ambiguous associations between religiosity and psychological adjustment. They cite that these findings are largely based on paper-and-pencil personality tests that are subject to a variety of possible psychometric and researcher biases (Bergin, 1983; Gartner, 1996). In contrast, many of the positive associations have been observed on " 'real life' behavior events that can be directly observed and reliably measured" (Gartner, 1996, p. 201). The preponderance of current evidence points to a beneficial influence of religion on psychological and social functioning.

However, few scholars would assert that all forms of religion are healthy or beneficial. Some religious beliefs, practices, and manifestations are clearly dysfunctional and even pathological, such as purported demonic possession, scrupulosity (obsessive overconcern for one's sinfulness), religious delusions and compulsions, and mass suicides of religious cult members (Galanter, 1996; Meadow & Kahoe, 1984; Meissner, 1996). Furthermore, abuses of religious leadership and principles can occur, leaving adherents disillusioned or injured (Benyei, 1998).

Unfortunately, most research on mental health and faith has been correlational. Therefore, although we know that the two constructs are usually positively related, we know little about what factors moderate or mediate their relationship. Future research in the area needs to address several sets of potential moderators and mediators to better explain *how* mental health and faith are related. First, the impact of social involvement warrants scrutiny. It may well be that participation in an organized religion enhances social support, which is a known buffer of stress and pathology (Joiner & Coyne, 1999). Less common than the pervasive but indirect benefit of socializing are direct services or charities provided by some churches to members experiencing economic or emotional distress. Informal pastoral counseling may also alleviate psychological or emotional distress. Second, variables related to self-disclosure should be examined. It may be that the norms of certain faith communities sanction (or, oppositely, stigmatize) the admission of personal limitations, thus creating a forum for self-disclosure that has been associated with positive outcomes (Pennebaker, 1997). Testimonials, public speaking opportunities, and other group processes may encourage individuals to process emotional content in supportive settings, similar to group therapy (McRae, Carey, & Anderson-Scott, 1998). Third, cognitive strategies may play a role. Spiritual perspectives may have the effect of increasing hopefulness and optimistic beliefs, which are widely known to enhance psychological functioning (e.g., M. Seligman, 1990). It may be that individuals who express a faith in principles or in powers that cannot be proven are simply more ready to suspend disbelief/doubt than are others. Similarly, religious practices may sometimes create a positive distraction from ruminative or self-critical thinking (Nolen-Hoeksema, 1991). It may also be that spirituality supports a perspective on the value of life and on passage of time that is conducive to mental health (e.g., Carstensen, Isaacowitz, & Charles, 1999). Finally, issues of behavioral congruence should be examined. It may be that individuals who report high levels of faith are also more likely to report personal behavior that matches their expectancies/values. Such congruence between one's beliefs and actions is predictive of mental health (Maddux, 1995). In sum, investigation of these and other potential moderating and mediating variables will be necessary for future scholarship to effectively integrate issues of faith with racial-cultural psychology and counseling.

Integration of Religion and Spirituality with Racial-Cultural Psychology and Counseling

From a historical perspective, scholars working in the 1950s and 1960s to advance a multicultural agenda and those interested in integrating religious and spiritual issues into psychology and counseling had the same goal: to gain wider recognition and respect in the field and, eventually, to change the profession itself. During the 1970s and early 1980s, when mainstream psychology began to openly acknowledge some of its major errors and omissions (racial inequities and injustices, etc.), arguments supporting spirituality and religion also gained some audience (Richards & Bergin, 1997). Despite these similar aims and despite the similar historical struggle to overcome biases in the larger field, the development of literature specific to religious and spiritual issues was for many years separate from and parallel to the literature advocating multicultural and racial-cultural perspectives. The two literatures were characterized by separate scholarly networks, professional associations, journals, and to some degree worldviews. Nevertheless, there were notable exceptions to this general trend.

Beginning primarily in the 1960s, articles began to appear on the unique mental health contexts of individuals from specific cultural-religious groups (e.g., North African Muslims, Jamaican Rastafarians). These types of articles provided information useful to psychological practice, but they were mostly opinion papers and rarely contained empirical data. The number of articles and book chapters of this kind steadily increased in number during the 1970s and 1980s, and they remain common in the current literature (e.g., Garrett, 1999; Baez & Hernandez, 2001).

However, some articles appearing in the 1980s and early 1990s went beyond describing spiritual and religious issues of specific racial and cultural groups to advocate changes in the field itself, coupled with an open acknowledgment of issues of faith generally (e.g., Bishop, 1992). This type of advocacy increased substantially through the late 1980s to mid-1990s, when empirical reports and papers by scholars already recognized for their work in the multicultural literature began to take up the issue. For example, Courtland Lee (Lee, Oh, & Mountcastle, 1992) wrote on indigenous healing methods and on the spiritual and religious influences that need to be considered by counselors in their work. Similarly, Clemmont Vontress (1996) reported on the relevance of traditional spiritual forms of healing in Africa and on existential approaches to treatment. Nancy Boyd-Franklin (1989, 2003) addressed the salience of religious issues in African American families. These and other authors strengthened the sense of credibility behind such scholarship efforts.

Among the major contributions of the late 1980s and early 1990s was the work of Linda James Myers (1988). Grounded in an African worldview, Myers's optimal theory takes an explicitly spiritual perspective of psychology: "Human beings are the expression of what can be defined as energy, spirit, consciousness, or god/goddess" (L. J. Myers & Speight, 1994, p. 103). Optimal theory asserts that each individual is part of a much larger whole, a unified consciousness that includes past and future generations. Optimal theory therefore emphasizes interrelatedness and interdependence as the foundation for mental health. From this perspective, dysfunction and distress occur when individuals fail to recognize their connections with others, becoming fragmented as they base their identity and worth on external criteria such as material possessions. In sum, optimal theory translates traditional African perspectives on life and healing into contemporary psychological terms, infusing psychotherapy and counseling with insight rich with wisdom collected over centuries. Optimal theory has been used to develop a model of identity development (L. J. Myers et al., 1991) and to advocate for a shift of emphasis in multicultural approaches to treatment, training, and research (Speight, Myers, Cox, & Highlen, 1991). Clearly, optimal theory and the similar African-centered models of Akbar (1995) and Philips (1990) represent the potential for scholars to effectively combine cultural and spiritual perspectives that inform psychology and counseling.

During the late 1990s, more and more authors joined the chorus of publications advocating the integration of issues of faith into racial-cultural psychology and counseling. Special issues of *Multicultural Counseling and Development* and *Counseling and Values* addressed the overlap of racial-cultural and spiritual themes, and the journal *Mental Health, Religion, and Culture* was created to serve increased scholarship in the area. At the same time, the number of presentations on the topic at national professional conventions increased exponentially. For example, D. W. Sue, Bingham, Porche-Burke, and Vasquez (1999) identified spirituality as a basic dimension of humanity, one of the five major themes of the first National Multicultural Conference and Summit. They affirmed that "understanding that people are cultural and spiritual beings is a necessary condition for a psychology of human existence" (p. 1065), thus confirming the place of spirituality in the multicultural revolution.

Scholarly books on the topic began to appear in the late 1990s, among them Mary Fukuyama and Todd Sevig's *Integrating Spirituality into Multicultural Counseling* (1999) and P. Scott Richards and Allen Bergin's edited *Handbook of Psychotherapy and Religious Diversity* (2000). Fukuyama and Sevig present a comprehensive overview of the topic, using the multicultural literature as a foundation. They cover differences in religious and spiritual worldviews across racial groups, and they parallel competencies for working with racial issues to competencies for working with issues of faith. The process of spiritual development and specific spiritual techniques for working with clients are detailed. Most important, they provide models of training and practice that made religious and spiritual issues explicit. Richards and Bergin's *Handbook* provides descriptions of 12 religious groups found in North America, along with chapters specific to the faith issues of four racial-cultural groups. Each chapter provides concrete, specific information on a denomination, including unique mental health issues, attitudes toward psychotherapy, and attitudes toward potentially problematic issues of perfectionism, sexuality, abortion, substance use, and so on. Specific racial-cultural influences on spirituality are detailed, as are relevant historical, political, and social factors that contribute to the heterogeneity of beliefs within each group.

In addition to these major contributions, textbooks on multicultural and racial-cultural psychology and counseling have begun to devote chapters to religious and spiritual issues (e.g., Pedersen, Draguns, Lonner, & Trimble, 2002; Smith, 2004; Trusty, Sandhu, & Looby, 2002). The number of journal articles on the topic is also increasing exponentially. Nevertheless, despite the increase in professional interest, very few empirical studies have examined the interactions among race, culture, faith, and mental health (Richards & Bergin, 2000). This is a glaring deficiency in the field.

Moreover, most of the extant research on religion and mental health has been done with European and European American Protestants and Roman Catholics. Thus, the research findings of a positive relationship between religiosity/spirituality and mental health have been based largely on samples of Whites and Christians. Clearly, major problems of external validity need to be overcome (S. Sue, 1999). And despite ample anecdotal evidence that faith beliefs and faith communities are a benevolent influence in many other racial groups (e.g., Garrett, 1999; Mbiti, 1990; Richards & Bergin, 2000), additional research studies are needed to confirm or refute the rationale for integrating spiritual and religious issues with racial-cultural psychology and counseling.

RATIONALE FOR INTEGRATING SPIRITUAL AND RELIGIOUS ISSUES WITH RACIAL-CULTURAL PSYCHOLOGY AND COUNSELING

As emphasized in many recent publications, there are several compelling reasons for integrating spiritual and religious issues in racial-cultural psychology and counseling (e.g., Fukuyama & Sevig, 1999). First, such an approach represents global demographics. In North America, the vast majority of people hold spiritual convictions, with most affirming the importance of those beliefs to their lives and well-being (Gallup, 1995). The same trend typifies most world populations (Keller, 2000; O'Connor, 1998). Spirituality appears to be central to the experiences of most humans. However, even if spirituality and religion were valued by a small minority of the population, other compelling reasons would remain.

Second, an approach that incorporates spiritual and religious variables better reflects client self-understanding and client cultural/historical/social contexts (Fallot, 2001) than one that does not. Accurate understanding of context is invaluable for psychological research and practice (Slife, Hope, & Nebeker, 1999). Nevertheless, present practices often overlook important contextual issues, often to the detriment of groups not adequately represented in the literature (Smith, 2004; S. Sue, 1999). There are thousands of religious and spiritual perspectives represented across the globe, yet we have only begun to address this fundamental element of human experience. We need research representative of spiritual contexts and religious diversity (Fukuyama & Sevig, 1999; Richards & Bergin, 2000). As such research increases, the external validity of extant theories and research results will become clearer, with perhaps more accurate models developing over time. Improving understanding of people's experiences and perspectives would also allow the field to reach many who are not adequately represented by current mental health practices. Additionally, it could improve efforts to increase empowerment, social justice, and community building (Kloos & Moore, 2000), all aims of racial-cultural psychology and counseling.

Third, an approach that values spiritual and religious experience is rooted in meaning and making meaning, processes of interpreting reality that are fundamental to mental health (Rhi, 2001; S. Taylor, Kemeny, Reed, Bower, & Gruenewald, 2000). Some theorists go so far as to call the process of making meaning the foundation for all psychological inquiry (e.g., Richardson, Fowers, & Guignon, 1999). Spiritual and religious teachings emphasize this process of deriving meaning from life's experiences, from the global existential questions of Where did I come from? Why am I here? and Where am I going? to the specific lessons or principles derived from pain and suffering during any given moment. As has been noted, "Religious cultures are the most powerful factors that modify the individual's attitudes toward life, death, happiness and suffering" (Rhi, 2001, p. 573). Spirituality and religion are primary mechanisms for meaning making that are inseparable from perceptions of wellness for many individuals (Cook & Kelly, 1998; Young, Cashwell, & Woolington, 1998). Individuals whose spiritual or religious beliefs are not acknowledged or respected may therefore experience counseling as confusing or even harmful.

Fourth, an approach that incorporates spiritual and religious contexts is not only grounded in the lived experience of the individual, but it also makes possible a shared foundation on which universal experiences may be comprehended. Thus, it speaks to both sides of the emic/etic conundrum (e.g., L. J. Myers & Speight, 1994; Speight et al., 1991). Spiritual beliefs tend to be quite personal and intimate; they often constitute the essence of one's uniqueness or the perceived core of one's being. Yet most spiritual beliefs emphasize the spiritual nature of *all* of existence, and it is often assumed that spirituality is a reality that impacts all people, whether or not they acknowledge it (Cook & Kelly, 1998). Spiritual beliefs attempt to cultivate a profound respect for the individual by emphasizing that each person shares the same ultimate reality as all other individuals (e.g., we are all a part of the fabric of nature, all children of God), providing a both/and perspective rather than an either/or categorization. In sum, a spiritual approach provides a perspective that may be portrayed as a relational web that transcends the emic/etic dichotomy: An individual is of great worth *because* of connections to others and to a power greater than self (Smith & Draper, 2004).

Implied in the previous point is a fifth benefit of taking a spiritual perspective. Most spiritual or religious tenets tend to shift the focus of inquiry or intervention away from the self and away from individualistic values that do not facilitate emotional growth and happiness, offering instead a more collectivist perspective that does (e.g., D. G. Myers, 2000). As research has shown, self-focused attention predicts decreased well-being and negative affect (Flory, Raikkonen, Matthews, & Owens, 2000), and excessive self-focus is a common symptom for nearly all mental illnesses (Ingram, 1990). In opposition to self-focus, many religious and spiritual tenets emphasize the importance of service, giving, and responsibility to others and the environment, along with the need to transcend self-focused desires and actions.

Thus, spiritual and religious perspectives can serve as a buffer against the harmful effects of self-preoccupation.

Sixth, race and culture moderate how spirituality and religion are interpreted and expressed (e.g., Höllinger & Smith, 2002; G. Miller, Fleming, & Brown-Anderson, 1998). Racial and cultural groups have unique ways of viewing and practicing even similar religious doctrines and spiritual teachings. Therefore, "the counseling process requires continued research regarding how people experience spirituality across cultures" (Ingersoll, 1998, p. 156). In particular, people in situations of pervasive hardship or distress and people who have relatively less access to other coping resources gravitate to spiritual and religious methods of coping (Pargament, 1997). For example, in North America spirituality and religious beliefs and practices are endorsed more by Blacks than by Whites (R. Taylor, Mattis, & Chatters, 1999). Effective mental health treatment therefore recognizes that "spiritual or religious issues are often embedded within the issues that bring many racial and ethnic minority clients to counseling" (Constantine, 1999, p. 179). Yet people of Color often fear that their spiritual and religious beliefs will be misunderstood by mental health professionals (Cinnirella & Loewenthal, 1999). Because racial-cultural psychology and counseling advocates the cause of oppressed peoples, it can play an important role in training professionals to understand and respect spiritual and religious issues, particularly as they relate to clients who are coping with adversity.

Seventh, religion and spirituality are fundamental aspects of human *diversity,* representing sources of both intergroup conflict and intergroup collaboration. In North America alone, there are hundreds of religious and spiritual groups, and this represents only a small portion of the remarkable diversity across the globe (Keller, 2000). Nevertheless, diversity is frequently a source of conflict. Intolerance of religious or spiritual differences characterizes North American history (Carnes, 1995) and intergroup conflicts throughout the world. Conflict has repeatedly been instigated and perpetuated by religious differences (e.g., Protestant and Roman Catholic colonizers versus indigenous peoples). Addressing spiritual and religious contexts is therefore necessary to increase intergroup respect and to combat oppression based on religious differences. Moreover, differences in religious and spiritual beliefs often parallel differences of race or culture. Racial-cultural counseling and psychology can provide a forum for increasing mutual respect among all people, particularly those whose spiritual or religious differences fall along racial lines.

Eighth, integrating spirituality into treatment has potential to augment the effectiveness of that treatment by strengthening the therapeutic alliance and drawing on existing client resources (Richards & Bergin, 1997). Some clients may not feel comfortable speaking openly about their spiritual beliefs or experiences with acquaintances or friends. Thus, a therapist who enables clients to express their personal ways of finding meaning can potentially facilitate additional interpersonal growth and trust. Furthermore, increased understanding of a client's spiritual perspective may help the therapist access resources with the potential to heal. Particularly for a client already grounded in a specific religious or spiritual orientation, the practices, principles, and people associated with that orientation can be used to inform and augment treatment. It has been observed that "organized religious communities are the largest untapped resources for aiding the therapeutic process with religious clients" (Bishop, 1992, p. 181).

Finally, study of spiritual and religious methods of healing can inform psychological theory and practice (Kloos & Moore, 2000; Lee et al., 1992; L. J. Myers, 1988; Richards & Bergin, 1997). Although psychology has discovered many useful principles that can facilitate wellness and healing, psychology has a short history compared with religious and spiritual forms of healing. The wisdom of ages has shaped the practices and traditions of faith in many cultures across the world to enhance coping, resilience, and healing (e.g., Garrett, 1999; Lee et al., 1992). Psychology has only begun to consider the potential healing power of faith. Yet such efforts must first address several potential obstacles to the integration of spiritual and religious perspectives in psychology.

POTENTIAL OBSTACLES IN INTEGRATING FAITH PERSPECTIVES INTO RACIAL-CULTURAL PSYCHOLOGY AND COUNSELING

Despite the compelling rationale presented in the recent literature to integrate religious and spiritual perspectives into psychology and counseling, recent authors have also raised several concerns and pointed to obstacles with the potential to retard the growth of the field if they are not openly acknowledged and addressed (e.g., Fukuyama & Sevig, 1999; Funderburk & Fukuyama, 2001; Richards & Bergin, 1997, 2000). These obstacles include the historical factors reviewed earlier, perceived conflicts between religious and spiritual issues and the values and practices of the mental health profession, and pragmatic concerns related to conducting research on a topic that is complex and abstract. These obstacles and related concerns that have been raised in the professional literature are briefly summarized in this section.

Obstacles Described in the Literature That Are Grounded in Historical Factors

As noted previously, several historical factors have contributed substantially to restricting discussion of spiritual and religious issues in psychology and counseling. Therefore, removing contemporary obstacles to integrating issues of faith in psychology and counseling requires that these factors be acknowledged. The most pernicious of these factors include (1) a focus that either magnifies or minimizes the negative aspects of spirituality and religiosity, (2) interpretations of science that conflict with the essence of faith, and (3) lack of professional training on the topic.

Magnification or Minimization of Negative Coping Styles and Harmful Religiosity

Not all religious and spiritual practices are healthy (Richards & Bergin, 1997). In some cases, zealous devotion can cause excessive and unproductive shame, entrench mechanical rituals to the point of compulsion, restrict intellectual exploration, or reinforce fatalistic perceptions that undermine a need to improve social conditions

(Gotterer, 2001). Witch hunts, the transitory euphoria of religious revival meetings, possession syndromes among folk religionists, and a host of questionable to clearly negative mental health outcomes can be associated with spiritual practices or religious dogmas (Rhi, 2001). People can unproductively blame God for their problems, demonstrate excessive dependence on rituals or leaders, or engage in various other forms of negative coping detailed elsewhere (Pargament, 1997). Clinicians and researchers may therefore raise legitimate concerns about *how* certain spiritual or religious practices and doctrines are interpreted and acted out. For example, because religious language and imagery tend to be abstract and symbolic, clinicians should appropriately monitor their emphasis on religious themes with clients who have a history of delusional or magical thinking (Fallot, 2001). In such cases, "the area between providing validation and a reality check can be blurry" (Gotterer, 2001, p. 191).

Rather than deal with this complexity, some scholars and clinicians have artificially reduced the blurriness of the topic by either critically magnifying the negative aspects of religion to the point of obscuring the positive aspects (Freud, 1927) or else naïvely focusing on the positive aspects and minimizing potential negative aspects (see Smith et al., 2003). Optimal practice and research will expend effort to determine when clients warrant validation or a reality check through careful assessment of the degree to which the style of religious coping is both helpful and potentially harmful for the client. Furthermore, because negative religious coping styles often represent dysfunction in other areas of the client's life, this information can augment effective treatment and referrals. Therapists can help clients identify both helpful and harmful consequences of their beliefs and actions without inappropriately magnifying or minimizing those consequences (Richards & Bergin, 1997).

Narrow Interpretations of Empiricism

The scientist-practitioner model of training and the philosophy of empiricism from whence this model is derived are meant to help mental health professionals remain as objective as possible, replacing personal beliefs and values with empirical data. This emphasis on observable data has led some to conclude that science and religion are strictly incompatible (e.g., National Academy of Sciences, 1984). Therefore, suspicion of any claim to knowledge not based on the five senses may still impede serious scholarship in the area (Slife et al., 1999). However, as so many theorists have shown in recent years, religion and science can be quite compatible, particularly once researchers and scholars recognize that empiricism is not immune from human values, nor can it provide truly objective data (Bergin, 1980; Haque, 2001; Richards & Bergin, 1997). Religion and spirituality can be objectified to a certain extent, but can also be considered within narrative and dialectic frameworks (Slife et al., 1999).

Need for Professional Training

Unless current research and theory regarding religion and spirituality becomes infused in graduate school curricula, the future will be much like the past. Practitioners can be expected to practice only within the bounds of their competence, and without additional training practitioners may not be competent to address the spiritual and religious issues presented by their clients (Fukuyama & Sevig, 1999; Souza, 2002). At present, even "multicultural" education does not sufficiently inform students about religious or spiritual issues (Ribak-Rosenthal & Kane, 1999). A survey of APA-accredited clinical psychology programs found that only 57% of multicultural courses explicitly include issues of faith (Brawer, Handal, Fabricatore, Roberts, & Wajda-Johnson, 2002). This same survey found that only 17% of training programs make a systematic effort to address the topic, and most address it only superficially or on a strictly intellectual level. Nevertheless, because an understanding of a client's experience of faith, similar to experience with race, entails emotive and experiential awareness, care must be taken in the development of training models and texts to provide more than superficial coverage of the topic.

Even though professional standards are being revised to specifically include competence in spiritual and religious diversity (W. R. Miller, 1999), very few training models have been developed (Souza, 2002; Speight et al., 1991), a deficit that limits the likelihood of systematic implementation. Treatment models that explicitly integrate spirituality and mental health (e.g., L. J. Myers et al., 1991; J. E. Myers, Sweeney, & Witmer, 2000; Richards & Bergin, 1997) have not yet become widely acknowledged and adopted. Thus, even though some psychologists are already using spiritual interventions in psychotherapy (Richards & Potts, 1995), many lack even a basic knowledge of minority religious groups (Ribak-Rosenthal & Kane, 1999). In sum, making spirituality one of the major themes of a racial-cultural psychology (D. W. Sue et al., 1999) entails a substantial increase in training initiatives.

Obstacles Discussed in the Literature That Relate to Value Conflicts

At another level, certain values and beliefs prevalent in the field present obstacles to the integration of issues of faith into racial-cultural psychology and counseling. These potential conflicts are partly due to historical influences in psychology, but they are also partly due to the influences of contemporary Western culture. They include several sources of bias against organized religion that often remain implicit in discussions of the topic. For racial-cultural psychology and counseling to integrate religious and spiritual issues, these biases must be addressed.

Materialistic Values

Values of materialism embedded throughout all aspects of contemporary society conflict with many spiritual principles and religious teachings. Devotion to technology, wealth, and personal recognition characterize both North American society and the mental health professions. In such a climate, spiritual and religious tenets that contradict materialism and material explanations of human behavior may be suspect because they go against the grain of popular thinking (Rhi, 2001). "The notion of spirituality is [seen as] irrelevant to everyday life or has a specious image projected onto it by our materialistic culture" (Gotterer, 2001, p. 191).

The "Religiosity Gap"

Several surveys have shown that mental health professionals, psychologists in particular, are notably less likely to endorse religious tenets than are members of the general public (e.g., Shafranske, 2000). This so-called religiosity gap (Fallot, 2001, p. 83) may account for the reluctance of some clinicians to address clients' religious experiences in their practice. Gotterer (2001) has noted that clinicians' reactions to the topic of religion can roughly be broken down into three types:

> (a) those who are spiritual and/or religious but able to acknowledge others' beliefs; (b) those uncertain about religious and spiritual beliefs and wary of entering into this territory; and (c) those turned off altogether by either religion and spirituality, or religion in particular. (p. 191)

To overcome the effects of the religiosity gap as a potential barrier to integrating issues of faith in psychology and counseling, professionals should explicitly recognize their own personal values regarding spirituality and religion. For example, therapists who have had negative personal experiences with religious institutions or their leaders can work through their own negative feelings so as to effectively assist others in working through their issues.

Dichotomizing Religion versus Spirituality

Although only 48% of psychologists report that religion is important to them, 73% strongly endorse the importance of spirituality (Shafranske, 2000). Not surprisingly, this emphasis on spirituality over religion is also prevalent in the mental health literature, which tends to draw a clear distinction between religiosity and spirituality. Many authors seem to prefer speaking about spirituality, ostensibly because it is a broader concept and lacks the baggage associated with specific institutions (Fallot, 2001). Metaphorically, it is as if spirituality is the substance worthy of attention, while religion is but one of many ways one can attempt to capture that substance in a container of a particular shape and size. The container (religion) is assumed irrelevant, as long as the substance (spirituality) is addressed. Spirituality, as commonly understood in Western culture, is essentially an intrapersonal and highly subjective (i.e., *psychological*) experience.

However, perspectives emphasizing the differences between spirituality and religion are less common in cultures in which the distinctions between the social aspects of religion and the psychological aspects of spirituality are not always clear (Carr, 2000; Mbiti, 1990; O'Connor, 1998). Even in Western cultures, where many individuals reject religion but embrace spirituality, the two constructs overlap substantially (Hill et al., 2000). Religious devotion often involves intensely personal and private experiences or practices; more to the point, among some individuals and groups, their religion can be practiced as *a way of life* that is internalized and assumed to address a universal essence, not merely as a set of external social prescriptions. Unfortunately, by drawing a clear distinction between spirituality and religiosity, psychologists may unintentionally minimize the values and experiences of certain clients, particularly those who view life in more holistic and less dichotomous terms. As has been noted:

> [A] sharp and judgmental separation between [religion and spirituality], especially for counselors, is neither sound nor constructive. . . . To omit either, to artificially separate

them, or to confuse their special meanings would be to distort or trivialize the deep and diverse religious/spiritual attitudes that so many people hold and bring to counseling. (Kelly, 1995, pp. 7–8)

Concerns about Intrusiveness

Some clinicians may feel that addressing spiritual issues with clients feels too intrusive or that it violates social norms that tend to avoid discussion of religious topics (Fallot, 2001; Gotterer, 2001). Indeed, clients' spiritual and religious experiences may be difficult topics to discuss openly. However, therapy commonly addresses other difficult topics, such as racial dynamics, sexuality, abuse, and a host of undesirable behaviors embarrassing to the client. Thus, it is questionable why issues of faith receive special exclusion from therapy. To remove this potential barrier, the possibility that therapists' personal discomfort with spirituality and/or religion can be projected onto clients should be explored (Souza, 2002).

Concerns about Imposition of Values

Throughout recorded history, people in positions of power have foisted their religious and spiritual beliefs and practices on others. With that context in mind, it has been argued that professionals who discuss issues of faith with clients or who use spiritual interventions are in danger of imposing their own values on clients (e.g., Richards & Potts, 1995; L. Seligman, 1988). For example, when a client adheres to atheism, it is possible that a therapist who holds strong religious convictions may directly or indirectly attempt to change the client's atheistic values. This is a serious concern that may lead some professionals to avoid addressing spiritual issues in therapy altogether.

Without question, incorporation of spiritual perspectives into psychotherapy brings value issues to the foreground (Richards & Bergin, 1997). However, there is currently no evidence that therapists who integrate faith issues into treatment are more likely to impose their values on clients than are other therapists. In fact, some have argued that therapists who make their values explicit in therapy (rather than leaving them implicit) are less likely to impose their values on clients (Bergin, 1980, 1991; Bergin, Payne, & Richards, 1996; Richards & Bergin, 1997). Nevertheless, it is important to emphasize that all therapists have a responsibility to monitor their own values and to avoid imposing their own values on clients (American Counseling Association, 1995). In light of the reality that many people approach life from a spiritual perspective (Keller, 2000), this injunction could include monitoring the promotion of secular values among therapists who insist on excluding spiritual issues from treatment (Bergin, 1980).

Conflicting Political Agendas

Religious groups sometimes identify themselves closely with a political party or with a clear political agenda (e.g., the Fundamentalist Right in the United States, Protestants and Catholics in Northern Ireland). When those political agendas conflict with psychological research or with the personal values of a psychologist, organized religion can become a source of tension in therapy. Unfortunately, there is a tendency to dismiss religion in general because of the political motives of a few groups (e.g., defamation of Islam based solely on the actions of a few extremists) and a similar tendency to treat all religious groups as if they share the same characteristics (Queener & Martin, 2001). Generalized bias against certain religious traditions may influence some professionals to perceive all organized religion as oppressive or to continue to denounce specific sects long after they have changed their official policies and practices.

Patriarchy and Sexism

As has been noted by Funderburk and Fukuyama (2001), "Spirituality and religion are imbedded in patriarchal structures" (p. 7). Men have traditionally been the leaders of spiritual and religious movements, with women frequently excluded from public recognition and organizational authority. Women may therefore feel invisible or disrespected in patriarchal organizational structures. They may feel encouraged to keep silent, sacrifice themselves for the benefit of men, and inhibit their natural inclinations and desires, all emphases that conflict with the tenets of feminism. Nevertheless, feminist approaches to therapy have acknowledged the integral nature of spirituality and the intrinsic benefits of faith, particularly a faith rooted in relational and egalitarian structures that minimize the harmful effects of sexism (Funderburk & Fukuyama, 2001).

Oppression and Racism

Throughout recorded history, religion has been used to justify subjugation and tyranny but has also inspired liberation and equality. It has contributed to widespread oppression but also to worldwide charitable relief efforts and mutually beneficial intergroup exchange. It has aided in the fight against racial segregation in public institutions, yet religious institutions themselves have been and continue to be highly racially segregated. In addressing the complex and contradictory associations between religion and racial prejudice, Gordon Allport's observation of nearly 50 years ago is still true: "Some people say the only cure for prejudice is more religion; some say the only cure is to abolish religion" (1954, p. 444). This contradiction and the lingering impact of racial injustices present an obstacle to the integration of spiritual and religious issues into racial-cultural counseling that warrants an examination of the relevant research literature.

Following the horrors of the Holocaust, researchers investigating the complex association of religion and racism came to the perhaps ironic conclusion that individuals who accepted an organized religion were more prejudiced in their racial attitudes than were nonreligious individuals (e.g., Adorno, Frenkel-Brunswik, Levinson, & Sanford, 1950). This finding was replicated across several studies (Gorsuch & Aleshire, 1974), although many of them were limited in external validity and in methodological rigor (Scheepers, Gijsberts, & Hello, 2002).

In explaining why religion may actually increase racial prejudice, Allport asserted that "the chief reason why religion becomes the focus of prejudice is that it usually stands for more than faith—it is the pivot of the cultural tradition of the group" (1954, p. 446). Original religious teachings are misinterpreted and modified over time to match cultural contexts (Rhi, 2001). Allport pointed out that this blending of cultural and religious/spiritual beliefs often leads to the presumption that social values hold the same sacrosanct status as faith values. When this occurs, it becomes fairly easy to distort and abuse religious/spiritual principles (Davies, 1988), a distortion that may then serve as a front for those seeking power at the expense of others. Religious values mixed with cultural values represent fundamental sources of power and privilege frequently associated with political agendas (e.g., Servin & Torres-Reyna, 1999), as noted above. Religious teachings that in their original form advocated mutual respect and goodwill therefore can become corrupted into tools for manipulation or exploitation.

In addressing this important topic, Allport (1954) also proposed that religion influences people (and their racial biases) in two seemingly incompatible ways because there are two distinct types of motivations for religious practice. First, there are *extrinsics,* who use religion for their own ends, ranging in magnitude from desires to simply expand social circles to desires for power or wealth. Second, *intrinsics* devoutly seek individual and, ultimately, world peace through internalizing positive, pro-social values.

This intrinsic-extrinsic paradigm of religious orientation is perhaps the most widely examined theoretical framework in the literature (Donahue, 1985). However, much of the research based on it has been contradictory or inconclusive, suggesting a possible curvilinear relationship. For example, several researchers have found no linear relationship between degree of religious/spiritual commitment and racial attitudes (e.g., Boivin, Darling, & Darling, 1987; Boivin, Donkin, & Darling, 1990). However, others have found that strong, but not nominal, intrinsic religious commitment is associated with lower levels of prejudice (e.g., Fulton, 1997; Ponton & Gorsuch, 1988). Thus, although moderate support for Allport's (1954) theory has been provided, it is now clear that the relationship between religious/spiritual variables and racist attitudes depends on the context (Cygnar, Jacobson, & Noel, 1977; Griffin, Gorsuch, & Davis, 1987; Jackson & Hunsberger, 1999). Important moderators include age, educational level, degree of geographical religious homogeneity, and the type of religiousness being assessed (e.g., Scheepers et al., 2002). Specifically, older and less educated populations tend to endorse more religious beliefs than do younger and more educated populations, but they also endorse more racist beliefs than do younger and more educated populations (for reasons unrelated to religion). Similarly, geographic areas with high religious homogeneity tend to have more racial bias than regions with religious heterogeneity. The type of religious activity being measured also influences the association: Behavioral adherence to religious doctrines is associated with racial tolerance, whereas religious particularism is associated with racial prejudice. In sum, the association between religiousness and racism is complex because there are many factors that moderate and mediate the relationship. Depending on the context, religion can increase tolerance or intolerance. This complexity will need to be considered carefully in efforts to integrate spirituality and religion into racial-cultural psychology and counseling, such that moderating factors and the politicization of religion are openly acknowledged and considered in connection with the faith professed by individuals.

Pragmatic Obstacles for Future Scholarship

At another level, an obstacle to integrating issues of faith into racial-cultural psychology and counseling is the current dearth of quality research and theory specific to the topic. Unless quality work becomes more prevalent, the movement will disappear in a few short years. Three obstacles that could prevent the movement from flourishing are lack of interdisciplinary collaboration, failure to address the native complexity of the topic, and failure to develop a consistent and precise lexicon to describe spiritual and religious experiences and conditions.

Interdisciplinary Collaboration

As described in the foregoing review of the literature, until only recently much of the research and theory concerning spirituality and religiosity has developed separately from efforts to promote racial-cultural psychology. Researchers across disciplines have rarely interacted, largely keeping to their own journals and professional associations. Thus, many of the efforts by scholars to integrate issues of spirituality and religion into racial-cultural psychology and counseling have tended to lack rigor or depth. Most publications on the topic are opinion papers; empirical research is scarce. We have yet to see widely recognized theoretical models of human development, personality, pathology, and so on that explicitly address issues of faith. Therefore, some scholars have simply taken existing models from the racial-cultural literature and applied them to spiritual and religious issues (e.g., the construct of "White privilege" altered to "Christian privilege," models of racial identity development modified into models of spiritual identity development). The field might advance more quickly if, rather than alter racial-cultural theories to fit religious and spiritual issues, efforts focused on increased collaboration with anthropologists, family scientists, political scientists, psychologists, sociologists, and religious scholars already grounded in theory and research specific to spiritual and religious issues.

Complexity

Like mental health and culture, religiosity and spirituality are exceedingly complex. Underlying this complexity is the fact that religious and spiritual behaviors, like culture and mental health, are multiply determined. For example, even observable behaviors such as church attendance are moderated and mediated by many factors (age, education, physical ability, upbringing and previous experiences, perceptions of religious leaders, social skills, personal motivations, etc.), most of which are frequently ignored by researchers to the extent that church attendance alone may be falsely assumed to equate with level of religiosity. Further compounding the complexity is that there are multiple aspects of religiosity, including attitudinal (e.g., doctrinal beliefs), behavioral (e.g., orthodoxy), relational (e.g., prayer and worship), and perceptual (e.g., God image). Examination of religiosity, therefore, requires that moderators and mediators be specified, with a clear description of the *type* of religiosity to be assessed. As research efforts improve in specificity, the results will be more valid and more useful in informing theory and practice. Nevertheless, amid the resulting reductionism aimed at improving specificity for purposes of measurement and analysis, care must be taken to maintain open dialectics that provide the essential context for empirical inquiry (Slife et al., 1999).

Linguistic Difficulties

As has been noted, "a challenging aspect of research in the realm of spirituality is the ineffable quality spiritual experiences have that render their symbolization with language very difficult" (Ingersoll, 1998, pp. 161–162). Simply put, language is sometimes inadequate to convey spiritual content. In clinical settings, a client may therefore have difficulty describing spiritual experiences (Souza, 2002) much in the same way he or she might have difficulty describing the taste of a flavorful ethnic food to a friend who is unfamiliar with that particular cuisine. Adjectives such as spicy, sweet, and sour may give a general impression of the flavor and may even allow the listener to categorize it as being similar to or different from familiar foods. However, any description of personal experience will be both subjective and imprecise, leaving the hearer with a fuzzy impression and the speaker with a sense of mild frustration. This is particularly true when attempting to describe a religious or spiritual experience, where terms such as peaceful, loving, and joy represent emotive states that are very general and do not convey distinctions between an experience specifically perceived as *spiritual* versus any other positive event. Thus, research in the area faces some difficulty in using terms that have sometimes been inconsistent and/or imprecise. For example, the terms *faith development, faith maturity,* and *spiritual maturity* have all been used to describe similar processes, with different authors attributing their own unique variations to the definition and assessment of each (e.g., Hill & Hood, 1999). Similarly, despite their widespread use, concepts such as spiritual well-being, fundamentalism, and extrinsic religiosity have been disputed and subdivided by various authors (e.g., Batson & Ventis, 1982; Malony, 1977; Richards & Bergin, 1997).

A related potential difficulty comes from construct overlap. Many descriptions of core spiritual values, embodied in terms such as hope and connectedness (Cook & Kelly, 1998; Ingersoll, 1998), are hard to distinguish from definitions of wellness. Few scholars would argue that spiritual health and mental health are the same construct. Most of the research literature assumes that faith positively influences wellness. Nevertheless, overlap in definitions could account for research affirming a positive association between mental health and spirituality, rather than any causal processes. This issue clearly warrants clarification because interpretation of research findings will depend completely on how faith is operationally defined.

However, just because a topic is difficult to define does not mean that it cannot be defined. It is possible to examine spirituality with scientific rigor (Bergin, 1980). Despite imprecise language, dozens of measures of spirituality and religious involvement have been shown to be psychometrically robust (Hill & Hood, 1999). And although there is certainly need for greater specificity, people do seem to understand what is meant by the global terms *spiritual* and *religious*. We therefore take the perspective that faith can be described with some consistency, just as food taste can be described, so long as the terms have similar meanings across people and are sufficiently specific. Future research needs to develop a consistent and specific expanded lexicon to better address how faith, mental health, and culture intersect and influence one another. Simultaneous with the development of such terms is the development of quality theories that articulate the intersections between race and culture. To that end, the following section provides an overview of some basic interactions between faith and culture, with accompanying recommendations for future theory development and empirical research.

THE INTERSECTIONS OF FAITH AND CULTURE: FRUITFUL AREAS OF THEORY DEVELOPMENT AND EMPIRICAL RESEARCH

Although psychological theories specific to race and culture and specific to religion and spirituality have been developed over the past several decades, only a few scholars have considered the overlap and interactions between these related sets of variables (e.g., Fukuyama & Sevig, 1999; L. J. Myers, 1988). A central assertion of these scholars is that cultural mores and spiritual or religious expressions of faith are intricately intertwined, each influencing the other in myriad ways. In some societies, such as contemporary European nations, this mutual influence is minimal or predominantly in the direction of culture influencing religion (Höllinger & Smith, 2002). For example, many Protestant Christian denominations have altered their official policies and practices to conform with social norms, such as in the ordination of women to church offices. In other societies, such as contemporary North African nations, the influence can be quite notable in the opposite direction: religion strongly influences culture. For example, public laws on alcohol consumption reflect the teachings of Islam. In societies with high religious homogeneity, this mutual influence of culture and religion is generally accepted (e.g., Thailand), while in societies with religious heterogeneity it can be a source of conflict (e.g., Sri Lanka). Paralleling these social processes are equivalent psychological processes, such that within any given group an individual may or may not experience a significant influence or internal conflict due to factors of this sort. Acknowledging these potential influences and interactions at both the societal and individual level can facilitate improved understanding of societies' and individuals' identities, motivations, values, and so on. In short, improved understanding of others' worldview and well-being will come as scholars develop and refine theoretical models inclusive of both faith and culture.

Fundamental to the development of integrated models is an understanding of the ways culture and religion/spirituality can serve similar psychological functions. Both culture and faith provide individuals with a template to contextualize most aspects of life, allowing for comprehension amid chaos (Cook & Kelly, 1998; Hong, Morris, Chiu, & Benet-Martinez, 2000). Both religion and culture provide meaning and a predictable social structure, making them relevant to and indeed inseparable from psychological inquiry. Both influence not only the way mental health is perceived and treated but also the way people act and see themselves generally. An optimal approach to theory development, therefore, considers not only the relevance of an individual's internalized spiritual and cultural meanings to mental health symptoms (e.g., Bishop, 1992), but also the impact of such meanings on an individual's identity, motivations, and values.

Identity

Both religion/spirituality and culture provide a context in which individuals can compare and contrast their own attributes and experiences with those of others who are similar and dissimilar. Through such comparisons and contrasts, children and adolescents develop their basic identity (Erikson, 1985). Because identity is developed in relation to others, it can serve as an important buffer against distress. That is, individuals who see themselves in terms of cultural and religious/spiritual groups perceive themselves as belonging to larger collectives, a shared identity that can provide emotional resources and the security of knowing that one is not alone.

Motivation

One's perspective of self and others has clear implications for one's actions. Faith and culture shape behavior. They both hold the promise of rewards for certain behaviors and punishments for others. They both provide for proximal and distal outcomes that can be consequential and pervasive. Thus, culture and faith are among the strongest motivators for group behavior.

The influence of culture and faith in motivating a group is most notably demonstrated in cases of intergroup conflict, such as those in contemporary Indonesia, Bosnia, Sri Lanka, Northern Ireland, and Tibet, where religious differences rouse millions. Multiple examples from across the globe and across history could also be cited. Similarly, at the individual level, a person who perceives a threat to her or his culture and/or faith mobilizes defenses if her or his identity seems to be under attack.

Additionally, cultures and faiths also motivate groups and individuals to higher achievement and to resilience in the face of opposition. For example, the history of Jewish peoples demonstrates how cultural and theistic motivations have maintained collective group identity for approximately 3,000 years. For an individual, a cause worth sacrificing for in times of peace is often worth dying for in times of oppression.

Values

Culture and faith provide identity and motivation because they inform values. They give life flavor and texture, which can then be shared and affirmed. They shape social structures that model and reify normative action and discourse, with even language becoming an act of values preservation. Culture and faith allow for judgment and, by extension, internalization, labeling what is bad or good, defining what is "me" or "not me." In short, both faith and culture define what is health, what is illness. They define a person's or a group's psychology.

Cultural and faith values tend to be similar within a given individual or group because unresolved contradictions between culture and religion, although sometimes present, are usually minimized or dismissed. Through processes that reduce cognitive dissonance (Festinger, 1957), when one's faith and culture are at odds, an individual will tend to modify one or the other. For example, an individual may have to choose between a cultural expectation/ceremony that involves alcohol consumption and a religious prohibition of alcohol. A person can value only so many things, and the most salient values are preserved. Once internalized, values become a schema through which life is seen. They provide the individual with a perspective of a world created in her or his own image. Cultural and faith values impress themselves on the external world, but such is usually useful and even necessary (Hong et al., 2000; Richardson et al., 1999).

It is hoped that an increase in scholarly attention to the kinds of relationships described here will spur the much needed development and refinement of psychological theories integrating race, culture, and faith to enhance our understanding individuals' and groups' worldviews and well-being. And although some existing models have begun to address these issues (e.g., L. J. Myers, 1988), future research can clearly facilitate exploration and then confirmation of ways in which faith and culture combine to influence mental health and wellness.

Recommendations for Future Research

Repeated assertions of the need to conduct research investigating possible relationships between cultural and spiritual/religious contexts appear in the current literature (e.g., Bishop, 1992; Constantine, 1999; Fukuyama & Sevig, 1999; Richards & Bergin, 2000). Yet, even across a variety of sources, several consistent themes can be distilled.

First, research is needed into ways counseling and psychotherapy can be made more compatible with faith perspectives (Braun-Williams, Wiggins-Frame, & Green, 1999). Because faith beliefs and faith practices have such a strong influence on many people and because faith values may sometimes conflict with values advocated in the mental health professions, a tendency to openly mistrust psychological treatment may be noted among religious individuals (e.g., Cinnirella & Loewenthal, 1999). Moreover, some religious traditions view mental illness as a deserved punishment from supernatural sources, so treatment that responds to issues of stigmatization should be investigated. Similarly, because some cultures make little distinction between spiritual and mental health, the effectiveness of interventions that incorporate full physical/emotional involvement or specific spiritual methods can be investigated relative to traditional "talk therapies" (e.g., Wiggins-Frame, Braun-Williams, & Green, 1999). Case studies that inform the integration of spiritual perspectives into treatment (e.g., Shimabukuro, Daniels, & D'Andrea, 1999) can help to refine such practices, which can then be assessed via traditional outcome research methodologies.

Related to this compatibility issue is a second area for future research: the need to identify unique mental health issues of specific religious/spiritual groups and subgroups. Animists, ethnic religionists, and spiritists of African, Asian, and Latin

American origin, along with Jains, Sikhs, and Zoroastrians, are among those whose beliefs and practices are likely to be misunderstood by North American mental health practitioners. But misunderstanding is also likely with religious groups that are more prevalent, such as Hindus and Muslims. Research and other publications that help clarify unique symptom patterns, common differential diagnoses, and typical expectations relevant to mental health and therapy are needed (Richards & Bergin, 2000).

Third, study should be undertaken of the benefits of collaboration with local spiritual organizations and leaders (e.g., Kloos & Moore, 2000). Such collaboration can involve simultaneous treatment by a spiritual leader and a therapist or the establishment of effective referral networks. (For an example service delivery model, see Queener & Martin, 2001.) Because clergy are typically viewed with reverence and may exert great community influence, research specific to improving pastoral counseling efficacy may also be of benefit.

Fourth, the potential of faith traditions to buffer against negative influences such as racism should be studied. It may well be that an active faith shared in public settings with members of the same racial group facilitates a sense of protection or refuge from a larger society that does not share similar values and that oppresses racial differences. Similarly, because opportunities to gain social status are often limited for oppressed groups, the degree to which religious involvement serves to create an internal system of recognition and value could be explored (Boyd-Franklin, 1989).

Fifth, the process of spiritual and religious identity development needs to be articulated, particularly in relation to racial identity development, acculturation, and other racial/cultural factors known to influence therapy process and outcome (Carter, 1995). Although tentative models of spiritual identity have been proposed (e.g., Poll & Smith, 2003), research is clearly needed to refine these models and to specify their utility in clinical settings.

A sixth topic for future research concerns the efficacy of collectivistic versus individualistic approaches to mental health treatment. Because spiritual beliefs frequently emphasize the importance of connectedness and responsibility to others, treatment approaches that emphasize interpersonal interdependence can be developed and tested with populations who typically express these values. Treatments that emphasize a relational perspective (Smith & Draper, 2004) and that explicitly involve clients' support systems, including extended family, can be compared with traditional individual counseling.

Seventh, an alternative to professionally driven research agendas may be found in collaborative action research partnerships (e.g., Kloos & Moore, 2000), possibly an optimal way to meet local needs and at the same time reveal reforms that should be considered in our professional practices. Such research grounded in the experience of individuals and groups has a unique potential to inform psychological theory and practice.

Finally, and perhaps most important, the rationale and obstacles presented earlier in this paper for integrating faith perspectives into racial-cultural psychology and counseling should be addressed through ongoing, systematic empirical efforts.

Researchers need to specify the types of religiosity and spirituality that promote mental health while also addressing the types that yield negative consequences (e.g., Smith et al., 2003). Researchers need to assess the effectiveness of integrating faith perspectives into professional training programs (Souza, 2002). They should also address the conflicts that may hamper future work in the area, including issues of racial segregation and racism in religious institutions, disagreement over the politicization of religious tenets, and differences in materialistic versus spiritual perceptions of well-being. They should use research designs that can address the innate complexity of spirituality and religion, including assessment of variables that potentially moderate or mediate the association with mental health, such as time perspective, perceptions of stressful events and emotional pain, opportunities for and beliefs about emotional disclosure, social support, and behavior/belief congruency, each of which is also influenced by cultural factors. To address this complexity effectively, scholars will need to collaborate with colleagues in other disciplines and work toward the development of a systematic lexicon for describing and assessing spiritual experiences. Finally, although several studies using predominantly European American samples have documented that therapy inclusive of spiritual and religious content is just as effective as secular therapy and is particularly effective with religious clients (McCullough, 1999), additional work is necessary to confirm these findings across other cultural and racial groups.

Future scholarship on these and similar topics can improve our understanding of how race, culture, faith, and mental health interact. Racial-cultural psychology and counseling have the potential to affirm faith as a fundamental aspect of human nature (D. W. Sue et al., 1999). But there is much work to be done. Although we know a great deal about reducing distress and promoting wellness, there are many potentially helpful and harmful influences of spirituality and religion on mental health that we are only just beginning to document and understand.

REFERENCES

Adorno, T. W., Frenkel-Brunswik, E., Levinson, D. J., & Sanford, R. N. (1950). *The authoritarian personality.* New York: Harper & Row.

Akbar, N. (1995). *The community of self* (Rev. ed.). Talahassee, FL: Mind Productions.

Allport, G. W. (1950). *The individual and his religion.* New York: Macmillan.

Allport, G. W. (1954). *The nature of prejudice.* Cambridge, MA: Addison-Wesley.

American Counseling Association. (1995). *Code of ethics and standards of practice.* Alexandria, VA: Author.

Argyle, M., & Beit-Hallahmi, B. (1975). *The social psychology of religion.* London: Routledge.

Baez, A., & Hernandez, D. (2001). Complementary spiritual beliefs in the Latino community: The interface with psychotherapy. *American Journal of Orthopsychiatry, 71,* 408–415.

Batson, C. D., Schoenrade, P., & Ventis, W. L. (1993). *Religion and the individual: A social-psychological perspective.* New York: Oxford University Press.

Batson, C. D., & Ventis, W. L. (1982). *The religious experience: A social-psychological perspective.* New York: Oxford University Press.

Benyei, C. R. (1998). *Understanding clergy misconduct in religious systems: Scapegoating, family secrets, and the abuse of power.* New York: Haworth.

Bergin, A. E. (1980). Psychotherapy and religious values. *Journal of Consulting and Clinical Psychology, 48,* 75–105.

Bergin, A. E. (1983). Religiosity and mental health: A critical reevaluation and meta-analysis. *Professional Psychology: Research and Practice, 14,* 170–184.

Bergin, A. E. (1991). Values and religious issues in psychotherapy and mental health. *American Psychologist, 46,* 394–403.

Bergin, A. E., Payne, I. R., & Richards, P. S. (1996). Values in psychotherapy. In E. Shafranske (Ed.), *Religion and the clinical practice of psychology* (pp. 297–325). Washington, DC: American Psychological Association.

Bishop, D. R. (1992). Religious values as cross-cultural issues in counseling. *Counseling and Values, 36,* 179–191.

Boivin, M. J., Darling, H. W., & Darling, T. W. (1987). Racial prejudice among Christian and non-Christian college students. *Journal of Psychology and Theology, 15,* 47–56.

Boivin, M. J., Donkin, A. J., & Darling, H. W. (1990). Religiosity and prejudices: A case study in evaluating the construct validity of Christian measures. *Journal of Psychology and Christianity, 9,* 41–55.

Boyd-Franklin, N. (1989). *Black families in therapy: A multisystems approach.* New York: Guilford Press.

Boyd-Franklin, N. (2003). *Black families in therapy: Understanding the African American experience* (2nd ed.). New York: Guilford Press.

Braun-Williams, C., Wiggins-Frame, M., & Green, E. (1999). Counseling groups for African American women: A focus on spirituality. *Journal for Specialists in Group Work, 24,* 260–273.

Brawer, P. A., Handal, P. J., Fabricatore, A. N., Roberts, R., & Wajda-Johnson, V. A. (2002). Training and education in religion/spirituality within APA-accredited clinical psychology programs. *Professional Psychology: Research and Practice, 33,* 203–206.

Carnes, J. (1995). *Us and them: A history of intolerance in America.* Montgomery, AL: Teaching Tolerance, Southern Poverty Law Center.

Carstensen, L., Isaacowitz, D., & Charles, S. (1999). Taking time seriously: A theory of socioemotional selectivity. *American Psychologist, 54,* 165–181.

Carr, W. (2000). Some reflections on spirituality, religion, and mental health. *Mental Health, Religion, and Culture, 3,* 1–12.

Carter, R. T. (1995). *The influence of race and racial identity in psychotherapy.* New York: Wiley.

Cinnirella, M., & Loewenthal, K. (1999). Religious and ethnic group influences on beliefs about mental illness: A qualitative interview study. *British Journal of Medical Psychology, 72,* 505–524.

Constantine, M. G. (1999). Spiritual and religious issues in counseling racial and ethnic minority populations: An introduction to the special issue. *Journal of Multicultural Counseling and Development, 27,* 179–181.

Cook, E. P., & Kelly, V. (1998). Spirituality and counseling. *Counseling and Human Development, 30,* 1–16.

Cygnar, T. E., Jacobson, C. K., & Noel, D. L. (1977). Religiosity and prejudice: An interdimensional analysis. *Journal for the Scientific Study of Religion, 16,* 183–191.

Davies, A. (1988). *Infected Christianity: A study of modern racism.* Montreal, Canada: McGill-Queen's University Press.

Donahue, M. J. (1985). Intrinsic and extrinsic religiousness: Review and meta-analysis. *Journal of Personality and Social Psychology, 48,* 400–419.

Ellis, A. (1971). *The case against religion: A psychotherapist's view.* New York: Institute for Rational Living.

Erikson, E. H. (1985). *Childhood and society* (2nd ed.). New York: Norton.

Fallot, R. D. (2001). The place of spirituality and religion in mental health services. *New Directions for Mental Health Services, 91,* 79–88.

Festinger, L. (1957). *A theory of cognitive dissonance.* Evanston, IL: Row, Peterson.

Flory, J., Raikkonen, K., Matthews, K., & Owens, J. (2000). Self-focused attention and mood during everyday social interactions. *Journal of Personality and Social Psychology Bulletin, 26,* 875–883.

Freud, S. (1927). *The future of an illusion.* Garden City, NY: Doubleday.

Fowler, J. W. (1981). *Stages of faith: The psychology of human development and the quest for meaning.* San Francisco: Harper.

Fulton, A. S. (1997). Identity status, religious orientation, and prejudice. *Journal of Youth and Adolescence, 26,* 1–11.

Fukuyama, M., & Sevig, T. (1999). *Integrating spirituality into multicultural counseling.* Thousand Oaks, CA: Sage.

Funderburk, J., & Fukuyama, M. (2001). Feminism, multiculturalism, and spirituality: Convergent and divergent forces in psychotherapy. *Women and Therapy, 24*(3/4), 1–18.

Galanter, M. (1996). Cults and charismatic groups. In E. Shafranske (Ed.), *Religion and the clinical practice of psychology* (pp. 269–296). Washington, DC: American Psychological Association.

Gallup, G. (1995). *The Gallup poll: Public opinion in 1995.* Wilmington, DE: Scholarly Resources.

Garrett, M. T. (1999). Understanding the "medicine" of Native American traditional values: An integrative review. *Counseling and Values, 43,* 84–98.

Gartner, J. (1996). Religious commitment, mental health, and prosocial behavior: A review of the empirical literature. In E. Shafranske (Ed.), *Religion and the clinical practice of psychology* (pp. 187–214). Washington, DC: American Psychological Association.

George, L. K., Larson, D., Koenig, H. G., & McCullough, M. E. (2000). Spirituality and health: What we know, what we need to know. *Journal of Social and Clinical Psychology, 19,* 102–116.

Gorsuch, R., & Aleshire, D. (1974). Christian faith and prejudice: A review and interpretation of research. *Journal for the Scientific Study of Religion, 13,* 281–307.

Gotterer, R. (2001). The spiritual dimension in clinical social work practice: A client perspective. *Families in Society: Journal of Contemporary Human Services, 82,* 187–193.

Griffin, G. A. E., Gorsuch, R. L., & Davis, A. (1987). A cross-cultural investigation of religious orientation, social norms, and prejudice. *Journal for the Scientific Study of Religion, 26,* 358–365.

Haque, A. (2001). Interface of psychology and religion: Trends and developments. *Counselling Psychology Quarterly, 14*, 241–253.

Helms, J. E., & Cook, D. A. (1999). *Using race and culture in counseling and psychotherapy: Theory and process.* Boston: Allyn & Bacon.

Hill, P., & Hood, R. (Eds.). (1999). *Measures of religiosity.* Birmingham, AL: Religious Education Press.

Hill, P., Pargament, K., Hood, R., McCullough, M., Swyers, J. P., Larson, D. B., et al. (2000). Conceptualizing religion and spirituality: Points of commonality, points of departure. *Journal for the Theory of Social Behaviour, 30*, 51–77.

Höllinger, F., & Smith, T. B. (2002). Religion and esotericism among students: A cross-cultural comparative study. *Journal of Contemporary Religion, 17*, 229–249.

Hong, Y., Morris, M. W., Chiu, C., & Benet-Martinez, V. (2000). Multicultural minds: A dynamic constructivist approach to culture and cognition. *American Psychologist, 55*, 709–720.

Ingersoll, R. E. (1998). Refining dimensions of spiritual wellness: A cross-traditional approach. *Counseling and Values, 42*, 156–165.

Ingram, R. E. (1990). Self-focused attention in clinical disorders: Review and conceptual model. *Psychological Bulletin, 107*, 156–176.

Jackson, L. M., & Hunsberger, B. (1999). An intergroup perspective on religion and prejudice. *Journal for the Scientific Study of Religion, 38*, 509–523.

James, W. (1936). *The varieties of religious experience.* New York: Modern Library. (Original work published 1902)

Joiner, T. E., & Coyne, J. C. (1999). *The interactional nature of depression.* Washington, DC: American Psychological Association.

Jung, C. G. (1933). *Modern man in search of a soul.* New York: Harcourt, Brace & World.

Keller, R. (2000). Religious diversity in North America. In P. S. Richards & A. E. Bergin (Eds.), *Handbook of psychotherapy and religious diversity* (pp. 27–55). Washington, DC: American Psychological Association.

Kelly, E. W. (1995). *Religion and spirituality in counseling and psychotherapy.* Alexandria, VA: American Counseling Association.

Kloos, B., & Moore, T. (2000). The prospect and purpose of locating community research and action in religious settings. *Journal of Community Psychology, 28*, 119–137.

Koenig, H. G., McCullough, M. E., & Larson, D. B. (2001). *Handbook of religion and health.* New York: Oxford University Press.

Lee, C., Oh, M., & Mountcastle, A. (1992). Indigenous models of helping in nonwestern countries: Implications for multicultural counseling. *Journal of Multicultural Counseling and Development, 20*, 3–10.

Maddux, J. E. (Ed.). (1995). *Self-efficacy, adaptation, and adjustment: Theory, research, and application.* New York: Plenum Press.

Malony, H. N. (Ed.). (1977). *Current perspectives in the psychology of religion.* Grand Rapids, MI: Eerdmans.

Maslow, A. (1964). *Religion, values, and peak experiences.* Columbus: Ohio State University Press.

May, R. (1982). *The will and spirit: A contemplative psychology.* San Francisco: Harper & Row.

Mbiti, J. S. (1990). *African religions and philosophies* (2nd ed.). Portsmouth, NH: Heinemann.

McCullough, M. E. (1999). Research on religion-accommodative counseling: Review and meta-analysis. *Journal of Counseling Psychology, 46,* 92–98.

McRae, M. B., Carey, P., & Anderson-Scott, R. (1998). Black churches as therapeutic systems: A group process perspective. *Health Education and Behavior, 25,* 778–789.

Meadow, M. J., & Kahoe, R. D. (1984). *Psychology of religion: Religion in individual lives.* New York: Harper & Row.

Meissner, M. W. (1996). The pathology of beliefs and the beliefs of pathology. In E. Shafranske (Ed.), *Religion and the clinical practice of psychology* (pp. 241–267). Washington, DC: American Psychological Association.

Miller, G., Fleming, W., & Brown-Anderson, F. (1998). Spiritual Well-Being Scale: Ethnic differences between Caucasians and African Americans. *Journal of Psychology and Theology, 26,* 358–364.

Miller, W. R. (1999). *Integrating spirituality into treatment: Resources for practitioners.* Washington, DC: American Psychological Association.

Myers, D. G. (2000). The funds, friends, and faith of happy people. *American Psychologist, 55,* 56–67.

Myers, J. E., Sweeney, T. J., & Witmer, J. M. (2000). The wheel of wellness counseling for wellness: A holistic model for treatment planning. *Journal of Counseling and Development, 78,* 251–266.

Myers, L. J. (1988). *Understanding an Afrocentric world view: Introduction to an optimal psychology.* Dubuque, IA: Kendall/Hunt.

Myers, L. J., & Speight, S. L. (1994). Optimal theory and the psychology of human diversity. In E. Trickett, R. Watts, & D. Birman (Eds.), *Human diversity: Perspectives on people in context* (pp. 101–114). San Francisco: Jossey-Bass.

Myers, L. J., Speight, S. L., Highlen, P. S., Cox, C. I., Reynolds, A. L., Adams, E. M., et al. (1991). Identity development and worldview: Toward an optimal conceptualization. *Journal of Counseling and Development, 70,* 54–63.

National Academy of Sciences. (1984). *Science and creationism: A view from the National Academy of Sciences.* Washington, DC: Author.

Nolen-Hoeksema, S. (1991). Responses to depression and their effects on the duration of depressive episodes. *Journal of Abnormal Psychology, 100,* 569–582.

O'Connor, B. B. (1998). Healing practices. In S. Loue (Ed.), *Handbook of immigrant health* (pp. 145–162). New York: Plenum Press.

Oxford English dictionary. (2002). Retrieved June 18, 2002, from http://www.oed.com.

Pargament, K. I. (1997). *The psychology of religion and coping.* New York: Guilford Press.

Payne, I. R., Bergin, A. E., Bielema, K. A., & Jenkins, P. H. (1991). Review of religion and mental health: Prevention and the enhancement of psychosocial functioning. *Prevention in Human Services, 9,* 11–40.

Pedersen, P. B., Draguns, J. G., Lonner, W. J., & Trimble, J. E. (2002). *Counseling across cultures* (5th ed.). Thousand Oaks, CA: Sage.

Pennebaker, J. (1997). *Opening up: The healing power of expressing emotions* (Rev. ed.). New York: Guilford Press.

Philips, F. B. (1990). NTU psychotherapy: Afrocentric perspective. *Journal of Black Psychology, 17,* 55–74.

Poll, J., & Smith, T. B. (2003). The spiritual self: Toward a conceptualization of spiritual identity development. *Journal of Psychology and Theology, 31,* 129–142.

Ponton, M. O., & Gorsuch, R. L. (1988). Prejudice and religion revisited: A cross-cultural investigation with a Venezuelan sample. *Journal for the Scientific Study of Religion, 27,* 260–271.

Queener, J., & Martin, J. (2001). Providing culturally relevant mental health services: Collaboration between psychology and the African American church. *Journal of Black Psychology, 27,* 112–122.

Rhi, B. (2001). Culture, spirituality, and mental health: The forgotten aspects of religion and health. *Psychiatric Clinics of North America, 24,* 569–579.

Ribak-Rosenthal, N., & Kane, C. (1999). Minority religious practices: The need for awareness and knowledge. *Counseling and Values, 43,* 142–152.

Richards, P. S., & Bergin, A. E. (1997). *A spiritual strategy for counseling and psychotherapy.* Washington, DC: American Psychological Association.

Richards, P. S., & Bergin, A. E. (Eds.). (2000). *Handbook of psychotherapy and religious diversity.* Washington, DC: American Psychological Association.

Richards, P. S., & Potts, R. W. (1995). Using spiritual interventions in psychotherapy: Practices, successes, failures, and ethical concerns of Mormon psychotherapists. *Professional Psychology: Research and Practice, 26,* 163–170.

Richardson, F. C., Fowers, B. J., & Guignon, C. B. (1999). *Re-envisioning psychology: Moral dimensions of theory and practice.* San Francisco: Jossey-Bass.

Scheepers, P., Gijsberts, M., & Hello, E. (2002). Religiosity and prejudice against ethnic minorities in Europe: Cross-national tests on a controversial relationship. *Review of Religious Research, 43,* 242–265.

Seligman, L. (1988). Invited commentary: Three contributions of a spiritual perspective to counseling, psychotherapy, and behavior change. *Counseling and Values, 33,* 55–56.

Seligman, M. E. P. (1990). Why is there so much depression today? The waxing of the individual and the waning of the commons. In R. E. Ingram (Ed.), *Contemporary psychological approaches to depression: Theory, research and treatment* (pp. 1–9). New York: Plenum Press.

Servin, G., & Torres-Reyna, O. (1999). The polls—trends: Religion and politics. *Public Opinion Quarterly, 63,* 592–621.

Shafranske, E. (2000). Beliefs and training of psychotherapists. In A. E. Kazdin (Ed.), *Encyclopedia of psychology* (Vol. 7, pp. 46–48). Washington, DC: American Psychological Association.

Shimabukuro, K. P., Daniels, J., & D'Andrea, M. (1999). Addressing spiritual issues from a cultural perspective: The case of the grieving Filipino boy. *Journal of Multicultural Counseling and Development, 27,* 221–239.

Skinner, B. F. (1971). *Beyond freedom and dignity.* New York: Knopf.

Slife, B., Hope, C., & Nebeker, R. S. (1999). Examining the relationship between religious spirituality and psychological science. *Journal of Humanistic Psychology, 39,* 51–58.

Smith, T. B. (Ed.). (2004). *Practicing multiculturalism: Affirming diversity in counseling and psychology.* Boston: Allyn & Bacon.

Smith, T. B., & Draper, M. (2004). Understanding individuals in their context: A relational perspective of multicultural counseling and psychotherapy. In T. B. Smith (Ed.), *Practicing multiculturalism: Affirming diversity in counseling and psychology* (pp. 313–323). Boston: Allyn & Bacon.

Smith, T. B., McCullough, M. E., & Poll, J. (2003). Religiousness and depression: Evidence for a main effect and the moderating influence of stressful life events. *Psychological Bulletin, 116,* 614–636.

Souza, K. Z. (2002). Spirituality in counseling: What do counseling students think about it? *Counseling and Values, 46,* 213–217.

Speight, S. L., Myers, L. J., Cox, C. I., & Highlen, P. S. (1991). A redefinition of multicultural counseling. *Journal of Counseling and Development, 70,* 29–36.

Strommen, M. (Ed.). (1971). *Research on religious development: A comprehensive handbook.* New York: Hawthorn.

Sue, D. W., Bingham, R., Porche-Burke, L., & Vasquez, M. (1999). The diversification of psychology: A multicultural revolution. *American Psychologist, 54,* 1061–1069.

Sue, S. (1999). Science, ethnicity, and bias: Where have we gone wrong? *American Psychologist, 54,* 1070–1077.

Taylor, R., Mattis, J., & Chatters, L. M. (1999). Subjective religiosity among African Americans: A synthesis of findings from five national samples. *Journal of Black Psychology, 25,* 524–543.

Taylor, S., Kemeny, M., Reed, G., Bower, J., & Gruenewald, T. (2000). Psychological resources, positive illusions, and health. *American Psychologist, 55,* 99–109.

Trimble, J. E. (2000, August). *Spiritual affinity and its influence on acculturation and ethnic identification.* Presidential address given at the 108th annual convention of the American Psychological Association, Washington, DC.

Trusty, J., Sandhu, D. S., & Looby, J. (Eds.). (2002). *Multicultural counseling: Context, theory and practice, and competence.* Huntington, NY: Nova Science.

Vontress, C. E. (1996). A personal retrospective on cross-cultural counseling. *Journal of Multicultural Counseling and Development, 24,* 156–166.

Watson, J. B. (1924). *Behaviorism.* New York: Norton.

Wiggins-Frame, M., Braun-Williams, C., & Green, E. L. (1999). Balm in Gilead: Spiritual dimensions in counseling African American women. *Journal of Multicultural Counseling and Development, 27,* 182–192.

Worthington, E. L., Jr., Kurusu, T. A., McCullough, M. E., & Sandage, S. J. (1996). Empirical research on religion and psychotherapeutic processes and outcomes: A ten-year review and research prospectus. *Psychological Bulletin, 119,* 448–487.

Young, J. S., Cashwell, C. S., & Woolington, V. J. (1998). The relationship of spirituality to cognitive and moral development and purpose in life: An exploratory investigation. *Counseling and Values, 43,* 63–69.

PART II

Critical Issues in Racial-Cultural Research, Measurement, and Ethics

CHAPTER 10

Cultural Psychology: Its Early Roots and Present Status

Juris G. Draguns

CULTURE: ITS CONCEPTIONS IN ANTHROPOLOGY AND PSYCHOLOGY

Classical and Current Definitions

Culture is an inclusive and complex concept. Over more than a century, it has proved to be exceedingly difficult to define, fuzzy at its outer boundaries and elusive at its core. At the dawn of cultural anthropology, Edward Burnett Tylor (1871/1958) introduced culture as "that complex whole which includes knowledge, belief, art, morals, law, custom, and any other capabilities acquired by man as a member of society" (p. 1). Tylor construed culture as the link between individual human beings and their society, understood as "a group of people who occupy a particular territory and speak a common language not generally understood by the neighboring people" (Ember & Ember, 1996, p. 21). Society, then, refers to an organized aggregate of interacting persons and culture, to their shared skills and cognitions.

Tylor's statement unleashed a torrent of definitions that has not stopped to this day. Kroeber and Kluckhohn (1963) listed and analyzed 164 such statements. Their effort culminated in the following integrative formulation:

> Culture consists of patterns, explicit and implicit, of and for behavior acquired and transmitted by symbols, constituting the distinctive achievements of human groups, including their embodiments in artifacts; the essential core of culture consists of traditional (i.e., historically derived and selected) ideas and especially their attached values; cultural systems may on the one hand be considered as products of action, on the other as conditioning elements of further action. (p. 361)

In contrast to the length and complexity of the preceding statement, Herskovits (1948, p. 17) pithily captured the essence of culture by defining it as "the man-made part of the environment." Ember and Ember (1996, p. 20) appended the following specification: "For something to be considered cultural, it must be learned as well as shared."

In Hofstede's (1991) view, cultures provide mental programs for feeling, perceiving, thinking, and acting and thereby constitute "software of the mind" (p. 5). As Brislin (2000) asserts, culture enables people to fill in blanks in their percepts and impressions on the basis of culturally shared and assumed knowledge. Nobles (1985) described cultures as patterns for interpreting reality and providing general designs for living. He differentiated surface features, exemplified by language, customs, beliefs, and values, and a deeper level, consisting of fundamental worldviews and meanings.

Triandis (1972) proposed the concept of subjective culture to investigate "the way people categorize experience, their ideas about correct behavior, the way they view other people and groups of people, and the way they value entities in their environment" (Triandis, 1994, p. 87). Techniques have been developed for conducting research on meaningful social behavior in its specific cultural complex and for answering such questions as What kinds of behavior does the concept of hospitality imply for a guest in Greece and a host in Peru? What are the perceived antecedents and consequences of restoration of freedom in Poland, Portugal, the Philippines, and South Africa?

Dimensions of Culture

Culture originated as a qualitative concept, descriptive and explanatory but neither measurable nor comparable. Over the past four decades great strides have been made in identifying cultural traits that lend themselves to bicultural, multicultural, and worldwide comparisons.

A major landmark in this respect is Hofstede's (1980) study of work-related attitudes conducted on an unprecedented grand scale. In 50 countries and three more supranational regions, a total of 116,000 employees of a multinational corporation participated in this research. On the basis of multivariate analyses, four factors were extracted which Hofstede labeled power distance, individualism-collectivism, uncertainty avoidance, and masculinity-femininity. It is important to emphasize that these four dimensions refer to the characteristics of cultures and not of individuals. Therefore, they should not be equated or confused with personality traits.

The relationship between Hofstede's (1980) axes of cross-cultural comparison and psychological characteristics of persons in various cultures remains a promising topic of empirical investigation. In relation to individualism-collectivism (Triandis, 1995, 1996), research has yielded a multitude of findings. The status of individualism-collectivism as a construct capable of differentiating cultures and correlated with numerous psychological indicators on the individual level is well established, although questions remain as to the interpretation of the accumulated research findings (Kagitcibasi, 1997). For the other three variables identified by Hofstede, cultural differences have been hypothesized in the domains of schooling (Hofstede, 1991), subjective well-being (Arrindell et al., 1997), psychiatric symptomatology (Draguns, 1990), and psychotherapy (Draguns, 1997). As yet, these extensions of Hofstede's concepts into the areas of education and mental health have not been put to a rigorous and systematic test. Recently, however, Snider (2003) was able to demonstrate that Chinese counselees differed from their Australian and

American counterparts in their preferred counselors' interventions. Specifically, he found that the predominant determinant of counselees' preference was power distance among the Chinese, egalitarianism among the Australians, and individualism among the Americans.

Subsequently, Hofstede (1991, 2001) added a fifth cultural dimension, based not on factor analysis but on explicit Confucian tenets which allegedly animate economic growth in East Asia. Originally referred to as Confucian dynamism and more recently renamed long-term orientation, this construct has differentiated Chinese, Korean, and Japanese groups from Europeans and North Americans, whose expectations were geared to short-term rewards. Additional cultural dimensions are exemplified by activity versus passivity as a modality for dealing with challenges and stresses of living; by tightness, defined as a multiplicity of cultural rules and restrictions; and by cognitive complexity, characterized by a great many specific and differentiated social roles (Triandis, 1995).

Self in Culture

In the past two decades, formulations based on clinical observation (e.g., Roland, 1988) and research evidence (e.g., Markus & Kitayama, 1991) have converged in describing culturally distinctive self-experience. In individualistic cultures, the self is experienced as an autonomous, self-contained entity; in collectivistic cultures, as interdependent and open to social influence and penetration. An individualistic self erects boundaries between the person and other human beings in his or her environment; a collectivistic self builds bridges to other people (Chang, 1988). Conceivably, distinctive features of self-experience may be ascertained for Hofstede's other three dimensions as well (Draguns, 1997).

Ethnicity as Culture?

In culturally pluralistic societies, such as those of North America, ethnocultural groupings, based on race and/or national origin, are often regarded as discrete cultural categories. Phinney (1996), however, proposed to view ethnicity as a multidimensional, quantitative characteristic and identified three variables that should be assessed: concordance of values, attitudes, and behaviors with those that are considered normative for the ethnic group in question; choice of ethnic self-designation and identity; and experiences with the outgroup, often negative, that impress an ethnic designation on a person. Each of these aspects is potentially measurable by means of scales of identity and values as well as by measures of acculturation to the mainstream or dominant culture. Thus, ethnicity overlaps with culture, but should not be equated with it.

Emergence of Global Culture

Customarily, culture has been defined in relation to a specific time and place, which was shared by a finite number of people belonging to a tribe or a nation. This traditional concept of culture is being challenged by the rapid process of globalization throughout the world and by the consequent emergence of a worldwide culture. In contrast to most other cultures, global culture is not geographically delimited, and no definition for global culture has as yet been proposed. When such a definition is formulated, it will have to incorporate the pervasive connectivity among cultures, the emergence of mixed or hybrid cultures, the increasing pull toward uniformity (Hermans & Kempen, 1998), and the dynamic and dialectical relationship of global convergence to the attempts of the peoples around the world to preserve their distinctive cultural identities (Marsella, 1998).

Another challenge that facilitates the emergence of a world community is posed by the urgent, yet intractable problems on a planetary scale, from environmental degradation to global terrorism. Such problems can be tackled and eventually resolved only by a worldwide cooperative effort that would be fostered by an emerging sense of global solidarity and, eventually, global identity.

CONTRIBUTIONS FROM ANTHROPOLOGY

Culture and Psychology

Early descriptions of cultures did not emphasize psychological characteristics. The concerns of psychology and anthropology began to converge when two eminent anthropologists, Franz Boas and Bronislaw Malinowski, recognized the complementarity of the two disciplines. Two of Boas's students, Ruth Benedict and Margaret Mead, pioneered the investigation of psychological phenomena in their cultural context. Benedict (1934) described the patterns of the American Indian cultures she studied and related them to the personality types she identified. Mead (1928) described the experience of adolescence in Samoa, allegedly free of restrictions on sexual expressions. Her data may have been flawed (see Freeman, 1983) and her conclusions sweeping. However, she forged a link between anthropological observations in the field and psychological concepts that had hitherto been studied only in the psychologist's own cultural milieu, such as gender roles and socialization experiences.

On the foundation of early culture and personality research, Ralph Linton (1945), a cultural anthropologist, and Abram Kardiner (1945), a socially oriented psychoanalyst, proposed a division of effort, with psychoanalysts providing concepts and hypotheses and anthropologists supplying observations in the field, especially on such socialization experiences as weaning, toilet training, and control of childhood sexuality. The objective of this joint effort was expected to be the delineation of the modal personality, supposedly prevalent in a given social milieu.

In general, the yield of information collected in this manner turned out to be less conclusive than the proponents had hoped. More outspoken, Bruner (1974) pronounced the culture and personality approach a "magnificent failure" (p. 395). In retrospect, Bruner's negative conclusion appears to be too sweeping. Two possible exceptions to his critical characterization of the culture and personality endeavor are the thorough multimethod study of the relationship between socialization experience and adult personality in Alor in Indonesia by DuBois (1944) and Benedict's (1946) analysis of the major themes of Japanese culture and of their psychological implications. The noteworthy feature of the latter study is that it was conducted at a distance, during World War II, when there was no access to Japan. Still, in the judgment of more recent evaluators (cf. LeVine, 2001), Benedict succeeded in capturing some of the pivotal features of Japanese social interaction and personal values.

More recently, LeVine (2001) has corrected some widespread misconceptions about the culture and personality studies. Contrary to representation in a number of sources, the theoretical stance of the culture and personality investigators was pluralistic rather than monolithic, and psychoanalysis was only one of the psychological currents in the movement. Culture and personality researchers did not neglect individual differences in the culture, and the postulates of modal personality or national character were never universally accepted. Linking cultural features with psychological characteristics was the principal concern of the culture and personality scholars, and this area of inquiry continues to be pursued by several current strands of cultural investigation in psychology, psychiatry, and anthropology.

Psychological and Cognitive Anthropology

The concerns of the culture and personality pioneers were eventually absorbed into the broader framework of psychological anthropology. Psychological anthropologists are committed to the investigation of behavior and experience in their cultural context (Hsu, 1972). The orientation of contemporary psychological anthropologists is more pluralistic than that of the proponents of the culture and personality movement. As a group, they are more concerned with the place of meaningful psychological manifestations within their cultural framework than with simple stimulus-response sequences (Bock, 1999, 2000). Psychological anthropologists decry the excesses of positivism and operationalism and caution against the acceptance of the claims of universality of findings based on exported procedures and measures, even when such findings are processed by multivariate statistical techniques. Psychological anthropologists focus their interest on subjective experience rather than on overt behavior, and their research preference is for flexible and individualized methods rather than large-scale standardized and uniform procedures.

Another point of contact between anthropology and psychology is cognitive anthropology that addresses the question "What material phenomena are significant for people of some cultures and how do they organize these phenomena?" (Tyler, 1969, p. 3). Its emphasis is on the cognitive operations of people in their environment. A similar objective is posited for ethnoscience, such as ethnobotany and ethnomedicine, which strive to reconstruct folk classifications and explanations of different natural phenomena from a within-culture perspective (cf. Jahoda, 1982).

Human Research Area Files: Archival Anthropological Data for Worldwide Comparisons

Human Research Area Files (HRAF) is a repository of rigorously coded field reports and ethnographies gathered by anthropologists for over 150 years, making it possible to compare quantitatively and statistically hitherto incomparable qualitative cultural data. For worldwide or hologeistic comparisons, each culture included in the HRAF sample is considered a unit, and correlations are ascertained for the entire set of cultures. For over 40 years, numerous studies on psychological variables have been performed with this store of data, for example, Rohner's (1986) series of hologeistic investigation of parental warmth across the world in relation to its consequences later in the child's life.

HRAF was designed to maximize the range of variety in its sample of cultures. As a result, the interrelated cultures of the modern nation-states of Europe, North America, and Asia are minimally represented, while small, traditional, and isolated cultures are included well beyond their weight in numbers (Barry, 1980). In the HRAF sample of 400 coded cultures (Textor, 1967), only 11 cultures pertain to the nations and ethnic groups of Europe, and in the more intensively utilized probability sample of 60 cultural units, only three European cultures are found: Lapps, Serbs, and Highland Scots (Barry, 1980). In neither compilation is there any representation of such major European cultures as those of France, Germany, Italy, Russia, or Spain. However, for purposes of ascertaining functional relationships over the entire range of human adaptation, HRAF remains a unique and invaluable resource.

Interaction of Anthropology and Psychology

Although the modi operandi of psychological and cognitive anthropologists are different from those of psychologists, the relationships across the disciplinary lines are not antagonistic. The major problem is the mutual isolation of the two disciplines, not any acrimony between them. The Society for Cross-Cultural Research provides a forum for researchers in both fields and thereby presents opportunities for interdisciplinary dialogue. In Jahoda's (1982, p. 266) words, "There is a close kinship between psychology and anthropology, and we have much to learn from each other." An eventual integration of cross-cultural research by anthropologists and psychologists can be envisaged.

THE EXPANDING ROLE OF PSYCHOLOGY IN THE STUDY OF CULTURE

Wilhelm Wundt, the founder of experimental psychology, devoted the last 20 years of his life to the development of *Völkerpsychologie* (Wundt, 1911), literally, "psychology of the peoples," or better, ethnopsychology. Proceeding from his conviction that the experimental method was inapplicable to the study of complex cultural phenomena, he immersed himself in the investigation of such products of cultures as languages, myths, and customs. This effort did not provoke much resonance during Wundt's lifetime, and it virtually stopped after his death. Thus, Wundt did not inaugurate cross-cultural psychology, although he pioneered the recognition of the importance of the interface between culture and psychology and indirectly promoted its eventual investigation.

A contemporary of Wundt, W. H. R. Rivers, an experimental psychologist at Oxford University, went further and can be credited with being the first experimental investigator of psychological phenomena outside of his own culture. Rivers joined the anthropological expedition to the Torres Straits and succeeded in collecting data on sensory functioning of Trobriand Islanders off northern Australia.

In particular, his findings on the magnitude of visual illusions have stood the test of time and have retained their relevance (Jahoda, 1982, 1990).

Cross-Cultural Psychology: Its Origins and Characteristics

Between the early landmarks of research by Wundt and Rivers and the 1970s, cross-cultural ventures by psychological researchers remained episodic, isolated, and discontinuous. Although good research was sometimes conducted, no coherent body of cross-cultural findings emerged. In the 1960s, increased stirrings of cross-cultural curiosity and awareness came to be felt, with a somewhat larger number of psychologists engaging in a concerted pursuit of research objectives.

The efforts of a growing band of psychologists active in cross-cultural research coalesced at a meeting in Hong Kong in 1972 at which the International Association for Cross-Cultural Psychology was founded. Over three decades, the objectives, methods, and tasks of cross-cultural psychology have crystallized. Its aspirations and characteristics have been described as:

> the study of similarities and differences in individual psychological functioning in various cultural and ethnic groups; of the relationships between psychological variables and socio-cultural, ecological, and biological variables; and of changes in these variables. (Berry, Poortinga, Segall, & Dasen, 1992, p. 2)

In light of this definition, cross-cultural psychology is centrally concerned with the comparison of psychological variables across cultures, and with the sociocultural and environmental antecedents and determinants of behavior. The overriding ambition of cross-cultural psychologists is to blend the methodological acumen of contemporary psychological research at its best with the sensitivity to those cultural factors that may affect or distort such comparison.

The key concept that has emerged in this quest is equivalence, defined as the comparability of scores or responses obtained in two or more cultures (van de Vijver, 2001). Physically identical stimuli may not be equivalent across cultures in meaning or demand characteristics. Take, for example, the picture of a smiling face, which in one culture may connote friendliness, in another submissiveness, and in a third ridicule. The statement "I often prefer to stay alone for hours, away from my friends and family" may be an acceptable expression of a need for privacy in an individualistic culture; in a collectivistic milieu, the same test item may be viewed as indicative of social withdrawal. Other threats to equivalence may come from the context in which testing takes place or an experimental procedure is administered. In many cultures in which psychological methods of data gathering are little known, even routine questions may generate substantial stress. The resulting arousal may accentuate culturally determined attitudes of compliance, reticence, resistance, and resentment and may in turn affect the responses produced, thereby rendering the stimuli less equivalent. Frequently, the several aspects of equivalence exercise a pull in divergent directions and present the cross-cultural researcher with a dilemma. For example, is it more important in a specific situation to assure the psychical identity of the stimuli or to attend to their equivalence in valence and meaning? In their striving to assure equivalence, contemporary cross-cultural investigators have come up with ingenious solutions that help them approximate, if not always attain, equivalence. By comparison with their less reflective predecessors, they bring to the task a greater awareness of the complexities inherent in comparing human behavior and experience across cultures.

Similarly, the dual objectives of comparison of several cultures and of untangling the interrelationship of variables within one culture often diverge in cross-cultural research. Another choice with which cross-cultural investigators are confronted is that between etic and emic orientations. The former term, etic, refers to a comparison between two or more cultures by means of a concept that is presumed to be universally applicable; the latter term, emic, describes immersion into a phenomenon distinctive of or indigenous to a specific culture (Berry et al., 1992; Segall, Lonner, & Berry, 1998). Berry (1969) pointed out that in embarking on research in another culture, a researcher often cannot help but start with an emic concept from his or her own culture, which, on being transferred, becomes an imposed etic. In the optimal case, purified of the accretions from a culture of origin, it acquires the status of a derived etic, valid and applicable in both cultures. What is to be avoided is an assumed etic, one that naïvely holds that the concepts within one's own culture are universally applicable and that such constructs as anxiety and hostility can be studied by means of American measures everywhere.

During its brief history, cross-cultural psychology has been largely slanted toward etic investigations, although a smaller amount of emic research has also been pursued. In the process, major progress has been made in developing modes of comparison that are realistic and appropriate for members of all cultures participating in such research. Moreover, over the past decade, cross-cultural psychologists have concentrated on culturally sensitive investigations of the interrelationship of phenomena within a culture. The concepts employed in many of these studies are universal or etic, but the context within which they are observed is unique or characteristic of a given culture. Thus, emic and etic are no longer construed as mutually exclusive categories; rather, they are flexibly employed and creatively integrated. In a schematic form, Figure 10.1 represents the various choices and courses of action open to investigators of the interplay of psychology and culture. The two approaches admit of switching and hold open the possibility of eventual integration. For example, in the *Handbook of Chinese Psychology* edited by Bond (1996), findings of emic, etic, and mixed studies have been integrated into a coherent body of knowledge. More dimly on the horizon, there is the prospect of cross-cultural data contributing to the formulation of universal laws of psychology, an important aspiration ever since the pioneering contributions of Wundt and Rivers (Jahoda, 1990; Segall et al., 1998), perhaps in relation to the role of parental warmth (Rohner, 1986) in human socialization and individuation.

As a research enterprise, cross-cultural psychology remains methodologically oriented and ethically slanted. Great emphasis is placed on the control of variables through experimentation, utilization of fortuitous real-life circumstances, and complex and flexible statistical procedures. The greatest achievements of cross-cultural psychology have been the identification and vigorous study of dimensions

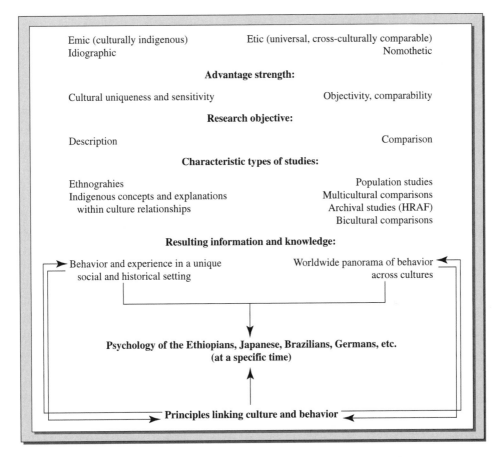

Figure 10.1   Cultural research in psychology: contrasting options.

of behavior that vary across cultures. The global construct of culture has been "un-packaged" (Betancourt & Lopez, 1993, p. 634), that is, broken down to specific and measurable characteristics, such as religiosity. No longer is culture being treated as an indivisible and complex whole. Instead, specific strands of cultural influence are being identified, sometimes in the form of cultural dimensions and syndromes (Triandis, 1996).

An Alternative Approach: Cultural Psychology

Under the banner of cultural psychology, a number of theoreticians and researchers have reacted against several characteristics of cross-cultural psychology. The basic controversy between these two camps revolves around the conceptualization of culture. Many cross-cultural researchers set out explicitly to investigate the influence of culture on behavior (cf. Brislin, 2000). In their view, culture can be clearly separated from the person. Cultural psychologists, however, view culture and behavior as inextricable. Therefore, they regard it as futile to study culture as though it were an external independent variable and to investigate behavior as a dependent variable.

Instead, Cole (1996) recommends concentrating on the study of individuals over time in their sociohistorical context and to regard them as active agents in their environment.

There is a special affinity between cultural psychology and developmental orientation, and cultural psychologists have excelled in conducting intensive case-based studies in a naturalistic setting (e.g., Valsiner, 1997). The culturalist approach is imbued with skepticism toward cross-cultural comparisons. In the culturalist view, behavior torn from its context loses meaning. Moreover, such attempts run the risk of comparing what is intrinsically incomparable and of yielding trivial or uninterpretable results in the process. It is apparent that cultural psychologists gravitate toward emic approaches in formulating problems, gathering observations, and coming to grips with the meaning of their findings. Moreover, culturalists refuse to draw a hard and fast line between their modus operandi and the qualitative methodologies more commonly associated with the humanities.

In the writings by culturalists, a sharp distinction is articulated between the cross-cultural and culturalist approaches of studying cultures and persons, and contrasts are emphasized. There is, however, one topic of investigation that holds out the prospect of convergence and perhaps of eventual integration. Both kinds of investigators accord central importance to the self; important contributions to the interlacing of self and culture have been made in the mainstream of cross-cultural psychology (Markus & Kitayama, 1991) and by investigators who are committed to a qualitative, phenomenological study of the self in its unique cultural context (Boesch, 1975, 1991; Kimura, 1995).

Indigenous and Ethnic Psychologies

Cultural psychology has much in common with the indigenous psychologies that are emerging in various parts of the world, perhaps in response to globalization (Marsella, 1998). Proponents of indigenous psychology (Kim & Berry, 1993) emphasize the uniqueness of various cultures and often consider personal and cultural characteristics as interwoven and inseparable. They are impressed with the less than perfect fit between the psychological systems imported from Europe and North America and the psychological reality of the countries outside of these regions. Díaz-Guerrero (1994) in Mexico and Enriquez (1990) in the Philippines have attempted to identify the characteristic themes of their respective cultures and to pinpoint recurrent traits. They have often tapped into the reservoir of local terms of psychological relevance and have studied their implications, connotations, and links to overt action. Thus, in Mexico, such terms as *simpatia, respeto, amor propio,* and *tristeza* have been proposed for psycholinguistic investigation (Diaz-Loving & Draguns, 1999). Indigenous psychology dips into local sources of psychological insight, and its aspiration is to construct a psychological system on the foundation of local concepts. At the same time, the incorporation of indigenous psychologies into an integrative and universal psychology has been envisaged as an ambitious and at this time remote goal (Berry & Kim, 1993). However, the thrust of indigenous psychology remains predominantly emic.

The burgeoning enterprise of racial and ethnic psychology in Canada, the United States, and elsewhere aims to recapture the investigation of ethnic groups for their own members. Early studies of African Americans, American Indians, and other groups were typically undertaken by behavioral and social scientists of other races. Current racial-cultural psychologies endeavor to provide an inside perspective of the characteristic phenomena of behavior and experience of the major racially distinctive components of the North American population. This effort eschews racial or ethnic comparisons, is more emic than etic in its conceptualization, and is centered on the phenomenon of identity, defined by Phinney (1996, p. 919) as "the subjective sense of group membership." Racial-cultural psychologists are interested not so much in the modal identities within a racial group as in meaningful variation among its members, associated, for example, with the salience of racial self-designation (Phinney, 1996). Among African Americans, Cross (1991) and Helms (1990) studied emically both racial identity and its variability across the life span.

Racial psychologists have been understandably reluctant to posit group characteristics in order to avoid their being misconstrued as stereotypes. Cautiously, however, Marin and Marin (1991) identified interdependence and crystallized gender roles as being prevalent among Hispanic Americans. Similarly, Uba (1994) pointed to the maintenance of harmonious relationships and fulfillment of interpersonal obligations as important strivings among Asian Americans, and Bennett (1994) listed generosity and cooperation among the prominent values of American Indians. On the level of deep structure, underlying but not coextensive with personal traits, the Afrocentric paradigm (Myers, 1992) hypothesizes continuity between traditional African cultural themes and psychological characteristics of contemporary African Americans, perhaps in the form of a holistic orientation, spontaneous self-expression, emphasis on synthesis, access to intuition, and strong communal ties. The same characteristics have emerged as prominent personality components among contemporary African populations (Okeke, Draguns, Sheku, & Allen, 1999).

Ethnicity and Race: An Attempt at Clarification

The concepts of ethnicity and race overlap in the view of the man or woman in the street. Betancourt and Lopez (1993) maintain that, in cross-cultural discourse, race has given way to ethnicity as an independent variable. This position is vigorously contested by several African American psychologists (Carter, 1995; Cross, 1991; Helms, 1990, 1996) who assert that race remains an important social construct, with far-reaching social consequences.

There is virtual consensus among social and behavioral scientists that race does not exercise a direct influence on behavior, but rather does so through socially shared experiences, both current and historical. There is widespread agreement that race, as the term is used in current American discourse, does not refer to a biologically determined category (Carter, 1995; Fish, 2002; Pinderhughes, 1989). Homo sapiens does not have any distinct subspecies (Fish, 2002). Race, then, is a socio-political designation based for the most part on visible physical characteristics. Historically and politically, it has served to maintain a hierarchical order among several "races." Imposition of this hierarchy culminated in the oppression and enslavement of persons based on race and obstructed and impeded the advancement and integration of persons belonging to an allegedly subordinate and inferior race. The effects of discrimination, oppression, and genocide continue to reverberate to this day.

In the case of African Americans, this externally imposed categorization has been counterbalanced by intragroup solidarity, and oppression has led to resistance and self-assertion (Allen, 2001). A negative, externally imposed label has been transformed into a positive, self-construed identity. Cross (1978, 1991) has traced this transformation through its several stages: (1) pre-encounter, characterized by de-emphasis on and devaluation of anything African in characteristics and heritage; (2) encounter, marked by acceptance of and comfort with the African aspects of experience; (3) immersion-emersion, encompassing a turbulent period of emphatic acceptance and glorification of everything African, without, however, incorporating it into oneself; (4) internalization, during which turbulence subsides and the African features of outlook and behavior are accepted calmly and as a matter of course; and (5) internalization-commitment, in which the newly internalized African American identity leads to engagement and action on behalf of the African American community. This sequence has been extensively tested and generally confirmed.

Helms (1990, 1996) distinguished sharply racial identity from ethnic identity, the former resulting from the history of subordination and oppression, the latter from the shared heritage transmitted through socialization. Moreover, racial designation is based predominantly on visible characteristics and pertains to broader categories (Carter, 1995). African, Asian, Hispanic, and Native Americans are examples of racial labels. Ethnic groups are principally defined on the basis of national origin and ancestral language, as exemplified by such terms as American, Mexican, Jamaican, Puerto Rican, Filipino, and Japanese. A special case concerns the category of Hispanic Americans, which is in part based on visible characteristics, but is more fundamentally determined on the basis of linguistic and historical heritage. Cross's (1978, 1991) five stages describe the transformation from an externally imposed label to a badge internalized with pride. Carter has provided case illustrations and research data on how this process is facilitated in the course of psychotherapy. Moreover, the progression continues. Philogène (1999) has studied the change in self-designation from Black to African American and has construed it as the emergence of a new social representation, which "allows society to shift from race to culture" (p. 154).

A special situation obtains in the case of historic traumata endured by some of the American minority groups, such as the enslavement of the ancestors of many African Americans, which not only inflicted unspeakable suffering, but attempted to obliterate cultural heritage. Have any threads of African culture been preserved despite this violent uprooting? Parham (1989) and Jones (1988) have identified some potential reflections of African cultural influence in such characteristics as interdependence, improvisation, rhythm, oral expression, and spirituality. In a recent large-scale study of African American self based on structural equation modeling, Allen (2001) concluded that "African Americans of all classes seem to embrace a worldview that is more collective, less competitive, more group-oriented, less material, and as such quite distinct from the well-documented European American worldview" (p. 175). Moreover, Allen contended that there is a detectable continuity between the values endorsed by contemporary African Americans and the prevailing ethos of traditional Africa.

TRANSCULTURAL PSYCHIATRY

There are parallels between the history of investigation of abnormal behavior and the divergent trends of cross-cultural and cultural psychology. The origins of the field go back to Emil Kraepelin, the founding father of scientific psychiatry, who anticipated the importance of social and cultural factors in psychiatric manifestations and inaugurated the study of depression in such locations as Algeria and Indonesia (Jilek, 1995). It was, however, not until the 1960s that the collection and comparison of observations on abnormal behavior within and across cultures became a cumulative and continuous undertaking, thereby bringing transcultural psychiatry into being (Murphy, 1982). It has been a multidisciplinary enterprise in which anthropologists, epidemiologists, psychologists, and sociologists have participated from the very start.

The field bifurcated into a more traditional segment concerned principally with the distribution of universal diagnostic psychiatric categories across cultures and a more emically oriented current of thought aimed at comprehending psychiatric disorders within their unique sociocultural context. The major contribution of traditional transcultural psychiatry has been in the form of multinational studies of schizophrenia, depression, and alcoholism under the aegis of the World Health Organization (1979, 1983; see Tanaka-Matsumi & Draguns, 1997; Tseng, 2001). On the basis of this research, the core syndromes found in all regions of the world were identified, and the axes of cultural variation were established in precipitating stressors, symptom manifestation, and prognosis.

The proponents of the new transcultural psychiatry, such as Kleinman (1991), construe distress and disability as personal experience within a cultural rather than within a diagnostic category, especially when the categorization is imported from the West. In China, Kleinman (1982) proceeded from this perspective in disentangling the nexus of somatic symptoms, depressive experiences, and cultural constraints.

Like cultural psychologists, the proponents of the new contextual psychiatry never tire of asserting that psychiatric complaints cannot be fully understood except in the interplay of culture and person. Information gathered in both of these frames of reference was reviewed in relation to the major racial groups of the United States (Draguns, 2000). It documents a few racial differences in the distribution of mental disorders between racial groups and highlights the importance of regarding complaints and symptoms as social transactions. To this end, the diagnostician's perspective should always be explicitly taken into account in assessing the patient. A grievous error that culturally informed clinicians have learned to avoid is confounding deviance with disturbance (Draguns, 2001) and imputing psychopathology to a person just because his or her actions appear bizarre when they are torn out of their cultural context.

CULTURE AND PSYCHOLOGY: CURRENT STATE AND FUTURE PROSPECTS

In the space allotted, it is impossible to do justice to the complexity and variety of the culturally relevant results in psychology. For more systematic information on the current state of knowledge, the interested reader is referred to a number of recent sources (Adler & Gielen, 2001; Berry, Dasen, & Saraswathi, 1997; Berry, Poortinga, & Pandey, 1997; Berry et al., 1992; Berry, Segall, & Kagitcibasi, 1997; Brislin, 2000; Gardiner, Mutter, & Kosmitzki, 2002; Matsumoto, 2001; Tseng, 2001). In lieu of systematic and integrative conclusions, an admittedly subjective and unintentionally arbitrary listing is offered of the accomplishments and prospects of the several fields that have jointly contributed to the current state of this multifaceted field:

- Major strides have been made in assuring the equivalence of concepts, stimuli, and contexts across cultures. With verbal stimuli, such as questionnaires, the sequence of translation, back-translation, and resolution of disagreements is well established (Brislin, 2000). Cross-cultural psychology has left behind the legacy of "safari research" in exporting mindlessly measures and procedures and not paying heed to their cultural relevance or appropriateness. At the same time, researchers realize the differential pull exercised by the several kinds of equivalence and are prepared to compromise and improvise in the quest for realistic resolutions of such dilemmas.

- Culture is no longer invoked as an amorphous global concept, nor is it simultaneously regarded as both an object of investigation and a source of explanation for its results. On a conceptual and empirical basis, a number of indicators and dimensions have been identified. A prominent example is the construct of individualism-collectivism, simultaneously a cultural variable and a source of a multitude of correlates. In addition to the already proposed cultural traits and syndromes, new ones will no doubt be identified and investigated, while the store of findings pertaining to the dimensions introduced will continue to grow and to be sifted.

- A major focus of developmental research has been on Piaget's stages of cognitive progression (Gardiner et al., 2000; Segall, Dasen, Berry, & Poortinga, 1999). Piaget described and conceptualized these stages of development at a specific point in space and time, in Switzerland in the 1920s and 1930s. Cross-cultural researchers have tested the applicability and universality of Piaget's stages. Their cumulative results point to the virtual constancy of the succession of these stages around the world, although their pace and duration have been found to vary across cultures. In line with Vygotsky's (1978) sociocognitive orientation, cross-cultural researchers have demonstrated that parent-child interactions in the earliest stages of infancy exercise an influence on the child's cognitive growth differently across cultures. Presence versus absence of schooling has a major impact on the child's subsequent development, both cognitively and socially (Brislin, 2000). In a subtler way, the mode and style of teaching also leave a mark, as does the nature of adult and peer models and interaction among them. This list could be continued, but the major point has been made: Cultural variations in childhood experience are a major fountainhead of far-reaching psychological characteristics later in life.

- After decades of relative neglect following the demise of the culture and personality movement, culturally oriented study of personality has acquired a new lease on life (Church & Lonner, 1998; Lee, McCauley, & Draguns, 1999). Studies of personality construction within and across cultures have emerged, and a major focus of this effort has been the recognition of the self as a key concept at the interface of person and culture (Triandis, 1994). In a universalistic frame of reference, an important development has been the extension of the Neo-Personality Inventory (Revised Neo PI-R) to a variety of cultures and language communities (McCrea, 2000). The five basic dimensions of Neuroticism, Extraversion, Openness, Agreeableness, and Conscientiousness have proved remarkably robust across languages and cultures, even though there appear to be partial exceptions to this rule, for example, in Mexico (Rodrigues de Diaz & Díaz-Guerrero, 1997).

- Three fundamental cultural value dimensions have been identified on the basis of a standardized survey conducted in 56 countries (Smith & Schwartz, 1997). They represent the characteristic choices in various cultures of conservatism versus autonomy, hierarchy versus egalitarianism, and mastery versus harmony. Proceeding emically, an international team of researchers (Chinese Culture Connections, 1987) has investigated explicitly Chinese values grounded in Confucian ethics and demonstrated their applicability in wide-ranging comparisons, on par with Hofstede's (1980) four statistically derived factors.

- The classic study by Ekman and Friesen (1971) demonstrated the ability of human beings, regardless of culture, to recognize facial expressions of seven basic emotions: anger, contempt, disgust, fear, happiness, sadness, and surprise. In emotional display, however, Matsumoto (1991) established differences between individualistic and collectivistic cultures, mediated by power distance and outgroup versus ingroup membership. Thus, universal and culturally influenced components of human emotional experience interact in a complex pattern that is beginning to be mapped.

- In regard to the behavior of men and women, Best and Williams (1997, p. 199) concluded that the manner in which relationships between men and women are organized and the way in which the two sexes relate to one another are remarkably similar in nature across social groups. Indeed, the biological differences between the sexes can be amplified or diminished by cultural practices and socialization, making gender differences in roles and behaviors generally modest but in some cases culturally important.

Differentiation of gender roles probably occurs in all cultures, but differs greatly in its nature and extent.

These and many more findings provide the stepping stones for the application of culturally oriented psychology in a variety of practical activities, prominently exemplified by counseling individuals in culturally diverse settings. With the help of a variety of current specialized sources (e.g., Aponte & Wohl, 2000; Carter, 1995; Gielen, Fish, & Draguns, 2004; Helms & Cook, 1999; Pedersen, Draguns, Lonner, & Trimble, 2002; Sue & Sue, 1999), immersion into culturally oriented psychology in its several facets, and personal openness to the experience of other cultures, providers of human services hold the promise of becoming more culturally sensitive and thereby more effective.

REFERENCES

Adler, L. L., & Gielen, U. P. (Eds.). (2001). *Cross-cultural topics in psychology* (2nd ed.). Westport, CT: Praeger.

Allen, R. I. (2001). *The concept of self: A study of Black identity and self-esteem.* Detroit, MI: Wayne University Press.

Aponte, J. F., & Wohl, J. (Eds.). (2000). *Psychological intervention in cultural diversity* (2nd ed.). Boston: Allyn & Bacon.

Arrindell, W. A., Hatzichristou, C., Wensink, J., Rosenberg, E., van Twillert, B., Stedema, J., et al. (1997). Dimensions of national culture as predictors of cross-national differences in subjective well-being. *Personality and Individual Differences, 23,* 37–53.

Barry, H. (1980). Description and uses of the Human Relations Area Files. In H. C. Triandis & J. W. Berry (Eds.), *Handbook of cross-cultural psychology: Vol. 1. Theory and method* (2nd ed., pp. 445–478). Boston: Allyn & Bacon.

Benedict, R. (1934). *Patterns of culture.* New York: Mentor.

Benedict, R. (1946). *The chrysanthemum and the sword.* Boston: Houghton Mifflin.

Bennett, S. (1994). The American Indian: A psychological overview. In W. J. Lonner & R. S. Malpass (Eds.), *Psychology and culture* (pp. 35–39). Boston: Allyn & Bacon.

Berry, J. W. (1969). On cross-cultural comparability. *International Journal of Psychology, 5,* 119–128.

Berry, J. W., Dasen, P. R., & Saraswathi (Eds.). (1997). *Handbook of cross-cultural psychology: Vol. 2. Basic processes and human development* (2nd ed.). Boston: Allyn & Bacon.

Berry, J. W., & Kim, U. (1993). The way ahead: From indigenous psychologies to a universal psychology. In U. Kim & J. W. Berry (Eds.), *Indigenous psychologies: Research and experience in cultural context* (pp. 277–280). Newbury Park, CA: Sage.

Berry, J. W., Poortinga, Y. H., & Pandey, J. (Eds.). (1997). *Handbook of cross-cultural psychology: Vol. 1. Theory and method.* Boston: Allyn & Bacon.

Berry, J. W., Poortinga, Y. H., Segall, M. H., & Dasen, P. R. (1992). *Cross-cultural psychology: Research and applications* Cambridge, England: Cambridge University Press.

Berry, J. W., Segall, M. H., & Kagitcibasi, C. (Eds.). (1997). *Handbook of cross-cultural psychology: Vol. 3. Social behavior and applications* (2nd ed., pp. 291–326). Boston: Allyn & Bacon.

Best, D., & Williams, J. (1997). Sex, gender, and culture. In J. H. Berry, M. H. Segall, & C. Kagitcibasi (Eds.), *Handbook of cross-cultural psychology: Vol. 3. Social behavior and applications* (2nd ed., pp. 163–212). Boston: Allyn & Bacon.

Betancourt, H., & Lopez, S. R. (1993). The study of culture, ethnicity, and race in American psychology. *American Psychologist, 48*(6), 629–637.

Bock, P. K. (1999). *Rethinking psychological anthropology* (2nd ed.). Prospect Heights, IL: Waveland Press.

Bock, P. K. (2000). Culture and personality revisited. *American Behavioral Scientist, 44,* 32–40.

Boesch, E. E. (1975). Psychologie de la connaissance de soi [Psychology of self-knowledge]. In *Symposium de l'Association de psychologie scientifique de langue française* (pp. 99–119). Paris: Presses Universitaires de France.

Boesch, E. E. (1991). *Symbolic action theory and cultural psychology.* Berlin, Germany: Springer-Verlag.

Bond, M. H. (Ed.). (1996). *Handbook of Chinese psychology.* Hong Kong: Oxford University Press.

Brislin, R. W. (2000). *Understanding culture's influence in behavior* (2nd ed.). Fort Worth, TX: Harcourt, Brace and Jovanovitch.

Bruner, J. S. (1974). Concluding comments and summary of conference. In J. L. M. Dawson & W. J. Lonner (Eds.), *Readings in cross-cultural psychology* (pp. 389–394). Hong Kong: University of Hong Kong Press.

Carter, R. T. (1995). *The influence of race and racial identity in psychotherapy: Toward a racially inclusive model.* New York: Wiley.

Chang, S. C. (1988). The nature of self: A transcultural view: Part I. Theoretical aspects. *Transcultural Psychiatric Research Review, 25*(3), 169–204.

Chinese Culture Connection. (1987). Chinese values and the search for culture-free dimensions of culture. *Journal of Cross-Cultural Psychology, 18,* 143–164.

Church, A. T., & Lonner, W. J. (Eds.). (1998). Personality and its measurement in cross-cultural perspective. *Journal of Cross-Cultural Psychology, 29*(Whole), 1–270.

Cole, M. (1996). *Cultural psychology: A once and future discipline.* Cambridge, MA: Belknap/Harvard.

Cross, W. E., Jr. (1978). The Thomas and Cross models of psychological nigrescence: A literature review. *Journal of Black Psychology, 5,* 13–31.

Cross, W. E., Jr. (1991). *Shades of Black: Diversity in African-American identity.* Philadelphia: Temple University Press.

Díaz-Guerrero, R. (1994). *Psicologia del méxicano: Descubrimiento de la etnopsicologia* [Psychology of the Mexican: Discovery of ethnopsychology] (6th ed.). Mexico City: Trillas.

Díaz-Loving, R., & Draguns, J. G. (1999). Culture, meaning, and personality in Mexico and in the United States. In Y. T. Lee, C. R. McCauley, & J. G. Draguns (Eds.), *Personality and person perception across cultures* (pp. 103–126). Mahwah, NJ: Erlbaum.

Draguns, J. G. (1990). Culture and psychopathology: Toward specifying the nature of the relationship. In J. J. Berman (Ed.), *Nebraska Symposium on Motivation, 1989: Cross-cultural perspectives* (Vol. 37, pp. 235–277). Lincoln: University of Nebraska Press.

Draguns, J. G. (1997). Abnormal behavior patterns across cultures: Implications for counseling and psychotherapy. *International Journal of Intercultural Relations, 21,* 213–248.

Draguns, J. G. (2000). Psychopathology and ethnicity. In J. F. Aponte & J. Wohl (Eds.), *Psychological intervention and cultural diversity* (2nd ed., pp. 40–58). Boston: Allyn & Bacon.

Draguns, J. G. (2002). Universal and cultural aspects of counseling and psychotherapy. In P. B. Pedersen, J. G. Draguns, W. J. Lonner, & J. E. Trimble (Eds.), *Counseling across cultures* (5th ed., pp. 29–50). Thousand Oaks, CA: Sage.

DuBois, C. (1944). *The people of Alor.* Minneapolis: University of Minnesota Press.

Ekman, P., & Friesen, W. (1971). Constants across cultures in the face and emotion. *Journal of Personality and Social Psychology, 17,* 124–129.

Ember, C. R., & Ember, M. (1996). *Cultural anthropology* (8th ed.). Saddle River, NJ: Prentice-Hall.

Enriquez, V. G. (Ed.). (1990). *Indigenous psychology: A book of readings.* Quezon City, Philippines: Akademya Ng Sikolohiya Pilipino.

Fish, J. M. (2002). A scientific approach to understanding race and intelligence. In J. M. Fish (Ed.), *Race and intelligence* (pp. 10–30). Mahwah, NJ: Erlbaum.

Freeman, D. (1983). *Margaret Mead and Samoa: The making and unmaking of an anthropological myth.* Cambridge, MA: Harvard University Press.

Gardiner, H. W., Mutter, J. D., & Kosmitzki, C. (2002). *Lives across cultures: Cross-cultural human development* (2nd ed.). Boston: Allyn & Bacon.

Gielen, U. P., Fish, J., & Draguns, J. G. (2004). *Handbook of therapy, healing, and culture.* Mahwah, NJ: Erlbaum.

Helms, J. E. (1990). *Black and White racial identity: Theory, research, and practice.* Westport, CT: Greenwood.

Helms, J. E. (1996). Toward a methodology for measuring and assessing racial as distinguished from ethnic identity. In G. R. Sodowsky & J. C. Impara (Eds.), *Multicultural assessment in counseling and clinical psychology* (pp. 143–193). Lincoln, NE: Buros Institute of Mental Measurements.

Helms, J. E., & Cook, D. A. (1999). *Using race and culture in counseling and psychotherapy: Theory and process.* Boston: Allyn & Bacon.

Hermans, H. J. M., & Kempen, H. J. G. (1998). Moving cultures: The perilous problems of cultural dichotomies in a globalizing society. *American Psychologist, 53,* 1111–1120.

Herskovits, M. (1948). *Man and his works.* New York: Knopf.

Hofstede, G. (1980). *Culture's consequences: International differences in work related values.* Beverly Hill, CA: Sage.

Hofstede, G. (1991). *Cultures and organizations: Software of the mind.* London: McGraw-Hill.

Hofstede, G. (2001). *Culture's consequences: Comparing values, behaviors, institutions, and organizations across nations* (2nd ed.). Thousand Oaks, CA: Sage.

Hsu, F. L. K. (1972). *Psychological anthropology.* Cambridge, MA: Schenkman.

Jahoda, G. (1982). *Psychology and anthropology: A psychological perspective.* London: Academic Press.

Jahoda, G. (1990). Our forgotten ancestors. In J. J. Berman (Ed.), *Nebraska Symposium on Motivation. Vol. 37: Cultural perspectives* (pp. 1–40). Lincoln: University of Nebraska Press.

Jilek, W. G. (1995). Emil Kraepelin and comparative sociocultural psychiatry: European. *Archives of Psychiatry and Clinical Neuroscience, 245,* 231–238.

Jones, J. M. (1988). Racism in Black and White: A bicultural model of reaction and evolution. In P. Katz & D. Taylor (Eds.), *Eliminating racism: Profiles in controversy* (pp. 137–157). New York: Plenum Press.

Kagitcibasi, C. (1997). Individualism and collectivism. In J. W. Berry, M. H. Segall, & C. Kagitcibasi (Eds.), *Handbook of cross-cultural psychology: Vol. 3. Social behavior and applications* (2nd ed., pp. 1–50). Boston: Allyn & Bacon.

Kardiner, A. (1945). *The psychological frontiers of society.* New York: Columbia University Press.

Kim, U., & Berry, J. W. (1993). *Indigenous psychologies: Experience and research in cultural context.* Newbury Park, CA: Sage.

Kimura, B. (1995). *Zwischen Mensch und Mensch* [Between one human being and another] (H. Weinhendl, Trans.). Darmstadt, Germany: Akademische Verlaganstalt.

Kleinman, A. (1982). Neurasthenia and depression: A study of somatization and culture in China. *Culture, Medicine, and Psychiatry, 6,* 117–189.

Kleinman, A. (1991). *Rethinking psychiatry: From cultural category to personal experience.* New York: Free Press.

Kroeber, A. L., & Kluckhohn, C. (1963). *Culture: A critical review of concepts and definitions.* New York: Vintage.

Lee, Y. T., McCauley, C. R., & Draguns, J. G. (Eds.). (1999). *Personality and person perception across cultures* (pp. 3–22). Mahwah, NJ: Erlbaum.

LeVine, R. A. (2001). Culture and personality studies, 1918–1960: Myth and history. *Journal of Personality, 69,* 603–617.

Linton, R. (1945). *The cultural background of personality.* New York: Appleton Century Crofts.

Marin, G., & Marin, B. (1991). *Research with Hispanic populations.* Newbury Park, CA: Sage.

Markus, H. R., & Kitayama, S. (1991). Culture and the self: Implications for cognition, emotion, and motivation. *Psychological Review, 98*(2), 224–253.

Marsella, A. J. (1998). Toward a "global-community psychology": Meeting the needs of a changing world. *American Psychologist, 53,* 1282–1291.

Matsumoto, D. (1991). Cultural influences on facial expressions of emotion. *Southern Communication Journal, 56,* 128–137.

Matsumoto, D. (Ed.). (2001). *Handbook of culture and psychology.* New York: Oxford University Press.

McCrea, R. R. (Ed.). (2000). Personality traits and culture: New perspectives on some classic issues. *American Behavioral Scientist, 44,* 3–157.

Mead, M. (1928). *Coming of age in Samoa.* New York: Morrow.

Murphy, H. B. M. (1982). *Comparative psychiatry.* Berlin, Germany: Springer-Verlag.

Myers, L. J. (1992). Transpersonal psychology: The role of the Afrocentric paradigm. In K. H. Burlew, W. C. Banks, H. P. McAdoo, & D. A. Azibo (Eds.), *African American psychology: Theory, research, and practice* (pp. 5–17). Newbury Park, CA: Sage.

Nobles, W. W. (1985). *Africanity and the Black family: The development of a theoretical framework*. Oakland, CA: Institute for the Advanced Study of Black Family Life and Culture.

Okeke, B., Draguns, J. G., Sheku, B., & Allen, W. (1999). Culture, self, and personality in Africa. In Y. T. Lee, C. R. McCauley, & J. G. Draguns (Eds.), *Personality and person perception across cultures* (pp. 139–162). Mahwah, NJ: Erlbaum.

Parham, T. A. (1989). Cycles of psychological nigresecence. *Counseling Psychologist, 17,* 187–226.

Pedersen, P. B., Draguns, J. G., Lonner, W. J., & Trimble, J. E. (Eds.). (2002). *Counseling across cultures* (5th ed.). Thousand Oaks, CA: Sage.

Philogène, G. (1999). *From Black to African American: A new social representation*. Westport, CT: Praeger.

Phinney, J. S. (1996). When we talk about American ethnic groups, what do we mean? *American Psychologist, 51,* 918–927.

Pinderhughes, E. (1989). *Understanding race, ethnicity, and power: The key to efficacy in clinical practice*. New York: Free Press.

Rodrigues de Diaz, M. L., & Díaz-Guerrero, R. (1997). ¿Son universales los rasgos de la personalidad? [Are personality traits universal?]. *Revista Latinoamericana de Psicologia, 29,* 35–48.

Rohner, R. P. (1986). *The warmth dimension: Foundations of parental acceptance theory*. Newbury Park, CA: Sage.

Roland, A. (1988). *In search of self in India and Japan*. Princeton, NJ: Princeton University Press.

Segall, M. H., Dasen, P. R., Berry, J. W., & Poortinga, Y. H. (1999). *Human behavior in global perspective: An introduction to cross-cultural psychology* (2nd ed.). Boston: Allyn & Bacon.

Segall, M. H., Lonner, W. J., & Berry, J. W. (1998). Cross-cultural psychology as a scholarly discipline: On the flowering of culture in behavioral research. *American Psychologist, 53,* 1101–1110.

Smith, P., & Schwartz, S. (1997). Values. In J. W. Berry, M. H. Segall, & C. Kagitcibasi (Eds.), *Handbook of cross-cultural psychology: Vol. 3. Social behavior and applications* (2nd ed., pp. 77–118). Boston: Allyn & Bacon.

Snider, P. D. (2003). *Exploring the relationship between individualism and collectivism and attitudes towards counseling among ethnic Chinese, Australian, and American university students*. Unpublished doctoral dissertation, Murdoch University, Perth, Australia.

Sue, D. W., & Sue, D. (1999). *Counseling the culturally different: Theory and practice* (3rd ed.). New York: Wiley.

Tanaka-Matsumi, J., & Draguns, J. G. (1997). Culture and psychopathology. In J. W. Berry, M. H. Segall, & C. Kagitcibasi (Eds.), *Handbook of cross-cultural psychology: Vol. 3. Social behavior and applications* (2nd ed., pp. 449–491). Boston: Allyn & Bacon.

Textor, R. B. (1967). *A cross-cultural summary*. New Haven, CT: Human Research Area Files Press.

Triandis, H. C. (1972). *The analysis of subjective culture*. New York: Wiley.

Triandis, H. C. (1994). *Culture and social behavior*. New York: McGraw-Hill.

Triandis, H. C. (1995). *Individualism and collectivism*. Boulder, CO: Westview.

Triandis, H. C. (1996). The psychological measurement of cultural syndromes. *American Psychologist, 51,* 407–415.

Tseng, W. S. (2001). *Handbook of cultural psychiatry.* San Diego, CA: Academic Press.

Tyler, S. A. (Ed.). (1969). *Cognitive anthropology.* New York: Holt, Rinehart and Winston.

Tylor, E. B. (1958). *Primitive culture.* New York: Harper. (Original work published 1871)

Uba, L. (1994). *Asian Americans: Personality patterns, identity, and mental health.* New York: Guilford Press.

Valsiner, J. (1997). *Culture and the development of children's action* (2nd ed.). New York: Wiley.

van de Vijver, F. (2001). The evolution of cross-cultural research methods. In D. Matsumoto (Ed.), *The handbook of culture and psychology* (pp. 77–97). New York: Oxford University Press.

Vygotsky, L. (1978). *Mind in society.* Cambridge, MA: Harvard University Press.

World Health Organization. (1979). *Schizophrenia: An international follow-up study.* New York: Wiley.

World Health Organization. (1983). *Depressive disorders in different cultures: Report of the WHO collaborative study of standardized assessment of depressive disorders.* Geneva, Switzerland: Author.

Wundt, W. (1911). *Völkerpsychologie* [Psychology of peoples]. Leipzig, Germany: Englemann.

CHAPTER 11

The Role of Socialization in Cultural Learning: What Does the Research Say?

Benjamin P. Bowser

Much has changed since Margaret Mead's (1928) fieldwork in Samoa that first suggested to American readers that a non-Western culture should not be dismissed as simply primitive, that cultural differences were real and well worth studying. Since then, every non-Western society on the planet has been transformed in some way by technologies, wars, and the development of a world economy dominated by the West. All that is foreign and "primitive" has now drawn much closer to us in social and political time and space; people from these worlds live and work in the United States, and events in their home countries are part of our daily news. The new world economy has made what used to be separate worlds dependent on each other as markets and sources of labor and vital natural resources.

All of these changes have subtly affected the relationship between socialization and cultural learning in the production of American psychology and sociology. This chapter looks at cultural socialization as a sociology of knowledge by pointing out the external influences over time that have changed researchers' thinking about their work. An outdated American concept of race is one of these influences that has served as a barrier in advancing theory and research in cultural socialization. The failure of psychologists to fully conceptualize race as a cultural rather than physical or nonspecific factor has led to an impasse in American mainstream social psychology. Finally, this chapter estimates the scientific potential for exploring cultural socialization both with and without a cultural concept of race. But first, the essential question must be outlined: What is it that social and behavioral scientists are curious about and wish to study? Then a clarification of the definitions and components of cultural socialization are in order.

ESSENTIAL QUESTIONS

In all observed human societies, culture is taught and learned and humans exhibit extraordinary facility in learning complex languages, customs, and motor skills and retaining and working from huge knowledge bases. The socialization of children is the most obvious example (Leiderman, Tuklin, & Rosenfeld, 1977). Humans are not born knowing their culture, nor are children able to demonstrate culture just as an outcome of advancing physical development. New members must be taught culture; it cannot be learned simply by virtue of birth, race, or proximity. Furthermore, what is learned is not one-dimensional or acquired step-by-step. Knowledge, skills, attitudes, beliefs, social roles, and experiences are gained in different ways, at different times, and at different rates within and across cultural systems (Whiting & Whiting, 1975, p. 174). Some members learn more of one thing, while others learn more of other things. When place, timing, and circumstances are taken into consideration, "cultural learning" is a virtual natural laboratory of all the complex ways that humans have devised to teach and to learn densely complex materials across all human mental and physical capacities.

With all these variations in teaching and learning, what are the different ways to teach and to learn, and when and under what conditions can learning occur best? If the answers to these questions were known, it could potentially revolutionize all levels of education: We could improve parenting, knowing precisely what would be effective and when, and we could teach and learn foreign languages and cultures much more efficiently, just to name a few benefits. Acquiring such knowledge is an extraordinary opportunity and a challenge. So what, then, is "cultural socialization"?

Culture

There are over 164 definitions of human culture (Kroeber & Kluckholm, 1952). Each definition attempts to explain the same core reality. Over thousands of years of relative isolation from one another, groups developed their own languages and hundreds of customs and have collectively experienced events and coded them in their language, history, and folklore. The results are over 45 distinct ethnic cultures in Western Europe, 144 in Central West Africa, and 76 in the precolonial southeast of North America, which includes the Caribbean (Price, 1990). Here, "ethnic" is defined as historical land-based groups who developed distinct cultures and who may or may not now define themselves as such (pp. 8–9). It is estimated that prior to the twentieth century there were worldwide approximately 3,432 distinct ethnic cultures of taken-for-granted attitudes, beliefs, values, and expectations regarding appropriate behaviors. Each of the 164 definitions of culture emphasizes different aspects of these 3,432 cultural systems. But do not look for these ethnic cultures in the present system of 189 political states. Most of these ethnic cultures have been absorbed into large national states, where one or more ethnic cultures politically dominate. The assimilation of ethnic groups into national states and then of these national states into transnational markets is one of the least studied trends in the world today. Fewer than half of these ethnic cultural systems still exist.

Socialization

Like culture, socialization has over 40 definitions, each making subtle distinctions (Wentworth, 1980). What they all describe is the learning of already established culture: taken-for-granted attitudes, beliefs, values, and expectations. Whether the learner is a child or an adult, at the beginning of learning he or she is unfamiliar with the culture and is without a role and place. The learner then goes through the socialization process. Later, the learner emerges with basic knowledge and training as an initiate and with a role and place in his or her new society (Handel, 1988). Again, there are potentially hundreds of ways to describe how and when this process takes place, how long it goes on, and what is emphasized at different points. Furthermore, there are various levels of learning. In formal learning, one consciously learns words, meanings, and knowledge systems, such as language and history. But formal learning is only a small part of cultural socialization. Most socialization is informal and sub-conscious learning where one acquires affective behaviors, "body language," senti-ments, and hundreds of unwritten expectations about appropriate behavior. Like culture, the many definitions of socialization describe different aspects of the so-cialization process. There is gender socialization, maternal and paternal socializa-tion, political socialization, religious socialization, emotional socialization, racial socialization, and more.

Toward an Explanation of Behavior

Neither culture nor socialization is a theory, though many behavioral and social sci-entists describe them as such. Culture and socialization are mainly descriptive con-cepts; to be theories, they must explain hypothetical relationships between factors and predict behaviors. More precisely, culture and socialization are vital components of an implicit working theory underlying the work of social psychologists; culture is the content, and socialization is the process by which that content is learned. Both are independent variables that lead to two specific dependent outcomes: distinct indi-vidual cultural psychologies and distinct group identities and social norms. In the first outcome, individuals with one or the other "cultural psychology" have differ-ences in the way they conceptualize reality and problems. There will also be differ-ences in the expression of affect and expectations regarding their and others' behavior. In the second outcome, individuals become members of social groups and learn appropriate group behaviors and internalize group identities.

Culture and socialization are interactive with one another. Thus, individuals can be different because of differences in their cultures, but they can also be different be-cause of differences in their socialization. Even within the same culture, people can be different psychologically and socially if they acquire the same culture through dif-ferent socialization processes. Between different cultures, personalities and social norms are further distinguished through different socialization processes. Having different personalities and social norms is not insignificant or simply a point of cu-riosity. The rest of the theoretical model asserts that different personality and re-lated social norms then lead to different attitudes and behaviors. Ultimately, people will behave differently and expect others in their group to behave according to group norms because of these differences.

When researchers talk about culture and socialization, they are making reference to the dynamics of the model in Figure 11.1. Here is the science and why studies of culture and socialization are important. The central theoretical hypothesis is this: There is a direct connection between culture and socialization that defines the range of socially acceptable personalities and social norms. Personalities and social norms then influence the selection and shaping of specific individual attitudes and group expectations that characterize a culture as distinct from others. Individual attitudes

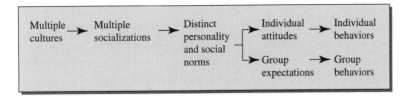

Figure 11.1 Transition of culture to individual and group behaviors.

and group expectations then provide cognitive "road maps" for prescribed individual and group behaviors. If we are able to better understand the dynamic relationship between culture and socialization that produces differences in personality and social norms, then we are further along in understanding variations in social behavior. With the central culture and socialization model clearly spelled out, it calls attention to another aspect of socialization: Is it possible that the relation between culture socialization and personality behavior is reciprocal? That is, in theory, can differences in personality, social norms, and behavior impact socialization and ultimately culture? In the model, this would mean that the arrows go backward as well from individual and group behaviors to impact culture. This point of reciprocity in socialization is revisited later because it is a way to better understand some changes in contemporary world society.

How has this basic theoretical framework specifying the relationship between culture and socialization been advanced in recent decades, and what role, if any, has race played in advancing this science? Psychological studies in the United States are a logical starting point given the primacy of American psychology in the study of socialization.

THE AMERICAN MAINSTREAM

Discussions of socialization go back to the turn of the past century in American psychology and sociology, and the concept has been used in all of the evolving theories since then (Wentworth, 1980). There were discussions of socialization in pre-World War II human ecology, where its content was sought in the environment (Hawley, 1950). Rising delinquency and other forms of social deviance that characterized increasingly urban society were explained by socialization into subcultures (Rubington & Weinberg, 1996). That is, the sources of deviance were not necessarily in the individual personality or biology of the deviant; he or she was taught lower-class toughness, criminal values, and so on. Deviant behaviors were products of disordered environments. Thus, the way to improve human behavior was to improve the environment (Howard & Scott, 1981). At the time, this was a progressive idea in comparison to earlier biological determinism. In social Darwinism and ecologicalism, socialization was viewed as a straightforward, one-dimensional process; there were no subtleties or variations about it.

By the 1950s, it was already apparent that major changes in American family life were developing (Baumrind, 1980). The 1950's assumption that America had become a middle-class society due to postwar affluence was shattered by the realization that there was still poverty in the nation. The civil rights movement also called attention to racial segregation and inequality. Behavioral and social scientists shifted their attention to efforts to explain poverty and racial inequality. At first, "Negro" children were compared with Whites on virtually every conceivable basis. As other minority groups (Native Americans, Mexican Americans) also demanded relief from racial discrimination, poverty, and civil disenfranchisement, they too were studied. The decades from 1960 well into the 1980s were the period of the racial comparative study. Many careers were established in doing these studies. These new studies were progressive in that now Blacks, Hispanics, Native Americans, and Asians were no longer ignored and treated as if they did not exist. But there were severe limits in this work, reflecting back to pre-1960's thinking. When minorities were compared with Whites, with the exception of Chinese and Japanese Americans, they were deficient in virtually every way and showed greater deviance than Whites (Howard & Scott, 1981). They were less intelligent, had lower cognitive ability, could not delay gratification, were more external, were dominated by lower-class personalities, were sexually active and pregnant earlier, could not read as well, and so on. By focusing on alleged deviations from the mainstream, these types of studies failed to provide systematic information about what was normal, everyday, and organized.

Controversy arose not about the specific comparative differences, but over explanations of these differences. Some explained the inequities as due to racial discrimination, but in time, the most influential view pointed to each group's culture and socialization. The new bottom lines were cultures of poverty, disordered families, "shadows of slavery," welfarism, and ghetto mentalities. Again, socialization was used as a simple learning process, but this time it was related to racial differences due to minority group subcultures. In time, with growing national conservatism and a sense that the racial inequalities were self-imposed, the number of racial comparative studies in psychology and sociology declined in mainstream journals and books.

An interesting point of history for this period is that the comparative racial research was never viewed as part of the mainstream of either psychology or sociology (Betancourt & Lopez, 1993). It was criticized for having weak theoretical foundations. That is, racial discrimination was never directly measured in research, nor were any of the deficient and deviant subcultures shown to exist. Like the racial divisions in American society, the comparative racial research was its own subfield, separate from and inferior to the real sociology and psychology. The mainstream was the place to find more theoretically and scientifically vigorous research regarding socialization. But sympathetic reviews of post-1980's mainstream social psychology found serious problems there as well (Brislin, 1983; Cushman, 1990; Kagitcibasi & Berry, 1989; Segall, 1986).

PROBLEMS IN THE MAINSTREAM: UNIVERSALS?

In hundreds of studies of American childhood and adolescence from 1960 through the early 1980s there were a series of repeated themes. In the first, most variation in behavior was found due to age, sex differences, and parent socialization (Whiting &

Whiting, 1975). It was assumed that there is a universal developmental sequence that children pass through to adulthood. The sequence and timing differ from person to person and for young men and young women. Therefore, there are age- and gender-appropriate behaviors; underneath the sequencing and timing is biological maturation. The role of parents was to maximize their children's development within the context of their maturation. It was essential to provide maximum physical and social stimulation in order for a child to maximize his or her potential. When a child's behavior was not age- or gender-appropriate, it pointed to problems with parenting.

Second, individuation was assumed to be the final stage of appropriate child development. That is, the underlying biological and psychological motivations for human growth and maturation are to reach a point where one can be self-actualized, living, working, acting, and thinking on one's own as an individual (Baumrind, 1980). Children were expected to grow up, be able to take care of themselves financially, emotionally, and physically, and move away and live independent lives. Continued deep emotional ties and directedness from family were indications of incomplete self-actualization.

Third, adolescence is a period of testing limits, identity confusion, shifting allegiance from parents and family to peers, and of general physical and social awkwardness. It is a psychosocially and physiologically necessary period characterized by challenges to parents and ambivalence about self and society (Goodman, 1970, p. 2). A consensus emerged that authoritarian responses to adolescence are the least effective and potentially damaging to the teen's development because they are alienating and deny opportunities for self-actualized development. The most effective response is to gently guide the teen through this period—to be more permissive. Teens will come out of adolescence as they mature and establish their personal and social identity.

Fourth, mothers play essential nurturing roles in the physical and emotional rearing of children. The consistency with which mothers nurture is thought by many to have a biological basis, despite variations in environment (Leiderman et al., 1977). While the father's role is not as well anchored in nature, it too must be played out in the life of children if they are to be balanced and well-adjusted adults. Children must have their biological mother and father; surrogates do not have the same authority, bonding with the child, or motivation to rear children as do their biological parents.

Fifth, cognitive ability is the most important intelligence. The central ability to survive, function, and thrive in modern society is cognitive, that is, the ability to quickly perceive abstract information and principles, retain these, and then use abstractions to solve complex problems. One view is that this ability is not normally distributed by race (Hernstein & Murray, 1994), countered by the assertion that it is (Blau, 1992). Unlike the other fundamentals, cognitive ability is measurable and comparative across all groups.

Finally, adult development is the endgame and objective of all the learning, changing, and physiological development. Once a person is fully grown, independent, and a productive member of society, his or her socialization is complete despite continued environmental influences (Baumrind, 1980). It is fascinating to read studies of socialization until the 1980s and to see how they were focused almost exclusively on children and adolescents.

Physiologically driven sequencing and timing of maturity, individuation as a physical and psychological goal, the necessity of turmoil in adolescence and nonauthoritarian parenting, the necessity of biological parents, the primacy of cognitive intelligence, and the end of socialization are six points that were thought to be fundamental to human psychology. They were the lessons learned from decades of research and observation, and they were thought to be virtually universal. So it was not only appropriate, it was advancing science to establish these points as standards by which individuals and groups could be compared. These points are to this day the bread and butter of counseling psychologists, the standards by which social workers evaluate families and children, and the measures of good parenting.

Because science confirmed these understandings, they were not only thought to be true for American society, but there was an early sense that one could reasonably expect to find these universals in all other societies and cultures as well. In retrospect, socialization had been advanced; it was no longer a simple "black box," where the content to be learned and individual learner went into one end and came out the other side socialized in that content. Individual variations at the end of socialization used to be due to environment and parenting; now there was a continuum from optimal to retarded socialization practices at different stages in a child's and adolescent's development. It was the same black box, but now it had a continuum of compartments, stages, and gates. Now variations were due to not only environment and parenting; there were also essential variations in environment and parenting that had to match changes in physiological development (Whiting & Whiting, 1975).

Emerging Crises

The presumptions that the nuclear-biological family is the only family form that results in effective parenting and that parenting is deficient without one or the other biological parent were central to comparative studies of White and Black families (Weinstein, Goodjoin, Crayton, & Lawson, 1990). African Americans pointed out that extended families also played important roles in children's psychosocial development and could provide emotional support and guidance if one or both biological parents were missing. Also, cognition as the only important intelligence came under criticism in racial comparative studies (Berry, 1984). Cognitive ability was thought to be predictive of success in college and was a gateway to admissions. Of course, Whites on average had more intelligence than any other group, but because these critiques were in racial comparative studies, they were not taken as serious issues in mainstream social psychology.

Where these points struck home in mainstream social psychology was with regard to social class differences (Cashmore & Goodnow, 1986; Kagitcibasi & Berry, 1989, p. 496). Variations in cognitive ability, family form, parenting styles, and general socialization outcomes have been observed among Whites and Blacks, and the variations have been accounted for by social class differences (Adey & Shayer, 1994; Blau, 1992). There were also social class variations in the extent to which the universals were evident among minority groups. For example, research repeatedly found that White, Japanese, and Chinese parents considered early stimulation to be very important, and that the family was the center of their children's education. In contrast, Mexican and African American parents were alleged to not value early stimulation and believed that it was the school's job to educate their children (Kagitcibasi, 1996, p. 31). The problem here is inadequate attention to both social class and culture. When income, education, and occupation were used to control for social class, the cultural differences within and between social classes within ethnic groups were accounted for. The parents who believed in early stimulation and home-centered education were culturally middle class, while those who did not were closer in cultural orientation to the working and lower class (p. 31). There have been attempts to identify these other class-race factors in national data (Wagenaar & Coates, 1999).

A blow that went straight to the heart of postwar socialization research came from cross-cultural studies. The universals that intracultural factors such as race and social class could not address came into question. The timing and sequencing of maturation attributed to physiological growth was often different in non-European societies: Children showed psychological maturity earlier, and physiological growth was not as closely matched to psychological maturity as thought in the West (Whiting & Edwards, 1988). In non-Western society, people did not have the same need to separate themselves from their family. Ego and self were less valued; maintaining extended family, community, and other lifelong social groups was more important and thought to be fundamental to normal adult adjustment and support. In these pro-social worlds, children were far more perceptive and capable of maturity much earlier than the Western middle class believes (Goodman, 1970). Adolescence was not necessarily a period of turmoil and conflict. In fact, childhood itself has not been a universal life stage throughout most of human social history (Aries, 1962). Teens had progressive responsibilities, were called on to nurture others, played important family roles, and carried them out without challenge or question. Parents were authorities but rarely had to exercise their authority.

Furthermore, in non-European societies, parenting was flexible and shared by other members of the extended family; children were not completely dependent on their biological parents. And cognitive intelligence was not the only kind of intelligence. Intelligence was socially defined in many ways and was different depending on the culture; intelligence was also skill in communications with others, sensitivity toward others' feelings and unexpressed needs, and the ability to quickly memorize a great deal of material in detail. If cultural differences were real and large and if abilities developed differentially in adaptation to these differing cultural contexts, then differences in test performance were not due solely to differences in level or amount of intellectual development (Berry, 1984). Ironically, most of the research on variations in intelligence was done in Africa (Mundy-Caste, 1974). Finally, adult maturation was not the end of socialization. It became increasingly evident both inside and outside of Western societies that socialization into new roles and experiences continued long after adolescence. Variations in adult behaviors attributed to aging were in fact new role socialization (Rossi, 1994). While one's body aged, becoming middle-aged, elderly, being a grandparent, and so on were learned roles.

The cross-cultural observers expressed it best: All the learned lessons that were thought to be universals are in fact Western middle-class cultural presumptions. Furthermore, they are not simply Western and middle class; they are expressions of the American middle class (P. Greenfield & Cocking, 1994, p. x; Howard & Scott, 1981). American social psychology is both a reflection and a reinforcement of the individualistic Western ethos, where the line is drawn very narrowly and sharply between self and nonself (Kagitcibasi, 1996, p. 55). Furthermore, what distinguishes minority cultural groups from the mainstream in the United States is that they value interdependence more than dependence as central cultural scripts. In contrast, the mainstream values independence over dependence (Greenfield & Cocking, 1994, p. 7). The cross-cultural work literally called into question the core of American social psychology regarding socialization and left the field in crisis. Many seemingly straightforward assumptions about human psychological functioning have not resulted in consensus about universality among qualified scientists (Shweder & Sullivan, 1993). What is universal and not more adequately explained by culture differences? The whole enterprise had to be rethought, integrating scattered islands of research where findings from diverse inquiries are compared and challenge ongoing inquiry (Anastasi, 1992).

REFLECTING BACK: IMPACT OF RACE

Why did questions posed primarily from cross-cultural evidence have such an impact after 1980 but not before? The content of the challenges to the universals was all there as early as 1928 in Margaret Mead's *Coming of Age in Samoa* as well as in the Human Relations Area Files of 300 cultures (Brislin, 1983). The evidence challenging the universals was also all there in the pre- and post-World War II ethnographies of foreign cultures. It made a difference after 1980 and not earlier because of the emerging status of non-Western cultures. South Americans, Koreans, Japanese, East Indians, Chinese, Mexicans, Middle Easterners, and South Africans are all players in the world community. They are now trade partners, competitors, investors, and industrialists. They are also culturally different. There are now many more people traveling back and forth, living in and comparing these cultures, who are exposing underlying structures (Swiderski, 1991). Also, there are now social psychologists from these other cultures who can see and write about the extent to which social psychology is biased by its Western and American middle-class assumptions. Furthermore, foreign societies are no longer considered quaint, exotic, points of curiosity, and inferior to the West.

Prior to 1980, it was believed that there was nothing to learn from less "developing" cultures that reflected back on middle-class America. In fact, one should go to great lengths to ignore race, ethnicity, and religion—cultural factors (Broude, 1995). All that mattered was that these foreign worlds would eventually become Western and middle class. Another reason why the cross-cultural research was not taken seriously was because the American concept of race confounded cultural differences. American social psychologists, using their national concept of race, were subtly biased against realizing that cultural differences both in and outside of the United States reflected back on their work and general assumptions about society and human personality. It prevented them from seeing that they had created a social psychology in their own class and culture image.

Race in the American Culture

Although the recognition of physical differences between people can be traced to ancient times, the social construction of a superior "White people" based on Europeans and of an inferior "Negro" or "Black people" based on Africans is recent (Drake, 1987; Snowden, 1983). Race as a peculiarly American institution was invented by colonial North Carolina and Virginia legislators in the 1700s to distinguish European from African laborers in order to reduce the number and severity of slave rebellions (Allen, 1994; Cecil-Fronsman, 1992). One had to be a property owner to vote, and a wealthy one to be in the legislature. Owners of the largest labor-intensive plantations created fabulous wealth. These were the men who bought African slaves and "hired" European indentured servants on virtually lifelong contracts. Initially, there was little distinction between Africans and Europeans in the planters' minds; Africans and Europeans often did the same work and even lived in the same dwellings. Because the planters were a very small percentage of the population and their slaves and European laborers were the majority, work slow-downs and stoppages and outright rebellions were common and severely threatened the plantation economy and social order. African slaves and European servants were united in these uprisings. The solution was to separate the two by elevating Europeans and reducing the status of Africans. Laws were passed in the key southern legislatures of Virginia and North Carolina creating unequal "racial" groups.

What did these laws do? Europeans were called "White" and forbidden to do the same work as African slaves. Their contracts were reduced and they were forbidden to live with or marry Africans. Africans were henceforth slaves, called "Negroes" (Blacks), and were denied the same rights as Europeans. More important, these statuses could be easily recognized by skin color. These unequal and color-coded statuses were enforced by law, and violations were severely punished. It worked. There were still revolts, but their number and severity were reduced; the plantation system was preserved; and soon poor Whites were vested in a system that provided them with higher relative status and superiority. The unique American racial system was born.

It took almost 200 years after the invention of American races to end the southern plantation system with the Civil War, but its cultural by-product of physically defined races lived on through the reconstruction of the South. Jim Crow racial separation and formal laws and customs reinforcing White superiority lasted right up to 1965; only the formal and public trappings of this system were outlawed by the 1964 Civil Rights Acts. But this nation's informal life is still struggling with the legacy of racism—White superiority and Black and other racial group inferiority (Jaynes & Williams, 1989). Where the legacy of slavery and American racism is particularly evident is in the continued use of the very same concept of race defined by colonial legislatures over 300 years ago.

The American concept of race separates people based on their physical appearance and presumes underlying and unequal biological differences. Thus, any observed differences between races in behavior, intelligence, and any other capability must be due to some natural differences (Gates, 1997; Gossett, 1997). It should be pointed out that racism was not a part of precolonial Western history and culture; quite the contrary, Greeks and Romans held Africans in high esteem (Snowden, 1983). Biological explanations of racial differences came under severe criticism in the past century, after they were used as the ideological basis of Nazi genocide during World War II. It is no coincidence that the Nazis and White supremacists who instituted the South African apartheid system studied and modeled their social systems after American Jim Crow (Kuhl, 1994). It is also no coincidence that some American Whites are still very much concerned with preserving "racial purity."

What does any of this have to do with socialization and culture in social psychology? The answer is *everything* in the context of the American concept of race. After the Nazi and apartheid reflections of American racism and the embarrassment of Jim Crow, it is no longer polite or politically correct in the American middle class to attribute racial differences to biology. But no alternative has been offered. Physical differences between races are still evident and seem to still be the basis of inequalities in education, health, crime, and so on. The way to deal with the confusion about race and the need for politeness is to simply not attribute racial differences to nature. Just do not think about it; ignore it. Partition race off as a troublesome subarea of study that someone else may be able to resolve. The result is an impasse in thinking about race. But what is the resolution, and what really are racial differences?

The differences that Americans see and attribute to race are really cultural. Racial differences are cultural differences (Anthias, 1992; Reynolds, 1992; Shanklin, 1994). The American physical concept of race is nonsense except for the fact that it is believed to be real. The extent to which it is believed is the extent to which Americans are locked into a fundamentally racist logic. There is no such thing as a "White," "Black," or any other color race. Blacks and Whites do not have distinct gene pools, and the genes that produce differences in skin color, hair texture, and so on are relatively few and minor (Graves, 1993). And after hundreds of years of sexual mixing, no "race" can claim that it is distinct or pure. In which case, what use is the concept of race, and how has it affected the study of socialization in social psychology?

The American concept of race has retarded the study of socialization and culture in social psychology. As long as people of Color in the United States and in other parts of the world were seen as another race, thinking about the content and process of socialization stopped. Virtually no attention was given to values and cultural differences among people of the same race in the same community. With race as a primary identifying factor, the existence of stable (middle-class) and disorganized (culture of poverty) households within the same poor community could not be adequately explained (Goodman, 1970, p. 100). Race is more important and salient than culture, so much so that subtle and important variations between people are missed. It is no coincidence that most comparative cross-cultural specialists reject the concept of race altogether and view it appropriately as a uniquely American affliction that is being exported to the rest of the world (Berry & Annis, 1988; Kagitcibasi, 1996).

Race as Culture and the New Socialization

There are a number of initiatives to reconstruct the culture and socialization nexus in social psychology without the American middle-class universals. First, it was necessary to eliminate race. J. W. Berry (1994) asserted that a more accurate term for a race or minority group is "ethnocultural" group. This puts the emphasis right where it belongs: on culture, not race, color, or subordinate status. Berry (1988) also posited in the late 1960s that development and socialization in different cultures may originate as adaptations to different ecological-economic conditions. The stage was set for a break from the American concept of race and American middle-class universals.

Urie Bronfenbrenner (1972) restates Berry and recalls Erik Erikson by suggesting that variations in ecological contexts condition cultural variations and subsequently result in variations in individual and group behaviors (Douvan, 1997). People respond to their environment by creating systems of survival (culture). These social systems then have to be responded to along with the environment. The relationship between environment, culture, and groups and individuals having to manage both is dynamic. The environment changes, then responses to the social system change the culture, and the results are changes in group-specific normative behaviors. As a general theory, this conceptual construct partly explains variations in behavior within and across cultural groups, whether in New York City or Islamabad, and without middle-class American universals.

Closely related to Bronfenbrenner's construct is Cigden Kagitcibasi's (1996) explanation of "social relatedness." She points out that a great deal of cross-cultural anthropology and psychology focuses on cultural differences and presumes Malinowski's thesis that each culture is unique. Many cultures have more commonalities than differences, she notes, and it might be more fruitful to trace their commonalities if one's objective is to find universal propositions. In which case, the focus should be on relatedness. In effect, she proposes a new search for universals, but this time without starting with American society as the measuring stick.

In the context of ecology and relatedness, Tallman, Marotz-Baden, and Pindas (1983) propose a redefinition of socialization that is sensitive to cultural differences and consistent with symbolic interaction, social exchange, and social learning theories. Socialization is:

> A process in which individuals living in a given social context learn, through interactions with each other, the particular identities extant within their social context and the ways to establish, maintain, and transform such identities. (p. 25)

This definition restates the relationship among learning, social interaction, and identity. What is new is the potential of social actors to transform the identity they are socialized into. This process of redefinition was illustrated in the authors' methodologically innovative study of comparative samples of intact families consisting of both parents and their 12- to 15-year-old sons and daughters. The settings were the industrial cities of Zacapu in Mexico and the Twin Cities (Minneapolis and St. Paul) in the United States. The hypothetical question was, How do parents in different cultures prepare their children for the future? To show how parents in different cultures addressed this problem, the authors had to compare three units of analysis: community social structure, parent-child relationships, and the individual child. The investigators developed a 1.5-hour game simulation to measure parent-adolescent social interaction, in which they asked parents and their adolescents to plan a child's career over a hypothetical 10-year period. During the game, observers recorded game choices and coded family interactions, allowing a measure of socialization. To factor in variations in social structure, sample families in different social strata from each site were recruited to play the same family game. The game had various conditions of success and failure and simulated different conditions of social change. Inferences were drawn from comparisons of family-adolescent problem solving and selections of solutions between strata within each culture and between cultures.

This is also one of the first studies that seriously compared Mexicans and Americans without using middle-class America as the only standard of comparison. Mexicans were compared with North Americans not as a race but as a cultural group, where the experience of poverty in both the United States and Mexico informs and shapes personality and behavior (McLoyd & Flanagan, 1990).

The transition in thinking from universals to greater appreciation for social context is also modeled in the work of Whiting and Edwards (1988). They attempted to code changes in social context within and across six cultures in a mix of agricultural villages and small cities in Liberia, Kenya, India, Mexico, the Philippines, Japan, and the United States. In all six cultures, the ecological settings in residential communities were described in detail, sample families were drawn from local village censuses, and samples of children were systematically observed. The focus of observation was on who the children interacted with (what family and nonfamily relations) and the quantity of interaction. The children observed were lap children (0 to 2.5 years), knee children (2.6 to 3.5 years), and yard children (3.6 to 5.5 years). The detailed observational notes were sent from each site to Cambridge, Massachusetts, where they were coded. Cultures themselves constituted different environments that produced variations in socialization.

There was nothing in Whiting and Edwards' (1988) study that called into question a central finding in Whiting and Whiting's (1975) earlier findings. Children and relationships that scored high on nurturance, had major responsibility of caring for other children, and scored low on need for independence and dominance came from societies with a relatively simple socioeconomic structure. There was little or no occupational specialization and little class variation and they had a localized kin-based political structure. In contrast, children who were high on egoism and low on nurturance came from societies with occupational specialization, centralized government, and social stratification (Whiting & Whiting, 1975, pp. 174–176). One should not conclude from this work that as foreign societies industrialize, the extended family and communities become passé (S. Greenfield, 1973). There is evidence of extended families persisting in urbanized and industrial Brazil, Canada, parts of England, and Japan (Anderson, 1975), not to mention among cultural minorities in the United States.

Over a decade later, Beatrice Whiting and Carolyn Edwards (1988) attempted to offer an even more complete and flexible analysis of the children's learning environments and their response to it. They pointed out that psychology tends to conceptualize socialization too narrowly on the modeling, teaching, and reinforcing behaviors of teachers and parents, without consideration for the surrounding complex of social interactions and routine activities that critically support this adult interaction. So they did not analyze age, sex, and cultural differences in children's activities and companions as simply the result of developmental changes of socialization pressure by parents, other caregivers, and teachers. They analyzed these differences as outcomes (dependent factors) in the process of socialization. In other words, the factors in the older notion of socialization were looked at as outcomes of broader social and environmental influences. Furthermore, when one considers socialization in a historical context and in the rest of the world, what needs explanation are trends in the West, and in particular, the United States. What are the consequences of children being increasingly brought up by schools, television, peer groups, babysitters, and day care centers rather than by parents and extended kin? It has been posited that children are no longer the center of American family life and are sacrificed for parents, despite nationalistic American assertions otherwise (Bronfenbrenner, 1972; Lasch, 1979).

Advancements on the Margins

The above are examples of exciting work looking at the relationship between socialization and culture without the prior biases. Cross-cultural psychology now reflects the most dynamic area of study in cultural socialization. One might say rightfully so. But again, it had to first free itself from the American race anchor and the American middle-class biases that were elevated to universals. There is another angle to this development: Although cross-cultural work is rich and has exciting possibilities, there is no parallel effort in the United States to relook at domestic races as ethnocultural groups within mainstream social psychology.

There should be a new look at the socialization of American ethnocultural groups, focusing on their varied physical and social ecologies. This would include a careful look at the strategies by which people respond to mainstream American culture as well as their own ethnocultural group. This work should also be comparative, searching for relatedness. What do ethnocultural groups have in common, and why, and what are the bases of their differences? While mainstream social psychology is still very much without direction regarding culture and socialization, there is potential for the new focus evident on the margins of the mainstream. There are occasional articles on race and socialization that are rarely cited; many of these articles are in ethnic studies journals, and it is in these marginalized articles that there is a serious and sustained attempt to look at cultural socialization in the United States.

It is important to speak of this work on the margins as having potential. This is because the socialization work that looks at race and socialization also continues to use the American concept of race. But their use of race is reactive to the mainstream and is in fact an attempt to humanize race within socialization by showing variations in behavior generally attributed to race as outcomes of social and eco-nomic conditions. For example, socialization of racial identity (being consciously aware of and claiming a specific racial membership) was found to be significantly related to the encounter stage of ethnic identity and, for African Americans, pre-dictive of lower classroom grades (Marshall, 1995). Based on in-depth case studies, another researcher found that racial socialization among Blacks was primarily as-sociated with traumatic experiences with Whites and other Blacks (Thomas, 1998). On the other hand, Black adolescents who were more religious were less stigma-tized by their racial identity than those who were not religious (Brega & Coleman, 1999). African American parents have to employ a variety of strategies to socialize their children with regard to race. What African Americans tell their children and when is critical (Hughes & Chen, 1999). There are attempts to isolate these tactics and determine the effectiveness and outcome of each (Thomas & Speight, 1999; Thompson, 1994) as part of cultural resilience in response to social environmental challenges (McCubbin, 1998).

African Americans are not the only subjects of racial socialization research. Mexican Americans also have to devise ways to socialize their children into their racial identity. What tactics work without leading to counterracial prejudice (Bernal & Knight, 1993; Quintana & Vera, 1999)? For a recent anthology of read-ings on socialization among American racial-ethnic groups, see Garcia and Hur-tado (1995) and Smith and Jackson (1989), and for a survey of issues among ethnic groups in Canada, see Berry and Annis (1988).

If there is a theme that runs through most of this work, it is that races are cultures within the context of the larger American society. One can argue whether or not the American concept of race is worth transforming or can be transformed given its racist history and underlying roots. But there is yet to be a conscious and systematic attempt in this literature to fully look at each racial group as ethnocultures.

Racial socialization research articles outline findings and issues within each "race" and show sensitivity to variations in identity, values, attitudes, beliefs, and behavior within the group. In this sense, they are showing ethnocultural content. But when racial groups are compared race by race and race by ethnic group, this sensitivity is often curtailed. Whites, Blacks, Native Americans, and Hispanics are compared among themselves, where one side of the comparison is undifferentiated. That is, one side of the comparison is not differentiated with regard to social class or intra-group cultural variations. Ironically, research on White racial identity and socialization is the rarest of all. White racial socialization is either considered a mystery or nonexistent, and the second greatest mystery is Euro-American ethnic identity and socialization (Betz & Fitzgerald, 1993). In one rare article, a re-searcher got White second-, fourth-, and sixth-graders to talk about their parents' racial socialization in some detail (Davilla, 1999). Other work asked whether Black, White, and biracial children communicated differently because of their dif-fering identities and statuses (Socha & Diggs, 1999). They do, and the differences are striking.

"Only when Americans realize that what they believe in is cultural will they re-alize that what African Americans and Native Americans experience is cultural"

(Kim, 1991, p. 23). This is true as well with regard to Whites' concept of themselves and people of Color's knowledge of European Americans.

IMPLICATIONS FOR SCIENCE

This review suggests that after almost a century of effort, the science of cultural socialization in the United States does not yet have a series of verified propositions, as initially thought. It has been the limited worldviews, American and middle class, of most of the past century's students of socialization that have been demonstrated in most of the field's prior work. In addition, the American concept of race has further compromised efforts to understand cultural socialization by shutting off from view much of the variability and subtlety of the social interactions that go into socialization of Whites as well as people of Color. For science to advance, at minimum scientists from a variety of cultural backgrounds and experiences must make conscious efforts to move beyond one another's cultural and class biases. These scientists should be both domestically and internationally diverse and should work closely together in a new century of research. The goal here is not simply to continue to assimilate researchers into a single national class culture, but to intentionally explore the worlds they are familiar with and have access to, making for rich and creative comparative analyses. But such teams of scientists with such variations in cultural experiences and backgrounds will not just happen; such a new generation will have to be intentionally cultivated and then supported.

Teams of diverse investigators could better explore the extent to which the relations among culture, socialization, personality, and behavior are direct (Figure 11.1) or interactive. That is, the socialization influences that shape persons and groups not only go from culture to socialization to the individual and group; there is a reverse flow of influence from the individuals and groups back to change culture. The past assumption was that culture is relatively stable and requires generations to change. In which case, culture is a very powerful independent variable. The key to better understanding culture, then, is to better understand socialization, because the variability in culture's influence is due to variations in socialization.

The research of Tallman et al. (1983) is unique in that it illustrates that parents are not uncritical conduits of culture, where cultural influences flow unimpeded from parents to children. Others have noted the environmental basis of parents' selective emphasis (Harkness & Super, 1996). Parents pick and choose which aspects of their culture they will emphasize and, in doing so, vary the transmission of their national, religious, and ethnic cultures to their children. In time, these parents change the culture they learned, because their children learn only part of what their parents learned. Subtly, the culture is changed. The next generation (grandchildren) will undoubtedly do the same, further impacting the original cultural systems. In which case, culture is no longer an anchor, a constant, or a given from which behavior could be predicted if we better understood socialization. Our ability to see the decentralization and reconstruction of culture by each generation is undoubtedly an outcome of the rapid social change that is now affecting human societies throughout the world.

To study and understand the relationships between increasingly fluid cultures and socialization requires a very different social psychology. Lessons from cross-cultural psychology suggest the first challenge: We must realize that socialization cannot be understood by "narrowly focusing on the teaching, modeling, and reinforcement behaviors of teachers and parents without consideration of the surrounding complex of social interactions and routine activities that critically support these adult interactions" (Whiting & Edwards, 1988, p. 2). The ecology of socialization research must be broadened, especially beyond the individual, to families and community as primary units of analysis (Szapocznik & Kurtines, 1993). Advancements will require conceptualization and testing of more complex relationships between the learner and his or her immediate family, extended family, close and casual friends, teachers, and even neighbors (Brooks-Gunn et al., 1993). We should no longer assume who are the primary and secondary socialization agents, or for that matter, that they are human and not also television personalities, pop stars, and recording artists. Profound and long-lasting influence on the learner can come from almost anywhere.

The following questions arise from a more broadly conceived effort: Are there hierarchies of relational influences? Do socializing agents compete for influence? Under what circumstances does one or the other relationship become more or less salient? Are the influences of multiple relationships over time cumulative, or are they episodic? How do parents and other socialization agents use their cultural knowledge to creatively shape and test new coping behaviors to address new challenges for themselves and their children? Whiting and Edward (1988) have shown how such questions can be answered across national cultures using a combination of qualitative and quantitative techniques. Qualitatively, children were observed in their home and community settings; observers noted who they interacted with and what they did in these interactions. Then, quantitatively, the number of interactions were counted and the interactions categorized and statistically analyzed by nonobserving team members. Such mixed methods comparing domestic ethnic-racial groups within and between social class divisions could generate new insights in socialization and culture in the United States as well.

Several major suppositions from past research still stand as feasible hypotheses for future research. The first is that there are links between psychological maturation and developing physiology. This is a hypothesis that should be aggressively explored in a more open and inclusive research framework that considers multiple social environmental influences. Goodman (1970) posits that the link between psychological and physiological maturation is not as strong as most Americans believe; the potential for perception and maturity of American children is grossly underestimated. Cross-cultural researchers also have noted the absence of the presumed necessary adolescent turmoil and earlier maturity of children in overseas communities (Goodman, 1970; Mead, 1928; Whiting & Whiting, 1975).

Second, can variations in the social environments where socialization occurs be classified? The principle that cross-cultural social environments are unique and relative to one's own environment may have been a useful and necessary corrective to the past century's presumption of Western cultural superiority and racism. A problem is that this principle precludes exploring commonalities and consistencies of social and psychological environments across human cultures. Much of the cultural socialization research of the past century was devoted to the study of cultural differences. We need a new and complementary approach that also explores relatedness—similarities and consistencies across cultures (Kagitcibasi, 1996). The goal of this approach is not to conclude that everyone is the same. It is to more accurately and systematically understand where cross-cultural similarities and differences are and why they are where they are. In which case, we might better understand the similarities and differences in how various groups of, for instance, Japanese and European American parents approach socialization and education in comparison with different groups of African American and Mexican American parents. But to do this requires in-depth knowledge of the variations within as well as between these ethnic groups.

A third hypothesis is that socialization works as a series of developmental stages or gates that learners must pass through in proper order to be well-adjusted and effective adults. Parents and teacher have believed that they must work within these developmental constraints because of children's limited capacity. In effect, children have well-known and bounded psychological plasticity. Variations across cultures show that humans are much more flexible than expected—in the West. Children as social learners are capable of more mature, perceptive, and insightful behavior than is normally recognized in the middle-class Western world.

Race as Culture to Improve Science

The place where studies of culture, socialization, and race need the greatest retooling is in the United States. If we relook at American society with race as a cultural rather than a quasi-physical phenomenon, we literally have to redo the past century of socialization studies. There is the potential to better understand American culture and socialization and to do more rigorous comparative analyses. In the context of race as culture, race is a historical and cultural factor that is more or less salient in each social actor's life. That is, people vary in the extent to which they are socialized into one, the other, or some combination of "racial" cultures. Thus, what makes White Americans White is not their skin color or some other innate physiological property, but their culture. The same applies for all other "racial" groups. This means Blacks can be and are more or less White, Whites can be more or less Black, and so on. The old prescriptive racial divisions that were unchanged regardless of a person's perception, socialization, and self-identification, never really existed outside of what most Americans have been taught to believe about race. In looking at the race myth, we can ask questions about the inner workings of (American) culture and personality that we have not been able to ask before.

How are Americans socialized into their ethnic and racial identities? Are race and ethnicity different identities? What is the content of each ethnic and/or racial culture—how would they be accurately described? What role and difference do these identities make for personality development? Do these identities ever conflict with one another? Are ethnic and/or racial cultures waning, increasing, or simply changing? What commonalities (relatedness) exist across racial and ethnic groups? These are not questions to be answered only by self-identified ethnics and racial minorities. Put another way: How are children socialized to be White, especially by parents and others who never directly discuss or recognize being White? Learners in other "races" are more or less conscious and more or less intentional in their racial socialization. What difference does either conscious or unconscious racial-ethnic identity make in personality development and individual and group behavior? Are racial and ethnic cultural differences minor relative to social class differences? Are social classes the same for all ethnic and racial groups, or does each racial and ethnic group have its own social class system? The answers to the latter questions have enormous implications for whether we have accurately compared groups in the prior decades of research.

These new questions are not limited to race relations or ethnic studies. Exploring these questions contributes to the central research model and ultimately to better understanding and predicting individual and group behavior. By penetrating the race barrier, we open up the enormous variety of peoples and socialization processes existing in the United States today, not only among people of Color but among European Americans as well. The importance and necessity of cross-cultural research in the United States and comparatively across national cultures become evident.

Research open to exploring the full ecology of social relationships and influences is consistent with the work called for by Bronfenbrenner (1972), Berry and Annis (1988), and Kagitcibasi (1996). By exploring race as a cultural factor, we have to go beyond Whites and Blacks as undifferentiated aggregates varied only by social class. Once we get into the ethnic and cultural content of social learners' lives, the architecture of varied and complex cultural psychologies will become apparent and should be more fruitful predictors of behavior.

Perhaps it is as Mark Baldwin (1902) proposed at the turn of the past century: Children come to know themselves only as a consequence of social interaction with others, and not by any other way (p. 23). But we might now add that what people bring to these interactions and how they process and respond to them have the potential to change the social interactions and create new ways.

REFERENCES

Adey, P., & Shayer, M. (1994). *Really raising standards: Cognitive intervention and academic achievement*. New York: Routledge.

Allen, T. W. (1994). *The invention of the White race. Vol. 1: Racial oppression and social control*. London: Verso.

Anastasi, A. (1992). A century of psychological science. *American Psychologist, 47*(7), 842–846.

Anderson, M. (1975). Family, household and the industrial revolution. In M. Anderson (Ed.), *Sociology of the family*. Hammondsworth, England: Penguin.

Anthias, F. (1992). Connecting "race" and ethnic phenomena. *Sociology, 26*(3), 421–438.

Aries, P. (1962). *Centuries of childhood*. New York: Alfred Knopf.

Baldwin, J. M. (1902). *Social and ethical interpretations in mental development*. New York: Macmillan.

Baumrind, D. (1980). New directions in socialization research. *American Psychologist, 35*(7), 639–652.

Bernal, M. E., & Knight, G. P. (Eds.). (1993). *Ethnic identity: Formation and transmission among Hispanics and other minorities.* Albany: State University of New York Press.

Berry, J. W. (1984). Towards a universal psychology of cognitive competence. *International Journal of Psychology, 19,* 335–359.

Berry, J. W. (1994). An ecological perspective on culture, ethnicity, and ethnic psychology. In E. Trickett, R. Watts, & D. Birman (Eds.), *Human diversity: Perspectives on people in context.* San Francisco: Jossey-Bass.

Berry, J. W., & Annis, R. C. (Eds.). (1988). *Ethnic psychology: Research and practice with immigrants, refugees, native peoples, ethnic groups and sojourners.* Amsterdam: Swets and Zeitlinger.

Betancourt, H., & Lopez, S. R. (1993). The study of culture, ethnicity, and race in American psychology. *American Psychologist, 48*(6), 629–637.

Betz, N., & Fitzgerald, L. (1993). Individuality and diversity: Theory and research in counseling psychology. In L. Porter & M. Rosenzweig (Eds.), *Annual review of psychology* (Vol. 44, pp. 343–381). Palo Alto, CA: Annual Review Press.

Blau, Z. (1992). *Black children/White children: Competence, socialization, and social structure.* New York: Free Press.

Brega, A., & Coleman, L. (1999). Effects of religiosity and racial socialization on subjective stigmatization in African-American adolescents. *Journal of Adolescence, 22*(2), 223–225.

Brislin, R. W. (1983). Cross-cultural research in psychology. In M. Rosenzweig & L. Porter (Eds.), *Annual review of psychology* (Vol. 34, pp. 363–400). Palo Alto, CA: Annual Review Press.

Bronfenbrenner, U. (1972). *Two worlds of childhood: US and USSR.* New York: Simon & Schuster.

Brooks-Gunn, J., Duncan, G. J., Klebanov, P. K., & Sealand, N. (1993). Do neighbors influence child and adolescent development? *American Sociological Review, 99*(2), 353–395.

Broude, G. (1995). *Growing-up: A cross-cultural encyclopedia.* Denver, CO: ABC-CLIO.

Cashmore, J. A., & Goodnow, J. (1986). Influences on Australian parents' values: Ethnicity versus socioeconomic status. *Journal of Cross-Cultural Psychology, 17,* 441–454.

Cecil-Fronsman, B. (1992). *Common Whites: Class and culture in antebellum North Carolina.* Lexington, MA: University Press of America.

Cushman, P. (1990). Why the self is empty: Toward a historically situated psychology. *American Psychologist, 45*(5), 599–611.

Davila, R. (1999). White children's talk about race and culture: Family communications and intercultural socialization. In T. Socha & R. Diggs (Eds.), *Communication, race, and family* (pp. 91–104). Mahwah, NJ: Erlbaum.

Douvan, E. (1997). Erik Erikson: Critical times, critical theory. *Child Psychiatry and Human Development, 28*(1), 15–21.

Drake, St, C. (1987). *Black folk: Here and there.* Los Angeles: University of California, Los Angeles, Center for Afro-American Studies.

Garcia, E., & Hurtado, A. (1995). Becoming American: A review of current research on the development of racial and ethnic identity in children. In W. Hawley & A. Jackson (Eds.),

Toward a common destiny: Improving race and ethnic relations in America (pp. 163–184). San Francisco: Jossey-Bass.

Gates, N. (1997). *The concept of race in natural and social science.* New York: Garland Press.

Goodman, M. (1970). *The culture of childhood: Child's-eye views of society and culture.* New York: Columbia University, Teachers College Press.

Gossett, T. F. (1998). *Race: The history of an idea in America.* New York: Oxford University Press. (Original work published 1963)

Graves, J. L. Jr. (1993). Evolutionary biology and human variation: Biological determinism and the myth of race. *Sage Race Relations Abstracts, 18*(3), 3–34.

Greenfield, P., & Cocking, R. (Eds.). (1994). *Cross-cultural roots of minority child development.* Hillsdale, NJ: Erlbaum.

Greenfield, S. (1973). Industrialization and the family in sociological theory. In D. Schulz & R. Wilson (Eds.), *Readings on the changing family.* Englewood Cliffs, NJ: Prentice-Hall.

Handel, G. (Ed.). (1988). *Childhood socialization.* New York: Aldine de Gruyter.

Harkness, S., & Super, C. (Eds.). (1996). *Parents' cultural belief systems: Their origins, expressions, and consequences.* New York: Guilford Press.

Hawley, A. (1950). *Human ecology: A theory of community structure.* New York: Ronald Press.

Hernstein, R. J., & Murray, C. (1994). *The bell curve: Intelligence and class structure in American life.* New York: Free Press.

Howard, A., & Scott, R. (1981). The study of minority groups in complex societies. In R. Munroe & B. Whiting (Eds.), *Handbook of cross-cultural human development* (pp. 113–154). New York: Garland STPM Press.

Hughes, D., & Chen, L. (1999). When and what parents tell children about race: An examination of race-related socialization among African American families. *Applied Developmental Science, 1*(4), 200–214.

Jaynes, G. D., & Williams, R. M. (Eds.). (1989). *A common destiny: Blacks and American society.* Washington, DC: National Academy Press.

Kagitcibasi, C. (1996). *Family and human development across cultures: A view from the other side.* Mahwah, NJ: Erlbaum.

Kagitcibasi, C., & Berry, J. W. (1989). Cross-cultural psychology: Current research and trends. In M. Rosenzweig & L. Porter (Eds.), *Annual review of psychology* (Vol. 40, pp. 493–532). Palo Alto, CA: Annual Review Press.

Kim, U. (1991). Discussion. In P. M. Greenfield & R. R. Cocking (Eds.), *Continuities and discontinuities in the cognitive socialization of minority children.* Proceedings of a Workshop, DHHS, Public Health Service, ADAMHA, Washington, DC.

Kroeber, A. L., & Kluckholm, C. (1952). *Culture. Part III: Papers of the Peabody Museum of Harvard University.* Cambridge, MA: Harvard University Press.

Kuhl, S. (1994). *The Nazi connection: Eugenics, American racism, and German national socialism.* New York: Oxford University Press.

Lasch, C. (1979). *The culture of narcissism.* New York: Norton.

Leiderman, P. H., Tuklin, S., & Rosenfeld, A. (Eds.). (1977). *Culture and infancy: Variations in the human experience.* New York: Academic Press.

Marshall, S. (1995). Ethnic socialization of African American children: Implications for parenting, identity development, and academic achievement. *Journal of Youth and Adolescence, 24*(4), 377–397.

McCubbin, H. (1998). *Resiliency in African American families.* Thousand Oaks, CA: Sage.

McLoyd, V., & Flanagan, C. (Eds.). (1990). *Economic stress: Effects on family life and child development* (No. 46). San Francisco: Jossey-Bass.

Mead, M. (1928). *Coming of age in Samoa.* New York: Morrow.

Mundy-Castle, A. (1974). Social and technological intelligence in Western and non-Western cultures. In S. Pilowsky (Ed.), *Culture in collision.* Adelaide: Australian National Association of Mental Health.

Price, D. (1990). *Atlas of world cultures: A geographic guide to ethnographic literature.* Newbury Park, CA: Sage.

Quintana, S., & Vera, E. (1999). Mexican American children's ethnic identity, understanding of ethnic prejudice, and parental ethnic socialization. *Hispanic Journal of Behavioral Sciences, 21*(4), 387–405.

Reynolds, L. (1992). Retrospective on "race": The career of a concept. *Sociological Focus, 25*(1), 1–14.

Rossi, A. (Ed.). (1994). *Sexuality across the life course.* Chicago: University of Chicago Press.

Rubington, E., & Weinberg, M. (Eds.). (1996). *Deviance: The interactionist perspective.* Boston: Allyn & Bacon.

Segall, M. H. (1986). Culture and behavior: Psychology in global perspective. In M. Rosenzweig & L. Porter (Eds.), *Annual review of psychology* (Vol. 37, pp. 523–564). Palo Alto, CA: Annual Review Press.

Shanklin, E. (1994). *Anthropology and race.* Belmont, CA: Wadsworth.

Shweder, R. A., & Sullivan, M. (1993). Cultural psychology: Who needs it? In L. Porter & M. Rosenzweig (Eds.), *Annual review of psychology* (Vol. 44, pp. 497–523). Palo Alto, CA: Annual Review Press.

Smith, J. O., & Jackson, C. (1989). *Race and ethnicity: A study of intracultural socialization patterns.* Dubuque, IA: Kendall Hunt.

Snowden, F. (1983). *Before color prejudice.* Cambridge, MA: Harvard University Press.

Socha, T., & Diggs, R. (1999). *Communications, race, and family: Exploring communications in Black, White, and biracial children.* Mahwah, NJ: Erlbaum.

Swiderski, R. (1991). *Lives between cultures: A study of human nature, identity, and culture.* Juneau, AK: Denali Press.

Szapocznik, J., & Kurtines, W. M. (1993). Family psychology and cultural diversity: Opportunities for theory, research, and application. *American Psychologist, 47,* 400–407.

Tallman, I., Marotz-Baden, R., & Pindas, P. (1983). *Adolescent socialization in cross-cultural perspective: Planning for social change.* New York: Academic Press.

Thomas, A. (1998). Racism, racial identity, and racial socialization: A personal reflection. *Journal of Counseling and Development, 77*(1), 35–38.

Thomas, A., & Speight, S. L. (1999). Racial identity and racial socialization of African American parents. *Journal of Black Psychology, 25*(2), 152–172.

Thompson, V. (1994). Socialization to race and its relationship to racial identification among African Americans. *Journal of Black Psychology, 20*(2), 175–189.

Wagenaar, T., & Coates, T. (1999). Race and children: The dynamics of early socialization. *Education, 120*(2), 220–240.

Weinstein, M., Goodjoin, R., Crayton, E., & Lawson, C. (1990). Black sexuality: A bibliography. *Sage Race Relations Abstracts, 1*(3), 4, 38, 56.

Wentworth, W. (1980). *Context and understanding: An inquiry into socialization theory.* New York: Elsevier.

Whiting, B., & Edwards, C. (1988). *Children of different worlds: The formation of social behavior.* Cambridge, MA: Harvard University Press.

Whiting, B., & Whiting, J. (1975). *Children of six cultures: A psycho-cultural analysis.* Cambridge, MA: Harvard University Press.

CHAPTER 12

Acculturation: Current and Future Directions

Eric L. Kohatsu

Acculturation is a complex and widely used construct in racial-cultural psychology and has undoubtedly impacted the research and clinical applications of the field in significant ways. According to Carter (1995), a race-based approach in psychology emphasizes the central importance of race and is the "superordinate locus of culture through which cultural groups are identified" (p. 259). In addition, race is the primary factor that impacts an individual's experience in a socioracial group, defines the extent of social exclusion and inclusion, and shapes culture through the sociopolitical history of racial groups and intergroup dynamics (e.g., Carter, 1995, 1997). The reality of most people living in the United States is that race exerts a powerful impact on many facets of their experience, including acculturation (Helms, 1990; Helms & Cook, 1999). Given the premises of race psychology as presented in this *Handbook* and discussed above, this chapter offers a race-based perspective on the current use and future trends in the acculturation research tradition.

The conceptual basis of acculturation has frequently been confounded with ethnicity, ethnic identity, and racial identity. As used in this chapter, *ethnicity* refers to the "national, regional, or tribal origins of one's oldest remembered ancestors and the customs, traditions, and rituals . . . handed down" (Helms & Cook, 1999, p. 19). "Ethnic identity" refers to individuals' strong attachments to their *ethnic* group. In addition, Casas and Pytluk (1995) defined ethnic identity as "one's knowledge of personal ownership or membership in the ethnic group, and the correlated knowledge, understanding, values, behaviors, and proud feelings that are direct implications of that ownership" (p. 159). In contrast, *racial identity* refers to the process in which individuals overcome internalized racism and achieve a self-affirming and positive collective identity based on a realistic understanding of their socioracial group's sociopolitical history and culture (e.g., Helms, 1995, 2001; Helms & Cook, 1999).

Grounded in a race-based framework and in these defined terms, the current chapter critically evaluates the acculturation research in the context of racial-cultural psychology by exploring (1) the various ways researchers have defined and conceptualized acculturation, (2) the associated methodological and measurement problems in investigations of acculturation, (3) a brief overview of the research on acculturation issues with racial-cultural groups in the United States, and (4) the intersections of acculturation with racial-cultural-based psychology. I also offer recommendations for future research and applications of acculturation.

CONCEPTUALIZATIONS AND DEFINITIONS OF ACCULTURATION

One of the predominant themes in the acculturation literature has been the consistent lack of consensus in defining the term (e.g., Celano, 1986; Kohatsu, 1992). Researchers have used the term acculturation in different ways and often in conjunction with other constructs, such as assimilation, ethnic identity, and ethnicity (Kohatsu, 1992, 1996). What makes defining acculturation so difficult is that there are multiple levels in which acculturation can take place. For example, examining acculturation at the group level could involve analyzing differences among refugees versus immigrants.

Nonetheless, three trends can be noted in the acculturation literature regarding defining the term (Kohatsu, 1992). In the oldest and most widely used definition, acculturation is a linear and unidimensional process involving the accommodation of the nondominant/migrant culture to the dominant host culture (e.g., Berry, 2003; Kohatsu, 1992; Sue, Mak, & Sue, 1998). The linear approach basically involves the individual's learning to adopt to the cultural patterns of the host or dominant culture, usually White culture. Implicitly, the definition embraces the idea that immigrants or nondominant group members lose their respective ethnic culture while adopting to the dominant host culture. Thus, the linear approach conceptualizes acculturation on a single continuum, ranging from high nondominant cultural identification to complete adoption of White culture. According to the unidimensional perspective, acculturation is defined as the extent to which a nondominant group member adopts the dominant White culture while simultaneously discarding his or her original culture.

The unidimensional approach to defining acculturation has in recent years been surpassed by a multidimensional approach. The so-called dominant group and nondominant group cultures are seen as coexisting independent systems. That is, each culture is conceived as a single continuum and individuals theoretically can vary in their acceptance of and adaptation to the two cultures independently (e.g., Cuellar, Arnold, & Maldonado, 1995; Kohatsu, 1992). Thus, each individual can maintain a certain level of involvement or noninvolvement in both cultures simultaneously. The multidimensional approach defines acculturation as the individual's process of learning about and adopting White cultural values, beliefs, attitudes, and behaviors into his or her self-concept and the degree to which the person maintains his or her own ethnic culture (or other ethnic cultures) through adherence to cultural values, beliefs, attitudes, and behaviors (Kohatsu, 1992).

The third approach has not generated as much research. Here, acculturation is defined as the acceptance or rejection of a prescribed set of cultural traits (e.g., Keefe & Padilla, 1987; Kohatsu, 1992). Individuals can maintain certain cultural traits (i.e., characteristics) from their original cultural group and discard others. Similarly, an individual can maintain certain traits from the dominant White culture and discard others. Each cultural trait can be measured independently of other traits. The trait approach can be defined as the delineation of specific cultural characteristics from the dominant culture and the nondominant culture that the migrant/nondominant group individual adopts.

Generally speaking, most researchers seem to endorse acculturation as a process of "change that occurs as a consequence of continuous, first-hand contact of two or more distinct cultural groups" (Roysircar-Sodowsky & Maestas, 2000, p. 133). The change in cultural values, attitudes, beliefs, and practices of both the immigrant/ nondominant group and the host culture, as a result of the contact, is what most acculturation researchers have focused on. A specific definition, from the multidimensional approach, is adopted in this chapter: Acculturation refers to the individual's process of learning about and adopting White cultural values, beliefs, attitudes, and behaviors into his or her self-concept (Kohatsu, 1992). Acculturation also involves the degree to which the person maintains his or her own ethnic culture (or other ethnic cultures) through adherence to cultural values, beliefs, attitudes, and behaviors (Kohatsu, 1992). Thus, the general definition adopted in this chapter describes acculturation at the individual or psychological level (Birman, 1994).

Although not widely researched, it has been suggested that acculturation applies primarily to first-generation immigrant/nondominant group individuals (Roysircar-Sodowsky & Maestas, 2000). An implicit notion in the acculturation research is that individuals who are second generation and on are not so deeply affected by the acculturation process; for these individuals, issues of ethnic identity become more salient (Roysircar-Sodowsky & Maestas, 2000). However, it is suggested in this chapter that psychological acculturation occurs in immigrant/nondominant group individuals regardless of generational level, albeit in different ways and at different rates (Casas & Pytluk, 1995).

Casas and Pytluk (1995) suggested that the psychological and social changes that take place in the acculturation process depend on the unique characteristics of the individual, the degree of intensity and importance ascribed to cultural contact between groups, and the actual numbers of nondominant and dominant groups. Thus, the experience of acculturation presumably can be highly variable among individuals of a particular immigrant/nondominant group and likewise across various immigrant/nondominant groups. Similarly, the sociocultural and racial environments in which acculturation takes place can also determine the quality of acculturation for any given individual (Birman, 1998; Birman Trickett, & Vinokurov, 2002). In short, researchers have not paid much attention to the specific sociocultural and racial environments and their influences on the acculturation process among nondominant and dominant group members.

Further, in understanding acculturation, it is important to note that some researchers have distinguished between acculturation and enculturation. Generally, enculturation refers to a process by which the individual is socialized in his or her own ethnic group's culture. That is, enculturation entails learning about one's own ethnic group's culture (Casas & Pytluk, 1995). In addition, enculturation "describes the influences on behavior exerted by the culture in which one develops, and which does not involve cultural change" (Birman, 1994, p. 261). Enculturation, then, represents one aspect of the acculturation process from a multidimensional perspective.

Acculturation is frequently used interchangeably with assimilation, as if they were synonymous terms. Nonetheless, according to some researchers, assimilation is not the same as acculturation (e.g., Helms & Cook, 1999). Assimilation refers to the acceptance and inclusion of a particular racial-cultural group by the dominant (White) group into the societal structure (Helms & Cook, 1999). In other words, assimilation entails the acceptance of a particular group into the social structure established by Whites/dominant group members in this country regardless of the extent to which the group maintains or discards its original culture. Assimilation pertains to the societal status of an individual in terms of "the extent to which he or she is accepted in personally relevant social environments" (p. 126) by the dominant group members.

A critical element in the conceptual understanding of acculturation is that unlike racial identity and other race-based psychological constructs, acculturation has usually not addressed the psychological processes that an individual undergoes in internalizing racism or dealing with oppression (Kohatsu, 1992). In other words, issues of racism and oppression are not an integral component of most acculturation models (Kohatsu, 1992). However, a number of racial-cultural psychologists have argued that race has indeed been a powerful factor that has affected the psychological and social well-being of many people in the United States and as such needs to be addressed (e.g., Carter, 1997; Thompson & Carter, 1997). Therefore, it is vital to clearly distinguish the conceptual boundaries of acculturation, racial identity, and ethnic identity in psychological research and practice.

Similarly, many studies in the past have confounded acculturation with ethnic identity and racial identity (Kohatsu, 1992; Roysircar-Sodowsky & Maestas, 2000). For instance, it was common for researchers to assess acculturation by employing either a racial or an ethnic identity measure and vice versa (e.g., Roysircar-Sodowsky & Maestas, 2000). This confounding occurred both on a conceptual as well as on a measurement level. Such imprecision in the conceptualization and measurement of acculturation has contributed significantly to the continued misuse of this cultural construct and to the misunderstanding of race-based psychological constructs.

One outcome of using acculturation interchangeably with other racial-cultural variables is that the research in this area has obscured the importance of sociorace-related variables and processes. As Kohatsu (1992) suggested, researchers often assumed that acculturation superseded other constructs such as racial identity. Consequently, rather than conceptualizing acculturation within a broader framework of other factors composing one's identity, acculturation was treated as the primary variable influencing a nondominant group member's sense of self when residing in a society in which dominant group members are culturally different.

SCALES AND MEASUREMENT ISSUES

Scales

Much of the empirical work done on acculturation issues in the United States has focused on Latinos and Asians (e.g., Kim & Abreu, 2001; Roysircar-Sodowsky & Maestas, 2000). More recently, theories of acculturation and its corresponding measurement have been extended to other racial-cultural groups, such as African Americans, American Indians, and White Americans (e.g., Birman & Trickett, 2001;

Landrine & Klonoff, 1994; Snowden & Hines, 1999). Several reviews of acculturation measures have been published (Kim & Abreu, 2001; Roysircar-Sodowsky & Maestas, 2000; Zane & Mak, 2003), and prevailing themes, partly based on these reviews, regarding the measurement of acculturation in the context of a race-based psychological approach is the focus of this section. First, a brief discussion of the major measures used in acculturation research is presented.

The majority of acculturation measures used in earlier research were unidimensional instruments; these scales assessed acculturation on a single continuum, ranging from high endorsement of the dominant culture at one end to high endorsement of one's original culture at the other end. According to Kim and Abreu (2001), 18 unidimensional scales were developed from 1978 to 1996 to assess acculturation among Latinos. Measures such as the Behavioral Acculturation Scale (BAS; Szapocznik, Scopetta, Kurtines, & Aranalde, 1978), Acculturation Rating Scale for Mexican Americans (ARMSA-1; Cuellar, Harris, & Jasso, 1980), and the Short Acculturation Scale for Hispanics (SASH; Marin, Sabogal, Marin, Otero-Sabogal, & Perez-Stable, 1987) exemplify the kinds of measures that were used in examining acculturation issues with Latinos. In addition, other unidimensional acculturation scales, such as the Suinn-Lew Asian Self-Identity Acculturation Scale (SL-ASIA; Suinn, Rickard-Figueroa, Lew, & Vigil, 1987), Navajo Family Acculturation Scale (NFAS; Boyce & Boyce, 1983), and the African American Acculturation Scale (AAAS; Landrine & Klonoff, 1994) were developed for use with specific socioracial groups. As a specific example of these unidimensional acculturation measures, the SL-ASIA (Suinn & Ahuna, 1992) is a 21-item measure that assesses language use, friendship choice, food preference, media preference, participation in cultural activities, identity, and generation level/geographic region. Responses to all items are summed and the mean score is calculated, resulting in highly acculturated (White American cultural orientation = 5), bicultural (3), or low acculturated (Asian identified = 1) ratings of Asian individuals.

What seems to be common among these unidimensional acculturation scales is that behaviors were used most frequently to determine acculturation levels. For example, the ARMSA-I (Cuellar et al., 1980) is a 20-item scale that assesses language familiarity and usage, ethnic interaction, cultural heritage, generational proximity, and ethnic pride and identity. Approximately 70% of the items in the ARMSA tap into the behavioral aspects of acculturation (Kim & Abreu, 2001).

In contrast, multidimensional measures of acculturation are far less common and less widely used. Examples of multidimensional acculturation measures include the Acculturation Rating Scale for Mexican Americans-II (ARSMA-II; Cuellar et al., 1995), Bidimensional Short Acculturation Scale (BSASH; Marin & Gamba, 1996), Bicultural Involvement Scale (BIS; Szapocznik, Kurtines, & Fernandez, 1980), Cultural Lifestyle Inventory (CLSI; Mendoza, 1989), Asian/Anglo Acculturation Scale (AAAS; Kohatsu, 1992), and the Bicultural Scale for Puerto Ricans (BSPR; Cortes, Rogler, & Malgady, 1994). In contrast to unidimensional scales, multidimensional acculturation measures assess acculturation along several presumably independent domains, such as the extent of acculturation to the dominant White culture and the degree of acculturation to one's original/nondominant culture.

For instance, the ARSMA-II consists of two subscales: a 17-item Mexican orientation scale (MOS) and a 13-item Anglo orientation scale (AOS). As a multidimensional scale, the summed scores from the MOS and the AOS can be derived and interpreted as separate factors. Further, on the MOS, 76% of items are behavioral, and on the AOS, approximately 85% of items are behavioral (Kim & Abreu, 2001).

Another example of a multidimensional measure is the Anglo-Asian Acculturation scale (AAAS; Kohatsu, 1992). The AAAS consists of two (counterbalanced) 20-item scales; the Asian scale measures acculturation to Asian culture and the Anglo scale measures acculturation to White American culture. Items assess acculturation in terms of cognitions (e.g., adherence to cultural values), behaviors (e.g., ease of communicating with Whites), and emotions (e.g., pride in being Asian). Two separate scores are derived (Asian and White acculturation scores), and internal consistencies of the two scales are consistently high (ranging in the .80s to .90s; Kohatsu, 1992).

Measurement Issues

The majority of empirical work and development of acculturation scales has been based on a unidimensional model of acculturation, such as the development of the ARMSA-I, SL-ASIA, and associated research (e.g., Kim & Abreu, 2001). As mentioned previously, implicit in this measurement approach is the notion that to be acculturated to the dominant White culture in the United States, the immigrant/nondominant group individual has to discard his or her ethnic culture due to the presumed superiority of the dominant culture (Abe-Kim, Okazaki, & Goto, 2001; Kim & Abreu, 2001; Kohatsu, 1992). In spite of advances made in the theory and measurement of multidimensional acculturation (e.g., Kim & Abreu, 2001), researchers have persisted in using a unidimensional approach and its corresponding measures. Such a persistent adherence to a unidimensional conceptualization of acculturation at some level reflects scientific racism in that it implicitly values the dominant White American culture as the standard to be upheld. Thus, this approach does not do justice to the strength of the cultures of immigrant/nondominant groups in the United States.

In addition, the majority of the existing acculturation measures have focused on assessing overt behaviors. As calculated by Kim and Abreu (2001), more than 50% of the items in 85% of the scales they reviewed were behavioral; 36% of the instruments contained behavioral items exclusively. Behavioral items focused on such factors as preferences for spoken language and media, participation in cultural activities, as well as friendship and food choices (Kim & Abreu, 2001). In addition, measures that rely on a unidimensional model of acculturation tended to strongly favor behavioral items. This emphasis on behaviors has resulted in the exclusion of other indicators of acculturation, such as values (Kim & Abreu, 2001).

For those measures that incorporate variables other than behaviors, the lack of precision in defining those variables is problematic. Constructs such as identity and cultural identity have been widely used in measuring acculturation (Kim & Abreu, 2001; Kohatsu, 1992). Yet, the ways researchers define and use such variables in the research is unclear (Roysircar-Sodowsky & Maestas, 2000). Kim and

Abreu attempted to provide a framework for categorizing the dimensions in acculturation; one of the dimensions discussed was cultural identity, which they defined as "attitudes toward indigenous and dominant groups (e.g., feelings of shame toward the indigenous culture and pride toward the dominant group)" (p. 420). On closer examination of the definition, this domain of acculturation appears to overlap conceptually with racial identity and other sociorace-based constructs. Certainly, this conceptualization of acculturation borders closely on what is captured by current racial identity theories (e.g., Helms & Cook, 1999) in its emphasis on a sociopolitical understanding of group membership. For example, in Helms's conceptualization of the Conformity racial identity ego status, a person of Color devalues his or her own socioracial group and idealizes the dominant White culture (Helms & Cook, 1999). Thus, Kim and Abreu's conceptualization of cultural identity appears to overlap with Helms's racial identity model in its underlying definitions.

Although the conceptualization of acculturation has become more complex (i.e., multidimensional) in recent years, the corresponding scales of these models have not followed suit. Many existing acculturation measures used in research are unidimensional (e.g., ARMSA-I, SL-ASIA) and continue to be widely used (e.g., Kim & Abreu, 2001; Kohatsu, 1992; Suinn & Ahuna, 1992; Suinn & Gillian, 1995). To the detriment of the field, multidimensional measures (e.g., ARMSA-II) tend to be less widely used in favor of the outdated unidimensional scales. Hence, in spite of the emerging body of work using multidimensional measures, the results of these studies are not comparable with the empirical studies using unidimensional scales (e.g., Kim & Abreu, 2001). What is especially problematic is that several former unidimensional scales have been updated by adding items that presumably transform these instruments into multidimensional measures (e.g., SL-ASIA; Ponterotto, Baluch, & Carielli, 1998). But researchers need to be careful about how the instruments are scored and what the scores represent in these so-called updated acculturation scales. Although the presumably updated instrument may appear to be multidimensional, it still functions as a unidimensional measure in the way it is scored and interpreted (Abe-Kim et al., 2001).

Another major theme in the acculturation research is that acculturation varies depending on the specific context/environment in which the individual functions at a given moment (Birman, 1998; Birman, Trickett, & Vinokurov, 2002). A particular kind of acculturation may be adaptive in one context but may not be in another. Therefore, in measuring acculturation accurately, it would be helpful for researchers to measure levels of acculturation in each specific context (e.g., school, home, public versus private places) because the outcomes will be different (Birman, 1998; Sasao & Sue, 1993). In other words, different contexts vary in the kind of acculturation style that is adaptive to that particular context/environment. Although empirical support for this facet of acculturation is lacking, Birman found that different kinds of acculturation were related to perceived competence in different contexts among immigrant Latino adolescents. For example, Hispanicism (i.e., degree of acculturation to Hispanic culture) predicted positive perceptions of social acceptance by Latino peers, whereas Americanism (i.e., degree of acculturation to White

American culture) predicted positive perceptions of social acceptance by non-Latino peers.

One problematic issue in the measurement of acculturation is the persistent intermixing of different domains (e.g., values, behaviors) in computing an acculturation score. For example, identity questions are often combined with behavioral items in obtaining an acculturation score. These composite scores are difficult to interpret because of the confounding of different domains of acculturation in a single composite score (Kim & Abreu, 2001). Another problematic issue is that most acculturation scales fail to measure the differential experiences of prejudice and discrimination among the various socioracial groups. For example, in a recent review of 22 acculturation measures, Zane and Mak (2002) found that less than 13% of items in just three scales accounted for perceived prejudice and discrimination.

ACCULTURATION RESEARCH ON SOCIORACIAL-CULTURAL GROUPS

Acculturation and its relationship to other psychological variables has been studied with each of the racial-cultural groups in the United States. Much of the research has focused on Latinos and Asians, although the empirical work on African Americans, American Indians, and White Americans continues to develop. In this section, analyses of the themes in the research with each of these socioracial groups are presented through the lens of a race-based psychology. The lack of consistency in defining acculturation and the vast differences in measuring acculturation in any given study make a comparative analysis and conclusion a daunting task. Due to the instrument problems noted above, this section of the chapter focuses on predominant themes that are common to the different models and measures of acculturation used in studying acculturation issues among the different racial-cultural groups. This section briefly highlights the acculturation research on Latinos, Asians, African Americans, Native Americans, and White Americans and concludes with a discussion of language issues.

Latinos

Beginning in the early 1970s, the majority of the research on acculturation focused on Latino groups, predominantly Mexican, and continued to expand in many different directions (e.g., Rogler, Cortes, & Malgady, 1991; Roysircar-Sodowsky & Maestas, 2000). Given the vast number of empirical studies, dissertations, and theses that have examined acculturation issues among various Latino ethnic groups, a comprehensive analysis of this large body of work is beyond the scope of this chapter. Nonetheless, predominant themes and observations culled from this vast body of literature are discussed.

Generally speaking, the relationship between acculturation (usually defined and measured in a unidimensional manner) and mental health among Latinos is not clear, and there are conflicting findings in the research. For instance, Rogler et al. (1991) proposed that there are positive, negative, and curvilinear relationships between acculturation and mental health-related variables. Studies have supported a positive relationship (e.g., Masten, Penland, & Nayani, 1994; Neff & Hoppe, 1993; Rogler et al., 1991), a negative relationship (e.g., M. A. Burnam, Hough, Karno, Escobar, & Telles, 1987; Gonzalez & Cuellar, 1983), and a mixed/inconclusive relationship (e.g., Canabal & Quiles, 1995; Cuellar & Roberts, 1997) between acculturation and mental health-related variables. For example, positive relationships were found between acculturation and self-esteem, somatization, and alienation (Cuellar, 2000). As stated earlier, unless there is some sort of uniformity in the conceptualization and measurement of acculturation, the growing body of research will become increasingly more difficult to interpret and draw conclusions from. That is, studies utilizing a unidimensional model and/or measure with those that employ a multidimensional measure do not lend themselves well to useful comparisons and interpretations given their differences.

Numerous studies have also been conducted analyzing the relationships between acculturation and counseling and personality-type variables, such as counselor credibility, self-esteem, ethnic identity, depression, type of preferred counseling, use of drugs/substance abuse, global self-worth, family competence, well-being, coping strategies, alienation, perceived stress, traditional sex roles, and knowledge of AIDS (e.g., Bell & Alcalay, 1997; Birman, 1998; Carvajal, Photiades, Evans, & Nash, 1997; Cross & Canul, 1994; Cuellar, 2000; Cuellar, Nyberg, Maldonado, & Roberts, 1997; Cuellar & Roberts, 1997; Cuellar et al., 1980; Fraser, Piacentini, Rossem, Hien, & Rotheram-Borus, 1998; Gil, Wagner, & Vega, 2000; Hovey, 2000; Hovey & Magana, 2000; Olmedo, Martinez, & Martines, 1978; Phinney & Flores, 2002; Pomales & Williams, 1989; Saldana, 1994). Keeping in mind the conceptual and measurement problems already discussed, it can tentatively be stated that the majority of these studies have generally demonstrated a significant link between acculturation and counseling-type variables in ways that appear to be consistent with acculturation theories. That is, empirical work has provided support for the proposed relationships between acculturation and the above-mentioned variables that makes sense in the context of unidimensional or multidimensional acculturation models/ theories. Depending on which domain of acculturation was examined, relationships found were either positive, negative, or curvilinear in ways that, for the most part, seem to be logically related to acculturation theories (Rogler et al., 1991). For example, acculturation to White culture was related to high levels of minority stress, depression, and positive self-perceptions of competence with American peers. In contrast, acculturation to Latino culture was related to preferences for nondirective counselors (Rogler et al., 1991). In addition acculturation was also positively related to ethnic identity (affirmation and belonging, ethnic identity achievement, and ethnic behaviors), and predicted a positive self-perception of competence in relating to Latino peers (e.g., Rogler et al., 1991).

Very few of the studies done on Latino acculturation addressed variables that are race-based. Among the exceptions, researchers either included a race-based variable in their conceptual model (e.g., perceived discrimination) or actually tried to empirically test its relationship to acculturation (e.g., Holleran, 2003; Sodowsky, Lai, & Plake, 1991). For example, Sodowsky et al. examined sociocultural variables such as perceived discrimination that moderate acculturation among Latinos and

Asians. They found that first-generation participants perceived significantly higher levels of prejudice and were less acculturated than second-, third-, or fourth-generation participants. However, such studies are the exception to the rule; for the most part, acculturation studies do not include specific race-based constructs in the design.

Asian Americans

Following closely in the footsteps of the research on Latino acculturation, the work on Asian American acculturation has struggled with many of the same kinds of problems and issues in terms of conceptualization and measurement. As Kohatsu (1992, 1996) noted, acculturation research on Asians has been fraught with the following problems: (1) researchers tend to rely on a unidimensional model of acculturation; (2) studies overuse unidimensional measures of acculturation, such as the SL-ASIA; and (3) few existing models of acculturation have employed Asian-specific cultural elements; instead, researchers tend to borrow models/measures developed on Latino groups and simply transpose the instrument to work with Asians.

For example, an overwhelming majority of the acculturation studies on Asian Americans have used the SL-ASIA, which is based on the Cuellar et al. ARMSA-I (e.g., Atkinson & Gim, 1989; Atkinson, Lowe, & Matthews, 1995; Ponterotto et al., 1998; Tata & Leong, 1994). Reliance on such an outdated measure and model has not advanced the research on acculturation among Asian Americans. While the ARMSA-II (a multidimensional acculturation scale) has been in use for several years now, the SL-ASIA has not followed suit in improving its validity (e.g., Ponterotto et al., 1998).

Similar to Latino/Hispanic acculturation research, researchers have examined acculturation in relation to a wide range of counseling, mental health, and personality-type variables among Asian samples (e.g., Atkinson & Gim, 1989; Atkinson et al., 1995; Ponterotto et al., 1998; Roysircar-Sodowsky & Maestas, 2000; Tata & Leong, 1994; Tracey, Leong, & Glidden, 1986),including attitudes toward professional help, coping strategies, utilization of mental health services, help-seeking behavior, family conflicts, stress, orientation to group counseling, depression, reporting distress, educational issues (e.g., GPA, academic performance, adjustment), perceived racial discrimination, openness to discussing personal issues with counselors, tolerance of cultural stigma toward mental health professionals, cultural adaptation, Big Five personality factors, language usage, changes in traditional cultural values, self-esteem, career counseling, anxiety, assertiveness, and perceptions of interpersonal and institutional racism (e.g., Abe-Kim et al., 2001; Anderson et al., 1993; Iwamsa & Kooreman, 1995; Kohatsu, 1992; Lee, Choe, Kim, & Ngo, 2000; Lee & Liu, 2001; Leong, 2001; Leong & Chou, 1994; Leong, Wagner, & Kim, 1995; Roysircar-Sodowsky & Maestas, 2000; Ryder, Alden, & Paulhus, 2000).

These variables have been found to relate to acculturation in ways that are fairly consistent with acculturation models. For example, higher levels of acculturation to White culture were found to be predictive of positive attitudes toward group counseling and mental health services, and highly acculturated children negatively perceived traditional parental roles and expectations. Again, an important caveat are the complex problems involving different models and measures make such summary statements at best tentative.

Reflecting a similar trend in acculturation research overall, there are few studies on Asian American acculturation that offer insights from a race-based perspective (e.g., Kohatsu, 1992; Liu, Pope-Davis, Nevitt, & Toporek, 1999; Sodowsky et al., 1991). One of the earliest studies was Kohatsu's work, which examined multidimensional acculturation and racial identity together in predicting anxiety, assertiveness, and awareness of institutional and interpersonal racism among Asian Americans in racial interactions with Whites. Unlike most studies, which relied on the Suinn-Lew scale, Kohatsu's work utilized a multidimensional model and measure of acculturation (i.e., Asian-Anglo Acculturation Scale) and employed a specific framework (e.g., Personal Identity and Reference Group Orientation variables) to analyze racial identity and acculturation. Relative to racial identity, acculturation was a significantly less robust predictor of personality type (e.g., anxiety, assertiveness) and racism (e.g., perceptions of interpersonal and institutional racism) variables. Thus, acculturation and racial identity are distinctly separate processes in light of the large differences in predicting anxiety, assertiveness, and awareness of interpersonal and institutional racism. However, acculturation does play a role, albeit presumably small, in interacting with race-based constructs (Kohatsu, 1992).

In a similar vein, Liu et al. (1999) used both a unidimensional (SL-ASIA) and a multidimensional measure (Asian-Anglo Acculturation Scale) of acculturation in their study to predict prejudicial attitudes toward members of nondominant racial groups and women. They found that higher acculturation to White culture and stronger identification with Asian culture predicted lower levels of prejudicial attitudes. Although this study had minor problems with some of the measures used, it does provide a current example of the incorporation of a race-based approach to expand the understanding of acculturation.

Stemming from the preceding discussion, the research on acculturation on Latinos and Asians share a number of similarities: lack of uniformity in the conceptualization, definition, and particularly the measurement of acculturation; problems in interpreting such a disparate and conflicting body of work; and the lack of addressing acculturation from a race-based perspective. In research with African Americans and Native Americans, there are significantly fewer similarities relative to the other two socioracial groups.

African Americans

Generally, acculturation was interpreted as not being applicable to African Americans because of the widespread perception that African Americans are not a recent immigrant group and because of the historical legacy of slavery in the United States. More important, it has been proposed that mainstream psychology has regarded African Americans as a group of people without a culture, and primarily a racial and not a cultural/ethnic group (Landrine & Klonoff, 1994; Snowden & Hines, 1999). In spite of this inherent scientific racism in psychology, a substantial body of work has emerged on articulating the core aspects of African culture that are the bedrock of an African American psychology (e.g., Jones, 1991; Landrine &

Klonoff, 1994). These core cultural elements are the foundation of the research on African American acculturation. An important caveat to this discussion is that the recent work that has emerged on African American acculturation can provide important insights on understanding acculturation from a race-based psychology in that the influences of race are much more apparent than in the previously discussed models and measures of acculturation. Be that as it may, several researchers have recently developed acculturation models and measures to be used with African American samples (e.g., Klonoff & Landrine, 2000; Landrine & Klonoff, 1994, 1996; Snowden & Hines, 1999).

One of the significant models and measures of African American acculturation, the AAAS-R (African American Acculturation Scale-Revised), is based on eight key factors: traditional African American religious beliefs and practices, preferences for things African American, interracial attitudes (e.g., attitudes toward Whites and racism), family practices, health beliefs and practices, cultural superstition, segregation, and family values (Klonoff & Landrine, 2000). On careful examination of the descriptions of these domains and their corresponding questionnaire items, it is striking that the AAAS domains account for the long-standing influence of race on the cultural beliefs and practices of Africans in the United States. That is, these African-based cultural beliefs and practices have persisted despite the historical legacy of racism toward African Americans. In essence, the influence of racial factors are accounted for in the cultural elements of the model. For instance, the item "I don't trust most White people" in the Interracial attitudes subscale clearly assesses degree of racial mistrust, resulting from White racism, among African Americans.

In contrast, the other major trend (and model) in acculturation research on African Americans took a different approach from the one adopted in the development of the AAAS. Snowden and Hines (1999) adapted a Latino acculturation instrument and tested the modified scale with a large sample of African Americans. Unlike the AAAS, Snowden and Hines's 10-item acculturation scale assessed media preferences, social interaction patterns, and race-related attitudes. It remains to be seen how valid and reliable this unidimensional scale is with African American samples.

Reflecting the acculturation research on Latinos and Asians, the work on African American acculturation has shown similar relationships to various psychological variables. For instance, acculturation (e.g., as measured by the AAAS) has been linked to coping strategies with stress, type of social support, depression, food attitudes and eating disorders, knowledge of AIDS transmission, engagement in risky sexual behavior, and alcohol consumption (e.g., Hines, Snowden, & Graves, 1998; Klonoff & Landrine, 1997, 1999, 2000; Snowden & Hines, 1998). Generally speaking, the relationships found in the studies do seem to support the validity of acculturation with African Americans. More specifically, some of the findings are as follows: (1) higher levels of acculturation to African American culture were related to abstention from alcohol consumption; (2) men who reported low levels of acculturation to White culture (traditional) were more likely to engage in risky sexual behavior; (3) women who had low levels of acculturation (to White culture) were found to drink heavily, whereas Black women who had high levels of acculturation (to White culture) engaged in risky sexual behaviors; (4) Blacks who smoked more frequently were more traditional (acculturated to Black culture); and (5) more acculturated Blacks (to White culture) tended to blame themselves (coping strategy) for psychological problems, whereas more traditional Blacks (acculturated to Black culture) tended to deny problems (coping strategy).

From a race-based perspective, few studies have explicitly examined the interface between race-based variables and acculturation (e.g., Pope-Davis, Liu, Ledesma-Jones, & Nevitt, 2000; Thompson, Anderson, & Bakeman, 2000). Pope-Davis et al. examined the relationships between racial identity and acculturation in an African American sample. Both Preencounter and Immersion statuses significantly predicted African American acculturation. For example, the stronger a Black person endorsed Immersion attitudes, the higher the level of African American acculturation. Conversely, the stronger a Black person endorsed Preencounter attitudes, the lower the level of Black acculturation. Pope-Davis et al. suggested that a relationship does exist between acculturation and racial identity and, consequently, may belie the proposition that these constructs are separate processes. The critical point made in this study was that acculturation does not exist independent of sociorace and racism, hence, supporting the basic premise in a race-based psychology.

Native Americans

Significantly less empirical work has been published on acculturation issues among Native Americans (e.g., Berry, Winthrob, Sindell, & Mawhinney, 1982; Choney, Berryhill-Paapke, & Robbins, 1995; Garrett & Pichette, 2000; Guinn, 1998; Oetting, Swaim, & Chiarella, 1998; Zimmerman, Ramirez-Valles, Washienko, Walter, & Dyer, 1996). The scant research on acculturation among American Indians reflects a familiar trend, namely, lack of consensus on defining acculturation, intermixing of different approaches, and conflicting findings. For instance, acculturation to either Indian or White culture among American Indian samples was not found to be related to preferences for counselors (Bennett & BigFoot-Sipes, 1991; Bennett, Big-Foot, & Thurman, 1989), yet analogue studies found the opposite effect regarding acculturation (e.g., BigFoot-Sipes, Dauphinais, LaFromboise, Bennett, & Rowe, 1992). Given the scarcity of sound empirical research on acculturation with Native Americans, it is difficult to make sense of this construct from a race-based perspective. It is important to mention in passing that Choney et al. (1995) strongly recommended that racial identity does not apply to American Indians due to tremendous cultural variations between tribes, the primacy of identifying with a specific tribe as opposed to racial group, and the important influences of religion. Nevertheless, there may or may not be convergence in race-based psychological constructs and acculturation for American Indians.

White Americans

As stated previously, much of the research in cross-cultural psychology has focused on individuals from nondominant socioracial groups. The current body of research on acculturation among White Americans can be categorized into three distinct domains: (1) studies comparing Whites with a socioracial minority group and applying acculturation to only the socioracial minority group (e.g., Park & Harrison, 1995); (2) studies comparing Whites with a socioracial minority group and measuring acculturation similarly in both groups (e.g., Franco, 1983; Frey, 2001; Marin et al., 1987; Montgomery, 1992); and (3) studies analyzing acculturation in a specific White ethnic group (e.g., Birman & Trickett, 2001; Birman & Tyler, 1994). Generally, most of the research has tended to fall into domain 1, although studies utilizing approaches in domains 2 and 3 are becoming more prevalent. It seems that an underlying assumption in the comparative empirical work on acculturation is that this construct applies only to socioracial minority groups and is not an important process to address among White Americans. A brief overview of the research in the latter two domains is now presented.

An important development in the research on acculturation has been to focus on specific immigrant White ethnic groups as they acculturate to American culture. For example, three primary aspects of acculturation (behavioral, language, and identity) were examined among Soviet Jewish refugees in the United States (Birman & Trickett, 2001; Birman et al. 2002; Birman & Tyler, 1994). What is particularly noteworthy in Birman's work is that acculturation to both White American and Russian culture were examined with Soviet Jewish refugees. Birman and Trickett's comprehensive study analyzed acculturation among Soviet Jewish refugees; both adolescents and parents were surveyed. Briefly, acculturation to American culture was found to be related to decreasing acculturation to Russian culture overall across most of the acculturation domains. Russian parents retained a more Russian orientation across the three dimensions of acculturation, whereas the adolescents were more American-oriented with respect to language and behavioral acculturation. However, Russian-language fluency for parents was maintained over time, whereas, surprisingly, Russian identity acculturation was maintained among the adolescents. As Birman and Trickett suggested, acculturation seems to progress at different rates for different age groups along different dimensions.

Regarding domain 2, studies have been conducted to examine acculturation between a nondominant socioracial group and a White American sample using the same model and measure (e.g., Franco, 1983; Frey, 2001; Marin et al., 1987; Montgomery, 1992). For example, Frey explored the relationships among acculturation, worldviews, and ratings of dissociative experiences between White American and international students (South American, Southeast Asian, and South Asian). For the White American participants, acculturation and self-reported childhood abuse were significant predictors of nonpathology (normal dissociation experiences). Moreover, the more the White American participants were acculturated to White American culture, the more they viewed culturally influenced dissociation as disturbing.

Overall, studies in domain 2 suggest that acculturation is a multifaceted process that is composed of multiple dimensions that may not be adequately addressed by researchers (Franco, 1983). Needless to say, more studies like those cited above need to be conducted to further uncover the complexities of acculturation and to fine-tune models and measures of this process for White Americans. It cannot be assumed that acculturation unfolds in similar ways and that it occurs within identical dimensions for Whites as it does for other racial-cultural groups.

Language Issues

The role of language may be another fruitful area to examine, indirectly, the interconnections between acculturation and race-based psychology. Undoubtedly, one of the most widely used factors in measuring acculturation has been language, particularly among Latinos and Asians (e.g., Birman & Trickett, 2001; Negy & Woods, 1992; Roysircar-Sodowsky & Maestas, 2000). According to Roysircar-Sodowsky and Maestas, assessing language was an important trend in the acculturation research from the 1970s to 1980s and from the late 1980s to the present. Language has been such an important factor that in many studies, it has frequently been used as a proxy to indicate levels of acculturation among immigrants (Negy & Woods, 1992).

Although an in-depth analysis of language issues is beyond the scope of this chapter, suffice it to say that Birman and Trickett (2001) pointed out that many studies tended to assess either language usage or language preference as an indicator of acculturation. However, the actual use of an ethnic/cultural language may be a function of the demands of particular environments (e.g., home versus school), whereas language preference appears to reflect the identity structure of acculturating individuals (Birman & Trickett, 2001). Nonetheless, numerous studies have demonstrated that there are differential effects on language acculturation among immigrant children and adults (e.g., Birman & Trickett, 2001; Tran, 1990).

It is suggested that one intersection between language in the acculturation process and race-based psychology is that environmental presses often dictate the process of language usage and preferences for immigrant individuals. On the one hand, the social, political, and cultural pressures from the larger macroculture regarding language (i.e., use of standard English) are an integral component of the acculturation process. On the other hand, an immigrant's low facility with the English language can be the source of a "cultural marker" that may lead to discrimination, racism, and stereotyping for that individual (e.g., Kohatsu et al., 2000). Therefore, an immigrant's feeling of competence in the majority culture's language has been connected to his or her cultural identity and other psychological outcomes/correlates, such as self-esteem (e.g., Noels, Pon, & Clement, 1996; Tran, 1990). More studies are needed to explore socioracial-related variables that interact with language usage and second-language acquisition in the acculturation process.

Summary

Acculturation has been a dominant force in the research on racial-cultural groups and continues to grow in complexity. Although it is difficult to make any kind of overall summary statement, Shen and Takeuchi (2001) provide compelling insights into the research on acculturation that applies to the discussion in this chapter. For example, studies that demonstrated a positive link between acculturation and mental health variables tended to have smaller sample sizes, analyzed specific groups, and did not account for confounding variables, such as socioeconomic status (Shen & Takeuchi, 2001). In contrast, empirical work that showed no relationship or mixed results usually had much larger sample sizes and controlled for these confounding variables. Therefore, the critical factors that seem to affect how research has been conducted on acculturation include sample characteristics, conceptualization of acculturation, how acculturation is measured, and what mental health variables were analyzed (Rogler et al., 1991; Shen & Takeuchi, 2001). There may be additional variables that mediate the effects of acculturation, and such factors need to be examined more closely. Clearly, race could be an influential factor that exerts influence on acculturation, both directly and indirectly.

CONCEPTUAL CONNECTIONS BETWEEN ACCULTURATION AND RACE-BASED PSYCHOLOGY

Interestingly enough, few researchers have examined, either empirically or theoretically, the relationship between acculturation and other race-based psychological constructs. Given the historical evolution of acculturation being conceptualized as a culture-centered construct, it makes some sense that such analysis has not taken place. Nonetheless, the reality of most people living in the United States is that sociorace, for example, exerts a tremendous influence on many facets of their experience, including acculturation (Helms, 1990; Helms & Cook, 1999).

An alternative approach to acculturation is to analyze it as a process that takes place within the larger context of sociorace-related (race) factors. As Helms (1994) suggested, there are two types of culture in the United States: microcultures and a macroculture. The macroculture is the dominant EuroAmerican culture; microcultures are the various ethnic cultures that immigrant/nondominant groups brought with them or maintained. Hence, sociorace is the larger context that acculturation takes place in and it significantly influences the process of cultural acquisition. Exactly how sociorace and other race-based constructs influence the acculturation process is not clear, but some of the potential areas of convergence are as follows. One important caveat to this discussion is that the impact of sociorace is complex and consists of many interacting factors. Addressing such complexity in its entirety is beyond the scope of this chapter.

One possible area of convergence is that sociorace provides the press for individuals (particularly of Color) to acculturate to the dominant EuroAmerican culture. It seems reasonable to suggest that one aspect of acculturating to EuroAmerican culture entails learning about the rules of the system in place and how to survive in the midst of such rules. Therefore, it is not only the overt EuroAmerican cultural values, attitudes, and so on that individuals learn about and adopt in the acculturation process, but also understanding what resources one has access to or not in the system. That is, one learns the mechanics of the system and how to survive within such an inequitable system. Learning to negotiate the dominant culture's system is an aspect of the acculturation process that has not been addressed in the research.

Another area of convergence is that sociorace, albeit indirectly, also presumably provides the press on immigrant individuals to enculturate. As documented in the acculturation research, in many nondominant cultures maintaining one's culture provides a buffer against the stress of acculturating to the dominant EuroAmerican culture (e.g., Helms & Cook, 1999). This buffer mechanism may be activated by the acculturative stress stemming from learning about EuroAmerican culture. However, maintaining one's original culture may be a protective mechanism against the prohibitive psychological and social costs that the dominant White culture exerts on immigrants/nondominant individuals on a continual basis.

Clearly, existing models of acculturation may be somewhat simplistic in that the larger sociopolitical forces that impinge on the acculturation process may not be accounted for. Rather, it may be more feasible to examine acculturation in its larger sociopolitical context by factoring in the interaction between the cultural acquisition process per se and sociorace. This interaction component (i.e., acculturation and race) is generally neglected in the current theories of acculturation and should be incorporated. By doing so, it may provide additional insights into the psychological outcomes of the acculturation process among socioracial and cultural groups. In a somewhat similar vein, Birman (1994) suggested that the experiences of nondominant cultural communities, including oppression, form the backdrop in which individual acculturation takes place. This backdrop provides the individual with choices about what path to take in the acculturation process (Birman, 1994).

One method for accounting for the multitude of factors and dimensions that impact acculturation may be to examine it in tandem with racial identity and ethnic identity processes in nondominant group members (e.g., Alvarez, Kohatsu, Liu, & Yeh, 1996; Kohatsu et al., 2000). All three essential components tend to operate simultaneously in many racial-cultural individuals (particularly among Latinos and Asians), and understanding the cultural adjustment of such individuals requires examining all three components. That is, acculturation may be more meaningful if analyzed in conjunction with racial identity and ethnic identity together rather than in isolation (e.g., Alvarez et al., 1996; Birman, 1994). In short, it may be more fruitful to further the research in acculturation by thinking about and measuring this construct from a race-based perspective. In so doing, researchers will be able to better account for the complex relationships between the larger racial context and acculturation. It is in these intersections that researchers will find the most meaningful information about the acculturation-related experiences of individuals from various racial-cultural groups.

Acculturation and race-based constructs may also converge in the way some researchers have conceptualized a more contextual (i.e., environmental) approach to acculturation (e.g., Cabassa, 2003; Sasao & Sue, 1993). As discussed previously, current work on acculturation posits that a person may shift his or her acculturation level from context to context as each particular environment may require a specific kind of cultural adaptation (e.g., from school to home). Such a context-driven approach to understanding acculturation reflects a similar phenomenon in racial identity (Helms & Cook, 1999). It may be precisely racially related stressors in the environment that lead to shifts in modes of cultural adaptation. Consequently, an individual's ability to shift cultures may be a requirement for survival in unfriendly racial and cultural environments (Helms & Cook, 1999). Therefore, understanding race-related stressors in specific environments can lead to a deeper understanding of the shifts in cultural adaptation in acculturating individuals.

In sum, although researchers have not examined the possible points of convergence between acculturation and race-based constructs, there are a number of areas where they interface. It is in these areas of interface that acculturation research could benefit the most in expanding the understanding of this complex process.

FUTURE DIRECTIONS AND CONCLUSION

To summarize the discussion in this chapter, I offer a few suggestions for researchers to consider in improving the knowledge base in acculturation. First, the future of acculturation research hinges on an expansion of the current conceptual models of acculturation. Researchers need to go beyond the unidimensional models (and measures) of acculturation and shift their paradigms to multidimensional perspectives and measures. Specifically, a more contextual/ecological approach that is multi-dimensional and accounts for the variety of sociocultural environments that people function in on a daily basis is one direction that would enhance the understanding of the acculturation process. Factoring in situationally specific aspects of accultur-ation would add conceptual sophistication to current models. Granted, this is not an easy task to accomplish, but it is a necessary advance for acculturation researchers.

Second, one underlying premise of this chapter is that research on acculturation could benefit from incorporating a race-based perspective in the theory and mea-surement of this variable. Delving into the complex relationships, at a micro-level, whether direct or indirect, that race-based constructs (e.g., racial identity) have with acculturation can only enrich the current conceptual models of this construct. Advocating such a change complements and reflects a more contextual approach to acculturation as well.

Third, as discussed previously, researchers tended to examine acculturation as in-dependent from other macro-level social processes and factors that impact the di-verse environments that most individuals and local communities interact with on a daily basis (Sasao & Sue, 1993). Researchers can enhance the understanding of ac-culturation by accounting for these multiple intersecting variables (e.g., racism, dis-crimination). One approach is to incorporate a race-based perspective in analyzing acculturation by including, for example, racial identity variables when examining ac-culturation. Unraveling the complex relationships between acculturation and race-based constructs will add a deeper dimension to the understanding of acculturation.

To conclude, the most widely used definitions and measures of acculturation ap-pear to have very little interaction with or relevance for a race-based psychological approach. Clearly, the effects of cultural contact and the resulting changes in cul-ture were kept in isolation from the larger social forces operating in many cultural environments. In essence, most acculturation models and measures, particularly unidimensional ones, seemed to ignore the very context in which acculturation takes place for racial-cultural individuals.

Acculturation is a complex, multifaceted phenomenon, and the research in this area has unveiled just a small portion of the complexity. Unfortunately, psycholo-gists seem wedded to the same models (predominantly unidimensional) and scales and endlessly replicate the same problems in studying acculturation. Such a trend appears particularly true of the research in Asian American acculturation. Re-search in acculturation needs to expand to unravel the multiple layers that charac-terize acculturation. It is anticipated that as the research continues to develop, more sophisticated models and instruments will emerge. The most fruitful developments can take place in exploring the interface between race-based psychology and acculturation due to the pervasive impact that race has on all racial-cultural individuals.

Contextualizing acculturation in a race-based psychology will add a deeper and more meaningful dimension to the work in this area. Rather than avoiding the powerful meanings and consequences that investigation in race-based constructs generates, it would behoove acculturation researchers to incorporate racial factors that are more pertinent to the very people they are attempting to understand. Examining the points of convergence between race-based psychology and acculturation will bring researchers that much closer to the real complexity of the experiences that individuals have in acculturating across different contexts in the United States.

REFERENCES

Abe-Kim, J., Okazaki, S., & Goto, S. G. (2001). Unidimensional versus multidimensional approaches to the assessment of acculturation for Asian American populations. *Cultural Diversity and Ethnic Minority Psychology, 7*(3) 232–246.

Alvarez, A., Kohatsu, E., Liu, W., & Yeh, L. (1996, February). *Rethinking Asian Pacific American racial identity: Distinctions between racial and ethnic identity.* Paper presented at the meeting of the Winter Roundtable on Cross-Cultural Counseling and Psychotherapy, New York.

Anderson, J., Moeschberger, M., Chen, M. S., Kunn, P., Wewers, M. E., & Guthrie, R. (1993). An acculturation scale for Southeast Asians. *Social Psychiatry and Psychiatric Epidemiology, 28*(3) 134–141.

Atkinson, D. R., & Gim, R. H. (1989). Asian-American cultural identity and attitudes toward mental health services. *Journal of Counseling Psychology, 36*(2), 209–212.

Atkinson, D. R., Lowe, S., & Matthews, L. (1995). Asian American acculturation, gender, and willingness to seek counseling. *Journal of Multicultural Counseling and Development, 23*(3) 130–138.

Bell, R. A., & Alcalay, R. (1997). The impact of the wellness guide/guia on Hispanic women's well-being-related knowledge, efficacy beliefs, and behaviors: The mediating role of acculturation. *Health Education and Behavior, 24*(3), 326–343.

Bennett, S. K., & BigFoot-Sipes, D. S. (1991). American Indian and White college student preferences for counselor characteristics. *Journal of Counseling Psychology, 38*(4) 440–445.

Bennett, S. K., BigFoot-Sipes, D. S., & Thurman, P. J. (1989, August). *American Indian client preferences for counselor attributes.* Paper presented at the annual meeting of the American Psychological Association, New Orleans, LA.

Berry, J. W. (2003). Conceptual approaches to acculturation. In K. Chun, P. Organista, & G. Marin (Eds.), *Acculturation: Advances in Theory, Measurement, and Applied Research* (pp. 17–37). Washington, DC: American Psychological Association.

Berry, J. W., Winthrob, R. M., Sindell, P. S., & Mawhinney, T. A. (1982). Psychological adaptation to culture change among the James Bay Cree. *Le Naturaliste Canadien, 109,* 965–975.

BigFoot-Sipes, D. S., Dauphinais, P., LaFromboise, T. D., Bennett, S. K., & Rowe, W. (1992). American Indian secondary school students' preferences for counselors. *Journal of Multicultural Counseling and Development, 20*(3) 113–122.

Birman, D. (1994). Acculturation and human diversity in a multicultural society. In E. J. Trickett, R. J. Watts, & D. Birman (Eds.), *Human diversity: Perspectives on people in context* (pp. 261–284). San Francisco: Jossey-Bass.

Birman, D. (1998). Biculturalism and perceived competence of Latino immigrant adolescents. *American Journal of Community Psychology, 26*(3), 335–354.

Birman, D., & Trickett, E. J. (2001). Cultural transitions in first-generation immigrants: Acculturation of Soviet Jewish refugees, adolescents and parents. *Journal of Cross-Cultural Psychology, 32*(4), 456–477.

Birman, D., Trickett, E., & Vinokurov, A. (2002). Acculturation and Adaptation of Soviet Jewish Refugee Adolescents: Predictors of Adjustment Across Life Domains. *American Journal of Community Psychology, 30*(5), 585–607.

Birman, D., & Tyler, F. B. (1994). Acculturation and alienation of Soviet Jewish refugees in the United States. *Genetic, Social, and General Psychology Monographs, 120*(1), 101–115.

Boyce, W. T., & Boyce, J. C. (1983). Acculturation and changes in health among Navajo boarding school students. *Social Science Medicine, 17,* 219–226.

Burnam, M. A., Hough, R. L., Karno, M., Escobar, J. I., & Telles, C. A. (1987). Acculturation and lifetime prevalence of psychiatric disorders among Mexican Americans in Los Angeles. *Journal of Health and Social Behavior, 28,* 89–102.

Cabassa, L. (2003). Measuring acculturation: Where we are and where we need to go. Hispanic. *Journal of Behavioral Sciences, 25*(2), 127–146.

Canabal, M. E., & Quiles, J. A. (1995). Acculturation and socioeconomic factors as determinants of depression among Puerto Ricans in the United States. *Social Behavior and Personality, 23,* 235–248.

Carter, R. T. (1995). *The influence of race and racial identity in psychotherapy: Toward a racially inclusive model.* New York: Wiley.

Carter, R. T. (1997). Race and psychotherapy: The racially inclusive model. In C. E. Thompson & R. T. Carter (Eds.), *Racial identity theory: Applications to individual, group, and organizational interventions* (pp. 97–107). Hillsdale, NJ: Erlbaum.

Carvajal, S. C., Photiades, J. R., Evans, R. I., & Nash, S. G. (1997). Relating a social influence model to the role of acculturation in substance use among Latino adolescents. *Journal of Applied Social Psychology, 27*(18), 1617–1628.

Casas, J. M., & Pytluk, S. D. (1995). Hispanic identity development: Implications for research and practice. In J. G. Ponterotto, J. M. Casas, L. A. Suzuki, & C. M. Alexander (Eds.), *Handbook of multicultural counseling* (pp. 155–180). Thousand Oaks, CA: Sage.

Celano, M. (1986). *Acculturation, adjustment, and length of residence of Vietnamese refugees.* Unpublished doctoral dissertation, University of Maryland, College Park.

Choney, S. K., Berryhill-Paapke, E., & Robbins, R. R. (1995). The acculturation of American Indians: Developing frameworks for research and practice. In J. G. Ponterotto, J. M. Casas, L. A. Suzuki, & C. M. Alexander (Eds.), *Handbook of multicultural counseling* (pp. 73–92). Thousand Oaks, CA: Sage.

Chun, K., & Akutsu, P. (2003). Acculturation Among Ethnic Minority Families. In K. Chun, P. Organista, & G. Marin (Eds.), *Acculturation: Advances in theory, measurement, and applied research* (pp. 95–119). Washington, DC: American Psychological Association.

Chun, K., Organista, P., & Marin, G. (2002). *Acculturation: Advances in theory, measurement, and applied research.* Washington DC: American Psychological Association.

Cortes, D. E., Rogler, L. H., & Malgady, R. G. (1994). Biculturality among Puerto Rican adults in the United States. *American Journal of Community Psychology, 22,* 707–721.

Cross, H. J., & Canul, G. D. (1994). The influence of acculturation and racial identity attitudes on Mexican-Americans' MMPI-2 performance. *Journal of Clinical Psychology, 50*(5), 736–745.

Cuellar, I. (2000). Acculturation and mental health: Ecological transactional relations of adjustment. In I. Cuellar & F. A. Paniaguia (Eds.), *Handbook of multicultural mental health: Assessment and treatment of diverse populations* (pp. 45–62). New York: Academic Press.

Cuellar, I., Arnold, B., & Maldonado, R. (1995). Acculturation rating scale for Mexican Americans-II: A revision of the original ARMSA scale. *Hispanic Journal of Behavioral Sciences, 17,* 275–304.

Cuellar, I., Harris, L. C., & Jasso, R. (1980). An acculturation scale for Mexican American normal and clinical populations. *Hispanic Journal of Behavioral Sciences, 2*(3), 199–217.

Cuellar, I., Nyberg, B., Maldonado, R. E., & Roberts, R. E. (1997). Ethnic identity and acculturation in a young adult Mexican-origin population. *Journal of Community Psychology, 25*(6), 535–549.

Cuellar, I., & Roberts, R. E. (1997). Relations of depression, acculturation, and socioeconomic status in a Latino sample. *Hispanic Journal of Behavioral Sciences, 19*(2), 230–238.

Franco, J. N. (1983). An acculturation scale for Mexican American children. *Journal of General Psychology, 108,* 175–181.

Fraser, D., Piacentini, J., Rossem, R. V., Hien, D., & Rotheram-Borus, M. J. (1998). Effects of acculturation and psychopathology on sexual behavior and substance use of suicidal Hispanic adolescents. *Hispanic Journal of Behavioral Sciences, 20*(1), 83–101.

Frey, M. L. (2001). Differences in acculturation, worldviews, and ratings of dissociative experiences: A cross-cultural comparison of White American students and international students from developing nations. *Dissertation Abstracts International, 61*(7-B), 3841.

Garrett, M. T., & Pichette, E. F. (2000). Red as an apple: Native American acculturation and counseling with or without reservation. *Journal of Counseling and Development, 78*(1), 3–13.

Gil, A. G., Wagner, E. F., & Vega, W. A. (2000). Acculturation, familism, and alcohol use among Latino adolescent males: Longitudinal relations. *Journal of Community Psychology, 28*(4), 443–458.

Gim Chung, R., Kim, B., & Abreu, J. (2004). Asian American Multidimensional Acculturation Scale: Development, factor analysis, reliability, and validity. *Cultural Diversity & Ethnic Minority Psychology, 10*(1), 66–80.

Gonzalez, R., & Cuellar, I. (1983). Readmission and prognosis of Mexican American psychiatric inpatients. *Revista Interamericana de Psicologia, 17,* 81–96.

Guinn, B. (1998). Acculturation and health locus of control among Mexican American adolescents. *Hispanic Journal of Behavioral Sciences, 20*(4), 492–500.

Helms, J. E. (Ed.). (1990). *African American and White racial identity.* New York: Greenwood Press.

Helms, J. E. (1994). The conceptualization of racial identity and other "racial constructs." In E. J. Trickett, R. J. Watts, & D. Birman (Eds.), *Human diversity: Perspectives on people in context* (pp. 285–311). San Francisco: Jossey-Bass.

Helms, J. E. (1995). An update of Helms's White and people of Color racial identity models. In J. G. Ponterotto, J. M. Casas, L. A. Suzuki, & C. M. Alexander (Eds.), *Handbook of multicultural counseling* (pp. 181–198). Thousand Oaks, CA: Sage.

Helms, J. E. (2001). An update of Helms's White and people of Color racial identity models. In J. G. Ponterotto, J. M. Casas, L. A. Suzuki, & C. M. Alexander (Eds.), *Handbook of multicultural counseling* (2nd ed., pp. 181–198). Thousand Oaks, CA: Sage.

Helms, J. E., & Cook, D. A. (1999). *Using race and culture in counseling and psychotherapy: Theory and process.* Boston: Allyn & Bacon.

Hines, A. M., Snowden, L. R., & Graves, K. L. (1998). Acculturation, alcohol consumption and AIDS-related risky sexual behavior among African American women. *Women and Health, 27*(3), 17–35.

Holleran, L. K. (2003). Mexican American youth of the Southwest Borderlands: Perceptions of ethnicity, acculturation, and race. *Hispanic Journal of Behavioral Sciences, 25*(3), 352–369.

Hovey, J. D. (2000). Acculturative stress, depression, and suicidal ideation in Mexican immigrants. *Cultural Diversity and Ethnic Minority Psychology, 6*(2), 134–151.

Hovey, J. D., & Magana, C. (2000). Acculturative stress, anxiety, and depression among Mexican farmworkers in the Midwest United States. Journal of Immigrant Health, 2 (3), 119–131.

Iwamsa, G. Y., & Kooreman, H. (1995). Brief Symptom Inventory scores of Asian, Asian-American, and European-American college students. *Cultural Diversity and Mental Health, 1*(2), 149–157.

Jones, R. L. (1991). *Black psychology* (3rd ed.). Berkeley, CA: Cobb & Henry.

Keefe, S. E., & Padilla, A. M. (1987). *Chicano ethnicity.* Albuquerque: University of New Mexico Press.

Kim, B. S. K., & Abreu, J. M. (2001). Acculturation measurement: Theory, current instruments, and future directions. In J. G. Ponterotto, J. M. Casas, L. A. Suzuki, & C. M. Alexander (Eds.), *Handbook of multicultural counseling* (2nd ed., pp. 394–424). Thousand Oaks, CA: Sage.

Klonoff, E. A., & Landrine, H. (1997). Distrust of Whites, acculturation, and AIDS knowledge among African Americans. *Journal of Black Psychology, 23*(1), 50–57.

Klonoff, E. A., & Landrine, H. (1999). Acculturation and alcohol use among Blacks: The benefits of remaining culturally traditional. *Western Journal of Black Studies, 23*(4), 211–216.

Klonoff, E. A., & Landrine, H. (2000). Revising and improving the African American Acculturation Scale. *Journal of Black Psychology, 26*(2), 235–261.

Kohatsu, E. L. (1992). The effects of racial identity and acculturation on anxiety, assertiveness, and ascribed identity among Asian American college students. *Dissertation Abstracts International, 54*(02-B), B54/2.

Kohatsu, E. L. (1996, May). *Conceptualization and measurement of acculturation versus racial identity: A critical analysis.* Paper presented at the 68th annual meeting, Midwestern Psychological Association, Chicago.

Kohatsu, E. L., Dulay, M., Lam, C., Concepcion, W., Perez, P., Lopez, C., et al. (2000). Using racial identity theory to explore racial mistrust and interracial contact among Asian Americans. *Journal of Counseling and Development, 78,* 334–342.

Landrine, H., & Klonoff, E. A. (1994). The African American Acculturation Scale: Development, reliability, and validity. *Journal of Black Psychology, 20*(2), 104–127.

Landrine, H., & Klonoff, E. A. (1996). *African American acculturation: Deconstructing race and reviving culture.* Thousand Oaks, CA: Sage.

Lee, R. M., Choe, J., Kim, G., & Ngo, V. (2000). Construction of the Asian American Family Conflicts Scale. *Journal of Counseling Psychology, 47*(2), 211–222.

Lee, R. M., & Liu, T. H. (2001). Coping with intergenerational family conflict: Comparison of Asian American, Hispanic and European American college students. *Journal of Counseling Psychology, 48*(4), 410–419.

Leong, F. T. L. (2001). The role of acculturation in the career adjustment of Asian American workers: A test of Leong and Chou's (1994) formulations. *Cultural Diversity and Ethnic Minority Psychology, 7*(3), 262–273.

Leong, F. T. L., & Chou, E. L. (1994). The role of ethnic identity and acculturation in the vocational behavior of Asian Americans: An integrative review. *Journal of Vocational Behavior, 44,* 155–172.

Leong, F. T. L., Wagner, N. S., & Kim, H. H. (1995). Group counseling expectations among Asian American students: The role of culture-specific factors. *Journal of Counseling Psychology, 42*(2), 217–221.

Liu, W. M., Pope-Davis, D. B., Nevitt, J., & Toporek, R. (1999). Understanding the function of acculturation and prejudicial attitudes among Asian Americans. *Cultural Diversity and Mental Health, 5,* 317–328.

Marin, G., & Gamba, R. (1996). A new measurement of acculturation for Hispanics: The Bidimensional Acculturation Scale for Hispanics (BAS). *Hispanic Journal of Behavioral Sciences, 18,* 297–316.

Marin, G., Sabogal, F., Marin, B. V., Otero-Sabogal, R., & Perez-Stable, E. J. (1987). Development of a short acculturation scale for Hispanics. *Hispanic Journal of Behavioral Sciences, 9*(2), 183–205.

Masten, W. G., Penland, E. A., & Nayani, E. J. (1994). Depression and acculturation in Mexican-American women. *Psychological Reports, 75,* 1499–1503.

Mendoza, R. H. (1989). An empirical scale to measure type and degree of acculturation in Mexican-American adolescents and adults. *Journal of Cross-cultural Psychology, 20,* 372–385.

Montgomery, G. T. (1992). Comfort with acculturation status among students from South Texas. *Hispanic Journal of Behavioral Sciences, 14,* 201–223.

Neff, J. A., & Hoppe, S. K. (1993). Race/ethnicity, acculturation, and psychological distress: Fatalism and religiosity as cultural resources. *Journal of Community Psychology, 21,* 3–20.

Negy, C., & Woods, D. J. (1992). The importance of acculturation in understanding research with Hispanic-Americans. *Hispanic Journal of Behavioral Sciences, 14*(2), 224–227.

Noels, K. A., Pon, G., & Clement, R. (1996). Language, identity, and adjustment: The role of linguistic self-confidence in the acculturation process. *Journal of Language and Social Psychology, 15*(3), 246–259.

Oetting, E. R., Swaim, R. C., & Chiarella, M. C. (1998). Factor structure and invariance of the orthogonal cultural identification scale among American Indian and Mexican American Youth. *Hispanic Journal of Behavioral Sciences, 20*(2), 131–154.

Olmedo, E. L., Martinez, J. L., & Martines, S. R. (1978). Measure of acculturation for Chicano adolescents. *Psychological Reports, 42,* 159–170.

Park, S. E., & Harrison, A. A. (1995). Career-related interests and values, perceived control, and acculturation of Asian-American and Caucasion-American college students. *Journal of Applied Social Psychology, 25*(13), 1184–1203.

Phinney, J., & Flores, J. (2002). "Unpacking" acculturation: Aspects of acculturation as predictors of traditional sex role attitudes. *Journal of Cross-Cultural Psychology, 33*(3), 320–331.

Pomales, J., & Williams, V. (1989). Effects of level of acculturation and counseling style on Hispanic students' perceptions of counselor. *Journal of Counseling Psychology, 36*(1), 79–83.

Ponterotto, J. G., Baluch, S., & Carielli, D. (1998). The Suinn-Lew Asian Self-Identity Acculturation Scale (SL-ASIA): Critique and research recommendations. *Measurement and Evaluation in Counseling and Development, 32*(2), 109–125.

Pope-Davis, D. B., Liu, W. M., Ledesma-Jones, S., & Nevitt, J. (2000). African American acculturation and Black racial identity: A preliminary investigation. *Journal of Multicultural Counseling and Development, 28,* 98–112.

Rogler, L. H., Cortes, D. E., & Malgady, R. G. (1991). Acculturation and mental health status among Hispanics. *American Psychologist, 46*(6), 585–597.

Roysircar-Sodowsky, G., & Maestas, M. V. (2000). Acculturation, ethnic identity, and acculturative stress: Evidence and measurement. In R. H. Dana (Ed.), *Handbook of cross-cultural and multicultural personality assessment* (pp. 131–171). Mahwah, NJ: Erlbaum.

Ryder, A. G., Alden, L. E., & Paulhus, D. L. (2000). Is acculturation unidimensional or bidimensional? A head-to-head comparison in the prediction of personality, self-identity, and adjustment. *Journal of Personality and Social Psychology, 79*(1), 49–65.

Saldana, D. H. (1994). Acculturative stress: Minority status and distress: Hispanic. *Journal of Behavioral Sciences, 16*(2), 116–128.

Sasao, T., & Sue, S. (1993). Toward a culturally anchored ecological framework of research in ethnic-cultural communities. In E. Seidman, D. Hughes, & N. Williams (Eds.) [Special issue: Culturally anchored methodology], *American Journal of Community Psychology, 21,* 705–728.

Shen, B., & Takeuchi, D. T. (2001). A structural model of acculturation and mental health status among Chinese Americans. *American Journal of Community Psychology, 29,* 387–418.

Snowden, L. R., & Hines, A. M. (1998). Acculturation, alcohol consumption, and AIDS-related risky sexual behavior among African American men. *Journal of Community Psychology, 26*(4), 345–359.

Snowden, L. R., & Hines, A. M. (1999). A scale to assess African American acculturation. *Journal of Black Psychology, 25*(1), 37–47.

Sodowsky, G. R., Lai, E. W., & Plake, B. S. (1991). Moderating effects of sociocultural variables on acculturation attitudes of Hispanics and Asian Americans. *Journal of Counseling and Development, 70,* 194–204.

Sue, D., Mak, W. S., & Sue, D. W. (1998). Ethnic identity. In L. C. Lee & N. W. S. Zane (Eds.), *Handbook of Asian American psychology* (pp. 289–323). Thousand Oaks, CA: Sage.

Suinn, R. M., & Ahuna, C. (1992). The Suinn-Lew Asian Self-Identity Acculturation Scale: Concurrent and factorial validation. *Educational and Psychological Measurement, 52*(4), 1041–1047.

Suinn, R. M., & Gillian, K. (1995). The Suinn-Lew Asian Self-Identity Acculturation Scale: Cross-cultural information. *Journal of Multicultural Counseling and Development, 23*(3), 139–151.

Suinn, R. M., Rickard-Figueroa, K., Lew, S., & Vigil, P. (1987). The Suinn-Lew Asian Self-Identity Acculturation scale: An initial report. *Educational and Psychological Measurement, 47,* 401–407.

Szapocznik, J., Kurtines, W. M., & Fernandez, T. (1980). Bicultural involvement and adjustment in Hispanic-American youths. *International Journal of Intercultural Relations, 4,* 353–365.

Szapocznik, J., Scopetta, M. A., Kurtines, W. M., & Aranalde, M. A. (1978). Theory and measurement of acculturation. *Interamerican Journal of Psychology, 12,* 113–120.

Tata, S. P., & Leong, F. T. L. (1994). Individualism-collectivism, social-network orientation, and acculturation as predictors of attitudes toward seeking professional psychological help among Chinese Americans. *Journal of Counseling Psychology, 41*(3), 280–287.

Thompson, C. E., & Carter, R. T. (1997). *Racial identity theory: Applications to individual, group, and organizational interventions.* Hillsdale, NJ: Erlbaum.

Thompson, P. C., Anderson, L. P., & Bakeman, R. A. (2000). Effects of racial socialization and racial identity on acculturative stress in African American college students. *Cultural Diversity and Ethnic Minority Psychology, 6*(2), 196–210.

Tracey, T. J., Leong, F. T. L., & Glidden, C. (1986). Help seeking and problem perception among Asian Americans. *Journal of Counseling Psychology, 33*(3), 331–336.

Tran, T. V. (1990). Language acculturation among older Vietnamese refugee adults. *Gerontologist, 30*(1), 94–99.

Zane, N., & Mak, W. (2003). Major approaches to the measurement of acculturation among ethnic minority populations: A content analysis and alternate empirical strategy. In K. Chun, P. Organista, & G. Marin (Eds.), *Acculturation: advances in theory, measurement, and applied research* (pp. 39–60). Washington, DC: American Psychological Association.

Zimmerman, M. A., Ramirez-Valles, J., Washienko, K. M., Walter, B., & Dyer, S. (1996). The development of a measure of enculturation for Native American youth. *American Journal of Community Psychology, 24*(2), 295–304.

CHAPTER 13

Work: Cultural Perspectives on Career Choices and Decision Making

Nadya A. Fouad and Angela M. Byars-Winston

> *Work is a necessary evil to be avoided.*
> —Mark Twain
> *It is your work in life that is the ultimate seduction.*
> —Pablo Picasso

The quotations above portray two dramatically different conceptions about work in people's lives. For some individuals, work is indeed an activity to be tolerated for the sake of a paycheck. Clearly, though, there are others for whom work is a source of identity. For these individuals, work may provide not only substantial monetary gain but also great personal satisfaction and reward. Common sense might suggest that employers, parents, and teachers would want workers with passion and commitment to the job, and in fact, U.S. society may be based on having more workers like Picasso than like Twain. But who is likely to be the latter worker, and who is likely to be the former? This chapter focuses on what we know about how people choose their work, and what we know about the factors that have gone into their decision-making processes about work and career.

We begin our chapter with four fundamental premises. First, we assume that individuals are employed in a social context of a work environment, and that the work environment is part of the social fabric of a community, which in turn becomes part of the gross national product of the country. This grossly oversimplified process highlights that individuals work in a social context, the work they do is defined in that social context, and the contributions of that work are evaluated in that social context (Carter & Cook, 1992).

Our second premise is that all decisions about career and work take place within a sociocultural context. In other words, individuals make work and career decisions in the context of their families and social environments. Career and work decisions, then, are influenced by the family's worldview and salient cultural values (Fouad & Brown, 2000). For some, that means familial influence will lead them to be highly achieving and attending to individual goals; for others, it means attending to collective, familial goals (Fiske, Kitayama, Markus, & Nisbett, 1998).

Our third premise is that for some people, work decisions are not active choices, but rather a compromise between the opportunities available and the talents they can bring to the environment (Blustein, 2001; Fitzgerald & Betz, 1994; Fouad, 2001; Fouad & Byars, 2002; Miller, 1999).

Underlying these three premises is our fourth premise, that all work and career behavior is reciprocally influenced by culture. We suggest that one's cultural worldview, upbringing, and cultural perspectives about the appropriate role of work in life influence the work choices one makes. We also propose, however, that the work and career choices available are influenced by culture. In some cases, culture provides opportunities (e.g., entering a family business or having a legacy to pay for college); in other cases, culture acts as a barrier (e.g., racism). Based on the above premises, for the purposes of this chapter, we use the term "vocational psychology" to capture the person-environment transactions of work-related behavior, highlighting both the psychological and sociological aspects of work in people's lives.

Our goal in this chapter is to focus on what we know about the role of culture in work and career choices, to examine the gaps in our knowledge of culture and work, and to propose a framework for further research in the area. We begin first by gaining an understanding of the demographic diversity of work in the United States.

DEMOGRAPHIC DIVERSITY OF WORK

Work in the United States is increasingly done by a racially and ethnically diverse group of people. In the 2000 U.S. census (U.S. Bureau of the Census, 2001), in which individuals were allowed to indicate more than one racial/ethnic affiliation, individuals 18 or younger were more likely to identify with two or more racial/ethnic minority affiliations. The data indicate that about two out of three U.S. individuals identified as White, which is 9% fewer than in 1990 (Brewer & Suchan, 2001). The United States, as predicted, is more racially and ethnically diverse than ever before in its history. Of the remaining one third, approximately 13% indicated they were African American, 1.5% identified as American Indian or Alaskan Native, 4.5% as Asian American/Pacific Islander, 13% as Hispanic/Latino, and about 7% indicated "other" race.

The greatest increase in number was among individuals identifying as Asian American/Pacific Islander and Latino/Hispanic. This is most likely due to both immigration rates and higher fertility rates. For example, the census data (U.S. Bureau of the Census, 2001) indicated that 35% of Hispanics were less than 18 years old, compared to 26% of all the U.S. population. Brewer and Suchan (2001) mapped changes in racial/ethnic diversity in the United States, providing evidence that racial/ethnic diversity is now in each state of the country and not just limited to the border and coastal states.

These data have implications for the workforce. It is axiomatic that the workforce is becoming increasingly racially and ethnically diverse. A study of the changes in the workforce by a committee of the National Research Council (NRC, 1999) showed that, in fact, diversity (in terms of age, sex, race, and education) is occurring in nearly all occupational groups. The committee indicated that this increased diversity will influence the context and perhaps content of jobs, but declined to speculate how this might occur.

The NRC results, however, defined diversity broadly, and an examination of labor market data indicates that racial/ethnic diversity is not distributed equally across occupational groupings. The Bureau of Labor Statistics (BLS, 2002) provides data on selected race or ethnic affiliations (Black, White, Hispanic origin) in a variety of areas. Blacks and Hispanics are underrepresented in many professional occupations, such as executive, administrative, and managerial specialties (7.9% and 5.1%, respectively); engineers, architects, and surveyors (5.3% and 3.5%, respectively); natural scientists (4.8% and 2.8%, respectively); and physicians, dentists, and veterinarians (5.0% and 4.1%, respectively). Conversely, Blacks and Hispanics are overrepresented in other, lower-paying positions. For example, Blacks are 25% of the dieticians, social workers, communications workers, correctional institution officers, and shoe sales workers, and are 30% of guards, 36% of postal workers, and 32% of licensed practical nurses. Hispanics are 38% of the butchers, textile sewing machine operators, and concrete finishers, and 40% of the house cleaners in the United States. The differences become clear in the effect on median wages, as Blacks earned 80% and Hispanics earned 68% of the median weekly wage that Whites did. For all three racial/ethnic groups, men earned more than women. When examining the most extreme differences across gender and race, Hispanic women earned 56% of the median weekly wage earned by White men.

While race and ethnicity matter in the kind of work people do, it also matters in their search for employment. Unemployment status differs markedly across racial/ethnic categories. For 2000 and 2001, unemployment rates for Whites were 3.5% and 4.2%, while unemployment rates for Blacks were 7.6% and 8.7%, and were 5.7% and 6.6% for Hispanics. Because 2001 was a year characterized by a number of economic downturns, it is interesting to note reasons for unemployment. Whites and Hispanics were much more likely to be unemployed due to temporary layoff (17.5% and 16.8%, respectively) than were Blacks (10.1%) (U.S. Department of Labor, 2002). A 1996 U.S. Bureau of the Census study provided some insight into racial/ethnic differences for not working. When examining the top three reasons for not working, Whites indicated they could not work because they had a disability (21.9%), were taking care of children (25.3%), or were retired (17.6%), while Blacks were most likely to indicate they had a disability (32.3%), were taking care of children (18.1%), or were unable to find work (13.7%). The top three reasons for Hispanics not to work included taking care of children (30%), going to school (22.3%), and illness (14.5%).

The data provided here indicate that the occupational landscape is not equal. Race and ethnicity make a difference in occupational choice, income, ability to work, and opportunity to work. However, we do not know why or how this difference occurs, yet understanding why is important in providing greater work and occupational equity. Counseling strategies may need to focus on boosting individual esteem and efficacy in choice, or, rather than individual counseling interventions, we may need to focus on social justice strategies to provide greater equity in career opportunities. The next section explores the theoretical perspectives about career choices and provides a brief overview of the empirical support for these theoretical constructs; most of these studies were conducted with European Americans. We follow with a review of empirical support for the cultural validity of the theoretical constructs, summarizing what we know about the constructs for racial/ethnic groups other than European Americans. Finally, we present suggestions for expanding our knowledge base about career development across cultural groups and our recommendations for future work.

GENERAL THEORETICAL FRAMEWORKS

What are the forces that shape an individual's career development and eventual career choice? How does one develop an interest in a particular career or field of work versus other fields? What accounts for how a person remains satisfactorily employed in a given position? These are some of the questions with which vocational psychology scholars have grappled for over 50 years. Although multiple theories and models have emerged, there are three overarching theoretical perspectives that have garnered sustained attention in the field; trait-factor, developmental, and social cognitive approaches. These theories focus on the development and content of career choice and interests. Given space constraints, we limit our brief review to the examination of these theories. Other theories and models, such as D. Brown (2002) and D. Brown and Crace's (1996) value-based model; Mitchell and Krumboltz's (1996) social learning theory; Peterson, Sampson, Lenz, and Reardon's (2002) cognitive information processing model; and Young, Valach, and Collin's (2002) constructionist perspective, have added further insight into the complexity of factors involved in career development processes and outcomes. The reader is directed to these sources for further detail on the respective theories and models. The reader is also referred to Swanson and Gore (2000) for a recent review of vocational theory and research.

Trait-Factor Theories

Early vocational psychologists were greatly influenced by the study of individual differences. This influence highlighted the fact that individuals have unique combinations of abilities, interests, and aptitudes, collectively referred to as traits, and that these traits are useful in matching people with skill requirements, or factors, of potential jobs. The degree of match between a person and job skill requirements constitutes congruence. People with a stronger congruence between their individual traits and the skill requirements of a job are more likely to flourish in and be satisfied with their job than those with weaker congruence. One of the significant contributions of this theoretical perspective to vocational psychology is the concept of career personality. Holland (1997), a major leader in trait-factor theory, postulated six career personality types: realistic, investigative, artistic, social, enterprising, and conventional, often referenced as the RIASEC types. These types are differentiated by their orientation to working with people (i.e., social and enterprising), ideas (i.e., investigative, artistic), or data and things (i.e., conventional and realistic). Holland hypothesized that the six types are spatially arranged on a hexagon, termed the Holland or RIASEC hexagon. He furthered asserted that those types that are adjacent to each other on the hexagon are more similar (e.g., conventional and enterprising) than those that are on opposite corners (e.g., realistic and enterprising), and that the distance, termed calculus, between these types is equal. These RIASEC types can also characterize work environments. As people tend to be interested in careers that are congruent or similar to their personality type, career choice is seen as an expression of one's personality in the world of work.

Within the trait-factor approach is the theory of work adjustment (TWA), proposed by Lofquist and Dawis (1991; Dawis, 2002). This is one of the few theories focusing on how individuals adjust to work after making a career choice and entering a given job position. Similar to Holland's (1997) theory of career choice, TWA proposes that work satisfaction occurs when an individual's needs are met by the reinforcers of a given job position (e.g., security, autonomy, advancement or promotion opportunities). People are likely to stay in jobs (tenure) when they perceive that their needs are being met and they, in turn, meet the requirements of the job. Analogous to the concept of congruence, the degree of match between workers' needs and work reinforcers is termed correspondence. The process of achieving and maintaining correspondence is known as work adjustment. TWA purports that adjustment is an ongoing process.

Empirical findings tend to support the congruence concept. For example, Hansen and Sackett (1993) found a high degree of congruence between career interests (e.g., using RIASEC typology) and choice of college majors, and Oleski and Subich (1996) and Spokane, Meir, and Catalano (2000) found a significant relationship between congruence and job satisfaction.

In sum, trait-factor theories focus more on the content of career choice than on the process of how traits (e.g., abilities, interests, aptitudes, values) develop. Common to all trait-factor approaches is the centrality of the interaction between a person and his or her environment, termed person-environment fit. Trait-factor theories emphasize the need for individuals to develop their traits and then select work environments congruent to those traits.

Developmental Theories

These theories focus on the myriad factors (biological, psychological, sociological, and cultural) that influence career choice, adjustment to careers, and eventual withdrawal from formal work. As these theories rest on general principles of human development, the primary assumption is that career development is a process that occurs over the life span. As such, these perspectives emphasize stages and important career-related tasks typically associated with various developmental ages.

One of the most influential developmental theories was proposed by Super (1953, 1990; Savickas, 2002). He considered the environment in which individuals live and the various roles they assume in their family, community, work, and other settings. These roles provide a context in which developmental career stages unfold. Super proposed the term vocational (or career) maturity to indicate the degree to which individuals had completed relevant developmental tasks and acquired the competencies necessary at each career stage to achieve effective career growth (Zunker, 1998). As career maturity was originally tied to completion of tasks at prescribed, appropriate age levels, it implicitly suggested "immaturity" if a person failed to complete a given career task at an expected age (e.g., crystallizing one's career interests by age 18). A more recent articulation of career maturity, career adaptability, was proposed to focus on how well individuals manage various career developmental issues, like transitions, across their life span, regardless of age (Goodman, 1994; Savickas, 1997).

Central to Savickas (2002) assumption of career development is the process of developing and implementing a vocational self-concept. He asserted that self-concept is how individuals view themselves and their context, resulting from a combination of individuals' biological and personality characteristics (e.g., needs, values, interests, aptitudes), the social roles they hold, and evaluations made about how others view them.

Overall, the basic tenets of developmental theories emphasize the importance of social and environmental factors on an individual's career development. Research supports the influence of these factors, for instance, familial variables such as attachment, on the career exploration process (e.g., Blustein, 1997).

Social Cognitive Theory

The cognitive revolution in psychology sparked the development of social learning and social cognitive theories of career development. These theories stress the role of cognitive processes, learning, and modeling involved in career choices, interest development, and career-related outcomes (e.g., goals, decision making). Based on the work of Bandura (1977, 1997), social learning and social cognitive theories espouse the concept of triadic reciprocity, that individuals' behavior dynamically and bidirectionally interacts with environmental (e.g., social support) and personal (e.g., belief systems) factors. The concept of personal agency is important in these theoretical perspectives relative to how individuals direct their efforts to achieve a desired goal, such as a chosen career.

Social cognitive theory (Bandura, 1986; Lent, Brown, & Hackett, 2002) places great emphasis on self-regulatory cognitions, namely, self-efficacy beliefs and outcome expectations. Self-efficacy beliefs largely determine what career interests develop and the eventual career choice for an individual, as do outcome expectations. Interests persist for activities in which individuals feel competent and believe they can succeed, and conversely, interests decline in areas where perceived competence is lacking. Career goals develop out of our interests, and we are more likely to exert effort to reach those goals in areas where we feel confident. Outcome expectations, too, influence interest formation and choice goals. For instance, when an individual expects positive consequences as a result of pursuing a given career path (e.g., prestige, respect from others, economic security), he or she is more likely to perceive that goal as desirable and develop greater interest in achieving it. Based on these concepts, career interests and career choice goals result from individuals' beliefs about the perceived likelihood of their success in that career and the desirable outcomes of pursuing that career. Social cognitive career theory (Lent et al., 2002), based on social cognitive theory, also acknowledges the influence of contextual factors on career-related processes and outcomes. The individual often experiences these contextual factors as either environmental supports or barriers to his or her career choice (e.g., social support, financial constraints, labor market trends impacting availability of work). Such factors can affect and moderate the career-related choices that one makes.

Strong predictive relationships have been found between self-efficacy beliefs and outcome expectations and career-related interests and goal intentions (e.g., Fouad & Smith, 1996; Lopez, Lent, Brown, & Gore, 1997). New studies are investigating how contextual factors impact the development of career goals and choices (Lent, Brown, & Hackett, 2000). Overall, a growing body of empirical research is providing support for the utility of social cognitive perspectives for understanding career development.

Theoretical developments in vocational psychology have been primarily concerned with the processes and outcomes involved in career development: the dynamics, developmental sequences, and precipitating factors that lead to career interests and choices and the results of such interests and choices once an individual has acted on them. Despite a rich history of theorizing about career choice and development, Krumboltz (1994) noted, "Our psychological theories are as good as we know how to make them so far, but in all probability they are far short of being accurate" (p. 11).

One of the areas in which inaccuracies are evident in vocational theories is their relevance to and validity for culturally diverse individuals. In particular, examination of the career development and behavior of racial/ethnic minorities has often been absent in vocational psychology research, with White Americans constituting the model racial/ethnic group studied (Byars & McCubbin, 2001). Specific criticisms against career theories as a result of the predominance of largely monocultural samples (i.e., White Americans) highlight that the construction of these theories is based on White, middle-class males and White American values, ignoring the unique sociopolitical realities and related psychological experiences of racial/ethnic minorities (Carter & Cook, 1992). Given the general exclusion of racial/ethnic minority worldviews and samples in the generation of vocational theory and research, the degree to which the constructs and assumptions in dominant career theories and models accounts for the career behavior of non-White Americans remains challenged. Examination of the cultural validity of career theories across diverse racial/ethnic groups may increase our understanding of the meaning of work for a broader range of individuals.

SUPPORT FOR RACIAL/ETHNIC MINORITY GROUPS

In this section, we turn our attention to support for the constructs highlighted above across cultural groups. We were interested in determining whether the constructs function the same across cultural groups, as well as whether the proposed relationships among constructs are similar across groups. Following a process we used earlier (Fouad & Byars, 2002), we identified the empirical articles with the keywords race/ethnicity/culture and various permutations of career aspirations, career interests, and career choices. These key words included career aspirations, career expectations, career choices, career interests, career self-efficacy, career goals, career supports, career barriers, career decisions, and career congruence. We limited our review to the past decade, identifying those articles published after 1991. We reviewed empirical articles, rather than reviews or conceptual articles.

Once we identified the empirical articles, we selected those articles that had race or ethnicity as the independent variable, and the career variables listed above as the dependent variable. Because we were interested in comparing results across studies, we calculated the effect sizes for each study, rather than relying on the statistical significance of results reported by authors because the latter is influenced by sample size. Effect sizes are indicators of the strength of relationships among variables and thus signify practical significance (Cohen, 1992; Thompson, 2002). Cohen suggested a scale to indicate the strength of the effect size. He calculated that the difference between independent means (signified by d) may be small (.2), medium (.5), or large (.8); the correlation (r) may be small (.1), medium (.3), or large (.5), or, in multivariate analyses, R^2 may be small (.02), medium (.15), or large (.35). Although the use of effect size is APA policy, in most cases, authors did not report effect sizes. Thus, we were able to use only articles in which effect sizes were provided, or in which the means and standard deviations were available for us to calculate effect size.

The articles we chose for review are summarized in Table 13.1. In the first column we identify the major career constructs of career aspirations, interests, career choice, decision-making process, and supports/barriers. The second column contains the authors' operational definition of the construct (e.g., "What do you do as a career?" for aspirations) and how race/ethnicity was operationalized (e.g., self-report, acculturation, or racial identity). The third column contains the sample population in the study (e.g., African American and White college students). The fourth column has the authors' names and date of publication, and the final column has the effect size. Results of the studies are explained briefly in the following section.

Aspirations

The first set of studies we reviewed examined the influence of race/ethnicity on career aspirations. An implicit, if not explicit, hypothesis in these studies is that differences in work choices may be a result of differences in the aspirations, or career dreams, that individuals have early in life. Several investigators examined differences in students' responses to "What do you want your career to be?" Other researchers studied potential factors (e.g., traditionality of choice, money, interest area) related to those aspirations.

Researchers in the first group of studies asked an open-ended question to determine career aspiration, coded the response, and then examined differences between ethnic groups (Arbona & Novy, 1991; Leung, Ivey, & Suzuki, 1994; Mau & Bikos, 2000; Murrell, Frieze, & Frost, 1991). Regardless of the coding system used, effect sizes for differences between groups were relatively small. In fact, as examined more fully by Fouad and Byars (2002), most studies showed greater differences between men and women than between ethnic groups.

Table 13.1 Summary of Studies and Effect Sizes

	Operational Definition: Dependent and Independent Variables	Sample	References	Effect Size
Aspirations a. Between-group Differences	Open-ended question, self-report	Mexican American, African American, and White college freshmen	Arbona & Novy, 1991	.17
	Open-ended question, self-report	African American and White women college students	Murrell, Frieze, & Frost, 1991	.001
	Occupations list, self-report	Caucasian and Asian American college students	Leung, Ivey, & Suzuki, 1994	.16
	Open-ended question, self-report	Asian American, African American, Hispanic, and White high school students	Mau & Bikos, 2002	.03
b. Within-group Differences	Open-ended question, racial identity	African American college students	Evans & Herr, 1994	.16
	Ethnic-traditionality of choice, acculturation	Asian American college students	Tang, Fouad, & Smith, 1999	.23
	a. Gender traditionality and acculturation; b. Prestige level and acculturation	Mexican American high school students	Flores & O'Brien, 2002	a. .23, b. −.17
	Parent occupational level	African American college students	Chung, Loeb, & Gonzo, 1996	.3
	Math career aspiration, racial identity	African American college students	Gainor & Lent, 1998	.14
Interests	Strong Interest Inventory, self-report	Hispanic, White, and African American middle school students	Davison, Aviles, & Spokane, 1999	.06
	Strong Interest Inventory, self-report	African American, Asian American, Caucasian, Native American, and Hispanic professionals	Fouad, Harmon, & Hansen, 1994	Social: .25 Artistic: .21

240

Table 13.1 *Continued*

	Operational Definition: Dependent and Independent Variables	Sample	References	Effect Size
	Strong Interest Inventory, self-report	African American, Asian American, Caucasian, Native American, and Hispanic students and professionals	Fouad, 2002	.02
	a. Self-directed search themes (RIASEC), self-report; b. Interest themes, acculturation	Asian American and Caucasian	Park & Harrison, 1995	a. R: .14, I: .11, C: .32; b. S: .2, E: .18, I: -.15, C: −.14
Choice	a. Individualistically oriented achievement, acculturation; b. Collectively oriented achivement, acculturation	Asian American college students	Lew, Allen, Papouchis, & Ritzler, 1998	a. −.15 b. .20
	a. Extrinsic work values, self-report; b. Security values, self-report; c. Power work values, self-report; d. People work values, self-report; e. Self-expression work values, self-report	Asian American and White college students	Leong, 1991	a. .25 b. .16 c. .15 d. .08 e. .02
	Factors influencing choice, self-report	African American, Asian American, Caucasian, Native American, and Hispanic college students	Perrone, Sedlacek, & Alexander, 2001	.2

(continued)

241

Table 13.1 *Continued*

	Operational Definition: Dependent and Independent Variables	Sample	References	Effect Size
	Interviews of factors considered important in career choice, self-report	African American, Asian American, Caucasian, and Hispanic college students	Teng, Morgan, & Anderson, 2001	.09
Supports/barriers a. Barriers	a. Perception of discrimination, self-report; b. Perception of opportunities for African American students, self-report; c. African Americans' perception of discrimination and opportunities	African American and White college students	Chung & Harmon, 1999	a. .35 b. .68 c. −.63
	Open-ended question about barriers about a. ethnic identity, b. family, c. study skills, self-report	African American, Asian American, Caucasian, Filipino, and Hispanic college students	Luzzo, 1993	a. .33 b. .13 c. .12
	Questionnaire about barriers to attending college due to a. ethnicity, b. family, self-report	Mexican American and White high school students	McWhirter, 1997	a. .35 b. .09
	Questionnaire on a. career-related barriers, b. educational barriers, self-report	European American and combined ethnic group college students	Luzzo & McWhirter, 2001	a. .27 b. .15
b. Supports	Questionnaire on coping with barriers	European American and combined ethnic group college students	Luzzo & McWhirter, 2001	.16

Table 13.1 *Continued*

	Operational Definition: Dependent and Independent Variables	Sample	References	Effect Size
	Questionnaire on a. readiness to go to college, b. confidence admitted to college, SES	Minority high school students	Olszewski-Kubilius & Scott, 1992	a. .23 b. .26
Decision-making process	Career Maturity Inventory, self-report	Asian American and White college students	Leong, 1991	.18
	Career Maturity Inventory, self-report	African American, Asian American, Caucasian, Filipino, and Hispanic college students	Luzzo, 1992	.14
	Questionnaire of attributions for decision making, self-report	African American and Caucasian high school students	Powell & Luzzo, 1998	.10
	Career Maturity inventory a. involvement in decision making, b. appropriateness of choice, self-report	African American and Caucasian high school students	Westbrook & Sanford, 1991	a. .28 b. .25
	Career Maturity Inventory a. knowledge of world of work, b. factors in decision making, self-report	Mexican American and Caucasian high school students	Lundberg, Osborne, & Minor, 1997	a. .4 b. .34
	Career decidedness, college rank	African American women	McCowan & Alston, 1998	.2
	Career decidedness, self-report	Asian American and White college students	Leong, 1991	.16

(continued)

Table 13.1   *Continued*

Operational Definition: Dependent and Independent Variables	Sample	References	Effect Size
Questionnaire of attributions for decision making, self-report	African American and Caucasian high school students	Powell & Luzzo, 1998	.1
Career Decision Scale, self-report	African American and Caucasian high school students	Rojewski, 1994	.01
Career decision-making self-efficacy, self-report	White and minority urban/suburban high school students	C. Brown, Darden, Shelton, & Dipoto, 1999	.17
Career decision-making self-efficacy, self-report	White and minority college students	Gloria & Hird, 1999	.13
a. Career decision-making self-efficacy, b. Career commitment, self-report	White and Black college students	Chung, 2002	a. .27 b. .28

Several investigators were more interested in examining differences within racial/ethnic groups. Chung, Loeb, and Gonzo (1996), Evans and Herr (1994), and Gainor and Lent (1998) were interested in within-group differences for African American students. Racial identity was not highly related to career aspirations, but Chung et al.'s study showed that father's occupational level does have a relationship to aspirations. Flores and O'Brien (2002) and Tang, Fouad, and Smith (1999) examined the influence of acculturation on traditionality of choice, showing that level of acculturation is related to traditionality of choice for minority college students.

These studies, collectively, show a small relationship between career aspirations and influences on career goals and race/ethnicity. Thus, we cannot explain differences in occupational choice by the differences in hopes and dreams for careers.

Interests

Evident in the theoretical models examined earlier is the importance of vocational interests in career choice. Savickas (1999) examined the diverse perspectives about interests and the various roles that interests play in vocational choice. We adopt here his definition that interests "form a consistent, persistent, and stable dispositional response tendency, which increases one's readiness to attend to and act upon a particular group of environmental stimuli" (p. 51). Embedded in this definition are several ideas that are viewed as critical to vocational choice. First, interests are seen as traits that are stable over time. Second, interests are seen as characteristic ways of responding to the environment. Third, interests help to determine to which environmental stimuli a person will respond. Interests may be seen as a collection of traits used to model the response to the environment. Thus, interests are an important component in vocational choice because, although the theories discussed earlier differ in their perspectives on how this occurs, vocational choice is envisioned as the fit between the person and the environment.

Research before 1991 on racial group differences in interests began early in the 1970s by simple examination of mean differences in interest scores. However, research on racial/ethnic group differences in interests since 1991 has focused on the structure of interests underlying these differences as well as on large-scale studies of interest profiles. Most of these studies, using sophisticated structural analyses, do not lend themselves to a calculation of effect size. However, they are important enough in our understanding of differences in vocational interests among groups that this literature is briefly summarized in this section. We finish the section with a discussion of the few studies for which effect sizes could be calculated.

Scholars who have examined the structure of interests across groups have essentially tested the cultural validity of Holland's (1997) theory. Revisions of the major interest inventories in the 1990s provided large, culturally diverse samples. These enabled researchers to examine whether Holland's six themes are found in the same order around the hexagon (or circle) across groups. In a more stringent test of his calculus assumption, researchers have also tested whether the themes are equidistant from each other.

In general, though they have shown gender differences, studies done with multidimensional scaling techniques showed that racial/ethnic groups had the same circular ordering of the Holland themes on the Strong Interest Inventory for African American, Hispanic, Asian American, and Caucasian professionals (Fouad & Dancer, 1992; Fouad, Harmon, & Borgen, 1997) and college students (Hansen, Collins, Swanson, & Fouad, 1993; Hansen, Sarma, & Collins, 1999; Hansen, Scullard, & Haviland, 2000; Swanson, 1992). One exception to these findings was a study by Haverkamp, Collins, and Hansen (1994), who found the circular ordering on the Strong Interest Inventory for Asian American college students was RIASCE, rather than RIASEC, as predicted by Holland (1997). Day and Rounds (1998), however, also found invariance across ethnic groups in a large sample (N = 49,450) of ethnically diverse high school students who took the American College Testing (ACT) program's Unisex ACT Interest Inventory.

The results of these studies indicated similarity across groups in the circular ordering of Holland's (1997) themes around the hexagon, although none of the studies indicated support for the strict calculus assumption that all themes are equidistant around the hexagon. However, most of the researchers reached a conclusion similar to that of Day and Rounds (1998), that "people of different ethnicities and sexes hold the same cognitive map of the world of work when the structures of their preferences are examined" (p. 734).

Several studies have examined mean differences in interest scores, most with the intention to evaluate the appropriateness of use of interest inventories across cultures. Davison Aviles and Spokane (1999) and Park and Harrison (1995) investigated racial/ethnic group differences in interests of students, finding that differences were small. Fouad, Harmon, and Hansen's (1994) study, with older, more established professionals, replicated the few ethnic group differences on the six General Occupational Theme scales. In a follow-up study, Fouad (2002) compared a group of career clients, primarily students, from the same ethnic group with the professionals and also found a small effect size for differences among ethnic groups; greater within-group than between-group differences were found.

In summary, researchers who have examined ethnic group differences in vocational interests have found that, when differences exist, effect sizes are small. Thus, differences in variance in interests are not explained by racial group affiliation. However, as Fouad (2002) noted, the interest inventories used to assess interests are either designed to eliminate differences between groups (i.e., the UNIACT), or the inventories do not include items that may tap differences in preferences for activities across racial/ethnic groups. For example, a review of items in the 1994 revision of the Strong contained no "collectivistic" items, on which racial/ethnic groups may be expected to differ (Fiske, Kitayama, Markus, & Nisbett, 1998).

Career Choice

The literature reviewed thus far indicates that racial/ethnic groups do not differ in the careers to which they aspire, and they do not differ in the interests they express. But clearly, there are differences in the careers chosen, for as we noted earlier, all racial/ethnic groups are not equally represented in the occupational landscape. In this section, we review the empirical literature on factors that may be related to differences in vocational choices: the content of choices, including supports and perception of barriers to career choices, and the processes of making career choices, including self-efficacy of decision making about careers, career maturity, and vocational identity.

Content of Choice

Two studies examined influences on career choices for Asian Americans. Lew, Allen, Papouchis, and Ritzler (1998) and Leong (1991) examined differences in Asian American values, the latter also comparing them to Whites. Both studies showed that the differences had relatively small effect sizes. Perrone, Sedlacek, and Alexander (2001) were interested in racial/ethnic group differences in factors influencing occupational choices. Their findings indicated a small relationship between ethnicity and factors influencing career choice goals, with Caucasians more likely to indicate intrinsic interest as a factor in choice, and higher earnings more a factor for African Americans, Asian Americans, and Native Americans. Teng, Morgan, and Anderson (2001) also found negligible differences between ethnic groups in factors that students indicated were important in their career.

This literature suggests that there is a small effect size between career choice and various factors related to occupational choice. Individuals appear to be incorporating the same types of information in their choices and are influenced by the same types of values regardless of ethnic group affiliation. When there are differences, there are more within-group than between-group differences.

Barriers/Supports

As we noted earlier, there are quite real barriers to the participation of racial/ethnic minority individuals in the workplace. A number of studies have focused on the perception of barriers and perceptions of lack of opportunities as possible reasons for differences in occupational choices; others have focused on facilitators or supports of vocational choice.

Chung and Harmon (1999) were interested in the perceptions of occupational discrimination for African American college students by both African American and White students. They found marked differences in perceptions, with Whites perceiving less discrimination than African American students and African Americans perceiving fewer opportunities for African Americans than White students. They also examined the relationship between African American students' perception of discrimination and perception of occupational opportunities for African Americans, finding a large effect size.

Luzzo (1993) and McWhirter (1997) have also focused on career barriers, each using a different scale, then working together using McWhirter's Perceptions of Barriers Scale (Luzzo & McWhirter, 2001). All three studies found that minority students were more likely than Whites to perceive barriers due to race or ethnicity. In Luzzo and McWhirter's study, for example, the largest difference between ethnic groups was found in the item "In my future career, I will probably be treated differently because of my racial/ethnic background." Luzzo and McWhirter also found that perceptions of ability to cope with barriers (coping efficacy) differed across groups, with minority students having lower self-efficacy in coping with barriers than White students.

Other researchers have examined supports for career and educational choices. Olszewski-Kubilius and Scott (1992) found that although there was a difference between high- and low-income minority students in their perceptions that they were ready to go to college and their confidence that they would be admitted to college, with those in higher income brackets more confident, there were no differences in wanting to go to college, feeling it was important to go to college, or family support and encouragement for attending college.

The studies in this section indicate that racial/ethnic minority students do perceive barriers to accomplishing their educational and occupational goals. As we noted earlier, labor market data indicate that barriers to equal employment do in fact exist. These barriers are more than mere perceptions on the part of racial/ethnic minority students; they are part of the reality of making career choices. Conversely, White students are less likely to view barriers, either for themselves or for racial/ethnic minority students. This becomes problematic in changing the real occupational barriers for racial/ethnic students: Those White individuals more likely to be in positions of power to influence change are least likely to view the need for change to reduce barriers.

Career Decision-Making Process

The final group of studies that examined race/ethnicity in career-related constructs focused on the processes involved in making career decisions. These include confidence in one's ability to make a career decision, or career decision-making self-efficacy, and career maturity, which is completing the developmental tasks for a particular career stage.

Investigations of race differences in career maturity have been confounded with concerns about the measurement of career maturity, which is a possible explanation for marked differences in results. Three studies (Leong, 1991; Luzzo, 1992; Powell & Luzzo, 1998) showed negligible effect sizes for racial/ethnic group differences in career maturity of college and high school students, and two studies (Lundberg, Osborne, & Miner, 1997; Westbrook & Sanford, 1991) found moderate effect sizes.

Investigators have also examined racial/ethnic group differences in decidedness, or the inverse, career indecision. Four studies in this area found very small effect sizes in career decidedness. For example, career decidedness was not related to racial identity for African American women, though, as predicted by developmental theory, college senior women are more career-certain than are freshmen women (McCowan & Alston, 1998). Others have not found ethnic or racial differences in career decidedness (Leong, 1991; Powell & Luzzo, 1998; Rojewski, 1994).

Thus, although there have been mixed results about career maturity, there appear to have been few differences found in career decidedness. To investigate potential causes for these findings, researchers examined racial/ethnic differences in confidence related to making a career decision (or self-efficacy). Studies have either shown no racial/ethnic group differences (C. Brown, Darden, Shelton, & Dipoto, 1999) or small differences, with White students showing more self-efficacy (Gloria & Hird, 1999) and African American students (Chung, 2002) scoring higher on career decision making self-efficacy. Chung found that African American students in his sample also scored higher in career commitment.

The studies in this section show that confidence in career decision making also does not account for the differences in occupational choice among racial/ethnic groups. Overall, the studies we have reviewed show that the strongest differences between racial/ethnic groups appear to be related to perception of opportunities and discrimination, rather than to aspirations, interests, decision-making skills, or confidence.

SUMMARY

The changing demographics of the U.S. population challenge the feasibility of traditional career theories. Patterns of occupational segregation and other inequities persist in how and where people work and the resulting income earned. As many career theories were developed without consideration of the cultural context influencing these work patterns (Hall, 1997), primary constructs of focus (e.g., interests, choice, decision making) have generally been de-contextualized from the cultural processes affecting those constructs (e.g., perceived support, barriers). Gysbers, Heppner, Johnston, and Neville (1998) identified five key tenets that have typified theory development in vocational psychology: (1) individuality and autonomy to choose careers is of primary importance in career development; (2) an individual is economically affluent to make a given career choice; (3) the structure of career opportunity is open and available to all who work hard; (4) work occupies an important and central aspect in people's lives; and (5) career development is a linear, orderly, and rational process. Collectively, these assumptions do not accurately reflect the reality of work for a majority of people, regardless of racial or ethnic group affiliation.

Our review of vocational research illustrates that the dominating constructs and ideas about career are culturally bound and, as such, are better understood in light of the cultural contexts in which the career-related behaviors occur. We support a social ecological view of work in which culture occupies a primary role in theoretical propositions, attending to the cultural relevance of key ideas and constructs and also reflective of the realities of work. As Savickas (1994) observed, contemporary career theories often exclude "the work experience of the diverse groups that populate our country and ignor[e] the frustrations of individuals with lower SES" (p. 237). In contrast to the notions of linearity in most career theories, careers often include discontinuities in work patterns and do not generally follow a fixed course (Savickas, 2001). They do not fit conceptually with how people think about career "paths" or "transitions." Although no one theory is sufficient in itself (Hackett, Lent, & Greenhaus, 1991; Super, 1992), we encourage research that better captures the dynamic and contextual nature of people-work interactions and adaptations.

Without question, the occupational landscape in the United States is not equal, and career patterns cannot be explained solely by differences in career aspirations. However, it is clear that at least part of these differences can be attributed to the perceived and actual barriers that some racial/ethnic groups encounter in realizing their career aspirations. Improved theorizing is needed to better capture relative processes, outcomes, and discontinuities in how people perceive, prepare for, enter into, and maintain work so that career interventions are more effective with diverse groups (Helledy et al., in press). Based on the literature we have covered, we suggest the following methodological, theoretical, and construct considerations in future research:

- Examine the relationship between perceptions of barriers, real barriers, and the construction people put on the barriers to understand how to help create systemic change that will really be effective in creating equitable opportunities for all. This must include ways to counteract both real barriers and the perception of barriers, as both internal and external factors reduce individuals' options.
- Conduct interdisciplinary (e.g., with anthropology, sociology) studies. Our review of vocational research reveals little variance (small to moderate effect sizes) in career constructs using extant analytic tools and methodological approaches. It is unclear whether there are indeed no cultural differences or whether our studies

have not been designed to uncover the differences that may exist. Interdisciplinary research may reveal different cultural constructs heretofore excluded in vocational research that may better examine cultural influences involved in processes and outcomes of career development.

- Focus on the impact of perceived structures of opportunity. Earlier in this chapter, we posed the question of whether vocational psychology should focus on building individuals' efficacy to make desired career choices or on promoting greater equity in opportunities for work. Again, our findings in the current review suggest that greater attention should be paid to the social and institutional structures that constrain and facilitate access to work, given the impact of perceived career barriers for some racial/ethnic groups. Such a focus highlights the need for systems-level examinations of the context of work.

- Attend to the realities of work. We do not know why race/ethnicity makes a difference in income or ability to work, perhaps because our theories are not designed to answer those questions. Generally, career theories give no central consideration to why these differences occur—only consideration for how work should evolve for "mainstream" society. Emerging research (e.g., Chung & Harmon, 1999) indicates that people do not differ greatly in their occupational dreams and aspirations but in their expectations to realize those aspirations, which seem to be informed by perceptions of barriers. That is, optimal vocational functioning is restrained by contextual oppression (Fitzgerald & Betz, 1994). We encourage additional constructs that examine the meaning and locus of choice given environmental factors that restrain career development.

REFERENCES

Arbona, C., & Novy, D. M. (1991). Career aspirations and expectations of Black, Mexican American, and White students. *Career Development Quarterly, 39,* 231–239.

Bandura, A. (1977). Self-efficacy: Toward a unifying theory of behavioral change. *Psychological Review, 84,* 191–215.

Bandura, A. (1986). *Social foundations of thought and action: A social cognitive theory.* Englewood Cliffs, NJ: Prentice-Hall.

Bandura, A. (1997). *Self-efficacy: The exercise of control.* New York: Freeman.

Blustein, D. L. (1997). The role of work in adolescent development. *Career Development Quarterly, 45,* 381–389.

Blustein, D. L. (2001). Extending the reach of vocational psychology: Toward an inclusive and integrated psychology of working. *Journal of Vocational Behavior, 59,* 171–182.

Brewer, C. A., & Suchan, T. A. (2001). *Mapping Census 2000: The geography of U.S. diversity.* Washington, DC: U.S. Government Printing Office.

Brown, C., Darden, E. E., Shelton, M. C., & Dipoto, M. C. (1999). Career exploration and self-efficacy of high school students: Are there urban/suburban differences? *Journal of Career Assessment, 7,* 227–237.

Brown, D. (2002). The role of work and cultural values in occupational choice, satisfaction, and success: A theoretical statement. *Journal of Counseling and Development, 80,* 48–56.

Brown, D., & Crace, R. K. (1996). Values in life role choices and outcomes: A conceptual model. *Career Development Quarterly, 44,* 211–223.

Byars, A. M., & McCubbin, L. D. (2001). Trends in career development research with racial/ethnic minorities: Prospects and challenges. In J. G. Ponterotto, J. M. Casas, L. A. Suzuki, & C. A. Alexander (Eds.), *Handbook of multicultural counseling* (2nd ed., pp. 633–654). Thousand Oaks, CA: Sage.

Carter, R. T., & Cook, D. A. (1992). A culturally relevant perspective for understanding the career paths of visible racial/ethnic group people. In H. D. Lea & Z. B. Leibowitz (Eds.), *Adult career development: Concepts, issues, and practices* (2nd ed., pp. 192–217). Alexandria, VA: National Career Development Association.

Chung, Y. B. (2002). Career decision-making self efficacy and career commitment: Gender and ethnic differences among college students. *Journal of Career Development, 28,* 277–284.

Chung, Y. B., & Harmon, L. W. (1999). Assessment of perceived occupational opportunity for Black Americans. *Journal of Career Assessment, 7,* 45–62.

Chung, Y. B., Loeb, J. W., & Gonzo, S. T. (1996). Factors predicting the educational and career aspirations of Black college students. *Journal of Career Development, 23,* 127–135.

Cohen, J. (1992). A power primer. *Psychological Bulletin, 112,* 155–159.

Davison Aviles, R. M., & Spokane, A. R. (1999). The vocational interests of Hispanic, African American, and White middle school students. *Measurement and Evaluation in Counseling and Development, 32,* 138–148.

Dawis, R. V. (2002). Person-environment correspondence theory. In D. Brown (Ed.), *Career choice and development* (4th ed., pp. 427–464). San Francisco: Jossey-Bass.

Day, S. X., & Rounds, J. (1998). Universality of vocational interest structure among racial and ethnic minorities. *American Psychologist, 53,* 728–736.

Evans, K. M., & Herr, E. L. (1994). The influence of racial identity and the perception of discrimination on the career aspirations of African American men and women. *Journal of Vocational Behavior, 44,* 173–184.

Fiske, A. P., Kitayama, S., Markus, H. R., & Nisbett, R. E. (1998). The cultural matrix of social psychology. In D. T. Gilbert, S. T. Fiske, & G. Lindzey (Eds.), *The handbook of social psychology* (4th ed., Vol. 2, pp. 915–981). New York: Wiley.

Fitzgerald, L. F., & Betz, N. E. (1994). Career development in cultural context: The role of gender, race, class, and sexual orientation. In M. L. Savickas & R. W. Lent (Eds.), *Convergence in career development theories* (pp. 103–118). Palo Alto, CA: Consulting Psychologists Press.

Flores, L. Y., & O'Brien, K. M. (2002). The career development of Mexican American adolescent women: A test of social cognitive career theory. *Journal of Counseling Psychology, 49,* 14–27.

Fouad, N. A. (2001). The future of vocational psychology: Aiming high. *Journal of Vocational Behavior, 59,* 183–191.

Fouad, N. A. (2002). Cross cultural differences in vocational interests: Between group differences on the Strong Interest Inventory. *Journal of Counseling Psychology, 49,* 283–289.

Fouad, N. A., & Brown, M. (2000). Race, ethnicity, culture, class and human development. In S. D. Brown & R. W. Lent (Eds.), *Handbook of counseling psychology* (3rd ed., pp. 379–410). New York: Wiley.

Fouad, N. A., & Byars, A. M. (2002). *The cultural context of work.* Unpublished manuscript. University of Wisconsin-Milwaukee.

Fouad, N. A., & Dancer, L. S. (1992). Cross-cultural structure of interests: Mexico and the United States. *Journal of Vocational Behavior, 40,* 129–143.

Fouad, N. A., Harmon, L. W., & Borgen, F. H. (1997). Structure of interests in employed male and female members of U.S. racial-ethnic minority and nonminority groups. *Journal of Counseling Psychology, 44,* 339–345.

Fouad, N. A., Harmon, L. W., & Hansen, J. C. (1994). Cross-cultural use of the Strong. In L. W. Harmon, J. C. Hansen, F. H. Borgen, & A. C Hammer (Eds.), *SII applications and technical guide* (pp. 255–280). Palo Alto, CA: Consulting Psychologists Press.

Fouad, N. A., & Smith, P. L. (1996). A test of a social cognitive model for middle school students: Math and science. *Journal of Counseling Psychology, 43,* 338–346.

Gainor, K. A., & Lent, R. W. (1998). Social cognitive expectations and racial identity attitudes in predicting the math choice intentions of Black college students. *Journal of Counseling Psychology, 45,* 403–413.

Gloria, A. M., & Hird, J. S. (1999). Influences of ethnic and nonethnic variables on the career decision-making self-efficacy of college students. *Career Development Quarterly, 48,* 157–174.

Goodman, J. (1994). Career adaptability in adults: A construct whose time has come. *Career Development Quarterly, 43,* 74–84.

Gysbers, N. C., Heppner, M. J., Johnston, J. A., & Neville, H. (1998). Empowering life choices: Career counseling in cultural contexts. In N. Gysbers, M. Heppner, & J. Johnston (Eds.), *Career counseling: Process, issues, and techniques* (pp. 31–54). Boston: Allyn & Bacon.

Hackett, G., Lent, R. W., & Greenhaus, J. H. (1991). Advances in vocational theory and research: A 20-year retrospective. *Journal of Vocational Behavior, 38,* 3–38.

Hall, C. C. I. (1997). Cultural malpractice: The growing obsolescence of psychology with the changing U.S. population. *American Psychologist, 52,* 642–651.

Hansen, J. C., Collins, R. C., Swanson, J. L., & Fouad, N. A. (1993). Sex differences in the structure of interests. *Journal of Vocational Behavior, 42,* 200–211.

Hansen, J. C., & Sackett, S. A. (1993). Agreement between college major and vocational interests for female athlete and non-athlete college students. *Journal of Vocational Behavior, 43,* 298–309.

Hansen, J. C., Sarma, Z. M., & Collins, R. C. (1999). An evaluation of Holland's model of vocational interests for Chicana(o) and Latina(o) college students. *Measurement and Evaluation in Counseling and Development, 32,* 2–13.

Hansen, J. C., Scullard, M. G., & Haviland, M. G. (2000). The interest structures of Native American college students. *Journal of Career Assessment, 8,* 159–172.

Haverkamp, B. E., Collins, R. C., & Hansen, J. C. (1994). Structure of interests and Asian-American college students. *Journal of Counseling Psychology, 41,* 256–264.

Helledy, I., Fouad, N. A., Gibson, P., Henry, C., Harris-Hodge, E., et al. (in press). The impact of cultural variables on vocational psychology: Examination of the Fouad and Bingham (1995) culturally appropriate career counseling model. In R. T. Carter (Ed.), *Handbook of racial-cultural psychology and counseling: Training and practice* (Vol. 2). Hoboken, NJ: Wiley.

Holland, J. L. (1997). *Making vocational choices: A theory of vocational personalities and work environments* (3rd ed.). Odessa, FL: Psychological Assessment Resources.

Krumboltz, J. D. (1994). Improving career development theory from a social learning perspective. In M. L. Savickas & R. W. Lent (Eds.), *Convergence in career development theories* (pp. 9–31). Palo Alto, CA: Consulting Psychologists Press.

Lent, R. W., Brown, S. D., & Hackett, G. (2000). Contextual supports and barriers to career choice: A social cognitive analysis. *Journal of Counseling Psychology, 47,* 36–49.

Lent, R. W., Brown, S. D., & Hackett, G. (2002). Social cognitive career theory. In D. Brown (Ed.), *Career choice and development.* (4th ed., pp. 255–311). San Francisco: Jossey-Bass.

Leong, F. T. (1991). Career development attributes and occupational values of Asian American and White American college students. *Career Development Quarterly, 39,* 221–230.

Leung, S. A., Ivey, D., & Suzuki, L. (1994). Factors affecting the career aspirations of Asian Americans. *Journal of Counseling and Development, 72,* 404–410.

Lew, A. S., Allen, R., Papouchis, N., & Ritzler, B. (1998). Achievement orientation and fear of success in Asian American college students. *Journal of Clinical Psychology, 54,* 97–108.

Lofquist, L. H., & Dawis, R. V. (1991). *Essentials of person-environment correspondence counseling.* Minneapolis: University of Minnesota Press.

Lopez, F. G., Lent, R. W., Brown, S. D., & Gore, P. A. (1997). Role of social-cognitive expectations in high school students' mathematics-related interests and performance. *Journal of Counseling Psychology, 44,* 44–52.

Lundberg, D. J., Osborne, W. L., & Minor, C. U. (1997). Career maturity and personality preferences of Mexican American and Anglo-American adolescents. *Journal of Career Development, 23,* 203–213.

Luzzo, D. A. (1992). Ethnic group and social class differences in college students' career development. *Career Development Quarterly, 41,* 161–173.

Luzzo, D. A. (1993). Ethnic differences in college students' perceptions of barriers to career development. *Journal of Multicultural Counseling and Development, 21,* 227–236.

Luzzo, D. A., & McWhirter, E. H. (2001). Sex and ethnic differences in the perception of educational and career related barriers and levels of coping efficacy. *Journal of Counseling and Development, 79,* 61–67.

Mau, W., & Bikos, L. H. (2000). Educational and vocational aspirations of minority and female students: A longitudinal study. *Journal of Counseling and Development, 78,* 186–194.

McCowan, C. J., & Alston, R. J. (1998). Racial identity, African self-consciousness, and career decision making in African American college women. *Journal of Multicultural Counseling and Development, 26,* 28–38.

McWhirter, E. H. (1997). Perceived barriers to education and career: Ethnic and gender differences. *Journal of Vocational Behavior, 50,* 124–140.

Miller, V. M. (1999). The opportunity structure: Implications for career counseling. *Journal of Employment Counseling, 36,* 2–12.

Mitchell, L. K., & Krumboltz, J. D. (1990). Krumboltz's learning theory of career choice and counseling. In D. Brown & L. Brooks (Eds.), *Career choice and development* (3rd ed., pp. 233–280). San Francisco: Jossey-Bass.

Murrell, A. J., Frieze, I. H., & Frost, J. L. (1991). Aspiring to careers in male- and female-dominated professions: A study of Black and White college women. *Psychology of Women Quarterly, 15,* 103–126.

National Research Council. (1999). *The changing nature of work: Implications for occupational analysis.* Washington, DC: Author.

Oleski, D., & Subich, L. M. (1996). Congruence and career change in employed adults. *Journal of Vocational Behavior, 49,* 221–229.

Olszewski-Kubilius, P. M., & Scott, J. M. (1992). An investigation of the college and career counseling needs of economically disadvantaged, minority gifted students. *Roeper-Review, 14,* 141–148.

Park, S. E., & Harrison, A. A. (1995). Career-related interests and values, perceived control, and acculturation of Asian-American and Caucasian-American college students. *Journal of Applied Social Psychology, 25,* 1184–1203.

Perrone, K. M., Sedlacek, W. E., & Alexander, C. M. (2001). Gender and ethnic differences in career goal attainment. *Career Development Quarterly, 50,* 168–178.

Peterson, G. W., Sampson, J. P., Lenz, J. G., & Reardon, R. C. (2002). A cognitive information processing approach to career problem solving and decision making. In D. Brown (Ed.), *Career choice and development.* (4th ed., pp. 373–426). San Francisco: Jossey-Bass.

Powell, D. F., & Luzzo, D. A. (1998). Evaluating factors associated with the career maturity of high school students. *Career Development Quarterly, 47,* 145–158.

Rojewski, J. W. (1994). Career indecision types for rural adolescents from disadvantaged and nondisadvantaged backgrounds. *Journal of Counseling Psychology, 41,* 356–363.

Savickas, M. L. (1994). Measuring career development: Current status and future directions. *Career Development Quarterly, 43,* 54–62.

Savickas, M. L. (1997). Career adaptability: An integrative construct for life-span, life-space theory. *Career Development Quarterly, 45,* 247–259.

Savickas, M. L. (1999). The psychology of interests. In M. L. Savickas & A. R. Spokane (Eds.), *Vocational interests: Meaning, measurement, and counseling use* (pp. 19–56). Palo Alto, CA: Davies-Black.

Savickas, M. L. (2001). The next decade in vocational psychology: Mission and objectives. *Journal of Vocational Behavior, 59,* 284–290.

Savickas, M. L. (2002). Career construction: A developmental theory of vocational behavior. In D. Brown (Ed.), *Career choice and development* (4th ed., pp. 149–205). San Francisco: Jossey-Bass.

Spokane, A. R., Meir, E. I., & Catalano, M. (2000). Person-environment congruence and Holland's theory: A review and reconsideration. *Journal of Vocational Behavior, 57,* 137–187.

Super, D. E. (1953). A theory of vocational development. *American Psychologist, 8,* 185–190.

Super, D. E. (1990). A life-span, life-space approach to career development. In D. Brown & L. Brooks (Eds.), *Career choice and development: Applying contemporary theories to practice* (2nd ed., pp. 197–261). San Francisco: Jossey-Bass.

Super, D. E. (1992). Toward a comprehensive theory of career development. In D. Montross & C. Shinkman (Eds.), *Career development: Theory and practice* (pp. 35–64). Springfield, IL: Thomas.

Swanson, J. L. (1992). The structure of vocational interests for African-American college students. *Journal of Vocational Behavior, 40,* 144–157.

Swanson, J. L., & Gore, P. A. (2000). Advances in vocational psychology: Theory and research. In S. D. Brown & R. W. Lent (Eds.), *Handbook of counseling psychology* (3rd ed., pp. 233–269). New York: Wiley.

Tang, M., Fouad, N. A., & Smith, P. L. (1999). Asian Americans' career choices: A path model to examine factors influencing their career choices. *Journal of Vocational Behavior, 54,* 142–157.

Teng, L. Y., Morgan, G. A., & Anderson, S. K. (2001). Career development among ethnic and age groups of community college students. *Journal of Career Development, 28,* 115–127.

Thompson, B. (2002). Statistical, practical, and clinical: How many kinds of significance do counselors need to consider? *Journal of Counseling and Development, 80,* 64–71.

U.S. Bureau of the Census. (1996). *Survey of income and program participation, April–July 1996.* Available from U.S. Census Bureau Web site: http://www.census.gov.

U.S. Bureau of the Census. (2001). *U.S. Census 2000, summary files 1 and 2.* Available from U.S. Census Bureau Web site: http://www.census.gov.

U.S. Bureau of Labor Statistics. (2002). *2002 occupational employment statistics.* Retrieved June 2002, from http://www.bls.gov.

Westbrook, B. W., & Sanford, E.-E. (1991). The validity of career maturity attitude measures among Black and White high school students. *Career Development Quarterly, 39,* 199–208.

Young, R. A., & Valach, L., & Collins, A. (2002). A contextualist explanation of career. In D. Brown (Ed.), *Career choice and development* (4th ed., pp. 206–254). San Francisco: Jossey-Bass.

Zunker, V. G. (1998). *Career counseling: Applied concepts of life planning* (5th ed.). Pacific Grove, CA: Brooks/Cole.

CHAPTER 14

Psychotherapy Process and Outcome from a Racial-Ethnic Perspective

Jairo N. Fuertes, Catarina I. Costa, Lisa N. Mueller, and Mindy Hersh

Psychologists, counselors, and mental health researchers have suggested that psychosocial and psychocultural influences among U.S. populations, including racial and ethnic groups as well as recent immigrants, should be considered in the conceptualization, delivery, and evaluation of mental health services (Sue & Sue, 1999, 2003). Theorists have made an inextricable connection between identity and race, ethnicity, and culture. Theorists have also conceptualized a connection between race, ethnicity, and culture and various constructions and behavioral norms of psychological health and well-being (Trickett, Watts, & Birman, 1994). Yet, despite the conceptual advances relating race, ethnicity, and culture to psychological health and well-being, a review of the empirical literature in counseling and psychotherapy indicates psychological factors that are informed by race, ethnicity, and culture (viz., of an emic nature) have not been incorporated in the literature. This is a serious limitation in the knowledge base, as it has now been determined that significant disparities exist in mental health and quality of mental health care service delivery for racial and ethnic minority populations in the United States.

In 2001, the surgeon general of the United States released a thorough report addressing the state of mental health for the country's ethnic and racial minorities in which the disparity in the quality of mental health care for underserved minority patients was exposed (U.S. Department of Health and Human Services, 2001). No longer can mental health professionals overlook the essential role that culture plays in the experiences that this fast-growing population faces when they seek mental health treatment in various service settings, such as hospitals and community mental health clinics. The report revealed that for the four minority U.S. populations investigated (African Americans, American Indians and Alaskan Natives, Asian Americans and Pacific Islanders, and Hispanic Americans), a multitude of mental health needs are being grossly insufficiently met due to culturally insensitive services. In addition to receiving less care for mental health concerns, minority populations also tend to receive poorer quality care. The surgeon general asserted that "culture counts," in that it influences the way people view, physically experience, and seek help for mental illness.

For the current chapter, we reviewed the relevant literature on counseling process and outcome, with specific emphasis on the race, ethnicity, and cultural background of clients/patients. We selected articles, chapters, and books on the topic of counseling in general as well as the more specific field of cross-cultural/multicultural counseling. We provide a critical review of this literature and point to limitations as well as possibilities with respect to the study and treatment of mental health issues for racial, ethnic, and cultural minority groups in the United States. We offer specific suggestions as to how counseling process and outcome research can be analyzed and conducted from a racial-ethnic perspective.

We define race and ethnicity as conceptualized by the editor of this *Handbook:* "race as reflected in skin color, physical features, and its sociopolitical use, and ethnicity as pertaining to one's country of origin and loosely connected to one's heritage and family background" (Carter, personal communication, April 2000). For the sake of clarity, we note that our focus is on ethnic and racial factors, particularly with respect to the four major nondominant groups in the United States: African Americans, Hispanic Americans, Asian Americans, and Native Americans. Despite the focus on these four groups, we attempt at later points in the chapter to discuss issues and points related to counseling process and outcome in a way that may be relevant to the broader field of counseling, including concerns that may apply to other cultural minority groups in the United States as well as White Americans. The chapter deals with the counseling of individuals who are adults, and we refer the reader to other chapters in either volume of this *Handbook* that focus on other counseling populations and treatment modalities (e.g., children, groups, and families).

Our review of the literature included a perusal of the latest editions of three major books in the field, the *Handbook of Counseling Psychology* (Brown & Lent, 2000), the *Handbook of Multicultural Counseling* (Ponterotto, Casas, Suzuki, & Alexander, 2001), and the *Handbook of Psychotherapy and Behavior Change* (Bergin & Garfield, 1994, 2003). We conducted a computer search of PsychINFO from 1971 to 2000 using various combinations of key terms, such as counseling, therapy, psychotherapy, race, ethnicity, process, and outcome. Our review of the literature also included manual searches for multicultural psychotherapy literature of the past six years in the following journals: *Journal of Counseling Psychology, Journal of Multicultural Counseling and Development, Journal of Consulting and Clinical Psychology, Journal of Counseling and Development, Cultural Diversity and Ethnic Minority Psychology,* and *Psychotherapy.* The reader should note that we utilize the terms counseling, therapy, psychotherapy, and treatments interchangeably in the chapter, all of which refer to the practice of psychological helping.

REVIEW OF THE LITERATURE

Outcome Research

The present section addresses three general questions about counseling outcome by reviewing the meta-analytic literature on this topic. The first question is whether counseling is effective for nondominant racial-ethnic populations in the United States, particularly in comparison to U.S. White populations. The second question is whether specific treatments are equally effective across racial and ethnic groups in the United States. The third question examines whether and how race and ethnicity have been incorporated in the research that has examined outcome in counseling. In our conceptualization of outcome, we borrow Hill and Williams's (2000) definition: "changes that occur directly or indirectly as a result of therapy" (p. 670).

A meta-analysis is an analysis of an analysis, a review of the literature that examines the statistical results reported in a number of studies on the same topic. The primary statistic calculated is effect size, which is a standard index of the strength between two variables (cf. Cohen, 1992). The most recent meta-analysis on outcome research was by Wampold et al. (1997), who conducted a meta-analysis of "bona fide" therapies (see Wampold et al. for the list of seven criteria used to determine bona fide status) by examining 114 studies published between 1970 and 1995. Their study attempted to build on previous meta-analyses of psychotherapy (Berman, Miller, & Massman, 1985; Robinson, Berman, & Neimeyer, 1990; Shapiro & Shapiro, 1982; Smith & Glass, 1977). Wampold et al. derived effect sizes only for studies that directly compared two or more treatments, they did not classify treatments into general types, and they included only analyses of bona fide psychological treatments. In addition, they controlled for treatment similarity and year of publication of the studies.

The effects obtained by Wampold et al. (1997) supported previous findings on the efficacy of psychotherapies. The bona fide psychotherapies examined were found to be largely equally effective, with comparison effect sizes in the range of .00 to .21. The type of therapy examined explained about 10% of the variance in effect sizes. In an additional analysis of effect sizes that included data from Lambert and Bergin (1994), Wampold et al. computed effect sizes between psychotherapy and no-treatment groups, the results of which also supported previous meta-analytic findings. Treated patients were .82 standard deviation units above the untreated patients. Thus, the average treated client is much better off than the average client who is not treated; whereas the average untreated client hovers around the 50th percentile of outcome, the average treated client scores at the 80th percentile, a 30% increase in outcome.

For the purpose of this chapter and to address the three general questions above, we randomly selected 21 of the 114 studies included in the Wampold et al. (1997) study and read them for a review. The 21 articles (see Appendix A) appeared in the following journals: *Journal of Counseling Psychology, Journal of Clinical and Consulting Psychology, Behavior Therapy,* and *Behavior Research and Therapy.* The selected studies were published between 1970 and 1995, and most of them focused on the effectiveness of specific psychotherapies and treatments on mood disorders and client's adjustment patterns.

Our review revealed that studies were conducted on a high percentage of White American clients. Of the 21 studies reviewed, the number of participants totaled 1,077. However, only four of the 21 studies selected identified the racial makeup of the samples, with one study identifying the sample as "predominantly White Anglo-Saxon." In the three remaining studies that provided specific information about their participant sample, the total number of nondominant racial or ethnic group participants identified was 81, including one study by Rodriguez and Blocher (1988) with 66 Puerto Rican women as its total sample. The rate of people of Color to total participants in the remaining two studies was 11%. Overall, the percentage of people of Color in the 21 studies that was documented was only 7.5. More important, not one of the 21 studies provided *any results* by race, ethnicity, or culture.

Given the random selection of the studies, we make the assumption that the participants in the 21 studies roughly represented the total participant pool that made up all the studies in the Wampold et al. (1997) data set. Consequently, their highly restricted samples and analyses limit their results and those of the meta-analysis to only White American populations. Thus, based on our review of the selected studies, analyzed in what is considered the best and most elegant meta-analytic study of psychotherapy outcome, we conclude that the effectiveness of counseling/psychotherapy treatments for nondominant racial and ethnic group members has not been established. Based on the meta-analytic evidence compiled by researchers in the field of counseling/psychotherapy thus far, the extent to which nondominant racial and ethnic Americans benefit from psychotherapy is not known, particularly in comparison to White Americans. It is also unknown whether there are differences in outcome for various nondominant racial and ethnic groups.

As part of our review of the meta-analytic literature, we examined other meta-analyses that have received considerable attention in the literature, and to an extent have shaped professionals' opinions about the effectiveness of psychotherapy with U.S. populations. Smith and Glass (1977) examined several variables associated with outcome, including the role of similarity between therapists and clients. They examined the results of 375 studies involving approximately 25,000 participants. The results of their analyses showed that similarity of ethnicity, age, and social level between client and therapist was associated with counseling outcome. However, Smith and Glass analyzed ethnicity, age, and social level as a group, and reported one significant correlation for the three factors combined ($r = -.19, p < .01$). The more similar clients and therapists were on ethnicity, age, and social level, the better the outcome. Of a total of 11 descriptive variables identified by Smith and Glass, therapist and client similarity was the second strongest correlation with outcome. However, the correlation between therapist-client similarity and outcome is difficult to interpret or appreciate as presented in their article. Was it age, social-level similarity, ethnic similarity alone, or their combined effect, that drove the significant finding? Twenty-six years later, the answer remains unclear.

Despite having modeled their later meta-analyses on many of the techniques and procedures of Smith and Glass (1977), Shapiro and Shapiro (1982) did not examine race or ethnic effects in their analyses of 143 outcome studies. They examined only client education, on the basis that "examination of the source studies suggested that the only relevant data available in most cases is the *client's educational level*"

(p. 585); however, education was not found to be significantly related to any of the effect sizes in their analyses. Berman et al. (1985) reviewed 25 studies that examined the efficacy of cognitive, desensitization, and mixed (cognitive-desensitization) treatments. They found the three treatments to be largely equally effective, but they did not examine their data set in terms of client race, ethnicity, or culture. They reported characteristics for their sample in terms of age, gender, and education, but none of these factors was analyzed in relation to effect size of outcome.

Robinson et al. (1990) examined the effects of psychotherapy on depression. They found that clients benefited from treatment for depression with psychotherapy as well as clients treated solely with medication. They found no differences in efficacy between psychotherapies in the treatment for depression. With respect to client variables, Robinson et al. examined client gender and age with respect to outcome and found no significant correlation. However, clients' race or ethnicity was not reported, and no analyses were conducted to examine differences on outcome. Lipsey and Wilson (1993) examined the efficacy of psychological, educational, and behavioral treatment by organizing the results from an impressively broad range of meta-analytic studies. They summarized the effect sizes of 302 meta-analyses, 296 of which produced positive effect sizes. The results of their compilation provided yet more evidence of the efficacy of psychological treatment and an array of educational and behavioral interventions. However, their findings were not examined in terms of the types of clients with which these are proven to be so effective.

After analyzing these meta-analytic studies of psychotherapy, it becomes possible to discuss the studies with respect to the variables of interest in this chapter: race, ethnicity, and cultural factors. The most striking aspect of these meta-analytic studies is that none of them reported characteristics of the samples or conducted analyses in terms of race, ethnicity, or cultural domains. The current Zeitgeist in the outcome research community can thus be characterized as assuming a basic homogeneity effect with respect to treatment populations. An implicit assumption made by many researchers is that treatments have universal applicability (Sue & Sue, 2003; Sue, Zane, & Young, 1994) across U.S. racial, ethnic, and cultural groups. The assumption of universality needs to be challenged and tested, given the undisputable fact of outcome disparities in mental health as outlined by the surgeon general. Until this is done, the limitations in population scope inherent in the major meta-analytic studies in our field represent a serious shortcoming of the outcome literature and of what is known about psychotherapy outcome.

To summarize our observations based strictly on a reading of the meta-analytic literature: At this point, it is unknown whether nondominant racial and ethnic group members benefit from therapy or whether they benefit from it as well as do White American participants. It has not been empirically established whether differences would be observed between and within racial and ethnic groups, or whether certain psychotherapies are more effective for people of Color across a variety of psychological and psychosocial problems. Last, the influence of race or ethnicity on outcome, or if similarities or differences along these domains are truly associated with outcome, has not been investigated.

Related Outcome Literature

In this section, we present observations gleaned from a review of the broader literature on outcome in psychotherapy. Seligman (1995) summarized the results from a *Consumer Reports* nationwide survey of counseling/psychotherapy clients. In terms of the main results reported, Seligman noted that of 426 people surveyed who responded feeling "very poor" prior to therapy, 87% reported feeling very good, good, or so-so after therapy. The survey results also showed that of 786 respondents surveyed who said they felt "fairly poor" prior to treatment, 92% were feeling very good, good, or at least so-so after therapy. Seligman also reported evidence for a dose-response effect with respect to treatment: The more therapy patients received, the better off they felt. This was true for clients in psychotherapy alone and for those receiving psychotherapy plus medication. All therapies did equally well, and psychologists, psychiatrists, and social workers did better in treatment of patients than marriage counselors and doctors. In his critique of the *Consumer Reports* study, Seligman addressed the strengths and weaknesses of effectiveness and efficacy studies in general, and the *Consumer Reports* research in particular. One important limitation, among many, noted by Seligman and others since, is in the demographics of the respondents, who were all highly educated and predominantly middle-class White Americans. The restricted sampling seriously limited the generalizability of the findings. The study did not report the race or ethnicity of the respondents or their therapists, or whether similarity was associated with outcome or satisfaction. However, Seligman noted that survey designs that are properly implemented hold promise as possibly answering the famous question, "Which treatments are most effective for which patients under what conditions?" (p. 453). We interpret his "properly implemented" statement to mean that the use of a more racially, ethnically, and culturally representative sampling of clients and their treatment providers in the U.S. population will provide our field with greater information about how therapy benefits racial, ethnic, and cultural minority group members.

Lambert and Bergin (1994) reviewed the outcome literature in psychotherapy, the result of which provided support for previous findings on the absolute and relative efficacy of psychotherapy. Among their findings, they reported dose-response patterns, which suggested that on average, about 50% of patients improved after eight sessions of psychotherapy, and about 75% improved after about six months (or about 26 sessions). They noted that in comparison to patients in no-treatment control conditions, psychotherapy patients tended to improve more quickly and retain their gains longer. Lambert and Bergin also provided excellent discussions on the topics of common factors and therapist skill/competence, both of which are relevant to the topic of the current chapter. Lambert and Bergin speculated that common factors evident in all psychotherapies probably account for substantial amounts of patient improvement. The reader is encouraged to read their chapter, in which the authors provide excellent taxonomies of common factors organized into support, learning, and action categories. Lambert and Bergin also provided an example of how specific techniques of different schools of psychotherapy relate to nonspecific change agents shared by all psychotherapies, including affective experiencing, cognitive mastery, and behavioral regulation. Excellent examples are provided of how specific techniques from various theoretical and technical traditions fit within the three change agents.

With respect to therapist skill and competence, Lambert and Bergin (1994) noted that three qualities seemed to discriminate more helpful from less helpful therapists. These qualities included therapist adjustment, skill, and interest in helping their clients; the "purity of the treatment" (p. 174) offered to the client; and the quality of the therapist-client relationship. Lambert and Bergin noted that these therapists' qualities generally explain about 9% (a medium effect size) of the variance in outcome. Lambert and Bergin did not discuss race or ethnicity as factors with respect to outcome, but clearly, their important ideas and observations have indirect implications for future outcome research (see also Bergin & Garfield, 2003). Those implications are discussed next, in the section entitled "Future Research Directions."

In a review of the outcome literature, Beutler, Machado, and Neufeldt (1994) reported that therapist variables classified as objective and therapy-specific (e.g., therapy style, specific therapist interventions) exerted the most powerful effects on outcome. They also noted that, surprisingly, therapist skill or competence had not been well researched. As part of their discussion, they cited a review of the outcome literature conducted by Moncher and Prinz (1991), who reviewed 359 treatment outcome studies and found that most studies failed to assess therapist competence and skill in relation to outcome. Beutler et al. cited only two studies, by Bennun and Schindler (1988) and Crits-Christoph, Cooper, and Luborsky (1988), that found a positive relationship between therapist skill and outcome. Beutler et al. made the important observation that therapist skill is relatively distinct from both experience level and therapist compliance with a therapy model. As part of their discussion of promising "subjective therapy variables," they noted therapist-client value and attitudinal similarity, which in their view influenced the quality of the therapy relationship, which in turn is concretely associated with outcome. Beutler et al. cited Smith, Glass, and Miller's (1980) significant therapist-client similarity findings with respect to outcome and noted, "It is unfortunate that so little outcome research on shared cultural beliefs has been conducted to date" (p. 242).

In a related chapter, Orlinsky, Grawe, and Parks (1994) cited a broader, more international literature linking psychotherapy process and outcome. They cited American and European research on therapist skill and outcome and concluded that an effect size of .20 exists between these variables. Despite the lack of research on therapist skill/competence, when studied, therapist skill yields results that can be considered the strongest "therapist variable" associated with outcome. To examine and critique the types of studies that have assessed therapist skill, we *randomly* selected 11 individual studies included in the literature review on therapist skill that was presented and examined by Orlinsky et al. in 1994 (see Appendix B). We examined the sample populations in the studies, as well as the specific client and therapist variables measured in the research. The articles reviewed appeared in the *Journal of Clinical Psychology, Family Process, American Journal of Psychiatry, Journal of Consulting and Clinical Psychology, Journal of Counseling Psychology,* and *Psychotherapy* between 1986 and 1992. Independent variables measured in the studies selected included professional skills such as trustworthiness, expertness, and level of treatment technique, and relationship skills such as counselor adaptability, sensitivity, and collaboration. Client variables included active participation, early termination, and collaboration.

Seven of the 11 studies reported finding positive relationships between different measures of therapist skill and treatment outcome. Among these, counselor's skill was a significant predictor of the therapy alliance, client premature termination, and improvement. However, of the 11 studies reviewed, only four mentioned participant ethnicity in their method section. Of these, only one study utilized a diverse group of participants (Hagborg, 1991), and the remaining three had samples of predominantly or completely White American participants. None of the studies examined differences in clients' perceptions of therapist level of skill or competence as a function of race or ethnicity.

From our review of the 11 studies and the broader literature on therapist variables cited above, we conclude that therapist skill/competence has not been well studied, even though it appears to be an important predictor of outcome. We also conclude that therapist skill or competence in working with nondominant racial or ethnic groups has not been examined at all, although we next cover literature that has examined or proposed at the theoretical level the construct of "multicultural competence" in counseling. Clearly, there is a need for outcome research that examines more precisely the role of therapist skill/competence in predicting outcome in counseling and psychotherapy, and an equally if not greater need for the study of therapist competence in multicultural counseling that involves U.S. nondominant racial and ethnic groups.

RELATED MULTICULTURAL LITERATURE

An important article relevant to the topic of this chapter is the work of Sue et al. (1994), who reviewed outcome and process research on psychotherapy with culturally diverse populations. Given the importance of that chapter to the current topic, we review their findings and present some of their important ideas here, but we refer the reader to the article for a more in-depth reading of its contents. The authors examined the extant empirical evidence on process and outcome research with African Americans, American Indians, Asian Americans, and Latino Americans (see also Zane et al., 2003).

Sue et al. (1994) noted that outcome has been studied largely in terms of utilization of treatment, dropout rates, and length of treatment. Direct assessments of counseling or treatment outcome with nondominant racial and ethnic groups have not been conducted, which makes it impossible to derive conclusions on the effectiveness or efficacy of treatment. Trends gleaned from the literature on utilization by Sue et al. pointed to overutilization patterns by African Americans and American Indians and underutilization by Latino and Asian Americans. Knowledge of services, accessibility, and use of the English language seem to be associated with utilization patterns, particularly for foreign-born populations. The reasons behind utilization of services are not well understood, but Sue et al. do hint at some of the pervasive and profound problems evident in respective racial and ethnic communities, including issues of poverty and education.

In terms of dropout rates and length of treatment, Sue et al. (1994) noted that the data have been inconsistent and unsystematically collected. However, overall patterns suggested that on average, nondominant racial and ethnic groups terminate prematurely from therapy (i.e., after one session) more frequently than Whites (50% versus 30%). For all racial and ethnic groups except American Indians, the evidence seems to point to benefits of counseling and psychotherapy. With African Americans, there are inconsistent findings; some suggested inferior benefits, but others suggested "no differences" in comparison to Whites. For Asian and Latino Americans, the results are fairly consistent in supporting benefits from treatment. Research with American Indians is severely lacking, but some research suggests benefits for substance abuse interventions. Sue et al. also noted that results of racial and ethnic matching were inconsistent with African Americans, but racial, ethnic, and language matching seem to be associated with number of sessions, decreased premature termination, and positive outcomes for Latino Americans.

Sue et al. (1994) pointed out that in terms of counseling process, the topics most frequently examined with nonclinical samples and via analogue and survey studies were client preferences and acculturation. Clients tended to prefer counselors who were racially and ethnically similar, but this is not the most important component in similarity (e.g., in comparison to values or attitude similarity). Sue et al. also noted that Asian Americans and Latino Americans tend to expect a more directive counseling style from helpers. However, they also noted that studies on the effect of acculturation are inconsistent, and due to methodological limitations results on the effects of acculturation, client preferences, and preferred counselor style were "premature" to interpret.

Sue et al. (1994) discussed specific methodological concerns with studies cited in their chapter. The concerns included a lack of specificity in the research questions examined, including the direct assessment of outcome and of culturally related process factors, the inconsistent use of terminology and labels, the use of nonclinical respondents, the use of homogeneous sample groups that ignored important within-group differences, and the selection of measurements that ignored culture-related outcomes. Most important, the authors discussed the lack of conceptual/theoretical models as a major constraint on process and outcome research with racially and ethnically diverse populations. We return to some of the observations made by Sue et al. in the section that deals with future research directions.

Another relevant and recent paper that examined and summarized the multicultural counseling literature was by Ponterotto, Fuertes, and Chen (2000). They found 16 models of multicultural counseling, all at various stages of development and most with little, if any, empirical support of their premises. However, two models were identified as having advanced conceptual reformulations and empirical scrutiny. The two models were the multicultural counseling competence model (Sue, Arredondo, & McDavis, 1992; Sue et al., 1998) and the racial identity and interaction model (Helms, 1984, 1990). Ponterotto et al., found nine studies that examined the value/efficacy of the multicultural competence model, and 40 studies that examined the racial identity model in counseling. With respect to the multicultural competence model, the review found significant work directed at refining the model and its measurement in counseling and supervision. The application of the model to counseling and supervision is very limited, but support was gleaned from several studies in informing culturally responsive behavior, suggesting that the model guides counselor behavior to be credible and consistent with the client's expectations. There is also support for use of the model in counselor training, primarily in increasing counselor cultural-racial self-awareness and openness and sensitivity to issues of human diversity.

With respect to the racial identity model, Ponterotto et al. (2000) found evidence that Black racial identity statuses were associated in theoretically predicted ways with psychological health, ethnic identity, and attitudes toward counseling. Research findings also suggested that White racial identity statuses were associated in theoretically predicted ways with psychological health, interracial comfort, and multicultural counseling competence. Research examining interactions in counseling has yielded theoretically predicted relationships between racial identity status and affective responses in counseling (Carter & Helms, 1992; Richardson & Helms, 1994), as well as between racial identity status of counseling participants and the quality of discussions about race and race-related issues (Carter, 1995).

Although we have discussed some process variables and topics in the present section, we follow the outcome research review by summarizing and critiquing a recent chapter by Hill and Williams (2000) that focused entirely on process research.

Process Research

Hill and Williams's (2000) contribution adequately describes the latest findings on process research in psychotherapy and provides a benchmark for developing future research ideas on the topic from a racial and ethnic perspective. Hill and Williams defined process as "overt and covert thoughts, feelings, and behaviors of both clients and therapists during therapy sessions" (p. 670) and distinguished between process variables and "input" and "extratherapy" variables. According to Hill and Williams, input variables refer to "characteristics of the clients and therapists (e.g., personality, demographics, expectations, theoretical orientation/worldview) and setting (e.g., physical arrangement of the room, agency versus private practice)" (p. 670). Extratherapy variables refer to events that occur outside of counseling, "such as the death of a relative or having a good support system" (p. 670). For the purposes of this chapter, we summarize the main findings from Hill and Williams regarding process research.

In terms of therapists, Hill and Williams (2000) described research on various therapist techniques in counseling, such as interpretation, confrontation, self-disclosure, paradoxical interventions, and homework assignments. According to these authors, some generalizations can be gleaned from the research. For example, studies showed that interpretations delivered when sought by the client or when the client is ready, in moderate depth, and specifically tailored for the client were most helpful. Also, findings showed that confrontations can lead to negative client reactions and defensiveness but in certain situations can also lead to client arousal and openness to persuasion. Clients often experienced therapist self-disclosure as helpful, as it led to increased client experiencing and promoted client insight. Self-disclosure also led to perceptions of the therapist as human, real, and to an improved therapy relationship. According to Hill and Williams, self-disclosure also led to clients feeling normal and assured, to a decrease in symptoms, and to greater liking of therapists. However, Hill and Williams pointed out that more needs to be known about the context in which these interactions are applied, including the role of mediating factors such as timing, mode of therapist delivery, and variations in types of clients.

In terms of clients, some research has been conducted on client involvement and resistance. Because observers usually rate both of these, Hill and Williams (2000) stated that these concepts serve to describe the nature of the counseling interaction rather than to predict other process or outcome factors. Hill and Williams noted that the concepts of involvement and resistance were limited by the inconsistencies in their operational definitions in different theoretical contexts. In addition, methodological differences in the way involvement and resistance were measured as well as their conceptual overlap complicate their study and application value.

Research regarding more covert client processes includes reactions, nondisclosures, and transference. Hill and Williams (2000) cited research from Thompson and Hill (1991) and Hill, Thompson, and Corbett (1992) in which therapist awareness and attention to positive and negative client reactions had an important influence on the helpfulness of therapist responses and interventions. According to Hill and Williams, future research needs to address the ways therapists assess client reactions as well as the reactions' effects on therapists. The research regarding nondisclosure also indicated a greater need for assessment of signs that indicated clients' failure to verbalize thoughts and feelings. The concept of transference is often defined and interpreted in multiple ways in the context of different theoretical orientations.

A client-therapist interaction variable of paramount importance in process research is the working alliance. Hill and Williams (2000) noted consistent research findings pointing to a moderate effect size between the alliance and outcome ($r = .26$). Consequently, studies have examined the phases of the alliance, therapist and client contributions to the alliance, and problems in the alliance, such as ruptures, misunderstandings, and impasses. Process research has also examined therapeutic events in counseling. These included helpful and unhelpful events and the progress by which clients developed insight and created meaning through counseling.

Hill and Williams (2000) noted that there was no lack of process research in the field for the past 15 years. They also believed process research has come a long way in becoming increasingly relevant to clinicians and useful in the practice aspect of the field. While we are indebted to Hill and Williams for their substantial contributions to process research and their premier chapter, we conclude that process research to date has been largely "color-blind." Process research has not examined how all the important variables and constructs discussed earlier manifest themselves or play out when client and therapist are of different racial or ethnic backgrounds. This is clearly a limitation of this research and a challenge for psychotherapy researchers to meet in the coming years.

Journal Search (1995 to 2000)

With respect to our review of seven major journals (*Journal of Counseling Psychology, Journal of Multicultural Counseling and Development, Journal of Consulting and Clinical Psychology, Journal of Counseling and Development, Cultural Diversity and Ethnic Minority Psychology, Counseling Psychologist,* and *Psychotherapy*) we found a total of 79 articles that related to counseling of adult individuals who were nondominant racial or ethnic group members. From these 79, we deleted 12 articles that were not related to personal-social counseling of adults (e.g., dealt with career issues or children). The purpose of the search was not to provide an extensive review of the literature, but to inform our views on the current state of process and outcome research from a racial and ethnic perspective. Due to space limitations, we do not list the specific articles obtained in the search and discuss our findings only in terms of general trends. The articles have been compiled in a separate list, which is available to readers on request.

The 67 articles reviewed tended to cluster around five broad areas. The first area contains articles that were theoretical in nature and presented models of multicultural counseling that emphasized the "how-to" component of counseling and were based largely on specific constructs, such as counselor and client racial identity, level of acculturation, worldview, and counselor multicultural competency. This cluster also includes articles that presented counseling approaches for use with specific racial or ethnic groups, such as African Americans, or specific subgroups, such as Cuban Americans or Korean Americans. The second area contained theoretical and research papers that discussed or advanced specific constructs intended or presumed to inform counseling. These papers examined the relationships between various constructs, such as racial identity and acculturation and cultural awareness and ethnic loyalty; advanced fairly novel constructs, such as acculturative stress and bicultural identification; or presented new measures, such as the Asian American Family Conflicts Scale and the Color-Blind Racial Attitudes Scale. The third area contained articles that examined clients' perceptions of or reactions to counselors or their preferences for counselors. For the most part, these studies included measures of client level of acculturation, racial identity, racial or ethnic background, universal-diverse orientation, and immigrant status. Many of the studies in the third area used fairly sophisticated analogue methodology that manipulated factors such as counselor bilingual speaking ability, speech accent, or approach to counseling, with the most popular outcome measure being perceptions of counselor's sensitivity, similarity, or credibility.

The fourth area contained articles that focused on counselor variables or skills, such as counselor multicultural competency, counselor worldview, or level of racial identity in conjunction with counselor's perceptions of client or use of clinical interventions. Articles included clinical attributions in diagnosis, effects of stereotypes on diagnostic ratings, and racial identity-level effects on counselor interracial comfort. The fifth area included articles that were more applied in nature, using actual clients and counselors in counseling and focusing more on clinical issues. The studies in this area incorporated constructs such as acculturation, acculturative stress, racial identity, worldviews, and biculturalism to examine and measure psychological correlates such as client perceived stressors, coping styles, fear of success, life satisfaction, self-esteem, perceived discrimination, and various clinical symptoms such as bulimia nervosa, depressive symptomatology, and HIV-related risk behaviors.

A review of these articles suggests that there have been many studies in the area of multicultural counseling, with the literature being both theoretical and applied and increasingly complex in both design and level of analysis. Advancements in model, theory, and construct development of a multicultural nature have the potential to provide counselors with both "a compass and a map" for conducting effective multicultural counseling. When properly used, they may help counselors be more attentive and sensitive to clients' experiences and to interpersonal nuances, such as the level of trust and the quality of the working relationship. The theoretical, model, and construct advances may also help counselors be more cognizant of prejudices, biases, and blind spots that may affect their clinical judgment. Last, the advancements may provide practitioners with an appreciation of how some racial and ethnic factors, such as acculturation, racial identity, and immigrant status, may relate to problems for clients, such as discrimination, stress, and depression.

Despite the conceptual developments in the literature, however, a more critical review of 67 studies reveals several limitations, as well as exciting opportunities for future research that have been set up by the conceptual advancements. The limitations of the present research and opportunities for future research are discussed next.

FUTURE RESEARCH DIRECTIONS

We have reviewed selected studies in the literature that examine outcome and process in psychotherapy. As we mentioned, one of our goals with respect to outcome was to answer three questions. We examined the literature for evidence to support the notion that therapy is effective for nondominant racial and ethnic populations in the United States, particularly in comparison to White American populations. We also examined whether treatments were equally effective across racial and ethnic groups in the United States. And we examined whether and how race and ethnicity have been incorporated in the research that has examined outcome in counseling.

As a result of the dearth of research that examines how race, ethnicity, and culture are incorporated into psychotherapy outcome, there is very little empirical evidence to answer the first two questions. Our review of the literature shows that meta-analyses conducted thus far included studies that have been conducted with almost exclusively Euro-American populations or have not identified the racial or ethnic makeup of the participant samples. Clearly, there is a need for meta-analytic evidence on how nondominant racial and ethnic clients fare in counseling. Studies that incorporate race, ethnicity, and culture into their variables would be best able to answer questions of counseling efficacy with these populations.

Another possible venue for answering our first two questions is the effectiveness approach employed in the *Consumer Reports* study and discussed by Seligman (1995) and by Bernal, Bonilla, Padilla-Cotto, and Perez-Prado (1998). As we mentioned earlier, Seligman noted that survey designs that are properly implemented (presumably at least in terms of sampling a more representative group of clients and their providers in the U.S. population) hold promise for answering the famous question, "Which treatments are most effective for which patients under what conditions?" (p. 453). To follow up on Seligman's suggestion, we think that a properly conducted effectiveness survey of counseling/psychotherapy that includes a representative sample of nondominant racial and ethnic clients may provide useful evidence about the effectiveness of counseling services to such populations in various settings and conditions.

Nevertheless, despite the lack of evidence from large-scale meta-analytic or effectiveness studies, reviews of the literature suggest that therapy is effective for nondominant racial and ethnic groups. The research studies obtained from our manual searches and identified as applied in the discussion above provide results that suggest that nondominant racial and ethnic group members are helped by counseling interventions across a variety of problems, including eating disorders, depression, and health risk behaviors. It is also our collective clinical experience that many of our clients who are nondominant racial and ethnic group members benefit from counseling. More important, the surgeon general's report included the following recommendation, based on the overwhelming evidence of the effectiveness of mental health interventions for those populations for whom quality of care is available: "Every person, regardless of race or ethnicity, should seek help if they have a mental health problem or symptoms of a mental disorder" (U.S. Department of Health and Human Services, 2001).

Based on our review of the literature, we arrive at the conclusion that there is a need for rigorous research that examines outcomes and how mental health care can be improved for racial and ethnic minority populations in the United States. Outcome variables that seem important to study include client premature termination, satisfaction, involvement, and gain in treatment. There is also a need for problem-based and symptom/diagnosis-oriented outcome studies that involve nondominant racial and ethnic group members, particularly as these groups, as documented in the surgeon general's report, are less likely to receive needed and adequate mental help and are underrepresented in mental health research (U.S. Department of Health and Human Services, 2001).

However, it is crucial that researchers incorporate relevant race/ethnicity measures to account for within-group heterogeneity in communities of Color, such as racial identity, acculturation, cultural group affiliation, and value orientation. Perhaps most important, even beyond the question of variables or populations, is the need for applied research that is from the field and involves actual clients and therapists engaged in counseling. Something that we have done well in the area of multicultural counseling is to conceptualize, theorize, survey students, and conduct analogue studies. While such work has been useful and necessary for practitioners, it is time for researchers to examine how theories, constructs, and ideas play out in actual counseling.

There is also a need for continued research on therapist variables. The topic that has received the greatest attention in recent years is counselor multicultural competency (Fuertes, Bartolomeo, & Nichols, 2001) and racial identity (Carter, 1995). Further research may be directed at studying how counselor multicultural competency facilitates the development of rapport in counseling, counselor and client involvement in therapy, client trust in counseling, client affective experiencing and insight, client satisfaction with therapy, and other variables (see Lambert & Bergin, 1994, for lists of process and outcome variables). Studies that examine the relationship between multicultural competencies and culture-bound or culturally relevant process and outcome indices (e.g., cultural mistrust, racial identity, acculturation stress, cultural self-understanding, amelioration of cultural conflict, internalized homophobia) seem especially needed and potentially useful. Future service delivery, counselor training programs, and research endeavors in the area of multicultural counseling and competence will be galvanized by data that demonstrate how multicultural competence relates to or explains important events in counseling.

Other therapist variables gleaned from the literature that seem important are therapist skill (traditional skill) and interpersonal adjustment. As we noted previously, it is very surprising that therapist skill has not been studied more in counseling research. This is especially surprising given the conclusion that some in our field have arrived at, namely, that therapist skill is irrelevant to counseling and that virtually anyone (or anything) can deliver counseling services (e.g., Christensen & Jacobson, 1994). This belief is perhaps due to clinicians, researchers, and consumers equating therapist experience, degree, and training with therapist skill, which is not accurate (Beutler et al., 1994). Thus, we believe that much more research should be directed at studying therapist skill, particularly with respect to expertness of technique, treatment modality, client population, and type and severity of treatment issue.

Therapist interpersonal adjustment also appears to be an important issue and distinct from therapist skill. In our opinion, therapist interpersonal adjustment may be related to personal qualities and skills of the therapist. These qualities and skills may relate, for example, to the therapist's being able to quickly size up the interpersonal nature of the situation (e.g., the client's perceptions of the therapist), or to being "street-smart," "wise" (Hanna, Bemak, & Chi-Ying Chung, 1999), emotionally intelligent, charismatic, or patient. These are possible characteristics of good therapists that might be studied empirically as part of a program of multicultural counseling research.

There is also a tremendous amount of research directed at the effects of similarity. A topic that emerged from our review of the literature was the role of similarity between client and therapist and its relationship to outcome. Although many studies have examined the effect of client-counselor similarity with respect to clients' perceptions and reactions, virtually no research has examined if and how similarity is associated with outcome. Beutler et al. (1994) noted, "It is unfortunate that so little outcome research on shared cultural beliefs has been conducted to date" (p. 242). Smith and Glass (1977) found similarity between therapist and client to be associated with effect size. Although the finding was difficult to interpret as presented in their article, it is certainly worth pursuing in future research. Researchers may examine which aspects of similarity are associated with initial perceptions, which might be associated with process issues such as trust and development of rapport in the relationship, and which aspects or dimensions of similarity, particularly as seen by the client, are truly associated with outcome. Research might also be directed at testing Trevino's (1996) model of counseling, which postulates process and outcome effects as a function of client-therapist worldview similarity and discrepancy.

Sue et al. (1994) discussed the lack of conceptual/theoretical models as a major constraint on process and outcome research with racially and ethnically diverse populations. The field of psychology is poised to study the role of multicultural counseling theory in an applied way. Recently, Ponterotto et al. (2000), and Fuertes and Gretchen (2001) reviewed 16 different theories and models of multicultural counseling. These authors observed that the conceptual and theoretical advances in the field have set the next stage in scientific development for the area of multicultural counseling, which is the empirical validation of these varied approaches to counseling.

As we have shown as part of our review of the literature, and as was recently suggested by Ponterotto, Costa, and Lin (2002), there is a great need for research that examines process in psychotherapy, and that does this with nondominant racial and ethnic clients and/or counselors. Multicultural process research might examine, for example, the effects of certain therapist interventions early in therapy in establishing or fostering a trusting and productive relationship with clients. Researchers might also examine how therapists intervene when ruptures in the therapy relationship appear, or when impasses and misunderstandings occur in their work with racial and ethnic minority clients. It seems particularly important to study, in a qualitative way, how counselors cope with ambiguity and difficult multicultural cases, and the process by which they decide to seek supervision or consultation for these difficulties. Therapist self-disclosure appears important to study, as this particular intervention has been found to be so powerful in eliciting client responses and perceptions of counselors.

With respect to clients, there seems to be a need to examine the role of clients' values and beliefs in accepting or evaluating therapist interpretations, suggestions, directives, and advice. The client's perspective is important in multicultural research (Fuertes et al., 2001), especially as it pertains to the role of factors such as racial identity, acculturation, cultural mistrust, hostility, or apprehension, and other culturally related variables that may influence or fuel reactions to or perceptions of counseling or counselors. As noted by Orlinsky et al. (1994), client cooperation versus resistance and client openness versus defensiveness demonstrate robust effects with counseling outcome.

APPENDIX A: ARTICLES INCLUDED IN THE WAMPOLD STUDY

Arnow, B. A., Taylor, C. B., Agras, W. S., & Telch, M. J. (1985). Enhancing agoraphobia treatment outcome by changing couple communication patterns. *Behavior Therapy, 16,* 452–467.

Borkovec, T. D., & Costello, E. (1993). Efficacy of applied relaxation and cognitive-behavioral therapy in the treatment of generalized anxiety disorder. *Journal of Counseling and Clinical Psychology, 61,* 611–619.

Chang-Liang, R., & Denney, D. R. (1976). Applied relaxation as training in self-control. *Journal of Counseling Psychology, 23,* 183–189.

Craske, M. G., Brown, T. A., & Barlow, D. H. (1991). Behavioral treatment of panic disorder: A two-year follow-up. *Behavior Therapy, 22,* 289–304.

Deffenbacher, J. L., Mathis, H., & Michaels, A. C. (1979). Two self-control procedures in the reduction of targeted an nontargeted anxieties. *Journal of Counseling Psychology, 26,* 120–127.

Deffenbacher, J. L., Story, D. A., Stark, R. S., Hogg, J. A., & Brandon, A. D. (1987). Cognitive-relaxation and social skills interventions in the treatment of general anger. *Journal of Counseling Psychology, 34,* 171–176.

Emmelkamp, P. M. G., & Wessels, H. (1975). Flooding in imagination vs. flooding in vivo: A comparison with agoraphobics. *Behavior Research and Therapy, 13,* 7–15.

Gormally, J., Varvil-Weld, D., Raphael, R., & Sipps, G. (1981). Treatment of socially anxious college men using cognitive counseling and skills training. *Journal of Counseling Psychology, 28,* 147–157.

Jerremalm, A., Jansson, L., & Ost, L. (1986). Individual response patterns and the effects of different behavioral methods in the treatment of dental phobia. *Behavior Research and Therapy, 24,* 287–596.

Holmes, D. P., & Horan, J. J. (1976). Anger induction in assertion training. *Journal of Counseling Psychology, 23,* 108–111.

Kipper, D. A., & Giladi, D. (1978). Effectiveness of structured psychodrama and systematic desensitization in reducing test anxiety. *Journal of Counseling Psychology, 25,* 499–505.

Michelson, L., Mavissakalian, M., & Marchione, K. (1988). Cognitive, behavioral, and psychophysiological treatments of agoraphobia: A comparison outcome investigation. *Behavior Therapy, 19,* 97–120.

Nicholas, M. K., Wison, P. H., & Goyen, J. (1991). Operant-behavioural and cognitive-behavioural treatment for chronic low back pain. *Behavior Research Therapy, 29,* 225–238.

Osterhouse, R. A. (1972). Sensitization and study-skills training as treatment for two types of test-anxious students. *Journal of Counseling Psychology, 19,* 301–307.

Rodriguez, M., & Blocher, D. (1988). A comparison of two approaches to enhancing career maturity in Puerto Rican college women. *Journal of Counseling Psychology, 35,* 275–280.

Shapiro, D. A., Barkham, M., Rees, A., Hardy, G. E., Reynolds, S., & Startup, M. (1994). Effects of treatment duration and severity of depression on the effectiveness of cognitive-behavioral and psychodynamic-interpersonal psychotherapy. *Journal of Consulting and Clinical Psychology, 62,* 522–534.

Thackwray, D. E., Smith, M. C., Bodfish, J. W., & Meyers, A. W. (1993). A comparison of behavioral and cognitive-behavioral interventions for bulimia nervosa. *Journal of Consulting and Clinical Psychology, 61,* 639–645.

Van Oppen, P., De Haan, E., Van Balkom, A. J. L. M., Spinhoven, P., Hoogduin, K., & Van Dyck, R. (1995). Cognitive therapy and exposure in vivo in the treatment of obsessive-compulsive disorder. *Behavior Research and Therapy, 33,* 379–390.

Williams, S. L., & Zane, G. (1989). Guided mastery and stimulus exposure treatments for severe performance anxiety in agoraphobics. *Behavior Research and Therapy, 27,* 237–245.

Zane, G., & Williams, S. L. (1993). Performance-related anxiety in agoraphobia: Treatment procedures and cognitive mechanisms of change. *Behavior Therapy, 24,* 625–643.

APPENDIX B: ARITICLES INCLUDED IN THE ORLINSKY STUDY

Bennun, I., Halhweg, K., Schindler, L., & Langlotz, M. (1986). Therapist's and client's perceptions in behaviour therapy: The development and cross-cultural analysis of an assessment instrument. *British Journal of Clinical Psychology, 25,* 275–283.

Crits-Cristoph, P., Cooper, A., & Luborsky, L. (1988). The accuracy of therapists' interpretations and the outcome of dynamic psychotherapy. *Journal of Consulting and Clinical Psychology, 56,* 490–495.

Gabbard, C. E., Howard, G. S., & Dunfee, E. J. (1986). Reliability, sensitivity to measuring change, and construct validity of a measure of counselor adaptability. *Journal of Counseling Psychology, 33,* 377–386.

Glass, L. L., Schnitzer, R. D., & Frank, A. F. (1989). Psychotherapy of schizophrenia: An empirical investigation of the relationship of process to outcome. *American Journal of Psychiatry, 146,* 603–608.

Green, R. J., & Herget, M. (1991). Outcomes of systemic/strategic team consultation: The importance of therapist warmth and active structuring. *Family Process, 30,* 321–336.

Grimes, W. R., & Murdock, N. L. (1989). Social influence revisited: Effects of counselor influence on outcome variables. *Psychotherapy, 26,* 469–474.

Hagborg, W. J. (1991). Adolescent clients and perceived counselor characteristics: A study of background characteristics, therapeutic progress, psychological distress, and social desirability. *Journal of Clinical Psychology, 47,* 107–113.

Holtzworth-Munroe, A., Jacobson, N. S., KeKlyen, M., & Whisman, M. A. (1989). Relationship between behavioral marital therapy outcome and process variables. *Journal of Consulting and Clinical Psychology, 57,* 658–662.

McNeill, B. W., Lee, V. E., & May, R. J. (1987). Perceptions of counselor source characteristics by premature and successful terminators. *Journal of Counseling Psychology, 34,* 86–89.

O'Malley, S. S., Foley, S. H., Rounsaville, B. J., Watkins, J. T., Sotsky, S. M., Imber, S. D., et al. (1988). Therapist competence and patient outcome in interpersonal psychotherapy of depression. *Journal of Consulting and Clinical Psychology, 56,* 496–501.

Svartberg, M., & Stiles, T. C. (1992). Predicting patient change from therapist competence and patient-therapist complementarity in short-term anxiety-provoking psychotherapy: A pilot study. *Journal of Consulting and Clinical Psychology, 60,* 304–307.

REFERENCES

Bennun, I., & Schindler, L. (1988). Therapist and patient factors in the behavioural treatment of phobic patients. *British Journal of Clinical Psychology, 27,* 145–150.

Bergin, A. E., & Garfield, S. L. (1994). *Handbook of psychotherapy and behavior change* (4th ed.). New York: Wiley.

Bergin, A. E., & Garfield, S. L. (2003). *Handbook of psychotherapy and behavior change* (5th ed.). New York: Wiley.

Berman, J. S., Miller, R. C., & Massman, P. J. (1985). Cognitive therapy versus systematic desensitization: Is one treatment superior? *Psychological Bulletin, 97,* 451–461.

Bernal, G., Bonilla, J., Padilla-Cotto, L., & Perez-Prado, E. M. (1998). Factors associated to outcome in psychotherapy: An effectiveness study in Puerto Rico. *Journal of Clinical Psychology, 54,* 329–342.

Beutler, A. E., Machado, P. P. P., & Neufeldt, S. A. (1994). Therapist variables. In A. E. Bergin, & S. L. Garfield (Eds.), *Handbook of psychotherapy and behavior change* (4th ed., pp. 229–269). New York: Wiley.

Brown, S. D., & Lent, R. W. (2000). *Handbook of counseling psychology.* New York: Wiley.

Carter, R. T. (1995). *The influence of race and racial identity in psychotherapy: Toward a racially inclusive model.* New York: Wiley.

Carter, R. T., & Helms, J. E. (1992). The counseling process as defined by relationship types: A test of Helms's interactional model. *Journal of Multicultural Counseling and Development, 20,* 181–201.

Christensen, A., & Jacobson, N. S. (1994). Who (or what) can do psychotherapy: The status and challenge of nonprofessional therapies. *Psychological Science, 5,* 8–14.

Cohen, J. (1992). A power primer. *Psychological Bulletin, 112,* 155–159.

Department of Health and Human Services. (2001). *Mental health: culture, race, and ethnicity.* A supplement to Mental Health: a report of the surgeon general. Available from http://www.surgeongeneral.gov/library/mentalhealth/cre/execsummary-1.html (1/29/04).

Fuertes, J. N., Bartolomeo, M., & Nichols, C. M. (2001). Future research directions in the study of counselor multicultural competency. *Journal of Multicultural Counseling and Development, 29,* 3–12.

Fuertes, J. N., & Gretchen, D. (2001). Emerging theories of multicultural counseling. In J. G. Ponterotto, J. M. Casas, L. A. Suzuki, & C. M. Alexander (Eds.), *Handbook of multicultural counseling* (2nd ed., pp. 509–541). Thousand Oaks, CA: Sage.

Hanna, F. J., Bemak, F., & Chi-Ying Chung, R. (1999). Toward a new paradigm for multicultural counseling. *Journal of Counseling and Development, 77,* 125–134.

Helms, J. E. (1984). Towards a theoretical explanation of the effects of race on counseling: A black and white model. *The Counseling Psychologist, 12,* 153–165.

Helms, J. E. (1990). *Black and white racial identity: Theory, research, and practice.* Westport, CT: Greenwood.

Hill, C. E., Thompson, B. J., & Corbett, M. M. (1992). The impact of therapist ability to perceive displayed and hidden client reactions on immediate outcome in first sessions of brief therapy. *Psychotherapy Research, 2,* 143–155.

Hill, C. E., & Williams, E. N. (2000). The process of individual therapy. In S. D. Brown, & R. W. Lent (Eds.), *Handbook of counseling psychology* (3rd. ed., pp. 670–710). New York: Wiley.

Lambert, M. J., & Bergin, A. E. (1994). The effectiveness of psychotherapy. In A. E. Bergin & S. L. Garfield (Eds.), *Handbook of psychotherapy and behavior change* (4th ed., pp. 143–189). New York: Wiley.

Lipsey, M. W., & Wilson, D. B. (1993). The efficacy of psychological, educational, and behavioral treatment: Confirmation from a meta-analysis. *American Psychologist, 48,* 1181–1209.

Lipsky, M. J., Kassinove, H., & Miller, N. J. (1980). Effects of rational-emotive therapy, rational role reversal, and rational-emotive imagery on the emotional adjustment of community mental health center patients. *Journal of Consulting and Clinical Psychology, 48,* 366–374.

Moncher, F. J., & Prinz, R. J. (1991). Treatment fidelity in outcome studies. *Clinical Psychology Review, 11,* 247–266.

Orlinsky, D. E., Grawe, K., & Parks, B. K. (1994). Process and outcome in psychotherapy: Nocheinmal. In A. E. Bergin, & S. L. Garfield (Eds.), *Handbook of psychotherapy and behavior change* (4th ed., pp. 270–376). New York: Wiley.

Ponterotto, J. G., Casas, J. M., Suzuki, L. A., & Alexander, C. M. (2001). *Handbook of multicultural counseling.* Thousand Oaks: Sage.

Ponterotto, J. G., Costa, C. I., & Lin, A. W. (2002). Research perspectives in cross-cultural counseling. In P. B. Pedersen, J. G. Draguns, W. J. Lonner, & J. E. Trimble (Eds.), *Counseling across cultures* (5th ed., pp. 395–420). Thousand Oaks, CA: Sage.

Ponterotto, J. G., Fuertes, J. N., & Chen, E. C. (2000). Models of multicultural counseling. In S. D. Brown, & R. W. Lent (Eds.), *Handbook of counseling psychology* (3rd ed., pp. 639–669). New York: Wiley.

Richardson, T. Q., & Helms, J. E. (1994). The relationship of the racial identity attitudes of black men to perceptions of parallel counseling dyads. *Journal of Counseling and Development, 73,* 172–177.

Robinson, L. A., Berman, J. S., & Neimeyer, R. A. (1990). Psychotherapy for the treatment of depression: A comprehensive review of controlled outcome research. *Psychological Bulletin, 108,* 30–49.

Seligman, M. E. P. (1995). The effectiveness of psychotherapy: The Consumer Reports study. *American Psychologist, 50,* 965–974.

Shapiro, D. A., & Shapiro, D. (1982). Meta-analysis of comparative therapy outcome studies: A reply to Wilson. *Behavioural Psychotherapy, 10,* 307–310.

Smith, M. L., & Glass, G. V. (1977). Meta-analysis of psychotherapy outcome studies. *American Psychologist, 32,* 752–760.

Smith, M. L. Glass, G. V., & Miller, T. I. (1980). *The benefits of psychotherapy.* Baltimore: Johns Hopkins University Press.

Sue, D. W., Arredondo, P., & McDavis, R. J. (1992). Multicultural competencies and standards: A call to the profession. *Journal of Multicultural Counseling and Development, 20,* 64–88.

Sue, D. W., Carter, R. T., Casas, J. M., Fouad, N. A., Ivey, A. E., Jensen, M., et al. (1998). *Multicultural counseling competencies: Individual and organizational development.* Thousand Oaks, CA: Sage.

Sue, D. W., & Sue, D. (1999). *Counseling the culturally different* (3rd ed.). New York: Wiley.

Sue, D. W., & Sue, D. (2003). *Counseling the culturally different* (4th ed.). New York: Wiley.

Sue, S., Zane, N., & Young, K. (1994). Research on psychotherapy with culturally diverse populations. In A. E. Bergin & S. L. Garfield (Eds.), *Handbook of psychotherapy and behavior change* (4th ed., pp. 783–817). New York: Wiley.

Thompson, B. J., & Hill, C. E. (1991). Therapist perceptions of client reactions. *Journal of Counseling and Development, 69,* 261–265.

Trevino, J. G. (1996). Worldview and change in cross-cultural counseling. *The Counseling Psychologist, 24,* 198–215.

Trickett, E. J., Watts, R. J., & Birman, D. (1994). *Human diversity: Perspectives on people in context.* San Francisco, CA: Jossey-Bass.

Wampold, B. E., Mondin, G. W., Moody, M., Stich, F., Benson, K., & Ahn, H. (1997). A meta-analysis of outcome studies comparing bona fide psychotherapies: "All must have prizes." *Psychological Bulletin, 122,* 203–215.

Zane, N. et. al. (2003). Research on psychotherapy with culturally diverse populations. In A. E. Bergin & S. L. Garfield (Eds.), *Handbook of psychotherapy and behavior change* (5th ed.). New York: Wiley.

CHAPTER 15

Race and Research Evidence

Chalmer E. Thompson, Caroline E. Shin, and Joy Stephens

In the annals of psychological science, there exist informed critiques of "race re-search"—the published work of early behavioral scientists and theorists whose clear aim was to prove the inferiority of non-Whites relative to Whites (e.g., Gould, 1996; Guthrie, 1976, 1998; Thomas & Sillen, 1972). In contrast to this formative body of research, recent reviews on race and ethnicity have shown that contrived evidence of human inferiority and superiority based on race differences has slackened consider-ably, though it is not entirely absent. Recent research on race and ethnicity has also shifted from skewed attention to African Americans to studies on the spectrum of groups deemed "racial," including Whites (e.g., Helms, 1994a; Jones, 1992; Sue, Zane, & Young, 1994). By removing obstructions to the research and, by inference, contesting mainstream definitions of race, contemporary researchers can increase our understanding of the construct and its complex impact on human development and functioning.

Yet, knowledge about race as a construct that influences psychological function-ing continues to be obstructed by narrow or confused assumptions about the meaning of race. In a treatise on research about race, Helms (1994a) contended that researchers frequently rely on research participants' reported race as the sole barometer with which to understand the variable or phenomenon (see similar treat-ments relative to race and/or ethnicity by Betancourt & Lopez, 1993; Jones, 1994; Yee, Fairchild, Weizmann, & Wyatt, 1993). Helms proposed that research would benefit from *direct assessments* of race, defined as measures or interview protocols that elicit participants' understanding about race and the meaning they ascribe to it. Critical researchers, too, have contended that research profits when investigators *approach* rather than *avoid* explorations about the social, ideological, and political meanings that people experience as they develop identities (Fox & Prilleltensky, 1997). Moreover, in the absence of direct assessments, researchers who use race solely as a nominal variable in their investigations can only speculate on the rela-tionship between said race and other variables (e.g., Blacks profit from therapy with Black as opposed to White therapists *probably* as a result of shared experiences of racism and/or culture; see also Thompson & Isaac, 2003). Proclivities to associate race with nominal categories reflect some collusion with the perspective that race is a fixed quality about people and not a social, dialectic construction embedded in sociopolitical contexts (Helms, 1992, 2002).

Achieving an understanding of race as relevant to psychologists is hampered also by the frequent use of race as synonymous with ethnicity (e.g., Carter & Pieterse, this *Handbook,* Volume One; Helms, 1992, 1994a, 1994b, 1995, 2001). Although both phenomena are knottily intertwined, the practice of equating the two compromises an understanding of each (Helms & Talleyrand, 1997). In contrast to ethnicity, race has been associated with social constructions influenced by racist ideology. These constructions also are influenced by and reiteratively influence the manner in which people operate within a hierarchy that proclaims differential levels of human worth based on race (Neville, Worthington, & Spanierman, 2001; Thompson, Murry, Harris, & Annan, in press; Thompson & Neville, 1999). We believe that researchers who separate the study of race from that of ethnicity are moving toward efforts to inform our understanding of the phenomenon as intimately linked to constructs like moral development and decision making, social agency, and cognitive complexity.

And yet another hindrance to understanding race is the tendency of researchers to employ the construct as something that can be simulated and, subsequently, reproduced and studied in a laboratory. In these studies, "minority" and "majority" groups are created and speculations are subsequently made by researchers about race (or rather, majority-minority status) as a "source of friction within society" (Helms, 1994a, p. 289). Although race undoubtedly shares qualities in common with other phenomena that emerge from oppressive environments, we propose that rather than starting with presumptions of commonalities about societal sources of friction, a more prudent strategy for researchers to pursue is to understand nuances of different forms of oppression. With this proposal in mind, we agree with Helms that findings from laboratory simulations that presume similarities between common elements of oppression and manifestations of racism have the potential of robbing an understanding of the particularistic qualities of race as a phenomenon (see also Gaines & Reed, 1995).

Changes in race research have occurred since the emergence of psychology as a science; there is room for optimism. But what *is* our understanding of race as relevant to the research and work of psychologists? and Why do some researchers continue to opt for definitions that often subtly mask or diminish its existence? We attempt to answer both questions in this chapter, first by offering a definition of race that can guide (and that has guided some) research about race. We propose that the second question—the observation that many researchers experience an apparent struggle to acknowledge and grasp race—relates to the interaction of individuals and sociopolitical structures and, hence, definitional issues concerning race. An understanding of how race poses constraints *as well as* creative challenges for researchers needs to be folded into our definition of race. Such an understanding bespeaks the complexities inherent in the construct and the related phenomenon, racism.

We also examine trends over the past 35 years in how researchers have studied race relative to personality development, experiences of the self and others, a range of behaviors with which psychologists concern themselves (e.g., help-seeking, health maintenance, coping, treatment compliance, termination), and generally any efforts that could lead to *change.* Therefore, we focused on reviewing research with some association with referent-group personality and/or (dis)inclinations toward individual, group, or structural change. Our motivation in selecting certain studies for review was to identify research that has the potential to inform applications or interventions in such settings as mental health centers, hospitals, schools, churches, and other organizations.

RACE AND BEHAVIORAL SCIENCE: TOWARD A DEFINITION

Spanning academic disciplines, it is generally agreed that race (1) is a social construction that has a basis in racist ideology that (2) continues to evolve in the absence of forceful, direct efforts to dismantle racism, its progenitor, at micro- and macrosystem levels and (3) is an aspect of identity that informs the ways individuals perceive themselves, others, and reality. We present brief explanations of each of these elements in the following.

Race Is a Historical and Cultural Construction
Based on Racist Ideology

Race is a construction with historical origins in racist ideology (e.g., Carter, 1995; Frederickson, 1988; Gould, 1996; Guthrie, 1998; Jones, 1992; Thompson & Carter, 1997). These ideologies served as the basis for Europeans and later Whites to impose notions about their own worth relative to those whom they oppressed and exploited. In the United States, for example, African, Asian, Latino/a, and Native Americans were considered to possess innate qualities that had bearing on their character, intellect, morality, and ultimately their worth as humans (Stanfield, 1994). Racist ideology did not originate in the United States (Smedley, 1993), and each societal context affected by it is constructed differently. Consequently, differences ostensibly occur in the ways racism is dramatized in societies and how racial groups behave toward one another interracially. Myriad forces are implicated in differences observed in racialized and colonized societies, including the extent of ethnic threat to resources (irrespective of scarcity); distinctiveness in the culture and/or phenotypical differences of people of different races; perspectives on the society's inhabitants by those of other nations, especially more industrialized ones; and the extent to which intermarriage of dominant and subordinate groups reflects an elevation or elimination of lower-status positions (e.g., Forbes, 1990; Mukarubuga, 2002; Smedley, 1993).

Race Evolves at Micro- and Macrosystem Levels

Contemplating the phenomena of race and racism in the United States, Forbes (1990) stated:

> We are not dealing with systems of denigration which came to an end ages ago but instead, with a continuing reality. And this reality is significantly structured by categories and concepts created during earlier years and often carried forward into our day by scholars, government officials, and popular media markers. (p. 9)

The persistent use of racial categories as innate, unquestioned, and relatively fixed qualities about people has unfolded in the United States and in colonized nations throughout the world (Fanon, 1968; Gould, 1996; Smedley, 1993).

Thompson et al. (in press) suggested that the failure to resolve issues of racism morphs into greater invisibility of Whites relative to other racial groups. This transcendence into invisibility is to distract dominant group members from the strain of equating their status with superior "goodness" and the recognition, often below the level of consciousness, that this equation is untrue. Institutional structures help support a denial of race as relevant to the lives of Whites and as essential *and* distortedly characterized in the lives of non-Whites. Whites who become aware of their socialization also learn to identify how these structures contribute to their feeling neutral and normal and, conversely, how "others" are constructed as "racial" and, by implication, less than, "exotic," and reduced of human complexity (see McIntyre, 1997; Neville et al., 2001). Internalized racism, conceived loosely as the adoption of racist ideology by non-Whites, entails some buying into the racialized messages conveyed in these institutional structures, as well as the personal and material rewards that are garnered in colluding in the societal context (e.g., Casas & Pytluk, 1995).

Hegemonic racism conveyed through institutions helps to support a socialization in which race is variously denied or essentialized as an aspect of the self. Psychological research can, but does not always, support trajectories of racist ideology. It commits acts of insensitivity and injustice by treating race as if it were a categorical quality of human existence. As van Dijk (1987) observed:

> Research [that denies the structural nature of racism in our societies] ignores and thereby confirms and reproduces the fact that both blatant and very subtle racism permeates *all* social and personal levels of our societies: from the decisions, actions, and discourses of the government or the legislative bodies, through those of the various institutions, such as education research, the media, health, the police, the courts, and social agencies, all the way down to everyday interaction, thought, and talk. (p. 15)

We want to make it clear that we are not advocating a wholesale eschewal of race as a categorical construct. We propose that how and why a person reports (or fails to report) his or her race is necessary to discerning that person's understanding of self and society (e.g., Root, 2001). Narratives have shown that people respond in a variety of ways to the imposition of race. In some cases, these responses include a rejection of the imposed categorization, particularly when the phenotypical qualities, such as the light skin and eye color of Whites, are not consistent with the qualities constructed as being aligned with said racial group, like the purity and homogeneity of the superior-designated group (e.g., Harris, 1995). Another problem of researchers using race as a categorical quality is that the investigators themselves might be instrumental in applying racial designations of participants based on the neighborhoods from which the participants are drawn and/or assumptions about subjects' identification based on appearance. How researchers apply labels also relates to their own experiences as racial beings and their perceptions of others based on unfounded data (Kwan, this *Handbook,* Volume One).

Race as a Perception of Self, Others, and Reality

In general, people in racialized societies learn to perceive and rationalize their own and others' positioning within a hierarchically arranged societal structure. *Racial socialization* refers to the process by which people learn about their role and the role of others in the drama. This process is not always acknowledged or recognized, but as noted by Carter (1995), "Given the social, political, and historical salience of race in our society, it seems reasonable to conclude that it is impossible to be socialized in this society without being presented with several opportunities to internalize beliefs and attitudes about one's racial group" (p. 42).

We believe that an important factor to understand about race is that the construction of the racial self is closely tied to the construction of the racial other. In fact, there is no construction of a racial aspect of the self without the construction of a racial aspect of others. So, when inordinate attention is directed to the study of subordinate-designated groups, our understanding about race's construction is restricted. The understanding of marginalized groups without an understanding of dominant group processes of this construction also supports the notion of race as relevant solely to non-Whites and the creation of Whiteness as invisible. It is possible, in fact, that with the limitations of the research in race in terms of how it is defined and the marginality that can be applied to people of Color who conduct that research, our understanding of race remains quite limited (Fine, 2000).

When race is treated as a differential quality of groups—as a denied quality of Whites and, by comparison, an essential quality of people of Color—there is a persistence in the dehumanization that began when racist ideology was instrumental to the quest by Europeans and Whites to take over land and other resources that belonged to those they considered to be unlike and inferior to them (see Thompson, in press; Thompson et al., in press). Dehumanization refers to divestiture of human qualities; when people are portrayed in ways that either minimize or overinflate qualities about themselves, they become entangled in and participate in cultivating a cycle of dehumanization.

Differences in how people perceive themselves racially are the by-product of reiterative processes involving the person and the context. How people perceive themselves is dependent on their perceptions of the race of others and the extent to which they may associate with the referent group that they "appear" to be associated with. Efforts to dissociate are multiple and include a rejection of the racial self, a diminution of race or racism, and, for people of Color, the creation of hierarchies within hierarchies for the purpose of elevating the self within the dehumanizing structure. Race has been referred to as a phenomenon that invokes moral deliberations: To participate in a structure of racism is ultimately to participate in the dehumanization of certain groups of people.

Finally, we propose that when attending solely to the negative impact of hegemonic racism, researchers present only a partial view of reality and the prospect of needed change. People can and do instigate needed and meaningful change even as they simultaneously fall into patterns of colluding in behaviors that perpetuate racism. Racism as a force is interwoven into all aspects of our reality and being;

consequently, the multiple manifestations of resistance, endurance, and working together are also part of the phenomenon (Helms, personal communication, 2003) and thus need to be acknowledged and understood.

Race: A Definition for Behavioral Scientists

To derive an understanding of race and, importantly, produce measures to create meaningful change in people, we propose that psychological researchers define race as follows: In popular society, race refers to a designation suggestive of differential worth of a person's cultural and biological heritage based on her or his association with a referent group. The designation of race consistently has defied logic about biological "purity" and is replete with inconsistencies and contradictions that can best be described as the result of perpetuating power differentials between Whites and non-Whites. The experiences that occur within this rubric of injustice and de-humanization are pertinent to psychological study and can be assessed by examining how people (1) construct perceptions about themselves racially relative to others who are racially similar and dissimilar, (2) experience and make meaning of racism in their respective community and in society at large, and (3) seek to evoke or not evoke changes in an unfair hierarchical structure based on race.

With the use of this definition as a guide, we believe that behavioral scientists can glean knowledge about psychological processes such as cognition and learning, emotional and psychological development, health maintenance, group/organizational behaviors, and personal and social agency that are informed by race. Lines of inquiry can direct attention to race as a variable that helps shape these processes by taking steps to learn about its meaning in people's lives. Investigators who incorporate this definition can go beyond comparison studies by beginning with the ways people self-identify, and then probe into the sources of this identification at personal and ecological levels. And rather than studying comparisons solely between those who identify themselves as White and those who identify as non-White (e.g., African American, Asian American/Pacific Islander, Native American), researchers can explore differences within and similarities between racial groups in terms of the individuals who compose them (e.g., between Mexican Americans who differ in complexion and levels of English fluency, among African and Caribbean American teens in transitioning urban communities, and between upper-middle-class and poor White families whose children attend the same school).

We turn next to a review of published research on race conducted in the past 35 years to determine what we currently know about race as a psychological construct.

RESEARCH ON RACE: JANUARY 1967 TO MARCH 2000

Using PsychINFO, we selected keywords—Asian Americans, African Americans/Blacks, Hispanic/Latino/a Americans, biracial Americans, Native Americans, White Americans, minorities, and race—and then combined each with a second set of keywords: counseling, psychotherapy, mental health, mental illness, racial identity, and acculturation. Our use of the word "race" was to identify studies that included other racial groups not already named, such as Arab Americans. We were interested in research that had greater potential for wide dissemination and fairly easy access and therefore excluded dissertations. We also limited the search to research conducted on people or communities within the United States. Another group of studies we eliminated from our search was validation studies of widely used clinical or intelligence tests; as a rather sizable segment of research, these seem to require a separate analysis of race research specific to mainstream concepts of personality.

Our search yielded a total of 426 research studies. We read the abstracts of each study to obtain data for the five questions below. When the abstract was not sufficient to glean information, we referred to the full-length article. These questions are:

1. What proportion of research is comparative versus noncomparative, and to what extent do investigators use race as noncategorical variables?

2. How much of the research is conducted in psychology versus nonpsychology journals?

3. What populations are being studied and in what contexts (e.g., college students, children, patients/clients; in contexts such as hospitals, college campuses)?

4. What is the racial composition of the research samples?

5. What proportion of studies are theory-driven or based on grounded theory procedures, and relatedly, what proportion of the theories are based on explanatory models about race specifically?

Below we report percentages of subgroups in five groups corresponding to the above set of questions.

Prevalence of Comparative Research on Race and Researchers' Inclination to Define Race as a Categorical Construct

We were interested in determining the proportion of studies in which research participants were compared to one another by race. The contrasting group of studies comprised investigations in which subjects identified themselves (or were identified) as sharing a similar race. In this contrasting group, we found that researchers examined qualities, trends, and behaviors of one particular racial group.

We also wanted to know the proportion of studies that defined race only as a categorical construct in contrast to definitions that were consistent with the one we described in the preceding section. Of the 426 studies we identified in our search, the majority ($N = 228$ or 54%) were comparative studies in which race was studied solely as a categorical variable. We labeled the second largest group of studies the no comparison/socioracial group; it comprised investigations in which no comparisons were made between groups and where matters of race were probed beyond nominal categories ($N = 83$ or 19.5%). The third largest group was composed of studies in which investigators made no comparisons, but where race was treated strictly as a categorical variable ($N = 63$ or 15%). These were the studies that examined issues pertinent to one or more groups without comparisons and where differences such as socioeconomic status, gender, attitudes, and help-seeking behaviors were explored.

The smallest number of studies, though not significantly less in number than the prior group, was the comparison/socioracial group, constituting 12% of the studies ($N = 52$).

It is important to note that a large number of studies, which we call the comparative/race-as-category group, were epidemiologic studies that described trends in the attitudes about and frequency and type of mental health service utilized or sought by different groups by self-identified race (e.g., Brown, Schulberg, Sacco, Perel, & Houck, 1999; Chamberlain et al., 2001; Mason & Gibbs, 1992). These studies offer important information that can promote further exploration into why different groups tend to rely on certain services over others based on factors that could relate to racial differences. Although relatively few in number, a subset of these epidemiologic studies began with nominal categories but went further to explore *why* different groups tended to patronize services or receive involuntary services as related to race (e.g., Shrout, Canino, & Bird, 1992; Takeuchi & Cheung, 1998; D. R. Williams, Takeuchi, & Adair, 1992). For example, Takeuchi and Cheung tested a stratification hypothesis to determine referral patterns among a large sample of Los Angeles outpatients. The stratification hypothesis referred to those issues of power differentials in society based on ethnicity and gender, and whether certain ethnic/gender groups were more likely to be coercively referred than others. In their racially and ethnically heterogeneous sample, the authors found that the stratification hypothesis was most applicable to African American men, who were more likely to be coercively versus voluntarily referred than other racial and gendered subsamples.

We consider the prevalence of comparison/race-as-category studies to be a problem when researchers fail to move beyond these investigations to examine the nuanced variations of self-identification. Explorations into these nuances can include tests of hypotheses of existing conceptualizations about race and race-related matters, such as the stratification hypothesis, then move to qualitative or mixed methods of research.

Prevalence of Studies on Race in Psychology versus Nonpsychology Journals

To determine how psychology and counseling-related journals fared in comparison to journals outside of these two disciplines in relation to research on personality and change, we calculated the proportion of research published in psychology versus nonpsychology journals. Those journals with the words psychology or psychological, psychotherapy or psychotherapeutic, psychoanalysis, counseling, mental health, behavioral science, vocational behavior, behavioral development, personality, behavior disorders, and perceptual and motor skills in the title were categorized as psychology or counseling-related journals. We identified journals in which the titles included the terms health (with the exception of health psychology), education, psychiatry, sociology, and student development, to the exclusion of the other cited words, as nonpsychology or noncounseling-related.

We found that the number of research studies in the two groups were about even: 208 (49%) of the studies were found in psychology and counseling-related journals, and 215 (50.5%) were found in nonpsychology and noncounseling-related journals. Based on these data, it would appear that psychology and nonpsychology-related journals publish studies involving race with similar frequency.

It would require an extensive review of articles to determine whether or not the quality of studies based on race differs in psychology and nonpsychology-related journals. Fish (2000) noted in his comparisons between psychology and anthropology that the two disciplines differ specifically in relation to the study of race. Indeed, Fish admonished psychologists for the prevalence of race research in which a biological perspective is implicated over a social constructionist one. To us, that psychology-related journals and nonpsychology-related journals publish race studies with similar frequency is not as worrisome as the possibility that at least a good deal of responsibility in crafting empirically and theoretically informed knowledge about race is not considered significant to psychological science and practice. An examination of the extent to which psychologists embrace race as a construct that informs psychological processes can perhaps occur by noting the frequency with which both psychology and nonpsychology journal articles draw from psychological research and theory to design studies or make interpretations about race or race-related phenomena.

Populations and Contexts Studied

The populations from which research participants were drawn varied widely, with 153 of the studies (36%) involving nonclinical adult samples (e.g., caregivers, single mothers, community dwellers, older adults) or persons varying in age. This latter group consisted of participants whose age ranged typically from early teens to elderly adults. The next most numerous group was composed of college students (93 or 22%), followed by patients or clients in hospitals or mental health settings (73 or 17%). Nonclinical adolescents were included in 32 studies, and nonclinical children under the age of 13 in 31 studies (about 1% each). The remaining groups, less than 1% of the total sample, consisted of professionals such as psychologists and physicians (20 studies), graduate and professional students (13 studies), prisoners (8 studies), and nonprofessional people who were employed in agencies or organizations (3 studies). Overall, the spectrum of participants by age and context appears to be relatively large.

We believe that the practitioners and the public can profit from examinations that do not merely draw subjects from different contexts, but that also provide creative measures to forge an understanding of persons as influenced by and influencing contexts. Studies that attempt to connect psychological functioning, for example, with qualities in familial, school, or community contexts can be valuable in elucidating personal and environmental constructions and the dramas that occur when people manage and form relationships as they also manage trajectories of racist ideology (see Thompson & Isaac, 2003). For example, Perry (2001) found that White adolescents at two schools, one predominantly White and the other a multiracial high school, constructed "cultureless" identities as a means to normalize their privileged racial status. Using ethnographic research, the investigator found differences in how these identities were constructed in the two contexts. Future research in which developmental, maturational, and contextual factors are studied in combination has the potential to reveal particularities as well as commonalities in how people form ideas and come to understand themselves and realities influenced by racism.

Racial Composition of Samples

Our primary interest in learning about the racial composition of research samples was to determine the frequency with which researchers focused solely on understanding one racial group or several, say, in comparison or "minority" studies. In the 426 studies, 287 (67%) involved the study of two or more racial/ethnic groups; 82 (19%) of the studies involved only African American informants, followed at a distant second by 21 involving only White American subjects, 18 involving Hispanic/Latino/a subjects, 17 involving Asian American subjects, and 1 involving Native American subjects. These last four racial groups were studied in fewer than 1% of these studies. In the studies where research samples were not compared on the basis of race or sociorace, several examined differences based on variables of gender, acculturation, attitudes, and so forth.

Comparison studies of racial groups have one potential limitation to their quest for racial understanding: Findings gleaned from the research may present more information about racial *differences* than about race per se. Hence, we propose that the finding that a large number of studies are comparison or minority studies is troubling, as is the paucity of racial/ethnic research on non-African Americans. Even as we put aside the issue of how race is studied relative to each racial group, we appear to be learning comparatively little about race, however defined, as opposed to racial differences.

Presence and Nature of Theory

We grouped studies together on the basis of (1) whether or not theoretical conceptualizations were implicated, either deductively or inductively, and (2) if theory was present, whether it related to racial issues. We uncovered three groups: theory, basis in Race; theory, basis not in race; and no theory. For the purpose of grouping studies, we defined theory as any explanatory framework the investigators used to impose coherence on the studied phenomenon/a.

In the majority of studies (256 or 60%), researchers did not attempt to test out or create theory. In terms of frequency, the theory, basis not in race group follows; here, researchers attempted to either create or test theory that did not relate specifically to race (95 or 23%). Seventy-one or 17% of the studies included some attention to theory development related to race (the theory, basis in race group) that was consistent with the operational definition we described earlier in this chapter.

Based on our search, we conclude that the psychological study of race is generally absent of theoretical development. This criticism has been directed at behavioral science in general (e.g., Hoshmand & Polkinghorne, 1992). Racial identity, cultural mistrust, and acculturation theories are the most prevalent of the conceptualizations used in the 71 studies conducted in the past 35 years. An emerging area is the study of color-blind attitudes and White privilege, which Neville et al. (2001) describe as based on the premise that in the United States, "people's nationalities have been *racialized,* that is, converted into superior and subordinate 'races' . . . and that White privilege and color-blind attitudes are products of this system" (p. 259). The authors point out that racial discourse in psychology has focused on the "disadvantaged," but that to understand the dialectic of racism, it is important to have a critical understanding of those who benefit most from the system.

Blacks and Whites were the groups most targeted for racial identity research and cultural mistrust, whereas Asian Americans and Hispanic/Latino/a Americans were most frequently targeted in acculturation studies. Although most of the racial identity research is based on measures developed by J. E. Helms, new measures and paradigms have been created (e.g., Casas & Pytluk, 1995; Cross & Vandiver, 2001). Summarizing a cross-section of studies based on Helmsian theory, we know from the research that racial identity attitudes have been shown to predict Whites' expression of racism (Carter, 1990), Blacks' psychological functioning (Carter, 1991), Whites' adherence to traditional work values (Carter, Gushue, & Weitzman, 1994), Blacks' life role domains (Carter & Constantine, 2000), and the influence of racial stereotypes on information processing among Whites (Gushue & Carter, 2000). Regarding counseling relationships, research using racial identity models has shown that cross-racial therapy interactions are of better quality when the counselors have resolved more of their own racial concerns than has the client (Carter & Helms, 1992); Black surrogate male clients' emotional reactions to counseling dyads comprising a therapist and a client with similar racial identity statuses were predicted by racial identity attitudes (Richardson & Helms, 1994); and racial identity attitudes predicted White counselor preferences for Whites and White male counselor preferences for Blacks (Helms & Carter, 1991). Most of the racial identity research has been conducted within the past 23 years.

Although largely concentrated on African Americans, new research is beginning to show more within-group examinations of the phenomenon of racial identity. For example, Cunningham (1997) examined differences among light-skin Blacks (those who report being perceived as "mixed," Latino/a, or White, and/or not feeling Black enough) and dark-skin Blacks not fitting the above categories, noting that the experiences of the two groups likely were based on their interactions with Whites and Blacks.

Cutrona, Russell, Hessling, Brown, and Murry (2000) examined characteristics of community, specifically cohesion and disorder, and their effects on the well-being of African American women. They found that neighborhood variables significantly related to individual risk and resource variables in the prediction of distress among the women in the sample. They employed trait-situation interaction theories while drawing on an informed understanding of the contextual influences that shape racial realities in African American women. This study is important because it creatively merges issues of context, psychological functioning, and theory. Similarly, Schulz et al. (2000) explored the experiences of unfair treatment and the concentration of households with incomes below the poverty level relative to the mental and emotional well-being of African American and White Detroit adult residents. They found that psychological distress and life satisfaction were significantly related to exposure to unfair treatment and below-poverty-level household concentration. They also found race effects operating in regard to race-based residential segregation. Both of these studies present intriguing methodologies and draw in direct evidence of contextual factors that influence experiences and mental health functioning.

Only two studies, both involving Black research participants, were based on psychotherapy and counseling processes related to race involving nonanalogue research designs. In one, Thompson and Jenal (1994) conducted a qualitative examination of quasi-counseling dyadic sessions involving Black self-identified female college students who were paired either with a White or a Black self-identified counselor. The students were asked to discuss their experiences at the campus, a major research university overwhelmingly populated by Whites, and counselors were instructed to approach all topics using "universal" parameters, that is, by viewing problems as relating to the students' allegiances absent of race. They found an emergent pattern in how both counselors and students behaved in the interactions. Consequently, although race was missing from the discourse, the investigators found evidence that race was one of several factors that related to the nature or quality of these interactions. The authors of the study noted that research on the processes that occur in actual counseling as therapists and clients work through issues of race can aid practitioners by supplying them with tools to conduct therapy with liberation and empowerment as goals.

CONCLUSIONS

P. J. Williams (1997) likened the contemporary struggle with race in the United States as a pantomime, whereby avoidance of the phenomenon seems necessary for people, especially Whites, to cope with the reality of racism. Williams speaks specifically about Blacks in the following passage, but the significance of other non-White groups in the configuration of an unjust structure seems fitting:

> If race is something about which we dare not speak in polite social company, the same cannot be said of the *viewing* of race. How, or whether, blacks are seen depends upon a dynamic of display that ricochets between hypervisibility and oblivion. Blacks are seen "everywhere," taking over the world one minute; yet the great ongoing toll of poverty and isolation that engulfs so many remains the object of persistent oversight. (p. 17)

We propose that acknowledgment of the perversities of race is a prudent first step to conducting systematic inquiries about this construction. We also propose that future race researchers need to be aware that investigations of race are likely to be difficult to conduct because people can become uneasy when talking about or even identifying themselves racially. Researchers who have not examined the reasons behind the discomfort may become discouraged when they try to approach investigations where matters of race and racism are raised. But if the discomfort and uneasiness is seen as a projection of a conditioning that silences or diminishes race for the purpose of erasing or minimizing the reality of racism, then the researcher will likely anticipate and be prepared for resistance. For example, investigators who examine the nuances of racism in society know that any racial markers in the research process (e.g., mention of "Asian American," a survey that explains that the research plans to explore racial differences, the inclusion of a measure of acculturation or discrimination) can prompt reactions from participants or would-be subjects. These prompts can also variously encourage or discourage participation. Consequently, knowing more about the impact of race and racism on the life experiences of participants can inform researchers of the challenges to collection of data.

Although not included in our search, we discovered two studies that point to challenges in research involving procedural considerations in achieving representative samples. Cannon, Higginbotham, and Leung (1988) found that efforts to recruit Black and White women who were not in professional, managerial, or administrative jobs and who worked in male-dominated occupations were quite difficult. Ross and Mirowsky (1984) found in their sample of White, Mexican, and Mexican American adults that acquiescence and giving socially desirable responses occurred more frequently among persons in lower socioeconomic positions, who are older, or who are of Mexican origin. How prone potential participants are to involving themselves in research is related to multiple factors, to be sure, but not the least of these are the class, gender, and racial structures engendered in how the research is conducted and who "owns" it.

Because of a reluctance by some to associate themselves racially, whether for fear of being stereotyped, exploited, or, more generally, perceived in a confined and segmented manner by investigators, it would seem that researchers need to approach their studies with regard to their own roles in society's hierarchy relative to their informants'. Thompson (2001) proposed that a helpful guideline for conducting research on race, irrespective of the research method, is to assume the stance of an ethnographer. In conducting their research, ethnographers need to engage in a continual process of reflection, locate their positions or statuses within the informants' contexts, and examine the biases that likely influence their perceptions of the data. Importantly, and as excellently elaborated by Fine (1994), the ethnographer explores the "self-other hyphen," thus reinventing the self and ensuring that the act of data gathering comports with the informants' quest to be understood. We contend that these practices constitute the thrust of research related to race and, for that matter, any research involving human subjects.

Excellent models of these ethnographic investigations can be found in the work of anthropologists, several of whom have studied race in interaction with social class, gender, and other aspects of the self. Some of the titles reflect this focus: *Making Meaning of Whiteness: Exploring Racial Identity with White Teachers* (McIntyre, 1997), *Codes and Contradictions: Race, Gender Identity, and Schooling* (Weiler, 2000), *Urban Girls: Resisting Stereotypes, Creating Identities* (Leadbeater & Way, 1996), and "Dialectics of Race and Nationality: Contradictions and Philadelphia Working-Class Youth" (Schneider, 1997). These studies present rich data for researchers as they forge into areas of personality development, inter- and intragroup interactions, and community influences on racial socialization. We also point to the fact that none of the studies that emerged in our search examined the interactions or attitudes of people by non-White racial group membership. In other words, we seem to have little research related to the dynamics that occur between, for example, Asian Americans and African Americans, or different Hispanic or Latino/a ethnic groups related to our operational definition. Further research should also explore the decision-making processes that occur with self-identification for all racial groups, including those potential participants who identify themselves as bi- or multiracial.

Finally, we believe that it is essential for researchers to expand their ideas about what constitutes *race research*. Earlier investigators tended overwhelmingly to collude with social climates in which overt, demeaning acts were openly sanctioned. These climates also helped to prevent investigators from thinking insightfully and behaving morally about their work and attendant investment in perpetuating an unfair system of stratification. When *race* was addressed as a topic of inquiry, it implied the study of non-Whites for the purpose of supporting the notion of human superiority/inferiority. But because the construct of race speaks to lived experiences of everyone residing in racialized societies, race research ought to include *any* investigation in which the meaning that people make of their sociopolitical existence can conceivably influence the range of variables that are considered to be within the realm of psychological science.

Perhaps in the future the majority of behavioral scientists will make use of racial terms with little or no hesitation when titling and writing research articles in which people of Color do not predominate as research subjects. We might also envision a future when most behavioral scientists not only adopt, but by necessity appreciate the sacrifice and depth of commitment of those who ponder, anticipate, and work through the very real strains that occur when matters of race are posed in investigations. We suggest humbly that such visions of the future of psychological research are probably likely to occur when societies themselves emulate *not* a utopic reality of empathetic understanding, but a commitment to *working through* the problems that contribute to dehumanization.

REFERENCES

Betancourt, H., & Lopez, S. R. (1993). The study of culture, ethnicity, and race in American psychology. *American Psychologist, 48*(6), 629–637.

Brown, C., Schulberg, H. C., Sacco, D., Perel, J. M., & Houck, P. R. (1999). Effectiveness of treatments for major depression in primary medical care practice: A post hoc analysis of outcomes for African American and White patients. *Journal of Affective Disorders, 53*, 185–192.

Cannon, L. W., Higginbotham, E., & Leung, M. L. (1988). Race and class bias in qualitative research on women. *Gender and Society, 2*, 449–462.

Carter, R. T. (1990). The relationship between racism and racial identity among White Americans: An exploratory investigation. *Journal of Counseling and Development, 69*, 46–50.

Carter, R. T. (1991). Racial identity attitudes and psychological functioning. *Journal of Multicultural Counseling and Development, 19*, 105–114.

Carter, R. T. (1995). *The influence of race and racial identity in psychotherapy: Toward a racially inclusive model.* New York: Wiley.

Carter, R. T., & Constantine, M. G. (2000). Career maturity, life role salience, and racial/ethnic identity among Black and Asian American college students. *Journal of Career Assessment, 8,* 173–187.

Carter, R. T., Gushue, G. V., & Weitzman, L. M. (1994). White racial identity development and work values. *Journal of Vocational Behavior, 44,* 185–197.

Carter, R. T., & Helms, J. E. (1992). The counseling process as defined by relationship types: A test of Helms' interactional model. *Journal of Multicultural Counseling and Development, 20,* 181–201.

Casas, J. M., & Pytluk, S. D. (1995). Hispanic identity development: Implications for research and development. In J. G. Ponterotto, J. M. Casas, L. A. Suzuki, & C. M. Alexander (Eds.), *Handbook of multicultural counseling* (pp. 155–180). Thousand Oaks, CA: Sage.

Chamberlain, D., Muntaner, C., Walrath, C., Nickerson, K. J., LaVeist, T. A., & Leaf, P. J. (2001). Racial differences in attitudes toward professional mental health care and in the use of services. *American Journal of Orthopsychiatry, 70,* 805–807.

Cross, W. E., Jr., & Vandiver, B. J. (2001). Nigrescence theory and measurement: Introducing the Cross Racial Identity Scale (CRIS). In J. G. Ponterotto, J. M. Casas, L. A. Suzuki, & C. M. Alexander (Eds.), *Handbook of multicultural counseling* (2nd ed., pp. 371–393). Thousand Oaks, CA: Sage.

Cunningham, J. L. (1997). Colored existence: Racial identity formation in light-skin Blacks. *Smith College Studies in Social Work, 67,* 375–400.

Cutrona, C. E., Russell, D. W., Hessling, R. M., Brown, P. A., & Murry, V. (2000). Direct and moderating effects of community context on the psychological well-being of African American women. *Journal of Personality and Social Psychology, 79,* 1088–1101.

Fanon, F. (1968). *Black skin, White masks.* New York: Grove Weidenfeld.

Fine, M. (1994). Working the self-other hyphen. In N. Denzin & Y. Lincoln (Eds.), *Handbook of qualitative research* (pp. 416–445). Thousand Oaks, CA: Sage.

Fine, M. (2000). "Whiting out" social justice. In R. T. Carter (Ed.), *Addressing cultural issues in organizations* (pp. 35–50). Thousand Oaks, CA: Sage.

Fish, J. M. (2000). What anthropology can do for psychology: Facing physics envy, ethnocentrism, and belief in "race." *American Anthropologist, 102,* 552–563.

Forbes, J. D. (1990). The manipulation of race, caste, and identity: Classifying Afroamericans, Native Americans and Red-Black people. *Journal of Ethnic Studies, 17,* 1–51.

Fox, D., & Prilleltensky, I. (1997). *Critical psychology: An introduction.* London: Sage.

Frederickson, G. (1988). *The arrogance of race: Historical perspectives on slavery, racism, and social inequality.* Middletown, CT: Wesleyan University Press.

Gaines, S. O., Jr., & Reed, E. S. (1995). Prejudice: From Allport to Du Bois. *American Psychologist, 50,* 96–103.

Gould, S. (1996). *The mismeasure of man* (Rev. ed.). New York: Norton.

Gushue, G. V., & Carter, R. T. (2000). Remembering race: White racial identity attitudes and two aspects of social memory. *Journal of Counseling Psychology, 47,* 199–210.

Guthrie, R. (1976). *Even the rat was white: A historical view of psychology.* New York: Harper & Row.

Guthrie, R. (1998). *Even the rat was white: A historical view of psychology.* Boston: Allyn & Bacon.

Harris, C. I. (1995). Whiteness as property. In K. Crenshaw, N. Gotanda, G. Peller, & K. Thomas (Eds.), *Critical race theory: The key writings that formed the movement* (pp. 276–291). New York: New Press.

Helms, J. E. (1992). Why is there no study of cultural equivalence in standardized cognitive ability testing? *American Psychologist, 47,* 1083–1101.

Helms, J. E. (1994a). The conceptualization of racial identity and other "racial" constructs. In E. J. Trickett, R. J. Watts, & D. Birman (Eds.), *Human diversity: Perspectives on people in context* (pp. 285–311). San Francisco: Jossey-Bass.

Helms, J. E. (1994b). How multiculturalism obscures racial factors in the therapy process: Comment on Ridley et al. (1994), Sodowsky et al. (1994), Ottavi et al. (1994), and Thompson et al. (1994). *Journal of Counseling Psychology, 41,* 162–165.

Helms, J. E. (1995). An update of Helms's White and people of Color identity models. In J. G. Ponterotto, J. M. Casas, L. A. Suzuki, & C. M. Alexander (Eds.), *Handbook of multicultural counseling* (pp. 181–198). Thousand Oaks, CA: Sage.

Helms, J. E. (2001). An update of Helms's White and people of Color identity models. In J. G. Ponterotto, J. M. Casas, L. A. Suzuki, & C. M. Alexander (Eds.), *Handbook of multicultural counseling* (2nd ed., pp. 181–198). Thousand Oaks, CA: Sage.

Helms, J. E. (2002). A remedy for the Black-White score disparity. *American Psychologist, 57,* 303–305.

Helms, J. E., & Carter, R. T. (1991). Relationships of White and Black racial identity attitudes and demographic similarity to counselor preferences. *Journal of Counseling Psychology, 38,* 446–457.

Helms, J. E., & Talleyrand, R. M. (1997). Race is not ethnicity. *American Psychologist, 52,* 1246–1247.

Hoshmand, L. T., & Polkinghorne, D. E. (1992). Redefining the science-practice relationship in professional training. *American Psychologist, 47,* 55–66.

Jones, J. M. (1992). Understanding the mental health consequences of race: Contributions of basic social psychological processes. In D. N. Ruble & P. R. Costanzo (Eds.), *The social psychology of mental health: Basic mechanisms and applications* (pp. 199–240). New York: Guilford Press.

Jones, J. M. (1994). Our similarities are different: Toward a psychology of affirmative diversity. In E. J. Trickett, R. J. Watts, & D. Birman (Eds.), *Human diversity: Perspectives on people in context* (pp. 27–45). San Francisco: Jossey-Bass.

Leadbeater, B., & Way, N. (1996). *Urban girls: Resisting stereotypes, creating identities.* New York: New York University Press.

Mason, M. A., & Gibbs, J. T. (1992). Patterns of adolescent psychiatric hospitalization: Implications for social policy. *American Journal of Orthopsychiatry, 62,* 447–457.

McIntyre, A. (1997). *Making meaning of Whiteness: Exploring racial identity with White teachers.* Albany, NY: State University of New York Press.

Mukarubuga, C. (2002). Rwanda: Attaining and sustaining peace. In G. Salomon & B. Nevo (Eds.), *Peace education: The concept, principles, and practices around the world* (pp. 229–236). Mahwah, NJ: Erlbaum.

Neville, H. A., Worthington, R. L., & Spanierman, L. B. (2001). Race, power, and multicultural counseling psychology: Understanding White privilege and color-blind racial attitudes.

In J. G. Ponterotto, J. M. Casas, L. A. Suzuki, & C. M. Alexander (Eds.), *Handbook of multicultural counseling* (2nd ed., pp. 257–288). Thousand Oaks, CA: Sage.

Perry, P. (2001). White means never having to say you're ethnic: White youth and the construction of "cultureless" identity. *Journal of Contemporary Ethnography, 30,* 56–91.

Richardson, T. Q., & Helms, J. E. (1994). The relationship of the racial identity attitudes of Black men to perceptions of "parallel" counseling dyads. *Journal of Counseling and Development, 73,* 172–177.

Root, M. P. P. (2001). Negotiating the margins. In J. G. Ponterotto, J. M. Casas, L. A. Suzuki, & C. M. Alexander (Eds.), *Handbook of multicultural counseling* (2nd ed., pp. 113–121). Thousand Oaks, CA: Sage.

Ross, C. E., & Mirowsky, J. (1984). Socially-desirable response and acquiescence in a cross-cultural survey of mental health. *Journal of Health and Social Behavior, 25,* 189–197.

Schneider, J. A. (1997). Dialectics of race and nationality: Contradictions and Philadelphia working-class youth. *Anthropology and Education Quarterly, 28,* 493–523.

Schulz, A., Williams, D., Israel, B., Becker, A., Parker, E., James, S., et al. (2000). Unfair treatment, neighborhood effects, and mental health in the Detroit metropolitan area. *Journal of Health and Social Behavior, 41,* 314–322.

Shrout, P. E., Canino, G. J., & Bird, H. R. (1992). Mental health status among Puerto Ricans, Mexican Americans, and non-Hispanic Whites. *American Journal of Community Psychology, 20,* 729–752.

Smedley, A. (1993). *Race in North America: Origin and evolution of a world view.* Boulder, CO: Westview.

Stanfield, J. H., II. (1994). Ethnic modeling in qualitative research. In N. K. Denzin & Y. S. Lincoln (Eds.), *Handbook of qualitative research* (pp. 175–188). Thousand Oaks, CA: Sage.

Sue, S., Zane, N., & Young, K. (1994). Research on psychotherapy with culturally diverse populations. In A. E. Bergin & S. L. Garfield (Eds.), *Handbook of psychotherapy and behavior change* (4th ed., pp. 783–817). New York: Wiley.

Takeuchi, D. T., & Cheung, M.-K. (1998). Coercive and voluntary referrals: How ethnic minority adults get into mental health treatment. *Ethnicity and Health, 3,* 149–158.

Thomas, A., & Sillen, S. (1972). *Racism and psychiatry.* New York: Carol.

Thompson, C. E. (2001, August). *Ethnography and psychotherapy research: Is there room at the inn?* Paper presented at the American Psychological Association convention, San Francisco.

Thompson, C. E. (in press). Psychological theory and culture: Implications for practice. In R. T. Carter (Ed.), *Handbook of racial-cultural psychology: Training and practice* (Vol. 2). Hoboken, NJ: Wiley.

Thompson, C. E., & Carter, R. T. (Eds.). (1997). *Racial identity theory: Applications to individual, group, and organizational interventions.* Mahwah, NJ: Erlbaum.

Thompson, C. E., & Isaac, K. (2003). African Americans: Treatment issues and recommendations. In D. R. Atkinson (Ed.), *Counseling American minorities* (6th ed., pp. 125–143). Boston: McGraw-Hill.

Thompson, C. E., & Jenal, S. L. (1994). Interracial and intraracial quasi-counseling interactions when counselors avoid discussing racial issues. *Journal of Counseling Psychology, 41,* 484–491.

Thompson, C. E., Murry, S. L., Harris, D., & Annan, J. R. (in press). Healing inside and out: Applying racial identity theory to a racially divided U.S. community. *International Journal of Counseling.*

Thompson, C. E., & Neville, H. A. (1999). Racism, mental health, and mental health practice. *Counseling Psychologist, 27,* 155–223.

van Dijk, T. A. (1987). Communicating racism: ethnic prejudice in thought and talk. Newbury Park, CA: Sage.

Weiler, J. (2000). *Codes and contradictions: Race, gender identity, and schooling.* Albany, NY: State University of New York Press.

Williams, D. R., Takeuchi, D. T., & Adair, R. K. (1992). Marital status and psychiatric disorder among Blacks and Whites. *Journal of Health and Social Behavior, 33,* 140–157.

Williams, P. J. (1997). *Seeing a color-blind future: The paradox of race.* New York: Farrar, Straus and Giroux.

Yee, A. H., Fairchild, H. H., Weizmann, F., & Wyatt, G. E. (1993). Addressing psychology's problems with race. *American Psychologist, 48,* 1132–1140.

CHAPTER 16

Psychological Functioning and Identity Development of Biracial People: A Review of Current Theory and Research

Marie L. Miville

In 2000, for the first time in U.S. history, biracial people were able to identify themselves as such in the national census. This event marked a substantial movement forward in the societal (political, legal, etc.) recognition of the rights and realities of biracial people. The United States has had a long and painful history with respect to racism and racial discrimination, and people of biracial descent have been affected by this history in a variety of ways. Examples of this historical impact include the use of the "one-drop rule" as a legal definition of racial heritage as well as laws passed by legislatures that made so-called interracial marriages illegal for many generations. The 2000 census marked a critical moment in which biracial people finally began to gain governmental legitimacy with respect to their rich and complex racial heritage. Indeed, according to the U.S. census, nearly seven million people checked more than one racial category, representing 2.4% of the population (Jones & Smith, 2001).

Given the sociohistorical context, it is not surprising that there has been a lack of research in the social sciences on biracial people. It is only within the past two decades that most theory and research describing the unique experiences of biracial people has been proposed and conducted. With the publication of several book-length works, beginning with *Racially Mixed People in America* (Root, 1992), pioneering researchers have recently been able to present a variety of themes, findings, methodologies, and theories regarding biracial people in a single forum. Such collective efforts have allowed for greater distribution of knowledge and ideas, providing direction for future research. Several conferences have been organized focusing on biracial people, and a number of social/political support groups for biracial people currently exist in many cities across the country (N. G. Brown & Douglass, 1996). As a result, the past decade has been particularly productive in the number and type of research studies conducted on biracial people.

This chapter reviews research that has been conducted on biracial people since 1992. A search of several databases in psychology, education, sociology/social work, and psychiatry yielded approximately 30 published studies focusing on this topic. Most of the studies examined psychological adjustment issues and identity development in biracial people. Methodologies used in the studies were predominantly qualitative in design, though more recently, quantitative approaches also have been used. Age groups of the studies may be categorized as child, adolescent, and young adult/adult, and the racial background of individuals has varied from a focus on biracial participants of one unique racial mix (e.g., Black/White) to biracial participants of a variety of mixtures (e.g., Black/White, Hispanic/White). Additionally, a number of authors have proposed theories of biracial identity development (reviewed by Kerwin & Ponterotto, 1995; Wehrly, Kenney, & Kenney, 1999); others maintain that existing racial identity development models are applicable to this group (Carter, 1995; Helms, 1995). Finally, several authors (Renn, 2000; Root, 1992, 1996) have described unique issues relevant to research design and methodology of studies focusing on biracial people that are described here briefly.

The current chapter uses the term *biracial* to refer to those individuals who are descended from two races (e.g., Black/White). The large majority of research reviewed here involves participants in this category. The term *multiracial* has been suggested more recently as including biracial people as well as people descended from more than two races (Root, 1996; Wehrly et al., 1999). However, given that few studies have focused on multiracial people, the term biracial generally is used here. Also, the term *racial identity* is used here to describe the psychological construct of identity based on racial group membership, and the term "race identity" refers to demographic race.

The chapter is organized in the following way. First, a very brief description of current race and racial identity models is given to provide a theoretical basis for some of the research that has been conducted. (although a large number of the studies seem to yield their own theories of identity development.) A review of current issues and difficulties in conducting research on biracial people follows. Then a review of studies on biracial people is arranged according to two primary topic areas: psychological functioning and identity development. Finally, the implications of this review for future research and theory development are identified.

THEORIES OF BIRACIAL IDENTITY DEVELOPMENT

Many scholars today agree that notions of race are socially constructed, not biologically derived (Helms, 1995; Root, 1999, 2002). Race exists as a psychological and social reality, daily affecting both monoracial and biracial people. Racial identity development (RID) models have been proposed that describe a series of strategies that both Whites and people of Color use to integrate racially oriented information. RID models (Cross, 1971, 1991; Helms, 1990, 1995) propose that individuals do not react identically to conditions of discrimination or privilege, but develop various schemas or strategies for interpreting these experiences. Helms (1995) and Carter (1995) proposed that RID models apply as well to biracial people. Some researchers (Fatimilehin, 1999; Miville, Baysden, & So-Lloyd, 1999) have provided evidence to support the validity of RID models in describing some aspects of racial identity development of biracial people.

Other authors contend that RID models do not capture the authentic experiences of biracial people in their identity development. Indeed, Root questions the "assumption of some universal process affecting identity development in general" (2002, p, 173), contending that such models are hierarchical and Eurocentric. Renn (2000) also states that it is impossible for biracial people to be "neatly separated for an Immersion experience" (i.e., involving oneself in one's racial community, p. 3), a key status of racial identity development. Instead, more recent models of biracial identity development emphasize the dynamic and situational nature of race identity for biracial people. For example, Root (1998, 1999) emphasizes an ecological approach that identifies a number of variables affecting race identity (e.g., cognitive processes, inherited influences, traits, social interactions with communities). Kich (1992) suggested that biracial people develop across three identity stages: Awareness of Differentness and Dissonance (ages 3 to 10); Struggle for Acceptance (age 8 to late adolescence); and Self-Acceptance and Assertion of an Interracial Identity (age 18 to adulthood).

Despite disagreements among scholars, common themes across race and racial identity models can be noted. Most important are the emphases on race as a social construction and identity development as nested in a social context affected by sociopolitical history. Further, although scholars generally agree that race identity and racial identity are developmental (i.e., change over time and with experience), current theories have moved away from describing invariant stages, instead emphasizing strategies of identification, affected by cognitive and affective processes and social interactions. Where theories apparently diverge is in their differing emphases on the dynamic interplay of variables and the recognition that biracial people can and do adapt a variety of positive and healthy ways of identifying themselves; that is, internalization or integration of identity is dynamic, fluid, and ongoing and is affected by such variables as physical appearance and language. It is important to examine how theory has been translated into research and to examine the research methods that currently are used in studies of biracial experiences.

ISSUES IN RESEARCH DESIGN AND METHODOLOGY

Theory and methodology are intricately linked, and the body of research on biracial people serves as a case in point. Much of the research on biracial people has been qualitative, reflecting many researchers' resistance to imposing a predetermined theory on participants. Renn (2000) argues:

> Adherence to a critical theory or constructivist approach within qualitative research . . . takes into account the epistemological and ontological perspectives that allow us to see race as socially constructed and the experiences of the multiracial people under study as only partially knowable by others. (p. 12)

She goes further to state:

> Because understandings and meanings of multiraciality are themselves born of [philosophical underpinnings of] a pluralist and relativist epistemology, these qualitative approaches are the preferred strategy to research in this area. (p. 12)

Unfortunately, the sole use of qualitative inquiry presumes that the experiences of biracial people cannot be meaningfully or accurately portrayed in quantitative designs and that there is a lack of common themes and understandings that defy the generation of theory meaningfully portraying or interpreting biracial experiences (i.e., the construct of racial identity development) at a collective level. Further, the sole use of qualitative inquiry implies that few to no generalizations regarding biracial people can be made, a current problem with the existing research (Rockquemore, 2002a).

Root (1992, 2002) outlined a number of methodological issues unique to research on biracial people. For example, with respect to sampling, Root noted that due to historical and demographic trends, biracial people are distributed nonrandomly in the United States and elsewhere, being more concentrated in certain regions such as Hawaii and the West, and less so in others. As a result, many studies tend to use nonrandom samples from regions with a larger biracial population. Further, identifying biracial participants can be difficult, and the use of surnames is not a generally effective means for doing so. Many studies use advertising and snowball methods to obtain participants, and thus selection bias is a problem with much research on biracial people. As well, the use of control groups has unique issues for this population, given the problem of defining who should serve as a control group (e.g., majority monorace people, minority monorace people). Thus, researchers must clarify what is being controlled for by using one or another control group. Generational issues are also of concern in sampling methods, in that the generation in which one grew up (both in real time and generation of being in the United States) necessarily affects identity development of biracial people. Types of samples are also of concern in the current research. Early studies apparently yielded findings showing that biracial people were psychologically vulnerable (see Gibbs, 2003). However, the use of nonclinical samples in the past decade has helped mitigate concerns about the at-risk nature of being biracial. Further, the use of college samples, while rich in nature, necessarily limits the generalization and credibility of the findings.

Renn (2000) provided several suggestions to mitigate concerns for conducting and presenting research on biracial people. She suggested that in conceptualizing research designs, researchers should "draw attention to the constructed nature of race in the context of other socially constructed categories and identities," such as gender (p. 12). Thus, Renn believes that research designs should investigate how race interacts with other socially constructed variables, rather than as a single variable. Another suggestion was for scholars to clearly state how terms related to concepts of race were being used in their project, rather than leaving to either the participant or the reader to create definitions of these terms. Renn also proposed the use of "disruptive gestures" (e.g., use of italics, quotation marks) in presenting data to draw the reader's attention to the use of racial terms in a research paper.

CURRENT RESEARCH ON THE PSYCHOLOGICAL FUNCTIONING OF BIRACIAL PEOPLE

The following section reviews research on the psychological functioning of biracial people. A common notion, even myth, about biracial people is that due to their unique or dual racial heritage (and the subsequent lack of a coherent or stable community), they are at risk of becoming confused or somehow maladjusted. Kerwin and Ponterotto (1995) described this as the stereotype of the "tragic mulatto" or "marginal person." Thus, one primary area of research emphasis has been the psychological functioning of biracial people.

For the most part, studies examining the psychological functioning of biracial people have used a more quantitative approach, given the nature of the question: How well-adjusted are biracial people? Studies typically utilize existing measures of psychological functioning, and some include control groups. Most studies reviewed here focus on either adolescents or adults; no published studies were found on adjustment of biracial children under age 12 (although two unpublished dissertations have been conducted on this population: Karasaki, 1998; Pierce, 1992).

Cauce et al. (1992) examined differences between 22 biracial adolescents from Seattle, ranging in age from 11 to 13, whose racial background was either African American/White or Asian American/White and a control group of African American children matched on age, year in school, gender, family income, and family composition. Cauce et al. decided to use a minority control group, versus a majority control group, because they felt that all participants thus would share the experience of being "non-White" in the larger community. Measures of family functioning (e.g., environment, attachment, family support, and child rearing), peer relations, self-esteem, life stress, and psychological adjustment were given to the 44 adolescents. T-tests did not reveal any significant differences between the biracial and control groups. Limitations of the study focused on small sample size, lack of geographical diversity, and selection bias in how the participants were recruited for the study.

Cooney and Radina (2000) also examined psychological adjustment issues among biracial adolescents (mean age = 16 years). They included adolescents from the National Longitudinal Study of Adolescent Health with the following racial backgrounds: 1,870 monoracial (White), 534 monoracial (racial/ethnic minority, including Black/African American, American Indian/Native American, Asian/Pacific Islander, and Hispanic), and 284 biracial adolescents (two or more of previous racial-ethnic classifications, as defined by parental responses). Nine indicators were used to assess depression, delinquent behavior, substance abuse, receipt of psychological counseling, being held back in school, being suspended or expelled, grade point average, problems encountered in school, and feelings about school for the past year. A series of bivariate and multivariate analyses were conducted, with males and females being analyzed separately. Significant effects for biracial status were found for both boys and girls on fewer than half of the measures. Biracial boys and girls were found to have higher rates of counseling use, grade retention, suspension or expulsion, depression (boys only), and delinquency (girls only). These findings were interpreted by the authors as indicating some risk of adjustment problems in biracial adolescents.

Milan and Keiley (2000) also examined personality functioning among biracial adolescents using the same database. Their sample included 272 self-identified biracial youth, 3,521 White/non-Hispanics, and 1,941 monoracial minority adolescents. The authors constructed variables from existing measures to assess parental relationships, depression, somatization, conduct problems, school-related behavioral problems, and self-worth. Alpha reliabilities for the constructed measures were all above .80, and a confirmatory factor analysis found the measures loaded on factors in predicted directions. One-way ANOVAs were used to examine differences among the three groups. Results indicated that biracial adolescents did not differ in their perceptions of family relationships. However, biracial children were found to have higher reports of conduct problems, school problems, somatization, and low self-worth. As Cooney and Radina (2000) found, these youth were most likely to have sought counseling (17% versus 13% minority and 10% White). Milan and Keiley interpreted these findings as indicating that biracial youth were somewhat psychologically vulnerable relative to monoracial adolescents.

Similarly, McKelvey and Webb (1996) explored psychological adjustment of Vietnamese Amerasians, using non-Amerasian siblings and unrelated, same-age Vietnamese immigrants as controls. The sample included 346 participants, of which 140 (40.5%) were Amerasians, 71 (20.5%) were non-Amerasian siblings, and 118 (34.1%) were unrelated similar-age Vietnamese immigrants. Ages ranged from 19 to 33. Participants completed the 25-item Hopkins Symptom Checklist (HSCL-25), which measures anxiety and depression, the Vietnamese Depression Scale (VDS), and a personal information sheet detailing alcohol and drug use, number of hospitalizations, social support, indices of childhood trauma, and adaptation to American life. A MANOVA and follow-up univariate ANOVAs yielded significant differences across the groups. Vietnamese Amerasians reported greater alcohol use, more hospitalizations, fewer years of education, more childhood trauma, greater perceived effects of trauma, and higher depression, as measured by the VDS. At the same time, Vietnamese Amerasians also were adapting to American life and enjoyed similar levels of social support to the other groups. McKelvey and Webb note that the findings demonstrate the resilience of Vietnamese Amerasians in the face of numerous obstacles present not only in the larger society, but in their families as well.

Mass (1992) examined the psychological adjustment and self-concept of 53 biracial (Japanese/White) and 52 monoracial Japanese American college students. The latter group was mostly third- and fourth-generation Japanese, with ages ranging from 18 to 42. Several questionnaires were used to assess Japanese American ethnic experiences, self-concept, personality functioning, acculturation, and ethnic identity. Follow-up interviews with 33 participants also were conducted. No statistical analyses were reported (a critical weakness with the published study), but Mass indicated that no significant differences were found regarding self-concept and personality functioning. However, biracial students were found to be less identified with being Japanese and were more acculturated. Limitations of the study include a small sample size and the lack of adequate descriptions of the statistical analyses used in the project.

Phinney and Alipuria (1996) examined the self-esteem of 47 biracial university students with a comparison group of 345 monoracial students, all of whom were U.S.-born. Approximately half of all participants (both monoracial and biracial) came from a racially diverse campus, while the other half attended a predominantly White university. Participants completed measures for racial self-label, parents' race/ethnicity, and self-esteem. One-way ANOVAs did not yield differences in self-esteem between the two groups. A second study on high school students also revealed no significant differences on, among other variables, grade point average and self-esteem. Limitations of the study include the confusing use of the term "multiethnic" (i.e., the categories appear to be race-based) and the use of participants the researchers labeled biracial who self-labeled as monoethnic.

A number of recent studies described in *Dissertation Abstracts International* have examined psychological functioning among biracial people (Adams, 1997; Buxenbaum, 1996; Cooke, 1998; Harrison, 1997; J. E. Jones, 2000; Karasaki, 1998; Mukoyama, 1998; Mur, 1999; Oliver, 2002; Pierce, 1992; Shepherd, 1997; Tremayne, 1998; Van Kirk, 2002; Zwiebach-Sherman, 1999). Space does not allow for a complete review of these studies, but findings generally did not reveal significant relations between being biracial and psychological functioning.

Together, these published studies portray biracial people as generally well-functioning (Cauce et al., 1992; Mass, 1992; Phinney & Alipuria, 1996), although at some psychological risk (Cooney & Radina, 2000; McKelvey & Webb, 1996; Milan & Keiley, 2000). Strengths of the studies are large sample sizes, use of a control group, and use of standardized instruments that allow for meaningful comparisons. However, a common criticism of most of these studies is that their findings were inconclusive as to how or why a biracial heritage plays a role in psychological adjustment or maladjustment. Indeed, a major limitation of Cooney and Radina, Milan and Keiley, and McKelvey and Webb is that racial identity (i.e., race as a psychological construct) was not a variable in any of these studies; instead, these studies used a self-identified biracial label (i.e., race as a demographic label). Future research must incorporate racial identity variables in conjunction with psychological functioning to establish a clearer relationship between psychological functioning and racial identity among biracial people.

CURRENT RESEARCH ON THE IDENTITY DEVELOPMENT OF BIRACIAL PEOPLE

Without a doubt, the topic of greatest interest to researchers of biracial people has been identity development. For the most part, studies on biracial identity have been qualitative in design, and the majority have sought to identify common themes from their participants that highlight the unique aspects of race and racial identity for biracial people. Only a few studies (Fatimilehin, 1999; Gillem, Cohn, & Throne, 2001; Miville et al., 1999) have examined racial identity of biracial people as defined by current RID models (Cross 1971, 1991; Helms, 1990, 1995). Other scholars attempted to build theories of race identity based on their participants' responses that described unique elements of development for biracial people (Collins, 2000; Kerwin, & Ponterotto, 1995; Kich, 1992; Root, 1992, 1996). The following sections describe biracial identity research examining racial identity and race identity across several age groups: children, adolescents, and young adults. For each study, the method and findings are briefly described, along with an evaluation and critique of the work.

Racial Identity

Fatimilehin (1999) conducted one of the few published studies thus far to use RID models to explore racial identity among biracial adolescents (Black Caribbean/White). The Black Racial Identity Attitude Scale (BRIAS; Parham & Helms, 1981, as cited in Helms, 1990), along with measures of racial socialization and self-esteem, were administered to 23 biracial participants, ranging in age from 12 to 19. Mean scores for Internalization were higher than for Pre-encounter, signifying that these participants had a positive racial identity. Internalization and claiming dual heritage both increased with age, implying that Internalization attitudes might be linked with pride in having dual heritages. Internalization also was positively correlated with self-esteem. Results provided initial support for the validity of RID models for biracial identity. However, a major drawback to the study is the small sample size, thereby limiting the power of the findings and restricting the range of BRIAS scores.

Miville et al. (1999) conducted a qualitative research design to examine how biracial identity development was similar and dissimilar to racial identity in general. Eight participants of varying racial backgrounds (ages ranging from 20 to 54) were interviewed in the following areas: experiences and memories of growing up; time or incident leading to initial awareness of being different; response to questions about race/ethnicity; important others for self-identification; cultural attitudes, beliefs, or practices; general observations about monoracial people and being biracial; and advice for parents raising biracial children. Transcripts were analyzed and coded by the authors, using a consensus model to derive a number of themes. Four major domains emerged from data analyses: encounters with racism, racial self-label/reference group orientation, the "chameleon" experience, and identity in context of people, places, and periods. Encounters as defined in RID models were found to be of two types: being a member of a racial/ethnic minority group, and being biracial (e.g., ambiguous racial appearance of participants, leading to "What are you?" question from others). Participants were found to simultaneously identify along a continuum of groups: as members of a particular racial/ethnic group (e.g., Chinese, Puerto Rican), as being biracial, and as being a person of Color or racial minority. The chameleon experience was characterized by social attitudes of acceptance toward others and flexible social boundaries. The authors concluded by noting that a number of themes paralleled those from RID models, particularly models applicable to people of Color. For example, participants described encounters with racism by their peers that were meaningfully internalized by participants as signifying their social status as a non-White person. Such experiences seemed to lead to a general identification with oppressed social group membership as a person of Color. As well, the development of racial identity over time (shifts and changes in self-label, peer groups) was apparent. Strengths of the study were the use of existing RID theory to shape the study and the consistent use of qualitative methodology and subsequent analyses to explore how racial identity defined by RID models existed for biracial participants. Limitations of the study included small sample size and use of participants from several racial backgrounds, with unique racial identity issues perhaps being missed as a result. The inclusion of participants from a predominantly White university also may have affected findings in that participants were in a social context that at times was overtly hostile toward people of Color, leading to the types of encounters experienced by participants.

Gillem et al. (2000) used a case study approach to explore racial identity development of two biracial (Black/White) individuals, Jacqueline and Adolphus. Using a semistructured interview format, the authors asked informants about their current identity; parent, family, and peer influences on their identity development; and their experiences of being biracial. Data were analyzed by a three-woman team, using a grounded theory analysis to identify themes. Like Miville et al. (1999), they found both participants to have encountered experiences in early adolescence, though they found some divergence between the two as to how subsequent immersion proceeded. One participant, Jacqueline, became immersed in Black student organizations while maintaining a voice of racial harmony and coming to embrace a biracial self-label. In contrast, the other participant, Adolphus, became involved in gang activities in high school and then attended a private university where he became conscious of both White and Black social worlds and uneasy about fitting in either. Based on these divergent experiences, the authors conclude that the Black RID model may not accurately represent the experiences of biracial people because it does not recognize the social complexity of adopting a biracial identity in a monoracially defined social world. Strengths of the study include a clear articulation of the constructs studied, along with a solid description of the methodology and data analyses. However, given that the study is based on two participants, it seems premature to discard RID models as being invalid for biracial people. As well, the findings of both Fatimilehin (1999) and Miville et al. indicate some parallel processes that exist between people of Color in general and biracial people in particular. To be sure, as Gillem et al. and Miville et al. note, the social context is crucial in formulating or hindering the development of a positive racial identity. Current social settings do not clearly support biracial Immersion experiences, often leaving individuals to choose one or another social group with which to socialize and identify.

Field (1996) examined a variable relevant to racial identity development, reference group orientation (RGO), "a pattern of behavior, interests, and values that is associated with a particular racial group" (p. 214), among 31 biracial (Black/White) adolescents. Field also included 31 White and 31 Black participants in her study to allow for comparisons. RGO has been noted by both Cross (1991) and Helms (1990) as being important to one's overall self-concept, particularly the congruence of RGO with actual racial group membership. Helms argued that adopting a White RGO might be linked with negative self-concept for African Americans. Field explored the relation of RGO and self-concept for biracial people. Measures of RGO (developed by Field), self-concept, and behavioral adjustment were completed by participants. MANOVAs were conducted to determine the relationship among self-identified race, RGO, self-concept, and behavioral adjustment. Race was significantly associated with RGO, and biracial youth had the most diverse RGO pattern (nearly even splits across Black, White, and bicultural RGOs). At the same time, biracial youth were found to be fairly similar to Black youth in their patterns of RGO, particularly in the prediction of self-concept. Thus, having either a Black or a bicultural RGO was linked with positive self-concept, whereas having a White RGO was linked with negative self-concept for both Black and biracial participants. Strengths of the study include use of control groups and standardized instruments. Limitations include lack of psychometric information on the RGO measure used in the study that served as a central variable. Field concluded that her findings supported Helms's contention that having a White RGO for both biracial and Black youth was linked to negative feelings about having a Black heritage. In contrast, both biracial and Black participants with a Black or bicultural RGO had positive feelings toward their Black heritage as well as a positive self-concept.

Race Identity in Children

Root's (1992) seminal work on biracial people in the United States featured several studies focusing on identity development that together ranged over the life span. A number of these have served as a basis for future research and theory building. For example, Jacobs (1992) examined identity development in children under 12 using a new doll-play instrument he developed. The instrument harkened back to the pioneering work by Clark and Clark (1939, as cited in Jacobs, 1992) that used doll choice among Black and White children. Jacobs drew on cognitive theories of Piaget and Kohlberg to focus on cognitive factors leading to the basis of race identity, such as color constancy. The doll-play instrument included 36 dolls varying in skin and hair color combination, racial features (Black, White, Asian), size/age, and sex. Children were interviewed on nine separate tasks regarding the dolls: free-play story, matching self to doll, self-identification, family identification, preference of sibling, preference of play, preference regarding like/dislike of dolls, sibling of light-brown boy doll, and constancy of race identity. By reviewing the interview data of 10 children (Black/White) ranging in age from 3 to 8 years (procedures for this were not outlined), Jacobs found four common factors relevant to race identity development in children: constancy of color, internalization of interracial/biracial label, racial ambivalence, and perceptual distortions in self- and family identifications. Jacobs proposed a three-stage model for biracial children: Stage I, Pre-Color Constancy involving play and experimentation with color; Stage II, Post-Color Constancy involving adoption of a biracial label and racial ambivalence; and Stage III, Biracial Identity. The study is innovative in design, and attempts were made to address some of the problems of interpretation of doll-choice designs inherent in the work of Clark and Clark (Cross, 1991). Central to these criticisms was accurately interpreting what doll choice meant to the participant. Many of the early doll studies presumed that positive or healthy attitudes about self necessarily predicted choice of same-race figures (versus no preference choice, which was indeed found for Black children). Jacobs attempted to mitigate these concerns in his study by using multiple race choices and both sexes for biracial participants (Black, White, Asian and male/female); thus, doll choice was not limited to skin color. As well, children were questioned across a broad range of themes for more accurate interpretation of their choices. A major drawback of the study, however, is that there is no description of the data collected (e.g., examples of self-statements, ratings of ambivalence), so the reader is unable to evaluate the findings. Also, the findings are based on only 10 children who differed in both age and cognitive functioning. Unfortunately, there do not seem to be follow-up studies using this design. Thus, although the study presents an interesting approach to examining race identity among young biracial children, insufficient information is presented to evaluate the design and implications of the findings.

D. J. Johnson (1992) also examined racial preferences among 62 biracial preschoolers ranging from 34 to 71 months, representing a mix of Black ($n = 28$), biracial (16), and White (18) children, using the short-form Preschool Racial Attitude Measure II (PRAM II). The PRAM II is an 18-item, two-choice measure that assesses racial and gender stereotyping, having a reliability of .80. Higher scores denote a pro-Black bias, middle-range scores reflect no preference, and lower scores denote a pro-White bias. Two-way ANOVAs by race and age revealed a main effect for age but not for race, and biracial children were not found to differ in level of bias from either White or Black children. However, trends in choices of bias supported a unique developmental pattern of biracial children across age; for example, at age 3, 80% of biracial children expressed a no preference bias, compared to 44% of White and 60% of Black children. The findings of the study are important in showing the unique development of racial preferences among biracial children. As well, the author's use of monoracial control groups and an assessment instrument, the PRAM II, allowed for examination of common and unique patterns between biracial and monoracial children.

Kerwin, Ponterotto, Jackson, and Harris (1993) conducted one of the best-known studies of race or racial identity of biracial children. The authors used a qualitative design involving semistructured interviews of nine biracial (Black/White) children, ages 5 to 16, and at least one parent. Interviews of children focused on "self-identity, use/nonuse of an interracial label, racial awareness, dual socialization, and the family's coping skills" (p. 223); parent interviews included "family's identity, use/nonuse of an interracial label, racial awareness of child or children, dual socialization, family's coping skills, developmental issues and problems, sociocultural factors, and the role of schools" (p. 223). Interviews were conducted by the lead author, a White woman, and data were compiled via the transcriptions of audiotaped interviews. Verbatim transcripts were then reviewed by a research team several times to identify major and minor themes. Triangulation of the data also occurred through the restatements of participant positions during the interviews. Parental themes focused on frustration with societal labels and uncertainty about use of labels by their children, preparing children for discrimination, and identifying locations potentially supportive of and open to their children's mixed racial heritage. Children's themes centered on varying responses to the use of labels, along with increased peer pressure to adopt a label with age, racial self-description, and encounters with racism leading to racial awareness. A major conclusion by the authors was that the data did not support a marginalized existence for biracial children, although there was "an increased sensitivity to the views, cultures, and values of the Black and the White communities and [the participants] perceived more commonalities than differences between them" (p. 228). Strengths of the study include the use of both children and parents and a rigorous methodology for both collecting and interpreting the data. Limitations of the study described by the authors include selection bias, leading to "overly optimistic findings," and reliance on verbal reports, also resulting in experiences being described in "an overly positive light" (p. 229). Although the authors defend well the small sample size, the nongeneralizability of the findings is a problem for researchers who wish to apply findings to a larger population.

Winn and Priest (1993) interviewed 34 biracial (mostly White/Black) children from 15 families, ranging in age from 8 to 20, using a 16-question format. Findings indicated that many participants felt conflicted about selecting one parent's racial identification over another; a large majority (82%) indicated they felt "obligated" to choose a monoracial designation and felt traitorous for excluding the parent's heritage with whom they did not identify. A third of participants expressed desire for their family to establish rituals celebrating their unique heritages. The majority seemed to indicate that they had positive racial self-concepts, though at the same time, they stated that their parents had not sufficiently prepared them to deal with the social realities of being biracial. The authors concluded that whatever combination of race identity descriptions biracial children adopt (i.e., monoracial or biracial), a key aspect is that these self-descriptions be positive; otherwise, these children will be at risk for developing psychological problems. Similar to the work of Kerwin et al. (1993), the authors used a snowball sample using personal contacts. However, the findings were less "positive," in that participants revealed their emotional struggles in developing their race identity. Unfortunately, the authors use a qualitative design, but then seem to present their data in only quantitative terms, reporting percentages of statement endorsements (e.g., percentage of participants who have rituals celebrating unique background). Given the small number of participants, such percentages are difficult to interpret without statistical analyses demonstrating their significance. Further, no consistent description of themes or meanings based on the interview data was presented. Thus, although the study focused on some interesting aspects of biracial identity development, there were not adequate data analyses present for the reader to evaluate.

Race Identity in Adolescents/Young Adults

Gibbs and Hines (1992) conducted a two-year research project involving interviews with 12 biracial (Black/White) adolescents and their families. The primary focus of the research was to explore race identity development, psychosocial adjustment, and parental perceptions of their children's adjustment. Families were identified via their involvement in a local interracial organization in San Francisco. Participants responded to questions from the Biracial Adolescent Psychosocial Interview developed by Gibbs that covered 12 areas of adolescent attitudes, behaviors, and experiences dealing with racial self-concept, race identity, and attitudes about being raised in an interracial family. Participants also were given measures of personality functioning and self-esteem. Parents completed a questionnaire related to their developmental and health history, school and social experiences, community support groups, family activities, and parental perceptions of the adolescent's attitude about being biracial. Findings were described as a series of conflicts adolescents expressed, including conflicts about racial/ethnic identity, social marginality, sexuality, autonomy and independence, and educational and career aspirations, along with general psychological adjustment. Most participants appeared to feel positive about themselves and their race identity, incorporating positive aspects of both Black and White backgrounds. Gibbs and Hines caution that unresolved race identity conflicts among biracial youth can lead to psychological problems. Strengths of the study include the use of both qualitative and quantitative methods (including standardized instruments) to create a richer portrait of the participants. As well, the first author's extensive clinical background provided a series of themes by which to categorize the data. Unfortunately, as with Winn and Priest (1993), the qualitative interview data are presented only in quantitative terms (i.e., use of percentages); a more useful approach might have been to additionally include statements of participants to illustrate the themes.

Tizard and Phoenix (1995) interviewed 58 biracial (White and African or African Caribbean) students in London, ranging in age from 14 to 18. Findings from the study revealed that most participants were very positive about their mixed heritage, stressing the advantages of being "special" and seeing things from both perspectives. Black and mixed peer groups were important to achieving a positive race identity. Problems with identity were linked with a strong affiliation to White people and, paradoxically, being told by their parents to be proud of being Black or of mixed parentage (the authors concluded that the latter was an effort by parents to mitigate the former). The authors concluded that participants, and biracial children in general, must have the "right to construct identities that are both Black and White" (p. 1409). As with Gibbs and Hines (1992) and Winn and Priest (1993), Tizard and Phoenix reported percentages about statements endorsed by participants (e.g., How do you feel about having one White and one Black parent?). However, the sample size was considerably larger and responses were statistically analyzed, for example, exploring the relations between race identity and parental messages. As well, participants were close in age, minimizing maturation effects.

U. M. Brown (2001) published a book describing her interviews of 119 biracial (Black/White) young adults from a variety of colleges in the Northeast (mean age = 21 years). Along with responding to the Brown Interracial Young Adult Interview (BIYAI), participants completed measures of self-esteem and physical appearance. The interview focused on racial identity (choice of racial category, conflict regarding the choice) and critical experiences growing up affecting race identity. Like previous studies, Brown noted variation and fluctuations in the race identity development of her biracial participants, along with a compartmentalization of public and private identities. Inclusion of the variable of physical appearance was a particular strength of Brown's work. Interestingly, although a number of scholars have noted the importance of physical characteristics in identity development (Root, 1992), few studies have actually included it as a variable. Brown found that physical appearance was related to race identity. Participants who were darker-complected were more readily recognized and accepted as Black by the larger social world, leading to more consistent reinforcement of their race identity. Lighter-skin participants experienced greater struggle with and adjustment to finding accep-tance by themselves and by others as a racial being (e.g., Black, White, or biracial). Brown found that some light-skin participants attempted to pass as White, gener-ally yielding mixed results regarding social acceptance, and often with high psy-chological costs. Other strengths of Brown's study are the inclusion of a large number of participants from a variety of colleges, use of standardized instruments of self-esteem and physical appearance, and presentation of psychometric informa-tion regarding the BIYAI. Sampling bias toward middle-class and more highly edu-cated participants was acknowledged by the researcher such that identity themes or conflicts for biracial people of different SES backgrounds were not represented.

The race identity studies described thus far have focused on biracial participants whose racial background was primarily Black/White. A few studies also have ex-amined race identity of biracial people from other racial backgrounds, though typ-ically, these participants have one parent who is White. For example, Newsome (2002) surveyed and interviewed 72 adolescents (one parent was White for all par-ticipants) in a racially diverse school in California (mean age of 15 years) to inves-tigate how parental and societal messages affect race identity among biracial youth. Survey questions centered on parental messages regarding racial differences, han-dling overt incidences of racial harassment, cultural home environment (cultural visibility of one or both races), availability of and comfort with extended family, race/ethnic classification, and peer group perceptions/reactions of race identity. Follow-up interviews focused on the individual's self-concept, family communi-cation, and societal factors, such as geographic region and peers. A latent content analysis was conducted to identify categories or themes among participant responses. Results revealed that family communication was generally supportive, though at times disconfirming. Maternal messages were found to be important in creating re-lational communication and ease. Regarding self-concept, most participants as-cribed to a culturally plural model and a "sense of sharing between the two group identities" (p. 153). Identities were found to be complex, however, in that 51 of 72 participants "identified themselves as being both their minority and majority racial identities" (p. 156). The authors concluded that participants embraced both identi-ties (minority/majority) and did not find these potentially competing group mem-berships to be "burdensome." The study was consistent in its use of qualitative methodology and the subsequent data analyses. As well, the focus on how identities are constructed via family and social messages was clearly linked with methodol-ogy used in the study. A limitation of the study, however, is the confusing use of the terms "race" and "ethnicity"; although the author early on acknowledged how these terms differ, they seem to be used interchangeably throughout.

Collins (2000) examined the race identity of 15 biracial adults (Asian/non-Asian, mostly White) using semistructured and open-ended interviews. Each participant was interviewed once in a session lasting one to two hours that was audiotaped and transcribed. Data were analyzed by the investigator using the constant comparable method to derive categories or themes. Overarching themes included self-evaluation (Who am I? or experiences with identity conflicts), confusion of categorization (Where do I fit?), belonging, infusion/exploration, situational use of identity, and resolution/acceptance/self-verification (positive assertion of identity). Based on these findings, Collins presented a biracial or double identity model composed of four developmental phases: (1) Questioning and Confusion, (2) Refusal and Suppression, (3) Infusion and Exploration, and (4) Resolution and Acceptance. The method and analyses were clearly and thoughtfully presented by Collins; however, as the author noted, further research must explore each theme more thoroughly. As well, it was not clear whether the themes and resulting model apply to all biracial people. Selection bias also is a limitation of the study.

In a groundbreaking study, Hall (1992) examined the race identity of biracial people of Black/Asian descent. Thirty participants in the study were recruited through newspapers and word of mouth in the Los Angeles area, and age of participants ranged from 18 to 32. Hall developed an Ethnic Identity Questionnaire, containing Likert-type items assessing demographic information, race identity choice, racial composition of neighborhood and friends, cultural knowledge, racial resemblance/appearance, political involvement, and perceived social acceptance by racial groups. Multiple regression analyses showed that the participants who chose a Black race identity were younger, had knowledge of Black culture, had predominantly Black friends, and perceived nonacceptance by Japanese American peers. Participants who chose an "other than Black" identity had opposite attributes: They were older, had less knowledge of Black culture and fewer Black friends, and felt accepted by Japanese Americans. Most ($n = 18$) participants had experienced a time in their life when they felt they needed to choose a race identity (Black or other). Hall concluded that "in spite of (or because of) all the detours and adjustments, the Black-Japanese in this study were well adjusted in their heterogeneous heritage. In fact, most found their biracialism and biculturalism to be assets" (p. 264). The study is important for its use of multiple factors that led to race identity choice (both personal and social variables), use of participants from a clearly specified racial background, and use of statistical analyses to determine the relations among the variables. Further psychometric information on the identity questionnaire, however, would help in evaluating its construct validity.

Phinney and Alipuria (1996) examined the race identity of 47 biracial (the predominant mix was White/Hispanic) and 345 monoracial university students and 194 biracial (the predominant mix was Black and/or Hispanic and other) and 696 monoracial high school students. One-fifth of the university sample spontaneously self-labeled as biracial, and the remainder identified monoracially. Biracial students from a predominantly White campus were more likely to describe themselves as White than biracial students from a racially diverse campus. Similarly, one-third of biracial high school students self-labeled as such, while the remainder self-labeled as monoracial. The high school sample was administered a measure of self-esteem and the 14-item Multigroup Ethnic Identity Measure (MEIM; Phinney, 1992) assessing three aspects of race identity: sense of belonging to and attitudes toward one's ethnic group, ethnic behaviors and customs, and ethnic identity achievement. The MEIM also assessed other-group attitudes. ANOVAs revealed no significant differences on the basis of sex, SES, or spontaneous self-label. As well, no differences were found in race identity scores of biracial and monoracial participants.

Some differences were found depending on type of racial mix; for example, biracial Hispanics had lower race identity scores (i.e., less positive attitudes) than monoracial Hispanics, and the opposite pattern was found for White biracial and monoracial participants. More positive race identity was significantly related to higher self-esteem for both biracial and monoracial participants. Important variables were the differential contexts (racial makeup of settings) and racial heritage affecting choice of self-labels. Thus, Black biracial participants tended to identify as Black, whereas Hispanic biracials did not necessarily identify as Hispanic. A major drawback to the study is the authors' confusing use of the terms "multiethnic" and "ethnic identity" to refer to their participants, which have been interpreted here as "biracial" and "race identity," respectively (e.g., Asian, Black, Hispanic, American Indian, and White). Strengths of the study are the large sample size, inclusion of comparison groups, and demographic information on settings.

Other studies have examined race identity from an ecological approach or as race identity is affected by social context. For example, in a series of studies combining qualitative and quantitative designs, Rockquemore and her colleagues (Rockquemore, 1998, 2002; Rockquemore & Brunsma, 2002) explored the meaning of the "biracial experience" and factors that influence race identity choices. Two specific variables were examined: social networks and physical appearance. Social networks were conceptualized as

> "push and pull factors" where individuals, located within a particular type of social network, may feel pulled toward one identity option because of positive experiences with one group and/or may feel pushed away from another identity option because of negative experiences. (p. 339)

Physical appearance represented

> a collection of cultural meanings that supply basic information to others and foster particular interpretations . . . appearances simultaneously *present* one's identity while also serving as the *source* of identity. (p. 340)

Participants were culled from university students in the Detroit, Michigan, area, of which 177 met the criteria for biracial (Black/White). Via responses to a race identity question, each respondent was classified as adopting one of the following biracial identities: singular (Black or White), border (identify as both, may be validated or unvalidated), protean (identify sometimes as one race and sometimes as the other, depending on the context), and transcendent (no definable race identity). Most (61%) identified as border, many of whom (nearly 40%) felt unvalidated in their identity choice by their social context. Only 13% chose a singular identity. The degree to which participants had negative experiences (push factors) with Blacks also predicted race identity, though negative experiences with Whites did not. Respondents with negative experiences with Blacks chose border identity, and those with positive experiences chose a singular Black identity. Feeling close to Blacks and Whites (pull factors) also related to racial identity in theoretically predicted directions: (1) feeling close to Blacks but not Whites predicted a singular Black identity, (2) feeling close to Blacks but closer to Whites predicted unvalidated border identity, (3) feeling closer to Whites than Blacks predicted validated border identity, and (4) feeling close to both Blacks and White predicted protean and transcendent identities. Further, although skin color rating was not predictive of identity, socially perceived appearance was. This latter finding contradicts earlier suppositions that phenotype determines identity; instead, "the reflexive, socially perceived self-understandings of appearance" (p. 350) predict race identity choice. The research conducted by Rockquemore is intriguing in its use of both qualitative and quantitative designs and theoretically derived social context variables to explain differences in racial identity choices. However, a drawback to the design is that several critical variables, including race identity choice and physical appearance, were derived from responses to a single item.

Twine (1996) also investigated social context as a variable significantly affecting race identity choices and development. She interviewed 16 biracial women, university students attending Berkeley, of Black ancestry identifying as biracial. These women had been raised in predominantly White households, neighborhoods, and schools. White mothers and middle-class privilege were attributed in the daughters' generally racially neutral identities. Challenges to these identities occurred upon encounters with overt racism beginning in puberty, when dating choices began. Essentially, adolescence marked the period in which the position of racial neutrality was lost, as White friends began pressuring the young women to date only Black men. Further shifts in identities occurred when participants began to attend the politically conscious campus of Berkeley, leading the young women to adopt a more racially aware framework. Strengths of the study include a contextual approach to exploring race identity development. However, as with other studies previously described, Twine does not describe her procedures for data analyses.

Contextual variables of race identity also were emphasized in recent research using ecological approaches to identity development by both Root (1998, 1999) and Renn (1999, 2003). Root conducted interviews of 20 sibling pairs (various racial backgrounds, mean age = 25) recruited from newspapers in the Seattle, Washington area. Criteria for inclusion were being at least 18 years of age and having a biological sibling willing to participate. Participants were sent questionnaires assessing background, body image, racial resemblance of self and sibling, racial experiences of being biracial, identity, and mental health. Two two-hour interviews followed, the first focusing on race and gender awareness and identity development, and the second focusing on describing their lives according to developmental stages. Four themes relevant to race identity development emerged: hazing, family dysfunction, increased racial integration in the structure of society, and other salient identities. The first two themes, hazing and family dysfunction, were viewed as detracting from healthy race identity development, leading to irrational color coding (i.e., race became associated with dysfunctional or abusive behaviors) and social distance. The findings were interpreted by Root as demonstrating the variability of race identity development in light of social context factors. An innovative aspect of the study is the use of siblings to help validate/triangulate interview data as well as to highlight individual variations that occur within the same family system. However, Root does not appear to describe her approach with analyzing the interview data. As well, selection bias via region is a limitation.

Renn (1999, 2003) involved 24 biracial university students using several data sources: individual interviews, written responses by participants, focus groups of three to four people, and analysis of archival data (e.g., field note observations about the campus) at each university. Data were analyzed by a three-member team who independently reviewed each transcript line by line to derive major codes and themes. Findings were interpreted via Bronfenbrenner's (1993, in Renn, 1999) model of ecological cognitive development. Emergent themes emphasized the search for new, previously undefined spaces on university campuses by these students. In particular, "specific person-environment interactions that happened in and among those spaces . . . contributed to [race] identity development" (p. 9). Several areas were found to be relevant: academic work, friendship groups, social life and dating, and campus activity involvement across a number of systems (micro-, meso-, and exosystems). As with previous researchers, Renn found that students claimed a variety of race identity classifications. Larger campus factors affecting race identity choices were the "size and location of the community of Color on campus and the impact of peer culture on the permeability of group boundaries" (p. 29). Strengths of the study include a theoretically derived research design and clear description of method and data analyses. Limitations of the study noted by the author include self-selection bias of participants (participants self-identified as biracial in order to be included) and type of setting (predominantly White campuses, highly selective, residential).

Several other published studies have used autobiographical approaches to understanding biracial identity development (e.g., Fukuyama, 1999; Gatson, 2003; Hall, 1992; Maxwell, 1998). Fukuyama described her own personal experience of growing up biracial, noting both developmental and contextual aspects affecting her identity development. Gatson used an autoethnographic approach to confront her Blackness, her Whiteness, and her biracialness. Both studies were unique in taking a more personal approach to understanding race identity, illustrating internal psychological processes that might point to future research. However, given the storytelling approach of both Fukuyama and Gatson, evaluation of the research methodology is not relevant; generalization of these works is not possible or appropriate.

A number of dissertations culled from *Dissertation Abstracts International* also have been conducted examining the race identity of biracial people. The majority of these projects have used qualitative or blended designs (Adermann, 2000; Basu, 2000; Buxenbaum, 1996; Coleman, 2001; Henriksen, 2001; Knaus, 2002; Marks, 2002; Martinez, 2001; Quintana, 1999; Ross, 1996; Saucedo, 2002; Storrs, 1996; Thompson, 1999; Tomoshima, 2000; van Blommestein, 2002), and others have attempted to examine identity using existing measures (Cooke, 1998; J. E. Jones, 2000; Ono, 2000). Space does not allow for a complete review of these studies, but many of the findings appear to converge on themes of fluidity and variations in the racial identity of biracial people, along with the importance of a supportive environment, beginning with family relations, for developing a positive racial identity.

CRITIQUE OF EXISTING RESEARCH AND IMPLICATIONS FOR FUTURE RESEARCH AND THEORY

As can be seen in the preceding review, research on biracial people has grown substantially since 1990 and includes both quantitative and qualitative designs, each with a variety of strengths and limitations. The use of qualitative designs has been promoted by several scholars in the study of biracial people. Both Root (2002) and Renn (2000) noted that given the unique stories of their biracial participants, these designs are the most effective means of studying this group. Generally, the themes described by researchers from such studies point to the fluidity, fluctuations, and variability in the race and racial identity development of biracial people. However, although the findings of many of these studies might be credible, a common problem with qualitative designs is their lack of generalizability (indeed, this is generally not the goal of qualitative studies). It is difficult to ascertain how themes found in one or another biracial participant group might help psychologists and other mental health professionals understand and assess identity development of biracial people in general. Thus, there is currently a need to incorporate designs that have potential for generalizing results (e.g., larger samples, use of control groups, use of standardized measures).

To be sure, the groundbreaking nature of much of the research on biracial people reviewed here must be acknowledged; as described earlier, research on biracial people brings a unique set of challenges to overcome to present information that is accurate and applicable to others (Root, 2002). Several problems were common among the studies reviewed here, including small, highly regional, and self-selected samples; lack of standardized instruments; lack of consistency in definitions of race identity variables; and lack of clarity or consistency regarding data analytic procedures (e.g., procedures of data analyses were not described). Most of the literature on psychological adjustment of biracial people did not use racial identity variables to assess impact of biracial identity on other aspects of functioning; instead, the label "biracial" was generally used as the independent variable. There also was confusion and lack of consistency regarding use of the terms *race, ethnicity,* and *culture*, making research findings difficult to interpret and apply elsewhere. Moreover, a key variable regarding the sociopolitical nature of race and racial identity, physical appearance (e.g., skin color, physical features), was measured by only a handful of studies reviewed in the chapter. Inclusion of this variable in future studies may add clarity to the effect of one's physical appearance in racial identity development of biracial people, as well as social acceptance or rejection in various racial/ethnic communities. Finally, much of the research reviewed here focused on adolescents and young adults, and thus little is known about life span issues affecting biracial people.

Interestingly, although a number of scholars have criticized the validity of racial identity development models for biracial/multiracial people, few studies have actually been conducted in this area. Indeed, in contrast to the criticism that RID models apparently do not account for race as a social construction, it is important to point out that RID models, and subsequent research using RID models, were among the first psychological theories to actually address race as a social construct. Cognitive strategies or statuses of RID models reflect qualitatively different constructions of race and thus seem to account for some variability inherent in racial identity development. Current RID models no longer posit an invariant stage-wise progress of racial identity development (Helms, 1995), instead focusing on the differing statuses used by both people of Color and White Americans in predicting psychological functioning (Carter, 1995). As well, although it is likely that RID models do not predict important aspects of racial identity of biracial people, they highlight critical commonalities of identity development for monoracial and biracial people (Helms, 1995). As noted by Miville and Helms (1996; Miville, Koonce, Darlington, & Whitlock, 2000), general common racial identity processes might be described as (1) Emergence/Conflicts of Identities and (2) Resolutions, either Internal or External. Thus, RID models do not necessarily preclude the development of more specific racial identity models for biracial people. At the same time, RID models identify critical common factors or processes that biracial people, along with people of Color in general, in the United States must negotiate in their development of a positive racial identity. Such processes relate to experiences with overt racism and finding supportive others in the community with whom to identify. Common processes of RID models based on privilege might also be examined for their validity and relevance with biracial people.

It would be more fruitful to use a both/and or blended approach in theorizing and researching race and racial identity of biracial people. It is reasonable to propose that there are aspects of racial identity development shared across people of Color (e.g., experiences of oppression/racism, exclusion, one-drop rule, social grouping, at-risk nature of being a person of Color in physical and psychological well-being) that are relevant to explore regarding their impact on biracial people. Similarly, issues of privilege affecting Whites also might be explored for their psychological impact on biracial people. The experience of being biracial is part of a larger sociopolitical context of racist policies affecting eople of Color and Whites. Logically then, there is likely some validity of RID models in understanding biracial people that points to further research at this time. RID research might explore not only identity development, but the impact of racial identity statuses on other aspects of psychological functioning. At the same time, the unique experiences and stories of biracial people must continue to be explored and articulated, for example, identifying unique sources of bias, conflicts, strengths, and resolutions. These experiences and processes include ambivalence and fluidity regarding social group and self-definitions, the search for an overarching community, crossing bridges/loosening social boundaries, and transcendence of or use of multiple racial labels as part of one's identity. Both qualitative and quantitative designs might be used to assess these areas. As well, given the current number of theories already existing on race and racial identity development of biracial people, it seems more useful at this time to test the validity and applicability of existing theories, whether they are RID or uniquely descriptive of biracial identity development, rather than create more theories on biracial identity development.

REFERENCES

Adams, J. L. (1997). Multiracial identity development: Developmental correlates and themes among multiracial adults. *Dissertation Abstracts International, 58*(5-B), 2662. (UMI No. 9731576)

Adermann, C. Y. (2000). A narrative approach to biracial identity development. *Dissertation Abstracts International, 61*(4-B), 2188. (UMI No. 9969184)

Basu, A. M. (2000). Biracial identity and social context. *Dissertation Abstracts International, 61*(4-B), 2268. (UMI No. 9969674)

Brown, N. G., & Douglass, R. E. (1996). Making the invisible visible: The growth of community network organizations. In M. P. P. Root (Ed.), *The multiracial experience: Racial borders as the new frontier* (pp. 323–340). Thousand Oaks, CA: Sage.

Brown, U. M. (2001). *The interracial experience: Growing up Black/White racially mixed in the United States.* Westport, CT: Praeger.

Buxenbaum, K. U. (1996). Racial identity development and its relationship to physical appearance and self-esteem in adults with one Black and one White biological parent. *Dissertation Abstracts International, 57*(5-B), 3430. (UMI No. 9630707)

Carter, R. T. (1995). *The influence of race and racial identity in psychotherapy: Toward a racially inclusive model.* New York: Wiley.

Cauce, A. M., Hiraga, Y., Mason, C., Agilar, T., Ordonez, N., & Gonzales, N. (1992). Between a rock and a hard place: Social adjustment of biracial youth. In M. P. P. Root (Ed.), *Racially mixed people in America* (pp. 207–222). Newbury Park, CA: Sage.

Coleman, N. L. (2001). Biracial identity development of individuals of African-American and European-American parentage. *Dissertation Abstracts International, 61*(5-B), 6162. (UMI No. 9992964)

Collins, J. F. (2000). Biracial Japanese American identity: An evolving process. *Cultural Diversity and Ethnic Minority Psychology, 6*(2), 115–133.

Cooke, T. I. (1998). Biracial identity development: Psychosocial contributions to self-esteem and racial identity. *Dissertation Abstracts International, 58*(10-B), 5669. (UMI No. 9812836)

Cooney, T. M., & Radina, M. E. (2000). Adjustment problems in adolescence: Are multiracial children at risk? *American Journal of Orthopsychiatry, 70*(4), 433–444.

Cross, W. E., Jr. (1971). The Negro-to-Black conversion experience: Toward a psychology of Black liberation. *Black World, 20*, 13–27.

Cross, W. E., Jr. (1991). *Shades of Black: Diversity in African-American identity.* Philadelphia: Temple University Press.

Fatimilehin, I. A. (1999). Of Jewel Heritage: Racial socialization and racial identity attitudes amongst adolescents of mixed African-Caribbean/White parentage. *Journal of Adolescence, 22*, 303–318.

Field, L. D. (1996). Piecing together the puzzle: Self-concept and group identity in biracial Black/White youth. In M. P. P. Root (Ed.), *The multiracial experience: Racial borders as the new frontier* (pp. 211–226). Thousand Oaks, CA: Sage.

Fukuyama, M. A. (1999). Personal narrative: Growing up biracial. *Journal of Counseling and Development, 77*(1), 12–14.

Gatson, S. N. (2003). On being amorphous: Autoethnography, genealogy, and a multiracial identity. *Qualitative Inquiry, 9*(1), 20–48.

Gibbs, J. T. (2003). Biracial and bicultural children and adolescents. In J. T. Gibbs & L. N. Huang (Eds.), *Children of Color: Psychological interventions with culturally diverse youth* (pp. 145–182). San Francisco: Jossey-Bass.

Gibbs, J. T., & Hines, A. M. (1992). Negotiating ethnic identity: Issues for Black-White biracial adolescents. In M. P. P. Root (Ed.), *Racially mixed people in America* (pp. 223–238). Newbury Park, CA: Sage.

Gillem, A. R., Cohn, L. R., & Throne, C. (2001). Black identity in biracial Black/White people: A comparison of Jacqueline who refuses to be exclusively Black and Adolphus who wishes he were. *Cultural Diversity and Ethnic Minority Psychology, 7*(2), 182–196.

Hall, C. C. I. (1992). Please choose one: Ethnic identity choices for biracial individuals. In M. P. P. Root (Ed.), *Racially mixed people in America* (pp. 250–264). Newbury Park, CA: Sage.

Harrison, P. M. (1997). Racial identification and self-concept issues in biracial (Black/White) adolescent girls. *Dissertation Abstracts International, 58*(4-B), 2123. (UMI No. 9728213)

Helms, J. E. (1990). *Black and White racial identity: Theory, research, and practice.* New York: Greenwood Press.

Helms, J. E. (1995). An update on Helms's White and people of Color racial identity models. In J. G. Poterooto, J. M. Casas, L. A. Suzuki, & C. M. Alexander (Eds.), *Handbook of multicultural counseling* (pp. 181–191). Thousand Oaks, CA: Sage.

Henriksen, R. C., Jr. (2001). Black/White biracial identity development: A grounded theory study. *Dissertation Abstracts International, 61*(7-A), 2605. (UMI No. 9980430)

Jacobs, J. H. (1992). Identity development in biracial children. In M. P. P. Root (Ed.), *Racially mixed people in America* (pp. 190–206). Newbury Park, CA: Sage.

Johnson, D. J. (1992). Racial preference and biculturality in biracial preschoolers. *Merrill-Palmer Quarterly, 38*(2), 233–244.

Johnson, T. P., Jobe, J. B., O'Rourke, D., Sudman, S., Warnecke, R. B., Chavez, N., et al. (1997). Dimensions of self-identification among multiracial and multiethnic respondents in survey interviews. *Evaluation Review, 21*(6), 671–687.

Jones, J. E. (2000). Multiethnic identity development, psychological adjustment, and parental attachment in adolescence. *Dissertation Abstracts International, 60*(10-B), 5227. (UMI No. 9948297)

Jones, N. A., & Smith, A. S. (2001). *Census 2000 brief: Two or more races, U.S. Census Bureau.* Retrieved May 30, 2003, from http://www.census.gov/prod/2001pubs/c2kbr01–6.pdf.

Karasaki, D. M. A. (1998). The self-esteem of preschool age biracial children as predicted by their racial identity, their parents' racial identity, and their parents' self-esteem. *Dissertation Abstracts International, 58*(10-A), 4081. (UMI No. 9812122)

Kerwin, C., & Ponterotto, J. G. (1995). Biracial identity development: Theory and research. In J. G. Ponterotto, J. M. Casas, L. A. Suzuki, & Alexander, C. M. (Eds.), *Handbook of multicultural counseling* (pp. 199–217). Thousand Oaks, CA: Sage.

Kerwin, C., Ponterotto, J. G., Jackson, B. L., & Harris, A. (1993). Racial identity in biracial children: A qualitative investigation. *Journal of Counseling Psychology, 40,* 221–231.

Kich, G. K. (1992). The developmental process of asserting a biracial, bicultural identity. In M. P. P. Root (Ed.), *Racially mixed people in America* (pp. 250–264). Newbury Park, CA: Sage.

Knaus, C. B. (2002). They are still asking the "What are you?" question: Race, racism, and multiracial people in higher education. *Dissertation Abstracts International, 63*(11-B), 3824. (UMI No. 9992964)

Marks, J. B. (2002). Multiracial women in psychology doctoral programs: A phenomenological investigation of their identities in graduate school. *Dissertation Abstracts International, 63*(1-B), 537. (UMI No. 3040103)

Martinez, L. (2001). A qualitative study of adolescents' reactions to being biethnic Mexican American/Euro-American. *Dissertation Abstracts International, 62*(5-B), 2492. (UMI No. 3015907)

Mass, A. I. (1992). Interracial Japanese Americans: The best of both worlds or the end of the Japanese American community? In M. P. P. Root (Ed.), *Racially mixed people in America* (pp. 265–279). Newbury Park, CA: Sage.

Maxwell, A. (1998). Not all issues are Black or White: Some voices from the offspring of cross-cultural marriages. In R. Breger & R. Hill (Eds.), *Cross-cultural marriage: Identity and choice* (pp. 209–228). Oxford, England: Berg.

McKelvey, R. S., & Webb, J. A. (1996). A comparative study of Vietnamese Amerasians, their non-Amerasian siblings, and unrelated, like-aged Vietnamese immigrants. *American Journal of Psychiatry, 153*(4), 561–563.

Milan, S., & Keiley, M. K. (2000). Biracial youth and families in therapy: Issues and interventions. *Journal of Marital and Family Therapy, 26*(3), 305–315.

Miville, M. L., Baysden, M. F., & So-Lloyd, G. (1999, August). *Multiracial identity development: An investigation of emerging themes.* Poster session at the annual meeting of the American Psychological Association, Boston.

Miville, M. L., & Helms, J. E. (1996, August). *Exploring relationships of cultural, gender, and personal identity among Latinos/as.* Poster presentation at the annual meeting of the American Psychological Association, Toronto, Ontario, Canada.

Miville, M. L., Koonce, D., Darlington, P., & Whitlock, B. (2000). Exploring the relationships between racial/cultural identity and ego identity among African Americans and Mexican Americans. *Journal of Multicultural Counseling and Development, 28,* 208–224.

Mukoyama, T. H. (1998). Effects of heritage combination on ethnic identity, self-esteem, and adjustment among American biethnic adults. *Dissertation Abstracts International, 59*(4-B), 1864. (UMI No. 9831033)

Mur, L. Y. (1999). An investigation of the relations between the psychological functioning and coping processes of interracial Black/White young adults and their racial identity outcomes. *Dissertation Abstracts International, 60*(1-B), 0403. (UMI No. 9917180)

Newsome, C. (2002). Multiple identities: The case of biracial children. In V. H. Milhouse, M. K. Asante, & P. O. Nwosu (Eds.), *Transcultural realities: Interdisciplinary perspectives on cross-cultural relations* (pp. 145–159). Thousand Oaks, CA: Sage.

Oliver, L. (2002). Multi-heritage identity: Self-identification, perceptions of others, and psychological well-being. *Dissertation Abstracts International, 63*(10-B), 4954. (UMI No. 3067907)

Ono, L. J. (2000). Parental relationships and ethnic identity of biracial European/Japanese American young adults. *Dissertation Abstracts International, 61*(5-B), 2818. (UMI No. 9973851)

Phinney, J. S. (1992). The Multigroup Ethnic Identity Measure: A new scale for use with diverse groups. *Journal of Adolescent Research, 7,* 156–176.

Phinney, J. S., & Alipuria, L. L. (1996). At the interface of cultures: Multiethnic/multiracial high school students and college students. *Journal of Social Psychology, 136*(2), 139–158.

Pierce, S. M. (1992). A study of biracial children and their self-concept and self-esteem. *Masters Abstracts International, 30*(1), 57. (UMI No. 1345890)

Quintana, E. D. (1999). Racial and ethnic identity development in biracial people. *Dissertation Abstracts International, 60*(3-B), 1313. (UMI No. 9924283)

Renn, K. A. (1999, April). *Space to grow: Creating an ecology model of bi- and multiracial identity development in college students.* Paper presented at the annual meeting of the American Educational Research Association, Montreal, Ontario, Canada.

Renn, K. A. (2000, April). *Tilting at windmills: The paradox of researching mixed-race.* Paper presented at the annual meeting of the American Educational Research Association, New Orleans, LA.

Renn, K. A. (2003). Understanding the identities of mixed-race college students through a developmental ecology lens. *Journal of College Student Development, 44,* 383–403.

Rockquemore, K. A. (1998). Between Black and White: Exploring the biracial experience. *Race and Society, 1,* 197–212.

Rockquemore, K. A. (2002). *Beyond Black: Biracial identity in America.* Thousand Oaks, CA: Sage.

Rockquemore, K. A., & Brunsma, D. L. (2002). Socially embedded identities: Theories, typologies, and processes of racial identity among Black/White biracials. *Sociological Quarterly, 43*(3), 335–356.

Root, M. P. P. (1992). Back to the drawing board: Methodological issues in research on multiracial people. In M. P. P. Root (Ed.), *Racially mixed people in America* (pp. 181–189). Newbury Park, CA: Sage.

Root, M. P. P. (1996). *The multiracial experience: Racial borders as the new frontier.* Thousand Oaks, CA: Sage.

Root, M. P. P. (1998). Experiences and processes affecting racial identity development: Preliminary results from the Biracial Sibling Project. *Cultural Diversity and Mental Health, 4*(3), 237–247.

Root, M. P. P. (1999). The biracial baby boom: Understanding ecological constructions of racial identity in the 21st century. In R. Hernandez-Sheets & E. R. Hollins (Eds.), *Racial and ethnic identity in school practices: Aspects of human development* (pp. 67–90). Mahwah, NJ: Erlbaum.

Root, M. P. P. (2002). Methodological issues in multiracial research. In G. C. N. Hall & S. Okazaki (Eds.), *Asian American psychology: The science of lives in context* (pp. 171–193). Washington, DC: American Psychological Association.

Ross, D. (1996). In their own words: Mixed-heritage children in the United States. *Dissertation Abstracts International, 56*(11-A), 4329. (UMI No. 9606555)

Saucedo, E. N. (2002). Profiles of Black Latinos in academe: The identity dilemma and the perception of self. *Dissertation Abstracts International, 63*(11-A), 3879. (UMI No. 3069848)

Shepherd, T. L. (1997). Beliefs and attitudes about biraciality and their relationship to psychological adjustment. *Dissertation Abstracts International, 571*(9-A), 4145. (UMI No. 9704930)

Storrs, D. A. (1996). Mixed race women: The construction and contestation of racial boundaries, meanings, and identities. *Dissertation Abstracts International, 57*(11-A), 4943. (UMI No. 9714508)

Thompson, C. A. (1999). Identity resolution in biracial Black/White individuals: The process of asserting a biracial identity. *Dissertation Abstracts International, 59*(12-B), 6498. (UMI No. 9915022)

Tizard, B., & Phoenix, A. (1995). The identity of mixed parentage adolescents. *Journal of Child Psychology and Psychiatry, 36*(8), 1399–1410.

Tomoshima, S. A. (2000). Factors and experiences in biracial and biethnic identity development. *Dissertation Abstracts International, 61*(2-B), 1114. (UMI No. 9963109)

Tremayne, K. J. (1998). The relationship between self-esteem, psychological adjustment and ethnic identity among biracial Japanese American/Caucasian American adults. *Dissertation Abstracts International, 58*(8-B), 4475. (UMI No. 9805040)

Twine, F. W. (1996). Brown skinned White girls: Class, culture and the construction of White identity in suburban communities. *Gender, Place, and Culture, 3*(2), 205–224.

van Blommestein, J. J. (2002). A racial journey with lived identities: The cumulative experience of individuals with Black-White parentage in a White-dominated society. *Dissertation Abstracts International, 64*(5-A), 1092. (UMI No. 3084058)

Wehrly, B., Kenney, K. R., & Kenney, M. W. (1999). *Counseling multiracial families.* Thousand Oaks, CA: Sage.

Winn, N. N., & Priest, R. (1993). Counseling biracial children: A forgotten component of multicultural counseling. *Family Therapy, 20,* 29–36.

Zwiebach-Sherman, C. (1999). Personal, community and familial influences on racial identification choice and positive psychological well-being among biracial adults. *Dissertation Abstracts International, 60*(5-B), 2414. (UMI No. 9929064)

CHAPTER 17

An Inquiry into the Measurement
of Ethnic and Racial Identity

Joseph E. Trimble

> *For there are nearly as many ways in which such identities, fleeting or en-*
> *during, sweeping or intimate, cosmopolitan or closed-in, amiable or bloody-*
> *minded, are put together as there are materials with which to put them*
> *together and reasons for doing so . . . answers people sometimes give to the*
> *question, whether self-asked or asked by others, as to who (or, perhaps,*
> *more exactly, what) they are—simply do not form an orderly structure.*
> —Clifford Geertz (2000, p. 225)

The words of the distinguished cultural anthropologist Clifford Geertz set the tone
and framework for the central theme of this chapter: The assessment and measurement of racial and ethnic identity is complicated and filled with many problems,
owing in part to the fact that human beings have multiple, intertwined identities
that influence one another in ways that are not fully understood. Multiple identities
come in many forms. No one is a member solely of a distinct racial or ethnic group,
just as no one is solely a man or a woman. All persons are members of particular
age groups and have particular sexual orientations. They may have disabilities. In
addition, they may follow vocations that provide them with unique role identities.
The enactment and nature of an individual's multiple identities can be influenced
by an individual's *lifeways* and *thoughtways,* which may be at variance with conventional expectations and proscriptions. A person's multiple identities, as well as
the sociocultural contexts in which these identities are enacted, must be factored
into the measurement of an identity construct. However, as we will see, most of the
research on the measurement of identity has been limited to the abstraction of race
and ethnicity at a social and psychological level of analysis; other dimensions of
identity are given less attention in the psychological literature.

In the past 20 years or so, considerable attention has been devoted to the measurement of ethnic and racial identity, although interest in the field extends back as
far as the late 1930s, with the seminal work of Eugene and Ruth Horowitz (R.
Horowitz, 1939; E. L. Horowitz & Horowitz, 1938). For the past hundred years or
so, according to the citations found in the *PsycINFO* electronic database, slightly

more that 4,623 articles have been written on ethnic and racial identity and related constructs; over 80% of them have been published since 1980. During the same period, close to 237 articles have been devoted to the measurement of racial and ethnic identity; this represents about 5% of the total articles devoted to the two constructs. Most of the articles are devoted to discussions about the constructs' meanings, uses, and implications in a variety of political, social, and psychological arenas of discourse and practice; few appear to be devoted to the actual social and psychological assessment of the constructs. Nonetheless, the accelerated interest in the field suggests that we must stop and take stock of the field's progress and its future directions. The growth in the field and the attendant methodological and procedural problems and theoretical debates point to the need for an inquiry in the measurement of these elusive constructs. To accomplish this goal, this chapter first provides a brief overview of the two constructs, including disparate and conflicting views on their relevance. Following this, attention is given to a review and summary of selected and representative measures currently in use and the theories underlying their development; a discussion of the measures is organized according to the level of measurement sophistication and precision employed by their developers. The last section of the chapter deals with selected measurement and methodological problems and issues associated with the conduct of research with distinct *ethnocultural* populations that are currently being voiced by theoreticians and researchers.

THOUGHTS ON THE ORIGINS OF IDENTITY AND RACIAL AND ETHNIC IDENTITY CONSTRUCTS

The term *identity* has Latin origins and is derived from the word *identitas;* the word is formed from *idem,* meaning "same." Thus, the term is used to express the notion of sameness, likeness, and oneness. More precisely, identity means "the sameness of a person or thing at all times in all circumstances; the condition or fact that a person or thing is itself and not something else" (Simpson & Weiner, 1989, p. 620). The psychoanalyst Erik Erikson (1968) undoubtedly has contributed to the ongoing debate in psychology and psychiatry about identity and its development and formation. According to Erikson, identity is located in the self or core of the individual and his or her communal culture; self-esteem and one's sense of affiliation and belongingness are deeply affected by the process. Furthermore, Erikson argued that identity is inextricably linked to self-understanding and therefore can be posited "as the academic metaphor for self-in-context" (Fitzgerald, 1993, p. ix). Erikson also maintained that the transformations from childhood through adolescence presented role clarification challenges that often created identity confusion. The confusion often emerged from interactions with peers and the context and situations youth face on a daily basis. Without a context, identity formation and self-development couldn't occur. Identity is a part of one's sense of self, and it enables if not permits individuals to respond to "the question, whether self-asked or asked by others, as to who (or, perhaps, more exactly, what) they are" (Geertz, 2000, p. 225).

Moynihan (1993) argues that identity is "a process located in the core of the individual and yet, also, in the case of his communal culture" (p. 64). It's a powerful phenomenon that strongly influences personality, one's sense of belonging, one's sense of sameness, and one's quality of life. To further an understanding of identity, most social and psychological theorists must contend with the concept of self. And to approach an understanding of the self concept, one is obliged to provide plausible if not substantial explanations for the following domains: physical traits and characteristics, personal experiences and their memory, personal behaviors, "what belongs to me and what I belong to," "the person I believe myself to be," and "who and what others tell me I am" (Cirese, 1985). Explanations for these domains consume volumes.

The term *ethnic* has Latin and Greek origins: *ethnicus* and *ethnikas* both mean nation. It can and has been used historically to refer to people as heathens. *Ethos* in Greek means custom, disposition, or trait. Ethnikas and ethos taken together therefore can mean a band of people (a nation) living together who share common customs.

Although the bulk of the social and behavioral studies circumscribed to the ethnic variables concentrate on the ethnic minority element, interest in ethnic phenomena in general actually is far more inclusive. Social science interest in ethnicity, especially as a potential explanatory variable, began in the late 1940s (see Cross, 1991; Juby & Concepción, this *Handbook,* Volume One; Katz & Taylor, 1988). Interest was fueled by at least two fundamental concerns: the contentious notion that the United States was a melting pot of different nationalities, ethnic groups, and religious affiliations and the then escalating abiding concerns about pluralism and integration. The era "witnessed an outbreak of what might be called 'ethnic fever,' " maintains Steinberg (1981, p. 3), in which "the nation's racial and ethnic minorities sought to rediscover their waning ethnicity and to reaffirm their ties to the cultural past." Integration and the melting pot notion were challenged, if not vilified; the melting pot notion was transformed from a perceived fact to a myth, and those who resisted integration were brought to their knees by civil rights legislation.

As a widely used construct to refer to types of people, *race* has multiple meanings and therefore is not an easy term to define. For example, Helms (1994) maintains:

> Ethnicity is often used as a euphemism for race, as well as for other sociocultural affiliations (such as religious and linguistic groups) [thus] it might better be defined as social identity based on the culture of one's ancestors' national or tribal group as modified by the demands of the CULTURE in which one's group currently resides. (p. 293)

To add to the complexity of the construct, Helms also maintains that "race has three types of definitions: (1) quasi-biological, (2) sociopolitical-historical, and (3) cultural. Each type may have relevance for how race becomes one of an individual's collective identities" (p. 297).

The race construct likely has it origins in the writings of ancient Greek historians and philosophers (see Sollors, 2002). According to the cultural anthropologist John Honigmann (1959), for example, Herodotus used the term *ethnea* to refer to humans who belong to different groups. Herodotus, however, did not base his classifications of humans on physical traits; thus, it's likely his term was synonymous with the term *ethnic group.* Use of physical traits and characteristics to define humans began in the 19th century, when the term *Aryan races* was first coined by Joseph de Gobineau (Honigmann, 1959).

Young (1999) traces the origin of the construct to Carolus Linnaeus, who maintained that "human beings come from four types: *Americanus, Asiaticus, Africanus,* and *Europeaecus*" (p. 219). Following Linnaeus, at some point physical anthropologists in the early twentieth century initiated a classification system by which humans where grouped into one of four races: *Mongoloid, Negroid, Australoid,* and *Caucasoid;* that classification system prevailed for the majority of the century. However, in the last quarter of the twentieth century the fourfold system fell from use, owing to problems associated with blood-gene groupings, race mixtures, and the inability to group humans into four or more discrete categories (Yee, Fairchild, Weizmann, & Wyatt, 1993). Moreover, on this point, Allport (1958) emphasized:

(1) except in remote parts of the earth very few human beings belong to a pure stock; and (2) most human characteristics ascribed to race are undoubtedly due to cultural diversity and should therefore be regarded as ethnic, not racial. (p. 111)

While there are calls from the social and behavioral science community for the elimination of the use of race as a labeling construct, there are compelling reasons for its continued use in the study of identity and identity development and formation (B. P. Allen & Adams, 1992; Yee et al., 1993). Few would seriously claim that racism and all its ugly and oppressive forms no longer exist; to eliminate the use of the race construct would obscure if not deny the racist experiences of millions of people who are subjected to it on a constant basis. To merely classify these experiences with the terms *prejudice* or *discrimination* takes away or obfuscates the painful sting of racism. Hence, to forcefully confront racism headlong race must be kept at the forefront of our vocabulary when discussing intergroup and interpersonal relations (Jones, 2003).

Race is a social construction, and although it has little, if any, use in classifying humans from a biological or anthropometrical perspective, it does have use as a social-political category (see Root, 1998, 2000). Helms and Cook (1999) emphasize the significance of the continued use of race because "we want to encourage consideration of the differential environmental significance of the various racial classifications as communicated through powerful societal socialization messages" (p. 30). Helms (2001) also firmly maintains that "racial identity theories do not suppose that racial groups in the United States are biologically distinct but rather suppose that they have endured different conditions of domination or oppression" (p. 181). Thus, for the eminent psychologist Janet E. Helms, racial identity:

refers to the psychological mechanisms that people develop to function effectively in a society where some people enjoy social and political advantage because of their ancestors' (presumed) physical appearances, but others suffer disadvantage and lower status for the same reasons. (Trimble, Helms, & Root, 2002, pp. 249–250; see Helms, 1996)

As an alterative to race, Helms recommends using *sociorace* to acknowledge "the fact that typically the only criteria used to assign people to racial groups in this country are socially defined and arbitrary" (p. 147). To emphasize her point, she contends that there are least nine characteristics that differentiate sociorace from ethnicity. In devising measurement approaches to assess identity, close attention should be given to the distinction between race and ethnicity, as they are different constructs. While research on ethnicity appears to dominate the literature, we must be mindful that as long as racism exists, the term race must continue to be used, if for no other reason than because there is no other word powerful or robust enough in the English language to truly capture the demeaning and debilitating experiences of those victimized by racists.

Combining the definitions and interpretations of identity, ethnicity, and race, it can be concluded that they mean or at minimum imply the sameness of a band or nation of people who share common customs and traditions; certain bands or nations may share common experiences born from oppression, domination, and colonialism. At one level of interpretation, the combined definition is sufficient to capture the manner in which identity is generally conceptualized and used to measure ethnocultural influences on its formation and development (see Trimble & Dickson, in press b). The psychologist Jean Phinney (1990) notes that there are "widely discrepant definitions and measures of ethnic identity, which makes generalizations and comparisons across studies difficult and ambiguous" (p. 500). Currently, the most widely used definition of the construct in psychology is the one developed by Phinney (1990, 2000, 2003): "Ethnic identity is a dynamic, multidimensional construct that refers to one's identity, or sense of self as a member of an ethnic group" (2003, p. 63). From her perspective, one claims an identity in the context of a subgroup that claims a common ancestry and shares at least a similar culture, race, religion, language, kinship, or place of origin. She adds:

> Ethnic identity is not a fixed categorization, but rather is a fluid and dynamic understanding of self and ethnic background. Ethnic identity is constructed and modified as individuals become aware of their ethnicity, within the large (sociocultural) setting. (2003, p. 63)

At another level, the term identity is almost synonymous with the term ethnicity, prompting some sociologists, such as Herbert Gans (2003), to suggest that identity is no longer a useful term.

BACKGROUND THOUGHTS ON ETHNICITY, ETHNIC IDENTITY, AND ETHNIC SELF-IDENTIFICATION

Ethnicity and race, or racial, are the principal cultural constructs used to measure identification, identity development, and identity formation, the three areas that subsume most of the literature in the field. The ethnic construct dominates literature themes; race or racial is limited to a few measures of the overarching identity construct. A few researchers argue for replacing the term race with ethnicity, and still others prefer to use the term *culture* to refer to the identity process ostensibly lodged in one's ethnocultural orientation and ancestral history. As psychosocial constructs, ethnic identity and ethnic self-identification are not without controversy, as there are varied views on their salience, relevance, stability, characteristics, and influences. Add to the discussion and debate that identity, whatever form it takes, is rarely static and immutable. To emphasize this point, Fitzgerald (1993) maintains that it is a mistake to think of identity as an unchanging entity, as "it is the illusion of unity that is still quite real with most people" (p. 32). Social categories and people are protean; they do not present an orderly structure that lends itself to measurement and comprehension.

In this section, selected social and psychological theories and perspectives are presented in summary form and reflected against the ethnic and racial identification events that occur in one's life. Two points must be made clear: (1) Provincial and theoretical attempts to explain and predict ethnic and racial identity are inconclusive and speculative, and (2) people do construct life stories for themselves that often are mutable, and the uncertainty of the story can be sufficient motivation for one to seek and find a portion of one's ancestral history to lend structure, meaning, and stability to one's life.

Ethnic identification and ethnic transformations are not solely private acts "but are usually if not predominantly public concerns, problematic situations, and issues of public contention as well as private debate" (Strauss, 1959, p. 26). Often, ethnic and racial identity declarations, especially those of mixed ethnic background, require external validation; thus, the judgments of others play a key role in the transaction (Root, 2000). People typically construct their identity in the context of their biological background and the sociopolitical context in which they are socialized. Moreover, people often construct autobiographies to place themselves in the social order and seek out settings and situations for confirmation (Harré, 1989). Hence, we find people constructing their identity and self-image to fit preferred sociocultural contexts and constructing the situations and contexts to fit the preferred image (Fitzgerald, 1993). Identity and all its derivatives are not static: People change, and their identity and sense of self change accordingly.

Social and psychological interest in ethnicity and identity has generated a prolific increase in journal articles and books on the subject. Few claim that ethnicity is a benign topic; some refer to it as the "new ethnicity" because it is viewed as divisive, inegalitarian, and racist (Morgan, 1981). On occasion, the mention of ethnicity and identity, especially in academic circles, sparks discussion about segregation and that without it, ethnicity would not survive. Sometimes the discussion turns to the possibility that Americans overemphasize and exaggerate the existence and beneficence of ethnicity (Yinger, 1986); such phrases as "imagined ethnicity" and "pseudo-ethnicity" are used interchangeably to refer to those who foist some ethnic factor to justify an action. In a related vein, when it comes to conducting research on ethnic factors, Gordon (1978) asserts, "Students of ethnicity run the risk of finding ethnic practices where they are not, of ascribing an ethnic social and cultural order where they do not in fact influence the person" (p. 151). Consequently, critics argue about some fanciful line that somehow separates ethnic influences from nonethnic ones. The argument begs the questions When can behavior, personality, values, attitudes, and so on be attributed to ethnic and racial factors? and If an ethnic or racial attribution is not possible or discernible, then what sociocultural and psychological influence can account for the phenomenon?

Greeley (1974) asks an important and related question: "Why . . . is ethnic identity important and useful for some Americans?" (p. 298). One relatively benign answer is that ethnicity serves as a convenient form of differentiation: Ethnic minorities can be differentiated from the dominant society and from one another (American Indians from African Americans, Puerto Ricans from Cuban Americans, Japanese Americans from Chinese Americans, etc.), neighborhoods and communities can be differentiated from one another (Navajo Nation reservation, Chinatown, Japantown, Little Italy, etc.), and it can serve to differentiate among and between individuals who do not appear to subscribe to a generalized normative behavioral diet that often occurs in stereotypic imagery, ethnic labeling, and the pejorative nomenclature of intergroup relations.

Ethnicity and ethnic identity are not likely to vanish. All countries differentiate their residents on some ethnic factor, and North America may well be an area where it is most prevalent. Barth (1969) argues that ethnic boundaries, especially for European immigrants, are more permeable in the United States than in less industrialized societies, but that the "ethnic distinctions are quite . . . often the very foundation on which embracing social systems are built" (p. 10). For many Americans, most notably the major ethnic minority groups, identity is the central core of their interpersonal system, and for a social support system to remain reasonably stable identity must be available, stable, and acceptable.

Several anthropologists, historians, psychologists, and sociologists have written extensively on ethnicity and ethnic and racial identity (for reviews, see Bernal & Knight, 1993; Carter, 1996; Cross, 1991; Harris, Blue, & Griffith, 1995; Helms, 1990, 1996; Steinberg, 1981; Thompson, 1989; Trimble, Helms, & Root, 2003; van den Berghe, 1981). The many theoretical positions embraced and advocated range from those that are lodged in individuals' experiences and worldview to those formed from a sociobiological perspective. Barth's (1969) perspective represents the former, where it is the native's worldview that defines relationships, boundaries, lifestyles, and thoughtways. The sociobiological perspective is most fervently represented by Pierre van den Berghe, who maintains that "ethnic and racial sentiments are extensions of kinship sentiments" (p. 18); thus, "decent . . . is the central feature of ethnicity" (p. 27). To support his argument, he asserts that "there exists a general predisposition, in our species as in many others, to react favorably toward other organisms to the extent that those organisms are biologically related to the actor" (p. 19).

A review of the various treatises written about ethnicity leads one to the inevitable conclusion that it is a complex subject. In its broadest form, it refers to "any differentiation based on nationality, race, religion, or language" (Greeley, 1974, p. 89). At a slightly more precise level, some theorists prefer the definition of ethnicity as "a collectivity within a larger society having real or putative common ancestry, memories of a shared historical past, and a cultural focus on one or more symbolic elements defined as the epitome of their peoplehood" (Schermmerhorn, 1969, p. 123). Using this definition, Greeley maintains that individuals can be classified "into groups on the basis of shared, observable traits to include shared physical characteristics, shared historical experiences, and shared religious identities" (p. 188). Note that the sociologist Andrew Greeley places an emphasis on using traits to classify individuals; presumably, individuals also use the traits to classify and identify themselves with a distinct ethnic group.

Another sociologist, Milton Yinger (1986), points out:

> Ethnicity has come to refer to anything from a sub-societal group that clearly shows a common descent and cultural background . . . to persons who share a former citizenship although diverse culturally . . . to pan-cultural groups of persons of widely different cultural and societal backgrounds who . . . can be identified as "similar" on the basis of language, race or religion mixed with broadly similar statuses. (p. 23)

Although the many components of Yinger's conceptualization are inclusive and indeed comprehensive as a starting point, he prefers to distinguish between groups by appealing to their unique social and biological characteristics. To form a more concise understanding of the influences of the two characteristics we must find a shared generic cohort of descendants who share recognizable and acknowledged geopolitical boundaries.

Geopolitical boundaries change as a result of political turmoil, colonialism, and globalization; consequently, individuals change their ethnic allegiance and identification as they move from one environment to another or their boundaries are rearranged (Arnett, 2002). Also, changes in affiliation and corresponding changes in the ethnic core can produce "pseudo-ethnicity" (or fictional ethnicity). An ethnic core may be exaggerated and contrived to form "imagined ethnicity," where the relationship between the primordial ethnic core and the emergent form is blended. Some understanding of the complexity can be found in defining "ethnic group," yet another elusive concept.

Definitions of ethnic identity vary according to the underlying theory embraced by researchers and scholars intent on tinkering with conceptual meanings. Social and behavioral science interest in identity focuses on discovering causal or correlational factors with other variables. To advance the discovery process, measurement scales are developed, tested, refined, and applied to scores of conditions, circumstances, and individuals. Even though ethnic identity is a process, many researchers approach the concept as though it were a static phenomenon. Moreover, without giving much serious thought to the topic, many researchers actually use ethnicity instead of ethnic identity, assuming that they are one and the same. They are not.

Often, ethnic identity is associated with one's presumed ethnic personality (see Devereux, 1975). In this context, one's personality is inferred from one's identity with an ethnic group. But, here again, identifiable cultural factors can influence personality development; however, inferring a similarity between identity and personality corrupts both constructs.

Typically, ethnic identity is an affiliative construct whereby individuals are viewed by themselves and by others as belonging to a particular group. An individual can choose to associate with a group, especially if other choices are available (i.e., the person is of mixed ethnic or racial heritage). Affiliation can be influenced by racial, natal, symbolic, and cultural factors (Cheung, 1993). Racial factors involve the use of physiognomic and physical characteristics; natal factors refer to "homeland" (or ancestral home) origins of individuals, their parents, and kin; and symbolic factors include those factors that typify or exemplify an ethnic group (e.g., holidays, foods, clothing, artifacts). Symbolic ethnic identity usually implies that individuals choose their identity; however, to some extent the cultural elements of the ethnic or racial group have a modest influence on their behavior (Kivisto & Nefzger, 1993). Cultural factors refer to the specific *lifeways* and *thoughtways* of an ethnic group and are probably the most difficult to assess and measure (see Cheung, 1993, for more details). In conceptualizing ethnic identity, racial, natal, symbolic, and cultural factors must be considered to achieve a full and complete understanding of the construct.

Cheung (1993) defines ethnic identification as "the psychological attachment to an ethnic group or heritage" (p. 1216) and thus centers the construct in the domain of self-perception. Saharso (1989) extends the definition to include social processes that involve one's choice of friends, selection of a future partner, perception of one's life chances, and the reactions of others in one's social environment. Both definitions involve boundaries by which one makes distinction about "self" and "other"; Saharso's definition extends the other's boundary to include an attribution component. An individual may strongly identify psychologically with an ethnic group; however, the strength and authenticity of the identity is contingent on the acceptance and acknowledgment of ingroup and outgroup members.

In 1990, Phinney summarized the ethnic identity literature that existed for adolescents and adults with an emphasis primarily on measurement and conceptualization. In prefacing her section on ethnic identity definitions, she states, "There is no widely agreed on definition of ethnic identity," and "the definitions that were given reflected quite different understandings or emphasis regarding what is meant by ethnic identity" (p. 500). Undoubtedly, social and behavioral scientists believe they have a general sense for the ethnic construct; some indeed are rather firm about their position (van den Bergh, 1981; Weinreich, 1986; Weinreich & Saunderson, 2003). Identity as a psychological construct, too, is the subject of considerable debate; however, the addition of *ethnic* to identity cast the debate and subsequent hodgepodge of opinion into another domain. In fact, about a quarter of the studies reviewed by Phinney were not built on a theoretical framework.

Several conceptual approaches to ethnic identity emphasize an individual level of analysis in which notions of identity formation and development are linked to one's self-concept. Much of the work in this area relies on Tajfel's (1982) theory of social identity. Tajfel basically maintains that one's social identity strongly influences self-perception and consequently should be the central locus of evaluation.

The strength and weakness of the self are largely determined from our status in our reference groups and how we assess outgroup members. When ethnicity and race form the nexus of an ingroup, then self-identity will be correspondingly influenced. Individuals' distinctive ethnic characteristics, however, can be restrictive, as they may reject "externally based evaluations of the ingroup" and therefore "may establish their own standards and repudiate those of the dominant outgroup" (Bernal, Saenz, & Knight, 1991, p. 135). Other responses are possible: Individuals might withdraw or choose to dissociate from the referent, thereby creating added psychological complications for themselves. Tajfel's social identity theory has generated considerable influence on ethnic identity research; some prefer to carry out the work under the ethnic self-identification rubric (see Helms, 1996; Phinney, 1990, 1992).

Ethnic self-identification and ethnic self-labeling typically are used interchangeably. Labeling involves the use of tags or markers to refer to and categorize groups and their members. Foote (1951) believes that labeling is proceeded by naming because in order for one to commit to an identity, one must accept the name ascribed to the group by others or one's own group's members. Both ingroup and outgroup members can use the same or variations of labels or names to refer to a specific ethnic group. For example, Buriel (1987) points out that numerous labels exist to refer to the Mexican-descent population in the United States; Mexican, Mexicano, Mexican American, Mestizo, and Chicano constitute most of the labels. Indeed, over the years, outgroup members coined a few pejorative and offensive labels to refer to those of Mexican descent, most of which are lodged in stereotypical, prejudicial, and racist thoughts. In fact, such belittling and deprecatory labels exist for all ethnic groups and all must be unequivocally rejected.

Ethnic labeling has a sociopolitical value and function, especially for census and demographic studies. At a superficial level, where generalizations about distinct cultural orientations are not used, ethnic labels serve a useful function. Typically, when labels are used, reference is not drawn to the deep culture of each group to explain similarities and differences. Data patterns are presented at a gross level to portray findings in the broadest manner possible. However, more often than not, researchers use ethnic labels to wittingly or unwittingly convey a deeper cultural meaning than the labels permit.

Ethnic self-identification is a distinct psychological variable and "refers to the description of oneself in terms of a critical ethnic attribute; that is, an attribute that defines more than merely describes the ethnic group" (Aboud, 1987, p. 33). In most social settings, use of one attribute may be sufficient; however, other settings may require the use of several related attributes for one to indicate the strength of one's identity. Vaughn (1987) views self-identification as a form of personal identity and differentiates the two from social identity. Personal identity "derives from a sense of self based on interpersonal comparisons" and social identity derives "from group membership" (p. 74). Rosenthal (1987) and Phinney (1990) view subjective identity as a starting point that eventually leads to the development of a social identity based on ethnic group membership. But Rosenthal adds that "ethnic identity arises in interaction and is a function not only of the individual and his or her relation to the ethnic group but of the group's place in the wider social setting" (p. 160).

Weinreich (1986) and Weinreich and Saunderson (2003) not only view self-identity as a starting point, they believe that identity formation and development refer to different identity states where different social contexts will influence the identity state and one's actions. Weinreich (1989) asserts:

> One's identity as situated in a specific social context is defined as that part of the totality of one's self-construal in which how one construes oneself in the situated present expresses the continuity between how one construes oneself as one was in the past and how one construes oneself as one aspires to be in the future. (p. 164)

Moreover, Weinreich maintains that ethnic self-identity is not a static process but one that changes and varies according to particular social contexts. Individuals may, for example, avoid situations where their identity is challenged, threatened, humiliated, and castigated; settings that favor the identity state are sought out and sustained whenever possible. Self-expression, maintenance of ethnic identity, and situated identities offer promise for understanding the complexities and dynamics of ethnic orientations through Weinreich's theory of identity structure analysis.

ETHNIC AND RACIAL IDENTITY MEASURES

With all of the theorizing and scholarly ramblings about the usefulness and appropriateness of the ethnic and racial constructs, one would think that considerable attention would have been devoted to their measurement and assessment. Such is not the case, as pointed out earlier. In fact, some theoreticians and writers on the subject believe that the measurement of ethnicity and race should be abandoned because the constructs' meanings are elusive and have pejorative, racist origins and implications (McKenney & Cresce, 1993; Stephan & Stephan, 2000). Moreover, universalistic-oriented scholars such as Werner Sollors (1989) maintain that *ethnicity is an invention* and that its continued use and measurement are divisive because most Americans have more in common with one another than differences (p. xx). Gans (1979) adds that in measuring ethnicity attitude, studies tend to overemphasize the importance ascribed to the construct; ethnic groups may have more in common with one another than distinct differences, but that small difference may be exaggerated because of the emotional importance placed on it by researchers and their participants.

Furthermore, adding to the problems associated with the constructs' measurement, Phinney (1990) notes that there are "widely discrepant definitions and measures of ethnic identity, which makes generalizations and comparisons across studies difficult and ambiguous" (p. 500). Additionally, Helms (1996) notes that there is a tendency for "researchers to collude with society in using concepts such as race, ethnicity or ethnic group, and culture as though they have a clear common meaning and are interchangeable" (p. 146). While criticisms about measurement vary from one theoretical camp to another, nonetheless numerous approaches and strategies have been devised and developed to measure the constructs, many of which mirror a variety of theories and social psychological perspectives. In this section, selected measures are summarized according to their theoretical emphasis, measurement approach, and themes. Critiques of the measures are not provided; however, comprehensive summaries and evaluations of numerous ethnic and racial measures can be found in the reviews by Helms (1996), Carter (1996), Burlew, Bellow, and Lovett (2000), Fischer and Moradi (2001), Kohatsu and Richardson (1996), and Cross (1991). These citations also contain extensive descriptions of numerous measures and scales not included in this section.

Social and behavioral science researchers rely on a variety of techniques and procedures that pose as measurement approaches. To answer the query posed by Geertz in the opening quotation—"who or, perhaps, more exactly, what they are"—some researchers will ask their respondents to specify their ethnic background, and on the basis of that one item, conclusions will be drawn about ethnic differences (or similarities) that are totally unjustified; still others will select subjects on the basis of surnames or physiognomic appearance and then proceed to generalize results to the total ethnic or racial population. Use of the latter procedures suggests that researchers are guilty of using an "ethnic gloss," that is, "an overgeneralization or simplistic categorical label of ethnic groups . . . that neglect[s] the unique differences found among individuals in various cultures or groups" (Trimble & Dickson, in press a). Indeed, measuring ethnic identity "is not a simple all or nothing proposition. Researchers have long recognized that a person's level or intensity of identification with a particular ethnicity can vary from a weak-nominal association to a strong-committed association" (Smith, 1980, p. 79).

Approaches to the measurement of ethnic and racial identity range from use of a single item (Richman, Gaveria, Flaherty, Birz, & Wintrob, 1987) to scales containing several dimensions (Carter, 1996; Helms, 1990, 1996; Phinney, 1992; Weinreich, 1986; Weinreich & Saunderson, 2003). Whatever measurement approach or technique one chooses to develop or use, one must factor in the following four domains of inquiry: (1) natality, where an emphasis is placed on ancestral genealogy, including parents, siblings, and grandparents; (2) subjective identification, where the respondent provides a declaration of his or her own ethnic or racial identity; this domain could be the most important of the four; Stephan and Stephan (2000, p. 549) argue that "the goal of assessment of race/ethnicity is accuracy from the perspective of the respondent, and that the accuracy of such a social construct can only be obtained by individual self-designation"; (3) behavioral expressions of identity, where respondents indicate their preferences for activities germane to their ethnic affiliation, such as foods, music, magazines, and books; and (4) situational or contextual influences, where the respondent indicates the situations that call for a deliberate expression of the ethnic affiliation, such as traditional ceremonies, interaction with family and peers, and neighborhood gatherings: the identity process. Figure 17.1 shows the four domains and the linkages between that enable individuals to fully express their ethnic self-identification (Trimble, 2000; Trimble et al., 2002). At minimum, scales and measures should attempt to capture the essence of each domain to provide a full and complete profile or silhouette of one's

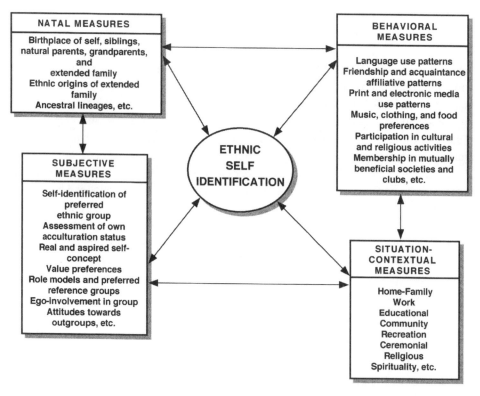

Figure 17.1   Ethnic self-identification measurement domains. *Sources:* From "Social Psychological Perspectives on Changing Self-Identification among American Indians and Alaska Natives," pp. 197–222, by J. E. Trimble, in *Handbook of Cross-Cultural and Multicultural Personality Assessment,* R. H. Dana, ed., 2000, Mahwah, NJ: Erlbaum; and "Social and Psychological Perspectives on Ethnic and Racial Identity," pp. 239–275, by J. Trimble, J. Helms, and M. Root, in *Handbook of Racial and Ethnic Minority Psychology,* G. Bernal, J. Trimble, K. Burlew, and F. Leong, eds., 2002, Thousand Oaks, CA: Sage.

identity. Helms (1996) adds to this suggestion by pointing out that measures at minimum should be tridimensional and include items to tap individual characteristics, own group affiliation, and outgroup relations.

In the next section, several assessment and measurement approaches are presented and summarized to illustrate the procedures social and behavioral scientists prefer to empirically examine ethnic and racial constructs. The section begins with the use of nominal procedures and progresses through to the use of complex and engaging measurement techniques and procedures.

ASSESSMENT AND MEASUREMENT APPROACHES AND TECHNIQUES

Before we turn to the summary, it is important to acknowledge the fact that there are numerous scales and measures in the literature designed for use with a diverse array of ethnic and racial populations. For example, a search of the electronic database *PsycINFO* yields articles describing scales to measure identity among Japanese, Chinese, American Indians, Native Americans, Blacks, African Americans, Hispanics, Puerto Ricans, Mexican Americans, Asians, Native Hawaiians, and Whites. Cross (1991) nicely summarizes a number of measures to assess Negro, Black, or African American identity. Additionally, several measures tap into multiracial, cross-racial, multicultural, multidimensional, and bicultural identity in the search results. On further inspection of the scales, one will note that virtually all of them are of the paper-and-pencil type, where respondents are asked to respond to forced-choice Likert-type scale alternatives (Stephan & Stephan, 2000; Trimble, 1991). A few of the scales do not represent a particular theoretical orientation; those that do follow a line of theoretical inquiry are derived from social and personal identity theory (Tajfel, 1982).

Nominal Measurement Approaches

Self-identification is a nominal procedure that, at best, provides an enumeration. The procedure also involves the fact that an individual is given a choice that is highly subjective. Some form of subjective criteria are used to decide which racial or ancestral category to choose; for those of mixed racial ancestry the choice may be more delicate than for those with an exclusive ancestry. With this procedure, typically, respondents are asked to place a check mark after an ethnic or racial category with which they most identify; in essence, they name or identify the ethnic or racial group provided them, and if it's not there they fill in a blank space, usually labeled "other." The results of the procedure permit the researcher to tabulate or cross-tabulate results; thus, numeration has its value, especially in census tallies and in political and social surveys, where one is not interested in attributing ethnicity to the outcome of a measured dependent variable.

Use of a nominal procedure for assessing race and ancestral heritage is no more evident than in the long-time efforts of the U.S. Bureau of the Census. The census bureau has been assessing racial backgrounds in some form or another since as far back as 1790. To capture the racial information, for example, from 1850 to 1970 the census asked for one's birthplace, the birthplace of parents, and language preferences (one's "native tongue"). In 1890, the U.S. Congress added racial items like "quadroon" and "octoroon" to tap mixed African American ancestry (to assess the "one drop" of black blood rule). The term "mulatto" was used in the mid-nineteenth century; it is still used in Puerto Rico to refer to people of mixed African and Euro-American ancestry. Eventually, after much protest, these offensive terms were eliminated from the forms. Beginning in 1900 the census forms used White, Chinese, and Japanese as the primary racial categories; in 1970 a Hispanic-origin question was added, and in 1980 there were four racial designations: Black, Asian American and Pacific Islander, American Indian, White, and an "other" category. To gather more in-depth racial information, an ancestral heritage question was added, asking the respondent to report beyond two generations.

If nothing else, use of different racial terms and questions has always been a problem for the census bureau. In an effort to settle the matter of what terms to use to refer to ethnic and racial groups at a federal level, the U.S. Office of Management and Budget (OMB) in 1976 imposed a standard of racial and ethnic categories to include White, African American, American Indian, Asian, and Hispanic; the imposition set a new item standard for the census bureau along with influencing how federal agencies and their representatives, researchers, educators, the media, and policy analysts referred to the country's racial and ethnic minority populations. Use of the categories contributed to virulent debates from all corners of the country; use of the terms is filled with controversy in part because of their instability, inaccuracy, and mutability.

During the 1990s, the census bureau debated use of a multiethnic question as there was growing pressure from researchers, scholars, and citizens about the lack of a category to designate mixed racial heritage. Several studies on multiracial identity fueled the debate. For example, Johnson et al. (1997) found that the addition of a multiracial category to a standard list of racial and ethnic groups produced significantly different response patterns when compared to a list that omitted the multiracial category. The researchers learned that respondents actually preferred the addition of a multiracial category. Johnson et al. amplify their findings by suggesting that "researchers make the minor modifications that would be necessary to enable the increasing numbers of multiracial persons in this country to identify themselves in social surveys and other data collection systems" (p. 683). Against the better judgment and recommendations of scores of activists and lobbyist groups and researchers, in 2000 the census bureau asked individuals to indicate all of the "races" of which they considered themselves a part. An individual could choose to indicate one race alone or could mark other races along with the single race category. Results from the survey showed that 2.4% of the U.S. population identified with two or more racial groups; the finding led the OMB to recommend that "responses that combine one minority race and white are allocated to the minority race" (OMB, 2000, Section II). The recommendation has caused quite a stir among many members of the prominent ethnic minority groups in the country.

Use of the multiracial item has created an array of contentious problems for all who rely on use of census outcomes (see Perlmann & Waters, 2002). The addition of the multiracial category presents complex tabulation and reporting problems for health care professionals, economists, demographers, social and behavioral scientists, and others who use racial categories for their work. In the research domain, if an investigator is interested in attributing an outcome to something about the deep culture of a racial or ethnic group, the multiracial or multiethnic category presents formidable attribution problems. For example, if a respondent claims that he or she is of White, American Indian, and African American background, what culture or ethnic group is most influential in forming and shaping that person's affective styles, behavior, and cognition? In the words of the demographer and former director of the census bureau Kenneth Prewitt (2002), the addition of the multiracial category represents a

> turning point in the measurement of race . . . the arrival of a multiple-race option in the census classification will so blur racial distinctions in the political and legal spheres and perhaps also in the public consciousness that race classification will gradually disappear. (p. 360)

Then again, he maintains, the new category may lead to further refinements of the construct. To the contrary, the sociologist Nathan Glazer (2002) believes the new census racial questions exaggerate the importance of the construct and asks, "But is . . . race so important a part of America that it deserves such prominence and detail?" (p. 22). As an alternative, Glazer recommends that the census form should seek race information only on African Americans, as

> they are less integrated in American society than any other large group . . . [and] they have a clear sense of their identity. When they answer the race question, one can depend on a high degree of reliability in the answer, as census research has shown. (p. 24)

No doubt the debate on the census bureau's use of the "check all that apply" question will continue well into the 21st century.

Variations on the Nominal Measurement Approach

Simple nominal ethnic and racial procedures for declaring affiliation and membership have limited use. Waters (1990) points out that the technique indeed affirms one's ethnic identity,

> but one cannot tell what this identity means to be an individual, how and why people choose a particular ethnic identity from a range of possible choices; how often and in what ways that ethnic identity is used in everyday life; and how ethnic identity is intergenerationally transferred within families. (p. 11)

To assess the deep meaning of ethnic identity the sociologist Mary Waters (1990) developed an engaging and well thought out interview schedule containing more than 100 pointed questions designed to explore the nature and meaning of ethnicity. Waters maintains that "one constructs an ethnic identification using knowledge about ancestries in one's background" and that "this information is selectively used in the social construction of ethnic identification within the prevailing historical, structural, and personal constraints" (p. 19). Although not a scale in the strict sense of the term, Waters's lengthy and orderly array of items allows an investigator to probe deeply into the meaning of a person's initial designation of his or her ancestry; she follows this question with one that explores the reason behind the reply. Waters's interview schedule moves through a carefully developed set of domains that assists the respondent in constructing an identity. The schedule begins with respondents making a nominal declaration of their identity and proceeds accordingly through the ordered sequence of questions and items. The interview protocol produces a script that requires considerable time and energy to analyze. The results undoubtedly generate a rich individual-centered profile, but Waters's schedule and research approach has its limitations, although she has used it successfully in her seminal research on identity.

Another approach to the study and assessment of identity relying on where one's initial nominal declaration is factored into the analysis is the research conducted by Deaux, Reid, Mizrahi, and Cotting (1999). Building their assessment strategy on a variant of Tajfel's social identity theory, the social psychologist Kay Deaux and her associates extend their work to include procedures and items that consider motivations for an identity claim, the functions that identity serves, the relationship between identity and subsequent behavior, and the links between a categorical definition and group motivation to explore the functions of social identification.

To initiate the inquiry, Deaux and her associates (1999) first asked respondents to sort through and rate a list of 64 identities. Results generated five properties, suggesting that individuals have interrelated multiple social identities; ethnicity is one of them. In a related procedure, the researchers asked respondents to select an identity from the list of 64 that was important to them and then respond to a series of questionnaire items that tapped the identity's importance for them; the items generated seven factors, including self-insight and understanding, intergroup comparison and competition, collective self-esteem, downward social comparison, and social interaction. The results demonstrate that identity is multifaceted and that different motives are salient for different forms of identity; ethnic identification may serve a different function from an identity with another facet of one's life and thus serve different needs. Most important, their work shows that the sole use of a nominal ethnic declaration is hardly sufficient to understand the functions of the label for the individual and group.

Multiple-Item Ethnic Identity Measures

Ethnic identity scales assume that people can readily identify with a group or even prefer to do so. In this instance, use of an item that asks people to check, list, or write in the name of the group with which they identify is a good starting point. In fact, many multiple-item identity scales start off with this question. Building her scale on Tajfel's social identity theory and the developmental stages advocated by Erikson, Jean Phinney's (1992) Multigroup Ethnic Identity Measure (MEIM) actually asks respondents to indicate their ethnic affiliation twice in her 15-item scale, once at the beginning and again in item 13, where respondents answer "My ethnicity is" by checking off one of seven ethnic categories, one of which is "other." Her widely used and well-known scale assesses self-identification through two dimensions derived from principal components, rotated factor analyses, ethnic identity, and other group orientation. Five items measure Affirmation/Belonging, seven items measure Ethnic Identity Achievement, and two measure Ethnic Behaviors. Item consistency measures obtained from a number of samples range from coefficient alphas of .77 to .92; construct validity measures are reasonably strong and are consistent with the item reliability outcomes (see Fischer & Moradi, 2001). The scale can be used to obtain a global overview measure of ethnic identity; additionally, one can obtain separate scores from the subscales.

Multigroup identity scales similar to the MEIM have been developed by Dunbar (1997) and Sevig, Highlen, and Adams (2000). The 21-item Personal Dimensions of Difference Scale (PDDS) developed by the psychologist Edward Dunbar examines seven categories of social group membership along three dimensions: ascribed group identity, personal empowerment via group membership, and perceived social support for group membership. Todd Sevig and his associates developed the Self-Identity Inventory based on optimal theory applied to identity development. The

71-item scale uses items from the California Psychological Inventory, the Belief Systems Analysis Scale, and the Social Desirability and Infrequency Scales to form six dimensions. Construct validity and item reliability measures fall within acceptable coefficient ranges. Both scales are useful variations of the MEIM; however, they probe different social and self-identity dimensions.

Multiple-Item Racial Identity Measures

Early in the 1990s, Burlew and Smith (1991) identified four ways that measures of racial identity could be classified to include (1) developmental, (2) Africentric, (3) group-based, and (4) racial stereotypes. Based on the development of several scales since that time, the psychologist A. Kathleen Burlew revised the categories to include (1) identity formation, (2) cultural connectedness, and (3) multicultural experiences that permit a more accurate grouping of a majority of the measures intended to tap racial identity (Burlew et al., 2000). The scales and theoretical perspectives presented in this section reflect the themes of these classifications.

In 1991, the psychologist William Cross published a landmark book on African American identity, where he laid out his theory of *nigrescence*. Along with a wonderful review of the research and commentary on African American identity, Cross provided data on three stages of a multistage nigrescence model: (1) Pre-encounter, (2) Immersion-Emersion, and (3) Internalization (see Cross, Parham, & Helms, 1991). In 1979, Cross developed a 54-item scale that captured the essence of the three stages that permitted him to empirically demonstrate that African American identity progresses through stages and that identity can be tracked accurately. His scale and multistage approach to assessing African American identity influenced the subsequent development of important and thought-provoking racial identity measures (see Burlew et al., 2000).

Cross revised his theory in 1995 to include expanded and more clearly defined nigrescence stages. To complement the refinement of his theory and provide an empirical tool to measure the stages, Cross and his associates developed the Cross Racial Identity Scale (CRIS; Cross & Vandiver, 2001). The development of the scale occurred over a five-year period and involved the assistance of multicultural experts and samples of African American college students. The full scale consists of 40 items, 30 of them targeted to assess six subscales that compose the main features of Cross's revised nigrescence theory; each of the subscales contains five items, accompanied by a seven-choice alternative rating scale. The six subscales are fairly independent of one another; thus, one is encouraged to aggregate scores for each subscale but interpret outcomes in the context of the full set of subscales. Reliability coefficients or alphas for the subscales are strong and on average range from .75 to .89. Exploratory and confirmatory factor analyses have been used to evaluate the factor structure of the subscales; results confirm the fit of the subscales to the six-factor model (see Cross & Vandiver, 2001). Also, Cokely (2002) provided empirical evidence in a study of racial identity attitudes and internalized racism to support Cross's revision of his nigrescence model.

Along with his seminal scholarly work on nigrescence theory and use of developmental stages in assessing identity progression, Cross and his associates recently offered an identity assessment approach that emphasizes "identity as operations, functions, negotiations, enactments or activities" (Cross, Smith, & Payne, 2002, p. 93). Developing a variant of Vygotsky's activity theory, Cross and his associates constructed situation-based case studies from narratives grounded in everyday transactions. Analyses of the narrative protocols from a sample of African Americans reveal that certain distinct "situation identity" patterns emerge:

> (a) identity protection transactions, or buffering; (b) an identity "on/off" switch, called code switching, that allows movement in and out of Black and non-Black cultural settings; (c) identity connectivity enactments that make transracial friendship possible; (d) identity belonging activities that promote a sense of bonding and attachment to the Black experience; and (e) identity individuation activities that sustain the boundaries of a person's individuality. (p. 105)

Cross is one of a few identity researchers to factor in situational influences in the measurement of ethnic and racial identification (see Figure 17.1).

The foremost and most cited racial identity scales center on the seminal and thought-provoking research of the psychologist Janet E. Helms. Helms and her associates developed their scales according to the five developmental stages model proposed by Cross and his associates; later, Helms (2001) modified her model to focus on statuses in lieu of stages because "statuses give rise to schemata, which are behavioral manifestations of the underlying statuses. It is schemata rather than the statuses per se that paper-and-pencil racial identity attitude inventories presumably assess" (p. 184; see Carter, 1996; Helms, 1996). Currently, the Helms racial identity measures tap 11 statuses in one form or another. The scales are grounded in the following themes:

> (a) one's racial identity develops in comparison to one's "contrast" racial group; (b) healthy identity development involves the abandonment of societal impositions of racial-self in favor of one's own personality relevant self-definition; (c) members of all of the socioracial groups develop racial identity by means of a sequential process in which increasingly more sophisticated differentiations of the ego evolve from earlier less mature statuses; and (d) qualitative differences in *expression* of racial identity statuses can be measured, but development must be inferred from responses to measures. (Helms, 1996, p. 155)

Two of Helms's widely used racial identity measures are summarized briefly; one should be mindful that her measures are undergoing constant revision owing to the prolific amount of research they have generated in the study of racial identity. The more prominent of her scales is the Form B revised version of the Black Racial Identity Attitude Scale (Helms, 1990). The 30-item scale uses 5-point Likert-type choice alternatives to assess the Pre-encounter, Encounter, Immersion-Emersion, and Internalization stages (now statuses). Reported reliability coefficients for the four stages/statuses range from alphas of .49 to .79 (Fischer & Moradi, 2001). Ponterotto and Wise (1987) found a three-factor solution using exploratory factor analysis with principal axis factoring and an oblique rotation solution that supported three dimensions of the subscales: Pre-encounter, Immersion-Emersion, and Internalization. Other factor analytic solutions performed on the scales support a four-factor solution. There are two other versions of her scale, the long form that contains 50 items and another version of the 30-item short form.

The 50-item White Racial Identity Attitude Scale (WRIAS) extends Helms's theoretical perspectives to White racial identity (Carter, 1996; Helms, 1996; Helms & Carter, 1990). She contends that as Whites become more racially conscious, they will progress through two phases, Abandonment of Racism and Defining a Nonracist White Identity; each of these phases contains stages/statuses that include Contact, Disintegration, Reintegration, Pseudo-independence, Immersion-Emersion, and Autonomy. Swanson, Tokar, and Davis (1994) treated the scale with factor analysis item reliability techniques and found a wide range of alpha coefficients; items from their subscale analysis generated coefficients from −.63 to .68. Other researchers report different reliability coefficients (see Helms, 1996). The factor analysis solutions provided by Swanson, Tokar, and Davis show little support for Helms's White racial identity model. Consequently, some researchers urge that users of the WRIAS proceed with caution (Fischer & Moradi, 2001). To the contrary, Helms (1996) argues that a scale can generate variable reliability coefficients (often called alphas) because (1) researchers may not have sampled adequately, (2) alpha coefficients are estimates of the interrelationship between items and factor dimensions and not a measure of homogeneity, and (3) reliability coefficients may underestimate the relationships in part because of the influence of situational variables. She contends that we must be careful in using reliability coefficients to make judgments about scale properties. "Reliance on coefficient alpha as the sole indicator of the interrelatedness of items," she maintains, "is probably premature when the possible limitations of this approach for evaluating the reliability of racial identity measures is considered" (p. 172).

Using variants of factor analysis, several researchers generated factor dimensions that challenged the various theoretical dimensions of Helms's racial identity scales (see Carter, 1996; Helms, 1996). Carter and Helms contest the use of factor analysis with the scales because the measures and their subscales are not intended to be unidimensional or homogeneous, the statistic cannot reveal the increasing complexity of subscales and their items, and the technique often assigns a single variable to many factors (called split loadings) and thus creates problems for interpreting the dimensional meaning of the item. Helms and Carter recommend use of cluster analysis because the statistic uses one source for partitioning the variance; the source then can be used to create groups. Carter treated the Black and White racial identity scales with cluster analysis and found support for the theoretical dimensions for the White scale; support for the Black version was found after the raw scores were transformed to percentile scores. His results suggest that cluster analysis may be a more appropriate statistic for use in identifying common item dimensions in racial and ethnic identity because "if distinct dimensions were to exist in the instruments, they should be discernible from scale configurations rather than item configurations" (Carter, 1996, p. 218).

Multiple Ethnic Identity Measures

Until recently, most of the published ethnic and racial identity measures tapped the major ethnic group self-identity of the respondent; that is, the respondent typically is asked to state or list one ethnic affiliation. However, as emphasized earlier, many respondents have more than one ethnic identity and some actually prefer to state their declarations with ethnic groups that are most salient for them. Indeed, results from the 2000 census, where people were given the option to "check all that apply" to the race question, support this preference. Some researchers were acutely aware of this preference and consequently developed measures on which respondents could declare their multiple ethnic or racial group preferences. Two of these measurement approaches are summarized in this section.

In 1991, psychologists Eugene Oetting and Fred Beauvais proposed the orthogonal cultural identification theory and a correspondent scale to assess cultural identity. Their approach is built on the belief that cultural identity or ethnic identity is not a linear phenomenon. Furthermore, they contend that cultural identity dimensions are independent of one another and that an increasing identification with one culture does not produce a decreasing identification with another culture. One could, for example, highly identify with two cultural or ethnic groups and, conversely, not identify with any group. Hence, the two researchers would argue that an individual could conceivably identify with two, three, and even four cultural or ethnic groups and not in the least be disoriented or confused about his or her cultural identification.

Oetting and Beauvais (1991) developed a full scale consisting of over 50 items that allows an individual to "independently express identification or lack of identification" with several cultural groups (p. 663). They claim that "in large-scale surveys of adults, only two basic items may be needed to assess identification with any one culture reasonably well: (1) Do you live in the . . . way of life? and (2) Are you a success in the . . . way of life?" (p. 664). Other items can be added to assess such factors as family identification and tradition, participation in cultural events, language preferences, and parental identification to expand the scale's measurement domains and its presumed effectiveness. In using the scale one does not have to rely on all of the full scale items; as few as 14 of the items have been proven to generate reliable outcomes.

Trimble (2000), using confirmatory factor analysis, tested a model of the American Indian version of the Oetting and Beauvais scale and generated seven factor dimensions derived from a 14-point Likert-type format. The confirmatory factor model was constructed from items to conform to three domains of a four-part ethnic measurement model, specifically natality, behavioral orientations, and subjective perceptions advocated by Trimble (1991, 1995; see Figure 17.1). The average item reliability or alpha coefficients for the items was .89; initially, the items formed three exploratory factor dimensions through use of a principal components analysis. The 14-item scale was administered to 846 self-identified American Indian youth in eight communities located in both reservation and nonreservation settings in the central southwestern region of the United States. Results reveal that 71% "all" or "nearly all" identified with the American Indian group. The results also indicate that some of the Indian self-identified youth identified to some degree with other groups (e.g., about 9% indicated that they "mostly" or "nearly all" identified as Anglo-White and 7% did so for the Spanish/Mexican American group). However, 11% indicated that they identified "little" or "not at all" as American Indian, yet these respondents self-identified nominally as American Indian.

Perceived ethnic self-identification of one's parents influences levels and degrees of identification among offspring. Results from Trimble's (2000) analysis revealed that the ethnic background of one or both parents varied but had an influence on the identity declarations of the respondents. Sixty-nine percent of the youths' mothers were seen as "all or nearly all" Indian as were 58% of their fathers. At the other extreme, the identity of some 9% of the mothers and 13% of the fathers was perceived as "not at all" Indian. Finally, the results reveal that 43% (360) of the youth who "all" or "nearly all" identified as American Indian indicated that their parents were also seen as identifying at the same level of intensity. Overall, an analysis of responses reveals that the youths' degree of identity varied considerably for close to 80% (846) of the respondents. Thus, one's parental ethnic background along with one's self-claimed affiliation with and attachment to an ethnic group can influence the degree to which one affiliates with an ethnic declaration to the extent that one may declare an affiliation with other ethnic groups, as Oetting and Beauvais's (1991) model and theory predict.

In the 1980s, the cross-cultural psychologist Peter Weinreich put forth his theory and measurement technique explicating identity structure analysis (ISA), a complex, highly sophisticated approach to assessing ethnic identity as well as identities with other facets of one's life; in effect, if one identifies with more than one ethnic or racial group to some degree, then that can be captured with the approach (Weinreich, 1986; Weinreich & Saunderson, 2003). ISA is grounded in psychodynamic developmental theory, personal construct psychology, appraisal theory, social constructionism, cognitive-affective consistency theories, and symbolic interactionist theoretical perspectives. According to Weinreich and Saunderson:

> ISA conceptualizes one's appraisal of social situations as involving one's interpretation of their significance to self's identity from moment to moment. Appraisal provides and records experiences of situations and events. (p. 20)

ISA can be custom-designed to measure identity in an idiographic or nomothetic framework through use of bipolar constructs; thus, the approach be can tailored for an individual as well as for groups. Indices can be constructed to measure such constructs as self-image (past, current, and ideal), values, role models, reference groups, empathetic identification, identification conflicts, evaluation of others, and a few other related identity domains.

The assessment of ethnic and cultural identity is an important feature of ISA. According to Weinreich:

> One's ethnic identity is defined as that part of the totality of one's self-construal system made up of those dimensions that express the continuity between one's construal of past

ancestry and one's future aspirations in relation to ethnicity. (Weinreich & Saunderson, 2003, p. 28)

One's construal of one's ethnic identity, too, is largely influenced by one's ancestral heritage and the history of the groups with which one identifies. Moreover, in the context of ISA, ethnic self-identity is not viewed as a static process but one that changes and varies according to particular social contexts. Individuals, for example, may avoid situations where their identity is challenged, threatened, humiliated, and castigated; settings that favor the identity state are sought out and sustained whenever possible.

ISA is an approach to the assessment and measurement of identity; hence one will not find a single multi-item scale available to study ethnicity. ISA uses a structured measurement procedure. To analyze the results produced by the theoretically based technique one must have access to a specialized computer program and the lengthy accompanying manual. For numerous reasons, the Identity Exploration software (IDEX) is a requirement to analyze Weinreich's approach to identity because it is based in ISA concepts and constructs (see Weinreich & Saunderson, 2003). Indeed, as a multi-item approach for the measurement of ethnic identity and identity in general, Weinreich's ISA sets the standard for comprehensiveness and inclusiveness. If a researcher is interested in exploring ethnic identities and affiliated identities in great detail, ISA offers wonderful opportunities; however, if one is interested in assessing identity in a survey questionnaire format, use of ISA is not recommended.

The scales summarized in this section and those described in the literature are not without criticism. Indeed, several researchers and scholars have subjected many of the measures and their corresponding theories to extensive scrutiny through use of cross-validation procedures, empirical testing, and theoretical speculation. For example, Root (2000) maintains that "the current models do not account for a range of ways in which people construct their core identities and determine the importance of race in them" (p. 214). Moreover, Root notes that "researchers have found no reliable method of extrapolating the core or breadth of one's identity from one context of identity or from a response to one question" (p. 212). She provides some thoughtful suggestions to accommodate several criticisms by focusing on the ecological influences on racial development that deal with inherited influences, traits, and social interactions with communities. Thus, it must be stated that before any of the ethnic and racial identity scales and theories are considered for use, one should carefully review the literature and factor in the observations and criticisms.

In the main, the fashionable mode of ethnic and racial identity scale and measurement development relies on use of self-report procedures and with variants of a forced-choice response alternative following Likert-type formats. A few assessment and measurement approaches use interview schedules and protocols such as those developed by Waters (1990) and Root (2000). Reliance on these formats can create measurement equivalence and item bias problems; these topics are discussed in the next section.

Because the measurement of ethnic and racial identity involves people from different cultural, racial, and ethnic backgrounds, they may not be all that familiar and cognitively resonant with self-report procedures and conventional approaches to scale development. Given this possibility, perhaps alternative approaches to assessing identity should be developed and considered. For example, to assess identity and cultural orientations Tsai, Chentsova-Dutton, and Wong (2002) recommend use of Q-sort techniques, sociometric tasks, and behavioral and emotional assessment techniques such as reactions to facial expressions. Tsai and her associates describe use of a 360-degree pie to evaluate the significance of roles of culturally different respondents; roles are viewed as components of identity and thus may be more appropriate for use with culturally different groups, such as Asian Americans. Additionally, use of unobtrusive measurement techniques, such as drawings, doll selection and play, role-play, psychodrama, and games and simulations, is worthy of exploration.

CULTURAL EQUIVALENCE, ITEM BIAS, AND MEASUREMENT CONSIDERATIONS

In this section, summary information is provided about the issues associated with the development and use of psychosocial scales for cultural-specific and cultural-comparative research. Debates abound on the influence of one's worldview in understanding and interpreting standardized tests and psychosocial scales (see Dana, 2000; Irvine & Carroll, 1980; Malpass & Poortinga, 1986; Trimble, Lonner, & Boucher, 1983; van de Vijver & Leung, 1997). Moreover, many cross-cultural psychologists contend that "comparing elements from differing societies leads to inadmissible distortions of reality" (Kobben, 1970, p. 584). Ethnic and racial comparative research using identity measures may be fraught with problems of "incomparability" and thus may lead researchers to draw conclusions about a finding that may not be valid or justified. Indeed, with some exceptions, most ethnic and racial identity measures cited in the literature have not factored in cultural equivalence and item bias possibilities.

Cultural Equivalence and Item Bias

In constructing and using measurement instruments in cultural-comparative or cultural-sensitive research, the investigator must give serious attention to issues of equivalence. The instrument's content, format, and metric style must be congruent with and comparable across the cultural groups selected for study. Researchers must provide hard evidence that the components of the measurement process meet the standards of functional, conceptual, metric, linguistic, and stimulus equivalence.

Cultural equivalence refers "to the problem of whether, on the basis of measurements and observations, inferences in terms of some common psychological dimension can be made in different groups of subjects" (Poortinga, 1983, p. 238). Most cross-cultural researchers agree that cultural equivalence can be examined by giving attention to the following concepts: functional equivalence, conceptual equivalence, stimulus equivalence, linguistic equivalence, and metric equivalence.

Although five types of cultural equivalence are used to discuss the concept, in an exhausted review of the literature on equivalence, Johnson (1998) identified 52 types; subsequently, he classified the types into interpretive and procedural summary categories. In his findings, Johnson pointed out that "in no other field of inquiry . . . has this seemingly elementary concept [equivalence] been assigned as many alternative meanings and disaggregated into as many components as in the field of cross-cultural research" (p. 2).

Embedded in the notion of equivalence is the fundamental tenet that comparisons between ethnocultural groups require that a common, if not identical, measurement and assessment process exist; stretched to the extreme, the principle holds that a universal process must be developed to demonstrate and assess ethnocultural group comparability. Consequently, to achieve functionality two or more behaviors must "pre-exist as naturally occurring phenomena" that are related or identical to a similar problem or circumstance; the behaviors must serve a similar function for both groups (Berry, 1969, p. 122). Conceptual and stimulus equivalence exists when the meaning of stimuli, concepts, methods, and so on are similar or identical for the culturally different respondents. The requirement for linguistic equivalence is similar, although the emphasis is placed on the linguistic accuracy of item translations. Metric equivalence or scale equivalence (Poortinga, 1975), probably the most technical and the most difficult to evaluate, "exists when the psychometric properties of two (or more) sets of data from two (or more) cultural groups exhibit essentially the same coherence or structure" (Berry, 1980, p. 10). Of the five equivalence types, metric or scalar has received the least amount of empirical attention, perhaps because it is the most technical and/or poorly understood. Yet, for the psychometrician it may be the most important concern. Before a measure can be used in ethnic and racial specific and comparative research it must first meet standards within the ethnocultural groups; then and only then can it be used between two or more groups. For example, use of forced-choice scale alternatives laid out in a linear manner may not fit with the cognitive and evaluative preferences of certain cultural groups; a Likert-type format may work for one group but not for another. Thus, the researcher must find a common metric or scalar measure to pursue comparative measurement studies.

Cultural equivalence is similar to item bias. Item bias deals with the similarity or dissimilarity of scale outcomes across ethnic and racial populations and thus is concerned with "the presence or absence of validity-threatening factors" (van de Vijver, 2000, p. 89). In drawing a distinction between the two constructs, van de Vijver and Poortinga (1997) assert that item bias is associated with construct, instrument, and method bias; item bias differs from cultural equivalence, in part, because the latter deals more with the outcomes than the factors that influence validity (see van de Vijver & Tanzer, 1997). Put in simpler terms, according to Byrne and Watkins (2003), "Bias refers to the presence of nuisance factors [and] equivalence refers to the implication of bias on score comparability" (p. 174).

Assessing Cultural Equivalence, Item Bias, and Invariance

Use of conventional scaling procedures in cultural-comparative research has introduced a number of methodological problems, especially in the use of a structured response format (Johnson, 1998). Mounting ethnographic evidence points to the following problems. First, researchers tacitly, and perhaps incorrectly, assume that the numeric intervals between choice alternatives on the continuum are equal and can be assigned an integer value. Second, the number of choice alternatives is presumed, perhaps also incorrectly, to represent the full range of categories that an individual would use to evaluate an item. Third, the dimensions of the scale items may not be truly comparable between cultural groups. Finally, the effects and the outcomes of the categorization process, difficult to define in any group, may be confounded by the possibility that not all cultural groups respond to stimuli in a linear manner.

Response styles of culturally different respondents create problems for scale and questionnaire construction and use. Consider the following findings I have accumulated from years of conducting field research with different ethnocultural groups. Traditional Alaska Eskimos (Inuit), certain elderly from the Iroquois Nations in northern New York, and first- and second-generation Korean Americans in southern California have difficulty responding to items that are accompanied with multiple choice alternatives set in fixed-order Likert-type formats. Samples of American Samoans in the South Pacific expressed unwillingness to complete a series of tests because they didn't understand the procedures. Bilingual Korean Americans were able to complete the scales but not without expressing their concerns. Samples of rural Chinese Americans residing in the southeastern area of the United States preferred to use three categories to evaluate test and survey items. For the items with "yes" and "no" alternatives many of the respondents chose not to respond. According to one local informant, a "no response" to this choice format could mean "yes" but not "no." Traditionally oriented Sioux (Lakota) American Indian children from two reservations in South Dakota were reluctant to complete certain questionnaire items because they wanted first to discuss their choices with others, especially family members. Choices required by tests and questionnaires are difficult to make in the absence of some perceived consensus; Lakota children are taught to respect the knowledge and wisdom of the community and, therefore, one should not act independently. And rural Mayan Indians in Central America have difficulty making very fine distinctions and discriminations in response to questionnaire items. Often, respondents will offer their own interpretations that don't necessarily fit the framework provided for the task. Other illustrations and examples could be provided. On the basis of these and other observations, several points emerge: (1) Not all cultural groups judge, evaluate, and assess stimuli in a linear manner; (2) the number of salient choice options can vary from individual to individual both within and between societal groups; (3) responses are difficult for some because they don't yet understand what the collective will accepts; (4) the conventional psychometric format common to paper-and-pencil tests and instruments may not work in all cultural and ethnic groups; and (5) the need to capture information through a paper-and-pencil approach may be inconsistent and unrelated to *emic* styles of information sharing (Trimble & Lonner, 1993).

In recent years, a number of cross-cultural researchers and psychometricians have put forth a variety of interesting statistical algorithms for assessing the presence of forms of cultural equivalence and culturally bound item bias (see J. Allen & Walsh, 2000). To assess metric equivalence, for example, some researchers have analyzed the scales or instruments with principal components or factor analysis. If the structural dimensions of instruments resemble one another, then, presumably, the scales are equivalent across groups. Strength of the factor-based scales for the respective groups serves as a partial criterion. Factor solutions have been expanded to include congruence coefficients and related manipulations to isolate the nature of the equivalence. Windle, Iwawaki, and Lerner (1987) and Nishimoto (1986), for example, used factor solutions to examine the metric equivalence of personality scales administered to Asian and non-Asian populations. In both studies, the factor solutions did not differ. However, the item composition and thus the factor meanings did vary.

Use of factor analysis in psychometric research and testing equivalence is not without criticism (Carter, 1996; Helms, 1996; Kline, 1983). The full range of arguments are multifold and, in some instances, compelling, and they are not included in this chapter. Nonetheless, three critical points should be made: (1) Factor solutions rarely fit the data completely in cultural-comparative research, due, for the most part, to nonrandom measurement and translation error and unspecified conceptual contributions to the obtained weights; (2) factor solutions are suggestive; and (3) data should be, at a minimum, at the interval level. Most scales and inventories use binary or ordinal-level response categories with presumed equality of the numerical distances between the alternatives; distortions can exist, thus eroding the strength of the correlation coefficients. Kim and Mueller (1978) point out that variables with limited categories are not compatible with factor analytic models. The most forceful critic, though, is Duncan (1984), who considers factor analysis a failure in the measurement field because, among other points, "We . . . see nothing more than a 'correlational' science of 'inexact constructs'" (p. 207).

A few cross-cultural researchers recommend use of covariance structural modeling (e.g., LISREL, EQS) or variants of confirmatory factor analysis (CFA) to test for equivalence (Poortinga, 1983; van de Vijver & Leung, 1997). There are limitations associated with the use of exploratory factor models; the advances in confirmatory factor modeling, however, appear to overcome these limitations. For example, in testing for measurement equivalence, Prelow, Tein, Roosa, and Wood (2000) and Spini (2003) used CFA algorithms and found that many of their scales and corresponding items were unstable across different cultural groups.

Use of item response theory (IRT) to assess cultural equivalence and item bias has produced interesting findings. Ellis, Becker, and Kimmel (1993) and Ellis (1995) used IRT to test the equivalence of the Trier Personality Inventory, originally developed for use in (then) West Germany. The differential item functioning (DIF) index showed that subsequent retranslations of original inventory items reduced the overall content and reduced error due to translations. Bontempo (1993) also used IRT on an individualism-collectivism scale to both demonstrate the efficacy of the procedure and test for translation bias. Use of IRT and corresponding DIF analyses can generate different item consistency outcomes where item bias is detected (Budgell, Raju, & Quartetti, 1995; Marshall, 2002). The lines of research show promise for using IRT to assess equivalence of measures, scales, and tests.

Another creative statistical technique for assessing instrument equivalence has been proposed by van de Vijver and Leung (1997). The approach calls for the use of a two-way analysis of variance where each item in a scale is examined for item bias. Score groups are formed based on the aggregate item summations on the scale. These groups then are analyzed with an analysis of variance statistic. Byrne and Watkins (2003) used the procedure with two culturally different groups to assess measurement invariance among items from a self-description questionnaire; their results indicated that there was evidence of measurement and structural invariance among four subscales of the full scales. Analysis of covariance and analysis of variance techniques should be used with caution, as Byrne and Watkins emphasize: "The fact remains that neither can fully explain all incidences of noninvariance" (p. 173).

A growing number of researchers recommend a form of latent trait analysis, especially when the scale contains binary scores. The Rasch (1960) one-parameter model can be used; however, Irvine and Carroll (1980) remind us that the model should be used "alongside traditional models as part of another method of looking at the same data" (p. 210). Rasch modeling and analysis is a powerful alternative to factor analysis and analysis of variance in assessing the properties of tests and psychosocial scales. According to Schumaker and Linacre (1996), "Factor analysis is confused by ordinal variables and highly correlated factors. Rasch analysis excels at constructing linearity out of ordinality and at aiding the identification of the core construct inside a fog of collinearity" (p. 470). Moreover, factor analysis is aggregate-based; thus, misfitting individuals are a problem and cannot be identified. Rasch modeling provides a fit for each respondent to the model statistics and plots respondents and items on the same real number line (scale) so that one can visualize if the cases have higher or lower self-esteem than the items are capable of finding; Rasch measurement modeling assumes that item estimates are sample-free and case estimates are item-free.

Use of Rasch modeling to assess cultural equivalence has not been that extensive. The few studies using the approach have found that use of negatively worded items with culturally unique populations creates scale problems and item interpretation (Gerber et al., 2002); item linguistic translation can create invariance in multinational focused scales (Leplege, Ecosse, & WHOQOL Rasch Project Scientific Committee, 2000); shorter versions of a scale can be constructed for use in cultural comparative research, but the longer version can be used with one cultural group without making any item adjustments (McInerney, Yeung, & McInerney, 2001); and gender status and self-defined ethnic group respondents influence scale invariance and item nonequivalence of short scales originally believed to be reliable (Trimble & Mahoney, 2002).

To close out this section attention must be give to the achievement of cultural equivalence through use of item linguistic translation procedures, as it is central to understanding the cultural equivalences of measures. Typically, researchers interested in using a measure with more than one ethnic or cultural group will use a *translation–back translation* (TBT) technique. The TBT technique is straightforward: A researcher first asks a bilingual person to translate the items into the language of the intended research population, then asks another linguist to translate the items back into the original language of the measure; items from the translated versions are compared and adjustments are made accordingly. The procedure is repeated until the versions match one another conceptually and functionally (Marin & Marin, 1991). Use of the conventional TBT technique is flawed and unreliable; thus, it is not recommended (Brislin, 1976; McGorry, 2000; van de Vijver, 2000).

Several interesting and plausible alternatives for assuring item and scale equivalence using translations have been proposed and empirically tested. Erkut, Alarcon, Coll, Tropp, and Garcia (1999) developed a dual-focus method that relies more on concept translations than straightforward word-for-word translations. Indigenous researchers are invited to join the full research team and together they work through the meanings of concepts intended for use in the measures. Similarly, Geisinger (1994) recommends use of an editorial board consisting of bilingual translators who have credentials similar to those of the researcher; both collaborate on the translation of items. Finally, Johnson (1998) identified some other interesting approaches to item and scale translations, including decentered translation, use of independent bilingual translators who develop alternative versions of the target measure, rank ordering of alternative versions of the measure in the source language, use of cognitive "thinkaloud" protocols, and facet analysis.

SUMMARY AND CONCLUSIONS

We come to the end of our inquiry into the measurement of ethnic and racial identity. The inquiry began with Clifford Geertz's observation that identities "simply do not form an orderly structure." Although his keen observation is not the central theme of this chapter, it sets a tone that the assessment and measurement of racial and ethnic identity is complicated and filled with many problems owing in part to the fact that human beings have multiple, intertwined identities that influence one another in ways that are not fully understood. The problems are compounded by the growing popularity of identity and the effect this has on its meaning. "As identity became more and more a cliché," maintains Philip Gleason (1983), "its meaning grew progressively more diffuse, thereby encouraging increasingly loose and irresponsible usage" (p. 931). The tone is consistent with Weinreich's contention that "a person's appraisal of the social world and its significance is an expression of his or her identity"; consequently, one can have multiple intertwined identities that shift according to a number of circumstances and situations (Weinreich & Saunderson, 2003, p. xix).

To approach the inquiry, the origins of the meanings of identity, ethnicity, and race were provided. When the derivations and meanings of the three constructs are combined, a loose definition emerges to indicate the sameness of a band or nation of people who share common customs and traditions; certain bands or nations may share common experiences born from oppression, domination, and colonialism. The chapter's inquiry focused primarily on how social and behavioral scientists attempt to measure *sameness*.

To extend the inquiry, a section was devoted to a summary of the thoughts and theoretical perspectives on ethnicity. Although there are several compelling definitions of the construct, ethnicity is not without controversy. Most scholars agree that ethnicity is a social construction. Some view it as an invention, a synonym for identity, symbolic, political, fictional, imagined, and pseudo or contrived. Ethnicity and race are linked to identity; however, the linkage is not straightforward as there are varying opinions on what is more salient and in need of emphasis to understand identity formation and development—ethnic identity or racial identity. Several scholars insist that the concept of the self must be factored into the discussions and theory building. Many have been influenced by the seminal work on social identity initiated by the social psychologist Henri Tajfel, who viewed the self as the core of the identity process.

With the summary background in hand, the inquiry turned to a review of several approaches and techniques to the measurement of ethnic and racial identity. The inquiry started off with a review of nominal approaches to self-identification such as those used recently by the U.S. Bureau of the Census; here again, use of nominal approaches to capturing race and ethnicity is not without controversy. Flowing from that section several measures were summarized illustrating multiple-item measures and those that attempt to capture multiple ethnic and racial identities.

Several important conclusions emerged from the section. First, valid and reliable measures of ethnic and racial identity must be grounded in theory or, at a minimum, on several fundamental propositions. Cheung (1991) reminds us that typically,

> ethnicity has been treated as no more than a self-evident, *ascriptive* quality, as have been sex and age. Operationally, ethnicity was always measured by one or a combination of a few objective indicators such as color, place of birth, and language, neglecting the subjective aspect of ethnicity. (p. 575)

Relying on a deconstructive perspective, the cultural anthropologist Dwight Heath (1991) argues that many of the assumptions and uses of ethnicity are garbled "and confused in a markedly inconsistent manner [and are] unlikely to yield further insights that are theoretically or conceptually helpful in terms of understanding how alcohol interacts with the human animal" (p. 610). Although both Cheung and Heath are highly critical of the measurement tendencies, they are quick to point out that some positive contributions have been made to the field of ethnicity, especially in the way the ethnic variable has been viewed in some studies.

Second, we must acknowledge the conclusion that the measurement of ethnicity is no small task, especially given the debate surrounding its theoretical foundations and its usefulness. Researchers must consider the "various cultural and structural dimensions of ethnicity" (Cheung, 1989, p. 72) and "distinguish between general aspects of ethnic identity that apply across groups and specific aspects that distinguish groups" (Phinney, 1990, p. 508). To accomplish this we must move away from viewing ethnic groups as homogeneous entities—in fact, there may be more heterogeneity within certain ethnic and racial groups than among the dominant groups in North American society (Cheung, 1993; Trimble, 1991).

The inquiry closed with a summary of the methodological and measurement problems inherent in the development and use of measures for ethnic and racial populations. Aspects of cultural equivalence and item bias were presented along with an assortment of statistical techniques that can be used to assess invariance and nonequivalence. Studies suggest that sole reliance on conventional and traditional psychometric approaches for establishing a measure's reliability and validity is insufficient and incomplete given advances in the use of latent structure analyses. Helms (1996) reminds us that "this closed-minded perspective frequently has led them [those who use alpha coefficients, interitem correlations, and factor analysis] to discount their own findings in support of racial identity theory" (p. 186). Translation of measures for use with linguistically different ethnic and racial populations is an area in need of serious review and exploration, too. Consequently, a short section was provided calling attention to potential sources of measurement error, item bias, and nonequivalence owing to the inability of researchers to reliably and accurately translate measures for use in cross-cultural settings. Use of the conventional translation–back translation technique is no longer recommended as it has been proven to create multiple sources of measurement error and cultural nonequivalence.

What emerges from the inquiry is uncertainty and ambiguity—uncertainty about the meanings of identity, ethnicity, and race; uncertainty about their usefulness in describing the U.S. population; uncertainty about a person's appraisal of the social world and its significance as an expression of self-identity; uncertainty about what theory best explains psychosocial dynamics, components, and processes; uncertainty about the cultural equivalence of measures and how best to control for cultural bias; uncertainty as to why ethnicity and race are given so much prominence in North America and in other parts of the world; and uncertainty about the applicability of the findings generated by the incongruent and inconsistent measures. Apart from accounting for demographic distributions, there are uncertainties about the causal relationship between ethnic and racial identity outcomes: Most empirical studies using ethnic and racial identity as a moderating or independent variable fail to predict anything of psychosocial importance such as drug and alcohol use, depression, adolescent delinquency, grieving, eating disorders, and suicide, among many other variables.

The inconsistencies and incongruities suggest that the field of ethnic and racial identity is in a condition of disorder and confusion. Weinreich and Saunderson (2003) summarized the confusion best when they asserted that it is "a kaleidoscope set of conceptualizations [where] methods of assessment of parameters of identity, deriving from disparate conceptualizations of self and identity, are often unrelated" (p. 361).

The inconsistencies, incongruities, and confusion in the field should not deter or dissuade the scholar and scientist from conducting further inquiry into the daunting topic. Quite the contrary. The field is not whimsical, patchy, or unsteady—it is in desperate need of structure and order. To accomplish orderliness and structure scholars are challenged and encouraged to engage further and deeper into the topic to sort out and smooth over the discrepancies and incongruities. A good starting point for a probing inquiry is the emergence of a multiracial or multiethnic classification category. In the cultural and ethnic comparative research realm, researchers typically rely on monoethnic or monoracial categories to test hypotheses about the contribution of one's cultural lifeways and thoughtways to some outcome variable or variable domain. What deep or surface cultural attributes will a multiethnic category permit? If a researcher is interested in discovering deep cultural or ethnic contributions to a cognitive learning style, for example, how will the contributions be disentangled from one's multiethnic worldview or orientation?

There is yet another challenge that most assuredly will press the wit, vigor, and intellect of those bent on advancing an inquiry into ethnic and racial identity. The number of ethnic and racial groups in North America is increasing, not declining—the pot is not melting and the populace does not appear to be assimilating at the rate many demographers and sociologists predicted. All over the world geopolitical boundaries are changing as a result of political turmoil, colonialism, and globalization; consequently, individuals are changing their ethnic allegiances and identities as they move from one environment to another or their boundaries are rearranged (Arnett, 2002). Indigenous groups are asserting sovereign rights and demanding recognition and access to their ancestral lands. Once suppressed voices are demanding their right to recognition. Consequently, the number of ethnic groups worldwide is increasing prominently and becoming more independent and visible; this presents new challenges for the field of ethnic and racial identity.

At the start of this chapter, our inquiry began with an observation by Clifford Geertz (2000), and so it is fitting that the inquiry close with another of his astute and speculative observations:

> As the world becomes more thoroughly interconnected, economically and politically, as people move about in unforeseen, only partially controllable, and increasingly massive, ways, and new lines are drawn and old ones erased, the catalogue of available identifications expands, contracts, changes shape, ramifies, involutes, and develops. (p. 225)

Accordingly, the only principled way we can meet the challenge posed by the enlarging catalogue is to engage in a thorough inquiry, all the while realizing that the world is constantly changing.

ACKNOWLEDGMENT

I want to take this occasion to express my sincere gratitude and appreciation to my graduate research assistant at Western Washington University, Ryan Dickson, who provided wonderful assistance in the identification and compilation of the chapter's references and thoughtful and helpful comments on various draft sections.

REFERENCES

Aboud, F. E. (1987). The development of ethnic self-identification and attitudes. In J. S. Phinney & M. J. Rotheram (Eds.), *Children's ethnic socialization: Pluralism and development* (pp. 32–55). Newbury Park, CA: Sage.

Allen, B. P., & Adams, J. Q. (1992). The concept of "race": Let's go back to the beginning. *Journal of Social Behavior and Personality, 7,* 163–168.

Allen, J., & Walsh, J. A. (2000). A construct-based approach to equivalence: Methodologies for cross-cultural/multicultural personality assessment research. In R. H. Dana (Ed.), *Handbook of cross-cultural and multicultural personality assessment* (pp. 63–85). Mahwah, NJ: Erlbaum.

Allport, G. W. (1958). *The nature of prejudice.* Garden City, NY: Doubleday Anchor Books.

Arnett, J. J. (2002). The psychology of globalization. *American Psychologist, 57*(10), 774–783.

Barth, F. (Ed.). (1969). *Ethnic groups and boundaries.* Boston: Little, Brown.

Bernal, M. E., & Knight, G. P. (Eds.). (1993). *Ethnic identity: Formation and transmission among Hispanics and other minorities.* Albany: State University of New York Press.

Bernal, M. E., Saenz, D. S., & Knight, G. P. (1991). Ethnic identity and adaptation of Mexican American youths in school settings. *Hispanic Journal of Behavioral Sciences, 13*(2), 135–154.

Berry, J. W. (1969). On cross-cultural comparability. *International Journal of Psychology, 5,* 119–128.

Berry, J. W. (1980). Introduction to methodology. In H. C. Triandis & J. W. Berry (Eds.), *Handbook of cross-cultural psychology: Vol. 2. Methodology* (pp. 1–28). Boston: Allyn & Bacon.

Bontempo, R. (1993). Translation fidelity of psychological scales: An item response theory analysis of an individualism-collectivism scale. *Journal of Cross-Cultural Psychology, 24*(2), 149–166.

Brislin, R. W. (1976). *Translation: Applications and research.* New York: Wiley.

Budgell, G. R., Raju, N. S., & Quartetti, D. A. (1995). Analysis of differential item functioning in translated assessment instruments. *Applied Psychological Measurement, 19*(4), 309–321.

Buriel, R. (1987). Ethnic labeling and identity among Mexican Americans. In J. S. Phinney & M. J. Rotheram (Eds.), *Children's ethnic socialization: Pluralism and development* (pp. 134–152). Newbury Park, CA: Sage.

Burlew, A. K., Bellow, S., & Lovett, M. (2000). Racial identity measures: A review and classification system. In R. H. Dana (Vol. Ed.), *Handbook of cross-cultural and multicultural personality assessment: Personality and clinical psychology series* (pp. 173–196). Mahwah, NJ: Erlbaum.

Burlew, A. K., & Smith, L. R. (1991). Measures of racial identity: An overview and a proposed framework [Special issue]. *Journal of Black Psychology, 17,* 53–71.

Byrne, B. M., & Watkins, D. (2003). The issue of measurement invariance revisited. *Journal of Cross-Cultural Psychology, 34*(2), 155–175.

Carter, R. T. (1996). Exploring the complexity of racial identity attitude measures. In G. R. Sodowsky & J. C. Impara (Eds.), *Multicultural assessment in counseling and clinical psychology* (pp. 193–223). Lincoln, NE: Buros Institute of Mental Measurements.

Cheung, Y. W. (1989). Making sense of ethnicity and drug use: A review and suggestions for future research. *Social Pharmacology, 3*(1/2), 55–82.

Cheung, Y. W. (1991). Overview: Sharpening the focus on ethnicity. *International Journal of Addictions, 25*(5A/6A), 573–579.

Cheung, Y. W. (1993). Approaches to ethnicity: Clearing roadblocks in the study of ethnicity and substance abuse. *International Journal of Addictions, 28*(12), 1209–1226.

Cirese, S. (1985). *Quest: A search for self.* New York: Holt, Rinehart, & Winston.

Cokely, K. O. (2002). Testing Cross's revised racial identity model: An examination of the relationship between racial identity and internalized racialism. *Journal of Counseling Psychology, 49*(4), 476–483.

Cross, W. E., Jr. (1991). *Shades of black: Diversity in African American identity.* Philadelphia: Temple University Press.

Cross, W. E., Jr. (1995). The psychology of nigrescence: Revising the Cross model. In J. G. Ponterotto, J. M. Casas, L. A. Suzuki, & C. M. Alexander (Eds.), *Handbook of multicultural counseling* (pp. 93–122). Thousand Oaks, CA: Sage.

Cross, W. E., Jr., Parham, T. A., & Helms, J. E. (1991). The stages of black identity development: Nigrescence models. In R. J. Jones (Ed.), *Black psychology* (3rd ed., pp. 319–338). Berkeley, CA: Cobb & Henry.

Cross, W. E., Jr., Smith, L., & Payne, Y. (2002). Black identity: A repertoire of daily enactments. In P. B. Pedersen, J. G. Draguns, W. J. Lonner, & J. E. Trimble (Eds.), *Counseling across cultures* (5th ed., pp. 93–107). Thousand Oaks, CA: Sage.

Cross, W. E., Jr., & Vandiver, B. J. (2001). Nigrescence theory and measurement: Introducing the Cross racial identity scale (CRIS). In J. G. Ponterotto, J. M. Casas, L. A. Suzuki, & C. M. Alexander (Eds.), *Handbook of multicultural counseling* (2nd ed., pp. 371–393). Thousand Oaks, CA: Sage.

Dana, R. H. (Ed.). (2000). *Handbook of cross-cultural and multicultural personality assessment.* Mahwah, NJ: Erlbaum.

Deaux, K., Reid, A., Mizrahi, K., & Cotting, D. (1999). Connecting the person to the social: The functions of social identification. In T. Tyler, R. Kramer, & R. John (Eds.), *The psychology of the social self* (pp. 91–113). Mahwah, NJ: Erlbaum.

Devereux, G. (1975). Ethnic identity: Its logical foundations and its dysfunctions. In G. de Vos & L. Romanucci-Ross (Eds.), *Ethnic identities: Cultural continuities and change* (pp. 42–70). Palo Alto, CA: Mayfield.

Dunbar, E. (1997). The personal dimensions of difference scale: Measuring multi-group identity with four ethnic groups. *International Journal of Intercultural Relations, 21,* 1–28.

Duncan, O. D. (1984). *Notes on social measurement.* New York: Russell Sage Foundation.

Ellis, B. B. (1995). A partial test of Hulin's psychometric theory of measurement equivalence in translated tests. *European Journal of Psychological Assessment, 11*(3), 184–193.

Ellis, B. B., Becker, P., & Kimmel, H. (1993). An item response theory evaluation of the English version of the Trier Personality Inventory (TPI). *Journal of Cross-Cultural Psychology, 24*(2), 133–148.

Erikson, E. (1968). *Identity, youth, and crisis.* New York: Norton.

Erkut, S., Alarcon, O., Coll, C. G., Tropp, L. R., & Garcia, H. A. (1999). The dual-focus approach to creating bilingual measures. *Journal of Cross-Cultural Psychology, 30*(2), 206–218.

Fischer, A. R., & Moradi, B. (2001). Racial and ethnic identity. In J. G. Ponterotto, J. M. Casas, L. A. Suzuki, & C. M. Alexander (Eds.), *Handbook of multicultural counseling* (2nd ed., pp. 341–370). Thousand Oaks, CA: Sage.

Fitzgerald, T. K. (1993). *Metaphors of identity: A culture-communication dialogue.* Albany: State University of New York Press.

Foote, N. N. (1951). Identification as the basis for a theory of motivation. *American Sociological Review, 16,* 14–21.

Gans, H. (1979). Symbolic ethnicity: The future of ethnic groups and cultures in America. In H. J. Gans et al. (Eds.), *On the making of Americans: Essays in honor of David Riesman* (pp. 193–220). Philadelphia: University of Pennsylvania Press.

Gans, H. (2003, March 7). Identity. *The Chronicle of Higher Education,* pp. B4.

Geertz, C. (2000). *Available light: Anthropological reflections on philosophical topics.* Princeton, NJ: Princeton University Press.

Geisinger, K. F. (1994). Cross-cultural normative assessment: Translation and adaptation issues influencing the normative interpretation of assessment instruments. *Psychological Assessment, 6,* 304–312.

Gerber, B., Smith, E. V., Jr., Girotti, M., Pelaez, L., Lawless, K., Smolin, L., et al. (2002). Using Rasch measurement to investigate cross-form equivalence and clinical utility of Spanish and English versions of a diabetes questionnaire: A pilot study. *Journal of Applied Measurement, 3*(3), 243–271.

Glazer, N. (2002). Do we need the census race question? *Public Interest, 149,* 21–32.

Gleason, P. (1983). Identifying identity: A semantic history. *Journal of American History, 69*(4), 910–931.

Gordon, M. M. (1978). *Human nature, class, and ethnicity.* Oxford, England: Oxford University Press.

Greeley, A. M. (1974). *Ethnicity in the United States.* New York: Wiley.

Harré, R. (1989). Language games and the texts of identity. In J. Shotter & J. J. Gergen (Eds.), *Texts of identity* (pp. 20–35). Newbury Park, CA: Sage.

Harris, H. W., Blue, H. C., & Griffith, E. H. (Eds.). (1995). *Racial and ethnic identity.* New York: Routledge.

Heath, D. B. (1991). Uses and misuses of the concept of ethnicity in alcohol studies: An essay on deconstruction. *International Journal of the Addictions, 25*(5A/6A), 607–627.

Helms, J. E. (Ed.). (1990). *Black and White racial identity: Theory, research, and practice.* Westport, CT: Greenwood Press.

Helms, J. E. (1994). The conceptualization of racial identity and other "racial" constructs. In E. J. Trickett, R. J. Watts, & D. Birman (Eds.), *Human diversity: Perspectives on people in context* (pp. 285–311). San Francisco: Jossey-Bass.

Helms, J. E. (1996). Toward a methodology for measuring and assessing racial as distinguished from ethnic identity. In G. R. Sodowsky & J. C. Impara (Eds.), *Multicultural assessment in counseling and clinical psychology* (pp. 143–192). Lincoln, NE: Buros Institute of Mental Measurements.

Helms, J. E. (2001). An update of Helm's White and people of Color racial identity models. In J. G. Ponterotto, J. M. Casas, L. A. Suzuki, & C. M. Alexander (Eds.), *Handbook of multicultural counseling* (2nd ed., pp. 181–198). Thousand Oaks, CA: Sage.

Helms, J. E., & Carter, R. T. (1990). Development of the White Racial Identity Inventory. In J. E. Helms (Ed.), *Black and White racial identity: Theory, research and practice* (pp. 67–80). Westport, CT: Greenwood.

Helms, J. E., & Cook, D. A. (1999). *Using race and culture in counseling and psychotherapy: Theory and process.* Boston: Allyn & Bacon.

Honigmann, J. J. (1959). *The world of man.* New York: Harper & Row.

Horowitz, E. L., & Horowitz, R. E. (1938). Development of social attitudes in children. *Sociometry, 1,* 301–338.

Horowitz, R. E. (1939). Racial aspects of self-identification in nursery school children. *Journal of Psychology, 7,* 91–99.

Irvine, S., & Carroll, W. (1980). Testing and assessment across cultures: Issues in methodology and theory. In H. C. Triandis & J. W. Berry (Eds.), *Handbook of cross-cultural psychology: Vol. 2. Methodology* (pp. 181–244). Boston: Allyn & Bacon.

Johnson, T. P. (1998). Approaches to equivalence in cross-cultural and cross-national research. In J. A. Harkness (Ed.), *Zuma-nachrichten spezial* (pp. 1–40). Mannheim, Germany: Zentrum UmFragen Methoden Analysen.

Johnson, T. P., Jobe, J. B., O'Rourke, D., Sudman, S., Warnecke, R. B., Vhavez, N., et al. (1997). Dimensions of self-identification among multiracial and multiethnic respondents in survey interviews. *Evaluation Review, 21*(6), 671–687.

Jones, J. M. (2003). Constructing race and deconstructing racism: A cultural psychology approach. In G. Bernal, J. E. Trimble, A. K. Burlew, & F. T. Leong (Eds.), *Handbook of racial and ethnic minority psychology* (pp. 276–290). London: Sage.

Katz, P. A., & Taylor, D. A. (Eds.). (1988). *Eliminating racism: Profiles in controversy.* New York: Plenum Press.

Kim, J., & Mueller, C. (1978). *Factor analysis: Statistical methods and practical issues* [Sage University Paper series on Quantitative Applications in the Social Sciences, 07-001]. Beverly Hills, CA: Sage.

Kivisto, P., & Nefzger, B. (1993). Symbolic ethnicity and American Jews: The relationship of ethnic identity to behavior and group affiliation. *Social Science Journal, 30,* 1–12.

Kline, P. (1983). The cross-cultural use of personality tests. In S. Irvine & J. W. Berry (Eds.), *Human assessment and cultural factors* (pp. 337–352). New York: Plenum Press.

Kobben, A. (1970). Comparativists and non-comparativists in anthropology. In R. Naroll & R. Cohen (Eds.), *A handbook of method in cultural anthropology* (pp. 1282–1289). New York: Natural History Press.

Kohatsu, E. L., & Richardson, T. Q. (1996). Racial and ethnic identity assessment. In L. A. Suzuki, P. J. Meller, & J. G. Ponterotto (Eds.), *Handbook of multicultural counseling and assessment* (pp. 611–650). San Francisco: Jossey-Bass.

Leplege, A., Ecosse, A., & WHOQOL Rasch Project Scientific Committee. (2000). Methodological issues in using the Rasch model to select cross culturally equivalent items in order to develop a quality of life index: The analysis of four WHOQOL-100 data sets (Argentina, France, Hong Kong, United Kingdom). *Journal of Applied Measurement, 1*(4), 372–392.

Malpass, R., & Poortinga, Y. (1986). Strategies for design and analysis. In W. J. Lonner & J. W. Berry (Eds.), *Field methods in cross-cultural research* (pp. 47–83). Newbury Park, CA: Sage.

Marin, G., & Marin, B. V. (1991). *Research with Hispanic populations.* Newbury Park, CA: Sage.

Marshall, G. N. (2002). Differential item functioning in a Spanish translation of the PTSD checklist: Detection and evaluation of impact. *Psychological Assessment, 14,* 50–59.

McGorry, S. Y. (2000). Measurement in a cross-cultural environment: Survey translation issues. *Qualitative Market Research: An International Journal, 3*(2), 74–81.

McInerney, D. M., Yeung, A. S., & McInerney, V. (2001). Cross-cultural validation of the Inventory of School Motivation (ISM): Motivation orientations of Navajo and Anglo students. *Journal of Applied Measurement, 2*(2), 135–153.

McKenney, N. R., & Cresce, A. R. (1993). Measurement of ethnicity in the United States: Experiences of the U.S. Census Bureau. Challenges of measuring an ethnic world: Science, politics and reality. In *Proceedings of the Joint Canada–United States Conference on the Measurement of Ethnicity.* Washington, DC: U.S. Printing Office.

Morgan, H. W. (1981). *Drugs in America.* Syracuse, NY: Syracuse University Press.

Moynihan, D. P. (1993). *Pandaemonium: Ethnicity in international politics.* New York: Oxford University Press.

Nishimoto, R. (1986). The cross-cultural metric equivalence of Langner's twenty-two item index. *Journal of Social Service Research, 9*(4), 37–52.

Oetting, E. R., & Beauvais, F. (1991). Orthogonal cultural identification theory: The cultural identification of minority adolescents. *International Journal of Addictions, 25*(5A/6A), 655–685.

Office of Management and Budget, & Executive Office of the President. (1995). Standards for the classification of federal data on race and ethnicity; notice. *Federal Register, 60*(166), 44673–44693.

Perlmann, J., & Waters, M. C. (Eds.). (2002). *The new race question: How the census counts multiracial individuals.* New York: Russell Sage Foundation.

Phinney, J. S. (1990). Ethnic identity in adolescents and adults: Review of research. *Psychological Bulletin, 108,* 499–514.

Phinney, J. S. (1992). The multigroup ethnic identity measure: A new scale for use with diverse groups. *Journal of Adolescent Research, 7,* 156–176.

Phinney, J. S. (2000). Ethnic identity. In A. E. Kazdin (Ed.), *Encyclopedia of psychology* (Vol. 3, pp. 254–259). New York: Oxford University Press.

Phinney, J. S. (2003). Ethnic identity and acculturation. In K. Chun, P. B. Organista, & G. Marin (Eds.), *Acculturation: Advances in theory, measurement, and applied research* (pp. 63–81). Washington, DC: American Psychological Association.

Ponterotto, J. G., & Wise, S. L. (1987). Construct validity of the Racial Identity Attitude Scale. *Journal of Counseling Psychology, 34,* 218–233.

Poortinga, Y. (1975). Some implications of three different approaches to intercultural comparison. In J. W. Berry & W. J. Lonner (Eds.), *Applied cross-cultural psychology* (pp. 23–29). Amsterdam: Swets & Zeitlinger.

Poortinga, Y. (1983). Psychometric approaches to intergroup comparison: The problem of equivalence. In S. Irvine & J. W. Berry (Eds.), *Human assessment and cultural factors* (pp. 237–257). New York: Plenum Press.

Prelow, H. M., Tein, J., Roosa, M. W., & Wood, J. (2000). Do coping styles differ across sociocultural groups? The role of measurement equivalence in making this judgement. *American Journal of Community Psychology, 28*(2), 225–244.

Prewitt, K. (2002). Race in the 2000 census: A turning point. In J. Perlmann & M. C. Waters (Eds.), *The new race question: How the census counts multiracial individuals* (pp. 354–360). New York: Russell Sage Foundation.

Rasch, G. (1960). *Studies in mathematical psychology: I. Probabilistic models for some intelligence and attainment tests.* Oxford, England: Nielson & Lydiche.

Richman, J., Gaveria, M., Flaherty, J., Birz, S., & Wintrob, R. (1987). The process of acculturation: Theoretical perspectives and an empirical investigation in Peru. *Social Science Medicine, 25*(7), 839–847.

Root, M. P. (1998). Experiences and processes affecting racial identity development: Preliminary results from the biracial sibling project. *Cultural Diversity and Mental Health, 43*(3), 237–247.

Root, M. P. (2000). Rethinking racial identity development. In P. Spickard & W. J. Burroughs (Eds.), *Narrative and multiplicity in constructing ethnic identity* (pp. 205–220). Philadelphia: Temple University Press.

Rosenthal, D. A. (1987). Ethnic identity development in adolescents. In J. S. Phinney & M. J. Rotheram (Eds.), *Children's ethnic socialization: Pluralism and development* (pp. 73–91). Newbury Park, CA: Sage.

Saharso, S. (1989). Ethnic identity and the paradox of equality. In J. P. Van Oudenhoven & T. M. Willemsen (Eds.), *Ethnic minorities: Social psychological perspectives* (pp. 97–114). Berwyn, PA: Swets North America.

Schermmerhorn, R. A. (1969). *Comparative ethnic relations: A framework for theory and research.* New York: Random House.

Schumaker, R., & Linacre, J. (1996). Factor analysis and Rasch. *Rasch Measurement Transactions, 9*(4), 470.

Sevig, T. D., Highlen, P. S., & Adams, E. M. (2000). Development and validation of the self-identity inventory (SII): A multicultural identity development instrument. *Cultural Diversity and Ethnic Minority Psychology, 6,* 168–182.

Simpson, J. A., & Weiner, E. S. (1989). *The Oxford English dictionary* (2nd ed., Vol. VII). Oxford: Clarendon Press.

Smith, T. W. (1980). Ethnic measurement and identification. *Ethnicity, 7,* 78–95.

Sollors, W. (Ed.). (1989). *The invention of ethnicity.* New York: Oxford University Press.

Sollors, W. (2002). What race are you? In J. Perlmann & M. C. Waters (Eds.), *The new race question: How the census counts multiracial individuals* (pp. 263–268). New York: Russell Sage Foundation.

Spini, D. (2003). Measurement equivalence of 10 value types from the Schwartz Value Survey across 21 counties. *Journal of Cross-Cultural Psychology, 34,* 3–23.

Steinberg, S. (1981). *The ethnic myth: Race, ethnicity, and class in America.* New York: Atheneum.

Stephan, C. W., & Stephan, W. G. (2000). The measurement of racial and ethnic identity. *International Journal of Intercultural Relations, 24,* 541–552.

Strauss, A. L. (1959). *Mirrors and masks: The search for identity.* Glencoe, IL: Free Press.

Swanson, J. L., Tokar, D. M., & Davis, L. E. (1994). Content and construct validity of the White Racial Identity Attitude Scale. *Journal of Vocational Behavior, 44,* 198–217.

Tajfel, H. (1982). *Social identity and intergroup relations.* Cambridge, MA: Cambridge University Press.

Thompson, R. H. (1989). *Theories of ethnicity: A critical appraisal.* New York: Greenwood Press.

Trimble, J. E. (1991). Ethnic specification, validation prospects, and the future of drug use research. *International Journal of the Addictions, 25*(2A), 149–170.

Trimble, J. E. (1995). Toward an understanding of ethnicity and ethnic identity, and their relationship with drug use research. In G. Botvin, S. Schinke, & M. Orlandi (Eds.), *Drug abuse prevention with multiethnic youth* (pp. 3–27). Thousand Oaks, CA: Sage.

Trimble, J. E. (2000). Social psychological perspectives on changing self-identification among American Indians and Alaska natives. In R. H. Dana (Ed.), *Handbook of cross-cultural and multicultural personality assessment* (pp. 197–222). Mahwah, NJ: Erlbaum.

Trimble, J. E., & Dickson, R. (in press-a). Ethnic gloss. In C. B. Fisher & R. M. Lerner (Eds.), *Applied developmental science: An encyclopedia of research, policies, and programs.* Thousand Oaks, CA: Sage.

Trimble, J. E., & Dickson, R. (in press-b). Ethnic identity. In C. B. Fisher & R. M. Lerner (Eds.), *Applied developmental science: An encyclopedia of research, policies, and programs.* Thousand Oaks, CA: Sage.

Trimble, J. E., Helms, J. E., & Root, M. P. P. (2003). Social and psychological perspectives on ethnic and racial identity. In G. Bernal, J. E. Trimble, A. K. Burlew, & F. T. Leong (Eds.), *Handbook of racial and ethnic minority psychology* (pp. 239–275). Thousand Oaks, CA: Sage.

Trimble, J. E., & Lonner, W. J. (1993). *Is there a need for another type of cultural equivalence in cultural comparative research?* Paper presented at the International Test's Commission Conference on Test Use with Children and Youth: Pathways to Progress, Oxford, England, Oxford University, St. Hugh's College.

Trimble, J. E., Lonner, W. J., & Boucher, J. (1983). Stalking the wily emic: Alternatives to cross-cultural measurement. In S. Irvine & J. W. Berry (Eds.), *Human assessment and cultural factors* (pp. 259–273). New York: Plenum Press.

Trimble, J. E., & Mahoney, E. (2002). Gender and ethnic differences in adolescent self-esteem: A Rasch measurement model analysis. In P. D. Mail, S. Heurtin-Roberts, S. E. Martin, & J. Howard (Eds.), *Alcohol use among American Indians and Alaska Natives: Multiple perspectives on a complex problem* (National Institute on Alcohol Abuse and Alcoholism Research Monograph No. 37, pp. 211–240). Bethesda, MD: National Institute on Alcohol Abuse and Alcoholism.

Tsai, J. L., Chentsova-Dutton, Y., & Wong, Y. (2002). Why should researchers study ethnic identity, acculturation, and cultural orientation? In G. C. Hall & S. Okazaki (Eds.), *Asian American psychology* (pp. 41–65). Washington, DC: American Psychological Association.

van den Berghe, P. (1981). *The ethnic phenomenon.* New York: Elsevier.

van de Vijver, F. (2000). The nature of bias. In R. H. Dana (Ed.), *Handbook of cross-cultural and multicultural personality assessment* (pp. 87–106). Mahwah, NJ: Erlbaum.

van de Vijver, F., & Leung, K. (1997). *Methods and data analysis for cross-cultural research.* Thousand Oaks, CA: Sage.

van de Vijver, F., & Poortinga, Y. H. (1997). Towards an integrated analysis of bias in cross-cultural assessment. *European Journal of Psychological Assessment, 13,* 29–37.

van de Vijver, F., & Tanzer, N. K. (1997). Bias and equivalence in cross-cultural assessment: An overview. *European Review of Applied Psychology, 47,* 263–279.

Vaughn, G. M. (1987). A social psychological model of ethnic identity development. In J. S. Phinney & M. J. Rotheram (Eds.), *Children's ethnic socialization: Pluralism and development* (pp. 73–91). Newbury Park, CA: Sage.

Waters, M. C. (1990). *Ethnic options: Choosing identities in America.* Berkeley: University of California Press.

Weinreich, P. (1986). The operationalisation of identity theory in racial and ethnic relations. In J. Rex & D. Mason (Eds.), *Theories of race and ethnic relations* (pp. 299–320). Cambridge, England: Cambridge University Press.

Weinreich, P., & Saunderson, W. (Eds.). (2003). *Analysing identity: Cross-cultural, societal and clinical contexts.* New York: Routledge.

Windle, M., Iwawaki, S., & Lerner, R. (1987). Cross-cultural comparability of temperament among Japanese and American early and late adolescents. *Journal of Adolescent Research, 2*(4), 423–446.

Yee, A. H., Fairchild, H. H., Weizmann, F., & Wyatt, G. E. (1993). Addressing psychology's problems with race. *American Psychologist, 48*(11), 1132–1140.

Yinger, J. M. (1986). Intersecting strands in the theorization of race and ethnic relations. In J. Rex & D. Mason (Eds.), *Theories of race and ethnic relations* (pp. 20–41). Cambridge, England: Cambridge University Press.

Young, L. W., Jr. (1999). Race. In J. S. Mio, J. E. Trimble, P. Arredondo, H. E. Cheatham, & D. Sue (Eds.), *Key words in multicultural interventions: A dictionary* (p. 219). Westport, CT: Greenwood Press.

CHAPTER 18

Challenging Some Misuses of Reliability as Reflected in Evaluations of the White Racial Identity Attitude Scale (WRIAS)

Janet E. Helms

Almost 20 years ago, I published the first theory of White racial identity development in psychology (Helms, 1984), followed a few years later by the research version of the White Racial Identity Attitude Scale (WRIAS; Helms & Carter, 1990) and a self-help book for nonpsychologists (Helms, 1992). Prior to the introduction of my theory, many theorists and researchers investigated racial dynamics as they pertained to White people, but generally their perspectives were concerned with the manner in which White people perceived the "racial other" (i.e., racism) rather than the consequences to their conceptions of themselves (i.e., identity). Thus, there was an overabundance of theories and models pertaining to how White people perceived, felt about, or thought about people of Color—especially Black Americans. Some of these are summarized in Helms (1990).

However, in my Black-White model, I presented the idea that White people's conceptions of racial others were inexorably intertwined with their conceptions of themselves as White people. Moreover, I argued that identification or disidentification with the "Black other" was a critical dynamic (i.e., an introject) in White identity development. This proposition was not unique to me. For example, Carl Jung (1930), the psychoanalytic theorist, argued that the most negative aspects of White Americans' personalities (i.e., attitudes, behaviors, defense mechanisms) were influenced by their internalization of negative characteristics that he attributed to their having caught "the contagion" of being Black. He describes the process in the following quote:

> Now what is more contagious than to live side by side with a rather primitive people? Go to Africa and see what happens. When the effect is so very obvious that you stumble over it, then you call it "going black." But if it is not so obvious, then it is explained as "the sun." . . . But the defenses of the Germanic man [sic] reach only as far as consciousness reaches. Below the threshold of consciousness the contagion meets little resistance. Since the Negro [sic] lives within your cities and even within your houses, he also lives within your skin, subconsciously. Naturally, it works both ways. Just as every Jew has a Christ complex, so every Negro has a white complex, and every white American a Negro complex.

The Negro, generally speaking, would give anything to change his skin; *so, too, the white man hates to admit that he has been touched by the black.* (p. 196; emphasis added)

In psychoanalytic theory, the process by which a powerful entity (e.g., therapist, White people) influences and not consciously is influenced by a less powerful entity (e.g., client, Black people) is called, "mutual introjection." Jung did not argue that Blacks were the *only* racial group introject in the White American psyche. For example, he believed that Native Americans (i.e., Indians) were also an influence, but he was less precise in defining how their influence was manifested or whether it was positive or negative.

Nor did I argue that Blacks are the only influence on the racial identity development of White people (Helms, 1984). Because I do not believe that every group influences White identity development in the same manner, I expected that subsequent theorists would use my Black-White model to develop other models focused on the influence of other groups of people of Color on White identity development. Nevertheless, just as whether White people have internalized identical socialization experiences with respect to *all* racial groups is an empirical question, so too is my belief that "going Black" is one component of the psychodynamically complex White identity. To my knowledge, these two questions have been empirically studied only twice (Remy, 1993; Scarpellini-Huber, 1997).

As compared with the attitudes-toward-others models, what was unique about my perspective was that I proposed options by which White people could overcome the socialization that required them to maintain their self- and group esteem by directly or indirectly exploiting and subjugating people who were perceived as "not Whites." I suspect that the idea that one could recognize and overcome one's racist socialization is the aspect of my theory that continues to appeal to those who persist in using my theory and measure in spite of the barrage of advice that they should not do so (e.g., Behrens, 1997; Behrens & Rowe, 1997; Fischer & Moradi, 2001; Tokar & Swanson, 1991).

Something—perhaps Jung's "Negro complex"—about the idea that White people's not necessarily conscious socialization with respect to Black people influences who they are as White people mightily distressed some mostly White theorists. This distress served as a catalyst for anti-Helms and/or intended replacement theories of White identity. These included Rowe and associates' (Rowe, Behrens, & Leach, 1995; Rowe, Bennett, & Atkinson, 1994) and LaFleur and associates' (Behrens & LaFleur, 2002; LaFleur, Rowe, & Leach, 2002; Leach, Behrens, & LaFleur, 2002) White consciousness models and Ponterotto's (1988) training model. The anti-Helms theorists generally agree that their alternative perspectives are "conceptually cleaner" (Fischer & Moradi, 2001, p. 352), "less unclear" (Rowe et al., 1995, p. 225), and subject to higher levels of "testability" (Leach et al., 2002) than mine. However, there have been no empirical studies that support these assertions, as relevant measures seem to be in a state of perpetual closeted development.

Also, other authors have pointed out that there is considerable overlap between Helms's model and its successors (Block & Carter, 1996; Thompson, 1994). Moreover, my model appears to serve a heuristic function because many practitioners and researchers have continued to explore and expand on the constructs that I proposed in spite of detractors' advice that they not do so. Scott and Robinson's (2001) "Key Model," an attempt to integrate White male identity and White racial identity, is such a theoretical elaboration.

MEASURES OF WHITE IDENTITY

In addition to stimulating the quest for replacement White identity models, my (Helms, 1984, 1990) conceptual model also directly served as a catalyst for Claney and Parker's (1989) White Racial Consciousness Development Scale (WRCDS) and indirectly as a measure of Choney and Behrens's (1996) Oklahoma Racial Attitudes Scale (ORAS-P).

WRCDS

Claney and Parker's (1989) WRCDS is the only alternative, independently developed measure of my racial identity constructs. Thus, one would have expected it to be welcomed into the research arena because it is a well-known measurement principle that the availability of multiple measures of a construct allows researchers to separate measurement effects from the constructs being measured (e.g., Campbell & Fiske, 1959).

Nevertheless, the WRCDS has been used in only one subsequent study, perhaps because naïve researchers and/or the developers of the WRCDS took Choney and Rowe's (1994) antiscientific condemnation of the measure seriously. Based on their single psychometric study of the WRCDS, Choney and Rowe advised the following:

> [Practitioners and researchers] should disregard any findings resulting from the use of the WRCDS. Service providers should also refrain from using the WRCDS in their assessment procedures. In addition, researchers not only should avoid using the instrument in future investigations but also might consider critically examining the measurement properties of the RIAS-W [*sic*] before investing more resources in the examination of White racial identity. (p. 104)

It is surprising to me that the journal editor and reviewers permitted Choney and Rowe to offer such daunting advice, given that science progresses by studying and using constructs rather than by "not studying" and "not using" them. Moreover, it is clear that Choney and Rowe had difficulty being objective about the merits of the WRIAS given that they felt compelled to denigrate it even in a study in which it was not their ostensible focus. Suffice it to say that I hope researchers will disregard Choney and Rowe's advice (and similar advice) about use of the WRCDS as well as their advice with respect to the WRIAS.

ORAS-P

My model and measure indirectly influenced the development of the ORAS-P (Choney & Behrens, 1996) in two ways, both stimulated by its authors' beliefs that Blacks are not a reference or contrast group in White identity development. First, to my surprise, I discovered that the original version of the ORAS-P contained several items adapted from the WRIAS, with "minority" substituted for "Black." Second, the ORAS-P authors intended their measure to be used in assessing constructs reflective of their "undeniable reality [that] White people say things and act in ways that seem to reflect a variety of attitudes toward racial/ethnic minorities" (Rowe et al., 1995, p. 225). Accordingly, they argued that rather than regarding these attitudes as a reflection of an underlying " '[White] racial identity,' we chose to treat attitudes [toward minorities] as the primary phenomena of interest" (Rowe et al., 1995, p. 225).

Thus, if Rowe et al. (1995) are taken at their word, then the ORAS-P should be considered a measure of types of racism (i.e., attitudes toward other racial groups) rather than a measure of Whites' consciousness of their own intra- or interracial dynamics per se. Consequently, the WRIAS and the WRCDS are currently the only two extant measures of White racial identity. With perhaps two recent exceptions (Kyle, 2001; Mueller & Pope, 2001), independent researchers have not conducted psychometric studies of the ORAS-P. Moreover, although the cadre of ORAS-P developers have engaged in multiple studies of the White identity measures derived from my model, actually more than I have, I could not find any published evidence that they have studied their own measure in such depth.

Given the alleged overlap among the constructs in Rowe et al.'s (1994) model of Whites' attitudes toward minorities, which they have labeled "White consciousness," and my model of White identity stages/statuses (Block & Carter, 1996; Pope-Davis, Vandiver, & Stone, 1999; Thompson, 1994), it is likely that the same criticisms that are leveled against the measures developed from my theoretical perspective, the WRCDS and WRIAS, will also be true for the ORAS-P if it is subjected to the same kinds of critical psychometric scrutiny from independent researchers.

MEASUREMENT-RELATED THEMES

Nevertheless, the purpose of this chapter is not to refute the charges that my constructs and, consequently, my measures of them are inaccurate; I have done so elsewhere, apparently to no avail (e.g., Helms, 1996, 1997, 1999). However, I will summarize some of the reoccurring measurement themes as to how to interpret my theory, about which anti-Helms critics and I disagree, as well as resources where the reader can obtain point-counterpoint arguments for herself or himself. My reason for summarizing these measurement themes is that one's position with respect to each of them has implications for how one studies or uses measures of racial identity constructs generally and mine specifically.

The first theme concerns whether my racial identity constructs and, therefore, measures of them are supposed to be interdependent. I have argued that I designed the constructs to be interrelated. It is a developmental model; consequently, the identity constructs are hypothesized to evolve out of one another. Moreover, I have argued that each individual potentially manifests some level of each of the identity statuses, ranging from none at all to a maximum level, and, consequently, should not be classified on the basis of single scale scores. That is, racial identity constructs and, therefore, measures of them interact with one another.

In more formal psychometric terminology, the scales are interrelated or multicollinear because the constructs are so related in real life. People who use sensitizing schemas (Reintegration, Disintegration) do not tend to also use repressing strategies (Contact, Pseudo Independence, Autonomy). Therefore, scores on scales with similar repression-sensitizing themes will be positively correlated with other within-theme scales and negatively correlated with oppositional themes. This is inevitable given the nature of the constructs.

However, multicollinearity does not necessarily signify redundancy in measurement, as most users of the WRIAS have assumed. A case in point is that test takers' scores on verbal and mathematics tests of mental abilities typically are so highly correlated as to be considered multicollinear if the same criteria that are used to evaluate the WRIAS were used to evaluate ability tests. Yet one rarely hears that scores on one type of ability test should be substituted for the other.

Nevertheless, it is the case that scores on the WRIAS scales or items should not be studied as if they reflect independent or orthogonal constructs because they do not. In virtually all of my writings about my White racial identity theory from the beginning (e.g., Helms, 1984, 1996, 1997), I theorize that successive stages/statuses of White identity evolve from prior ones, and, consequently, measures of more than one of the relevant constructs must be interrelated. However, critics believe that evidence of interrelatedness of WRIAS scale scores necessarily is evidence of poor theorizing (Behrens, 1997; Fischer & Moradi, 2001; Tokar & Swanson, 1991), and persist in testing models in which scores on the scales are supposed or constrained to be independent. There seems to be nothing that I can do to encourage them to use alternative measurement paradigms.

Another theme concerns whether samples differ with respect to racial identity characteristics. Pro-Helms theorists and I believe that they do (e.g., Carter, 1996; Helms, 1997). Anti-Helms theorists believe that all samples should respond identically (e.g., Behrens, 1997; Behrens & Rowe, 1997; Fischer & Moradi, 2001), and, as a result, they interpret empirical evidence of heterogeneity in samples' responses to items as being indicative of serious flaws in the WRIAS or the theory on which it is based. Interestingly, I found no study of the WRIAS in which the researchers attributed their failure to find support for their hypotheses to faulty hypotheses rather than "problems" with the "reliability" of the WRIAS. Thus, in the eyes of most WRIAS researchers, the only way to demonstrate the merits of the WRIAS is for their hypotheses to be confirmed, regardless of the characteristics of their samples.

It should be noted, however, that it is a well-known measurement principle that "the characteristics of the participants involved in a measurement situation will affect the score variability and, subsequently, the measurement reliability in the situation" (Yin & Fan, 2000). Presumably, if this principle has merit for nonracial measures, then it is also true with respect to studies incorporating the WRIAS. Consequently, it is just possible that researchers ought to reconsider their hypotheses when the evidence obtained from the WRIAS does not support them rather than automatically revising the WRIAS on a study-by-study basis, as has become common practice.

A third theme concerns whether it is appropriate to use scores obtained from the WRIAS to assess individuals given that "convergent validity" evidence is allegedly stronger than reliability evidence. I argue that it is appropriate given that evidence of validity is "the most fundamental consideration in developing and evaluating tests" and "[it] is the interpretations of test scores required by proposed uses that are evaluated, not the test [WRIAS] itself" (American Educational Research Association [AERA], American Psychological Association [APA], & National Council on Measurement in Education [NCME], 1999, p. 9). Nevertheless, Behrens (1997) developed the concept of "validity paradox" to explain why confirmatory validity evidence across studies should be disregarded with respect to the WRIAS, a perspective that has been readily adopted by anti-Helms theorists (Fisher & Moradi, 2001; Leach et al., 2002), as well as novice researchers. Yet the paradox seems to apply only to the WRIAS, not to measures that yield similar psychometric data such as the ORAS-P (Choney & Behrens, 1996, p. 235; Kyle, 2001; Pope-Davis et al., 1999).

CHAPTER FOCUS

Much of the condemnation of my theory has occurred in response to researchers' beliefs that the WRIAS scales do not behave in a manner that is consistent with their understanding of psychometric theory and their unwillingness to consider my interpretations of my own theory and measure. Although I have offered many suggestions about how to use psychometric theory more appropriately to study the WRIAS or conduct research using it (Helms, 1996, 1997, 1999), these recommendations have been summarily dismissed. For example, Behrens's (1997) meta-analysis of reliability coefficients is often cited as evidence of the "psychometric unsoundness" of the WRIAS, but my meta-analysis (Helms, 1999), which provides an alternative interpretation, is virtually never cited, or, if cited, its measurement implications are not well understood.

Rather than presuming malicious intent, however, I assume that what appears to me to be anti-Helms favoritism or White group racial solidarity occurs because critics of the WRIAS (e.g., Behrens, 1997) identify themselves as psychometricians or are so identified by others, whereas I am not (e.g., Tokar & Swanson, 1991). Alternatively, perhaps researchers simply do not understand that when interscale variances, covariances, and, therefore, Cronbach alpha coefficients are interdependent (i.e., correlated), as I demonstrated (Helms, 1999), then all statistical and psychometric procedures that presume independent measurement errors (e.g., reliability, factor analysis, structural equation models) are potentially nonsensical. Under such circumstances, it is particularly ridiculous to use WRIAS reliability coefficients to correct WRIAS interscale correlations, as Behrens did, because the measurement errors for the reliability and correlation coefficients are correlated.

Nevertheless, much of the evaluation of the WRIAS and, therefore, White racial identity theory has been based on interpretations of psychometric data that are not consistent with contemporary psychometric theory (e.g., AERA et al., 1999; Wilkinson & APA Task Force on Statistical Inference, 1999). Various authors have discussed the prevalence of misuse and misinterpretations of reliability data with respect to other personality measures (Caruso, 2000; Vacha-Haase, 1998). However, the focus of my discussion is researchers' misapplications of reliability theory as they pertain to the WRIAS specifically because I believe that race evokes strong emotions that may have prevented researchers from recognizing the extent to which they have engaged in poor science with respect to the WRIAS and, for that matter, the WRCDS and ORAS-P. In the latter case, poor science has taken the form of advocating for the use of the measure in the absence of virtually any published reliability or validity evidence (e.g., LaFleur et al., 2002), whereas in the case of the WRIAS and possibly the WRCDS, it has taken the form of protesting their use in spite of such evidence (e.g., Behrens, 1997).

In this chapter, I have chosen to focus explicitly on issues of reliability because researchers have often misinterpreted the adage "A test [score] cannot be valid unless it is reliable" to mean that WRIAS data should be discarded if certain reliability coefficients are not obtained. However, such misinterpretations camouflage wider misuses of reliability data. I discuss some general misuses of reliability theory and illustrate or discuss how each has been manifested with respect to the WRIAS.

"IT IS NOT THE TEST THAT'S RELIABLE"

Concern about researchers' erroneous belief that reliability coefficients should be interpreted as characteristics of tests rather than test scores has been expressed consistently in the psychometric literature (Pedhazur & Schmelkin, 1991; Wilkinson & Task Force on Statistical Inference, 1999). Such distorted beliefs are inherent in researchers' and practitioners' statements to the effect that "tests are reliable" or, in the case of the WRIAS, "tests are not reliable" based on the size of obtained reliability coefficients.

Some themes that reflect such misuses or misunderstandings of reliability data are summarized in Table 18.1 with respect to White identity measures. The themes are roughly categorized according to common misuses that I discuss subsequently. Two authoritative resources for psychologists specifically point out that attribution of reliability to tests rather than to test scores is incorrect and nonscientific interpretation of reliability data. They are the *Standards for Educational and Psychological Testing* (AERA et al., 1999) and *Statistical Methods in Psychology Journals: Guidelines and Explanations* (Wilkinson & APA Task Force on Statistical Inference, 1999). *Testing Standards* provides guidelines for developing and using tests, whereas Wilkinson et al. provide guidelines for describing one's research design.

Testing Standards (AERA et al., 1999) provides the following general definition of reliability: "The extent to which test scores for a group of test takers are consistent over repeated applications of a measurement procedure and hence are inferred to be dependable, and repeatable for an individual test taker" (p. 180). This definition implies that reliability inheres in test scores (i.e., participants' responses) rather than the test (e.g., the WRIAS) itself.

Table 18.1 Summary of Reliability Misinterpretations

Reliability Induction or Inferring Reliability from Prior Studies

"The RIAS-W measures Contact, Disintegration, Reintegration, Pseudo-Independence, Immersion/Emersion, and Autonomy statuses. *Reliability estimates range from .55 to .74, on the Contact stage and the Disintegration stage*" (Watt, Robinson, & Lupton-Smith, 2002, p. 97).

"Coefficient alpha reliability coefficients reported by Helms and Carter (1991) were .55, .77, .80, .71, and .67, in Study one, and .67, .76, .75, .65, and .65, in Study 2, for Contact [,] Disintegration, Reintegration, Pseudo-Independence, and Autonomy scales, respectively" (Pope-Davis, Vandiver, & Stone, 1999, p. 72).

"Bennett et al. (1993) reported internal consistency reliability coefficients (Cronbach's alpha) of .72, .80, .79, .77, .82, .75, and .68 for the Reactive, Conflictive, Integrative, Dominative, Dependent, Dissonant, and Avoidant subscales, respectively" (Pope-Davis, Vandiver, & Stone, 1999, p. 72).

"In three separate reliability studies, Helms and Carter (1990) cited reliabilities of .55 to .67 for Contact, .75 to .77 for Disintegration, .75 to .82 for Reintegration, .65 to .77 for Pseudo-Independence, and .76 to .74 for Autonomy" (Taub & McEwen, 1992, p. 442).

Reliability Imputation

"This study was designed to investigate the reliability and validity of the WRIAS" (Alexander, 1992, p. 62).

"As the WRIAS began to see widespread use in the 1990s, questions regarding *its* reliability and validity began to emerge" (Leach, Behrens, & LaFleur, 2002, p. 72).

"Reliability analyses of the WRIAS were conducted to examine Hypothesis 2, that the derived scales are reliable" (Mercer & Cunningham, 2003, p. 226).

Use of Specified and Unspecified Rules of Thumb

"While Disintegration and Reintegration had acceptable levels of reliability, the other three subscales' reliabilities appeared quite weak" (Alexander, 1992, p. 63).

"Because the test-retest reliability coefficients for the RIAS-B and WRIAS were both below the .70 minimum for temporal stability, they should not be considered stable personality traits" (Lemon & Waehler, 1996, p. 82).

"Two independent evaluations [two citations] of the psychometric properties of the ORAS-P supported this contention [in that each] investigated the *reliability coefficients of the scales,* the interscale correlations, and the factor structure. *The alpha coefficients were adequate,* ranging from a low of .62 for Avoidant to .85 for the Dependent Scale" (Leach, Behrens, & LaFleur, 2002, p. 75).

"Previous investigations [three citations] have *reported suboptimal coefficient alphas for some WRIAS subscales, particularly the Contact subscale*" (Constantine, 2002).

Confusing Psychometric Studies with Assessment Studies

"Unfortunately, we must echo Behrens's (1997) call to exercise extreme caution when using the WRIAS for group-level analyses. (Carter, 1996, and Helms, 1996, recently have advocated use of the [*sic*] profiles with individuals, though they still recommended comparing individual data to norms.)" (Fischer & Moradi, 2001, p. 352).

Note: RIAS-B is the Black Racial Identity Attitude Scale, WRIAS is the White Racial Identity Attitude Scale, and ORAS-P is the Oklahoma Racial Attitudes Scale–Preliminary. Italics within quotations were added for emphasis.

Wilkinson and APA Task Force on Statistical Inference (1999) make the linkage between reliability and sample characteristics more explicit. They summarize the correct use of reliability coefficients as follows:

> It is important to remember that *a test is not reliable or unreliable. Reliability is a property of the scores on a test for a particular population of examinees* (Feldt & Brennan, 1989). Thus, authors should provide reliability coefficients of the scores for the data being analyzed even when the focus of their research is not psychometric. Interpreting the size of the observed effects requires an assessment of the reliability of scores. (p. 2, emphasis added)

When researchers wrongfully assume that reliability is a stable property of tests, they tend to erroneously report the results of their reliability analyses as well. Some of these wrongful practices include (1) reliability induction, inferring reliability from previous studies rather than conducting one's own reliability analyses; (2) assuming that reliability coefficients are "inadequate" according to some specified or unspecified standard (e.g., .70) without conducting tests of significance or computing confidence intervals; (3) assuming homogeneity of sample characteristics such that all samples are supposed to respond in the same manner regardless of their characteristics; and (4) misconstruing the relationships between reliability and validity coefficients. Each of these misuses can be illustrated with respect to interpretation of data derived from studies of the WRIAS.

Both Behrens (1997) and Helms (1999) studied the issue of confidence intervals and Cronbach alpha coefficients reported for WRIAS scale scores. So, that issue is not investigated in the present study. In this chapter, I focus primarily on the extent to which researchers have engaged in errors in reporting reliability data and the extent to which such reporting practices have contributed to wrongful conclusions about the WRIAS. Specifically, using meta-analytic data, I investigated the following questions: How often did researchers report (1) reliability coefficients, (2) WRIAS interscale correlations, and (3) indices of sample characteristics (e.g., standard deviations, means)? Also, I examined whether reporting practices differed by type of study (e.g., dissertations versus journal articles). In addition, given that Behrens's study has been deemed the definitive study of the WRIAS, I also examined whether reporting practices improved following his study.

With respect to induction studies per se (i.e., studies in which researchers inferred reliability from previous studies), I examined the extent to which sample characteristics matched the characteristics of the study from which reliability was inferred. Finally, to illustrate why use of reliability rules of thumb might contribute to misleading results, I examine in some detail reliability and validity data provided by Steward, Boatwright, Sauer, Baden, and Jackson (1998). Their study was selected because they were among the few authors who actually reported reliability information for the WRIAS and some other measure.

Originally, I also had intended to incorporate studies of the ORAS-P when examination of them would have served to highlight a conundrum in White identity/attitude measurement generally. However, the four studies that I was able to obtain in which the ORAS-P was used did not report enough psychometric data to make their inclusion plausible (Choney & Behrens, 1996; Kyle, 2001; Mueller & Pope, 2001; Pope-Davis et al., 1999).

REPORTING ERRORS

One type of error occurs when researchers assume that reliability is a stable property of tests and, as a consequence, do not report reliability coefficients for their sample. This type of error may take one of two forms: not mentioning reliability at all and induction (i.e., inferring reliability from previous researchers' studies). Although the first type is worth a brief discussion, for the most part, the meta-analytic data available to me did not permit me to tell whether reliability coefficients were missing because the researchers did not mention reliability or because they inferred reliability data from elsewhere. Of course, one could go back to the original sources to obtain this information if desired, but the exact reason why the data were missing did not seem particularly important for purposes of this chapter.

Not Mentioning Reliability

The most egregious type of misattribution of reliability to tests is the failure of researchers to mention reliability at all in their empirical studies. When researchers commit this error, it is presumably because they do not realize that evidence of reliability is important. In Behrens's (1997) study, which reviewers consider to be *the* authoritative evidence of the unsoundness of the WRIAS (Behrens & Rowe, 1997; Fisher & Moradi, 2001; Leach et al., 2002), Behrens committed this error twice in his second study (Behrens, 1997). If researchers followed his example, one might expect to find similar omissions in studies following his in which the WRIAS was used.

In my extended replication of Behrens's (1997, study 1) meta-analysis of Cronbach alpha coefficients, I reported that 18.4% of the 38 studies used in my analyses did not report reliability coefficients for the WRIAS scales. However, it was not clear whether these were instances in which reliability was not mentioned at all or was explicitly inferred from previous studies. Either of these is considered a poor practice, although not mentioning reliability is slightly worse than inferring it from previous studies.

Nevertheless, 18% is a rather small percentage of not reporting relative to other studies of reliability coefficients involving other measures (e.g., Vacha-Haase, 1998). For example, Vacha-Haase reported that 65.8% of the 628 studies that included an administration of the Bem Sex Role Inventory did not provide any information about the reliability of the researchers' data. Perhaps this finding attests to WRIAS researchers' increasing awareness that attention to reliability of measurements is desirable, even though the researchers may not necessarily interpret their reliability data correctly.

Reliability Induction

Inferring reliability of one's present measurements from reliability coefficients that were reported in previous studies is a more common error than not mentioning it at all. Vacha-Haase, Kogan, and Thompson (2000) have coined the concept of "reliability induction" to refer to the process of "*explicitly* referencing the reliability coefficients from *prior* reports as the sole warrant for presuming the score integrity of entirely *new* data" (p. 512, emphasis in the original). They also recommended some strategies for comparing new studies to the prior inducted studies to determine whether such induction is plausible.

The practice of reliability induction is problematic because it presumes, rather than demonstrates, that characteristics of the sample used in the cited study necessarily characterize the new sample, which, of course, is not plausible. Leach et al. (2002) rightly criticized Brown, Parham, and Yonker (1996), Carter, Gushue, and Weitzman (1994), Parks, Carter, and Gushue (1996), and Taub and McEwen (1992) for inducting reliability from Helms and Carter's (1990) data. However, they praised the work of Pope-Davis and colleagues (1999), even though the research team engaged in reliability induction with respect to *both* the WRIAS and the ORAS-P. Thus, the authors leave the impression that reliability induction is a poor practice when it pertains to evaluations of the WRIAS, with which they disagree, but does not matter in studies that confirm their own impressions.

Helms and Carter's (1991) study was cited as the authority for Pope-Davis et al.'s (1999) WRIAS induction, and Bennett, Atkinson, and Rowe (1993), an apparently unpublished paper presentation, were the authoritative source for the ORAS-P induction. Because I did not have access to the Bennett et al. study and the ORAS-P seemingly has not been used in many other accessible studies, I could not investigate the extent to which reliability induction was appropriate where it was concerned. Also, Pope-Davis et al. used item parcels rather than the original individual WRIAS or ORAS-P items and, as a consequence, only limited comparisons of the characteristics of their sample to Helms and Carter's (1990) sample(s) could have been conducted.

In addition to the WRIAS reliability induction studies cited by Leach et al. (2002), I also located induction studies by Carter (1990) and Watt, Robinson, and Lupton-Smith (2002). These studies could not be used to examine induction with respect to the specific study cited by the authors because Watt et al. cited ranges of reliability coefficients for the WRIAS scales, which they attributed to a theoretical article in which no reliability data were reported (i.e., Helms, 1984) and Carter used his 1988 dissertation as the source of his induction. Consequently, only a small number of studies were available that used the same authoritative source as the focus of their reliability induction.

Therefore, I decided to operationally define induction as the extent to which reliability coefficients were not reported. This leaves one to infer that the reason they were not reported is because the researcher cited someone else's reliability information, although, in fact, the inference might be incorrect. However, this conclusion does not seem too far-fetched given that the sources I was able to locate, as previously discussed, did induct from prior studies, albeit different ones. When studying induction, one compares studies with no reported reliability coefficients to the standard study from which reliability is inferred. In this case, I used Helms and Carter (1990) as the standard because it is the study that has been most frequently cited.

METHOD

The present study consisted of 64 potential sets of WRIAS Cronbach alpha coefficients. Some of the studies (n =38) were used in the Behrens (1997) and/or Helms (1999) combined data set. In addition, I conducted a search in the Psych-INFO database using "WRIAS" and "Helms." This search resulted in the additional 26 studies. Two other studies revealed by the search (DeSole, 2002; Jome, 2000) could not be obtained in time for this study and, consequently, are not included. I examined the abstracts for each of the PsychINFO sources that were identified and, if it was a description of an empirical study not contained in Behrens or Helms, I attempted to obtain the full original version of the study. Some studies contained reliability coefficients for more than one subgroup (e.g., different experimental groups) and, consequently, contributed more than one set of data (e.g., Miyatake, 1998). Others did not use the WRIAS and, consequently, contributed no data (e.g., Mueller & Pope, 2001).

The new studies used in these analyses are marked with asterisks in the reference list. Because I intended to examine reliability reporting errors as a major focus of this study, empirical studies involving the WRIAS were included even if they did not report any reliability or interscale correlation coefficients, which was not the case for either Behrens (1997) or Helms (1999).

RESULTS

Tables 18.2a and 18.2b summarize the characteristics of the studies with respect to Cronbach alpha coefficients, standard deviations, means of scores on the WRIAS scales, and other descriptive information pertaining to the samples investigated.

General Reporting Practices

In the data set as a whole, sample size was the only data that 100% of the studies reported. A total of 11,234 (presumably) White respondents completed some form of the WRIAS. Samples ranged in size from a low of 16 to a high of 506 (mean = 175.53, SD = 119.244). If researchers had used standard or common reporting practices, more than enough data would have been available to evaluate how respondents' characteristics interacted with their responses to the WRIAS items.

Table 18.2a   Summary of Descriptive Information for Referent and Comparison Studies

Scale	Referent Study			Comparison Studies		
	Alpha	Mean	SD	Alpha	Mean	*SD*
Contact	.55	30.90	4.17	.15–.68	31.58	4.39
Disintegration	.77	25.06	6.42	.39–.87	22.74	5.30
Reintegration	.80	25.07	5.89	.38–.88	21.62	5.32
Pseudo independence	.71	36.08	5.04	.33–.93	36.12	4.49
Autonomy	.67	33.71	4.79	.28–.76	37.58	4.28

Table 18.2b   Summary of Reference and Comparison Studies' Descriptive Statistics

Characteristic	Comparison Study (%)
Type of Sample	
College Students*	55.9
College and Graduate Students	11.8
Graduate Students	26.5
Practitioners	2.9
Practitioners and Graduate Students	2.9
Geographic Region	
East-Northeast*	15.6
Mid-Atlantic	9.4
South	12.5
Midwest	40.6
West-Northwest	15.6
Miscellaneous	9.3
Type of Study	
Dissertation	50.0
Journal	45.0
Book chapter*	3.1
Unpublished paper	1.6

Note: Number of comparison studies was 34 (type of sample), 32 (geographic region), and 64 (type of study). Asterisks indicate characteristics of Helms and Carter's (1990) referent study.

However, only 68.8% ($n = 44$) of the studies reported alphas for each of the five WRIAS scales. An additional 3.1% ($n = 2$) reported alphas for four of the five WRIAS scales and 28.1% reported no reliability coefficients. In the two cases missing only one alpha coefficient, Davidson (1991) actually reported Cronbach alphas for scores on the Contact scale in her two studies, but they were based on a modified version of the scale.

In addition to the possible problem of induction (i.e., inferring reliability), coefficients seemed to be missing for a variety of reasons, some of which may be unique to researchers' use of the WRIAS. Examples of improper reporting practices with respect to reliability were as follows: Some authors seemingly calculated reliability for the total inventory rather than the individual scales (e.g., Miyatake, 1998; Snider, 2000), inferred reliability from a multivariate analysis of variance of the individual inventory items (Look, 1997), combined scales in a manner that they believed Behrens had recommended or that seemed to make sense to them, or substituted "Hispanics" for "Blacks." Each of these reporting practices made the study's results not directly comparable to the WRIAS data that Helms and Carter (1990) reported.

Also, in the sample as a whole, 64.1% ($n = 41$) reported standard deviations for each of the five scales, but 29.7% ($n = 19$) reported none. In one case, Utsey and Gernat (2002), a Cronbach alpha coefficient was reported for scores on the original Autonomy scale, but standard deviations and interscale correlations were reported only for their revision of the Autonomy scale. Some authors reported standard deviations for subgroups in their samples (e.g., men and women) but reliability coefficients based on the total sample. In these cases, I computed sample-weighted standard deviations using Glass and Hopkins's (1996, pp. 72–73) formula.

It was also the case that only 64.1% ($n = 41$) reported means for their samples on each of the WRIAS scales, whereas 29.7% ($n = 19$) did not. Thus, although reporting practices with respect to the WRIAS were generally better than those of previous studies of other measures reported in the literature, they were still cause for considerable concern. Moreover, given that studies that reported one type of data (e.g., Cronbach alpha coefficients) did not necessarily report other types of data (e.g., standard deviations), it was difficult to manage missing data for the intended analyses.

General Sample Composition

With respect to sample composition, the average percentage of women in the samples across the studies ($n = 31$) for which this information was available was 62.71 ($SD = 14.32$). Almost equal percentages of the 62 studies were dissertations (50%) or journal articles (45.2%). More than half of 32 of the studies (56.3%) used samples of undergraduate college students exclusively, whereas another 6.3% used mixtures of graduate and undergraduate students. Another nine (14.3%) used graduate student samples exclusively. Of the 32 studies for which the sample's geographic origins could be ascertained, the largest percentage (40.6%) was from the Midwest.

Pre- and Post-Behrens (1997) Studies

I compared studies conducted before Behrens's (1997) study to those conducted afterward with respect to reliability reporting practices. For these comparisons, a study was coded 1 if it was conducted in 1997 or before (i.e., before or in the same year as Behrens's study) and 0 if it was conducted after 1997.

Fifty WRIAS studies were conducted in the seven years preceding Behrens's study, whereas 14 have been conducted in the almost six subsequent years. It is not clear whether this noticeable decline can be attributed to Behrens directly. Of the reporting practices and sample characteristics examined, only the reporting or lack of reporting of standard deviations was significantly related to when the study was conducted ($n = 64$; chi square [$df = 2,1$] = 6.551; $p < .038$). Of the 41 studies that reported all five standard deviations, 85.4% ($n = 35$) occurred prior to Behrens's study, whereas only 12.2% ($n = 5$) occurred afterward. On the other hand, for the 19 studies in which no standard deviations were reported, the relevant percentages were 57.9% (before Behrens) and 42.1% (after Behrens).

Induction Study

In addition to sample size ($n = 506$), Helms and Carter (1990) reported means, standard deviations, gender composition, type of sample (i.e., students), and geographic region of the sample used in their normative study. It was also possible to infer type of publication (i.e., book chapter) from their report. The characteristics of Helms and Carter's sample are summarized in Tables 18.2a and 18.2b. Each of these dimensions was examined with respect to the total data set prior to conducting the induction study.

Preliminary comparisons to Helms and Carter's (1990) original large-sample reliability study indicate that the samples in subsequent studies differed markedly on most dimensions from their sample. However, an explicit induction study makes these comparisons more explicit. As previously mentioned, Vacha-Haase et al. (2000) defined a methodology for examining the extent to which researchers' generalization of reliability information from prior studies to their own studies was justified.

The induction aspect of the present study focused on those studies for which all five Cronbach alpha coefficients were not reported ($n = 18$). When the data were continuous, I compared them to Helms and Carter's data by subtracting the data in the inducting sample from the respective value as reported by Helms and Carter. This information, which is discussed subsequently, is summarized in Table 18.3 for sample characteristics.

Sample Characteristics

Variability

In general, Cronbach alpha reliability coefficients are larger when sample heterogeneity is high. I compared the standard deviations of each of the five scales to its counterpart as reported in Helms and Carter by subtracting the value reported in the invoking study from the values reported by Helms and Carter. Thus, if a sample's standard deviations perfectly matched those reported by Helms and Carter, the obtained value would be zero. A negative value signifies that the inducting sample was more variable with respect to the relevant standard deviation and, consequently, might have resulted in larger reliability coefficients than those reported by Helms and Carter if they had been calculated. Positive values indicate that Helms and Carter's samples were more variable than the inducted samples and, potentially, may have yielded larger reliability coefficients than the invoking researchers would

Table 18.3 Induction Study: Deviations Relative to Helms and Carter (1990) of the WRIAS Characteristics of Samples with Missing Alphas

Characteristics	N	Minimum	Maximum	Mean	SD
Contact SD	9	−2.65	1.57	−0.21	1.20
Disintegration SD	9	0.12	1.72	1.17	0.80
Reintegration SD	9	0.01	1.89	0.85	0.78
Pseudo Independence SD	9	0.47	2.14	1.03	0.45
Autonomy SD	9	−0.10	2.09	0.78	0.56
Contact mean	10	−3.46	0.68	−1.51	1.36
Disintegration mean	10	−5.55	6.74	1.77	3.31
Reintegration mean	10	0.57	7.49	3.89	2.37
Pseudo independence mean	10	−4.34	17.08	1.17	5.53
Autonomy mean	10	−6.04	−1.49	−4.31	1.28
Percent women	10	−16.80	17.00	3.70	12.43

have found. Henceforth I will refer to the Helms and Carter information as the "referent" or "standard."

The first five lines of the characteristics in Table 18.3 are summaries of the differences between standard deviations in inducting studies and referent standard deviations as previously described. Eighteen studies did not report any reliability information and, consequently, should have been summarized in this table. However, 50% of them were also missing standard deviations, and eight studies (44.4%) were missing mean scores for each of the WRIAS scales.

The invoking studies on average were slightly more variable with respect to the Contact standard deviation relative to the referent, but the referent was considerably more variable with respect to Disintegration, Reintegration, Pseudo Independence, and Autonomy. Of these latter four comparisons, the largest average disparity occurred for the comparisons of the standard deviations of the scores on the Disintegration scale of the referent study. This finding suggests that Helms and Carter's sample may have been dealing with issues of racial identity confusion to a greater degree than were other samples.

Mean Comparisons

The next five lines in Table 18.3 compare the means across studies to the referents. Higher negative values mean that the average level of the given racial identity schema in the comparison studies was higher than the respective referent mean; higher positive values signify the obverse. Zero values occur when means were equivalent.

On average, the referent sample had higher levels of Disintegration, Reintegration, and Pseudo Independence relative to the invoking samples. On the other hand, the invoking studies had higher levels of Contact and Autonomy than the referent sample. Autonomy displayed the largest mean disparity in favor of the invoking sample and Reintegration displayed the largest disparity in favor of the referent sample.

Thus, one might conclude that, on average, the samples in the studies following the referent study were both more naïve (Contact) and more sophisticated (Autonomy) with respect to racial identity development than the original sample. However, the original sample appears to have been more confused (Disintegration), racially biased (Reintegration), and intellectualized (Pseudo Independence) with respect to racial identity development. These interpretations are offered cautiously because the same samples were not included in both analyses.

Percentage of Women

Subtracting the percentages of women either reported by invoking researchers or computed from their descriptions of sample gender compositions from the referent percentage yielded positive values if the referent sample included more women than the induction studies, negative values if the induction studies contained more women, and zero values if they matched. Notice that in Table 18.2a, women were the largest percentage of respondents in the referent study. In general, it had a greater percentage of women than subsequent studies for which this information was available.

Summary

With respect to sample characteristics, the studies pursuant to Helms and Carter (1990) did not match the referent with respect to variability or average levels of scores. Nor were they equivalent in terms of sample composition, defined as percentage of women in the sample. Thus, it was inappropriate for inducting researchers to assume that either Helms and Carter's referent reliability data generalized to their samples or that their samples were necessarily relevant to Helms and Carter's findings.

Study Characteristics

The referent study was a book chapter. Of the inducting studies in the WRIAS data set none was a book chapter, 77.8% ($n = 14$) were dissertations, and the remainder, 22.2% ($n = 4$), were journal articles. Thus, they did not match on this dimension.

Helms and Carter reported that their data were collected in the eastern and northeastern United States. Researchers often did not report this information, but when they did, the geographic regions that they reported were coded. When they did not report where data were collected, the first author's geographic location was coded, if it could be discerned. Consequently, there is probably some error with respect to this information. Be that as it may, the largest percentage (21.1%) of the 18 inducting studies was from the Midwest. None was from the Northeast, although one each (i.e., 5.3%) was from the Mid-Atlantic or eastern United States. Consequently, inducting studies did not match the referent with respect to geographic location.

The referent sample consisted of university students attending predominantly White institutions in the East. Seven inducting studies (38.9%) used exclusively undergraduate samples, three (16.7%) used exclusively graduate students, and one study (5.6%) used practitioners. The other seven could not be classified on this dimension. Thus, of the inducting studies for which this information was available, the largest percentage did study college students.

Summary

In sum, in terms of the type of information one would typically expect to find in the Method or Results sections, studies that did not report Cronbach alpha coefficients also did not tend to report other descriptive information relevant to whether their results could be generalized to the referent study. In general, for those studies that did report relevant information, there was little indication that the data collection or reporting processes were equivalent to those reported by Helms and Carter.

Reliability and Validity

Many researchers have attempted to revise the WRIAS because they believed that the reliability coefficients that they obtained were "not adequate" (see Table 18.1). As previously noted, others have advised against using the measure in its entirety or specific scales because of "inadequate" reliability (e.g., Behrens, 1997; Choney & Rowe, 1994). However, the question of adequacy is a matter of validity rather than reliability. In this case, validity pertains to the intended use of scores obtained from the WRIAS scales. That is, decisions about what minimal levels of reliability a researcher or WRIAS user needs ought to be based on the level that is needed to answer a particular question. It might be useful to illustrate these points because they have been so frequently misconstrued in the literature in which the WRIAS has been used.

Determining Whether Reliability Is Adequate

Unless you have engaged in even more unusual psychometric practices than characterized, a researcher or WRIAS user's test scores will manifest some level of reliability. However, there is no single objective numerical standard for what constitutes "adequate" reliability. Nunnally (1967), who is often cited as the original source of contemporary reliability rules of thumb, said, "What a satisfactory level of reliability is depends on how a measure is being used . . . one saves time and energy by working with instruments that have only modest reliability, for which purpose reliabilities of .60 or .50 will suffice. . . . For basic research, it can be argued that increasing reliabilities beyond .80 is often wasteful" (p. 226). WRIAS researchers have mostly ignored his advice.

Instead, some WRIAS researchers have used .70 as their standard and appealed to one psychometric authority or another as their justification for doing so (e.g., Lemon & Waehler, 1996). However, none of these researchers actually statistically compared obtained reliability coefficients to their chosen standard to determine whether the obtained alpha coefficients differed significantly from .70. Fan and Thompson (2001) describe procedures for conducting such analyses. Also, more often than not, researchers do not report what standard they are using to judge the reliability or lack of reliability of their WRIAS scale scores.

Yet, even if the researchers had specified their standard(s) and used appropriate statistical techniques (e.g., confidence intervals, statistical tests) to determine whether the standard had been met, using rules of thumb to evaluate the reliability of scores is considered bad practice. Pedhazur and Schmelkin (1991) discuss this matter, "[We] point out to the inquirer that the matter [of deciding whether one's reliability is sufficient] is not one to be resolved by an authority decreeing that a given reliability coefficient is Kosher or not Kosher. . . . Rather, *it is for the user to determine what amount of error he or she is willing to tolerate, given the specific circumstances of the study* (e.g., what the scores are to be used for, cost of the study)" (pp. 109–110; italics were in the original).

Unfortunately, such advice may have been too imprecise for the researchers who have studied the WRIAS. Yet it is possible to use principles of classical test theory (CTT) to demonstrate how researchers may judge for themselves whether their obtained reliability coefficients are suitable for their intended purposes. The relevant principle is as follows: *Reliability coefficients set the ceiling for validity coefficients.* This principle underlies the adage that "tests [scores] cannot be valid unless they are also reliable."

Correlation coefficients between the WRIAS and another measure of some construct are one form of validity evidence, and correlations, in turn, can be transformed into other metrics such as the number of standard deviations (d) by which two groups' mean scores differ. So, for example, correlations between scores on the

WRIAS and scores on a scale that measures stages of intellectual development are validity coefficients (Steward et al., 1998). With respect to the WRIAS, the meaning of the reliability principle in this instance is that the square roots of the WRIAS reliability coefficients set the theoretical *upper* limits of the correlations (i.e., validity coefficients) between the WRIAS scales and some other measure with equivalent reliability. That is, although obtained validity coefficients or correlation coefficient(s) involving the WRIAS can be lower than the upper limit suggested by the product of the square root of the WRIAS and the other measure's reliability coefficients, they cannot be higher unless the wrong measurement model has been used to estimate reliability or chance factors are operating. If scores on the "other measure" (e.g., intellectual development) provide lower reliability estimates than the WRIAS on the same sample, then the other measure's reliability is responsible for attenuations in the correlation coefficients.

In case this explanation sounds like gibberish, Steward et al.'s (1998) study may be helpful. The authors investigated whether scores on the WRIAS could be predicted from scores on the Scale of Intellectual Development (SID; Erwin, 1983). More important for our purposes, the authors reported Cronbach alpha coefficients for all of the original WRIAS and SID scales, means and standard deviations (*SD*), as well as intercorrelations among scores for both sets of scales. Few authors are so conscientious in their data reporting procedures.

Reliability Ceilings

Table 18.4 summarizes Cronbach alpha (r_{xx}) coefficients for the scales comprising each measure in the fourth column. Thus, obtained alpha coefficients for the WRIAS ranged from .58 (Autonomy) to .78 (Pseudo Independence); alpha coefficients for the SID ranged from .70 (Empathy) to .79 (Dualism). Sometimes a researcher investigates relationships or correlations between WRIAS scores and some dependent variable for

Table 18.4   Using Steward et al.'s (1988) Cronbach Alpha Coefficients to Estimate Validity Ceilings

Scale	*M*	*SD*	Alpha (r_{xx})	Ceiling $(r_{xx}{}^{.5})$	*D*
WRIAS					
Contact	31.87	4.45	.60	.77	2.41
Disintegration	20.10	4.52	.68	.82	2.87
Reintegration	18.94	4.30	.67	.82	2.87
Pseudo independence	37.26	4.43	.78	.88	3.71
Autonomy	39.76	3.59	.58	.76	2.34
SID					
Dualism	42.39	8.56	.79	.89	3.90
Relativism	49.56	10.22	.68	.82	2.87
Commitment	34.51	6.49	.78	.88	3.71
Empathy	59.10	7.72	.70	.84	3.10

Note: WRIAS is the White Racial Identity Attitude Scale; SID is the Scale of Intellectual Development.

which reliability cannot be calculated. In Steward et al.'s study, age was such a variable. In such instances, if Steward et al. had wanted to determine a priori the value of the highest possible WRIAS-and-age correlation(s) that they could have obtained given the WRIAS reliability coefficients that they found, they would have calculated the square root of their reliability coefficients (i.e., $r_{xx}^{.5}$). (The same procedures would be used to answer such questions for the SID, although that measure is not the focus of this discussion.)

Thus, for example, to determine the highest possible correlation between WRIAS Autonomy and age, given its Cronbach alpha of .58, find the square root of .58, which as shown in the fifth column of Table 18.4 equals .76. Interpretation of the value of .76 is that it is the ceiling for correlation coefficients involving scores on the Autonomy scale when the obtained Cronbach alpha is .58. Therefore, using the principle that reliability sets the upper limit for validity, one would not expect to find a relationship between Autonomy and age greater than .76, if the two variables were strongly related.

Steward et al. actually obtained a correlation between Autonomy and age of −.17, which suggests that age and Autonomy were only weakly related in their study. However, rather than attributing this weak relationship to faults in the WRIAS (which Steward et al. did not do, but many other authors have done), we have to suppose that Autonomy and age must not have been related very much in the researchers' sample given that the obtained correlation could have been as high as ±.76, if the variables were strongly related. The validity ceilings (i.e., square roots of alpha coefficients) for the other variables are shown in Table 18.4 as well.

Considering that a correlation coefficient does not know where it comes from, it is possible to treat it as though it was derived from comparing the means between two groups (e.g., women, men; Blacks, Whites) to their combined standard deviation using procedures illustrated by Thompson (2002, p. 69). The results of these calculations are summarized in the last column of Table 18.4. Thus, the validity ceilings, because they are correlation coefficients albeit theoretical coefficients, can be transformed to theoretical between-group differences, in this case, the number of standard deviations that might be expected to separate group means (i.e., Cohen's d), given a particular reliability coefficient. For example, the validity ceiling of .76 for Autonomy is equivalent to a theoretical upper limit for d of about two and one-third standard deviations (i.e., 2.34).

By way of giving some meaning to this effect size, the so-called Black-White prototypical achievement gap on standardized tests is only one standard deviation, which is equivalent to a correlation of about .45. Therefore, based on their smallest Cronbach alpha coefficient, Steward et al. theoretically could have found sizable between-group differences with respect to Autonomy scores. They actually found a correlation of −.32 between gender and Autonomy, which is equivalent to a d of about two-thirds of a standard deviation (i.e., .68). Therefore, at the risk of being redundant, note that it was not the magnitude of the reliability of scores on the Autonomy scale that prevented Steward et al. from obtaining a higher difference between men and women's Autonomy scores.

Decisions about Adequacy

Another reminder is that because reliability of WRIAS scores may vary from sample to sample, theoretical validity ceilings may also vary, although the procedures for estimating ceilings will not. Nevertheless, given WRIAS reliability values of the size obtained by Steward et al., the individual researcher or WRIAS user must still decide whether they are of sufficient magnitude for her or his purposes. The researcher probably should not discard or engage in post-hoc revision of WRIAS scales in her or his study unless the theoretical validity coefficients (i.e., ceilings) or other effect sizes (e.g., *d*), derived from obtained WRIAS reliability coefficients, are smaller in magnitude than the validity coefficients that are commonly found in the researcher's area of inquiry.

For example, if Steward et al. had reviewed a body of literature in which correlations between the SID and some other variable exceeded the theoretical upper limits of the validity coefficients that their WRIAS scores could have provided (i.e., ranging from .76 to .88), then they arguably would have had a rationale for discarding or revising WRIAS scales for their sample. However, when researchers make a decision to change the WRIAS because their obtained reliability coefficients are not large enough for their intended purpose, then they should still provide full psychometric data and descriptions of their samples for the unaltered WRIAS scores so that subsequent researchers may conduct reliability generalization studies (Helms, 1999).

On the other hand, if the researcher's validity coefficients are lower than the estimated theoretical WRIAS validity coefficient limits, then the researcher should entertain the possibility that her or his hypotheses, rather than the WRIAS or White racial identity theory, are at fault. This is a possibility that rarely seems to occur to researchers when their hypotheses involving WRIAS scores are not supported.

Correcting Validity Coefficients for Attenuation

There are two reasons why "low" reliability coefficients might be problematic. One is that they may signal poor scale development; the other is that they might contribute to a high rate of Type II error (i.e., not finding significant or meaningful results when one should have). It is not true that "unreliable" WRIAS scale scores can cause artificial evidence of validity as Behrens (1997) contends. Random measurement error cannot correlate, which is what you have if you are claiming that WRIAS reliability is so low that the measure must never be used again.

With respect to the WRIAS, when researchers have not obtained their desired level of reliability, most researchers have assumed that the WRIAS is bad, validity evidence not withstanding, but they have ignored the possibility that, for whatever reason, they might not have had sufficient power in their designs to discover significant or meaningful relationships among their variables. Various psychometric theorists (e.g., Nunnally, 1967) have argued that if you believe that obtained correlations are too low because of imperfect reliability of obtained scores, then validity coefficients may be "corrected" for attenuation due to imperfect reliability. Nunnally (1967) observed: "One of the most important uses of the reliability coefficient is in estimating the extent to which obtained correlations [i.e., validity coefficients] between variables are attenuated by measurement error" (pp. 217–218).

In basic research, to correct a correlation for attenuation, the correction for attenuation is as follows: $r'_{ws} = r_{ws}/(r_{ww}r_{ss})^{.5}$. Still using Steward et al.'s data, r'_{ws} is the expected correlation between a WRIAS and SID scale if scores on them were perfectly reliable, r_{ws} is a correlation between a pair of WRIAS and SID scores, and r_{ww} and r_{ss} are respective reliability coefficients for scores on each of the measures. Table 18.5 illustrates the results of using the correction for attenuation formula to correct correlation coefficients (reported in the second column) that Steward et al. found.

The column labeled r_{both} shows what magnitude the researchers' correlations would have been if both the WRIAS and SID had yielded perfectly reliable scores. This is an estimate of how much the two types of characteristics (e.g., WRIAS Contact and SID Dualism) were actually related in Steward et al.'s study. Although it depends on your standards, it appears that three WRIAS scales (i.e., Reintegration, Contact, and Disintegration) shared small to moderate relationships with Dualism, for example, when their correlations were corrected for attenuation due to imperfect reliability.

The column labeled, r_{wrias}, shows the corrected correlations using only the square roots of WRIAS reliability coefficients in the denominator. Given that Steward et al. used WRIAS scores as dependent or criterion variables in their study, this column allows them to estimate the validity of scores on the SID. This type of correction would be used if one wanted to know how useful the SID would be in predicting racial identity scores if the WRIAS (i.e., the criterion) were perfectly reliable. These results pretty much parallel those obtained and shown for the double correction.

Correcting your results for attenuation due to imperfect reliability of the WRIAS and predictor or criterion measures in studies is another strategy that researchers may use to make objective decisions about the effectiveness of the WRIAS. Rather than relying on specific or nonspecific rules of thumb to decide how or whether to use the WRIAS, they might examine the corrected validity coefficients involving WRIAS scale scores, derived from their own data, and make their decisions accordingly. In this case, assuming that the researchers have used sound practices to obtain their WRIAS reliability coefficients, then low correlations do not reflect deficiencies in the WRIAS, but rather a lack of sufficiently strong relationships among their variables for the researcher's or test user's purposes.

DISCUSSION AND IMPLICATIONS

Treating reliability and validity coefficients as indicants of immutable properties of the WRIAS has become all too common, as has been the belief that whether or not the WRIAS should be used can be discerned from single studies. Researchers who actually computed their own reliability coefficients typically concluded that their individual study was definitive proof against the WRIAS if all of their hypotheses or understandings of how reliability coefficients should function were not supported. For their part, authors who did not compute their own reliability coefficients also attributed their failure to find support for their hypotheses to the WRIAS, even when, in many cases, they had modified the WRIAS based on their

Table 18.5 Correcting Steward et al.'s Validity Coefficients (Correlations) for Attenuation Due to Imperfect Reliability

Scale	Dualism			Relativism			Commitment			Empathy		
	r	r_{wrias}	r_{both}	r	r_{wrias}	r_{both}	r	r_{wrias}	r_{both}	r	r_{wrias}	r_{both}
Contact	.25	.32	.36	.01	.01	.01	.00	.00	.00	.00	.00	.00
Disintegration	.16	.19	.22	.09	.11	.13	.09	.11	.12	-.02	-.02	-.03
Reintegration	.30	.37	.41	.04	.05	.06	.01	.01	.01	-.07	-.09	-.10
Pseudo Independence	-.03	-.03	-.04	.16	.18	.22	.16	.18	.21	.16	.18	.22
Autonomy	.08	.11	.12	-.03	-.04	-.05	.10	.13	.15	.17	.22	.27

Note: The correlations (r) between WRIAS and SID scales were obtained from "The Relationships among Counselor-Trainees' Gender, Cognitive Development, and White Racial Identity: Implications for Counselor Training," by R. J. Steward, K. J. Boatwright, E. Sauer, A. Baden, and J. Jackson, 1998, *Journal of Multicultural Counseling and Development, 26,* p. 264; correlations are respectively corrected for imperfect WRIAS reliability coefficients (r_{wrias}) and imperfect WRIAS and SID reliability coefficients (r_{both}).

assumptions of how racial identity ought to be measured or their interpretations of Behrens's (1997) recommendations.

Ordinarily, given the number of published and unpublished studies in which the WRIAS has been used, it ought to be possible to conduct reliability generalization (RG) studies of the type advocated by Vacha-Haase (1998). In RG studies, one investigates the effects of sample characteristics on the magnitude of reliability coefficients across studies as a means of determining the factors responsible for their variability. With respect to the WRIAS, it was difficult to conduct a wrong type RG study because researchers engaged in a variety of unsystematic reporting practices that made it difficult to interpret their results meaningfully. According to Vacha-Haase, the wrongful practice of not reporting reliability coefficients and standard deviations appears to be fairly common with respect to other measures. So, the fact that these reporting errors occurred with respect to the WRIAS was to be expected.

Yet, researchers engaged in some reporting practices that made their data unusable in a wrong type RG analysis and may be peculiar to their use of the WRIAS. These included (1) inferring lack of reliability from multivariate analyses of the individual WRIAS items (Look, 1997); (2) changing one or more of the racial groups in the item stems (Snider, 2000); (3) conducting profile analyses without reporting the reliability coefficients on which the analyses were based (Levitt, 1995); (4) either using total scores or combining one or more scales (Martinez, 2000); and (5) revising scales on the basis of reliability coefficients obtained in one's own study without reporting either the original reliability coefficient or the standard deviation and/or interscale correlations associated with it (Davidson, 1991; Utsey & Gernat, 2002).

One problem associated with using flawed methodology and poor reporting practices in a single study, which I identified, is that it appears that subsequent researchers and reviewers who cite such studies have not evaluated research design sections of the cited studies with respect to reliability, but rather uncritically reiterate the relevant researcher's conclusions. As a result, poor methodologies and reporting practices with respect to the WRIAS have become institutionalized.

Nevertheless, in spite of the flawed reliability data that are available, it is possible to offer some tentative conclusions with respect to studies in which the WRIAS was used. First of all, the researchers who relied on reliability induction from the Helms and Carter (1990) study were probably not justified in doing so. The results in Table 18.3 suggest that the characteristics of their samples were not similar to those of Helms and Carter's sample on any of the dimensions that I investigated. Consequently, it is highly unlikely that they would have found the same reliability coefficients or validity data, given that both are dependent on sample characteristics. Some support for this inference can be found from examining the last two columns of Table 18.3. Contact was the most variable of the WRIAS scales in the inducting studies. On average, samples in these studies not only tended to express a higher mean level of Contact relative to Helms and Carter's sample ($M = -1.57$), but also were relatively less variable (SD Mean $= -0.21$), which might account for the tendency of some researchers to report low Cronbach alpha coefficients for the Contact scale.

In the words of Crocker and Algina (1986):

> Reliability is a property of the scores on a test for a particular group of examinees. Thus, potential test users need to determine whether reliability estimates reported in test manuals [or prior studies] are based on samples similar in *composition* and *variability* to the group for whom the test will be used. (p. 144, emphasis added)

If their admonition is appropriate for more established tests, then surely it also pertains to the WRIAS, a comparatively new measure.

Other than variability of scores, it was not possible to examine many characteristics of the studies in comparison to Helms and Carter (1990) because Helms and Carter did not provide detailed descriptions of their samples. Perhaps they have discovered the error of their ways and will do better in subsequent studies of the WRIAS. Nevertheless, they did describe the gender composition of their sample. Their normative sample was predominantly women (67%), in fact more so than the inducting studies on average. Subsequent studies too have tended to be based on predominantly female samples. There was no evidence that percentages of women were related to the size of reliability coefficients for the studies in which relevant data were available. However, it does seem desirable to begin to collect data on more male samples so that gender differences in White racial identity characteristics may be assessed.

There was no direct evidence that Behrens's (1997) study was responsible for the misuses of reliability discussed in the present chapter. Misuses were abundant prior to his study and they continued thereafter. The only two differences were that more studies were conducted in the years prior to his study and fewer studies reported indices of sample variability afterward. Nevertheless, reviewers as well as post-1997 doctoral researchers frequently cite Behrens as the source of their aberrant practices with respect to reliability theory. One cannot prove that fewer studies have been conducted because researchers and graduate students believe that Behrens proved the "psychometric unsoundness" of the WRIAS.

However, consider Steward et al.'s (1998) half-page justification for why they chose to use the WRIAS in their study:

> Some in the profession consider the use of this measure questionable based on item analysis results and the underlying assumption that the measure actually assesses the developmental nature of racial identity for White people (Behrens, 1997; Behrens & Rowe, 1997; Knox, 1996). However, we have chosen to use this measure for the very reasons that others have cited as reasons to do otherwise. First, the WRIAS is a relatively new scale. (p. 260)

Of the citations against which Steward et al. felt compelled to defend themselves, only one was a published empirical study (i.e., Behrens, 1997).

One cannot imagine novice researchers being able to defend their position as well as Steward et al. did. Moreover, it is doubtful that researchers would have to mount such a strident defense if the WRIAS were not a measure of White identity created by researchers who are not White. Thus, I fear that one consequence of imputing psychometric properties to the WRIAS instead of to scores on it, obtained from specific samples, under specific conditions is that researchers are being forced to prematurely abandon the study of White racial identity as I actually conceptualized it and replace it with others' beliefs about how I should have conceptualized it (e.g., Fischer & Moradi, 2001; Goodstein & Ponterotto, 1997).

Nevertheless, I reminded researchers that no single study can serve as sufficient evidence of the reliability or validity of the scores on the WRIAS in particular (Helms, 1997). Steward et al. (1998) also address this issue: "Although those who purport this measure's lack of utility may have some justification for moving on in measure development, we purport that the profession might be moving onward prematurely without additional investigation" (p. 260). Moreover, the reliability and validity analyses reported in Tables 18.4 and 18.5 support their admonition. Perhaps critics of the WRIAS and the theory on which it is based have had difficulty attending to such advice because the racial content that the WRIAS purportedly assesses tends to arouse strong emotions (e.g., Behrens, 1997; Behrens & Rowe, 1997) and they are in denial (i.e., the Contact schema in White racial identity theory) about the role of Black people in the psyche of White people in the United States.

Neale and Liebert (1986) also make the point that reliance on single studies is not a very fruitful strategy in a less emotionally laden context. They advise the following:

> No one study, however shrewdly designed and carefully executed, can provide convincing support [or nonsupport] for a causal hypothesis or theoretical statement[s]. . . . Too many possible (if not plausible) confounds, limitations on generality, and alternative interpretations can be offered for any one observation. . . . How, then, does social science theory advance through research? The answer is, by collecting a diverse body of evidence about any major theoretical proposition. (p. 290)

Their warning is as true of "expert researchers'" single studies as it is of one's own. It would be foolhardy to discourage development of instruments, such as the WRIAS, which might help Whites better understand the psychological effects of their racial histories on their collective consciousness, merely so that they can continue to deny the group's shared experience of "going Black."

REFERENCES

References marked with an asterisk were either new studies or modified studies added to the Behrens-Helms (1999) data set.

*Alexander, C. M. (1992). *Construct validity and reliability of the White Racial Identity Attitude Scale (WRIAS).* Unpublished doctoral dissertation, University of Nebraska, Lincoln.

American Educational Research Association, American Psychological Association, & National Council on Measurement in Education. (1999). *Standards for educational and psychological testing.* Washington, DC: American Educational Research Association.

Behrens, J. T. (1997). Does the White Racial Identity Attitude Scale measure racial identity? *Journal of Counseling Psychology, 44,* 3–12.

Behrens, J. T., & Rowe, W. (1997). Measuring White racial identity: A reply to Helms. *Journal of Counseling Psychology, 44,* 17–19.

Bennett, S. K., Atkinson, D. R., & Rowe, W. (1993, August), *White race identity: an alternative perspective.* Paper presented at the 101st Annual Convention of the American Psychological Association, Toronto, Canada.

Block, C. J., & Carter, R. T. (1996). White racial identity attitude theories: A rose by any other name is still a rose. *Counseling Psychologist, 24,* 326–334.

*Brown, S. P., Parham, T. A., & Yonker, R. (1996). Influence of a cross-cultural training course on racial identity attitudes of White women and men: Preliminary perspectives. *Journal of Counseling and Development, 74,* 510–516.

*Burkard, A. W., Ponterotto, J. G., Reynolds, A. L., & Alfonso, V. C. (1999). White counselor trainees' racial identity and working alliance perceptions. *Journal of Counseling and Development, 77,* 324–329.

*Burton, S. G. (1997). *The relationship between service-learning and racial identity of White college students: An exploratory study.* Unpublished master's thesis, University of Maryland, College Park.

Campbell, D. T., & Fiske, D. W. (1959). Convergent and discriminant validation by the multitrait-multimethod matrix. *Psychological Bulletin, 56,* 81–105.

Carter, R. T. (1988). An empirical test of a theory on the influence of racial identity attitudes on the counseling process within a workshop setting. *Dissertation Abstracts International, 49*(A), 431.

Carter, R. T. (1990). The relationship between racism and racial identity among White Americans: An exploratory investigation. *Journal of Counseling and Development, 69,* 46–69.

Carter, R. T. (1996). Exploring the complexity of racial identity attitude measures. In G. R. Sodowsky & J. C. Impara (Eds.), *Multicultural assessment in counseling and clinical psychology* (pp. 193–223). Lincoln, NE: Buros Institute of Mental Measurements.

*Carter, R. T., Gushue, G. V., & Weitzman, L. M. (1994). White racial identity development and work values. *Journal of Vocational Behavior, 44,* 185–192.

Caruso, J. C. (2000). Reliability generalization of the NEO Personality Scales. *Educational and Psychological Measurement, 60,* 236–254.

Choney, S. K., & Behrens, J. T. (1996). Development of the Oklahoma Racial Attitudes Scale—Preliminary Form (ORAS-P). In G. R. Sodowsky & J. C. Impara (Eds.), *Multicultural assessment in counseling and clinical psychology* (pp. 225–240). Lincoln, NE: Buros Institute of Mental Measurements.

Choney, S. K., & Rowe, W. (1994). Assessing White racial identity: The White Racial Consciousness Development Scale (WRCDS). *Journal of Counseling and Development, 73,* 102–104.

Claney, D., & Parker, W. M. (1989). Assessing White racial consciousness and perceived comfort with Black individuals: A preliminary study. *Journal of Counseling and Development, 67,* 449–451.

Cohen, J. (1988). *Statistical power analysis for the behavioral sciences* (2nd ed.). Hillsdale, NJ: Erlbaum.

*Constantine, M. G. (2002). Racism attitudes, White racial identity attitudes, and multicultural counseling competence in school counselor trainees. *Counselor Education and Supervision, 41,* 162–174.

*Coopwood, K. D. (2000). Black and White undergraduate resident university students' stages of intercultural sensitivity and racial identity at Indiana State University. *Dissertation Abstracts International, 63*(3-A), 877.

Crocker, L., & Algina, J. (1986). *Introduction to classical and modern test theory.* New York: Holt, Rinehart and Winston.

*Davidson, J. R. (1991). *Evaluation of an education model for race/ethnic sensitive social work and critique of the White Racial Identity Attitude Scale.* Unpublished doctoral dissertation, University of Texas at Arlington.

Desole, L. M. (2002). *Race in marital and family therapy: The relationship of racial identity attitudes to White family therapists' preferences regarding ideal family functioning.* Unpublished doctoral dissertation, Teachers College, Columbia University, New York.

Erwin, T. D. (1983). The Scale of Intellectual Development using Perry's scheme. *Journal of College Student Personnel, 24,* 6–12.

*Evans, K. M., & Foster, V. A. (2000). Relationships among multicultural training, moral development, and racial identity development of White counseling students. *Counseling and Values, 45,* 39–48.

Fan, X., & Thompson, B. (2001). Confidence intervals about score reliability coefficients: An *EPM* guidelines editorial. *Educational and Psychological Measurement, 61,* 517–531.

Feldt, L. S., & Brennan, R. C. (1989). Reliability. In R. L. Lean (Ed.), *Educational Measurement* (3rd ed., pp. 105–146). New York: Macmillan.

Fischer, A. R., & Moradi, B. (2001). Racial and ethnic identity: Recent developments and needed directions. In J. G. Ponterotto, J. M. Casas, L. A. Suzuki, & C. M. Alexander (Eds.), *Handbook of multicultural counseling* (2nd ed., pp. 341–370). Thousand Oaks, CA: Sage.

Glass, G. V., & Hopkins, K. D. (1996). *Statistical methods in education and psychology* (3rd ed.). Needham Heights, MA: Allyn & Bacon.

Goodstein, R., & Ponterotto, J. G. (1997). Racial and ethnic identity: Their relationship and their contribution to self-esteem. *Journal of Black Psychology, 23,* 275–292.

*Gulseth, S. D. (2002). *White racial identification as a predictor of prejudice in simulated criminal sentencing.* Unpublished doctoral dissertation, University of North Dakota, Grand Forks.

*Gushue, G. V., & Carter, R. T. (2000). Remembering race: White racial identity attitudes and two aspects of social memory. *Journal of Counseling Psychology, 47,* 199–210.

*Haskins, W. L. (1992). *The relationship of self concept to stages of White racial identity attitudes.* Unpublished doctoral dissertation, University of Oklahoma, Norman.

Helms, J. E. (1984). Toward a theoretical explanation of the effects of race on counseling: A Black and White model. *Counseling Psychologist, 12,* 153–165.

Helms, J. E. (1990). *Black and White racial identity: Theory, research, and practice.* Westport, CT: Greenwood Press.

Helms, J. E. (1992). *A race is a nice thing to have: A guide to being a White person or understanding the White persons in your life.* Topeka, KS: Content Communications.

Helms, J. E. (1996). Toward a methodology for measuring and assessing racial as distinguished from ethnic identity. In G. R. Sodowsky & J. C. Impara (Eds.), *Multicultural assessment in counseling and clinical psychology* (pp. 143–192). Lincoln, NE: Buros Institute of Mental Measurements.

Helms, J. E. (1997). Implications of Behrens (1997) for the validity of the White Racial Identity Attitude Scale. *Journal of Counseling Psychology, 44,* 13–16.

Helms, J. E. (1999). Another meta-analysis of the White Racial Identity Attitude Scale's Cronbach alphas: Implications for validity [Special issue: *Measurement and Evaluation in Counseling and Development*]. Special Issue: *Assessment and Race, 32,* 122–137.

*Helms, J. E., & Carter, R. T. (1990). Development of the White Racial Identity Attitudes Inventory. In J. E. Helms (Ed.), *Black and White racial identity: Theory, research, and practice* (pp. 67–80). Westport, CT: Greenwood Press.

Helms, J. E., & Carter, R. T. (1991). Relationships of White and Black racial identity attitudes and demographic similarity to counselor preferences. *Journal of Counseling Psychology, 38,* 446–457.

Jome, L. M. (2000). *Construct validity of the White Racial Identity Attitude Scale.* Unpublished doctoral dissertation, University of Akron, Akron, Ohio.

Jung, C. (1930, April). Your Negroid and Indian BEHAVIOR. *Forum, 83*(4), 193–199.

*Kyle, M. T. (2001). *Identity and racial attitudes of White undergraduate college students.* Unpublished doctoral dissertation, Our Lady of the Lake University, San Antonio, Texas.

LaFleur, N. K., Rowe, W., & Leach, M. M. (2002). Reconceptualizing White racial consciousness. *Journal of Multicultural Counseling and Development, 30,* 148–152.

*Leach, M. M., Behrens, J. T., & LaFleur, N. K. (2002). White racial identity and White racial consciousness: Similarities, differences, and recommendations. *Journal of Multicultural Counseling and Development, 30,* 66–80.

Lemon, R. L., & Waehler, C. A. (1996). A test of stability and construct validity of the Black Racial Identity Attitude Scale Form B (RIAS-B) and the White Racial Identity Scale (WRIAS). *Measaurement and Evaluation in Counseling and Development, 29,* 77–85.

*Levitt, M. J. (1995). *Intersections/missed connections: Racial and womanist identity in a group of Black and White women.* Philadelphia: Temple University Press.

*Look, C. T. (1997). *White racial identity: Its relationship to cognitive complexity and interracial contact.* Unpublished doctoral dissertation, Ball State University, Muncie, Indiana.

*Martinez, L. J. (2000). Affective correlates of White racial identity development. *Dissertation Abstracts International, 61*(6-B), 3284.

*Mercer, S. H., & Cunningham, M. (2003). Racial identity in White American college students: Issues of conceptualization and measurement. *Journal of College Student Development, 44*(2), 217–230.

*Miville, M. L., Gelso, C. J., Pannu, R., Liu, W., Touradju, P., Holloway, P., et al. (1999). *Appreciating similarities and valuing differences: The Miville-Guzman Universality-Diversity Scale.*

*Miyatake, R. K. (1998). *White racial identity attitudes as predictors of preference and credibility of African American, Asian American, and White female and male psychologists.* University of Maine–Orono.

Mueller, J. A., & Pope, R. L. (2001). The relationship between multicultural competence and White racial consciousness among student affairs practitioners. *Journal of College Student Development, 42,* 133–144.

Neale, J. M., & Liebert, R. M. (1986). *Science and behavior: An introduction to methods of research* (3rd ed.). Englewood Cliffs, NJ: Prentice-Hall.

*Neville, H. A., Heppner, M. J., Louie, C. E., Thompson, C. E., Brooks, L., & Baker, C. (1996). The impact of multicultural training on White racial identity attitudes and therapists' competencies. *Professional Psychology: Research and Practice, 27,* 83–89.

Nunnally, J. C. (1967). *Psychometric theory.* New York: McGraw-Hill.

*Ochs, N. G. (1994). The incidence of racial issues in White counseling dyads: An exploratory survey. *Counselor Education and Supervision, 33,* 305–313.

*O'Connor, M. M. (1999). *Relationship between counselor White racial identity development and key multicultural counseling processes.* Unpublished doctoral dissertation, Northern Arizona University, Flagstaff.

*Pack-Brown, S. P. (1999). Racism and White counselor training: Influence of White racial identity theory and research. *Journal of Counseling and Development, 77,* 87–92.

*Parks, E. E., Carter, R. T., & Gushue, G. V. (1996). At the crossroads: Racial and womanist development in Black and White women. *Journal of Counseling and Development, 74,* 624–631.

*Patterson, B. T. (1994). *Racial attitudes and inter-ethnic experiences of White university students: An exploration of the characteristics of racial attitude development.* Chapel Hill: University of North Carolina Press.

Pedhazur, E. L., & Schmelkin, L. P. (1991). *Measurement, Design, and Analysis. Hillsdale.* NJ: Erlbaum.

Ponterotto, J. G. (1988). Racial consciousness development among White counselor trainees: A stage model. *Journal of Multicultural Counseling and Development, 16,* 146–156.

Pope-Davis, D. B., Vandiver, B. J., & Stone, G. L. (1999). White racial identity attitude development: A psychometric examination of two instruments. *Journal of Counseling Psychology, 46,* 70–79.

Remy, L. A. (1993). *White racial identity: White college students' definition of self in relation to African-Americans, Hispanics, and Asian-Americans.* Unpublished master's thesis, University of Maryland, College Park.

*Richardson, T. Q., & Molarinaro, K. L. (1996). White counselor self-awareness: A prerequisite for developing multicultural competence. *Journal of Counseling and Development, 74,* 238–242.

Rowe, W., Behrens, J. T., & Leach, M. M. (1995). Racial/ethnic identity and racial consciousness: Looking back and looking forward. In J. G. Ponterotto, J. M. Casas, L. A. Suzuki, & C. M. Alexander (Eds.), *Handbook of multicultural counseling* (pp. 218–238). Thousand Oaks, CA: Sage.

Rowe, W., Bennett, S. K., & Atkinson, D. R. (1994). White racial identity models: A critique and alternative proposal. *Counseling Psychologist, 22,* 129–146.

Sabnani, H. B., Ponterotto, J. G., & Borodovsky, L. G. (1991). White racial identity development and cross-cultural counselor training: A stage model. *Counseling Psychologist, 19,* 76–102.

Scarpellini-Huber, J. M. (1997). Inter and intra-racial contact and affective reactions as aspects of recalled White racial identity socialization experiences. *Dissertation Abstracts International, 58*(B), 427.

Scott, D. A., & Robinson, T. L. (2001). White male identity development: The key model. *Journal of Counseling and Development, 79,* 415–421.

*Silvestri, T. J., & Richardson, T. Q. (2001). White racial identity statuses and NEO personality constructs: An exploratory analysis. *Journal of Counseling and Development, 79,* 68–76.

*Snider, B. R. (2000). *Bias in psychotherapy as it relates to the client's accent and counselors' racial identity development and universality-diversity orientation.* Unpublished doctoral dissertation, University of Oklahoma, Stillwater.

*Steward, R. J., Boatwright, K. J., Sauer, E., Baden, A., & Jackson, J. (1998). The relationships among counselor-trainees' gender, cognitive development, and White racial identity:

Implications for counselor training. *Journal of Multicultural Counseling and Development, 26,* 254–272.

*Swanson, J. L., Tokar, D. M., & Davis, L. E. (1994). Content and construct validity of the White Racial Identity Attitude Scale. *Journal of Vocational Behavior, 44,* 198–217.

*Taub, D. J., & McEwen, M. K. (1992). The relationship of racial identity attitudes to autonomy and mature interpersonal relationships in Black and White undergraduate women. *Journal of College Student Development, 33,* 439–446.

Thompson, C. E. (1994). Helms' White Racial Identity Development (WRID) theory: Another look. *Counseling Psychologist, 22,* 645–649.

Tokar, D. M., & Swanson, J. L. (1991). An investigation of the validity of Helms' (1984) model of White racial identity development. *Journal of Counseling Psychology, 38,* 296–301.

*Utsey, S. O., & Gernat, C. A. (2002). White racial identity attitudes and the ego defense mechanisms used by White counselor trainees in racially provocative counseling situations. *Journal of Counseling and Development, 80*(4), 475–479.

Vacha-Haase, T. (1998). Reliability generalization: Exploring variance in measurement error affecting score reliability across studies. *Educational and Psychological Measurement, 58,* 6–20.

Vacha-Haase, T., Kogan, L. R., & Thompson, B. (2000). Sample compositions and variabilities in published studies versus those in test manuals. *Educational and Psychological Measurement, 60,* 509–522.

*Watt, S. K., Robinson, T. L., & Lupton-Smith, H. (2002). Building ego and racial identity: Preliminary perspectives on counselors-in-training. *Journal of Counseling and Development, 80,* 94–100.

Wilkinson, L., & APA Task Force on Statistical Inference. (1999). Statistical methods in psychology journals: Guidelines and explanations. *American Psychologist, 54,* 594–604.

Yin, P., & Fan, X. (2000). Assessing the reliability of Black Depression Inventory scores: Reliabilty generalization across studies. *Educational and Psychological Measurement, 60,* 201–223.

CHAPTER 19

Racial-Cultural Ethical Issues in Research

Farah A. Ibrahim and Susan Chavez Cameron

This chapter provides an overview of the guidelines established by the federal government to control ethical, legal, and moral violations when conducting psychological research. In addition, historical ethical issues in research with racial-cultural nondominant groups in the counseling and psychotherapy domain are discussed. The current status of racial-cultural ethical research in counseling and psychotherapy is reviewed and the issues that still persist in spite of significant progress in the past 30 years are examined. A proposal to make research in counseling and psychotherapy more ethical is included.

In focusing on ethical racial-cultural research in psychology, two concerns are of critical importance. The first pertains to the use and discussion of the racial and cultural characteristics of a group. Such use assumes that all group members are similar to the group descriptors, which leads to erroneous assumptions about individuals in specific cultural groups. It has been repeatedly established by researchers that there is vast heterogeneity within racial-cultural groups, although the research literature tends to focus on differences between groups (Carter & Parks, 1992; Ibrahim & Kahn, 1987; Ponterotto & Casas, 1991; Sue, Zane, & Young, 1994; Vontress, 1988).

The second concern pertains to the notion of race. Although different races do not exist (i.e., all humans are of the same species: Homo sapiens), humans do have different physical characteristics that are socially significant and have historically been used to justify slavery and colonization (Cameron & Wycoff, 1998; Pope-Davis & Liu, 1998). The social-political construct of race in the United States and the rest of the world affects how people approach and utilize mental health and counseling services in the United States. Being physically or culturally different from the mainstream population also has implications for research on counseling process and outcome (Ibrahim & Ohnishi, 2001). Historically, social conditions for the racially and culturally different in the United States have been fraught with difficulties. These conditions affect trust among historically oppressed groups, a critical ingredient in counseling and psychotherapy (Cherbosque, 1987; White & Sedlacek, 1987). In addition, there is significant evidence in the counseling and psychotherapy literature that theories and strategies of counseling are more relevant to mainstream cultural value systems and ideologies (Ponterotto & Casas, 1991).

EFFORTS TO ESTABLISH GUIDELINES FOR ETHICAL RESEARCH: THE ESTABLISHMENT OF INSTITUTIONAL REVIEW BOARDS

For more than 50 years, research has been guided by a series of texts. In 1946, after the atrocities perpetrated by the Nazis were revealed, 23 Nazi physicians were charged with crimes against humanity in Nuremberg, Germany. Adopted as a judicial statement, the Nuremberg Code was published, which clearly outlines the requirements for conducting research. Originally consisting of six points defining ethical medical research, it was later revised and expanded to 10 points focusing on the importance of voluntary consent and the protection of human rights during medical experimentation and trials. First published in the United States in the *Journal of the American Medical Association* in 1946, the Code states:

> The voluntary consent of the human subject is absolutely essential. This means that the person involved should have legal capacity to give consent; should be so situated as to be able to exercise free power of choice, without the intervention of any element of force, fraud, deceit, duress, overreaching, or other ulterior form of constraint or coercion; and should have sufficient knowledge and comprehension of the elements of the subject matter involved as to enable him to make an understanding and enlightened decision. The latter element requires that before the acceptance of an affirmative decision by the experimental participants there should be made known to them the nature, duration, and purpose of the experiment; the method and means by which it is to be conducted; all inconveniences and hazards reasonably to be expected; and the effect upon their health or person which may possibly come from his participation in the experiment. The duty and responsibility for ascertaining the quality of the consent rests upon each individual who initiates, directs, or engages in the experiment. It is a personal duty or responsibility that may not be delegated to another with impunity.

The importance of the Nuremberg Code cannot be overstated. It was the first official document to define ethical conduct in research and is the basis for all subsequent codes and policies related to the protection and ethical treatment of all research participants.

In 1964, the Declaration of Helsinki (revised in 1975, 1983, 1989, 1996, and 2000) was passed by the World Health Organization. This text established the rules and regulations regarding biomedical research on humans. Although it emphasized the importance of informed consent, patient's rights, and investigator integrity, most important, it states, "The interests of society must not take precedence over that of the individual" (Karigan, 2001, p. 28).

Both of the previous documents originated outside the United States and though supported, they were not supported in earnest. In fact, it was not until after the details of the Tuskegee syphilis study were made public that a text was produced specifically protecting the rights of human subjects in this country. In 1974, Public Law 93-348, the National Research Act, was passed requiring the Department of Health and Human Services (DHHS) to establish federal regulations protecting human subjects. Also known as the Code of Federal Regulations, Title 45, Part 46, the National Research Act requires all institutions receiving federal funding for research to abide by these regulations, which not only govern the protection of human subjects and informed consent, but established institutional review boards (IRBs) and their guidelines, investigation procedures for medical devices, and the guidelines for good clinical practice in research.

The National Research Act led to the establishment of the National Commission for the Protection of Human Subjects of Biomedical and Behavioral Research (1979). Often referred to as the Belmont Report–Ethical Principles and Guidelines for the Protection of Human Subjects of Research, their report illustrated how ethical principles can be applied to research and called for more stringent protections for human subjects. As did the other texts, the Belmont Report emphasized the importance of respecting the participant's autonomy by requiring informed consent but expanded this coverage to include behavioral health research. It also gave emphasis to the importance of establishing IRBs.

The DHHS's Office of Protection from Research Risks at the National Institute of Health (NIH) oversees IRBs. The IRBs are entrusted with assuring the protection of vulnerable populations and facilitating more uniform protection of subjects with limited or questionable capacity to give consent (Applebaum & Rosenbaum, 1989; DeRenzo, 1994). Although there are many safeguards in place, and even when communities appreciate the potential value of research, the promises of protection made by IRBs do not appear to be sufficient in minimizing the fears in some academic circles or in communities of Color.

There are more than 5,000 IRBs in the United States, most of which are affiliated with hospitals or universities; some are also located in managed care organizations, for-profit entities, and state and federal agencies such as the NIH and Centers for Disease Control (CDC, 1998). According to Shamoo (1997), too much power is placed in the hands of IRBs that monitor research projects. Reportedly, IRBs often lack sufficient information with which to make judgments because members on the IRB are not always fully informed by the researchers regarding the true nature of the proposed research project. In particular, Shamoo challenges the research approval process, arguing that both an IRB and the DHHS allowed a fenfluramine study with young children to proceed despite data classifying fenfluramine as a neurotoxin that had been previously banned by the Federal Drug Administration.

In a report prepared by DHHS Inspector General June Gibbs Brown (1998), she supports community concerns regarding IRBs in addition to identifying four main problems with the IRB process. First, IRBs review too much, too quickly, with too little expertise. Second, there is minimal review of research once it has been approved. Third, IRBs tend to ignore conflicts that threaten their independence (for example, approving the use of fenfluramine with children despite evidence pointing to its neurotoxin effects). Fourth, little training is provided to investigators and board members. This concern regarding the IRB process was echoed by the Navajo and Mohawk Nations (American Indian Law Center, 1974) when both nations, somewhat jaded by past research transgressions, passed legislation banning all medical, behavioral, and social research within tribal lands unless permission to conduct the research is secured from respective tribal review boards. The use of tribal IRBs serves as a second layer, ideally better protecting the safety and welfare of tribal members. Other tribal nations have simply refused to participate in any research.

For research to be ethical, three principles established since World War II (Keith-Spiegel & Koocher, 1995) must be fulfilled: beneficence, justice, and autonomy. Beneficence means that ratios of benefits to risks are optimized and the process does not harm clients; justice implies that the benefits and burdens of the experimentation are equitably distributed. As for autonomy, clients must enter a study voluntarily and with informed consent. To give informed consent, clients must have the capacity and the ability to understand what it is they are agreeing to: they must possess the capacity to comprehend and evaluate what is being expected of them. According to some (e.g., Applebaum, Roth, Lidz, Benson, & Winslade, 1987; Grisso & Applebaum, 1995; Tankanow, Sweet, & Weiskopf, 1992), clients may have the ability to agree to participate in a research study, but yet be unable to fully comprehend the consequences of accepting a particular treatment intervention or medication, or the ability to evaluate options and the consequences of their choices. A client's ability to make a fully informed decision is further compromised when more complex information must be presented and understood. Furthermore, according to Winslow (1998), most consent forms are written either at or above college level. The implication here is that particularly vulnerable populations, such as the mentally ill, poor, indigent, and individuals and communities of Color that are educationally and economically disadvantaged, are at a decided disadvantage when giving informed consent because many are not able to appreciate the situation, the treatment choices, or the related consequences of their decision to participate. It is clear regarding any of the research cited in this chapter that, even with the protection of the IRB, adherence to these three principles is questionable at best.

HISTORICAL ETHICAL ISSUES IN RACIAL-CULTURAL RESEARCH IN COUNSELING AND PSYCHOTHERAPY

Historically, research on variables such as race, intelligence, and health has been characterized as racist, unethical, and ineffective (Bhopal, 1997; Sue, 1999). Sensitivity to ethical issues in research was heightened after the Nuremberg trials and the revelations that emerged about the horrifying misconduct of Nazi scientists (Wax, 1991). Also, the effects of racial prejudice and its influence on science were made evident by the Tuskegee experiment (Jones, 1992). It is critical for researchers to understand that much of the race-oriented science in the past was unethical, invalid, racist, and inhumane, although at the time it was considered to be very important (Bhopal, 1997). Bhopal notes that researchers and epidemiologists must heed warnings from psychology and anthropology, as these two professions played a leading role in racializing science. It is important to recognize that issues in psychology that confront racist assumptions are primarily raised by researchers who are from nondominant groups and researchers sympathetic to the cause of social justice who are courageous enough to point out how science was being used to maintain the status quo.

It is indeed impressive when one reviews the pioneering work of scholars who continue to debate and define counseling and psychotherapy research on nondominant groups. Although methodological and conceptual problems persist, the pioneers have continued to explore and define the issues and make significant contributions in this domain (Rogler, 1999; Sue, 1999). Sue et al. (1994) maintained that the historical research studies, although small and with particular cultural groups, advanced understanding of all human beings by providing research data on human variation as a result of culture; consequently, these studies strengthened psychology.

The historical issues in ethical racial-cultural research included concerns regarding the paucity of research focusing on racially and culturally different groups; the extension of research findings from White middle-class college students (originally all male) to explain all human behavior; lack of respect for different cultures and research showing various cultures and races as deficient on psychological variables without understanding the cultural context and the reasons for social norms or behaviors that differed from Western norms and behavior; the belief that counseling and psychotherapy theories and practices, structured and developed by mostly White males, are useful for all racial-cultural groups; and lack of understanding regarding cultural values and assumptions and their impact on the counseling process and outcome (Ponterotto & Benesh, 1988; Ponterotto & Casas, 1991; Rogler, 1999; Sue & Zane, 1987).

Gideonse (1977) notes that in a sexist society, it is impossible for science and scientists to not harbor sexist assumptions, including misogyny and self-hatred among women. We believe that the same argument applies to racist and classist societies and the resulting self-hatred among nondominant groups and the poor. Neither science nor researchers are value-free or even value-neutral. Researchers frequently believe that values and assumptions enter the research process only when subjective measures are employed and that science and scientists should be value-neutral. Gideonse reiterates Sherif's (1979) warning that social science cannot be separated from the confounding effects of human values, time, and the phenomenon of human consciousness. Campbell (2001) notes:

> Knowledge is socially distributed: what one takes for reality is embedded in a person's social reality. This social reality and the perceptions that emerge from it influence research methods including the topics selected, the design, the mode of data analysis, the sample, the measurement tools, and what conclusions are derived from the project. (p. 198)

Ibrahim (1989, 1999) supports this stance and has proposed that social science researchers (especially human service professionals) must clarify their values, beliefs, and assumptions or worldview prior to undertaking research in socially sensitive domains. Campbell showed that the topics selected for study, the processes used, and the results obtained can all obstruct or open up research on topics that are relevant to all or for specific groups only.

Casas (1985) highlighted that conceptually biased research paradigms are used in research with racial and ethnic nondominant groups. The outcome of such research is a perspective that labels a cultural-racial group as pathological, deviant, or culturally deficient. The issue of misdiagnosing and mislabeling is still relevant today, as evidenced by the number of articles addressing the same and similar concerns (Ponterotto & Casas, 1991; Rogler, 1999; Sue, 1999). Empirical research in the domain of counseling and psychotherapy with racial and cultural nondominant groups is still lacking (Bowser, this *Handbook,* Volume One; Rogler, 1999; Sue, 1999; Trimble, this *Handbook,* Volume One), although anecdotal scholarship exists. The research that exists on nondominant groups generally does not consider the contextual variables in understanding client behavior. In addition, available research overlooks the heterogeneity within groups, resulting in data that are as damaging as lack of knowledge and understanding: Stereotypes and global categorizations are perpetuated, for example, that all Asian Americans tend to behave a certain way, though there are between 15 and 57 different groups of Asian Americans. Further, research in the past focused on counseling and psychotherapy and relied mostly on analogue studies, due to the easy accessibility of samples (Atkinson & Schein, 1986; Casas, 1984; Fuertes, this *Handbook,* Volume One; Ponterotto, 1988; Sue, 1988, 1999).

Researchers in this domain have also been criticized for not collaborating with the populations and communities under study (Atkinson, Morten, & Sue, 1989; Ponterotto & Casas, 1991; Wax, 1991). Ethical research must involve the population that is being studied and should incorporate their cultural concerns and issues. It is critically important for research to provide meaningful data that can be used to make health decisions and to respect the community under study (Hernandez, 1979). Wax addressed the seriousness of conducting research without involving the community under study; he notes that this practice also leads to sharing information that has been gathered without adequate knowledge to give consent and shared without permission, an ethical violation. Awareness of the nature of socially sensitive issues such as culture, race, and gender is critical (Scarr, 1988). Sensitivity requires an understanding of the worldview, beliefs, values, and assumptions of cultural, racial, and gendered groups different from our own or the mainstream before embarking on a research study (Ibrahim, 1989).

A major criticism of the current research pertaining to counseling and psychotherapy is that it is generally conducted with no overarching framework to guide it (Casas & Vasquez, 1989; Ponterotto & Benesh, 1988; Ponterotto & Casas, 1991). Ponterotto and Casas (1991) presented a framework that outlined the variables that must be included in conducting research on racial-cultural groups. The first category addressed selection of personnel and professionals, their sociocultural characteristics and variables including beliefs, values, attitudes, and life experiences that must be understood and addressed in the counseling process. The second category focused on the sociocultural variables of the client. The last category addressed the interaction of client and counselor variables, including expectations, preferences, attitudes, and skills. Utilizing such a framework helps in establishing the cultural parameters of all involved in the process and will lead to culturally sensitive and client-specific interventions.

CRITICISM OF CURRENT RESEARCH OF RACIAL-CULTURAL VARIABLES IN COUNSELING, PSYCHOTHERAPY, AND PSYCHOLOGY

It is now generally accepted by the social sciences that human behavior is meaningful only when it is viewed in a sociocultural context (Segall, 1979). Segall, Lonner, and Berry (1998) postulated that psychology's lack of attention to the interrelationship of culture and behavior has created a gap in our understanding of how behavior is shaped. The conceptual issues regarding how behavior and culture are interrelated have not been adequately answered. Conceptual concerns pertain to absolutism and relativism and how these two schemas impact how research is conducted and how theory is built. In addition, the two dimensions of absolutism and relativism are derived from our cultural world; we are socialized in one cultural model or another, or a combination of absolutism and relativism, depending on the cultural context. Therefore, understanding the researcher's value system, that is, worldview, social context, and cultural group, becomes a critical part of the research paradigm.

After a systematic analysis of the published research literature on racial-ethnic topics reported in five counseling and psychotherapy journals, Ponterotto (1988) concluded that expressed criticisms and concerns were valid in seven areas:

1. Lack of a theoretical framework and lack of attention to contextual variables and cultural value systems (Casas, 1984, 1985; Ponterotto & Benesh, 1988). The lack of a theoretical and cultural framework does not allow for any specific theory or hypothesis to be carefully evaluated and retards the growth of science and literature in this domain.

2. Overemphasis on simplistic counselor and client process variables, with no regard for sociocultural variables that impact the counseling situation.

3. Inadequate focus on within-group differences.

4. Overuse of college populations as sample groups for most research conducted (46.3%).

5. Relying on psychometric instruments that are culturally limited. Of the 80 studies reviewed, only 31.3% used instruments that were specifically designed to be used with the nondominant population being studied.

6. Inadequate description of the socioeconomic levels of the samples.

7. Overreliance on paper-and-pencil outcome measures. Only eight studies out of the 80 reviewed used outcome measures that were not traditional paper-and-pencil instruments.

Three areas of criticism were not substantiated by Ponterotto's (1988) research. First, that racial-ethnic research in counseling relies to a large extent on experimental analogue research: Instead, it was found that 72% of the 80 articles reviewed included survey studies. Second, that researchers do not delineate the limitations of a study: Ponterotto found that 61.3% of the studies sampled discussed their limitations. Third, that sample size of most studies is inadequate: Ponterotto determined that this criticism was only partially valid.

Sue (1999) presented the current state of affairs in psychological research on race, culture, and bias. According to Sue, the quality, quantity, and funding for research on racial-cultural groups has been inadequate. He posited that one factor that has led to this inadequacy is how science is practiced within psychology. He noted that although research principles in psychology emphasize the importance of both internal and external validity, in practice psychology emphasizes internal validity. Because few psychological principles and methods have been validated on all racial-cultural groups available, researchers conducting studies on samples from these populations have a difficult time showing internal validity in their research. This lack of validation in psychological research has hindered the development of research on racial-cultural groups. Sue further noted that researchers continue to assume that findings obtained from one racial or cultural group can be generalized to other racial or cultural groups. He called this bias-based approach "selective reinforcement of scientific principles." According to him, substantial attention has been given to problems of internal validity in research, but relatively little attention is given to external validity (e.g., generalizability) as it pertains to the applicability of the findings to groups other than the ones under study (Helms, this *Handbook*, Volume One).

The lack of attention to external validity has negative implications for people of Color, specifically the poor, because their characteristic responses to stress, illness, dysfunction, and abuse may be different from those of the dominant race and gender and the privileged social class; this can lead to negative outcomes for racial-cultural nondominant groups, such as being labeled abnormal. Sue (1999) recommended that to develop a stronger knowledge base on racial-cultural nondominant groups, it is necessary that:

> (a) all research studies address external validity issues and explicitly specify the populations to which the findings are applicable; (b) different research approaches, including the use of qualitative and ethnographic methods be appreciated; and (c) the psychological meaning of ethnicity or race be examined in ethnic comparisons. (p. 1070)

CRITICAL ISSUES CONFRONTING RACIAL-CULTURAL ETHICAL RESEARCH

According to the surgeon general's report (DHHS, 2001), researchers conduct studies in non-White communities because they want their work to have an impact on resolving social programs, to guide policy, or to serve as a basis for programs that will improve the quality of life in these communities. Unfortunately, the outcome of most research has not benefited the communities that have been subjected to research with such high ideals. Historically, though with good intentions, solid methodology, and strong scientific backgrounds, researchers have conducted research with generally disastrous results for communities of Color. Academic and governmental research has been used to "prove" the inferiority of nondominant groups, to denigrate community and tribal practices, and to accentuate the negative or misrepresent the beliefs, norms, and cultures of the communities under study.

The most blatant of these abuses are best exemplified by three studies. The first, the Tuskegee syphilis experiment, was a 40-year study conducted by the U.S. Public Health Service from 1932 to 1972. In the Tuskegee study, 400 poor Black men with syphilis were left untreated in order for researchers to better understand the full course of the disease. Even when penicillin, a proven cure, became available in the 1950s, participants were actively deceived and denied treatment (Jones, 1992). A second example concerns Puerto Rican, Mexican, and Haitian women who, between 1956 and 1957, were used for the premarketing tests of birth control pills before a safe dosage was determined. These women of Color were neither warned about nor compensated for the effects or the potential side effects of the medications (Ad Hoc Women's Studies Committee against Sterilization Abuse, 1978; Connell, 1999). Although both of these studies are examples of past transgressions, unethical research practices are not a thing of the past. Beginning in 1989, in several areas of California, 1,500 children were given experimental measles vaccines as part of a government-sponsored trial. Not only were most of the participants from two nondominant groups, Latino and African American, but the parents of these infants and children were not informed that their children were part of a study that used unlicensed vaccines. The trials were conducted as a joint venture of Kaiser Permanente, the CDC and Johns Hopkins University, but were terminated two years later, when questions arose about the relation between the vaccine and the increased death rate among female infants who were in the study (Hilleman, 1998).

Researchers and "medical professionals continue to discriminate in their treatment practices on the basis of race and gender" (Berniker, 2000, p. 8588). The issues that concerned Berniker regarding race and gender discrimination were brought to the surface in the *New England Journal of Medicine* (Shulman et al., 1999). In a series of studies conducted by Shulman et al., it was clearly demonstrated that physicians give more credibility to a patient's complaint of chest pain (angina), and consequently refer him or her for cardiac catheterization, if the patient is a White male versus a Black female. Although the findings were alarming, in a similar study, this time conducted with medical students asked to rate cardiac patients' quality of life, the results were replicated (Rathore et al., 2000). In both studies, the physicians' and medical students' perceptions of patients' symptoms were affected by nonmedical factors, even though both Black and White patients presented with identical symptoms.

Despite continued efforts to educate the medical community regarding the need to provide equitable treatment to all patients, there are statistically significant disparities in the rate of referrals and treatment for people of Color and women for advanced medical care. It is clear, even in medicine, that factors such as race, culture, and gender are being used to make health care decisions. Although ethical guidelines in all health service occupations consider discrimination in the delivery of health care or unequal access to care unethical, the personal perceptions of the health care provider continue to determine how the patient or client is assessed and whether treatment interventions will be offered.

Similar abuses have also been a part of mental health research. Consider the following examples. In the spring of 1913, H. H. Goddard conducted studies on the feeble-mindedness of immigrants, the poor, and Negroes. In one of his studies, he "picked out the feeble-minded by sight" and administered IQ tests to immigrants at Ellis Island. Not surprisingly, of the Jewish, Hungarian, Italian, and

Russian immigrants sampled, an average of 82% were found to be feebleminded. Goddard's research results were used to deny entry to many of the would-be immigrants and were also used to successfully lobby Congress to pass the 1924 Immigration Act, severely limiting immigration from eastern and southern Europe (Cameron & Wycoff, 1998; Shaefer, 1990; Shipman, 1994). In 1916, a professor of psychology at Stanford University, Lewis M. Terman, after publishing the Stanford-Binet IQ test, claimed that mental deficiency was common in Spanish-Indian, Mexican, and Negro families (Shipman, 1994; Smedley, 1993).

These racial biases recently resurfaced with a vengeance in 1994, in Herrnstein and Murray's best-selling book, *The Bell Curve: The Reshaping of American Life by Difference in Intelligence.* The authors argued two points. First, based on social Darwinism, they contended that the poor underclass is simply a distillation of genetically inferior people. Second, stratification by social class is a by-product of inherited racial differences in IQ—with a small superiority for Asians when compared to Whites and a greater superiority of Whites when compared to African Americans. According to Gould (1996), for the authors to maintain their claim of the intellectual inferiority of the poor and of people of Color, they used "regression curves of their variables against IQ and parental socioeconomic status . . . in violation of all statistical norms" (p. 374).

IQ and achievement tests have been used in communities of Color with devastating effects. So great was the damage to the African American community that in a landmark decision, a California court banned the use of all IQ tests for the placement of African American children in special education, even if there was parental consent (*Larry P. v. Wilson Riles,* 1986). In this court hearing, it was clearly demonstrated that through the use of IQ and achievement tests, African American children were found to be below normal intelligence and placed in special education classes at rates far in excess of their White peers. The final court order banned the use of IQ tests with African American students for diagnostic purposes, in the assessment of learning disabilities, in the assessment of strengths and weaknesses, in the determination of goals and objectives, and in the development of comprehensive educational plans. Other school districts, such as those in New York, and Chicago, quickly followed suit, halting the use of IQ testing with African American children, and in some cases with children from other nondominant groups (Mercer, 1989).

Unfortunately, children are not exempt from abuses in mental health research. In two studies conducted in New York City, poor Hispanic and African American boys, 6 to 11 years old, most of whom were labeled with Attention Deficit Disorder, were administered the drug fenfluramine to identify biochemical markers in the brain for aggression and delinquency (Halperin et al., 1997; Pine et al., 1997). Fenfluramine is part of the drug combination fen-phen, which was banned by the Federal Drug Administration in 1997 because it frequently causes potentially fatal heart valve impairment (Connolly et al., 1997). The drug is also a known neurotoxin, a drug that causes death of brain cells (Barnes, 1989). The children in these studies, although not accused of any crimes or acts of delinquency, were the brothers of juvenile offenders in the New York City Probation System (Breggin & Breggin, 1994). It should be noted that since 1989, it was determined that fenfluramine has no positive effect on the behaviors of children (Donnelly et al., 1989), including children with autism (Stern et al., 1990).

Although there are many more examples that could be discussed, it is clear that a great deal of research, despite what the surgeon general would have us believe, is not conducted to "improve the quality of life in the community" (DHHS, 2001, p. 18). Instead, much research is conducted to serve the self-interests of the researchers, for example, to secure tenure or promotion or to support personal and/or common social prejudices. These allegations of self-interest are made more contentious given the recent allegations from the legal community charging research institutions with compromising health care. The current practice in many research institutions is to accept funding from corporate entities with a vested financial interest in the clinical findings (Campbell, 2001; Harrison, 1996; Wadman, 1997). According to Goldner (2000) and Kassirer (2000), research institutions receive grants and collect fees from contract research organizations, such as pharmaceutical companies, not only to conduct the research but also to identify and refer potential research participants for the studies (Goldner, 2000). According to these claims, "financial conflicts of interest have become pervasive in academic medicine" (Kassirer, 2000, p. 149). This expanding relationship between academia and industry is compromising health care by creating overt biases in favor of the funding agency.

THE BEST INTENTIONS

There are five basic problems confronting researchers working in communities of Color. First, there is the issue of historical distrust. Given the victimization and revictimization communities of Color have experienced at the hands of past researchers, many nondominant racial-cultural people are reluctant to participate in research or fail to see the value of research to themselves or their community. This is further aggravated when one considers that most of the research conducted in nondominant communities tends to be of interest to the larger society and is of little or marginal interest to the community under investigation. Even when nondominant communities of Color might be interested in a particular type of research, it is the communities of Color that endure all the burden of risk while a much broader population benefits from the findings. This is clearly demonstrated in the previous studies cited but most poignantly in the Tuskegee syphilis studies, which affected only Black men, and in the fenfluramine studies, which exposed poor African American and Latino children to a known neurotoxin. These historical abuses create uneasiness between academia and nondominant communities that further serves to undermine legitimate research efforts. For research to be considered ethical in communities of Color, researchers need to identify ways to include members from the community under study in the development of research questions and research designs. This would promote the development of trust between the two entities before researchers move in to collect data or to implement an intervention that the local community neither understands nor appreciates.

Linked to this distrust are issues of shame. For the most part, the findings generated from past research on communities of Color accentuated only the negative. Historically, through the use of research, communities and their membership have been identified as pathological, deviant, or deficient. Consequently, nondominant racial groups are reluctant to admit to particular problems and find it easier to simply ignore or deny pressing community problems rather than confront more devastating stigmas or negative stereotypes about their community. In short, to admit to given problems is to publicly "air dirty laundry." The result is that many of the pressing social problems confronting nondominant racial groups, such as juvenile violence, child abuse, domestic violence, and drug abuse, are minimally addressed, if addressed at all. Ethically, this falls under the principle Do not harm. Because harm has been done in the past, it is critical that all research involve the communities as co-researchers to move toward useful research endeavors that would facilitate the mental and physical health of the community.

The second basic problem confronting research in communities of Color pertains to the fact that sometimes, with the best intentions, researchers come into communities of Color attempting to honestly identify pressing physical or mental health issues only to revictimize the participants, leaving them more vulnerable to additional problems. When people in the community participate in studies, revealing intensely painful personal information, most soon discover that little or no funding is appropriated for actual service delivery. As a result, community members feel betrayed when they realize that so little changes for them or their community after researchers have collected the information they seek. The best example of this is demonstrated in the following story.

Believing that sharing their stories would lead to funding of treatment programs, many American Indian parents told of the devastation they and their children experienced as a result of being molested by Bureau of Indian Affairs teachers. As a result of the initial investigation, public hearings were held and Public Law 101-640 was passed (Canby, 1998). The law authorized funding for a study to establish a central registry, treatment programs for sexual offenders, and regional child abuse treatment centers for American Indians. Although lots of information and data were collected, very little funding was appropriated. Given such an experience and many others like it, many communities come to understand that, whether a Senate hearing or a research project, there is little or no remediation for problems once they are identified. This scenario also poses the ethical issue of not providing services after identifying severe trauma caused to a community. Essentially, if such a research project were to be funded, provisions must be made prior to data collection that in the final analysis services will be provided after the extent of the problems has been determined. Research that does not have such provisions should not be approved for funding or allowed by institutional review boards.

The third basic problem confronting research on communities of Color is that much of the research conducted serves to disempower the very community it seeks to serve (Sarason, 1972). When outside researchers come into a community as the experts, they imply an inability on the part of the community to self-identify community problems or to interpret the outcomes of programs they have developed to address an identified problem. This, coupled with the fourth problem—lack of cultural sensitivity, knowledge, or skills—further exacerbates an already complex problem (Sue, 1996). Because researchers are provided special access to community resources and sensitive information about the people in the community, there exists the potential for abuse. Most researchers are White, middle-class individuals (Keith-Spiegel & Koocher, 1995) who lack an understanding of the historical context in which these communities have existed or continue to exist in relation to the larger dominant communities that surround them (CDC, 1998; DHHS, 2001). Moreover, most of the researchers that represent the dominant culture are ignorant of the cultural traditions and mores of the communities they are studying, or their understanding is derived from textbooks and academic discourses that are conducted within the mainstream dominant culture's worldview; this alters the actual meaning of cultural traditions and mores, as no local interpreter is involved in the discourse. As a result, there is a greater likelihood for White middle-class researchers to assign their own personal values to the research findings (Keith-Spiegel & Koocher, 1995) and to draw conclusions and make recommendations from a culturally encapsulated or etic perspective. For American Indian communities, published information from the researcher's etic perspective has resulted in sensitive religious and cultural information being published without consent and out of context, and so misrepresenting them (American Indian Law Center, 1994). Such information has been used to further emphasize pathology in the specific American Indian community (Duran & Duran, 1995).

The issues of disempowerment and lack of cultural knowledge and skills creates a double bind for communities of Color with regard to research. Many, if not most, communities recognize the need to conduct research if they are to attract the outside funding necessary to address the more pressing social problems confronting them. Unfortunately, they also recognize that they lack the minority scholarship from within their community to conduct the research necessary to generate the monies. This makes communities of Color dependent on outsiders to conduct the very research they are ashamed to share with the outside world. Once again, for ethical research to be conducted in communities of Color it is critical to include the local leaders as bearers of knowledge that the academy or a research facility cannot have about local traditions and culture and to work with them as peers to resolve these pressing concerns and to make positive changes in the nondominant communities.

Issues of disempowerment and cultural incompetence are of further concern when the research is actually published. Because most of the researchers do not understand the complexities and diversity within the community being studied, according to LaFromboise, Trimble, and Mohatt (1990) there is a tendency to generalize across cultures, which in turn has a terrible impact on the larger community. Researchers unfamiliar with the within-group differences for a particular population are likely to unwittingly gloss over or minimize these differences. For example, a researcher conducting a study on the Navajo Reservation needs to be cognizant of and able to articulate the differences between Eastern and Western Navajo (the two groups are culturally different). Those conducting research in Hispanic communities must understand the cultural and value differences separating northern, central, and southern New Mexicans from Chicanos in East Los Angeles, Mexican Nationals in Indiana, and Cuban Americans in Miami.

The fifth issue confronting research in nondominant communities of Color is the inability of many people or communities of Color to truly give informed consent. Repeatedly, people of Color are persuaded to participate in research they don't fully understand or they are in a financial situation that puts them at risk for abuse. In the fenfluramine study previously mentioned, the parents received $100 and their children a $25 gift certificate to Toys R Us for participating in the study (Breggin & Breggin, 1994). In a poor community where monies and resources are slim, these types of "gifts" in exchange for participating are almost impossible to turn down. The same is true for the patients being recruited from a hospital emergency room during a psychiatric crisis: Is this individual able to fully exercise free choice or is he or she feeling subtly coerced? Ethical research, especially with nondominant groups, would not use coercion or bribes to induce people to participate. If a community chooses to participate it should be given some benefits as a group, especially if it is a poor community that needs support and services rather than a gift certificate to a toy store. Before starting research, full disclosure about the substances being tested and the risks involved must be provided to all in a language they can comprehend.

ENHANCING ETHICAL RACIAL-CULTURAL RESEARCH

Research influences the way people think and how decisions are made with regard to allocation of resources. According to the CDC (1998), research is a social activity, dependent on human interactions, with the goal of understanding the circumstances and reasons for variations in the human condition. If research is to truly be a social activity, as the CDC suggests, it must be fully embraced by communities of Color and the protection of ethical standards must be provided to the researchers and the communities that are engaged in the project. To be ethical, research must first become an inclusionary process, a collaborative partnership between the community and the researchers. The collaborative partnership must be fully participatory in establishing specific roles and responsibilities for both the researchers and the community by determining the level for involvement of each in the research project. As in any partnership, an explicit mechanism for dialogue, discourse, and participation for both groups must be established. It would include clarifying who has decision-making power and is responsible for the consequences.

A collaborative partnership will help ensure greater accountability. In a collaborative partnership, researchers are under the tutelage of community members and are better able to understand the nuances of the community and to be more respectful of the limitations on reporting findings. As a result, researchers would come to understand the cultural context in which problems have been generated. Researchers would develop a broader understanding of the unique social, cultural, and political dynamics of the community as they work in partnership with the community. This collaborative venture would also facilitate more accurate communication between the entities at various levels in the research process. Because communities would be able to provide their own interpretation of the results, consistent with the cultural assumptions, the accuracy of what is reported would be increased, ensuring that communities are not stigmatized by the results. These collaborative partnerships would in essence create a corrective screen because there would be multiple levels of accountability.

For collaborative partnerships to come to fruition the community that is the subject of research, not the researchers, must be given the exclusive right to determine what, if any, type of research will be conducted. Researchers need to understand that they are not the experts, but rather have an expertise to offer. When researchers enter a community of Color, they need to appreciate and value the expertise that already exists within that community and understand that they are invited guests and partners in research; the community holds the expertise and power of knowledge about its culture, social mores, beliefs, traditions, and way of life.

Second, for research to be ethical communities must directly benefit from the research findings. The quickest way to achieve this goal is to provide training, education, and employment opportunities for community members. This might include opportunities to work as co-investigator(s) with the principal investigators, to conduct interviews, or to serve as data managers. In addition, researchers already working in the community could offer technical assistance to community organizations interested in generating their own research. For communities that have successfully completed research projects, funding should be made available to address the identified problems. The best way to accomplish this goal would be to provide funding (from research funds obtained to conduct the research) in the form of planning monies, allowing communities to strategize and design intervention programs, and/or seed monies to initiate programs. Refunding of community projects could be based on outcome studies. Funding opportunities and working with the research investigators would serve to empower communities and community organizations.

Third, trust needs to be established between researchers and community participants; this is no small charge. To build trust there must be open and honest communication between the researchers and the community participants. Open communication requires that researchers work with community organizations to decrease bias and misunderstanding by educating individuals and community members regarding the value of research to all of them. It is also important for researchers to remember that a primary component of building trust is respect. Respect demands providing full informed consent at a reading level reflective of the average reading level of the community. It is crucial that researchers remember that it is one thing to require that information be given—it is quite another to ensure that the information is understood. Providing fully informed consent cannot be limited to the individual, but should include the community.

To build trust the researchers and the communities must share power and control. In most research institutions, the researcher owns the data. A paradigm shift needs to occur here so that there is joint ownership of the data, process, and results, meaning that the work belongs equally to the community and the researchers. When research projects are not shared between the community and the researcher, participants, especially those with issues of historical distrust, can and will mislead researchers. This is best exemplified by a story shared by a colleague of one of the authors (SCC). According to F. Detsoi (personal communication, August 23, 2001), she and a colleague were conducting a research project on maternal and infant health care in the eastern part of the Navajo Reservation. Detsoi is from eastern Navajo, and her research partner is non-Navajo. As they were conducting their research, the non-Navajo interviewed a small group of Navajo women about traditional childbirth practices. The women, sitting together, assured the non-Navajo researcher that Navajo women eat their placenta after delivering their babies. Alarmed and somewhat frightened by what she had learned, the colleague confronted Detsoi with her findings. As Detsoi listened to the story, it became clear to her that the interviewees did not trust the researcher and, at her expense and for their own amusement, simply lied/misinformed the researcher.

Fourth, researchers need to secure permission to work in the community. Often, researchers develop a research study, approach the IRB for approval, and then identify community individuals as participants. Partnerships created after all the research decisions have been made cannot be considered partnerships, nor does the situation instill trust or confidence in the researcher or the project. Here again, another paradigm shift is needed. Researchers need to make their expertise known to the community and work in partnership with the community to develop the community's research needs. It is also very important that communities of Color develop their own IRB rather than remain dependent on outside entities to protect them. This is not to imply that all researchers are corrupt or wish to do communities harm; the goal is to provide a second layer of protection to the community and, again, encourage the development of a collaborative working relationship between the researcher and the community.

With regard to securing permission from the community to conduct research, professional journals publishing research on racial and cultural nondominant groups should require the authors to provide proof of consent from the community in which the research was conducted. Proof of consent would serve three purposes: (1) It would strongly suggest to the readership that the research questions, assessment measures, and procedures used in the study were reviewed by a community board to determine cultural sensitivity and appropriateness; (2) it would serve to safeguard community taboos, cultural practices, and religious beliefs; and (3) it would give communities the opportunity to validate the research. It is recommended that research submitted for publication without prior approval from the community under study be rejected for publication, as it may be violating cultural norms and taboos about sharing information outside the community. This protection is needed for ethical and useful research findings for both communities of Color and the researchers.

Fifth, to conduct ethical research researchers must be willing to make long-term commitments to the community. The old method of "helicopter" research—dropping into a community, collecting data, and quickly exiting, leaving only a cloud of dust—is unacceptable and only contributes to and maintains the historical distrust.

If the medical, mental, and social problems confronting our communities are going to be effectively and holistically addressed, a public health approach to problem solving must be instituted.

The sixth, and most important, point is that research in communities of Color needs to be conducted to establish the norms within a particular community—not in contrast to the dominant culture. The dominant group cannot be the normative group for all racial and ethnic minority groups in the country; this only serves to reinforce the labeling of people of Color as pathological. Currently, in a mental health clinic, unless the practitioner is from that community, it is very difficult to determine with any certainly whether a behavior is culturally appropriate or inappropriate. Although stated in the Ethical Guidelines for both the American Counseling Association (1995) and the American Psychological Association (2002) that a client's socioeconomic and cultural experience must be considered when diagnosing mental disorders, in reality this cannot be done unless sufficient research is generated establishing baseline normative behaviors. In the *Diagnostic and Statistical Manual IV* (American Psychiatric Association, 1994, 2000) a cautionary statement is issued reminding clinicians that failure to understand the cultural frame of reference of clients may lead to misdiagnosing normal variations in behavior as psychopathology (Castillo, 1997). In short, without creating a normative base of behaviors for communities of Color, the assumptions a researcher has about the nature of people and of mental illness will directly impact how research is conducted and how behaviors are labeled.

GUIDELINES FOR FUTURE RESEARCH ON RACIAL-CULTURAL ISSUES IN PSYCHOLOGY, COUNSELING, AND PSYCHOTHERAPY

Table 19.1 summarizes all the recommendations that have been proposed for ethical racial-cultural research. This table includes previous and recent recommendations, culminating with the revision of the American Psychological Association revised ethical principles (2002).

Future Research Needs in Multicultural Counseling

More research is needed that focuses on multicultural and cross-cultural issues. This includes quantitative and qualitative research to create a sizable scientific data bank that will guide theory and allow for testing models that are currently available. Specific research is needed on the applicability of current counseling approaches to the diverse clients that counselors and psychologists are working with and will continue to work with in the future. Studies that focus on actual interventions are needed to create a balanced perspective between the lab and the field. Research studies must employ traditional scientific methods and qualitative analyses that will incorporate all the variables that must be considered when cultural, race, gender, social class, lifestyle, age, and disability differences exist (Gazda, Rude, & Weissberg, 1988; Gelso et al., 1988; Ponterotto & Casas, 1991).

Given the cultural dynamics of the United States, the history of racism, slavery, social exclusion (reservations), and internment, it is imperative that research start to identify the variables that affect people and groups over time, instead of

Table 19.1   Guidelines for Future Research on Racial-Cultural Issues in Psychology, Counseling, and Psychotherapy

1. Know and understand the ignoble history of race and science, especially as it pertains to research.
2. Recognize the worldview of the community of Color and its relevance to the researchers.
3. Obtain consent from the leaders and the people in the community, and the determine on what specific basis the consent was given.
4. Plan research projects conjointly by the community of Color and the researchers.
5. Clearly define race and culture variables. Clearly describe the characteristics of the study and the comparison group and the current racial-cultural coding used.
6. Recognize that data on variables such as race, social class, culture, ethnicity, and gender can play a pivotal role in increasing awareness of inequities and stimulating changes in policies.
7. In publishing, recognize what information would violate the confidentiality of the community of Color and the individuals within the communities. To whom should the information be disseminated? How should the information gained be made accessible to the local communities?
8. Editors must play a major role in developing and implementing a policy on the conduct and reporting of research on race, culture, and health.

Derived from "Is Research on Health Racist, Unsound, or Important to Science?" by R. Bhopal, 1997, *British Medical Journal, 314,* pp. 171–177; "The Contribution of Cultural Worldview to Generic Counseling and Psychotherapy," by F. A. Ibrahim, 1991, *Journal of Counseling and Development, 70,* pp. 13–19; "Transcultural Counseling: Existential Worldview Theory and Cultural Identity," pp. 23–55, by F. A. Ibrahim, in *Transcultural counseling,* second edition, J. McFadden, ed., 1999, Alexandria, VA: American Counseling Association; "Methodological Sources of Cultural Insensitivity in Mental Health Research," by L. H. Rogler, 1999, *American Psychologist, 54,* pp. 424–433; "Ethnicity as a Variable in Epidemiological Research," by P. Senior and R. S. Bhopal, 1994, *British Medical Journal, 309,* pp. 327–336; "Science, Ethnicity and Bias: Where Have We Gone Wrong?" by S. Sue, 1999, *American Psychologist, 54,* pp. 1070–1077; and "The Ethics of Research in American Indian Communities," by M. L. Wax, 1991, *American Indian Quarterly, p. 15,* 431–457.

accepting the culturally deficient model. Ponterotto and Casas (1991) propose a culturally pluralistic research perspective, echoing Gelso et al.'s (1988) perspective that (1) a semantically neutral terminology must be introduced into the multicultural literature; (2) this terminology and philosophy must emphasize the richness and value of cultural diversity and not discuss groups in terms of majority or minority (because "minorities" implies different from or less than the norm); (3) research must also focus on positive aspects of racial-ethnic groups, providing a balanced research agenda; (4) we must move away from a pure scientific model of research to using both quantitative and qualitative methodologies to derive a coherent context-based perspective on racial-ethnic communities; and (5) as stated earlier, research must be a respectful collaboration between researchers and communities.

REFERENCES

Ad Hoc Women's Studies Committee against Sterilization Abuse. (1978). *Workbook on sterilization.* Bronxville, NY: Sarah Lawrence College.

American Counseling Association (ACA). (1995). *Code of ethics and standards of practice.* Alexandria, VA: Author.

American Indian Law Center. (1974). *Model tribal research code* (2nd ed.). Albuquerque, NM: Author.

American Psychiatric Association. (1994). *Diagnostic and statistical manual of mental disorders IV-TR* (4th ed.). Washington, DC: Author.

American Psychiatric Association. (2000). *Diagnostic and statistical manual of mental disorders IV* (5th ed.). Washington, DC: Author.

American Psychological Association. (2002). *Ethical principles of psychologists and code of conduct.* Washington, DC: Author.

Applebaum, P. S., & Rosenbaum, A. (1989). *Tarasoff* and the researcher: Does the duty to protect apply in the research setting? *American Psychologist, 44,* 885–894.

Applebaum, P. S., Roth, L. H., Lidz, C., Benson, P., & Winslade, W. (1987). False hopes and best data: Consent to research and therapeutic misconceptions. *Hasting Center Report, 17,* 20–24.

Atkinson, D. R., Morten, G., & Sue, D. W. (1989). *Counseling American minorities: A cross-cultural perspective* (3rd ed.). Dubuque, IA: Brown.

Atkinson, D. R., & Schein, S. (1986). Similarity in counseling. *Counseling Psychologist, 14,* 319–354.

Barnes, D. M. (1989). Neurotoxicity creates regulatory dilemma. *Science, 243,* 29–30.

Berniker, J. S. (2000). Legal implications of discrimination in medical practice. *Journal of Law, Medicine, and Ethics, 28,* 588–594.

Bhopal, R. (1997). Is research on health racist, unsound, or important to science? *British Medical Journal, 314,* 171–177.

Breggin, P. R., & Breggin, G. (1994). *The war against children.* New York: St. Martin's Press.

Cameron, S. C., & Wycoff, S. M. (1998). The destructive nature of the term race: Growing beyond a false paradigm. *Journal of Counseling and Development, 76,* 277–285.

Campbell, P. B. (2001). Declaration of financial interests. *Nature, 412,* 751.

Canby, W. C. (1998). *American Indian law: In a nutshell.* St. Paul, MN: West Group.

Carter, R. T., & Parks, E. E. (1992). White ethnic group membership and cultural values preferences. *Journal of College Student Development, 33,* 499–506.

Casas, J. M. (1984). Policy, training, and research in counseling psychology. In S. D. Brown & R. Lent (Eds.), *Handbook of counseling psychology* (pp. 785–831). New York: Wiley.

Casas, J. M. (1985). A reflection on the status of racial- and ethnic-minority research. *Counseling Psychologist, 13,* 581–598.

Casas, J. M., & Vasquez, M. J. T. (1989). Counseling Hispanics. In P. B. Pedersen, W. Lonner, J. Draguns, & J. E. Trimble (Eds.), *Counseling across cultures* (3rd ed., pp. 156–176). Honolulu: University of Hawaii Press.

Castillo, R. (1997). *Culture and mental illness.* Pacific Grove, CA: Brooks/Cole.

Centers for Disease Control. (1998). *Building community partnerships in health research.* Atlanta, GA: Author.

Cherbosque, J. (1987). Differences between Mexican and American clients in expectations about psychological counseling. *Journal of Multicultural Counseling and Development, 15,* 110–114.

Connell, E. B. (1999). Contraception in the prepill era. *Contraception, 59,* 7S–10S.

Connolly, H. M., Crary, J. L., McGoon, M. D., Hensrud, D. D., Edwards, B. S., & Edwards, W. D. (1997). Valvular heart disease associated with fenfluramine-phentermine. *New England Journal of Medicine, 337,* 581–588.

DeRenzo, E. G. (1994). The ethics of involving psychiatrically impaired persons in research. *Institutional Review Board, 16,* 7–9, 11.

Donnelly, M., Rapoport, J. L., Potter, W. Z., Oliver, J., Keysor, C. S., & Murphy, D. L. (1989). Fenfluramine and dextroamphetamine treatment of childhood hyperactivity; Clinical and biochemical findings. *Archives of General Psychiatry, 46,* 205–212.

Duran, E., & Duran, B. (1995). *Native American postcolonial psychology.* Albany: State University New York Press.

Gazda, G. M., Rude, S. S., & Weissberg, M. (Eds.). (1988). Third national conference for counseling psychology: Planning the future [Special issue]. *Counseling Psychologist, 16,* 3.

Gelso, C. J., Betz, N. E., Friedlander, M. L., Helms, J. E., Hill, C. E., Patton, M. J., et al. (1988). Research in counseling psychology: Prospects and recommendations. *Counseling Psychologist, 16,* 385–406.

Gideonse, H. D. (1977, April). *Sex roles, inquiry and policy.* Paper presented at the annual meeting of the American Educational Research Association, New York.

Goldner, J. A. (2000). Dealing with conflicts of interest in biomedical research: IRB oversight as the next best solution to the abolitionist approach. *Journal of Law, Medicine, and Ethics, 28,* 379–404.

Gould, S. J. (1996). *The mismeasure of man.* New York: Norton.

Grisso, T., & Applebaum, P. S. (1995). The MacArthur Treatment Competence Study: III. Abilities of patients to consent to psychiatric and medical treatments. *Law and Human Behavior, 19,* 149–174.

Halperin, J. M., Newcorn, J. H., Kopstein, I., McKay, K. E., Schwartz, S. T., Siever, L. J., et al. (1997). Serotonin, aggression, and parental psychopathology in children with attention-deficit hyperactivity disorder. *Journal of the American Academy of Child and Adolescent Psychiatry, 36,* 1391–1398.

Harrison, R. (1996). Comments on disclosure of financial interest. *Journal of American Veterans Medical Association, 208,* 1962.

Hernandez, J. (1979). *Challenge to the sacred American cow.* Berkeley, CA: University of California Press.

Herrnstein, R. J., & Murray, C. (1994). *The bell curve: The reshaping of American life by difference in intelligence.* New York: Free Press.

Hilleman, M. R. (1998). Vaccines, human experimentation, and ethics in evolutionary perspective. *Developmental Biology Standard, 95,* 13–17.

Ibrahim, F. A. (1989). Response to "psychology in the public forum" on socially sensitive research. *American Psychologist, 44,* 847–848.

Ibrahim, F. A. (1991). The contribution of cultural worldview to generic counseling and psychotherapy. *Journal of Counseling and Development, 70,* 13–19.

Ibrahim, F. A. (1999). Transcultural counseling: Existential worldview theory and cultural identity. In J. McFadden (Ed.), *Transcultural counseling* (2nd ed., pp. 23–55). Alexandria, VA: American Counseling Association.

Ibrahim, F. A., & Kahn, H. (1987). Assessment of worldviews. *Psychological Reports, 64,* 163–176.

Ibrahim, F. A., & Ohnishi, H. (2001). PTSD and the minority experience. In D. Pope-Davis & H. Coleman (Eds.), *Intersection of race, class, and gender: Implications for multicultural counseling* (pp. 89–126). Thousand Oaks, CA: Sage.

Jones, J. H. (1992). *Bad blood: The Tuskegee syphilis experiment.* New York: Simon & Schuster Trade.

Karigan, M. (2001). Ethics in clinical research. *American Journal of Nursing, 101,* 26–31.

Kassirer, J. P. (2000). Financial conflict of interest: An unresolved ethical frontier. *American Journal of Law and Medicine, 27,* 149–162.

Keith-Spiegel, P., & Koocher, G. P. (1995). *Ethics in psychology: Professional standards and cases.* Hillsdale, NJ: Erlbaum.

LaFromboise, T. D., Trimble, J. E., & Mohatt, G. V. (1990). Counseling intervention and American Indian tradition: An integrative approach. *Counseling Psychologist, 18,* 628–654.

Mercer, J. R. (1989). Alternative paradigms for assessment in a pluralistic society. In J. A. Banks & C. A. McGee Banks (Eds.), *Multicultural education: Issues and perspectives* (pp. 289–304). Needham Heights, MA: Allyn & Bacon.

National Commission for the Protection of Human Subjects of Biomedical and Behavioral Research. (1979). *The Belmont report* (DHEW Publication No. 78-0013). Washington, DC: U.S. Government Printing Office.

Nuremberg Code. (1949–1953). *Trials of war criminals before the Nuremberg tribunal under control council law #10. Nuremberg, October 1946–April 1949.* Washington, DC: U.S. Government Printing Office. Available from www.ushmm.org/research/doctors/nuremberg_code.htm.

Pine, D. S., Coplan, J. D., Wasserman, G. A., Miller, L. S., Fried, J. E., Davis, M., et al. (1997). Neuroendocrine response to fenfluramine challenges in boys: Associations with aggressive behavior and adverse rearing. *Archives of General Psychiatry, 54,* 839–846.

Ponterotto, J. G. (1988). Racial/ethnic minority research in the *Journal of Counseling Psychology:* A content analysis and methodological critique. *Journal of Counseling Psychology, 35,* 410–418.

Ponterotto, J. G., & Benesh, K. F. (1988). An organizational framework for understanding the role of culture in counseling. *Journal of Counseling and Development, 66,* 237–241.

Ponterotto, J. G., & Casas, J. M. (1991). *Handbook of racial/ethnic minority counseling research.* Springfield, IL: Charles C. Thomas.

Pope-Davis, D. B., & Liu, W. M. (1998). The social construction of race: Implications for counseling psychology. *Counseling Psychology Quarterly, 11,* 151–62.

Rathore, S. S., Lenert, L. A., Weinfurt, K. P., Tinoco, A., Taleghani, C. K., Harless, W., et al. (2000). The effect of patient sex and race on medical students' ratings of quality of life. *American Journal of Medicine, 108,* 561–566.

Rogler, L. H. (1999). Methodological sources of cultural insensitivity in mental health research. *American Psychologist, 54,* 424–433.

Sarason, S. B. (1972). *The creation of settings and the future of societies.* San Francisco: Jossey-Bass.

Scarr, S. (1988). Race and gender as psychological variables. *American Psychologist, 43,* 56–59.

Segall, M. H. (1979). *Cross-cultural psychology: Human behavior in a global perspective.* Monterey, CA: Brooks/Cole.

Segall, M. H., Lonner, W. J., & Berry, J. W. (1998). Cross-cultural psychology as a scholarly discipline: On the flowering of culture in behavioral research. *American Psychologist, 53,* 1101–1110.

Senior, P., & Bhopal, R. S. (1994). Ethnicity as a variable in epidemiological research. *British Medical Journal, 309,* 327–336.

Shaefer, R. T. (1990). *Racial and ethnic groups* (4th ed.). New York: Scott, Foresman.

Shamoo, A. E. (1997). *Ethics in neurobiological research with human subjects.* Amsterdam: Gordon & Breach.

Sherif, C. W. (1979). Bias in psychology. In J. A. Sherman & E. T. Beck (Eds.), *The prism of sex: Essays in the sociology of knowledge* (pp. 35–58). Madison: University of Wisconsin Press.

Shipman, P. (1994). *The evolution of racism: Human differences and the use and abuse of science.* New York: Simon & Schuster.

Shulman, K. A., Berlin, J. A., Harless, W., Kerner, J. F., Sistrunk, S., Gersh, B. J., et al. (1999). The effect of race and sex on physicians' recommendations for cardiac catherization. *New England Journal of Medicine, 340,* 618–626.

Smedley, A. (1993). *Race in North America: Origin and evolution of a worldview.* Boulder, CO: Westview Press.

Stern, L. M., Walker, M. K., Sawyer, M. G., Odes, R. D., Babcock, N. R., & Spence, J. G. (1990). A controlled crossover trial of fenfluramine in autism. *Journal of Child Psychology and Psychiatry, 31,* 569–585.

Sue, S. (1988). Psychotherapeutic services for ethnic minorities: Two decades of research findings. *American Psychologist, 43,* 301–308.

Sue, S. (1996). Measurement, testing, and ethnic bias: Can solutions be found? In G. R. Sodowsky & J. C. Impara (Eds.), *Multicultural assessment in counseling and clinical psychology* (pp. 7–37). Lincoln, NE: Buros Institute of Mental Measurements.

Sue, S. (1999). Science, ethnicity and bias: Where have we gone wrong? *American Psychologist, 54,* 1070–1077.

Sue, S., & Zane, N. W. (1987). The role of culture and cultural techniques in psychotherapy: A critique and reformulation. *American Psychologist, 42,* 37–45.

Sue, S., Zane, N., & Young, K. (1994). Research on psychotherapy with culturally diverse populations. In A. E. Bergin & S. L. Garfield (Eds.), *Handbook of psychotherapy and behavior change* (4th ed., pp. 783–817). New York: Wiley.

Tankanow, R. M., Sweet, B. V., & Weiskopf, J. A. (1992). Patient's perceived understanding of informed consent in investigational drug studies. *American Journal of Hospital Pharmacy, 49,* 633–635.

U.S. Department of Health and Human Services. (1998). *Institutional review boards: A time for reform* (Report prepared by Inspector General June Gibbs Brown). Rockville, MD: Author.

U.S. Department of Health and Human Services. (2001). *Mental health: Culture, race, and ethnicity: A supplement to the mental health report of the surgeon general.* Rockville, MD: Author.

Vontress, C. E. (1988). An existential approach to cross-cultural counseling. *Journal of Multicultural Counseling and Development, 16,* 73–83.

Wadman, M. (1997, August 21). $100M payout after drug data withheld. *Nature, 388,* 903.

Wax, M. L. (1991). The ethics of research in American Indian communities. *American Indian Quarterly, 15,* 431–457.

White, T. J., & Sedlacek, W. E. (1987). White student attitudes toward Blacks and Hispanics: Programming implications. *Journal of Multicultural Counseling and Development, 15,* 171–183.

Winslow, E. (1998). Caring for patients with limited literacy. *American Journal of Nursing, 98,* 55–57.

World Medical Organization. (1996, December 7). Declaration of Helsinki. *British Medical Journal, 313*(7070), 1448–1449.

CHAPTER 20

The Decline of White Racial-Cultural Dominance in Counseling and Psychology: A Summary and Reflections on the Impact of Multiple Perspectives

Robert T. Carter, Alex L. Pieterse, and Bryant Williams

The chapters that compose Volume One of the *Handbook* collectively represent the work of psychologists and social scientists who have struggled to transform psychology from a monocultural White American scientific and applied discipline to a profession that includes multiple racial-cultural perspectives and worldviews. Although the hegemony of Western psychological concepts persists within the larger field of psychology, the theoretical developments and bodies of research reviewed in this volume provide confirmation that change is needed. It is apparent that the racial and cultural revolution in psychology has a long way to go. We believe that this is because it is difficult to consider the reality of people whose socialization and experience are different from one's own. From the perspective of oneself or one's own racial-cultural group it can seem axiomatic and self-evident that the filter one used to view one's experience and environment is shared by all of humanity. Cultural difference, when it has been addressed by the social sciences, has primarily focused on variations in dress and other physical manifestations of explicit customs that are readily apparent. It has been more difficult to discern the aspects of culture that are less visible, such as communication styles, thought patterns, and feelings. Therefore, we commend the tremendous effort of the contributing authors who have taken on the challenge of elucidating these veiled and unspoken aspects of race and culture.

The values, beliefs, and behaviors of White Americans and Western Europeans have actually never been the only norms by which other racial, ethnic, and cultural groups lived. However, through the imposition of power, the dominant group in our society has forced other racial-cultural groups to comply to Euro-American social, cultural, and psychological norms. The dominance of the American psychological perspective and its related practices has been revealed and appropriately labeled as oppressive, ethnocentric, and racist. The scholarship and research presented here is evidence of a continuing movement for change that allows and encourages scholars, clinicians, and researchers to argue for and subsequently develop and test theories that attempt to explain the fundamental role that racial-cultural factors play in human development, experience, and behavior.

The trajectory of the chapters in this *Handbook* has moved from the richly nuanced foundational definitions offered by Pedersen, Johnson, Juby, and Concepción; and Carter and Pieterse to the descriptions of the recent theoretical developments presented by Constantine and Wilton; Yeh and Hunter; Constantine, Watt, Gainor, and Warren; Kwan; and Smith and Richards; and finally to the extensive and thoughtful reviews of the research outlined by Draguns; Bowser, Kohatsu, Fouad, and Byars-Winston; Fuertes, Costa, Mueller, and Hersh; Thompson, Shin, and Stephens; Miville; Trimble; Helms; and Ibrahim and Cameron. These works highlight the transition that a portion of psychology is making to include a racial-cultural context. The transition to including race and culture into what is known about human development and behavior makes explicit the reality discussed by Johnson: that we live in a context that is shaped by a people's norms, values, meaning systems, and experience, which is usually referred to as culture. As the authors highlighted, in the United States this type of cultural variation occurs between and within racial groups.

In offering some concluding comments, the following discussion briefly highlights four themes that we believe underlie the chapters represented in this volume: the failure of traditional psychology, the need for clarity of definitions, the central role of identity, and a call for increased complexity and rigor in theoretical and research models. Last, we provide a comment on the current status and future direction of racial-cultural psychology as gleaned from these chapters.

THE FAILURE OF TRADITIONAL PSYCHOLOGY

Perhaps the most stinging critique of traditional psychology in recent years has been its limited consideration of the important influence of racial and cultural factors in the areas of human development, assessment and diagnosis, and therapeutic intervention (Multicultural Guidelines, 2003). In this volume the authors have aimed their critique at some of the core foundations of psychological scholarship. Their consistent charge is that in the areas of personal identity development, vocational psychology, psychotherapeutic process and outcome, socialization, and research methods and paradigms, traditional psychology has uniformly employed a White American perspective as a type of "one size fits all" approach. Specifically in reference to vocational theories, yet having equal applicability to other areas in the field of psychology, Fouad and Byars-Winston (this *Handbook,* Volume One) summarize the core argument:

> Specific criticisms against career theories as a result of the predominance of largely monocultural samples (i.e., White Americans) highlight that the construction of these theories is based on White, middle-class males and White American values, ignoring the unique sociopolitical realities and related psychological experiences of racial/ethnic minorities.

Furthermore, Carter and Pieterse (this *Handbook,* Volume One) describe the historical treatment of race in the field of psychology as frequently reflecting the racist ideologies of the time. Psychology's history of implicit and explicit racism legitimizes the need to focus on and reveal the entrenched and historical European and American notions of White superiority and the constitutive belief in the inferiority of other racial, ethnic, and cultural groups. While there is a recognition of the changing nature of the field leading to the incorporation of race as a psychological construct there also is a strong pull to hide race and treat it as a less visible aspect of cultural differences. Even as evidence demonstrates that racial disparities are prevelant is many aspects of American life. One's race predicts the quality of education, housing, health, health care, and other factors (DHHS, 2001). Ibrahim and Cameron's (this *Handbook,* Volume One) discussion of the inclusion of race and culture as ethical imperatives highlights the fact that much work still lies ahead—especially if racial-cultural concerns are to become part of the core of contemporary psychology and not simply an add-on in response to varied political, economic, and personal motivations.

THE NEED FOR CLARITY OF DEFINITIONS

It is not surprising given the inherent complexity of the human experience that definitions of racial-cultural concepts would be fraught with inconsistencies, contradictions, and a general lack of cohesion. The lack of clarity in the definitions of the core constructs of racial-cultural psychology (e.g., race, ethnicity, culture,) appears to have retarded both the appreciation and understanding of the concepts in the larger field. Two examples from the current volume highlight both the problem of obtaining clear definitions and the results associated with this lack of clarity. Kohatsu, focusing on acculturation, observes, "One of the predominant themes in the acculturation literature has been the consistent lack of consensus in defining the term. . . . Researchers have used the term acculturation in different ways and often in conjunction with other constructs, such as assimilation, ethnic identity, and ethnicity." Additionally, Thompson, Shin, and Stephens, in reference to race, note:

> Achieving an understanding of race as relevant to psychologists is hampered also by the frequent use of race as synonymous with ethnicity. . . . Although both phenomena are knottily intertwined, the practice of equating the two compromises an understanding of each.

As the *Handbook*'s contributors point out, the lack of clarity in the core constructs of the field creates innumerable problems. For instance, the use of race and ethnicity as interchangeable concepts has served to minimize many people's lived experience of the two as separate constructs. Carter and Pieterse (this *Handbook,* Volume One) demonstrate how race and ethnicity are actually quite distinct in their analysis of the terms' meanings. Additionally, Kwan (this *Handbook,* Volume One) provides a poignant example of the problem of using race and ethnicity interchangeably in his chapter on racial salience. He notes that for an Asian American in a predominantly White environment race is most likely salient, yet when the same individual transitions into a predominantly Asian American environment, his or her ethnicity transitions to the forefront. Additionally, because the field principally utilizes quantitative methodologies for gathering knowledge, which are deductive in nature, the lack of clarity of definitions can result in imprecise measures of the constructs and make it difficult to interpret research results. The works in this volume have addressed the issue of poorly defined constructs directly, through first outlining the history of inconsistency with which the core concepts have been presented and then by offering clear and concise definitions of the main constructs, such as race, ethnicity, and culture. We believe that clear and distinct definitions provide a sound foundation from which racial-cultural factors can enter the psychological discourse and subsequently form the basis of new theories and research.

THE CENTRAL ROLE OF RACIAL-CULTURAL ASPECTS OF IDENTITY

It becomes apparent in reading these chapters that the concept of racial-cultural identity and its multiple facets is integral in the field of racial-cultural psychology. Identity (knowing one's self) is also central in the lives of people, as it is a core question that everyone must confront. The theories of racial-cultural identity and their respective bodies of research that are discussed in these chapters have helped to shape and inform the paradigm of racial-cultural psychology. The perspective provided by a racial-cultural paradigm provides a more comprehensive lens with which to view human experience and behavior than has existed previously in psychology. The racial-cultural perspective of human experience and behavior is extremely complex because, as Kwan, Yeh, and Hunter; Helms; and Trimble note in their chapters, some of the reference groups to which one's identity is tied are no longer viewed as being static but are seen as being in flux and driven by the surrounding context. To add to the complexity of our thinking about racial-cultural identity, Helms introduces the notion that although racial groups are thought to be distinct and clearly demarcated, in actuality they are psychologically interrelated. To illustrate, Helms argues:

> In my Black-White model, I presented the idea that White people's conceptions of racial others were inexorably intertwined with their conceptions of themselves as White people. Moreover, I argued that identification or disidentification with the "Black other" was a critical dynamic (i.e., an introject) in White identity development.

Seen through the lens of racial-cultural psychology, the idea that maturity is equated with a fixed or unchanging identity loses it relevance and is replaced by concepts of racial-cultural identity whereby an individual retains and expresses identities associated with various reference groups. Additionally, as highlighted by Trimble, humans have multiple group memberships that are intertwined and reciprocal. The complexities associated with the experience of multiple reference group memberships have long been a part of the thinking in the social sciences, but historically they have been marginalized (Du Bois, 1903). The notion of multiple group identities is only now receiving more widespread theoretical and empirical attention, yet more complete understanding of the intersections of racial-cultural identities remains illusive. The notion of intersecting group-based identities expands our definition of what constitutes psychological health and points to the fact that the interpretation of human experience and behavior needs to take into consideration the racial-cultural context in which it is occurring.

A CALL FOR INCREASED COMPLEXITY AND RIGOR IN RESEARCH MODELS

Many of our colleagues will continue to criticize racial-cultural psychology's use of a relativistic (racially based, culturally grounded, and social constructionist) approach as being of limited utility due to its lack of universal applicability. However, it is important to recall that it was the idea that psychological concepts could be applied uniformly regardless of an individual's racial-cultural background that led to the development of the genetic deficiency and cultural deficit models (Pedersen, this *Handbook,* Volume One). For psychology to become more accurate and relevant as a science and practice, approaches that consider racial-cultural variation, such as qualitative research using adequate sample sizes and even purely ideographic methods (case studies), as reviewed in Miville's chapter (this *Handbook,* Volume One), are valuable because they have the potential to provide pertinent information about certain groups that could not be discovered through purely quantitative means. More important is the need to consider the limits of classical measurement theory and methods when investigating racial-cultural factors. It is likely that linear models do not accurately capture the complex and dynamic nature of racial-cultural factors. Non-linear strategies and methods that account and capture the complexity of racial-cultural variables are needed (Carter, 1996; Helms, 1996). Additionally, psychology's inclusion of diverse ways of knowing, as represented by the acceptance of multiple research methodologies, is indicative of at least a portion of the field's willingness to transform the discipline into a science that is psychologically appropriate and culturally relevant.

As noted by Helms (this *Handbook,* Volume One), racial cultural variables (e.g., racial identity) tend to be complex, interrelated and therefore interact with each other. Helms observes that many editors, reviewers, and researchers have violated traditional and classical or established methods of measurement and statistics to reject racial-cultural instruments, studies, and variables—a racist practice known by people of Color as shifting standards usually used to maintain the status quo. Helms argues against the practice of using shifting psychometric and methodological standards to assess racial-cultural constructs. More important, she argues for closer examination of the tendency to apply shifting standards to research focused on racial-cultural issues. In her chapter she reminds us to follow the standards for educational and psychological testing as outlined by various professional bodies with regard to the interpretation of psychometric data. Elsewhere, Helms (1996) has offered alternative approaches for measuring constructs that are interdependent. Highlighting the issue of measurement with racial-cultural variables, Trimble (this *Handbook,* Volume One) also draws attention to the fact that "Response styles of culturally different respondents create problems for scale and questionnaire construction and use"; further he notes, "[T]he need to capture information through a paper-and-pencil approach may be inconsistent and unrelated to *emic* styles of information sharing."

The *Handbook*'s authors present a strong argument for the need to develop and utilize research models and measurement strategies that more accurately reflect the intricacies of the impact of racial-cultural factors on social and psychological experience. It also should be noted that the call to rethink our current research paradigms with regard to racial-cultural issues is also an ethical argument. The disturbing historical data and description of current research approaches presented by Ibrahim and Cameron (this *Handbook,* Volume One) is a timely reminder of our ethical responsibility as psychologists and the need to hold research to standards of ethical practice. Finally, the chapters in Volume One have produced evidence of the ongoing rift between racial-cultural theory and the research designed to test those theories. We hope that the existence of this ongoing division serves as the basis for a call to greater urgency and more sustained focus on the examination of racial-cultural constructs in theory, research, and practice (Fuertes, Costa, Mueller, & Hersh, this *Handbook,* Volume One).

CURRENT IMPACT AND FUTURE DIRECTIONS

From our review and summary of the chapters in Volume One, it is evident that the racial-cultural emphasis has assumed a place of greater importance in the field of psychology. Scholars and clinicians are now able to incorporate racial-cultural variables with greater frequency and more sophistication in conceptual, empirical, and clinical domains. Additionally, there is now a growing recognition by professional bodies for the need to systematically understand the impact of race and culture on human development and behavior and to move beyond the myopia of dominant American thought (e.g., Multicultural Guidelines, 2003).

In regard to future directions, we stress the continuation of the field's current effort to understand the role of racial-cultural factors in human development, experience, and behavior. We encourage scholars of all disciplines to embrace the reality of race and culture as important and critical aspects of their theory and research on human experience. In addition, we have noted the gulf that lies between theory and research and recognize that a similar rift exists between research, training, and practice. The authors of this volume have presented many ideas that could serve as foundations for bridging the gap between theory and research in racial-cultural psychology, and we hope that these are implemented in the near future. We also hope that the theories presented in this volume will find concrete applications in training programs and clinical settings, such that racial-cultural psychology will continue its movement to becoming a core component of psychology. The use of culture and race as organizing principles and contexts would allow the field to approximate more closely the lived experiences of the individuals and groups that psychologists both serve and study and as such could go a long way at reducing inequities and disparities in health, mental health, and education.

Throughout this volume the authors have made explicit suggestions for how to address the many problems associated with traditional psychology and its reliance on the dominant American cultural perspective. Their recommendations regarding future directions for the theory and research of racial-cultural psychology provide a tangible bridge from which scholars, researchers, and practitioners can apply the concepts and research reviewed here to their respective areas of work. In summary, we offer a review of the authors' thoughts and recommendations, which we hope will serve as a guide as we continue the struggle to transform psychology into a racially based and culturally grounded science and applied discipline.

The authors of the initial chapters in Volume One, Pedersen, Johnson, Juby and Concepción, and Carter and Pieterse, document the conceptual confusion in racial-cultural psychology and each provides important guidance for the future. Pedersen reminds us of the force of racial-cultural and multicultural psychology for shaping and advancing our knowledge of human personality and behavior. He warns us to be vigilant about our cultural assumptions. Johnson leaves us with a definition and understanding of culture that should be used for future work: Culture is the context created and passed on through learned socialization processes. Therefore, culture sets the boundaries for meaning and communication. Juby and Concepción give guidance about how to define ethnicity and honor its unique meaning and significance, yet they warn us to be careful to not confuse it with other aspects of the self. If ethnicity is treated as country of origin, as Juby and Concepción suggest, it is distinct and as such it is possible to understand and study how ethnic group membership influences identity formation. Carter and Pieterse leave us with a way to understand the specific meaning of race. They suggest that race be treated as both a group and a psychological construct that is an aspect of the personality.

The chapters by Yeh and Hunter, Kwan, Smith and Richards, Bowser, Kohatsu, and Fouad and Byars-Winston chart how the self and various aspects of our lived experiences are shaped and affected by racial-cultural context. They help us see that it is imperative that we remain aware of the power of how we define ourselves and our experiences such that we are cognizant of the biases of our own racial-cultural context. Kwan and Kohatsu, in their respective chapters on racial salience and acculturation, demonstrate how these complex experiences are often important parts of our lives that have been obscured by the application of American and Western notions that hinder how we understand racial salience and acculturation. They instruct us that the future in these domains of inquiry will ask scholars to capture the complexity of human experience without de-emphasizing the reality of the physical and psychological elements of our daily lives. That it is important to take physical appearance into account in our models of personal, racial, and cultural identity was also emphasized by Miville in her review of the literature and research on biracial identity. How we look and the meaning that is assigned to our physical features have tremendous impact on how people categorize and subsequently respond to us, especially with respect to race and if we are biracial.

The fact that learning and work are essential and core parts our lives was highlighted by Fouad and Byars-Winston. More important, however, they note that we know little about how racial-cultural factors interact with the worlds of learning and work. We need more complex and thoughtful theory and research that capture all people's experiences in these areas.

Smith and Richards point out that we live in a society and culture in which religion is an important institution, yet the field of psychology has not integrated this aspect of life into our understanding of development and coping. It is critical that the future of racial-cultural psychology integrate spirituality and religion into its models (Constantine, Watt, Gainor, & Warren, this *Handbook,* Volume One; Constantine & Wilton, this *Handbook,* Volume One). With recognition that religion is also an area of life in America that is divided along racial-cultural lines and has been used as a justification for racial oppression and for cultural imposition.

As our models of human development and personality become increasingly more complex we must learn how to transfer this learning into our work with people in therapeutic contexts. As Fuertes, Costa, Mueller, and Hersh illustrate, we currently know very little about the role of racial-cultural factors in therapy. They suggest that we need to include the client's perspective in such areas as acculturation, cultural mistrust, and racial identity if we are to truly improve our understanding of how racial and cultural factors influence therapy.

Ibrahim and Cameron demonstrate that we have been neglectful with regard to upholding our ethical principles when working with communities of Color. These authors challenge us to join communities as researchers, rather than stand apart from them and treat people as objects. The future should see researchers learning through being flexible enough to utilize the ways of knowing of various people of Color as they join with them to develop and conduct research.

As we think about research in the future our contributors provide ways to avoid the pitfalls of the past (Draguns, this *Handbook,* Volume One) and warn us against seeing racial-cultural issues only through the lens of our American and Western cultural traditions. In this regard, Thompson, Shin, and Stephens, Trimble, and Helms call on us to question practices that might hamper our progress and hinder our ability as professionals to measure and study racial-cultural aspects of life and identity. Each chides us to use strategies that may be difficult to accept and embrace, yet each provides guideposts and maps that offer direction for how our research can have more power and significance.

There are many challenges ahead for racial-cultural psychology. There is also great promise.

REFERENCES

American Psychological Association. (2003). Guidelines on multicultural education, training, research, practice, and organizational change for psychologists. *American Psychologists, 58*(5), 377–402.

Carter, R. T. (1996). Exploring the complexity of racial identity attitude measures. In G. R. Sodowsky & J. C. Impara (Eds.), *Multicultural assessment in counseling and clinical psychology* (pp. 193–224). Lincoln, NE: Buros Institute of Mental Measurements.

Du Bois, W. E. B. (1903). *The souls of Black folk.* Chicago: A. C. McClurg.

Helms, J. E. (1996). Toward a methodology for measuring and assessing racial as distinguished from ethnic identity. In G. R. Sodowsky & J. C. Impara (Eds.), *Multicultural assessment in counseling and clinical psychology* (pp. 143–192). Lincoln, NE: Buros Institute of Mental Measurements.

Author Index

Subject Index

Acculturation, 207–225
  conceptualizations and definitions,
    208–210
  conclusions, 224–225
  definitions (ethnicity, ethnic identity, and
    racial identity), 207
  future directions, 224–225
  measurement issues, 212–214
  race-based psychology and, 222–224
  research on socioracial-cultural groups,
    214–222
    African Americans, 217–219
    Asian Americans, 216–217
    language issues, 221
    Latinos, 214–216
    Native Americans, 219
    White Americans, 219–220
  scales, 210–212
Acculturation Rating Scale for Mexican
  Americans (ARMSA-1), 211
Achievement stage, 96
Achievement tests, 400
Activity theory, 338
Adolescence development, 189–190
African American(s). *See also* Black racial
  identity:
  acculturation, 217–219
  Black racial identity development, 66, 265
  examples of behaviors of White people
    that induced African American
    students' experience of racial
    salience, 129
  historic traumata, 174–175

intragroup solidarity, versus externally
  imposed categorization, 174, 175
psychological responses to race and
  racism, 57–60
psychotherapy, 265
shifting shelf theory and, 87
socialization of racial identity, 198
social stratification, 47, 48–49, 50
African American Acculturation Scale
  (AAAS), 211
Ambiguity, tolerance of, 10
American Indians. *See* Native Americans
American mainstream, 187–199
  problems in, 188–192
  reflecting back: impact of race,
    192–199
    advancements on the margins,
      197–199
    race as culture and the new
      socialization, 195–197
    race in American culture, 193–194
Anthropology, 3, 163–168
  cognitive, 167
  culture and psychology, 166–167
  definitions (classical and current),
    163–164
  dimensions of culture, 164–165
  emergence of global culture, 165–166
  ethnicity as culture, 165
  Human Research Area Files (HRAF):
    archival data for worldwide
    comparisons, 167–168
  interactions of psychology and, 168